Now and Then
We Time Travel

ALSO BY FRASER A. SHERMAN
AND FROM MCFARLAND

*The Wizard of Oz Catalog: L. Frank Baum's
Novel, Its Sequels and Their Adaptations
for Stage, Television, Movies, Radio,
Music Videos, Comic Books,
Commercials and More* (2013; softcover 2005)

*Screen Enemies of the American Way:
Political Paranoia About Nazis,
Communists, Saboteurs, Terrorists and Body Snatching
Aliens in Film and Television* (2011)

*Cyborgs, Santa Claus and Satan:
Science Fiction, Fantasy and Horror Films
Made for Television* (2009; softcover 2000)

Now and Then We Time Travel

Visiting Pasts and Futures in Film and Television

FRASER A. SHERMAN

McFarland & Company, Inc., Publishers
Jefferson, North Carolina

LIBRARY OF CONGRESS CATALOGUING-IN-PUBLICATION DATA

Names: Sherman, Fraser A.
Title: Now and then we time travel : visiting pasts and futures in film and television / Fraser A. Sherman.
Description: Jefferson, North Carolina : cFarland & Company, Inc., Publishers, 2017. | Includes bibliographical references and index.
Identifiers: LCCN 2016053272 | ISBN 9780786496792 (softcover : acid free paper) ∞
Subjects: LCSH: Time travel in motion pictures. | Time travel on television. | Science fiction films—History and criticism. | Science fiction television programs—History and criticism. | Fantasy films—History and criticism. | Fantasy television programs—History and criticism.
Classification: LCC PN1995.9.T555 S54 2017 | DDC 791.43/615—dc23
LC record available at https://lccn.loc.gov/2016053272

BRITISH LIBRARY CATALOGUING DATA ARE AVAILABLE

ISBN (print) 978-0-7864-9679-2
ISBN (ebook) 978-1-4766-2643-7

© 2017 Fraser A. Sherman. All rights reserved

No part of this book may be reproduced or transmitted in any form or by any means, electronic or mechanical, including photocopying or recording, or by any information storage and retrieval system, without permission in writing from the publisher.

Front cover: Christopher Lloyd as Dr. Emmett Brown in *Back to the Future*, 1985 (Universal Pictures/Photofest)

Printed in the United States of America

McFarland & Company, Inc., Publishers
Box 611, Jefferson, North Carolina 28640
www.mcfarlandpub.com

To Mum, Dad, Tracy, Craig and Paige for family.
To Cindy and Roxanne for friendship.
To Dudley and Trixie, for being there.
To LeAnn, for everything.

Acknowledgments

This book wouldn't be as good as it is without the suggestions, advice and input of my friend and fellow movie buff Ross Bagby. Thanks, Ross, as always.

My friend Katherine Traylor helped me out by explaining Korean names.

Johannes von Moltke, Department of Germanic Languages and Literatures at the University of Michigan, gave me information I couldn't find anywhere else.

The Timelinks website (aetherco.com/timelinks) was an invaluable resources for suggesting movies and TV series that might otherwise have slipped through the cracks. The List of Time Travel Fiction on Wikipedia (en.wikipedia.org/wiki/List_of_time_travel_works_of_fiction) and epguides.com were also great places to find time travel-related material. My thanks to everyone who worked on them.

Table of Contents

Acknowledgments	vii
Preface	1
One. A Century of Screen Connecticut Yankees	7
Two. Time of the Time Machine	13
Three. Enjoying the Exotic: Travel from the Present to Other Times	20
Four. Bouncing Around Time, Getting Lost and Doing the Time Warp	47
Five. Strange Visitors from Another World: Travel to the Present from Other Times	64
Six. Changing History: When Time Is Up for Grabs	84
Seven. Shaping the Future by Changing the Past That Is Our Present	99
Eight. If I Knew Then What I Know Now: Changing Personal History	125
Nine. Love in a Time of Time Travel	164
Ten. Time Cops: Policing the Time Stream (or) Putting Right What Once Went Wrong	181
Eleven. Déjà Vu All Over Again: Time Loop Films	192
Appendices	201
Appendix I: Film Credits	202
Appendix II: Television and Direct-to-Video Series Credits	225
Appendix III: Television Specials	230
Appendix IV: Films and Television Series with Minor Time Travel Elements	231
Appendix V: The Rest of the World	235
Appendix VI: Interesting Short Films	240
Appendix VII: Movies About Parallel Lives	241
Appendix VIII: Time Travel Porn Films	242
Chapter Notes	243
Bibliography	244
Index	245

Preface

"People assume that time is a strict progression of cause to effect, but actually, from a non-linear, non-subjective viewpoint, it's more like a big ball of wibbly wobbly ... time-y wimey ... stuff."—*Doctor Who*, "Blink"

Time travel is an incredible fantasy.

Witness with your own eyes the marvels of ancient Greece or the nightmare of a hi-tech future dictatorship. Revisit the perfect summer from your childhood. Find out what would have happened if you'd taken that job, smiled at that girl, invested in that stock. See your dead wife one last time and tell her how much you love her. Finally understand what your dad was like when he was your age. Travel back to the past to prevent your country from losing a war, or from starting one. Come back from the future to the present to avert a dystopia.

Time travel has been the basis for more than 400 films and 150 television series, not to mention large numbers of individual TV episodes. In just the time I've been working on this book, six American time travel series, two web series and several films have appeared, plus more material overseas. Several other productions are in the works as I wrap up.

What's the appeal? Partly, it's the sheer flexibility time travel offers to tell a story. It can range from the epic (what if Germany won World War II?) to the personal (can you regain the love you lost?), from the comic (you relive the same awful day, over and over) to the tragic (you try and prevent your best friend's death but you fail). A time travel story can warn against a dark future, critique the present or mock the past. Among the recent TV series, *Hindsight* concerns a woman correcting her life choices of 20 years earlier; *Outlander* has a 1940s woman trapped in 1700s Scotland; *DC's Legends of Tomorrow* has a team of superheroes (and a couple of criminals) travel through time to stop an immortal villain.

Television and movies rarely deal with the method and process of time travel. It's simply a tool for telling the story. In many films and series, all it takes is a blow to the head or a sincere wish to break the time barrier. Even science fiction stories don't focus much on the physics or technical details: It's enough to show us the time machine and explain it with a few minutes of technobabble. The 2002 *The Time Machine*, for example, settles for a blackboard covered with impressive-looking equations.

Time Travel: The 1800s

Time travel fiction didn't start in the 19th century but the landmark works that form the roots of the subgenre were born then.

Charles Dickens' 1843 classic *A Christmas Carol* isn't exactly time travel—the ghosts show Scrooge visions of the past and future, but he can't interact with them. But it foreshadows many of the themes that time travel movies would develop: repenting your past, realizing your mistakes and learning your future is going to turn out very bad indeed. While Scrooge can't change events in other times, his new knowledge lets him avert his tragic future and live a long, happy life.

Mark Twain's *A Connecticut Yankee in King Arthur's Court* (1889) is unambiguously time travel, involving a Yankee engineer who gets hit on the head and wakes up in the age of King Arthur. Like *A Christmas Carol*, Twain's book contains ideas future time travel writers would revisit repeatedly. It mocks the ignorance of the past, satirizes the present and provides plenty of rollicking adventure and anachronistic humor. It also includes a plot element many movies would employ, the challenge of falling in love with someone from another time.

Yankee is time travel but it isn't science fiction. H.G. Wells' stories *The Chronic Argonauts* (1888) and *The Time Machine* (1895) presented time travel as a matter of physics and mathematics. (Wells wasn't the first to do so but his work was the one that had impact.)

Time travel fiction blossomed in the 20th century, and unsurprisingly the movies got in on the action. The first time travel film, now lost, was a 1910 adaptation of *Connecticut Yankee*. Two more adaptations followed in the next two decades, both employing an "it was just a dream" ending, as did 1933's time travel story *Turn Back the Clock*. *Berkeley Square* (1933) gave filmgoers a story where the time travel was real.

All those films were fantasy. Screen time travel by scientific means had to wait until 1947's *Brick Bradford* movie serial, followed by 1956's *World Without End*. Time travel showed up on radio—there were multiple adaptations of *The Time Machine*[1]—and in 1959 began appearing on TV on the classic anthology *The Twilight Zone*. In the decades since, it's become increasingly common in movies and television, and now online films and series.

Regardless of the medium or the method of time travel, stories about traveling through time have to deal with concepts and story problems more conventional narratives don't.

Causality

The power of fiction comes from characters living with the consequences of their actions.[2] Michael Corleone may regret joining the family business but he can't erase his decision to do so. Jay Gatsby can't undo Daisy's marriage to Tom Buchanan no matter how much he wants to. A time traveler, by contrast, can prevent a wedding that's already happened (*Before You Say "I Do," Peggy Sue Got Married*), take back their bad life choices (*Hindsight*) or refight a war that's already been lost (*Deep Blue Fleet*). If the time traveler fails, they can potentially try again and again until they succeed. For a time travel story to have any suspense, the writer has to prevent the protagonist from taking a mulligan.

The simplest solution is to limit the traveler to a single time jump. In films such as *Repeat Performance* and *Peggy Sue Gets Married*, the protagonist is sent back in time by some outside force, with no way to do it again if they fail to rewrite their past.

Another approach is to throw up obstacles against endless time traveling. The time machine might run out of fuel (*Back to the Future*) or get stolen (*The Time Machine*) or some law of physics prevents the traveler warning their past self what went wrong (*Juko's Time Machine*). Other stories assert that time resists changes, whether because of physical law, human choice or "destiny." Joan Leslie in *Repeat Performance* discovers destiny won't let her alter the previous year's events, but she can tweak the details. In *Turn Back the Clock*, Lee Tracy knows the stock market is going to crash in 1929, but he can't convince anyone else not to invest.

Some films do allow the time traveler to take a do-over. In *Running Against Time*, Robert Hays' efforts to prevent the Vietnam War (by preventing JFK's assassination) end up making the world worse. A final time jump prevents Hays from ever trying to change history, but this is presented as part of his personal arc: He hasn't cheated causality as much as he's gained the wisdom to accept the things he cannot change. On the other hand, *Superman* blatantly cheats by having Lois Lane die, then having the Man of Steel rewind time to save her.

Time-loop films such as *Groundhog Day* are a special case. There's no causality and no consequences for anything Bill Murray does—over-eating, smoking, suicide. After repeated days of causality-free living, Murray is desperate to get back to a life where his actions matter.

Logic

Time travel raises no end of contradictions and paradoxes, and the stories in this book rarely resolve any of them.

The classic conundrum is the grandfather paradox. If you go back in time and shoot your grandfather, you'll never be born; if you're never born you'll never travel back in time; if you never travel back, you'll never shoot your grandfather, so you'll be born after all.... In *Against Time*, for example, a drunken, depressed Robert Loggia travels back and averts a tragedy in his past. When we see him again at the end of the movie, he's happy, contented and never made the time trip—so how did his past change?

Some stories explain this by having the time traveler create an alternate timeline (e.g., *In Search of the Lost Future*) while the original history remains the same. The TV series *Continuum* rejects the paradox: Time travelers keep existing even if their past self dies. *Timecrashers* equips time travelers with tech to resist the effects of time changes. In fantasies, presumably magic negates the paradox. And of course, some stories simply ignore the issue.

Another logic challenge is showing the changes in the time stream. Theoretically, as soon as the past changes, the change should affect all future times. In screen time travel it often doesn't. In *Trancers*, the villain travels back to the 20th century to kill the ancestors of Los Angeles' 24th century leaders. Logically, the leaders should never have existed; instead, they exist up to the "same" moment their ancestors are killed, then they crumble into dust.

One challenge that time travel tales often fail is staying consistent with their own rules. In *Men in Black III*, a time travel device transports users physically into the past, until the plot requires it sends minds back instead. In *CSA*, the Confederacy wins the Civil War, history is transformed, but in 1960 Nixon and Kennedy still wind up competing for the White House.

Screen time travel often relies on symbolic or emotional logic rather than scientific. *Repeat Performance*'s time jump takes place on New Year's Eve, a night heavy in symbolism about the passage of time. The hero of *Before You Say "I Do"* makes his first time jump after a car accident, then returns home with another jump. In *Yesterday Was a Lie* and *In Search of the Lost Future*, the power to change history is limited by the characters' emotional desire to cling to the past.

Morality

Someone who murders a child and claims the child was evil and deserved to die is a deranged monster.[3] Someone who goes back in time and murders Hitler as a child is absolutely right that the kid's going to grow up evil. Knowing the future changes the rules (though you can still debate whether murdering pre–Nazi Hitler is the right choice).

To the people in the past, however, the traveler's actions will still look evil or irrational. In *The Flight That Disappeared*, the protagonists see themselves as patriotic Americans working on a missile project. They're understandably shocked when time travelers from the future brand them as future Hitlers whose super-missile will wipe out the world.

Changing history, as many screen time travelers try to do, raises further moral issues. In *Running Against Time*, Hays wants to end the Vietnam War to save his brother's life— but by doing so, he's altering the lives of millions of others. If JFK had lived, would he have fought for a civil-rights bill as President Johnson did? If not, is stopping the war worth continued segregation? Neither Hays nor the film brings up the possible downside.

This is why the time police of *Timecop*, *Trancers* and *Time Trax* exist, to prevent time travelers ruining other people's lives for their own benefit. Other movies, though, take the view that changing the past is acceptable, at least if you're a nice person. For example, by the end of *Back to the Future* Marty McFly has changed Biff Tannen's life for the worse (and he's undoubtedly changed other lives besides his parents') but he's the hero so nobody objects. Even when the sequels warn against changing history, the goal is to restore the altered timeline of the first film's end, not to bring back the original timeline of the movie's beginning.

Another issue with time changing is whether erasing something you've done means that ethically you're off the hook. Science fiction scholar Bud Foote has argued that if you can change what happens, you also change the morality: It didn't happen so you never did anything wrong.[4] By contrast, *Hindsight* creator Emily Fox says that if you did wrong, then changing the past doesn't excuse your actions.[5] Different screen stories take different views.

Relationships with Time

The relationship between people and time—their era, the era in which they arrive— is a big part of screen time travel. Characters who visit other times have to struggle to make sense of the new setting, and to make themselves understood. In *The Visitors*, medieval knight Jean Reno creates chaos in the present by his misunderstanding of everything;

Michael J. Fox in *Back to the Future* baffles a drug store clerk by asking for a Tab ("I can't give you a tab until you order!"). For some travelers, like Twain's Yankee, the past is a madhouse; for others, involuntarily trapped in another time, it's a prison or an exile.

The past can, however, be liberating for someone who's unhappy in their present. The standard arc for teen time travelers, and a number of adults, is that they're miserable and insecure, get hurled back in time, learn life lessons and return with new insight that lets them master their problems (e.g. *Forbidden Kingdom, Johnny Mysto* and *The Winning Season*). With other time travelers, it's their entire era they hate. Mark Harmon in *For All Time* loathes the present and falls in love with the supposed golden age of the late 1800s as much as the woman he meets there.

Time travel to the past also offers viewers a heaping load of nostalgia. *Back to the Future* is affectionate for the 1950s, *Hindsight* is heavy with 1990s nostalgia and *Der Trip* and *Spirit of 76* affectionately showcase fashions and attitudes of the 1970s. In the romance films *For All Time* and *Two Worlds of Jennie Logan,* the protagonists fall in love with the past as well as with their significant others.

What's in This Book

This book lists every time travel film and television series from the United States, the United Kingdom, Canada and Japan at time of writing. I've included noteworthy stories from the rest of the world in the body of the text and less memorable ones in Appendix V. (Worthiness has more to do with the time travel aspect than artistic merit.) I'm also including travel to alternate timelines, communication across time without physical travel and films where history gets changed without any actual time travel. I've watched everything I could find and noted my sources when a film or series was unavailable.

The films in each chapter are tied together by a particular aspect of time travel, including cross-time love, efforts to change history, visits to the past or future and time policing. Plenty of movies fit in multiple categories, so I've placed them wherever I think is most informative. The focus of my reviews is on the time travel elements of the film. I'm not going to attempt to point out every time paradox and illogical element, which could easily require another 100,000 words.

I have not included short films (anything running under an hour), though I've listed some in Appendix VI. I'm also not tackling individual episodes of non–time-travel television shows, such as fantasy or science fiction anthologies or series such as *Bewitched*, which had a number of time travel episodes. I include shows which are not primarily about time travel but do have it as a running element. In the first season of *Flash* (2014), for example, a villain from the future plays a major role. I have made exceptions to the rules when a story seemed worth it.

Films with a minor time travel aspect appear in Appendix IV. *Galaxy-Quest,* for instance, isn't a time travel film but time travel does play a key role in one brief scene. Films such as *Sliding Doors* that present a character whose choices create alternate time paths are in Appendix VII. Time travel porn films are in Appendix VIII.

I have excluded films and television series which do not fit the book even though some reference sources list them as time travel tales:

- Stories involving precognition, visions of the future or clairvoyant visions of the past.
- Time travel by suspended animation, enchanted sleep or the Einsteinian effects of faster-than-light travel.
- Stories of ghosts or reincarnations from past times.
- Tales about people with the power to stop time, such as *The Girl, the Gold Watch and Everything*.
- Documentaries about time travel or about time travel films, or documentaries that use time travel as the frame for an educational lecture about dinosaurs, ancient Egypt or whatever.
- Distorted time perceptions due to a character's mental issues.
- Stories where someone travels into a book or movie set in the past, such as *Teen Beach Movie* or *Lost in Austen*.
- Stories where someone magically becomes their younger or older self, but stays in one time.
- Movies about other dimensions that aren't alternate histories.
- Movies with "time" titles but no time travel. For instance, *Beastmaster 2: Through the Portal of Time* is actually a crossover to Earth from another dimension.
- "Movies" that are actually multiple TV episodes combined together.

As many SF writers have said, time travel makes a hash of our normal use of "now," "then" and "next" but I've done my best to keep the synopses clear. As part of that, I use "present," "past" and "future" in relation to when the movie was set; 2015 in *Back to the Future II* is "the future" for the characters, even though it's now in our past.

I've used English names for foreign films and series in the body of the book. The list of credits at the back includes the original foreign name, if there is one.

Now, onward, for time is wasting…

CHAPTER ONE

A Century of Screen Connecticut Yankees

"Tell me, was it the Wright Brothers who discovered radio?"—*Unidentified Flying Oddball* (1979)

Mark Twain's *A Connecticut Yankee in King Arthur's Court* has been filmed more than any other print time travel story, adapted more than twice as often as *The Time Machine*.

The original novel opens with a framing sequence in which an American tourist in England (presumably Twain himself) meets fellow American Hank Morgan. Hank astonishingly claims to have returned from a time trip to the age of chivalry and gives the tourist a centuries-old manuscript to prove it. The book tells how Hank, a foreman in a gun factory, was knocked out and woke up in sixth-century Camelot, though Twain gives the kingdom all the anachronistic knightly trappings his readers would have associated with Arthur.

The king sentences Hank to burn as a witch, but the engineer's pocket almanac reveals an imminent solar eclipse. Hank claims he can blot out the sun by magic and when the eclipse hits, Arthur submits and appoints the Yankee as his prime minister, "Sir Boss." Hank introduces Camelot to newspapers, schools, guns, bicycles and phones, and dreams of breaking the power of the monarch and the church (Twain's anti–Catholicism is very heavy-handed) in favor of a democracy. Tragically, while the Yankee is out of the country with his lady love Alisande, Camelot falls as it did in Malory's *Morte D'Arthur*. The church seizes power, plunges England back into ignorance and superstition and sends an army against Sir Boss's last fortress. Hank's hi-tech defenses kill thousands of knights but Merlin—despite being shown repeatedly as a powerless fraud—traps Hank in a magical sleep that lasts until the present. Upon finishing the manuscript, the tourist sees Hank pass away, to reunite with his wife and child in Heaven.

Like many classics, *Connecticut Yankee* can and has been interpreted multiple ways, including a critique of the South of Twain's day, an attack on 19th century nostalgia for chivalry, and as a commentary on colonialism. Reams have been written about Hank's implausible genius. Starting from scratch in a pre-technological society, he eventually manufactures guns, bicycles, phones and more. He also sets up a school system, a stock market and establishes the world's first newspaper.

Almost all screen adaptations tone down the book's message. Instead of Twain's scathing social criticism, movies take a similar view of monarchy to swashbuckler films. As film historian Jeffrey Richards says,[1] swashbucklers typically accept the principle that monarchy is a good system; you just have to replace the usurper with the true king or dispose of the evil counselor leading the king down the wrong path. Sir Boss' role in the movies isn't to institute democracy but to make Arthur the great king of legend.

None of the adaptations in this chapter use Twain's nineteenth-century protagonist. All film Hanks are twentieth-century characters, most of whom have a contemporary technical background such as radio engineer, rocket scientist or quantum physicist.

The first screen *Yankee* is a lost 1910 silent. Three reels survive from *A Connecticut Yankee in King Arthur's Court* (1921), a silent starring Harry Myers as wealthy Martin Cavendish. Martin loves his mother's secretary Sandy (Pauline Starke), but Mom wants him to marry rich. While Martin reads about the age of chivalry, a burglar clunks him on the head, and Martin wakes up in the sixth century. As in Twain he's captured, sentenced to death and escapes by predicting an eclipse. He falls for Alisande (Starke again) and pushes Camelot into the 20th century by introducing plumbing, telephones and automobiles. Sir Sagramore challenges him to a duel, but Martin triumphs (again as in Twain) by using a lasso to take the knight down. Martin wakes up and elopes with Betty.

In 1931's *A Connecticut Yankee*, radio engineer Hank Martin (Will Rogers) delivers equipment to a mansion stuffed to the rafters with weirdos. One of them, the mansion's owner (William Farnum), has built a radio to hear messages from the past, and successfully tunes in Arthur's court. After the requisite blow to the head, Hank arrives in Camelot and winds up in Arthur's (Farnum again) dungeon alongside Clarence (Frank Albertson), a commoner imprisoned for loving Princess Alisande (Maureen O'Sullivan).

After the eclipse trick turns Hank into Sir Boss, he begins mass-producing consumer goods, which he plans to sell by introducing advertising. He also hunts for an ancestor who supposedly lived in Camelot. Plans change when Morgan leFay (Myrna Loy) captures Alisande and Clarence: Hank learns Clarence is his ancestor, so Morgan executing him would be bad news. Sir Boss' rescue attempt ends up with him captured too, and his effort to seduce Morgan doesn't go any better. After Arthur's knights show up armed with modern weapons, a blow to the head sends Hank back to the present. He discovers the owner's time radio merely picked up a radio drama about King Arthur. Heading home, Hank discovers doubles of Clarence and Sandy hiding in his truck, trying to elope despite parental disapproval. Hank lends them the truck and walks home.

The 1949 musical *A Connecticut Yankee in King Arthur's Court* opens with Hank (Bing Crosby) in 1912 annoying a tour guide at Arthur's castle with his superior knowledge of Camelot and his claim he's spotted a bullet hole in one ancient suit of armor. Hank tells the castle's owner (Cedric Hardwicke) the usual tale of unconsciousness, his arrival in Camelot and becoming Sir Boss, though in this version he awes the court by lighting a match. With Sir Clarence Sagramore (William Bendix) as his assistant, Sir Boss builds a few gadgets, including a revolver, but has more impact on Camelot by teaching the court musicians swing. He also falls for Alisande (Rhonda Fleming) and uses a lasso to defeat her fiancé in combat.

Hank convinces Sagramore and Arthur (Hardwicke) to travel incognito with him and see how the commoners really live. Merlin (Murvyn Vye) contrives to capture and sell the trio into slavery, then imprisons Sandy as well. Hank uses the eclipse trick to escape, then fights his way to Sandy with the revolver before getting clubbed and waking in the present. Fortunately, the castle owner's niece is Sandy's double and, it's

"Sir Boss" (Bing Crosby) and Sandy (Rhonda Fleming) run into some knaves and varlets in the musical *A Connecticut Yankee in King Arthur's Court* (1949).

implied, her reincarnation. (See chapter nine for more discussion of the "exact double" romantic twist.)

A 1970 animated adaptation with Orson Bean as Hank stands out by drawing more heavily on Twain than any other version to date. Though little over an hour long, it includes scenes other versions skip, such as Hank blowing up Merlin's tower, Sir Boss going on a quest with Alisande and most significantly his dream of bringing England out of the Dark Ages centuries early. This time it's Merlin rather than the Catholic Church who rallies traditionalists to overthrow Sir Boss and undo all his work. When Hank finally wakes in the present, he wonders if he imagined it all. Then he finds a photo in the encyclopedia showing Arthur reading a newspaper while standing next to a motorcycle.

Bugs Bunny played considerably looser with the classic in the TV special *Bugs Bunny in King Arthur's Court* (1978) which the title credits refer to as "stolen" from Twain. (Bugs had previously visited Camelot in 1955's *Knight-Mare Hare*.) Bugs (Mel Blanc, who did all the voices) winds up in Camelot while tunneling to Georgia ("That's the last time I get directions from Ray Bradbury!") where he's captured by Sir Elmer of Fudde. Realizing which book he's in, Bugs pulls the eclipse trick to impress Arthur (Daffy Duck). As Sir Boss he builds a factory that sells armor to animals to protect them from hunters. Egged on by

Merlin (Yosemite Sam), Elmer challenges Bud to a duel that goes over the top as only Warner Brothers cartoons can. Before Elmer can finish Bugs off, the rabbit plucks Excalibur from the stone and becomes King Arth-Hare.

Unidentified Flying Oddball (1979) also plays fast and loose with Twain, but the results aren't as funny. NASA scientist Tom Trimble (Dennis Dugan) creates a robot look-alike, Hermes, to fly an experimental spaceship. A freak accident launches the ship across time to Camelot with both man and robot aboard. As Tom can't get out of his spacesuit, Mordred (Jim Dale) assumes he's a monster and captures him. Arthur (Kenneth More) sentences Tom to burn, but as the spacesuit is fireproof, Tom survives, proving himself a wizard.

Tom learns Mordred's crimes include imprisoning Alisande's (Sheila White) father to steal his lands and tries to help her. Between Hermes' abilities and the tech Tom cannibalizes from his spaceship, the scientist stays one step ahead of Mordred and eventually exposes him as a traitor. Mordred retaliates by allying with Merlin (Ron Moody) and sending an army against Camelot. Tom builds a flying chair with which he defeats the bad guys, and then he and Hermes return to the present with Sandy.

A Knight in Camelot (1998) cast Whoopi Goldberg as Dr. Vivian Morgan, whose gravity-wave experiment throws her back to Camelot. Unusually, she grasps in an instant what's happened rather than wondering why everyone's acting so medieval. After securing her position via the usual trickery, she begins modernizing Camelot and fighting against Arthur's (Michael York) acceptance of slavery. Her aide Clarence (Simon Fenton) makes Viv realize, however, that she's treating her own workers like slaves, which forces her to moderate her hard-driving attitude.

Although Viv fails to make any real technological changes to Camelot, she does bring the murderous knight Sagramore (Robert Addie) to justice for killing Clarence's family. She also convinces Arthur to become a more humane king. After Merlin (Ian Richardson) transports Viv home, he assures her that just as she's learned of honor from Camelot, so her influence on Arthur will make his kingdom a shining beacon of hope in the ages that follow. The scientist and the sorcerer set out into the universe to explore time and space together (Vivian is one of the names given to Merlin's lover).

Young Yankees in Camelot

Nineteen eighty-nine gave us Keshia Knight Pulliam as tween *Connecticut Yankee in King Arthur's Court* Karen Jones. When she wakes in the past after a fall from a horse, she has her backpack with her, and uses her Polaroid camera to prove she's a wizard. As Sir Boss, she makes mostly social changes, such as teaching the women martial arts. Her new friend Clarence (Bryce Hamnet) does the inventing, building bicycles based on her description. When traitors capture Arthur and Karen during the standard incognito trip, Clarence's bicycle squad saves them.

Mordred (Hugo E. Blick) subsequently imprisons Karen, Guinevere (Emma Samms) and Arthur (Stephen Gross) in a power grab. Arthur tells Karen that she's opened his eyes to Camelot's flaws, and promises that if he regains the throne, even peasants will be equal before the law. At their execution, Karen plays the eclipse card and saves the day, but Merlin

(René Auberjonois) plunges her into magical slumber. When she wakes in the present, she concludes it was all a dream, but a Polaroid photo of Merlin proves otherwise.

In *A Young Connecticut Yankee in King Arthur's Court* (1995), Hank Morgan's (Philippe Ross) ticket to Camelot is an electric shock from a friend's amplifier. This time Alisande (Polly Shannon) is a knight herself; she saves Hank from terrified peasants and takes him to Arthur's court. After the death sentence and eclipse trick, Hank sets himself up as "Sir Dude" and begins using the toolbox he brought with him to build a new amplifier so he can head home. In the meantime, he saves Lancelot (Ian Falconer) from a trap set by treacherous Ulrich (Jack Langedijk), gives Arthur (Nick Mancuso) oral sex tips, and wins Alisande's heart.

When Hank takes Arthur on a road trip to see how Ulrich and Morgan leFay (Theresa Russell) are oppressing the people, the villains capture them. Sandy and Lancelot save the day and Hank decides to stay in the past with Sandy. A fluke accident returns him to the present, where he discovers the new girl in school is Alisande's double and begins pursuing her.

Teen Calvin Fuller (Thomas Ian Nicholas) becomes *A Kid in King Arthur's Court* (1995) when Merlin (Ron Moody again) tries summoning a champion but instead pulls in Cal right after his humiliating strikeout in the big baseball game. In this version of Camelot, the scheming noble Belasco (Art Malik) is oppressing the people with extortionate taxes while hiding this from Arthur (Joss Ackland). A mysterious Black Knight steals the tax moneys back to give to the poor, Robin Hood–style. Cal falls for Arthur's daughter Kate (Paloma Baeza) but Belasco kidnaps Kate to force her sister Sarah (Kate Winslet) to marry him. Cal and Arthur go undercover as peasants, sneak into Belasco's fortress, and free Kate.

Belasco tries to win Sarah the old-fashioned way, at a tournament for her hand. The Black Knight defeats him, then unmasks as Sarah herself. Now that she's won the right to choose for herself, she picks her true love Cane (Daniel Craig). With Belasco beaten, Merlin sends Cal back to the moment before he struck out, and the kid's now confident enough to hit a homer. Better still, another player turns out to be Kate's double. (Cal is unattached at the start of the sequel, *A Kid in Aladdin's Palace*, covered in Chapter Three.)

The Evil Dead

Army of Darkness (1993) isn't a straight Connecticut Yankee retelling, but it's hard not to see Twain as a big influence. It's a sequel to *Evil Dead* and *Evil Dead II*; in those films, Ash (Bruce Campbell) and his friends struggled against demonic attacks unleashed by the Necronomicon, an occult text. Ash alone survives, though missing one hand, and at the end of *II* the book's power blasts him into the 1300s, packing a chainsaw and a shotgun. Local ruler Lord Arthur (Marcus Gilbert) captures Ash at the start of *Army of Darkness* and condemns him to death in a pit of monsters. After killing the monsters with the chainsaw, Ash uses his "bang stick" rather than an eclipse prediction to intimidate Arthur and his people.

Only the Necronomicon can send Ash home, so he sets out to find it. After battling various bizarre monsters, including an evil clone of himself, Ash retrieves the book, but without correctly using the charm he's been taught to neutralize it. Ash's clone leads an army of the dead to recapture the book, and the "deadites" kidnap Ash's lover Sheila (Embeth Davidtz). To save her, Ash develops modern technology such as gunpowder and a crude helicopter. (As Ash is just a sales clerk, it's an even more impressive achievement than Sir Boss.) Ash successfully leads Arthur's knights against the Deadites, then takes a magic potion that puts him to sleep until his own time. He returns to his old job. When a Deadite attacks the store, Ash kills it effortlessly.

The original ending would have awakened Ash in a post-apocalyptic future but Universal insisted on a happy conclusion.

CHAPTER TWO

Time of the Time Machine

"After all, he has all the time in the world."—The Time Machine (1960)

Alongside *Connecticut Yankee*, H.G. Wells' *The Time Machine* is the other founding novel of time travel fiction.

The book opens with the never-named Time Traveler explaining his theory of fourth-dimensional travel, then demonstrating a miniature time machine to his friends. A few days later, the Time Traveler, exhausted and in rags, meets them again. He tells them how he used a full-sized time machine to travel into a distant future where class warfare has divided humanity into the apathetic, free-spirited Eloi and the subterranean Morlocks, cannibalistic descendants of the working class. The Time Traveler befriends the Eloi Weena, but his recklessness leads to her death at the Morlocks' hands, and almost gets him killed too. After he finishes recounting his adventures, he heads back out into the time stream.

Like *Connecticut Yankee* this has a lot of pedantic lecturing. Unlike *Connecticut Yankee* it isn't insufferable because Wells' novel is shorter, and the Time Traveler much less brilliant than Sir Boss: He's frequently wrong, and admits even his theory of the Eloi-Morlock divide may be completely wrong.

The CBS radio series *Escape* aired an adaptation in 1948. In the first screen adaptation, a 1949 BBC dramatization, Russell Napier plays the Time Traveler who, after failing to convince his Victorian friends that he can transcend time, heads out in his time machine, with his travel marked by clock hands moving blurringly fast. He eventually arrives in AD 802,701, where things proceed as in Wells: He meets the Eloi, befriends Weena, but loses her to the flesh-eating Morlocks. After journeying further ahead to the end of Earth, the Time Traveler returns home. He wonders if the entire journey was a dream, until he finds a flower Weena gave him in one of his pockets.

Next came George Pal's classic 1960 adaptation, starring Rod Taylor as Herbert George. The book follows the novel fairly faithfully until the Morlocks capture Weena (Yvette Mimieux). George follows her into the Morlock tunnels, rescues her along with the other Eloi captives, and inspires the Eloi to shake off their apathy and fight. George uses fire to fend off the dark-dwelling Morlocks and ignites their tunnels, destroying the entire race. He returns to his own time to meet his friends, then heads back to Weena. George takes with him three books to help the Eloi rebuild civilization—but which three?

The tone of the film is sweetly charming and occasionally wistful. Here, unlike in the Wells novel, the nightmare future is the result of warfare rather than class warfare. Before making his big trip, George tells his best friend Filby (Alan Young) that he's leaving the present because he's sick of seeing science perverted to find new ways of killing people. His stops along the time stream include World War I, World War II and the 1966 nuclear war; in one stop he learns that Filby died fighting in World War I. The Morlocks descend from humans who hid underground to survive the 1966 war, though that doesn't really explain why they became cannibals.

The 1978 made-for-TV *The Time Machine* keeps the Pal film's anti-war theme but drops the charm, intelligence and quality. Megacorp scientist Neil Perry (John Beck) secretly uses his weapons research lab to build a time machine. His first jump lands him in supposedly comical adventures in the Old West. Then he visits the Eloi-Morlock future, saves Weena (Priscilla Barnes) and wipes out the Morlocks. He returns home to warn his bosses what continued warfare will do to the world, but their response is to order him to collect future weapons technology the company can sell. A disgusted Perry returns to the Eloi so he can use his genius to help humanity instead of hurting it.

The 2002 *The Time Machine* radically reworks Wells, even though it was directed by his grandson Simon. Alexander Hartedegan (Guy Pearce) is a brilliant Victorian physicist whose life changes when he sees his great love Emma (Sienna Guillory) murdered by a robber. Alex builds a time machine, goes back and saves her, only to see a horse trample her to death. Desperate, Alex travels into the future to learn from some more advanced era why he can't undo her death. (On the DVD commentary, Simon Wells says he should have justified Alex's desperation by implying many more rescue attempts.)

After repeated dead ends in multiple times, Alex arrives in a future where the Morlocks

Herbert George (Rod Taylor) rescues the Eloi Weena (Yvette Mimieux) from drowning, while her people stand by, in *The Time Machine* **(1960).**

look like Orcs and the Eloi resemble an idealized native tribe living in harmony with nature. When the Morlocks kidnap the Eloi Mara (Samantha Mumba), Alex enters their tunnels to confront the king Morlock (Jeremy Irons). The creature explains telepathically that when the moon exploded—something foreshadowed in earlier time jumps—the Morlock ancestors fled underground to escape the rain of rocks. He also explains that Alex can't save Emma because of the grandfather paradox: If Emma lives, Alex won't invent a time machine, so he can't save her, so she dies and he invents a time machine....

The Morlock is willing to let Alex leave in peace. Instead Alex uses the time machine's temporal distortion field to age the ruler to death. Alex rescues Mara, blows up his time machine, destroys the Morlock caverns and settles down with Mara in the Eloi's future Eden.

To date there have been two *Time Machine* film sequels. In the short *Time Machine: The Journey Back* (1993), George (Rod Taylor) returns to visit Filby as World War I begins. George tries to convince Filby to come to the future rather than fight, but Filby decides his duty to England takes precedence. As George leaves, he consoles himself with the thought that he can return and try again. After all, he has all the time in the world.

The 1984 German film *Return of the Time Machine* opens in 1925 with Dr. Erasmus Beilowski (Klaus Schwarzkopf) discovering a strange machine in an antiques store and recognizing it as the time machine Wells wrote about. He calls his friends and they spend an evening discussing the machine's potential. (According to what little information is

Herbert George (Rod Taylor) at bottom right watches the Morlocks enslave the Eloi in *The Time Machine* (1960).

With the Morlock tunnels sealed off, the Eloi can look forward to a future of peace.

available on the film, this parodies discussions of space travel's potential.) The group selects Wernesburger (Nikolas Lansky), a shy, broke factory worker, to be the guinea pig who takes the machine out into time for a spin.

Morlocks Without End: Variations on Wells

With its story of future humanity divided into sheep and mutant wolves, *World Without End* (1956) has a lot in common with H.G. Wells' *The Time Machine*. A long-standing legend says the Wells estate sued over the film, but there are no 1950s sources confirming that (at least none have turned up at time of writing). In any case, the film is a landmark, the first feature film where characters time travel by scientific means rather than magic.

A freak accident hurls a four-man rocket crew (including Rod Taylor, the future Herbert George) 500 years into the future. Nuclear war has split humanity into the grotesque, barbaric Mutates and the Eloi-like inhabitants of a subterranean city. The city's men are passive weaklings; the women are hot and not at all shy about hitting on the new arrivals.

Returning to the present is impossible. The rocket crew asks the city residents to help scavenge useful tools and equipment from the crashed ship, but the ruling council is too afraid of arousing the Mutates. Nor do they believe the astronauts' discovery that most of the surface dwellers are normal humans, oppressed by the Mutates. One councilor, Mories

(Booth Colman), also resents that Garnet (Nancy Gates) is more interested in the time travelers than in him. Mories turns the city against the spacemen, but the astronauts expose his treachery. Fleeing, Mories dies at the Mutates' hands. The spacemen kill the Mutate leader, then bring both cultures together on the surface. In a surprisingly moving ending scene, we see civilization rebuilding and children of both peoples studying together.

Two later movies portray a similar divide in humanity's future. In *Beyond the Time Barrier* (1960), Air Force pilot Bill Allison's (Robert Clarke) experimental plane gets hurled 64 years into the future (his record-setting speed, plus the speed of the Earth's movement through space, supposedly exceeded the speed of light). Earth has been contaminated by atomic tests, forcing most of humanity into space. Left behind are a last city of sterile humans and tribes of bald mutant savages.

The city dwellers hope to mate Allison with the still-fertile Trirene (Darlene Tompkins), but Allison wants to return to his own time and avert Earth's doom. He forms an alliance with other stranded time travelers to repair the plane for a flight home. When the moment comes, however, Bourman (John Van Dreelen), a man from the 1990s, tries to hijack the plane to return to *his* time. Trirene sacrifices herself to stop Bourman, after which Allison returns to the present. He's only been gone a few minutes, so his superiors don't believe his claims—except they can't explain (and neither does the film) why Allison aged 64 years in those brief moments.

Next came *The Time Travelers* (1964), in which four scientists see their experimental time scanner open an actual time gate. Danny (Steve Franken) steps through only to have bald, scarred mutants attack him. The others rush through to help, then the portal closes behind them. Once again time travelers discover mutants besieging a last human city, whose inhabitants hope to escape into Alpha Centauri. Willard (Dennis Patrick), one of the city leaders, tells the scientists they won't be coming along, as there's no time to recalculate the effect of their added weight on the rocket's fuel.

Between tedious lectures on the wonders of future science, the travelers work with the friendlier city dwellers to reopen the time portal. They've almost succeeded when the mutants swarm the city, massacring the humans before the rocket can be launched. The scientists open the portal and take the city survivors into the past, right at the start of the film. Unfortunately, they arrive out of synch, moving through time so fast the world is standing still. They pass back through the portal, arriving in a far future where the Earth is once again green.

Like *World Without End*, the animated *Time Kid* (2003) is more optimistic about uniting the two branches of humanity than Wells was. In 1902, brainy scholarship student Tom Spender (Michael Monroe Heyward) wants to hang with his elite classmates, even when they push him to dump a working-class friend. When Tom visits his widowed father Henry (Jerry Longe), he discovers a time machine in Dad's lab with a message saying Henry is trapped in the future.

Tom follows Henry into a future inhabited by the light-hearted, telekinetic Lumen and the bestial Sub-Men, who trap Lumens and use their brainpower to run their underground city. Tom and the Lumen Lira (Danielle Young) capture, then befriend the Sub-Man Zorog (Jon Kodera), who realizes the Lumen aren't the evil monsters his people believe. When the Sub-Men throw Tom in a cell with Henry, Zorog rescues the Spenders. After the Lumens use their mind-power to overcome the subterraneans, the two sides forge an uneasy peace. The Spenders return to 1902, but they materialize on a railroad they get out of the time machine right before a train demolishes it. Henry doesn't think he can rebuild it, but Tom tells him what's really important is building a better present. For starters, Tom rejects his snobby classmates in favor of his old chums.

The SyFy Channel's *Morlocks* (2011) keeps the idea of predatory mutates but throws the rest of Wells' novel out the window. Years ago, military researcher Radnor (David Hewlett) opened a wormhole into the future. The squad that went through never came back, so Radnor abandoned his research. Now Col. Wichita (Robert Picardo) informs Radnor that the military has opened a new wormhole. The platoon that went through lost the "latch" that can close the time gate, so the predatory Morlocks that dominate the future Earth can now crawl through time and attack us in the present.

Radnor leads a new team to the future and discovers the few survivors of the original time expedition. Although Radnor wants to research the Morlocks in hopes of preventing their future, the soldiers insist on finding the latch, then returning home.

Back in the present, Radnor and his ex, Angela (Christina Cole), discover Wichita's real agenda is to use Morlock DNA to cure his son's terminal cancer (code name Project E.L.O.I.). Radnor warns the colonel that E.L.O.I. could create the Morlocks, but the colonel doesn't care. Even after the Morlocks reopen the wormhole and swarm through, Wichita refuses to shut the gateway. Radnor successfully closes it by sending a bomb through it. The military finish off the remaining Morlocks; Radnor dies in the battle; as Radnor warned, Wichita's son begins mutating into the first Morlock.

H.G. Wells, Time Traveler

Time After Time (1979) is as far removed from *The Time Machine* as is *Morlocks* but it's a much better film. In 1893, H.G. Wells (Malcolm McDowell) reveals to his friends that he's built a time machine to visit the socialist utopia he anticipates by the late 20th century. Wells' friend Dr. Stevenson (David Warner) is none other than Jack the Ripper. Having committed his first murder in years, he uses the time machine to flee to the present before the police close in.

The time machine automatically returns to Wells, who's horrified at the thought of Jack butchering the future's pacifist innocents and time travels in pursuit. In 1979, he's even more horrified to discover a world that's not socialist, pacifist or utopian. When he catches up with Stevenson, who's begun a new killing spree, the doctor gloats that he's a much better fit for the modern world than Wells is. On the plus side, Wells takes comfort from meeting and falling for Amy (Mary Steenburgen), a banker who finds Wells charmingly old-fashioned.

Stevenson decides to time-jump away from Wells' interference, so he demands Wells give him the control key that will stop the machine returning to its creator. When the men fight for the key, Stevenson is apparently killed by a car. Wells is free to romance Amy, until he discovered Stevenson is still alive and killing. Worse, when Wells takes Amy into the future to prove he's a time traveler, they discover she's Stevenson's next victim. Wells tries to alert the cops, but his knowledge of the killings lands him in jail until after Amy is dead.

It turns out the victim was not Amy but a friend of Amy's. Stevenson captures Amy and demands the key in exchange for her life. Wells gives up the key, but rigs the time machine so that it hurls Stevenson through infinity, never to materialize again. Amy and Herbert return to the past, and the movie ends with a text note that Wells did indeed marry an American named Amy.

Wells again shows up as a time traveler in the 1990s TV series *Lois and Clark: The New Adventures of Superman*. In the second season episode "Tempus Fugitive," H.G. Wells (Terry Kiser) arrives at *The Daily Planet* on his way home from Earth's utopian 22nd century, a future built by Superman and his descendants. Wells tells Clark Kent (Dean Cain) that he needs gold to recharge his machine and head home before his 22nd century passenger, Tempus (Lane Davies), experiences the un-utopian world of the 1990s. Wells doesn't realize that Tempus is a sociopath who hates his own time and loves the crime and violence of present-day Metropolis. Tempus uses stolen gold to recharge the ship, then forces Wells to fly him back to 1966. That's when Superman's rocket crashed to Earth from Krypton, and Tempus plans to kill him with kryptonite, eliminating Tempus' own utopian time.

Wells leaves the blueprints for his time machine with Superman, who builds a duplicate. Superman and Lois (Teri Hatcher) arrive in 1966, but Superman fades away as baby Kal-El dies. Lois saves Kal, restoring the timeline, then Wells drops Tempus into a 19th century madhouse, just the "violent, hellish dystopia" Tempus wanted to live in. As Lois wasn't supposed to learn Superman's identity yet, Wells erases her and Clark's memories of the event.

Tempus returned to battle Superman, in one episode successfully erasing the Man of Steel from existence. But Wells is able to get a Superman from a parallel world to defeat Tempus and bring "our" Superman back to reality.

CHAPTER THREE

Enjoying the Exotic
Travel from the Present to Other Times

"That's what the present is—it's a little unsatisfying because life is a little unsatisfying."—*Midnight in Paris*

In *The Past Is a Foreign Country*, David Lowenthal says one of the reasons to travel into the past is "enjoying the exotic."[1] The protagonist of a time travel film, and by extension the viewer, gets to witness the wonder of long-gone ages or eras yet to come. You can sail with Blackbeard, hang with Hemingway, risk death by dinosaur, overthrow a tyrant or wallow in nostalgia. Even for involuntary time travelers exiled from their own time, being trapped in the past is often presented as a cool experience, like a tourist trip to Australia or Paris. Although the future in time travel stories is typically dystopian, the lure of the exotic is still present: *Samurai Jack*'s future Earth is a dystopia ruled by the demon Aku, but it's amazing to look at.

One of the first time travel films, *Berkeley Square* (1933) is the most emphatic that time travel is about exile rather than exoticism. Peter Standish (Leslie Howard) is a modern-day man who idealizes the Georgian era as the apex of culture and elegance. He believes that on the anniversary of the day his look-alike ancestor first entered the family home in 1784, they will somehow switch places—and of course, he's right. His views of the past, though, are wrong: people don't bathe more than once a month, they're superstitious and ignorant, and even the Prince of Wales thinks nothing of sneezing snot into his open hand. Despite being an expert on the era, Peter can't fit in. When he entertains people with *bon mots* from later eras, he only despises them for being impressed. After he makes it back to the present, he learns that his ancestor—a man who dreamed of the wonders of the future—was just as horrified by the 1930s (there's more on the movie in chapter nine)

Most of the movies in this chapter take a more upbeat tone.

Meet Famous Figures

The children's film *The Boy and the Pirates* (1960) introduces us to Jimmy (Charles Herbert), a pirate-crazy boy constantly searching the beach for buried treasure. Shortly after finding a strange bottle in the sand, he wishes he could be back in pirate times and presto, he finds himself aboard Blackbeard's (Murvyn Vye) ship. Abu (Joseph Turkel), the genie in the bottle, reveals that after five days of pirate adventures, Jimmy's wish expires

Three. Enjoying the Exotic

Helen (Heather Angel) enchants Lesley Howard in *Berkeley Square* (1933) but she can't reconcile him to "imprisonment for life in this filthy little pig-sty of a world."

and he will have to trade places with Abu. The only way out is to return the bottle to where he found it, and the ship is heading in another direction.

Blackbeard takes Jimmy in as a cabin boy and Jimmy begins to enjoy pirate life, except for that pesky deadline. Eventually Jimmy fakes a treasure map showing a legendary treasure on his home beach. This convinces Blackbeard to change course, and Jimmy makes it to shore with minutes to spare. After planting the bottle, the boy wakes up back in the present, wondering if he dreamed it all.

In *The Three Stooges Meet Hercules* (1962), the Stooges (Larry Fine, Moe Howard, Joe De Rita) are drug store clerks for the loathsome, bullying Dimsal (George N. Neise). Their friend Schuyler (Quinn Redeker), an inventor, is struggling to develop a time machine. The Stooges being the Stooges, they only have to tinker with the machine a few minutes before it hurls them, Schuyler and his girlfriend Diane (Vicki Trickett) back to a Greek battlefield in 900 BC. Their apparently divine materialization changes history, inspiring King Odius (Neise again) to triumph over Ulysses (John Cliff). When the guys realize they've helped the wrong side, they free Ulysses, but Odius' henchman Hercules (Samson Burke) captures them. The tyrant claims Diane as his bride and ships the guys to a slave galley.

Schuyler buffs up so much from his rowing that the Stooges can pass him off as Hercules. Schuyler wins their freedom by defeating a monster—the Stooges help in their unique way—then fights in the arena as Hercules to raise money for the return trip to Ithaca. The guys arrive in time to rescue Diane, overthrow Odius and inspire Hercules to become a hero instead of a thug. As the travelers head back to the present, Odius grabs onto the time machine, but falls off into the middle of a Wild West cowboys-and-Indians battle. Back in the present, the newly confident, muscular Schuyler gives Dimsal his comeuppance.

Cleopatra (1970), an avant-garde anime, opens in the future, as the alien Pasateli scheme to destroy Earth through the "Cleopatra plan." With no idea what that is, security chief Tarabahha (Yoshiro Kato) sends the minds of three agents back to Cleopatra's time to figure it out. They arrive in the midst of Cleopatra's (Chinatsu Nakayama) power struggles with Julius Caesar (Hajime Hana), entering the bodies of the slaves Lybia (Jitsuko Yoshimura) and Ionius (Nobuo Tsukamoto) and the leopard Lupa (Tsubame Yanagiya). There's a lot of scheming, off-the-wall animation (Caesar is a cigar-smoking political boss;

one sequence involves dancers modeled after 19th century French paintings) and multiple sex scenes, before Caesar is stabbed to death. His homosexual heir Octavian rejects Cleopatra and the legendary beauty commits suicide by asp. The agents realize the Cleopatra plan is to seduce and murder Earth's leaders. Armed with that knowledge, they return to their own time and stop the Pasateli scheme before it starts.[2]

In the Soviet hit *Ivan Vasilyevich Changes Occupation* (1973), scientist Shurik Timofeyev (Aleksandr Demyanenko) works on a time machine in his modern-day Moscow apartment. Officious building supervisor Ivan Vasilyevich (Yuri Yakovlev) complains the machine is an energy hog, but Shurik perseveres and opens a gate into the era of Ivan the Terrible (Yakovlev again). The tsar stumbles into the present while Vassilyevich and a burglar, George (Leonid Kuravlyou), fall into the past. A spear from a Tsarist guard smashes the machine.

In the past, George passes off Vasilyevitch as the tsar, though Ivan's stupidity constantly undermines the masquerade. In the present, Tsar Ivan explores the modern world and discovers Alexander's pretty wife Zina (Natalia Seleznyova) is having an affair with Yakin (Mikhail Pugovkin), who's about to break it off. Ivan, greatly taken with Zina, forces Yakin to change his mind to keep Zina happy. Things turn bad in both times: Ivan's army pegs Vasilyevitch as an imposter, and the police lock the tsar up as a lunatic. Alexander repairs his machine and restores everyone to the right era. At the end it appears the whole thing was a dream ... or was it?

The unsuccessful TV pilot *The Time Crystal* (1981) stars Chris Barnes as Bobby, a teenager who receives a pyramid crystal for his birthday. The crystal sends him back to the reign of Pharaoh Akhenaton (Kario Salem). Accepting Bobby as a divine messenger, the pharaoh lets the kid hang out with Akhenaton's brother Tutankhamen (Eric Greene).

It's a lucky break for Tut. Akhenaton has enraged the people by banning all religion except his monotheistic solar faith, and General Horembeb (Vic Tayback) plans to exploit that rage to seize the throne. Horembeb's allies poison Akhenaton, then hypnotize Tut into thinking he's a common slave. Bobby works with Tut's sister Baket (Olivia Barash) to free Tut from the spell. Tut retakes the throne and frees the people to worship the old gods again. Bobby returns home and discovers Baket's modern-day look-alike has moved in next door.

Played by Ken Campbell, *Erasmus Microman* (1988–9) was a mad scientist who dragged two kids (Nicholas Packard, Thea Redmond) along with him to meet history's great scientists, including Archimedes, Galileo and Darwin. In the second season, Microman pursued the villainous Dr. Dark (Lee B. McPlank) across time as he sought to drive the world back into a new dark age. This time the pedantry wasn't about people but inventions such as writing, maps, railroad and computers.[3]

Frankenstein Unbound (1990) opens in the near future, where Dr. Joseph Buchanan (John Hurt) has developed a particle beam for the U.S. military that causes its targets to vanish instantly. Buchanan dismisses the related time slips—people vanishing into other times, or appearing in the present—as an unimportant side effect. After a Mongol horseman attacks Buchanan on his drive home, the scientist and his AI-equipped car get drawn through a time slip to early 19th century Switzerland. Here he meets fellow scientist Victor Frankenstein (Raul Julia) and Mary Godwin (Bridget Fonda), the future Mary Shelley, author of *Frankenstein*. (In the Brian Aldiss source novel, Shelley and Frankenstein existed in separate timelines.)

Frankenstein's servant Justine (Catherine Corman) is on trial for murders committed by Frankenstein's Monster (Nick Brimble). Victor refuses to clear Justine, which would require accepting responsibility for the creature's actions. Buchanan tries unsuccessfully to save the girl from the hangman. Later, he becomes Mary's lover and gives Mary a copy of *Frankenstein*. While she's thrilled at her future success, she refuses to read it before she writes it. Buchanan discovers time has become completely unbound so there's no way back to his own time.

The Monster kidnaps and kills Victor's love Elizabeth (Catherine Rabett), then forces Buchanan to resurrect her using the car's power cells, so that she can become the Monster's bride. Buchanan uses the power cells to create another time slip, plunging him, Victor and the two monsters into an icy future. In the subsequent struggle, Victor and the Bride end up dead; the Creature flees into an underground complex, and Buchanan follows it. The computers recognize and respond to Buchanan, who destroys the Monster with the complex's laser equipment. Buchanan spies an underground city beyond the complex and heads there to learn what the future holds.

In the Canadian television series *Back to Sherwood* (1998), Robyn Hood (Aimée Castle) is a modern-day teen who discovers a magic talisman that sweeps her across time to the era of her ancestor, Robin Hood. The sorceress Brenan (Anik Matern) has captured Robin and Marian for Guy of Gisborne (Larry Day), leaving evil free to triumph. Robyn began traveling back to the past on a regular basis, working with the children of the Merry Men— Alana Dale, Joan Little, Phil Scarlet—to thwart Guy and Brenan.

The Ride (2003) is a surfing film in which arrogant surfing champion Dave Monroe (Scot Davis) drowns in present-day Hawaii and wakes up in 1911. He suffers the usual anachronistic confusion and meets the beautiful Lehua (Mary Paalani). He also meets Duke Kahanamoku (Sean Kaawa), a future Olympic gold medalist credited with introducing surfing to the rest of the world. Duke teaches Dave that surfing isn't about the money, the fame or the babes, it's about the joy of riding the waves, something Dave's forgotten in his climb to the top. Dave learns to love his life in the pre–Internet, pre-monetized surfing past with Duke and Lehua, but when he drowns again he returns to the present. He feels lost until he meets Lehua's great-granddaughter whose stories about Lehua show that the trip really happened.

In *Aladdin and the Adventure of All Time* (2000) we learn that after Aladdin's Arabian Nights adventures, the sorceress Scheherazade captured him and his princess, enslaved the sultan and hid the magic lamp in the present. When shy, book-loving Paige finds the lamp, she wishes Aladdin to her, which saves him from execution. Scheherazade steals the lamp back and hides it in another time, but the kids use her magic "sands of time" to hunt for it. Crossing time, they meet Henry VIII, Blackbeard and Cleopatra, none of whom fit the historical record (Blackbeard is a mild-mannered blond, for instance). Their encounter with the kids changes them. Aladdin and Paige confront Scheherazade in ancient Arabia, where Aladdin's wish turns Scheherazade into the wise, compassionate queen she's supposed to be. Returning to the present, Paige finds she's strong enough to stare down bullies and meets Al, an Arab student who's Aladdin's double.

The Winning Season (2004) shares *The Ride*'s sports nostalgia, in this case for the imagined golden age when pro baseball players worked for next to nothing because they loved the game. (Eliot Asimof's book *Eight Men Out* shows that golden age never existed.)

Joe (Shawn Hatosy), a pre-teen baseball fan, discovers an ultra-rare Honus Wagner cigarette card—a real collectible—in his elderly neighbor's (Kristin Davis) garage. His parents insist Joe give the card back to her, even though selling it would solve the family's money problems. Furious, Joe runs away from them right into 1909, the year Wagner (Matthew Modine) led the Pittsburgh Pirates to a World Series victory over the Detroit Tigers.

Joe meets Wagner and gets his autograph on the card, boosting its value. Even cooler, Joe gets to hang out with the baseball legend and his team. The guys accept that Joe is a time traveler but refuse to believe that 21st century ballplayers have a Hall of Fame and multi-million dollar salaries. Wagner gives Joe tips on batting techniques and self-confidence; Joe thinks he's repaying Wagner by driving his aristocratic girlfriend Mandy (Davis again) away so she won't distract Wagner from the game. After Detroit's Ty Cobb (William Lee Scott) steals the card, Joe agrees to keep Wagner from the next Series game in return for the card back. Joe repents at the last minute and takes the field in Wagner's uniform until his hero can return. They get the card from Cobb afterwards.

Once the series ends, Joe returns to the present. He discovers Mandy is his elderly neighbor, still broken-hearted from losing her man. A repentant Joe gives Mandy the card, which sends her back to 1909 to reunite with Wagner. At Joe's next game, the couple's happy ghosts watch as Joe uses Wagner's training to win.

In Woody Allen's *Midnight in Paris* (2011), Gil Pender (Owen Wilson) is a screenwriter and aspiring novelist visiting Paris with his fiancée Inez (Rachel McAdams). Pender's passion is for the Paris of the 1920s, when Hemingway and other American expats gave the city its artistic golden age. Walking alone at midnight, Gil is startled when a 1920s Peugeot pulls up and the passengers invite him along. Gil ends up hanging with F. Scott and Zelda Fitzgerald (Tom Hiddleston, Alison Pill) before the car returns him to the present. Next midnight, it happens again.

Gil becomes a friend of Hemingway (Corey Stoll), gets literary feedback from Gertrude Stein (Kathy Bates) and falls hard for the enchanting actress Adriana (Marion Cotillard). She finds his devotion to the 1920s amusing, as she thinks the true golden age for Paris was the 1890s "Belle Époque." Gil contemplates staying in the past with her (don't feel sorry for Inez—she's cheating on Gil back in the present) until the night a horse-drawn carriage takes them to the 1890s. After meeting Degas, Toulouse Lautrec and other artists of the era, Adriana decides to stay, even though those greats insist Paris hasn't had an artistic golden age since the Renaissance. Their words make Gil realize there is no golden age, only fantasies that compensate for disappointment about the present. He returns to his own time, breaks up with Inez, and settles down to live and write in Paris.

King Arthur puts in an appearance in a few time travel tales that are not *Connecticut Yankee*. The first was 1992's animated TV series *King Arthur and the Knights of Justice*. By the start of the first episode, evil Morgana (Kathleen Barr) and her Warlords have defeated and imprisoned Arthur and the Round Table, captured Guinevere and besieged Camelot. To set things right, Merlin (Jim Byrnes) summons the modern-day reincarnations of the heroes, quarterback Arthur King (Andrew Kavadas) and the Knights football team. Posing as their past incarnations, the Knights of Justice break the siege and rescue Guinevere. For the rest of the series, they thwarted Morgana's schemes while searching for the talisman that would free the Round Table and take them home.

In *Johnny Mysto Boy Wizard* (1997), Toran Caudell plays Johnny, an inept pre-teen stage magician. When he pesters the drunken conjurer Blackmoor (Russ Tamblyn) for tips, the hack gives Johnny what he pretends is a magical ring. The ring, however, really *is* magic. Johnny's act is a hit until he makes his sister disappear for real.

Searching for an explanation, Johnny and Blackmoor meet an old woman (Pat Crawford Brown) who tells them the ring once belonged to Merlin, and has been passed down in her family for centuries. The ring draws Johnny and Blackmoor back to Camelot, where evil Malfeasor (Michael Ansara) has stolen the ring from Merlin and conquered the kingdom. With the help of young Sprout (Amber Tamblyn) and the power of the ring, the two conjurers infiltrate Malfeasor's castle, where the usurper schemes "to turn all this earth into one rotten corpse." Johnny confronts Malfeasor, but their counterpart rings cancel each other out. Blackmoor finds Excalibur and uses it slay the black mage. Arthur knights the two time travelers and Sprout promises her descendants will hold the ring until it passes to Johnny. Back in the present, Johnny uses his new magic powers to partner with Blackmoor in a hit stage show.

Unusually, *The Excalibur Kid* (1999) shows the influence of T.H. White's *Once and Future King* instead of Malory or Twain: Morgause (Francesca Scorsone) is the villain; Merlin (François Klanfer) is a crotchety old man who lives backwards through time; there's a climactic magical duel between Morgause and Merlin. The protagonist, frustrated teen fencer Zack (Jason McSkimming), dreams of life in Camelot when good and evil were clear and everyone was noble and elegant. Arthur's sister Morgause uses that longing to pull Zack through time and trick him into drawing Excalibur out of the stone, believing King Zack will be easier to control than King Arthur.

Like Peter Standish in *Berkeley Square*, Zack soon becomes disillusioned with Arthurian food and table manners, and misses his old life. Zack works with Merlin on restoring Arthur to the throne but Arthur (Mak Fyfe) balks at the idea of becoming royalty. Eventually Zack's swordsmanship wins Arthur's respect. After they defeat Morgause, Merlin sends Arthur back to pull out the sword before Zack did, restoring history. Once Zack goes home, he forgets his time trip and can't understand why he's suddenly so happy with his life.

Time Trips to Prehistory

It's About Time (1966–67) was a TV sitcom in which a space capsule carrying astronauts Hector (Jack Mullaney) and Mac (Frank Aletter) ruptures the time barrier and lands in the Stone Age. The modern-day men must adapt to prehistoric life with the help of cave people Gronk (Joe E. Ross) and Shad (Imogene Coca) and their tribe. Midway through the one-season run, the astronauts figured out how to return home, bringing Shad, Gronk and their kids with them. The comedy for the rest of the season came from the Stone Age family adapting to the Space Age.[4]

In the anime *Age of the Great Dinosaurs* (1979), Jun (Chikao Otsuka), Remi (Hiroku Suzuki) and Chobi (Ichiro Nagai) are kids horrified by pollution and environmental degradation. A friendly ET gives them a UFO ride back to the age of dinosaurs, where they witness the decline of the saurians and the rise of humanity. A lone T. rex survives into human prehistory, but Chobi kills it to save a woman. Jun wonders if this proves man's destruction of nature is inevitable.[5]

In *Prehistoric Women* (1967), safari guide David (Michael Latimer) foolishly trespasses into the Land of the White Rhinoceros. The natives sentence him to death, but when he touches their rhino idol, a path opens into the past. David meets Saria (Edina Ronay), a blonde fleeing brunette Amazons led by the tyrannical Kari (Martine Beswick). Kari falls into instant lust for David, but he's repulsed by how brutally she treats her fair-haired slaves. Kari justifies her cruelty as payback for the way the blond tribe treated her before she led a slave uprising.

Saria asks David to work for the counter-revolution so he agrees to become Kari's lover. When he prepares to bed the queen, Saria, having fallen for him, protests and tells Kari what David really thinks of her. That gets David sentenced to the slave dungeons, only to have him rouse the slaves for a revolt against the brunette tyranny. The battle ends when the white rhinoceros appears and kills Kari. David returns to the present, where the rhino idol shatters, winning David his freedom. Back at camp, he discovers his new client's daughter is Saria's double.

Dinosaur Valley Girls (1997) is a mind-numbingly sexploitative film that might pass for a parody except it's completely unfunny. A Stone Age totem hurls martial arts film star Tony Markham (Jeff Rector) to the era in which dinosaurs co-existed with large-breasted, bikini-clad (except when they're topless) women harassed by a belligerent tribe of men. Neither tribe seems to understand sex but Tony soon explains it to the women, particularly Hea-Thor (Denise Ames). After some inter-tribal battles and dinosaur attacks, the two tribes get the whole sex thing figured out and everyone lives happily ever after.

Prehistoric Park (2006) was a follow-up to the docudrama series *Walking with Dinosaurs* in which a paleontologist travels through time to see dinosaurs in the wild. In this series, naturalist Nigel Marven begins bringing extinct life from the past to a zoo in the present—for example, capturing a T. rex before an asteroid strikes the Earth and wipes out the dinosaurs. The series looked at the causes of extinction events and the challenges of running a zoo stocked with prehistoric life.

In *100 Million BC* (2008), military researcher Frank Reno (Michael Gross) tells a Marine search-and-rescue team that years ago, his time travel experiments (based on the *Philadelphia Experiment* technology described in chapter four) stranded a Marine platoon in 70 million BC, including Frank's brother Erik (Christopher Atkins). Having perfected his technology, Frank leads the Marines into the past to bring the first team home. After multiple fights with dinosaurs, the two groups meet up and Frank sends everyone home, staying behind to seal the portal.

The seal doesn't work. A dinosaur appears in present-day LA, smashing buildings and shrugging off military ordnance. It's about to wipe out the Marines when young Frank (Dustin Harnish) materializes from 1950. It turns out Frank made it across time to contact his younger self and explain how to perfect the time machine. Young Frank sends the dinosaur home, then takes the Marines back to their own time, right after their original trip. Erik, who's fallen in love with one of their rescuers, stays in the present and seals the wormhole for good.

The time travelers of *Terra Nova* (2011) come from 2149, a dystopian, polluted, overpopulated world. When science discovers a wormhole 31 million years into the past, it begins sending volunteers on a one-way trip to "Terra Nova," a colony where humanity has the chance to start fresh. As Jim and Elizabeth Shannon (Jason O'Mara, Shelley Conn) discover after making the trip, Terra Nova isn't utopia: along with dinosaur attacks, personal conflict and disease, they have to cope with the Sixers, a rogue group from the sixth wave of colonists, living outside Terra Nova.

It turns out the Sixers are allied with Lucas (Ashley Zukerman), the embittered son of Terra Nova's leader Taylor (Stephen Lang). A technical genius, Lucas has figured out how to open a return gate to 2149. His backers send the Phoenix strike force to take over Terra Nova, then begin mining the area for ore to ship back to the future. Taylor, Jim and the other colonists realize the only way to choke off Lucas' supply of soldiers is to shut down the time gate so nobody else can come through. They succeed, but Lucas and Phoenix escape into the wilderness. In the final episode, Taylor and Jim discover, to their astonishment, that Phoenix have unearthed a ship's figurehead from the 1800s somewhere in the wilderness.

Irresponsible pre-teen Ernie (Pamela Adlon) goes *Back to the Jurassic* (2012)—actually the Cretaceous—when he visits his friend Max (Yuri Lowenthal) and spills soda on Max's father's (Fred Tatasciore) time machine. The machine swaps the boys and Ernie's sister Julia (Tara Strong) with a dinosaur egg belonging to the T. rex Tyra (Melanie Griffith), who assumes they're her new hatchlings. Tyra and the other dinosaurs are intelligent, though they and the kids don't share a common language.

Ernie has no wish to leave the awesome dinosaur age to return to his strict mother Sue (Jane Lynch) so he sabotages the time machine. That proves a mistake, as the monstrous Sarco brothers (William and Stephen Baldwin) kidnap the kids to their volcanic lair, hoping to lure Tyra there and then take over the valley. She shows up, the Sarcos take her down, and though Ernie fixes the time machine the kids won't abandon Tyra to save themselves. Sue and Max's dad, despite having to care for Tyra's real baby, manage to build a new time machine. They arrive in the past, distracting the Sarcos long enough for Tyra to beat them. Everyone returns to their home time.

The Classical World

Roman Scandals (1933) stars Eddie Cantor as Eddie, an amiable handyman in the U.S. community of West Rome. When he stands up to the wealthy Cooper (Willard Robertson), a hypocrite who plans to evict poor homeowners to line his own pocket, the police throw Eddie out of town. He gets hit on the head and dreams he's been transported back to ancient Rome, where he helps the heroic Josephus (David Manners) against the corrupt emperor Valerius (Edward Arnold). When he wakes up back in the present, he saves the homeowners by presenting evidence of Cooper's crooked dealings.

The 1944 British film *Fiddler's Three* has the sailor Tommy (Tommy Trinder), the Professor (Sonnie Hale) and Nora (Elisabeth Welch) hit by lightning at Stonehenge and hurled back to Nero's Rome. They get caught up in a scheme by the emperor (Francis L. Sullivan) and his scheming wife Poppaea (Frances Day) to murder Nero's mother and seize her fortune. Complications include Tommy dressing up as Carmen Miranda, Poppaea hitting on Tommy and the Professor and Tommy posing as prophets to escape death.

Norman's Awesome Experience (1987) is more tedious than awesome, as a mad scientist's experiment hurls physicist Norman (Tom McCamus), manipulative model Erika (Laurie

Paton) and her arrogant photographer Umberto (Jacques Lussier) to a rural village in the Roman era. Norman pulls a Connecticut Yankee, introducing soap, a telescope, fireworks and printing to the age, as well as falling in love with pretty Felix (Gabriela Salos). When the Romans attack, Norman holds them back until he and the villagers can escape in hot air balloons. They fly off and found Normandy, while Erika and Umberto, who sided with the invaders, end up Roman slaves.

Atlantis (2013–15) has modern-day Jason (Jack Donnelly) sliding through an underwater gate into a parallel world identical to the legendary lost continent. Jason becomes embroiled in two seasons of stock swashbuckling adventures, working with his friends Hercules (Mark Addy) and Pythagoras (Robert Emms) against scheming Queen Pasiphae (Sarah Parish). It turns out Jason is Pasiphae's son, taken to our world as a baby, but it doesn't make them get along any better.

The Arabian Nights

Eddie Cantor goes back in time again as Aloysius Babson in *Ali Baba Goes to Town* (1937). Pain meds leave Babson dreaming that he's been transported to Baghdad as "Ali Baba's son." The people are starving and ready to revolt, but Al saves the sultan's rule by launching programs based on the U.S. New Deal. Treacherous Prince Musah (Douglass Dumbrille) tries to seize the kingdom, but Al's cunning and his crazy antics stymie the usurper. Then Al wakes up back in the present.[6]

In the animated *Shazzan* (1967–68), American siblings Chuck (Jerry Dexter) and Nancy (Janet Waldo) discover two halves of an ancient ring with the word Shazzan written on the metal. When they join the halves together, it transports them back to the Arabian Nights and summons the genie Shazzan (Barney Phillips) to meet them. Shazzan tells the kids the only way home is to deliver his ring to its original owner, the Wizard of the Seventh Mountain. The search leads the two kids into confrontations with multiple evil tyrants and sorcerers, but Shazzan's power invariably saves the day.

Teens Yumi (Kumiko Nishihara) and Hayato (Yuuji Mitsuya) were stranded in Arabia in the anime *Time Travel Tondekeman* (1989–90). Tondekeman (Shigeru Chiba) is a kettle equipped with artificial intelligence and time travel capability. When the kids activate it, it drops them in the Arabian Nights, then falls into the clutches of the villainous Abdullah (Junpei Takiguchi). Abdullah uses Tondekeman to begin exploring and looting in other times. Hayato and Yumi, in cahoots with Prince Dandan (Akira Kamiya) and Princess Shalala (Rei Sakuma), work to stop him, whether that means visiting the Trojan War or Leonardo da Vinci's studio. In every age, their ultimate goal is to recover Tondekeman and return home.

A Kid in Aladdin's Palace (1997) was the sequel to *A Kid in King Arthur's Court* (see chapter one). After Cal (Thomas Ian Nicholas) accidentally frees Aladdin's genie (Taylor Negron), the djinn sends Cal back to the Arabian Nights. The usurper Luxor (James Faulkner) has placed Aladdin (Aharon Ipalé) in enchanted sleep and now seeks the lamp to secure his power. Joining forces with the thief Ali Baba (Nicholas Irons) and Aladdin's daughter Sheherezade (Rhona Mitra), Cal races to beat Luxor to the lamp. He succeeds, but Luxor steals it and sentences Sheherezade to death. Ali Baba and Calvin save her and defeat Luxor in the best sword-and-sandal style, then wake Aladdin. Cal returns to the present, whereupon Sheherezade uses the genie's power to join him.

Ancient China

Jason (Michael Angarano), the protagonist of *The Forbidden Kingdom* (2008), is a Boston teen obsessed with kung fu films. A local tough, Lupo (Morgan Benoit), pressures Jason into helping them rob the kindly old merchant Hop (Jackie Chan). In the course of the robbery, Lupo shoots Hop, then decides to kill Jason, a potential witness. An old staff in Hop's shop transports Jason back to ancient China. After Jason endures the usual anachronistic shocks, drunken martial artist Lu Yan (Chan again) tells the boy he must return the staff to the legendary Monkey King (Jet Li), imprisoned 500 years ago by the evil Jade Warlord (Collin Chou). A silent monk (Li again) and Golden Sparrow (Liu Yifei), who seeks revenge on the warlord, join the quest. In their journey, Jason learns martial arts, falls for Golden Sparrow and gains self-confidence.

When enemy warriors injure Lu Yan, Jason offers to trade the staff for Jade Warlord's immortality elixir. Jade Warlord double-crosses him, but Jason's friends get the elixir to Lu Yan, restoring him. In the subsequent battle, Jason frees the Monkey King, Jade Warlord kills Golden Sparrow and Jason destroys Jade Warlord. Returning home with new confidence and skills, Jason clobbers Lupo, then discovers Hop is actually Lu Yan, immortal and unharmed. Heading home, Jason meets Golden Sparrow's look-alike, which lets him skip the whole grieving process for his dead lover.

The Middle Ages

In *The Undead* (1957) hooker Diana (Pamela Duncan) reluctantly allows scientist Quintus (Val Dufour) and his former mentor (Maurice Manson) to place her under hypnosis so that she can recall her past lives. She flashes back to her life as Helene (Duncan again), framed as a witch and condemned to die because a real witch, Livia (Allison Hayes), wants Helene's lover Pendragon (Richard Garland) for herself. Diana prompts Helene to escape by seducing, then knocking out her jailer, after which Diana's mind merges into Helene's.

Quintus realizes that if Helene doesn't die when history says, it will erase all her future incarnations, including Diana. He uses the Diana-Helene mind-link to project himself physically into the past and tries to fix things. When Helene learns of the women who will never be born if she lives, she voluntarily goes to her death. Diana wakes up in the present, transformed to a better person by her life as Helene. Quintus, however, can't come back: With Helene dead, the mind-link is gone and he has no way out of the past.

In 1383 at the beginning of *Medieval Park* (1999), the would-be usurper Raykin (Marc Robinson) and his sorcerer Eurik (Claudiu Trandafir) narrowly escape the king's dungeons. Eurik casts a spell on the king's crest at the castle gate, allowing them to return across time to fight again. Now they have infinite time to prepare their next strike.

When a present-day theme park builds an exact duplicate of the castle, Eurik's magic merges the real and fake castles (it's unclear what Raykin gains by this). Four teenage park visitors get trapped in the castle along with a news crew covering the grand opening. Tediously incredulous at having time jumped, the kids free the sorcerer Percival (Paul Soles) from the dungeon and he explains everything. Together they thwart Raykin's plans, and then the time travelers return to the present.

Black Knight (2001) stars Martin Lawrence as Jamal Walker, an employee at a medieval-themed amusement park. A medallion found in the moat transports him back to the reign of corrupt King Leo (Kevin Conway); Jamal assumes everything he sees is an elaborate reenactment until he sees someone beheaded. Even so, when a lucky break makes him the king's right-hand man, Jamal seizes the chance for wealth and luxury. Victoria (Marsha Thomason), an attractive servant secretly working with a rebel movement, can't change his mind despite their mutual attraction.

Jamal's relationship with Leo soon turns sour and the time traveler is sentenced to death. After Victoria saves him, Jamal decides to use the medallion to return home, then decides it's time to stop taking the easy path. Assuming the role of the legendary Black Knight, he helps overthrow the tyrant. Jamal wakes up back in the present and meets Victoria's double, but gets transported back to ancient Rome when he falls into the moat again. (As he does it without the medallion, perhaps the time trip really was just a dream.)

Timeline (2003) opens with a dying man in the present gasping out the word "Castlegard." This is the location of an archaeological dig in France, financed by IT billionaire Doniger (David Thewlis), who's consistently able to direct archaeologist Johnston (Billy Connolly) to the best places to unearth artifacts. After a visit to Doniger, Johnston vanishes. His son Chris (Paul Walker), Johnston's assistant Marek (Gerard Butler) and the other diggers find evidence of Johnston's presence in the 14th century. When Chris confronts Doniger, the billionaire reveals his company's experimental teleporter opened a wormhole into 1357; Johnston went through, but didn't return. Chris and the other archaeologists go through the wormhole to rescue Johnston, but they're ambushed on arrival, and their return device is damaged.

Castlegard is English-held, French-besieged and the travelers are caught up in the war. Johnston has been imprisoned in the castle to make Greek fire (an astounding feat as the formula has been lost for centuries). Marek saves French noblewoman Claire (Anna Friel), which may change history as her death inspired the French to retake Castlegard. Ultimately the French take the castle. Marek stays in the past with Claire (concerns about changing history are conveniently forgotten), everyone else returns to the present and a freak wormhole accident hurls Doniger back to Castlegard to die.

Mysterious Museum (1999) begins in 1632 as the evil magus Falco (Adrian Neil) plots to obtain the powerful Polaris Jewel from a nearby village. The good wizard Darbin (Eugen Cristea) uses the jewel first, imprisoning Falco and his court in a painting. Darbin also puts the village into a second painting, for no discernible reason besides plot requirements.

In the present, siblings Kim, Ben and Casey (Brianna Brown, A.J. Trauth, Megan Lusk) visit a museum holding the paintings. During a storm, Ben and Kim are sucked into the village in the past, where they discover that Falco and his men are free and hunting the jewel. Casey helps them by drawing a wizard, then using the painting's magic to materialize the "Great M" (John Duerler) in the village. The Great M tells Ben that only the Polaris Jewel can send the kids home, and only if they use it before the storm ends. Further upping the stakes, Ben learns that Falco will use the jewel to conquer the 1600s, thereby rewriting history. Ben captures the jewel and re-imprisons Falco. The siblings return to the present, leaving the Great M to guard the jewel and the village.

In the Name of the King 2: Two Worlds (2011) is the sequel to a 2007 non-time travel fantasy film. Granger (Dolph Lundgren), a military veteran, is stunned when dark-clad assassins pop out of a time portal and try to kill him. Another time traveler, Elianna (Natalia Guslistaya), drags Granger through the gate into medieval times. Granger dodges more assassins—Elianna dies—and meets King Raven (Lochlyn Munro). The king sends him with the sorceress Manhatten (Natassia Malthe) to kill the Dark Mother (Christina Jastrzembska), a sorceress spreading plague through the kingdom. When Granger reaches her, he learns that Raven unleashed the plague to seize the throne. Granger is the true heir, hidden in the future to save him from Raven. Granger leads the Dark Mother's troops to defeat Raven's army, then returns home. Raven follows, seeking vengeance, but Granger kills him.

The third film in the series, subtitled *The Last Mission* (2014), follows a similar template. The protagonist Hazen (Dominic Purcell) is a mercenary carrying out a kidnapping in Bulgaria for the malevolent Avaylo (Marian Valev). He gets pulled back to medieval Bulgaria where Avaylo's ancestor Tervin (Valev again) tyrannizes the kingdom through his control of a dragon. Hazen joins the forces fighting Tervin, kills the tyrant, then returns to the present, followed by the dragon. The dragon conveniently kills Avaylo's mob and flies off; Hazen returns the kidnap victims to their family.

Feudal Japan

The samurai era of Japan has been a popular time travel destination for both U.S. and Japanese films. In *GI Samurai* (1979), a time slip drops Lt. Iba (Sonny Chiba) and his troops in the feudal era. They decide to get home by distorting history to the point the universe will have to yank them back to the present to preserve the timeline. To that end, they wage aggressive war on the rest of the nation, with breaks for infighting and womanizing. Some of the soldiers draw up a plan to ensure their return, but Iba rejects it: he's decided to stay in the war-torn era rather than return to the peaceful present. In the next battle, one of Iba's men frags him, after which the samurai massacre the modern troops, restoring history.

Fire Tripper (1985) effectively adapts one of manga artist Rumiko Takahashi's stories. In 15th-century Japan, a toddler, Suzuko (Sumi Shimamoto), vanishes from a burning cottage and reappears in the present. A couple adopts her and she forgets her past. Years later, after she and her friend Shu (Mayumi Tanaka) are caught in an explosion, Suzuko wakes in feudal Japan again, in a village besieged by bandits. The warrior Shukumaru (Yuu Mizushima) is the village defender, accompanied by his adopted sister Suzu. It turns out that Shukumaru is Shu, who arrived ten years earlier in the past, and Suzu is young Suzuko. When the bandits attack, Suzuku and Shukumaru take refuge in the future. Shu feels, however, that his duty lies in protecting the village, so they return to the past together and marry.

In *Teenage Mutant Ninja Turtles III* (1993), reporter April O'Neal (Paige Turco), the Turtles' confidante, handles an ancient Japanese scepter "simultaneously" with the 1603 samurai Kenshin (Henry Hayashi). The scepter trades them across time, leaving April helpless in the hands of Kenshin's warlord father Norinaga (Sab Shimono) and his ally, the

English mercenary Walker (Stuart Wilson). The Turtles use the scepter to follow April into the past, but lose it after they arrive. With 60 hours before they become trapped in the past, they join forces with Kenshin's lover, the rebel Mitsu (Vivian Wu). They win, even against Walker's Western artillery, and use the scepter to return with April to the present.

The anime *Inuyasha* (2000–04) begins when Kagome (Satsuki Yukino), a modern-day schoolgirl, falls down a well in her family's yard and emerges centuries in the past. Her arrival frees the half-demon Inuyasha (Kappei Yamaguchi), imprisoned years ago by his lover, Kagome's ancestor Kikyo (Noriko Hidaka), due to the schemes of the jealous man-demon Naraku (Toshihiko Nakajima). Kagome's arrival shatters the mystical Shikon Jewel Kikyo once guarded. Now Kagome and Inuyasha must race Naraku to recover the powerful shards. That struggle, with other menaces mixed in, kept the adventures going for 167 episodes, four movies and a sequel series, *Inuyasha: The Final Act* (2012).

In the final episode of *The Final Act*, the jewel spirits trap Kagome and Naraku within the assembled crystal where they will battle for eternity unless Kagome can find the wish that frees them. She does, by wishing the jewel out of existence, freeing her and sending Naraku to his rest. Kagome returns to the present, graduates from high school, then returns to the past to marry Inuyasha and study to become a priestess.

Haruka: Beyond the Stream of Time (2004) was one of several anime based on the same-name videogame. Schoolgirl Akane (Tomoko Kawakami) and her best friends—fiery Tenma (Tomokazu Seki) and insecure Shimon (Kouki Miyata)—are pulled back through time to ancient Japan. Akane is a chosen one, destined to be priestess of the dragon god; her guy friends are among the men who will serve as her Eight Guardians. Their mission is to find the magic talismans that will drive back the Oni clan, waging war on the government under the leadership of ruthless Akuram (Ryotaro Okiayu). After lots of moping and battles, Akane and her friends learn the Oni are victims of oppression, as much sinned against as sinning (unusual as most time travelers figure out instantly who the good guys are). Akane's destiny is to bring peace, not victory, and in the final episode, she succeeds. Akane also realizes she loves one of her companions, but the series ends without revealing which.

The ancient Japan of *Battle Girls: Time Paradox* (2011) is entirely populated by women. (This is rationalized as a parallel timeline, though the series never does explain how humanity reproduces.) While visiting an abandoned Shinto shrine, schoolgirl Hideyoshi (Rina Hidaka) is sucked back into the feudal era and becomes a retainer to the warlord Nobunaga (Megumi Toyoguchi). The general is determined to obtain the pieces of a magical crimson armor that will give its wearer the power to conquer Japan, but when she obtains it, Masamune (Yuka Hirata), Hideyoshi's teacher in the present, steals it.

Masamune tells Hideyoshi that uniting Japan under her clan, as her ancestors tried and failed to do, will fix all the problems of the centuries to follow. Instead the ruthless warlord Uesuhi Kenshin (Mariya Ise) steals the armor and becomes corrupted by its power. Nobunaga and her rivals join forces to defeat Kenshin, which makes the general and Masamune see they can never achieve unity through brute force. Masamune and Hideyoshi return to the present.

The Ambition of Oda Nobuna (2012) works a variation on the same premise. In this case the time traveler is a male, high schooler Yoshiharu (Takuya Eguchi), tossed back to a past where first-born women can lead their clans equally with men. Nobuna (Kanae Itou), the equivalent of Nobunaga, drafts Yoshiharu into her service. From that point the story is a fairly straight historical adventure, with Yoshiharu becoming the general's right hand—her lover in the final episode—as Nobuna fulfills her destiny and triumphs over various scheming rivals.

Like *Haruka*, the anime *Legend of the Millenium Dragon* (2011) acknowledges that time travelers can't always identify the good and bad guys of other eras. Jun Tendo (Kensho Ono), a shy schoolboy, is drawn back to the Hei'an period of Japan by the noble Gen'un (Nakamura Shidō II). Gen'un explains that the only way to save his city from the warlike Oni is for Jun to tap the power of his aristocratic bloodline by awakening and binding the water dragon Oroshi.

Jun awakens Oroshi, then meets Mizuha (Satomi Ishihara), an Oni girl his own age. The other Oni tell him the region was peaceful until the nobles drove the Oni off their land to build the city. The Oni also claim that Jun's power stems from their blood, not the nobility. Jun backs out of the war, but the power-hungry Gen'un unleashes sorcery against the Oni. Jun and Mizuha lead Oroshi to destroy Gen'un, which makes it possible to negotiate peace. Jun returns to the present, filled with new confidence.

Elizabethan England

In *Time Flies* (1944), British hustler Tommy (Tommy Handley) convinces his friend Bill Barton (George Moon) to invest $10,000 in Prof. McAndrew's (Felix Aylmer) time machine. While the professor shows his "time ball" to Bill and his skeptical wife Susie (Evelyn Dall), Tommy accidentally launches it on a time jump to the late 1500s. When the group takes a look around London, McAndrew "predicts" Elizabeth's (Olga Lindo) future death, which gets him sent to the Tower of London for treason. As the time ball can't fly home without him repairing it, Tommy wins over the queen by borrowing Sir Walter Raleigh's (Leslie Bradley) cloak to cover some mud she's about to walk over.

Tommy hopes to buy McAndrew's freedom by selling off rights to North America, which he claims to own. The Bartons pose as John Smith and Pocahontas with the same plan. The trio frees the professor, but the queen condemns them as witches to be burned at the stake. Instead, the travelers fly home once McAndrew makes the needed repairs. However they land three months late, which has the effect of temporarily turning them invisible.

Penelope Taberner (Sophie Thompson) becomes *A Traveller in Time* (1978) while visiting her relatives' Derbyshire farm. Penelope slips back in time to find herself in the Babington family's farmhouse on the same land, four centuries earlier. Passionate supporters of Elizabeth's imprisoned sister Mary of Scotland, the Babingtons plan to free her through a secret tunnel, then help her overthrow Elizabeth. Penelope knows the Babingtons will be captured and condemned as traitors, but she hopes to save them, even though some members of the family think she's a spy.[7]

The 1600s

In *Time Riders* (1991), motorcycle-riding scientist B.B. Miller (Haydn Gwynne) works on a time travel device in defiance of her skeptical superior, Crow (Clive Merrison). She brings an orphan boy, Ben (Kenneth Hall), forward from 1834, and Crow decides to take credit for it—once he's dissected and analyzed the boy to confirm it's true. Miller quickly adapts her time machine to fit on her motorcycle, takes Ben and drives with him into the past. Unfortunately they ride into 1645 and the English Civil War, so the Puritans who capture the duo assume they're witches. After multiple escapes from near-death and imprisonment, Miller and Ben recover the motorcycle and ride back to the present. They arrive slightly before Miller's initial experiment, so Miller decides not to undertake it. She then passes Ben off to Crow as her orphan nephew come to stay with her.

The title of *Lurid Tales: The Castle Queen* (1997) is wildly inaccurate as the sex is sedate and mostly off-screen. When college student Tom (Shannon Dow Smith) enters a video arcade, a beautiful woman straps him into a chair. Presto, he's on the estate of Lady Dorset (Kim Dawson) and her siblings Amy (Christi Harris) and Miranda (Betsy Lynn George). In the aftermath of the English Civil War, many powerful people would like to seize the Dorset land. The determined Amy, with Tom's help, launches projects ranging from prostitution to horse breeding to keep the family afloat and build their influence with the rich and powerful. Tom enjoys having sex with all three sisters until he's hung for a false charge of highway robbery. He wakes up in the arcade and goes back to his normal life.

The Pirates Who Didn't Do Anything (2008) is one of the *Veggie Tales* series of evangelical Christian children's movies in which the characters are anthropomorphic vegetables. Here, three busboys at a pirate-themed restaurant secretly feel that becoming real pirates would earn them some respect. They're magically transported back to the 1600s, where cruel Captain Robert the Terrible (Cam Clarke) has kidnapped Prince Alex (Yuri Lowenthal) as the first step to seizing the kingdom. The busboys find the courage within themselves to help Princess Eloise (Laura Gerow) rescue her brother and defeat Robert. When they return to the present, Robert follows. By defeating him in front of their co-workers, family and friends, the trio finally get the respect they want.

Georgian England

The Georgian House (1976) is a lost British TV series (only three episodes survive) in which students Dan (Spencer Banks) and Abbie (Adrienne Byrne) takes summer jobs at a museum in what was once the Georgian home of the wealthy Leadbetters. An African carving magically draws the students back to 1772, where Abbie finds herself taken for a visiting Leadbetter relative while Dan is a kitchen boy. The cause is Ngo (Brinsley Forde), a slave in danger of being sent back to the hell of England's Caribbean sugar plantations. Using his powers, Ngo brought Dan and Abbie to the past to help him return to Sierra Leone, after which he'll send them home. Abbie is eager to help; Dan's only desire is to return to the present. Together they begin working with Ngo, while trying to hide the truth about themselves from everyone else.[8]

The 1800s

Time Is the Enemy (1958) is another lost British TV show. All that's known about it is that a man (Clifford Elkin) discovers that a door in his house leads back to 1808 London, where he's accused of being a spy for Napoleon.[9] It's an exception in having an adult time traveler, as most of the protagonists in this section are children or teens.

For example, there's *The Amazing Mr. Blunden* (1972). This film opens in 1918, when solicitor Blunden (Laurence Naismith) arranges for widowed Mrs. Allen (Dorothy Allison) to become caretaker on an old estate, living there with her children Jim and Lucy (Garry Miller, Lynne Frederick). The kids encounter what they think are ghosts, but are actually time traveling orphans from 1818, Sara Latimer (Rosalyn Landor) and her brother Georgie (Marc Granger). Blunden himself is a ghost, seeking to atone for failing to help the Latimers.

The kids need help because their guardian's mother-in-law, Mrs. Wickens (Diana Dors), wants to kill them for their sizable inheritance. The kids realize her intentions, but none of the adults, including Blunden, believes them. Guided by Blunden, Jim and Lucy use the Latimers' potion to go back in time. Invisible to adults, they save Sara and Georgie. When the Allens return to the present, they discover Blunden's former legal firm has unearthed evidence the Allens descend from the Latimers. That gives Mrs. Allen title to the estate as well as a cash inheritance.

The Time Travelers (1976) was an unsuccessful Irwin Allen pilot for a series centered on a federal time travel project. Unlike Allen's *The Time Tunnel*, the tech works perfectly, which is a good thing for pathologist Clinton Earnshaw (Sam Groom): He's fighting a deadly plague threatening New Orleans and the only known cure was lost in the 1871 Chicago fire. Adams (Tom Hallick), a federal agent, escorts Earnshaw back through the time gate to find the cure.

The two men work with Chicago's Dr. Henderson (Richard Basehart) to fight the disease, and Earnshaw falls in love with Henderson's niece Jane (Trish Stewart). It begins to look like history is wrong and Henderson never found a cure. Then Earnshaw discovers a fungus in Henderson's homemade wine that generates a miracle antibiotic. Earnshaw tells Adams to take the wine to the present while he stays in the past with Jane, but she dies in the Chicago fire. Earnshaw returns to the present, heartbroken, but after the antibiotic stops the plague, Earnshaw signs on with the time project.

Moondial (1988) protagonist Minty (Siri Neal) no sooner goes to visit her elderly aunt (Valerie Lush) than her mum (Joanna Dunham) is involved in a car crash. Terrified that her comatose mother will die, Minty aimlessly wanders the grounds of a nearby manor house. She discovers a sundial that can open a gate to the 19th century, where she meets consumptive kitchen boy Tom (Tony Sands). Minty and Tom learn they've both seen another child, Sarah (Helena Avellano), who lives in the 1700s. The birthmark on Sarah's face makes her a target for abusive adults and bullying kids, so Tom and Minty take Sarah away with them. Back in the present, Minty watches the kids' ghosts go off together.

Brother Future (1991) stars Phill Lewis as TJ, a street hustler and cynic with no interest in black history until a car accident sends him to 1822 Charleston. Slave hunters seize TJ and sell him as a runaway, giving him a crash course in the horrors of slavery. TJ fights back in little ways, such as teaching a fellow slave, Josiah (Michael Burgess), to read, but a clairvoyant tells him he'll only go home when he does something truly noble. That moment comes when Josiah and his love Caroline (Akosua Busia) are caught up in Denmark Vesey's (Carl Lumbly) slave revolt. When the authorities arrest the conspirators, TJ sacrifices his life to get Josiah and Caroline to safety. He wakes up back home, inspired by Vesey's heroism to see that there are higher goals in life than self-interest.

The Ruby Ring (1997) opens with Lucy McLaughlin (Emily Hamilton) having the worst birthday ever: Her father's lost his job and so they're moving in with Emily's grandmother, leaving not only their home but Em's beloved horse. Granny (Jan Moffat) gives Emily a family heirloom, a magical ruby ring which can grant one wish. Emily wishes she were living in a big house with lots of servants and beautiful horses—and finds herself in nearby Langley Castle in 1896, as the new maid. Emily has only 24 hours to take her wish back, and it turns out she's lost the ring. With the help of Robert Langley (Christien Anholt), who finds the unconventional, rebellious servant quite charming, Emily hunts the ring as it passes between family members and ultimately into the hands of thieving groom Collins (Rutger Hauer). By the time Emily and Robert recover the ring, they've fallen in love, but Emily doesn't want to stay. She returns home, newly appreciative of how good her life is. And she visits Langley Castle and meets Robert's descendant (Anholt).

In *Tom's Midnight Garden* (1999), based on a Philippa Pearce book, Tom Long (Anthony Way) is staying with his aunt and uncle (Greta Scacchi, James Wilby) after his brother comes down with the measles. The stay looks to be miserable as the couple's apartment building—a remodeled manor house—has no other children and nowhere to play, and the elderly neighbor upstairs (Joan Plowright) frowns on noise. On the plus side, Tom discovers that when the grandfather clock in the hall strikes 13 in the dead of night, he can walk out of the building into the old mansion's Victorian garden, which is built over in the present. He's invisible to everyone except the lonely orphan Hatty (Florence Hoath); Tom and Hatty become friends, though she resents that from her perspective, Tom's nightly trips are months apart.

As Hatty grows up, she finds true love and eventually stops seeing Tom. In the present it turns out the upstairs neighbor is the aged Hatty, whose dreams of her youth drew Tom back in time with her. They talk about their lives since they last saw each other and the film ends with an adult, married Tom (Nigel Le Vaillant) watching wreckers demolish the apartment building. The BBC also serialized the story in a six-part 1989 adaptation and shorter versions in 1968 and 1974.

In *Time at the Top* (1999), young Susan (Elisha Cuthbert) accidentally triggers her blind neighbor's time travel device, turning their apartment building elevator into a time machine. It lets Susan out in 1881, where she meets fatherless young Victoria Walker (Gabrielle Boni), who fears that her impoverished mother Nora (Lynne Adams) is being romanced by a fortune hunter. Susan saves the family by letting the suitor discover there's no fortune to be had, which drives him away.

Susan and Victoria try various schemes to fix the Walker finances, from digging up a cache of gold coins (Susan knows where they'll be discovered in her own time) and going back to switch the late Mr. Walker's bad investments into 1800s growth stocks. After the Walkers become rich, Susan convinces her father (Timothy Busfield) to relocate to 1881—an easy decision when it turns out Nora is his late wife's exact double.

From Time to Time (2009) starts in 1944 where young Tolly Oldknow (Alex Etel) has gone to stay at his family's country estate, Green Knowe. (The movie is based on one of Lucy M. Boston's Green Knowe books.) Green Knowe is touched by the supernatural, and Tolly keeps finding himself a disembodied spirit in the past, visiting blind Susan (Eliza Bennett) and her best friend Jacob (Kwayedza Kureya) in the early 1800s. Between visits, Tolly's Granny (Maggie Smith) fills in the history of Susan and Jacob, and Tolly solves one family legend—a mysterious magical light is actually a flashlight he dropped in the past. Eventually Granny's stories inspire Tolly to find a lost family fortune, which saves Granny from having to sell Green Knowe.

In *Mary Shelley's Frankenhole* (2010–12), Castle Frankenstein is the nexus of a network of wormholes, the result of Victor Frankenstein's (Jeff Bryan Davis) new money-making endeavor. With the "frankenholes" stretching throughout time and space, anyone who needs the doctor's services can reach him. In the first episode, President Johnson goes back in time to have his brain placed in President Kennedy's resurrected body (Johnson figures he'll get laid more). In another episode, John Belushi's handler brings him to the lab so Frankenstein can immunize the actor against overdosing on drugs and booze. Unfortunately, Belushi seizes upon a vial of Dr. Jekyll's potion, drinks it and transforms into his less talented brother Jim. Dr. Moreau, Thomas Jefferson and Jesus all put in appearances over the two-season run.

The Lost Medallion: The Adventures of Billy Stone (2013) is a story that narrator Daniel (Alex Kendrick) tells to despondent residents of a children's foster home. Billy (Billy Unger), an archaeologist's son, and his best friend Allie (Sammi Hanratty) discover a valuable ancient medallion, drawing the attention of some crooks. When a panicked Billy wishes this had never happened, the medallion's magic sends him and Allie 200 years into the past. The kids help Prince Huko (Jansen Panettiere) save his kingdom from a usurper, after which Huko returns the kids to the present. History has changed and the thieves are now respectable archaeologists. Daniel tells the children that this shows that all you need for success is to trust in God's love.

The Old West

Timerider: The Adventure of Lyle Swann (1983) is a pointless exercise about the eponymous biker (Fred Ward) riding into the test site for a time travel experiment. Next thing Swann knows, he's in the 1870s, surrounded by people who seem terrified of his bike and his strange clothes. Female gunslinger Claire (Belinda Bauer) finds him fascinating and beds him at gunpoint. The outlaw Reese (Peter Coyote) steals the bike and kidnaps Claire. With the help of a lawman, Swann rescues both; then a helicopter from the time travel project arrives to drive Reese off. The chopper takes Swann home, without Claire, which the biker realizes is because she's his grandmother. If she leaves the past, his father won't be born.

After a couple of seasons as TV mountain man "Grizzly Adams," Dan Haggerty appeared as Jeremiah, a similar gentle giant, in *Grizzly Mountain* (1997). Dylan and Nicole (Dylan Haggerty, Nicole Lund) are the children of a Portland developer who plans to build on a nearby mountain as soon as a local tribe's lease expires. Exploring the area, the kids wander into a magical cave and emerge more than a century in the past. In this era Jeremiah, a mountain man who lives in harmony with nature, is fighting wealthy Burt (Perry Stephens), who wants to blow up the mountain to run a railroad into town. Burt's scheming lover Betty (Kim Morgan Greene) secretly salts the site with fool's gold, figuring she can make a fortune off the gold miners who'll flock to town.

The kids realize blowing up the mountain will destroy their route home, so they join forces with Jeremiah. Together they expose Betty's plot. Shocked, Burt cancels his plans and gives the lease to the tribe. When the kids' parents come through the time cave and learn about everything, Dad abandons his development dreams.

The time traveler in *Escape to Grizzly Mountain* (2000) is Jimmy (Miko Hughes), an orphan living with his adult sister Linda (Ellina McCormick). After Jimmy befriends Dudley, an abused grizzly cub at a fleabag circus, roustabout Charlie (Nik Winterhawk) tells him about the magic cave. Despite Linda's objections, Jimmy tries taking Dudley into the past, but the bear runs away just as Jimmy time jumps. After Jeremiah hears Jimmy's story, the mountain man reluctantly comes to the present to help find the bear. The mean-spirited circus owner, Molly (Cynthia Palmer), recaptures Dudley and has Jeremiah and Charley arrested when they try to free him. Jimmy convinces Linda his crazy time travel tale is true. The siblings reconnect for the first time since their parents' death, and Linda bails out the men. Jeremiah and Charley take Dudley away from Molly and back into the past, where Charley decides to stay.

At the start of *Durango Kids* (1999), a gang of outlaws pulls off a gold robbery in Ouray, Colorado, murdering watchman Bigalow (David Kirkwood). A century later, Bigalow's ghost secretly nudges a group of Durango middle-schoolers to realize the outlaws hid the gold in an old mine before dying in a shoot-out. The kids take a road trip to find the gold for themselves. Even with the help of older teen Sammy (Austin Nichols), it's a tough journey. When they enter the mine, they land in the past, right before the robbery. Even more surprising, their principal, Dudley (Larry Drake), is the town sheriff, having gone back in time to get the gold himself.

Sammy becomes preoccupied with flirting with Bigalow's daughter, but the other kids use their modern tech to thwart the gold rubbery. Dudley frames them as the bandits' accomplices, then takes the gold away for "safety"—actually to bury in the mine for recovery in the present—and the kids away to jail (actually for execution). Sammy rescues them and exposes Dudley, but Dudley's lover Jane (Melissa Berger) frees her man. Everyone winds up at the mine where the kids convince the bandits to bust Dudley and Jane for the reward money. Sammy decides to stay in the past for love, while the other kids make it back to the present.

In *Timeslingers* (2013), squabbling siblings Tom and Sarah (Taylor Locke, Carly Pope) are visiting a ghost town with their family when they suddenly time-jump back to the Old West. No sooner does friendly settler Johnny (Barna Moricz) take them in than they meet Jiffy (George Ilie), an ET child desperate to find his mother before their life-support systems run down. Sheriff Cane (Markus Parilo) seems willing to help, but he's secretly hoping to turn a profit by selling the mother to a freak show. When he captures her, the town panics upon realizing there's a monster in the jail.

Thanks to the kids, Mom gets her life-support in time. Tom convinces the townsfolk to stop being haters and help the aliens against the sheriff. The kids discover the aliens' tech caused their time jump, so after the ETs leave, Johnny—the new sheriff—places it where the kids will activate it in the present. The siblings return home, baffling their parents by not fighting.

The Twentieth Century

W.E. Johns' Biggles was a fictional British pilot whose adventures ran from World War I to the 1960s. In *Biggles* (1986), present-day New York businessman Jim Ferguson (Alex

Hyde-White) is suddenly yanked to 1917 (World War I), where he saves Biggles (Neil Dickson) from death on a secret mission in France. When Jim returns to the present, Raymond (Peter Cushing), Biggles' former commander, explains that Jim and Biggles are time twins, crossing time when each other is in peril. Raymond adds that such things happen far more often than people realize.

Biggles is currently in a lot of peril: Germany has built a sonic cannon that will win the war unless Jim helps Biggles preserves the real history (though as the cannon wasn't created by a time traveler, it would appear it *is* the real history). Jim's mysterious disappearances convince his fiancée Debbie (Fiona Hutchison) he's gone nuts, until she's drawn back with him. After they return to the present, Jim gets into trouble, which brings Biggles forward to save him. They end up stealing a helicopter and when they bounce back to 1917, the chopper comes along. Biggles uses it to destroy the cannon, then Jim returns to the present and marries Debbie. As the film ends, he's drawn back to the post–World War I era, where Biggles has been trapped in New Guinea by cannibals.

"Time Out," first segment of the anthology film *Twilight Zone: The Movie* (1983), stars Vic Morrow as Bill, a bitter bigot who believes non-whites are keeping real Americans like himself from success. Suddenly he finds himself a Jew in Nazi-occupied Paris, then the guest of honor at a Klan lynching, then a Vietnamese peasant fleeing from an American patrol. (Bill previously bragged about killing "gooks" in Korea.) Then he's back in World War II on a concentration camp train. He sees his friends outside the train in the present and screams for help. They can't see him and the train departs.... (The original plan for this story was that Bill would redeem himself by saving two Vietnamese children during a bombing raid, but Morrow's death while filming it changed that.)

AJ (Melora Stover), the protagonist of *Split Infinity* (1992), is a brainy high-school student whose only goal in life is making money and wearing the best clothes. Her parents and her wealthy grandfather (H.E.D. Radford) warn her that the only real wealth is people who care for you; AJ doesn't listen until she's knocked out and wakes up as her look-alike great aunt in 1929. AJ chafes against the strict discipline and sexism of the times, and misses her parents desperately now that they're decades away. A more immediate problem is that in 1929 her grandfather Frank is as avaricious as AJ, and he's determined to sell the family farm to invest in the stock market. AJ knows the market's going to crash and she's come to see that family land is more than an investment, so she tries talking him out of it. Frank goes ahead, invests, and loses the farm, but AJ raises enough money to keep the house. She returns to the present where she learns Grandpa used her stock tips to become wealthy and set up a foundation which funds a children's hospital.

In His Father's Shoes (1997) opens with Clay Crosby (Robert Ri'chard) baffled that his cancer-ridden father Frank (Louis Gossett, Jr.) stubbornly refuses to speak with *his* father Richard (Gossett again). Frank tells Clay the answer lies with one of Clay's grandmother's old postcards. After Frank dies, Clay puts on a pair of shoes a fortune-teller gave Frank and finds himself living his father's life in 1962. He continues being Frank until he takes the shoes off again.

As Clay travels back and forth to the past, constantly hunting the key postcard, he discovers that while Richard was devoted to his family, he was also frustrated and angry at the limits America placed on his generation of black men. That frustration led to the conflict that ultimate split Richard and Frank. When Clay meets his grandfather in the present,

Richard admits that he was proud of Frank. On Clay's final trip to the past, he discovers the postcard from his father to Clay's mother, spelling out Frank's feelings. It makes Clay understand his father in a way he never did before.

In *An Angel for May* (2002), Yorkshire pre-teen Tom (Matthew Beard) has been in emotional freefall since his parents' marriage fell apart. After his mother (Angeline Ball) tells Tom she's going to marry her new boyfriend (Hugo Speer), Tom runs away and stumbles through a hole in time into 1944. Here he befriends May (Charlotte Wakefield), who's been traumatized since a German bomb killed her family. Sam (Tom Wilkinson), the farmer who takes care of her, lets Tom stay when he sees May is happier around him.

Eventually Tom returns to the present, where he learns a firebomb destroyed Sam's farmhouse five days after he left; May was institutionalized, and in the present is a local bag lady (Anna Massey). Tom returns to the past too late to stop the bomb, but he saves Sam's daughter Alison (Julie Cox) from death by sharing his asthma inhaler. When he returns to the present, he discovers Alison was able to care for May, who's now a happily married senior. All of this matures Tom to the point that he can accept his mother's new marriage.

Austin Powers: The Spy Who Shagged Me (1999) was the second of three comedies about Austin Powers (Mike Myers), a super-spy who entered cryonic sleep in the late 1960s, then thawed out in the 1990s. In this film, Powers' arch-foe Dr. Evil (Myers) returns to 1969 to steal the super-spy's mojo—his hyper-sexed sex drive. Evil's henchmen encourage him to kill Powers in the past, or invest in the stock market, but instead the doctor builds a laser cannon on the moon to extort money from the United States. (A running joke in the films is that the villains never do things the easy way.)

Crippled in the present by the loss of his mojo, Powers follows Evil back to 1969, where he joins forces with (and beds) the CIA's Felicity Shagwell (Heather Graham). His superior, Basil Exposition (Michael York), tells Powers not to worry about the time paradoxes, "just enjoy yourself—and that goes for you," he adds, staring at the audience. On the moon, the two spies and Dr. Evil have a showdown, and Felicity dies. Powers uses Evil's time machine to go back and ally with his past self, save Felicity and destroy the laser. The two Austins and Felicity return to the present and settle down as a *ménage a trois*.

The Devil's Arithmetic (1999) opens with Jewish teenager Hannah Stern (Kirsten Dunst) reluctantly attending Passover with her family at Aunt Eva's (Louise Fletcher) house. Hannah asks Eva, a Holocaust survivor, about what she lived through—or about Eva's best friend, for whom Hannah was named—but Eva insists Hannah can never understand. When Hannah opens the front door as part of Passover ritual, she finds herself in a 1941 German village where she's taken in by Rivka (Brittany Murphy), a Jewish girl who believes Hannah is her cousin.

The Nazis take the village Jews, including Hannah, to a death camp. Largely ignorant of history, Hannah can't predict what's ahead, but she uses stories and fiction of the postwar world to keep the other prisoners' spirits up. Rivka vows that if she survives, she'll take a new name, Eva, from one of Hannah's stories, in the faith that the future really will be better for Jews. Hannah realizes Rivka is her aunt and she herself is the original Hannah; she's always been part of her family's history. When Rivka is sent to the gas chamber, Hannah takes her place, dies and wakes up in the present. She understands her aunt and her family history and vows she'll never forget it.

Three. Enjoying the Exotic 41

Sent back 60 years to a Jewish peasant village, Kirsten Dunst experiences the Holocaust first-hand in *The Devil's Arithmetic* (1999).

The U.K. series *Life on Mars* (2006–07) played up the cultural gap between present and past. After being struck by a car, Detective Inspector Sam Tyler (John Simm) wakes up in 1973. He's still a detective, newly assigned to work under Chief Inspector Gene Hunt (Philip Glenister), an arrogant sexist who thinks nothing of roughing up suspects or planting evidence. (The subtext to both this and the American remake is that such things are alien to 21st century policing.) Despite this, Sam finds himself liking Hunt and enjoying the squad's rawer, gut-instinct based policing instead of the computers and bureaucracy of his own time.

This is one of the few screen time travel tales that seriously questions the reality of the time trip. Has Sam truly traveled back 30 years or is he hallucinating (several weird visions suggest the latter)? If so, is he hallucinating in 2006 or is he in 1973 imagining he's from the future? In the final episode, Sam learns he's an internal affairs officer assigned to take DCI Hunt down. When Hunt makes a mistake that puts the entire squad in danger, Sam's superior Frank Morgan (Ralph Brown) tells Sam to let them die so that Hunt's career will be ended. Sam walks away from his friends and awakes in the present. But he's now haunted by the thought he let his friends die, and finds his old life tedious. His solution is to jump off a roof to his death, wake up back in 1973, save his team and settle into life in the past for good.

Gene Hunt returns in *Ashes to Ashes* (2008–10), wherein female detective Alex Drake (Keeley Hawes) gets shot and wakes up in 1981 as Hunt's new DI. Alex is familiar with the Tyler case so she concludes she's replicating Sam's fantasies, but as time goes on she becomes convinced her new world is real. In the last episode she and the viewers learn the truth: Alex and the rest of the squad are dead, working under Hunt (who's also dead) to resolve their issues before moving on as Sam has. Over Alex's protests, Hunt sends her to the next phase of existence, then returns to work with a new crop of departed spirits.

In the 2008 American *Life on Mars*, Sam Tyler (Jason O'Mara) is a New York cop, with Harvey Keitel as the hardnosed Hunt. This series played up nostalgia (fashion, music and political references) more heavily than the original, though it otherwise followed the same set-up until the final episode. It turns out this Sam is an astronaut in cryonic sleep during a 2035 trip to Mars, and everything he's experienced has been a programmed dream. As the ship arrives on the Red Planet, one astronaut notes their mission is a "gene hunt" for any DNA that would prove there was ... life on Mars.

One of several film spin-offs from the *Naruto Shippuden* anime series, *Naruto Shippuden the Movie: The Lost Tower* (2010) has the orphan ninja protagonist (Junko Takeuchi) and his team hunt the renegade Mukade (Ryuzaburo Otomo) into the ruined city of Loren. Mukade breaks the magic seal on the ley line under the city, tapping its chakra power and triggering an eruption that sucks Naruto 20 years into the past. Loren is still a thriving city, powered by chakra energy, and Naruto meets several ninjas from his clan there, one of whom may be his father.

Naruto and the other ninjas discover that teenage Queen Sara's (Saori Hayami) adviser is a disguised Mukade; Mukade murdered Sara's mother so he could manipulate the naive younger woman, tap the ley line energy and power an invincible robot army. Fighting them proves tough even for ninjas, but Sara closes the ley line, depowering the robots. The ninjas defeat Mukade, though the battle levels the city, and Naruto returns to the present with his memories erased, to avoid any time paradoxes.

The Immediate Past

Stephen King's The Langoliers (1995) starts off in familiar disaster-movie style as unstable businessman Toomey (Bronson Pinchot), a blind psychic girl (Kate Maberly), a British spy (Mark Lindsay Chapman) and other characters fall asleep on a cross-country flight. When they wake up, everyone else on board has vanished, including the pilot; passenger Engle (David Morse), a commercial pilot, takes over. When they land, it's at an eerie, empty terminal where sound doesn't echo, food is tasteless, clocks don't run and beer is flat.

Fellow passenger Bob (Dean Stockwell) formulates a bizarre (but accurate) theory that the plane slipped through a hole into the past, which is lifeless. Worse, it's being slowly eaten out of existence by creatures Toomey identifies with his childhood bogeymen, the Langoliers. The entities have no qualms about eating time travelers too, but the characters are able to pull off an escape back to the present in the nick of time. Several of the passengers don't make it home; Toomey, for example, ends up eaten by the Langoliers.

As *+1* (2013) opens, teens Jill (Ashley Hinshaw) and David (Rhys Wakefield) have just broken up. Later they attend the same wild party, along with their friends Teddy (Logan Miller) and Alison (Suzanne Dengel). An energy-charged meteor lands nearby and David and Teddy find themselves watching party scenes from earlier in the evening. David, having failed to make up with Jill, looks for her earlier self to try again, and succeeds. As the counterparts phase in and out, he keeps confusing the two Jills.

When the rest of the party realizes what's going on, open warfare breaks out as some of the partygoers try to kill their counterparts. The two Alisons become friends and start making out, then the timeslip wears off and they, and the other pairs, merge. (The fact that some duplicates are dead doesn't seem to affect anything.) David and Jill reunite, but more meteors are hurtling across the sky...

The Future Isn't What It Used to Be

The past in screen time travel can be exciting, nostalgic, romantic or adventurous. The future is exciting, but usually the way a volcanic eruption is exciting: amazing to watch, but you want to get somewhere safe as soon as possible. Usually the best anyone can hope for in these dystopian futures is personal happiness amidst the nightmare. *Freejack*'s protagonist finds wealth and love in the 21st century, but his world is still a polluted, oppressed mess. This may reflect general trends in SF films: H. Bruce Franklin says optimism and excitement about the future in early SF movies have faded in favor of negative future such as *Damnation Alley* (1977) and *A Boy and His Dog* (1975).[10]

In the 1950s, the bad future usually sprang from the aftermath of nuclear war, as in *World Without End* and *The Time Machine* in chapter two. Seventies stories such as *Timeslip* and *Idaho Transfer* focused on eco-catastrophe. More recent tales emphasize corruption and corporate takeover.

The British TV series *Timeslip* (1970) has tweens Simon (Spencer Banks) and Liz (Cheryl Burfield) discover an invisible barrier around an old naval base near their village. They find a hole in the barrier and crawl through into 1940, just as a Nazi strike force captures the base. Back in the present, sinister scientist Traynor (Denis Quilley) tells Liz's mum (Iris Russell)—who can follow Liz's adventures telepathically—that the kids can cross the barrier because they're young enough not to disbelieve in time travel.

Simon and Liz survive the attack because when they're outside their own time, they can't be killed. They try to return home, but stumble instead into a 1990 ice research station run by a clone of Traynor's mentor Devereaux (John Barron). Employed there is Liz's adult self (Mary Preston), a cold, rational woman scornful of her more emotional younger self. Devereaux's efforts to link his mind with the base computers have created serious technical glitches, and by the time the kids escape, everyone at the base is dead.

The kids arrive next in a different 1990, a technocratic Europe where Simon (David Graham) is a government toady and Beth is a Misfit, an artist living off the grid. The government's reckless experiments in terraforming Europe result in a massive heat wave that seems certain to destroy the continent. Liz and Simon travel back to the present in hopes of averting this apocalypse. They discover that Devereaux's experiments are at the root of everything; Traynor, for example, is a clone of the real Traynor, stripped of his ethics. Simon and Liz free the original Traynor, then the time slip sucks the clone away.

The clunky film *Idaho Transfer* (1973) focuses on a federal research project that's secretly sending its volunteers through time. The project's backers believe a worldwide ecological collapse is inevitable so sending people under 20—anyone older will die—into the future is humanity's only hope. After the latest time trip, the volunteers discover they can't return, possibly because the government has shut down the project. As the teens explore the landscape, which doesn't look very collapsed, Karen (Kelley Bohanan) becomes convinced she's pregnant. The others tell her that's impossible as time travel induces sterility (so how exactly will the human race survive?). Another volunteer begins killing people, so Karen uses the time machine to go back and try to prevent the murders. She fails. After a bewildering montage, she's captured by a family wearing the stereotypical shiny futuristic jumpsuits. The film seems to imply future humans survive by eating time travelers but it's almost as confusing as the montage.

Freejack (1992) is based on Robert Sheckley's *Immortality Inc.* in which a protagonist's consciousness is snatched into a future where mind transfer is a routine fact of life. Sheckley develops this brilliantly, the movie not so much. It's set 18 years in the future, an era implausibly so much more polluted than the present that the dying rich will pay to have their minds transferred to an uncontaminated body from the 1990s.

Body snatcher Vacendak (Mick Jagger) "freejacks" Alex Furlong (Emilio Estevez) into the future as a body for billionaire McCandless (Anthony Hopkins). Alex escapes and goes looking for his old lover Julie (Rene Russo), now a powerful businesswoman working for McCandless. After dodging Vacendak in action sequences, the couple learns that McCandless is in love with Julie and thinks moving into Alex's body would win her affection. McCandless finally captures Alex, but as the mind-swap machine activates, Julie destroys it, erasing McCandless' consciousness. Alex bluffs McCandless' underlings into believing the transfer went through, giving him access to McCandless' wealth and power. Vacendak spots the fraud, but likes Alex enough to go along.

A millennium from now in *Starship Girl Yamamoto Yohko* (1995–99), humanity settles territorial disputes with non-lethal space battles. Because human reflexes have deteroiated, the factions draw pilots from the past, such as videogamers Yamamoto (Minomi Takayama). Her space battles and rivalries with other pilots were among the plot-threads.

The stylishly animated *Samurai Jack* (2001–04) opens in feudal Japan, where a samurai (Phil LaMarr) wielding a magic katana battles the powerful demon Aku (Mako). The magic sword almost brings the warrior victory, but at the last instant Aku hurls him centuries into the future, an era when Aku rules Earth and is expanding his reach to the stars. "Jack" (as everyone calls him) doesn't have the power to beat Aku there, so he sets out to find a way back to the past. Along the way he helps ordinary people against demons, gangsters, robots and other menaces, while thwarting Aku's efforts to destroy him. The series ended with Jack still wandering the future, but a sequel series has been announced.

Based on a long-running DC Comics series, *The Legion of Super-Heroes* (2006–08) offered a jaunt into an upbeat, positive future. In the opening episode, the Legion—31st century superheroes—are badly beaten by their deadliest enemies, the Fatal Five. A handful of Legionnaires travel back to the present to recruit Superman to help them. Clark Kent (Yuri Lowenthal) hasn't become Superman yet, but he agrees to go up against the Five, who clobber him. A trip to the future's Superman Museum makes Clark realize what he's capable of and he rises to the occasion. As he can return to just seconds after he left the present, he stuck around with his new friends for two seasons of animated adventures, battling the Fatal Five and other criminals and keeping the future upbeat.

The Future Is Wild (2007–08) spun off from a speculative documentary series about how animals might evolve in a post-human world. C.G. (Ashley Peters) is a teen from 12,000 A.D., when Earth is in the grip of a devastating ice age. Sent through time to find a better home for humanity, she crashes in the 21st century where she meets Ethan (Marc Donato), Emily (Miranda Jones) and Luis (Taylor Abrahamse) who join her on her quest. Traveling millions of years into the future, the quartet copes with equipment malfunctions and other accidents, dodges futuristic life forms such as the land-dwelling megasquid and keeps hunting for a place humanity can call home.

And the Apes Shall Inherit the Earth

In *Planet of the Apes* (1968), astronaut Taylor (Charlton Heston) leaves Earth in 1972 and crashes after 18 months—but by the virtue of Einsteinian time-dilation, it's 2000 years later for the rest of the universe. He and his crew discover they've landed on a world of animalistic humans and intelligent talking apes, which at the end of the film (as most of you undoubtedly know) turns out to be Earth, A.D. 3972.

In the sequel *Beneath the Planet of the Apes* (1970), a second ship, hunting for Taylor's lost vessel, crashes on Earth in 3975. The sole survivor, Brent (James Franciscus), realizes his ship traveled through a time warp. (Contrary to events in the first film, it's implied that Taylor did too.) The friendly chimp scientists Cornelius (David Watson) and Zira (Kim Hunter) tell Brent that Taylor disappeared in the barren Forbidden Zone after mysterious fires and thunderbolts separated him from his lover, Nova (Linda Harrison). The scientists help Brent and Nova flee the gorilla military into the Zone, where Brent discovers what planet he landed on.

Psionic mutants capture the two humans, as they've already captured Taylor. Although the psis worship a nuclear warhead, they reject violence—but they don't think it's violent to torture the prisoners telepathically or force them to kill each other. Before the mutants can finish off the men, the apes attack. The mutants' psi attacks don't work as well on ape brains, so the gorillas massacre the mutants. Brent, Taylor and Nova die in the crossfire, but Taylor triggers the warhead as he dies, wiping out the entire world (though Cornelius and Zira made an *Escape from the Planet of the Apes*, as detailed in chapter seven)

In 1974 the franchise shifted to television with *Planet of the Apes*. Once again, two astronauts, Virdon (Ron Harper) and Burke (James Naughton), fly through a time warp, though they arrive a thousand years earlier than Taylor and Brent. Humans in this era are intelligent, but apes regard them as mental inferiors fit only for serfdom. As in the first two films, the idea humans ever equaled apes is a heresy so the presence of living proof greatly displeases ape leaders Zaius (Booth Colman) and Gen. Urko (Mark Lenard). With the help of the friendly chimp Galen (Roddy McDowall), the astronauts go on the run from Urko, helping out apes and humans along the way, but doing very little to change the oppression their fellow homo sapiens live under.

The cartoon *Return to the Planet of the Apes* (1975) was more engaging despite its stiff animation. In the opening episode, astronauts Jeff, Bill and Judy (Austin Stoker, Tom Williams, Claudette Nevins) test a time travel device that hurtles them further into the future than expected. The humans are animalistic again, while the apes have 20th century tech—TV, cars—and a history studded with names such as "William Apespeare." The astronauts, with the help of Cornelius and Zira (Edwin Mills, Philippa Harris), work to protect the humans and the mutant "Underdwellers"—the psis of *Beneath*—from genocidal Urko (Henry Corden). In the final episode, Cornelius presented the ape leaders with proof humans were once civilized, which the chimp optimistically assumes will lead to interspecies equality. As there was no season two, we can pretend he was right.

In the 2001 big-screen reboot *Planet of the Apes*, astronaut Davidson (Mark Wahlberg) sees an experimental spacecraft disappear into a magnetic storm along with its pilot Pericles, a genetically enhanced chimp. Entering the maelstrom to rescue Pericles, Davidson crash-lands in an ape-ruled future where humans are intelligent but slaves. With the help of the pro-human chimp scientist Ari (Helena Bonham Carter), Davidson leads a slave revolt and takes his people into the wilderness. There they discover a crashed space station, once staffed by genetically engineered apes, the ancestors of the future's ape-ocracy.

As usual, the ruling apes are desperate to cover up this history, so ruthless General Thade (Tim Roth) attacks the rebels. The battle goes against the humans until Pericles lands—apparently his ship took a slower wormhole—and greets Davidson with affection. The army treats this as a divine sign, though Thade chooses to die fighting. Davidson takes Pericles' ship back to the present, landing at the Lincoln Memorial—except it's the Thade Memorial, devoted to the general's heroic efforts to protect ape supremacy, and the cops who close in on Davidson are ape, not human.

CHAPTER FOUR

Bouncing Around Time, Getting Lost and Doing the Time Warp

"I'm not in control of my own destiny—it's a miracle I can control my own bladder."—*Between Time and Timbuktu*

Time travelers in the previous chapter mostly go from their home era to another and back, nothing more. The travelers in this chapter keep things livelier. They jump around to multiple destinations. They're lost and they can't choose their destination, or even return home. Or they stumble into a place where the laws of time no longer apply.

All Around Time

Some screen time travelers get to visit more than just one era. Usually all their destinations are in the past, but sometimes the future plays a part.

Where Do We Go from Here? (1945) stars Fred MacMurray as Bill Morgan, who's been rejected repeatedly as 4F when he tries to enlist in the military. After he frees the genie Ali (Gene Sheldon) from a magic lamp, the first of Bill's three wishes lands him in the Continental Army of 1776, where he volunteers as a spy for General Washington and almost gets shot. Then he wishes to join the Navy and becomes a sailor on Columbus' *Santa Maria*. After stopping a mutiny, Bill takes a sailboat to Manhattan Island, which he buys from the natives. Bill's third stop is New Amsterdam in the 1600s, where he meets Katrina (Joan Leslie), the double of his platonic friend Sally, and realizes he loves her. Bill and Ali prevent Katrina from marrying someone else, after which the trio returns to the present. Katrina turns into Sally and Ali finally gets Bill into the Marines.[1]

Captain Z-Ro (1955–56) introduced kids to the eponymous scientific genius (Roy Steffens), working in his secret "Fortress of Solitude" base on "experiments in time and space—to learn from the past, to plan for the future!" In one typical episode, Z-Ro shows his sidekick Jet (Bruce Haynes) how the discovery of gold at Sutter's Mill will transform a small growing community into a lawless, brawling town dominated by gold fever. One man resorts to murder to cover up the gold strike but Z-Ro intervenes to prevent the kill. He explains to Jet that for all the damage to Sutter's Mill, the gold rush was essential to shaping California history.

A much superior show, "Peabody's Improbable History" began in 1959 as a recurring segment on the *Rocky & His Friends* cartoon (later renamed *The Bullwinkle Show*). Peabody

(Bill Scott) is a bespectacled dog *and* a millionaire genius, the "puppy prodigy." After he adopts a boy, Sherman (Walter Tetley), he realizes their penthouse doesn't give Sherman room to exercise so he builds a time machine to give them easy access to open spaces. Each trip in the "Wayback Machine" introduces them to a point in history gone wrong: General Sherman can't march through Georgia because he doesn't have the money to cross a toll booth, Alfred Nobel has blown up his laboratory without inventing dynamite and so on. Invariably, Peabody's genius fixes things and episodes end with a painful pun. Fueled by the distinctive humor of creator Jay Ward and his staff, it's a real treat.

Like most big-screen adaptations of Ward's work, *Mr. Peabody and Sherman* (2014) failed to capture the charm of the original. After classmate Penny (Ariel Winter) bullies Sherman (Max Charles) over having a dog for a father, dog-hating social worker Grunion (Allison Janney) blames Sherman for the resulting fracas and vows to remove him from Peabody's (Ty Burrell) custody. When Sherman tries getting on Penny's good side by showing her the Wayback Machine, it ends up stranding her in ancient Egypt.

In *Mr. Peabody and Sherman* (2014) Ty Burrell and Max Charles are the voices of the "puppy prodigy" and his adopted son.

Peabody and Sherman save Penny from becoming King Tut's bride, head home but crash-land in the Renaissance. After Peabody gives Sherman a good talking-to, the boy runs off and joins the Greek army at Troy under Agamemnon. Peabody follows and apparently dies, so Sherman and Penny, who have become friends, try to erase the whole timeline. The end result, unfortunately, is duplicate Peabodys and Shermans running around in the present, triggering a massive time rift.

Grunion makes another attempt to take Sherman away, which provokes Peabody to bite her. That makes his legal situation worse, but fortunately Abraham Lincoln and George Washington appear through the time rift and give Peabody a presidential pardon. Peabody closes the rift, Grunion goes into the past with a love-smitten Agamemnon, and Peabody and Sherman finally forge a true father-son bond.

The Mr. Peabody and Sherman Show (2015) was a Netflix-streaming series in which Peabody (Chris Parnell) and Sherman (Max Charles) host a talk show from their penthouse. Along with a time trip each episode,

Four. Bouncing Around Time, Getting Lost and Doing the Time Warp 49

they cope with various mishaps (Peabody's trapped in an elevator, so Sherman has to handle the emcee duties), wacky neighbors and so on.

The Peter Potamus Show (1964) starred another anthropomorphic animal, hippo explorer Peter Potamus (Daws Butler). Accompanied by his monkey sidekick So-So (Don Messick), Peter traveled around in a balloon that could also travel across time. In the "America or Bust" episode, for instance, he escapes a storm by traveling to 1492. Here he helps Christopher Columbus quell a mutiny, find North America and negotiate peace with a native tribe. When the tribe decides for war, Peter unleashes his Hippo Hurricane Howler, a blast of super-breath which clobbers the tribe and convinces them to sign a treaty.

The protagonists of the oddball *Dimension 5* (1966) move to multiple times but only within an eight-week range, forward and back. Justin Power (Jeffrey Hunter) is an American spy working against the Dragons, a Chinese spy ring plotting to detonate an H-bomb in Los Angeles. Power and his partner Kitty Tsu (France Nuyen) have watch-like wrist devices that can shift them through time. When the Dragons assassinate a prisoner before he can talk, for instance, Powers goes back a couple of minutes and prevents the kill.

After determining where and when the shipment of bomb components will arrive, Justin and Kitty jump forward three weeks to intercept it. They find the shipment, get caught by the Dragons, but escape through time. Kitty, who was once raped by Dragon leader Big Buddha (Harold Sakata), gets captured trying to kill him for revenge. Then one of Big Buddha's own female agents kills him for no stated reason. Powers now tells Kitty that they'll have to jump back three weeks and live the events over again (this is as nonsensical as it sounds), but without repeating her mistake with Big Buddha.

In *Jimmy Green and His Time Machine* (1968), a puppet series from British TV, young Jimmy and a girl named Lettuce travel around time and space in "the best machine that ever has been," according to the theme song. That's about all anyone knows about it.

The stop-motion special *Rudolph's Shiny New Year* (1976) starts the moment Rudolph (Billie Mae Richards) finishes his famous ride guiding Santa's sleigh and returns to the North Pole. Father Time (Red Skelton) asks Rudolph to find Happy, the Baby New Year set to take office on January 1. After everyone made fun of his big jug-ears, Happy ran off, and if he doesn't return, December 31 will time-loop for eternity. Worse, the immortal vulture Eon (Paul Frees) is doomed to turn to ice on January 1, so he plans to prevent this by stopping Happy from becoming the New Year.

Hunting Happy takes Rudolph to the archipelago where old years retire to live on their own islands. After visiting one million B.C., 1023 (the year the fairy tales all happened) and 1776, Rudolph catches up with Happy only to have Eon carry the baby off. Rudolph reaches Eon's nest and convinces Happy that having a physical feature others make fun of shouldn't keep you down. Happy agrees to return and resume his duties, and Eon laughs so hard at the sight of the baby's ears that he melts his own cold heart, neutralizing the ice curse.

Fantasy Island (1977–84) stars Ricardo Montalban as Roarke, the enigmatic owner of the eponymous tropical resort where, for a price, visitors can have any fantasy granted. A number of these involved traveling in time: A young hoofer gets to dance with Bojangles Robinson, a prudish couple experience the traditional values of Puritan New England, a history teacher lives the life of a World War I flying ace. Like all of the fantasies shown on the series, the time trips involved a moral lesson. The teacher (Don Adams), for example, learns not to glamorize the horrors of war. A short-lived 1998 revival series with Malcolm McDowell as Roarke followed the same formula.

A Hitch in Time (1978) has school kids Paul (Michael McVey) and Fiona (Pheona McLellan) discover Prof. Wagstaff (Patrick Troughton) building a time machine. As the time platform can't bear his weight, the kids volunteer to test it. They want to visit Robin Hood, but get thrown into 1953, 1941 and other points in time instead. After the kids return, Wagstaff decides to time travel himself, trusting the kids to bring him home. No sooner does he step into time than an overbearing teacher (Jeff Rawle) discovers the machine and tries to drag the kids away. They fight back long enough to bring Wagstaff home, then the time machine turns the teacher into a teenager. Paul, Fiona and Wagstaff make one final jump which lands them back at the start of the movie.

Young Kay Harker (Devin Stanfield) becomes the guardian of the *Box of Delights* (1984) in an adaptation of John Masefield's novel. The box's magic powers include time travel. Kay protects the box from the villains hurting it, but it turns out his adventures were a dream.

In British TV's *Into the Labyrinth* (1981–82), children Phil (Simon Beal), Terry (Simon Henderson) and Helen (Lisa Turner) stumble across Rothgo (Ron Moody), a sorcerer imprisoned by his evil rival Belor (Pamela Salem). Rothgo sends the children through the labyrinth of time—looking rather like an ordinary rock garden—to recover the Nidus, a magic talisman that will give him power to defeat Belor. The kids bounce through various eras including Druidic England, the French Revolution and the Arabian Nights before recovering the Nidus. Belor kept scheming for two more seasons.

In *Kiteretsu Encyclopedia* (1988–96), pre-teen mechanical genius Eiichi (Toshiko Fujita) believes he's descended from the legendary genius Kiteretsu. Using Kiteretsu's designs he builds a robot, Korosuke, as his companion, and also a time machine with which he and Korosuke can voyage into the past (though he had plenty of adventures in the present).

A wax museum pops up overnight in *Waxwork* (1988) and the owner, Lincoln (David Warner), invites some local teens to tour it. Unhappily for them, the exhibits are actually time gates: China (Michelle Johnson), for example, stands too close to the Dracula tableau, gets sucked into the past and dies at Dracula's (Miles O'Keeffe) hands. Mark (Zach Galligan) and Susan (Deborah Foreman) escape the exhibits and learn from eccentric occultist Sir Wilfred (Patrick Macnee) that when each tableau has claimed a sacrifice in the present, Lincoln will have the power to bring on the apocalypse. Mark and Susan return to the museum, where Susan gets trapped. Mark faces a village of zombies but realizes he's safe as long as he doesn't believe in it. He frees Susan, only to be captured by Lincoln's acolytes. Sir Wilfred shows up with a literal pitchfork-wielding mob (though they have guns too) and everyone on both sides dies, except Mark and Susan. As the teens stagger away from the burning building, a zombie hand follows…

…and in *Waxwork: Lost in Time* (1992), the hand murders Susan's (now Monika Schnarre) abusive stepfather. The case against Susan looks ironclad, but a message from Sir Wilfred tells Susan and Mark how to travel through the time gates again, in the hope of finding evidence of their crazy story. ("If we can reanimate dead tissue, the prosecution's case goes out the window!") This time they visit Frankenstein's castle, an *Alien*-knockoff future, a haunted house (a parody of *The Haunting*) and an Arthurian realm. Wilfred's spirit explains these are all part of Cartagra, s spirit plane where God and Satan's chosen warriors battle in different ages—and that God has picked Mark as one of the warriors. Eventually Mark and Susan find the zombie hand and Mark sends Susan home to clear her name. She does, then returns to adventure with Mark in Cartagra.

Spinning off the *Back to the Future* trilogy (see chapter eight), the animated *Back to the Future* (1991–92) series assumes the time traveling Brown family—Doc (Dan Castellanata), Clara (Mary Steenburgen) and their kids—settled down in modern-day Hill Valley, hung out with Marty McFly (squeaky, ineffective David Kaufman) and locked horns with bullying Biff Tannen (Thomas F. Wilson). They also travel regularly through time—mostly the past—encountering other generations of Tannens and contending with them too. In "Roman Holiday," Marty is pressured into a chariot race with the arrogant Roman Bifficus with Marty's life at stake; in "Dickens of a Christmas," the Browns and Marty visit Victorian England where Ebenezer Tannen throws Clara in debtor's prison. But everyone always makes it back to the present in one piece.

The Halloween Tree (1993) was an animated TV special set in what looks vaguely like the 1930s. After young Pip falls ill with appendicitis, his friends are surprised to see him racing outside of town to a spooky old house, where he steals a pumpkin from a tree, then disappears. The house's owner, Moundshroud (Leonard Nimoy), pursues him, taking the other kids along and explaining Halloween iconography as they time-jump to Egypt (mummies), Stonehenge (witches), Notre Dame (gargoyles) and so on. Pip eventually runs out of steam and Moundshroud, whom the film implies is Death, takes the pumpkin, which holds Pip's life force. Pip's friends each offer a year off their life in return for Moundshroud giving Pip back his pumpkin, and the sinister figure agrees. When the kids return home, Pip is healthy.

Time Bokan (1975–2000) was another series that through the years ran in multiple incarnations: *Time Bokan Yattaman*, *Time Bokan Zendaman* and *Time Bokan: Royal Revival*. In the original opening episode, Prof. Kieda (Ryuuji Saikachi) invents the Time Bokan, a time travel mecha that resembles a tailed flying teapot. When he doesn't return from his initial time trip, his assistants Junko (Mari Okamoto) and Tanpei (Yoshiko Oota) go in search of him, landing first in prehistoric times. Hot on their tail are scheming Majo (Noriko Ohara) and her crooked crew, for the Bokan returned with a super-explosive jewel, a "dyamond," and Majo wants more of them. The bad guys take their own time travel robot into the past where it fights and loses against the Bokan. It was only the first of many colorful robot battles in different eras (and meetings with figures such as Dracula and Robin Hood) over the run of the series. After the professor returned home, the series rebooted several times with new crews of heroes and villains. *Royal Revival* pitted several teams of villains in competition against each other.

Time Warp Trio was a 2005 Discovery Kids! animated series based on the books by Jon Scieszka. Joe (Mark Rendall) receives a history book from his Uncle Joe as a birthday gift. As he and his friends Fred and Sam (Scott McCord, Darren Frost) glance at a picture of pirates, one of them wishes they could live the pirate life … and suddenly they're on a beach facing off against a very suspicious Blackbeard. After narrowly escaping typical perils of pirate adventures, they recover the book and return home.

This was only the beginning as the book carried the boys back into the past over and over. It also took them into the future to meet their descendants and fellow time travelers Jodie (Sarah Gadon), Freddi (Sunday Muse) and Samantha (Laurie Elliott). The series placed a lot of emphasis on learning history (Napoleon, Eric the Red, building the Brooklyn Bridge) along with the adventures.

Josh Kirby ... Time Warrior (1995) was a series of six direct-to-video kids adventures forming one story arc, with the first five films ending with a cliffhanger. Protagonist Josh (Corbin Allred) is an ordinary 14-year-old until 25th century scientists Zoetrope (Derek Webster) and Irwin 1138 (Barrie Ingham) show up at his house battling for one of the six segments of something called the Nullifier. Irwin explains the Nullifier is an indestructible weapon he scattered across time to prevent Zoetrope using it to wipe out the universe. Josh gets dragged along on Irwin's quest to stop Zoetrope from recovering the Nullifier, as does Azabeth Siege (Jennifer Burns), a gladiator from even further in the future.

Together the trio pursue Zoetrope into multiple eras and settings, including medieval times, a world of life-sized living dolls, Azabeth's home era and a cavern of mushroom people. They recover the Nullifier segments, at which point Irwin reveals he's really an agent of the 25th century's dictatorship. Zoetrope built the Nullifier to cancel the power of the government's deadly Decimator weapon; Irwin will prevent that by not only rescattering the pieces through time but turning them invisible as well. He abandons Josh and Azabeth, but Josh has learned he's a time warrior, with time travel powers of his own. Zoetrope and Azabeth sacrifice their own existence to charge up his powers, enabling Josh to reach the future, activate the Nullifier and break the dictator's power. He wakes up back in the present, wondering if he dreamed everything, but then he meets Azabeth's double, a new student at his school.

In the anime *Millennium Actress* (2001), the documentary maker Genya Tachibana (Shōzō Ilzuka) and his cameraman Ida (Masaya Onosaka) interview Fujiwara Chiyoko (Miyoko Shoji), a retired Japanese film star. In telling the men her story, Chiyoko unlocks her own memories of a young, anti-imperialist artist (Kōichi Yamadera) she fell in love with as a teenager. Her memories are strong enough to pull Ida and Tachibana into her past, both real events and scenes from her movies: one second Tachibana is watching Chiyoko quarrel with an older actor, the next she's a samurai princess whom he saves from a burning castle. Through it all, Chiyoko never stops searching for the painter, unaware that the military executed him.

The aging Chiyiko collapses mid-interview, and doctors confirm she hasn't long to live. She tells Tachibana she'll keep hunting her painter in the afterlife: even if she never finds him, it's the quest that defines her life.

In the 2015 Disney Channel's *Best Friends Whenever* series, teenage buddies Cyd (Landry Bender) and Shelby (Lauren Taylor) get caught in a lab accident that allows them to travel within their own lifetime (longer time jumps were riskier) by touching each other and thinking about when they want to be. Most of their time jumps focused on simple things, such as jumping to the future to learn the answers to a test, or jumping back to prevent a kitchen fire they started. Other adventures involved fixing harmful changes caused by previous time jumps, and preventing a future in which they wind up as a scientist's (Nora Dunn) guinea pigs.

My Time Machine Has a Glitch!

In 1962, TV's most famous time traveler appeared in *Doctor Who*, the longest-running SF TV show of all time. In the opening serial, "An Unearthly Child," London teachers Barbara (Jacqueline Hill) and Ian (William Russell) become curious about new student Susan Foreman (Carole Ann Ford), who mixes vast knowledge of history with ignorance of everyday life. When the teachers follow Susan to her home, they discover it's a police box (a phone booth for emergency police calls) sitting in a junkyard. Susan lives inside the box—which is bigger inside than outside—with her grandfather, the Doctor (William Hartnell)

Oh, and the box is a time machine, a TARDIS (Time and Relative Dimensions in Space), as the teachers discover when the disgruntled Doctor transports it away from London to the Stone Age. After perilous adventures with cavemen, they take off again, but the TARDIS is defective and can't take the teachers straight home. Instead, they visit ancient Rome, the Aztec Empire, the massacre of the Huguenots, and alien worlds where they battle menaces including the cyborg Daleks and the insectoid Zarbi. (The show was conceived as an educational vehicle for children but the SF aspect soon took over.) Eventually the Doctor left Susan in Earth's future and later dropped the teachers back in their own time. Other companions replaced them and the Doctor himself would regenerate, to be played by new actors.

No other screen time travelers have ever ranged as far across time and space as the Doctor in the TARDIS (at time of writing he controls his vessel much better). He met

Doctor Who (Peter Cushing) and his granddaughter Barbara (Jennie Linden) confront one of the merciless Daleks in *Doctor Who and the Daleks* **(1965). Unlike the TV show, "Who" really is the Doctor's last name.**

famous people (Dickens, Van Gogh, Agatha Christie), witnessed famous events (the French Revolution, World War II, the Siege of Troy) and traveled not only to Earth's future but entirely alien worlds. The Doctor has also appeared in three movies. *Doctor Who and the Daleks* (1965) and *Daleks' Invasion Earth 2150 AD* (1966) adapted the two storylines from the series, and starred Peter Cushing as Doctor Who. (In the TV series, "Who" is not his name.) In the American TV movie *Doctor Who* (1996), Paul McGann made his only appearance as the Doctor. After that the show lay fallow until the 2005 revival, which became a transatlantic hit.

Doctor Who also produced the spin-offs *K9*, *Torchwood* and *The Sarah Jane Adventures*, though only *K9* (2009) had enough time travel to be covered here (see chapter five).

The time-lost protagonists of *Journey to the Center of Time* (1967) were much less entertaining, as the movie bogs down with stock footage and interminable technobabble. When wealthy industrialist Stanton (Scott Brady) discovers the time travel research he's funding can't do more than peer 24 hours into the past, he threatens to cut off the cash flow. Scientists Manning (Anthony Eisley), Gordon (Abraham Sofaer) and White (Gigi Perreau) reluctantly agree to make a small time jump with Stanton, but their "time vault" freaks out and lands them in the far future, an Earth ravaged by war between humans and aliens.

After escaping the alien onslaught, the travelers try to fly the time-vault home but almost hit another vessel in the time stream. Stanton cold-bloodedly saves them by destroying the other ship with a laser, enabling the vault to land safely in the dinosaur age. After Gordon dies, Stanton selfishly uses the vault to head home alone. He learns too late that this is the very same vessel his past self destroyed, and he's unable to change that.

For no discernible reason, the vault rematerializes back in the past after Stanton's death. Manning and White return to the present only to discover their past selves frozen in time, minutes before the time vault took off (much like *The Time Travelers* in chapter two). Fearing the consequences of existing twice in the same moment, they return to the vault and head off into the unknown. Manning wonders if they'll be the Adam and Eve of some desolate future world.

Tony Newman (James Darren) and Doug Phillips (Robert Colbert) also faced a loss of funding at the start of TV's *The Time Tunnel* (1966–67). To prove their tunnel through time works, Tony sends himself through the experimental device and lands on the *Titanic*. The tunnel tech team (Lee Meriwether, John Zaremba) can't bring Tony back, so when he fails to convince the *Titanic* captain to change course, Doug follows Tony to the ship to help. By the time the *Titanic* goes down, the techies have figured out how to pull the guys back into the time stream, but only to drop them in a different era. In subsequent episodes Tony and Doug bounced from the Age of Arthur to the Old West to the distant future. Time paradoxes were brushed aside; even when Tony encounters Doug several years before they originally met, it doesn't affect anything. The series ended with the guys still lost in time. The 1994–95 *Alexei Sayle Show* parodied *Time Tunnel* in a series of sketches, *Drunk in Time*.

The theme song of *The Lost Saucer* (1975–76) tells how two 24th-century androids, Fum (Jim Nabors) and Fi (Ruth Buzzi), met young Alice (Alice Playten) and Jerry (Jarrod Johnson) while visiting to the 20th century. The androids invite the kids on board, but when the police show up to investigate, Fi and Fum take off in a panic. Trying to get Alice and

Jerry home, the saucer bounces through time from one weird world to another. Almost all their destinations were alien planets rather than future Earths. Typical for 1970s Saturday morning TV, their adventures provided viewers with life lessons. For instance, in the first episode the kids are arrested by an authoritarian culture where everyone has to have ID numbers on their faces. The take-away is that society shouldn't reduce people to numbers and data.

Another Saturday morning series, *The Fonz and the Happy Days Gang* (1980–82), turned characters from prime time's *Happy Days* into animated time travelers. As shown in the opening narration, Cupcake (Didi Cohn), a visitor from the future, kicks things off by crashing her time ship in 1957 Milwaukee. Arthur "Fonzie" Fonzarelli (Henry Winkler) successfully restarts the machine, but makes the mistake of boarding it with his dog Mr. Cool and his friends Richie (Ron Howard) and Ralph (Donny Most). Like the TARDIS and the Lost Saucer, once the machine takes off not even the Fonz's mechanical genius can make it return to Milwaukee. Instead, the protagonists bounce through the ages, confronting dinosaurs and cave people one week, invading robot armies or vampires the next. Fortunately, the Fonz can always save the day with his unflappable cool, mechanical know-how and his ability to seduce any woman from a cavewoman to a space empress.

Escape Through Time (1992) opens in the late 21st century as a counter-terrorist mission goes wrong. One team member escapes the trap by using a time-distorter ring and, as we later learn, lands in ancient Egypt. Centuries later, the ring winds up on the finger of high school student Jill (Jill Killinger). Criminals try to seize the ring, which sends Jill and her friend Kirsten (Kirsten Meyer) bouncing through time—the age of chivalry, the Old West, the future—with the crooks on their tail. The counter-terrorist team eventually meets the girls and realizes someday they'll be president and vice-president, so their survival is essential to history. The team saves the girls, and Jill and Kirsten finally make it home.

Red Dwarf (1988–2012) was an SF comedy about the ragtag band of losers lost in space aboard the Red Dwarf spaceship: low-comic roughneck Lister (Craig Charles), officious, obnoxious hologram Rimmer (Chris Barrie), a cat-evolved humanoid (Danny John-Jules) and various other characters who appeared for a season or two as the crew struggled to get back to Earth. While not a time travel show per se, a remarkable number of episodes involved time travel or visits to parallel worlds. In one, Lister changes his past so he doesn't go into space and becomes a multi-millionaire; Rimmer, left alone on the ship, selfishly changes things back. In another, Rimmer enters a parallel universe where his counterpart is an "old school," steely-eyed space hero. In the sixth season ender, the crew meet their future selves, veteran time travelers who've become so corrupt, they enjoy dropping in on Hitler for tea.

Let's Do the Time Warp Again

The PBS movie *Between Time and Timbuktu: A Space Fantasy* (1972) combined several Kurt Vonnegut stories into a single narrative. By winning a slogan contest for Blast-Off Cola (slogan and jingle contests were often parodied in film), Stony Stevenson (William Hickey) becomes a U.S. astronaut assigned to probe a "chronosynclastic infundibulum"—a time warp. After some acid-trip visuals, he finds himself bouncing through time to meet an amiable cult leader (Kevin McCarthy); meeting a scientist who can make water freeze even at 140 degrees; landing in a future world where anyone of superior ability is handicapped in the name of equality; and visiting Schenectady.

Stony ends up in the afterlife, accompanied by a recently dead girl named Wanda June (Ariane Munker). As she and other spirits celebrate their new existence, Death (Page Johnson), a Hitler look-alike, informs them there's no afterlife and makes everyone but Stony vanish. Stony replies that Death is just a manifestation of his imagination; to prove it, he makes Death disappears and brings everyone else back. The next second, Stony wakes up lying in mud on his own grave. After a brief conversation with God, he learns from the cemetery gardener (McIntyre Dixon) that the grave is empty: Stony's capsule returned to Earth without him, so his mother put up the memorial. A bemused Stony wanders off, singing to himself.

Terry Gilliam's *Time Bandits* (1981) has a disjointed sketch-comedy style that comes close to Gilliam's former show *Monty Python's Flying Circus*. Kevin (Craig Warnock), a British boy, discovers a group of tiny men busting out of his closet one night. Pursued by a giant head, they escape by creating a wormhole in the wall of Kevin's bedroom, unintentionally dragging Kevin through it with them. It turns out the sextet were former servants of God, demoted from creating plants to cosmic repairs after creating the world's worst tree: "It was 600 feet tall, bright red and smelled horrible." To get even, they stole a map that shows all the weak points in creation, points they can use to plunder time and space.

Accompanying the bandits, Kevin meets a height-obsessed Napoleon (Ian Holm), Robin Hood (John Cleese), a charming Agamemnon (Sean Connery) and almost drowning on the *Titanic*. Evil (David Warner) wants the map too, and tricks the bandits into entering his fortress. Kevin distracts Evil long enough for his friends to escape through a time gap and bring back tanks, cowboys, archers and others. Evil crushes them all but then God (Ralph Richardson) materializes and transforms Evil to stone. He reveals that He knew about the theft but saw it as a chance to test how Evil performed under pressure.

As the bandits, rehired into celestial service, depart with God, Kevin wakes up and finds his house on fire. When the fire chief arrives, he's a double for Agamemnon. Standing outside the house, Kevin finds photographs of his adventures, but also a fragment of petrified Evil. When his parents touch it, they explode, leaving Kevin alone.

Time Triangle

Several films make use of the concept of a specific place where time is out of joint. The most famous example is the Bermuda Triangle, which several films explain as a time rift.

The protagonists of *Fantastic Journey* (1977) didn't go looking for the secret of the Bermuda Triangle, but *it* found *them*. A mysterious glowing cloud sweeps over a charter fishing boat, which crashes on a vast tropical island. The island sits inside a vortex where multiple time zones co-exist ("Like a giant honeycomb if you will!"), so the travelers can stumble from a tribe of Arawaks into an Atlantean city, then meet a civilization of extraterrestrials or a party of Elizabethan pirates. The motley group of castaways (the cast changed as the series went along) including 23rd century healer Varian (Jared Martin), scientist Willoway (Roddy McDowall), pre-teen Scott (Ike Eisenmann), half-alien Liana (Katie Saylor) and Dr. Walters (Carl Franklin). They set out to find the one zone—possibly a mythical place—from which they can return to their own time. They never made it, but did run into plenty of strange and dangerous cultures and creatures along the way.

Edgar Rice Burroughs' The Land That Time Forgot (2009) has a Caribbean pleasure boat sucked through the Bermuda Triangle time warp to land on a prehistoric island of dinosaurs (Burroughs' book had dinosaurs, but no time travel) and castaways from various eras. A couple of other castaways steal the boat, so the newcomers have to ally with a Nazi submarine crew to escape. They eventually succeed, but Frost (C. Thomas Howell) misses the boat and stays behind. His wife Karen (Anya Benton) chooses to stay with him, and the film ends with them having a baby.

Jules Verne's Mysterious Island (2012) starts in 1865 with a handful of captured Union soldiers led by Harding (Lochlyn Munro) making a daring escape by balloon. The balloon passes through a hole in the sky—the Bermuda Triangle rift—and the passengers awake on a tropical island. The island contains humanoids in the jungle, a giant octopus off shore, and ships from all eras, including an airplane carrying present-day sisters Jules and Abby Fogg (Gina Holden, Susie Abromeit). The soldiers and the women meet Captain Nemo (W. Morgan Sheppard), who explains he developed a time machine to stop wars and injustices before they happened. Instead it created the time vortex that sucked in the *Nautilus* and continues trapping other vessels; the humanoids are Nemo's crew members, driven insane by being unable to leave. As the island volcano prepares to blow, Harding opens a second portal by recharging the time machine with lightning. The balloon escapes with the Foggs and the soldiers—Nemo, terminally ill, stays behind—but with no idea when or where they'll land.

In *Triangle* (2005), shipping magnate Benerall (Sam Neill) offers a team of researchers $5 million apiece if they can explain why his ships keep vanishing in the Triangle—and why one ship that did make it through claimed it encountered the *Nina*, the *Pinta* and the *Santa Maria*. The investigators discover the U.S. military's Philadelphia Experiment (see chapter five) created a time rift, which has been swallowing ships ever since. The military has a plan to close the rift, but Benerall's recruits realize it will do the reverse, ripping the rift open. The researchers convince the government to delay and let the Triangle close naturally. As the closure is retroactive, it's as if the Triangle never existed. In the new timeline, the investigators are living different, better lives, but have to struggle to adjust to the changes.

For the darkest and best Bermuda Triangle film, *Triangle*, see chapter eleven.

Rifts Elsewhere

My Science Project (1985) starts in the 1950s, with the Air Force disposing of a crashed UFO. Cut to 1985, when high schooler Michael Harlan (John Stockwell) discovers the ship's buried power source. With his best friend Latello (Fisher Stevens), Harlan determines that the device can send them forward in time and realizes he has a killer science project. When they demonstrate the machine, it creates a time warp around the school. The warp sucks in the science teacher (Dennis Hopper) and Harlan's girlfriend Ellie (Danielle von Zerneck), while materializing samurai, dinosaurs and other perils in the present. The guys have to fight through the danger, shut down the machine and bring Ellie and the teacher home.

In *House II: The Second Story* (1987), Jesse McLoughlin (Arye Gross) discovers his undead grandfather (Royal Dano) buried in the back yard of the family home, preserved by the Aztec crystal skull interred next to him. Unearthing the skull opens time gates around the house: Jesse and his buddy Charlie (Jonathan Stark) stumble into prehistory, then into an Aztec temple where they rescue "the Virgin" (Devin Devasquez). Gramps' old partner Slim (Dean Cleverdon), manifesting as another mummy, kills Gramps. Slim drags Charlie and the Virgin into the Old West where he hopes to trap Jesse and take the skull. Jesse destroys Slim, but the firefight brings down a swarm of cops. Jesse uses the skull a final time to travel back to the Old West for good, where he, Charlie and the Virgin set off for fresh adventures.

Lost in Space (1998) ineffectively reboots the 1960s TV series about a family lost among the stars. Here the Robinson family, including John (William Hurt), Maureen (Mimi Rogers) and estranged tween genius Will (Jack Johnson), leave an exhausted, over-crowded Earth to found a colony in space. A revolutionary group hires Smith (Gary Oldman) to destroy the Robinsons' ship, the *Jupiter II*, while the family is in cryosleep for the trip. Smith sabotages the ship, but the family wakes and saves the *Jupiter II* with a jump through hyperspace, landing on a planet rife with space-time distortions.

While the family waits for chance to relaunch the *Jupiter II*, John stumbles across the adult Will from 20 years ahead, alone on the planet except for a mutated Smith. Will has built a time machine so that he can save the Robinsons by preventing the launch. The original Smith shows up and tries to use the machine to go home. His future self kills him, after which John kills the mutate. Meanwhile, the *Jupiter II* has to take off without John to meet its launch window, but it crashes, killing everyone. Will sends John back in time to save the ship so the Robinsons make it off-world, lost in space but united as a family.

Sir Arthur Conan Doyle's The Lost World (1999–2002) was very loosely based on the classic Sir Arthur Conan Doyle adventure about an expedition that discovers living dinosaurs on a South American plateau. In this adaptation, Prof. Challenger's (Peter McCauley) expedition finds dinosaurs, apemen, cavemen, reptile men and Veronica (Jennifer O'Dell), the jungle-girl survivor of a previous expedition.

As the series progressed, the explorers learned that the plateau was rife with time distortions. In one episode, Challenger's experiments with a plateau energy source hurl him and his colleagues into 2033, where the Earth has been devastated by war. That gave the group an added incentive to find a way home, so they could prevent that future. In the final episode, the characters were trapped in different times, all facing lethal threats—conquistadores, human sacrifice, a malevolent computer—so Veronica, who'd learned she was the chosen guardian of the plateau, sacrificed herself to tap its power and save her friends. We'll never know if she succeeded.

In *Strange Days at Blake Holsey High* (2002–06), teen Josie Trent (Emma Taylor-Isherwood) arrives at the title boarding school assuming it'll be no different from any other she's attended. She changes her mind when her roommate Corinne (Shadia Simmons) gets sucked into a black hole (*Black Hole High* was a title for the series in syndication), landing 15 years earlier at the nearby Pearadyne research lab, right before it was destroyed in an explosion. Josie manages to bring Corinne home safely but the black hole continued warping reality around Blake Holsey. Usually it did this by reacting to people's emotions: When perfectionist Corinne can't accept a crappy day, for instance, the day keeps relooping until she learns to live with imperfection.

Corinne, Josie and the other members of the school science club learn that the Pearadyne explosion created the black hole, which ties in with a mysterious metal sphere Josie found, but later lost to sinister Victor Pearson (Lawrence Bayne) in the past. At the end of the third season, she reclaims the sphere from the past, only to return to a divergent timeline where Blake Holsey has been closed. In a three-part finale, the Science Club learns that Victor's wife (Jenny Cooper) originally came from the future to ensure that Victor acquired the sphere, which will lead to groundbreaking discoveries. Opposing her is Josie's father Avenir (John Ralston), who wants the sphere to create a nightmare future ruled by himself. Josie escapes the divergence and, with the Science Club, defeats her father, keeping history on track.

The tropical island setting of *Lost* (2004–10) was never an ordinary place, as the survivors of Oceanic Flight 815 found after they crashed there. The first few episodes included polar bears, monsters formed of black smoke and the occasional ghost; the survivors learn multiple groups have occupied the island, including at least one cadre of mad scientists. In the fourth season we learn that visitors to the island sometimes find their mind skipping randomly to other points in time. At the end of that season, an attack on the island prompts Ben (Michael Emerson), the leader of one of the rival groups, to activate an underground defense device. This transports the island away—and through time.

While six of the cast escaped and returned to the outside world for a few years, others bounced into the 1950s and the 1970s. Finally Jack Shepard (Matthew Fox), one of the "Oceanic Six" who escaped, becomes convinced their destiny is to return. Eventually he and several others make it back but to 1977. There Jack becomes convinced that if they detonate a nuke buried on the island, it will destroy the electromagnetic technology that brought the plane down. History will change and they'll never have crashed. In the sixth season it turns out that didn't work—everyone simply returns to the present for a final conflict unrelated to the time trip.

Dark Shadows, Deadly Times

In 1966, producer Dan Curtis conceived the daytime TV soap *Dark Shadows* as a Gothic drama in which orphan Victoria Winters (Alexandra Moltke) takes a job at the spooky old Collinwood Manor as a governess. She faced both soap problems—is one of the Collinses her birth mother or father?—and occasional supernatural threats. When the show tanked in the ratings, Curtis figured he had nothing to lose by having a 200-year-old vampire, Barnabas Collins (Jonathan Frid), freed from his sealed coffin. Ratings shot up and for the next five years the show threw all manner of supernatural thrills at the show's fans, including great chunks of time travel.

In episode 364, Victoria attends a séance and finds herself hurled back to 1795, the year Barnabas became undead. Responsible for that tragedy: Angelique (Lara Parker), maid to Barnabas' true love Josette (Kathryn Leigh Scott). A witch, she drives Josette and Barnabas apart. After Angelique marries Barnabas, he learns the truth about her and kills her. Angelique's dying curse turns him into a vampire, feeding on the citizens of nearby Collinsport until he's locked in the coffin. (In 1991, the prime-time *Dark Shadows* revival remade this plotline during its short run.)

In a later arc, the malevolent ghost of Quentin Collins (David Selby) kills young David Collins (David Henesy) and drives the rest of the family away in a reworking of Henry James' *The Turn of the Screw*. To set things right, Barnabas travels back to the 1800s, during Quentin's lifetime, and struggles to avert the chain of events—which involves lycanthropy and the black magician Count Petofi (Thayer David)—that turned Quentin into a vengeful spirit. As a result of Barnabas' intervention, Quentin doesn't die; a magical picture preserves him, Dorian Gray–like, into the present, alive. The haunting never happens.

In a later story, Barnabas travels into a parallel timeline, then returns to his own world, arriving in the 1990s. His family and friends are murdered or insane, the house is in ruins and a dead sorcerer controls the town. Barnabas makes it back to the present and struggles to prevent the tragedy, but the sorcerer, whose hate for the Collinses dates back 300 years, defeats him. Barnabas' only hope is to flee back through time to the 1600s and fight his enemy while he was alive. Barnabas triumphs, but Angelique—whom he's finally accepted as his one true love—dies in his arms.

With ratings sagging, Curtis switched to another parallel world setting where the alt-versions of Barnabas and Angelique finally had a happy ending. Had ratings picked up, the series would have continued with the new characters.

Land of the Lost

Saturday morning's *Land of the Lost* (1974–76) was a standout series that included scripts from SF authors Larry Niven, David Gerrold and Theodore Sturgeon. The opening credits tell how park ranger Rick (Spencer Milligan) and his kids Will and Holly (Wesley Eure, Kathy Coleman) are caught in an earthquake that hurls them through a dimensional gate. They land in another world populated by dinosaurs, the man-ape Pakuni and the insectoid Sleestak. It also draws in other visitors besides the Marshalls: a Civil War veteran, an Air Force pilot, the psionic Zarn (Marvin Miller), Holly's adult self and Enik (Walker Edmiston), an ancestor of the Sleestak.

The Marshalls struggle to survive, finding food and water without being eaten by dinos or captured by the Sleestak, who liked feeding prisoners to their monstrous god. Over the course of the first season, the Marshalls discovered Enik's people had built the Land as an artificial pocket universe before wiping themselves out. Enik wanted to go back in time and prevent that, but found it impossible to open a time gate out. He eventually realized that the Marshalls coming into the Land had created an imbalance: sending them home again would restore the balance and let Enik leave too. In the second season, however, the Marshalls were still in the Land. The forgettable third season had Rick escape but Uncle Jack Marshall (Ron Harper) gets sucked in to replace him.

In 1991, a revival series offered better special effects, but considerably less imagination and not much of a time travel element. Then in 2009 came the unimpressive big-screen version starring Will Ferrell as Rick, now a scientist with a crazy theory that humanity can

Will Marshall (Wesley Eure, right) and Holly Marshall (Kathy Coleman) of *Land of the Lost* (1974–77), with the insectoid Sleestak and the man-ape Pakuni against the jungle background.

tap time warps for power. He builds a prototype warp-tapper, but doesn't have the courage to test it. Then Holly (Anna Friel)—not his daughter but an admirer—shows up with a cave fossil imprinted with a modern cigarette lighter, proof that time warps exist.

Rick, Holly and spelunker Will (Danny McBride) explore the cave where Holly found the fossil and stumble into the Land, where dinosaurs swarm under suspension bridges and a crashed plane lies next to a Roman galley. Rick loses his prototype and Enik (John Boylan) tells the travelers that the Zarn (Leonard Nimoy) will use it to open a time warp back to Earth and lead the Sleestak in a war of conquest. After great effort, the travelers recovers Rick's gadget, only to learn too late that Enik is the real villain, using the image of the Zarn to manipulate the humans. Enik prepares to lead the Sleestak to Earth, but the good guys defeat him. Rick and Anna return home, while Will stays behind in the Land for more adventures. Back on Earth, Rick's evidence proves his theories and redeems his reputation.

Mental Shifts

In some movies, it's the mind rather than the body that's lost in time. For example, in Alain Resnais' *Je t'aime je t'aime* (1968), a research institute recruits failed suicide Claude Ridder (Claude Rich) as their time travel guinea pig, figuring he has nothing to lose. The plan is to send his mind back one year for one minute, but instead his consciousness becomes unmoored in time. Claude bounces randomly through the events of his recent life, particularly his nightmarish, dysfunctional relationship with the unstable, depressed Catrine (Olga Georges-Picot). As the lab is unable to recover Claude's mind, presumably he'll bounce around in his personal hell forever.

Slaughterhouse-Five (1972) adapts Kurt Vonnegut's picaresque story of Billy Pilgrim (Michael Sacks), a World War II POW who survived the Dresden firebombing to become a successful businessman and father. Later on, he's captured by the planet Trafalmadore, along with sex symbol Montana Wildhack (Valerie Perrine) who in a wildly sexist plot twist happily becomes Billy's lover. These events are told in random order because Billy's consciousness moves randomly through his life; for instance, he's already experienced his own death at the hands of disgruntled fellow POW Lazzaro (Ron Leibman). Time is fixed—the Trafalmadorians know they'll destroy the cosmos, but can't prevent it—so Billy can't alter anything. Eventually he learns to appreciate the happy times with Montana rather than becoming obsessed with his tragedies.

In *Premonition* (2007), Jim (Julian McMahon) dies in an auto accident, leaving his wife Linda (Sandra Bullock) struggling to hold things together. Then she wakes up to find Jim alive again and discovers it's actually several days before the accident. She bounces back and forth from past to present, and her confusion at living life out of sequence convinces her loved ones she's snapping from grief.

Linda learns Jim was contemplating an affair—they'd been drifting apart—and wonders if she should just let his death play out. Her priest (Jude Ciccolella) tells her to remember what she has faith in and fight for that, after which she confronts Jim about their relationship. Linda and Jim reconnect and make love, and the next morning Linda drives to the accident site to save him. In what the film assumes is a startling twist, it's Linda's arrival at the site that causes the accident. However, because of that night of love, Linda's now carrying his child.

A pretentious film, *Yesterday Was a Lie* (2008) throws in multiple shots of Dali's *Persistence of Memory* to prove how arty it is. Hoyle (Kipleigh Brown) is a hard-drinking detective still in pain after breaking up with Dudas (John Newton). A murder investigation again entangles her with Dudas and triggers *déja vu* flashes. "The singer" (Chase Masterson) tells Hoyle linear time is an illusion our minds impose on non-linear reality. A notebook involved in the murder case contains a formula that allows someone to change history by reordering the linear illusion.

It turns out that Dudas has the notebook, and Hoyle committed the murder while protecting him from someone who wanted it. Hoyle becomes convinced that Dudas is using the formula to make time repeat and hang on to their love. The Singer tells Hoyle that no formula can affect time—only love can do that, which proves Hoyle and Dudas' love is so strong, they should stay together. We end on a shot of the lovers dancing, but no clue whether it's past, present or future.

Shuffle (2011) stars T.J. Thyne as photographer Lovell Milo, whose unmoored mind one day is in his eight-year-old body, the next day his 90-year-old body, the next his 30. He has no idea which age is his real one and can't seem to remember anything about the parts of his future he's already lived. Despite this, he keeps meeting people who tell him his non-linear life is a gift, not a curse.

Milo discovers that he marries his lifelong best friend Grace (Paula Rhodes) in his mid-twenties. Shortly afterwards she's hit by a car; Milo's father (Chris Stone), a brilliant ER surgeon, is passed out drunk and unable to operate. After Grace dies, Milo cuts off all contact with his father. When Milo's one-night stand gets pregnant, he supports the baby but refuses to see the kid, for fear he'll be as bad at fatherhood as his own dad.

Grace's ghost appears and explains she triggered his time-jumping in the hope that showing him the future would stop his life collapsing. Restored by her love, Milo becomes a father to his son, marries again, reconnects with his father and lives a long, happy life. And in the afterlife, Grace is waiting.

Street vendor Chris (MacLeod Andrews), the protagonist of *Found in Time* (2012), has a mental glitch that causes him to black out and remember life out of sequence. What he doesn't know is that his girlfriend Jina (Kelly Sullivan) is a researcher studying whether Chris, unlike Billy Pilgrim, can actually change time when he's in the past. Ayana (Mina Vesper Gokal), who has the same mental state as Chris, starts hanging out with him, and now time begins to unwind. In various timelines, Chris kills Jina or doesn't, gets locked up in an asylum or doesn't and kills two cops to save a friend, or doesn't. Finally Chris averts most of the negative outcomes by changing time so that he and Jina never hook up. He and Ayana head off for adventures … unless it all took place in his head, which in this film seems possible.

CHAPTER FIVE

Strange Visitors from Another World
Travel to the Present from Other Times

> "We're not riding roughshod into an ancient culture where they ride in vehicles, blow each others' heads off, break into dorms and rape women and children!"
> —*Last Exit to Earth*

Most of the time travelers in the previous two chapters made the journey involuntarily. Travelers from the past and future coming to our time are almost always acting intentionally. They come from Then to Now to escape a pursuer, pursue an escapee or find some vital McGuffin. (Travelers whose goal is to find love or change history are covered in later chapters.) Like the previous two chapters, most or all of the futures here are unpleasant—radioactive wastelands or dystopian tyrannies.

Future Fiends

The Twonky (1953) turns Henry Kuttner's classic short story about oppression and thought control into a would-be wacky comedy. It begins when irascible professor Kerry (Hans Conried) discovers that his wife has bought him a TV set to keep him company while she's on a trip. That's annoying enough for TV-hating Kerry (1950s movies often took shots at the upstart medium), but it gets worse when the TV turns out to be a (very unconvincing) robot. It cleans the house, lights his cigarettes, prints money when he needs some, forces him to rewrite a lecture, and at one point tries renting him a hooker. Kerry reacts to all this like a sitcom character saddled with a nagging wife. Throughout the movie, Kerry loudly defends his right to make his own decisions, even bad ones (for example, he defends a woman's right to drive the wrong way on a one-way street).

After learning about the robot, Kerry's friend Trout (Billy Lynn) calls it a twonky, his childhood term for anything he didn't understand. Based on zero evidence, Trout correctly deduces the twonky has been sent to Kerry from the future to see if it can successfully control people's lives. He concludes that if they can destroy it, that may end the evil plan. Kerry finds the robot can defend itself from attack, so he contrives to dump it on the outskirts of town. When Kerry hitches a ride homeward, the twonky sneaks onto the back of the car. A truck rear-ends the car, smashing the robot and presumably saving the future from a dystopia of government-by-twonky.

The Adventures of Brisco County, Jr. (1993–94) was a tongue-in-cheek Western starring

Bruce Campbell as the eponymous Harvard-educated lawyer turned bounty hunter. In the first episode, murderous outlaw John Bly (Billy Drago) kills Brisco's sheriff father, then sets out to capture a mysterious Orb that can control men's minds and raise the dead. Hunting down Bly and his gang became Brisco's top priority.

Eventually Bly revealed he was from 500 years in the future, and the Orb would enable him to conquer his era when he took it home. A traveler from 25 centuries after Bly—the era that sent the Orb through time—warns Brisco that if Bly succeeds, he'll impose two millennia of oppression upon the world. Brisco kills Bly, saving both the Orb and Earth's future.

Based on Michael Crichton's novel, *Sphere* (1998) has a team of researchers (Liev Schreiber, Dustin Hoffman, Samuel L. Jackson, Sharon Stone) called in when the Navy finds a 300-year-old spaceship in the depths of the Pacific. The researchers discover it's an Earth ship that came through a wormhole from the future—implausibly the ultra-advanced tech is mid–21st century—carrying a mysterious, translucent ET sphere. Harry (Jackson) deduces that as the crew had no knowledge what would happen to them, the researchers are fated to die before filing a report.

When terrifying horrors attack the team, it appears Harry is right. Norman (Hoffman) realizes that the sphere has given the researchers the power to warp reality—the monsters are their own fears, brought to life. After the survivors escape to the surface, they command their new power to erase itself and wipe out their memories of what they found. The sphere promptly vanishes and the timeline is preserved.

Futurama: Bender's Big Score (2007) was the direct-to-video animated finale to the *Futurama* series. *Futurama* was the story of an interplanetary shipping crew that includes Fry (Billy West), a 20th century pizza delivery guy who fell into cryosleep and woke up a millennium in the future. In the movie, alien Internet scammers take over the shipping company and enslave Fry's robot co-worker Bender (John DiMaggio). The aliens discover that Fry has the formula for time travel tattooed on his butt, and use it to send Bender into the past and steal everything that's not nailed down. As the aliens' wealth grows, they worry that further changes to the timeline will hurt them more than help. They stop the thefts and decide to destroy the formula by destroying Fry's body.

Fry escapes back to 2000 AD, pursued by Bender, who in a *Terminator*-parody begins killing every Fry he can find. Due to a time paradox, Fry survives and rejoins his friends in the future. By this point the aliens have bought Earth itself, so they free Bender from their control and evict humanity. Fry is more depressed that his co-worker Leela (Katey Sagal) has found a new boyfriend, Lars (West again).

With the help of Santa Claus (don't ask), the Earth exiles counter-attack and destroy the alien fleet. The aliens try to deploy a super-weapon Bender stole for them, but the robot already stole the weapon back and uses it to finish off the aliens. Lars dies in battle and turns out to be another Fry counterpart. Everything's back to normal ... until Bender's meddling causes another paradox and wipes out the universe. (Don't worry, the series eventually returned.)

Villains from the Past

Bridge Across Time (1985) opens in 1888 as police chase Jack the Ripper (Paul Rossilli) onto London Bridge, where he apparently falls to his death, dislodging a brick from the parapet. The bridge is eventually moved to Arizona—a real-life 1968 event—and years later the missing brick is restored. When a woman accidentally bleeds on it, Jack materializes on the bridge in the present.

After the murders start, police detective Don Gregory (David Hasselhoff) deduces that the killer is a Ripper copycat (a remarkable feat as the murders don't resemble the original killings). Topping that show of brilliance, Don also determines that this is the real Ripper and that time travel is involved. The mayor (Lane Smith) orders Don to keep quiet rather than let talk of a serial killer hurt the town's tourist trade.

When a stranger (David Fox-Brenton) dies trying to destroy the bridge—there's no explanation who he is or how he knows Jack's secret—the town happily pins the murders on him. Don knows better and uses his girlfriend Angie (Stepfanie Kramer) to lure the Ripper into a trap. Jack outmaneuvers Don and plots to kill Angie on the bridge, so that her blood on the brick will send him back to his own time. At the last minute Don shoots the Ripper, which hurls Jack into the water along with the brick of destiny. Once again, his body vanishes.

Marching Out of Time (1993) is an obscure, possibly lost film (a few clips are available online) concerning a Nazi teleportation experiment designed to land troops in England. It crosses beams with scientist Memo's (Matthew Henerson) modern-day teleportation test in Venice, California. The Nazis materialize in the present, then return to the past with enough historical information to change the outcome of the war. Memo's neighbor Fred (Frederick Anderson) has to travel back to the past to recover the history books.

Pirates of the Plain (1999) offers a less unpleasant visitor, double-dealing 18th century pirate Captain Jezebel Jack (Tim Curry). After his crew throws the schemer overboard in an unearthly storm, he materializes in modern Nebraska, where he befriends Bobby (Seth E. Adkins), an imaginative nine-year-old. After Jack gets over his anachronistic confusion, he discovers Bobby's grandfather (Charles Napier) has an old, unreadable map showing the location of a fortune in silver buried by Jesse James. Jack understands the map's cryptic symbols and digs up the treasure with Bobby.

The storm sucks Jack's ship and crew through time to the farm. They fire cannons at the farmhouse but Jack and Bobby fight them off. The pirates capture Bobby and his mother (Dee Wallace Stone). Jack saves them by offering up the silver, but when he and his crew return to the past, the pirates discover Jack tricked them with tinfoil. Jack escapes back to the present and settles in with Bobby and his mom.

Ben 10: Race Against Time (2007) was a live-action film based on the animated *Ben 10* TV series. Ben Tennyson (Graham Phillips) has spent the summer battling aliens by using his omnitrix, which shapeshifts him into super-powered forms. But now that school's starting, he's back to being ordinary, though he gets a chance to destroy the alien Eon (Christien Anholt). Eon survives, and sets out to capture Ben and something called the Hands of Armageddon. Ben's grandfather Max (Lee Majors) reveals that the Hands of Armageddon brought Eon from his dying world through a time rift; Eon wants his entire race to follow. The Plumbers, an alien-fighting group that Max belongs to, took the Hands from Eon two centuries ago and closed the rift.

Eon captures Ben and uses the omnitrix to turn the boy into a younger Eon, powerful enough to use the Hands and reopen the rift. Ben overcomes Eon's control and deactivates the Hands, then destroys them and Eon.

Fox's TV series *Alcatraz* (2012) brought an army of crooks to the present, though nothing interesting resulted. In 1963, the entire inmate population of Alcatraz Prison vanishes overnight, the real reason the government closed down the prison. In 2012, the various cutthroats—bombers, bank robbers, serial killers—reappear and resume their criminal careers. Federal agent Hauser (Sam Neill) recruits Detective Madsen (Sarah Jones) and Alcatraz buff Diego Soto (Jorge Garcia) to hunt down the inmates. In between taking down the convict of the week, the trio discover the Alcatraz warden (Johnny Coyne) was behind the time traveling convicts. The series ended before the warden's agenda was revealed.

Pursued and Pursuers

In some stories, one time traveler arriving in the present brings another in hot pursuit.

In the BBC miniseries *Man Dog* (1972), teens Kate (Carol Hazell), Sammy (Jane Anthony) and Duncan (Adrian Shergold) see a man teleport. They investigate and discover the Group, refugees from a dystopian 26th century. Gala, the future's all-powerful secret police, wants the Group's time travel research in order to kill their enemies in the cradle. Instead, the Group fled to the present to plan for Gala's overthrow. The Group's time machine remained behind in the future, so the Gala commander Halmar (Jonathan Hardy) uses it to pursue the group. The title of the series refers to the Group punishing one member by transferring his mind into the girls' pet dog.

By stealing magic from others, medieval sorcerer Salatin (Brendan Dillon, Jr.) has become the mightiest of *The Lords of Magick* (1988). To cap off his career, he kidnaps Princess Lina (Ruth Zackarian), knowing that a child of royal blood will give him the power to rule everything. He then transports her to our present, confident that no one can follow, but sibling mages Michael (Jarrett Parker) and Ulric (Mark Gauthier) succeed. Although stunned by the 20th century's noise and automobiles, they enlist Tommy (David Snow), a wannabe magician, by promising to train him in magic. Salatin corrupts Ulric by preying upon his lecherous nature, but in the final showdown Ulric sacrifices himself to destroy Salatin. Michael and Lina return to the past, where Michael receives permission to resurrect his brother.

Out of Time (1988), an unsuccessful TV pilot, opens in 2088 when police work is a hi-tech profession thanks to the genius of 20th century inventor-detective Max Taylor (Bill Maher). Max's descendant Channing Taylor (Bruce Abbott) insists on using old-school, two-fisted policing to compete with his ancestor's towering legend, but this ruins the cops' plan to catch the murderous Marcus (Adam Ant). A time machine takes Marcus to 1988, where he plans to steal a miracle drug, and Channing is dragged along in the vortex.

Channing discovers the cops of 1988 consider Max a laughing stock for his fixation on gimmicks and gadgets. The two Taylors don't get along, but Pam (Rebecca Schaeffer), a waitress caught up in the hunt for Marcus, convinces them to work together. When the Taylors confront Marcus, he kills Max. Channing exhausts the time machine to jump back a few minutes so that Marcus dies instead. Now that he's stuck in the present, Channing joins forces with Pam and Max to fight crime.

Time Barbarians (1990) is the forgettable story of Doran (Deron Michael McBee), a barbarian king who entrusts his mate Lystra (Jo Ann Ayres) with a magic amulet. The malevolent Mandrak (Daniel Martine) rapes and murders Lystra, then flees to the present and becomes leader of a street gang. Doran follows and meets Lystra's present-day double, reporter Penny Price (Ayres). Doran eventually kills Mandrak, then heads home, promising Penny he'll never forget her (although he certainly got over Lystra's death fast).

Julian Sands is the *Warlock* (1991), an evil sorcerer captured by the witch hunter Redferne (Richard E. Grant) in late 1600s Massachusetts. Satan frees his servant and sends him to the present to collect three pieces of a grimoire that can unmake creation. While stealing the first part, the Warlock maliciously curses 20-year-old diabetic Kassandra (Lori Singer) so that she ages 20 years a day. Redferne arrives in the present (the film doesn't explain how) and tells Kass that to break the curse she must recover a piece of jewelry the Warlock stole from her.

Although the two heroes recover the bracelet and restore Kass's youth, they can't stop the Warlock from reassembling the full grimoire. Kassandra has learned that salt is kryptonite for witches, so she uses her insulin needles to inject the sorcerer with salt water. The Warlock dies, Redferne's spirit departs and Kass buries the grimoire in a salt flat. (*Warlock II* isn't a sequel and has no time travel element.)

The time travelers in *Future War* (1997) are future cyborg tyrants who collect slaves from the present. When one slave (Daniel Bernhardt) breaks free, the cyborgs pursue "the Runaway" with genetically engineered hunting dinosaurs (this is much less entertaining than it sounds). The Runaway finds refuge with Ann (Travis Brooks Stewart), an ex-hooker turned novitiate nun. Ann's connections in the underworld enable them to recruit the manpower and firepower to destroy the cyborg base. Free of pursuit, the Runaway decides to continue helping people by becoming a counselor at a rehab center.

In *Lancelot, Guardian of Time* (1997), the sorcerer Wolvencroft (John Saxon) kidnaps the young Arthur (Adam Carter) 15 years before he becomes king and takes him into the 20th century. If Wolvencroft tricks Arthur into drawing the Sword in the Stone in the present, the sorcerer can seize Excalibur from Merlin (Leonard Auclair). Merlin sends Lancelot (Marc Singer) to bring back Arthur and the legendary blade.

Arriving in the 20th century, Lancelot gets help from Katherine (Claudia Christian), a cynical writer who falls for the chivalric hero. Their first efforts against Wolvencroft fail, but when the moment to draw the sword arrives, Lancelot undoes Wolvencroft's time travel spell. All the medievals return to Camelot, Arthur draws the sword without harm and Lancelot destroys Wolvencroft. Back in the present, Katherine receives a magic ring from Lancelot that brings her to Camelot, where she marries him.

In the far future of *Megas XLR* (2004–05), humanity has lost a war to the alien Glorft. Commander Kiva (Wendee Lee) retrofits Megas, a captured alien mecha, to go back in time to a crucial point in the war and turn the tide. When Kiva launches Megas into the past, following in her own robot, the experimental time gate misfires. Megas lands in a 1930s New Jersey junkyard; 60 years later, Coop (David DeLuise) and Jamie (Steven Jayblum) find the robot and remodels it with a sports car for a head and a videogame hand control to work it. When Kiva arrives to claim Megas, she discovers that due to his modifications, nobody else can operate it, and the time travel circuits no longer work. While Kiva tries to repair them, she and the guys fight off Glorft attacks, battle other aliens and in one episode reclaim Megas from the New Jersey Department of Motor Vehicles.

In the 25th century of *Doomsday* (2015), Achilles (Alain Terzoli) is a loyal servant of humanity's cyborg overlords. By the start of the film, he's been infected with a fatal nanovirus that forces him to sabotage the cyborgs' defenses, allowing the Legion, the human resistance, to destroy them. (We later learn he was a sleeper agent for the Legion.) Hunted by the vengeful cyborg Erebus-7 (Richard Lawrence), Achilles flees into the past where he meets Cassie (Amy Pemberton) and Byron (Darren Jacobs). The couple treat Achilles as a mere annoyance until Erebus-7 blows up London, something the cyborg justifies as already part of history. After Rebus kills Byron, Achilles and Cassie flee. They meet Achilles' ancestor Dedra (Helen Soraya) and Cassie discovers that she herself eventually become the leader of the Legion. As history says Cassie lives a long time, it's physically impossible for Erebus to kill her. She destroys him, then kills Achilles to stop the virus from spreading.

From the Past with a Mission

In *The Visitors* (1993), a funny film from France, a witch's potion drives Count Godefroy (Jean Reno) to kill the father (Patrick Burgel) of his beloved Frenegonde (Valérie Lemercier). The wedding is off until a wizard offers Godefroy a potion that will send the count and his right hand Jacquasse (Christian Clavier) back in time to avert the fatal blow.

Oops. The potion sends both men into the present where they engage in lots of anachronistic slapstick to the bemusement of Godefroy's descendant Beatrice (Lemercier) and Jacquasse's decscendant (Clavier), a *nouveau riche* who now owns the count's castle. The time travelers learn they have a limited window to return to the past, after which they'll be stuck in the present and their descendants will cease to exist. Jacquasse has no interest in leaving a world where a commoner can live like a king, especially after he finds love with bag lady Ginette (Marie-Anne Chazel). Jacquasse' solution is to switch places with his descendant, who goes back in time with Godefroy and ends up in serfdom. Godefroy averts his father-in-law's death and marries Frenegonde.

Except in *The Visitors 2—The Corridors of Time* (1998) it turns out he doesn't: Jacquasse trading places with his descendant has jammed the time gate open, with side effects such as sucking out Frenegonde's father's life. The wedding is postponed and characters start jumping back and forth between the past and present, trying to set things right and engaging in more slapstick, but with less humor. Finally a frustrated Beatrice tricks Godefroy and Jacquasse into drinking the time travel potion again. As it wasn't properly mixed, the two men materialize in the French Revolution.

The American *Just Visiting* (2001) reuses Clavier and Reno (now named Andre and Thibaut), but gives their time trip a slightly different rationale: It's not the fair Rosalind's (Christina Applegate) father who winds up dead but Rosalind herself. When the botched spell lands Andre and Thibaut in the present, they meet the count's descendant Julia (Applegate) and her odious, two-timing boyfriend Hunter (Matthew Ross). Julia's personal-growth arc—learning Hunter's a jerk, having faith in herself, finding true love—takes up a fair amount of running time alongside the slapstick before Thibaut returns to the past and saves Rosalind. Andre stays behind—with sexy Tara Reid rather than a bag lady—and Hunter gets dragged to the past in his place.

New Zealand's *The Navigator: A Medieval Odyssey* (1988) also deals with culture shock, but for darker effect. It starts in mid–14th century Cumbria as the Black Death spreads across the land. Griffin (Hamish McFarlane), a village boy, has a vision revealing his village will be spared if they tunnel through to the far side of the Earth and place a new cross on the tallest church spire there. His brother Connor (Bruce Lyons) leads a digging party that emerges, though they don't know it, in 20th century New Zealand.

Although overwhelmed by the city's size and the traffic, the villagers befriend some foundry workers who agree to cast a cross from the copper the villagers brought with them. When they reach the church in Griffin's vision, the boy helps place the cross at the top, but falls to his death ... and wakes up. It turns out the whole trip was a vision, but it inspires the villagers to believe they're saved. Alas, Connor caught the plague while traveling and while he survived, he infected Griffin. The boy dies for real to save his village.

Arthur's Quest (1999) begins after Morgana (Catherine Oxenberg) murders Arthur's father. Merlin (Arye Gross) takes five-year-old Arthur and Excalibur to the present for safety; Caitlin (Alexandra Paul), a waitress, agrees to adopt Arthur until Merlin returns. A decade later, Arthur (Eric Christian Olsen) is a moody teenage misfit, alienated from everyone but Caitlin and his best friend Gwen (Katie Johnston). When Merlin returns, the boy refuses to believe any of his crazy talk about destiny, and the wizard's magic is too exhausted for him to prove his story.

When Morgana arrives in the present to steal Excalibur, Arthur realizes that Merlin's on the level. Arthur still doesn't want to get involved, but after Morgana kidnaps Caitlin, he joins forces with Merlin. Despite their efforts, Morgana finds and draws Excalibur from the stone where Merlin placed it. The sword, a force for good, shrivels Morgana's evil soul. Arthur and Merlin return to Camelot with Gwen and Caitlin, who's in love with Merlin. A history book reveals that Guinevere became Arthur's "vice king," Arthur invented the hamburger and Caitlin served as Camelot's secretary of state.

Time Changer (2002) starts in 1890, as colleagues of seminary teacher Russell Carlisle (D. David Morin) praise his new book, which advocates teaching secular morality separate from the authority of God's word. The one naysayer, Anderson (Gavin MacLeod), tells Carlisle this is literally a Satanic message because it fools secular people into thinking being good will get them into Heaven.

By a happy coincidence, Anderson has created a "singularity chrono-displacer" he uses to send Carlisle into the present to witness the damage of secularism. The professor discovers a future where stores sell sexy lingerie, prayer is outlawed in public schools (a conservative myth) and churches focus on social events rather than saving souls. Carlisle concludes that secularism has brought on the End Times. He returns to 1890 and rewrites his manuscript to reaffirm that Christianity is the only valid basis for ethics. Anderson meanwhile discovers his machine can't get him to the end of the 21st century, implying Judgment Day will happen by then ... but how much sooner?

The execrable *Clive Barker Presents Saint Sinner* (2002) opens in 1815, when the monk Tomas (Greg Serano) foolishly tampers with an occult talisman his order sealed away, thereby unleashing the succubi Munkar (Mary Mara) and Nakir (Rebecca Harrell). After they kill Tomas' best friend and use another artifact to escape into the present, the guilt-ridden monk follows them, carrying a holy dagger that can re-imprison them.

The succubi go on a killing streak and Tomas' attempt to track them makes him look like the guilty party (as happened to H.G. Wells in *Time After Time*). Detective Dressler

(Gina Ravera) believes Tomas' story and they begin hunting for someone holy enough to wield the dagger. Finally Tomas uses the dagger himself and destroys the demons. When he returns to the past, he dies; his tombstone describes him as a saint unaware of his own virtue.

From 1800s Japan comes the samurai *Izo* (2004) played by Kazuya Nakayama. After being crucified at the start of the film (this reflects the death of the real warrior Izo Okada), he appears in the present (he also pops up in World War II and other times). Izo spends most of the movie hacking up his enemies—part of some unexplained conspiracy, or representing social repression or something—and occasionally killing women and schoolchildren. Characters spout lots of pretentious dialogue ("Since I invested my emotions in your mitochondria, you have been the answer!") before the end, when the bad guys kill Izo only to have him apparently reborn.

Lucius (Hiroshi Abe), the protagonist of *Therma Romae—Roman Baths* (2012), is an unsuccessful architect specializing in public baths in Rome, AD 128. As he's struggling for a new, cooler idea, a time rift pulls him into a modern Japanese bath house. Lucius returns to Rome with innovative designs that make him a superstar. Emperor Hadrian (Masachika Ichimura) assigns his pet bath projects to Lucius. Fortunately Lucius keeps returning to Japan—which he assumes is some Roman slave province—and returning with more new concepts. (Executing 21st century designs with Roman technology often produces hysterical results.) Lucius also meets Mami (Aya Ueto), an aspiring manga artist awed by the Roman's thews.

Despite his success, Lucius feels he's just an imitator. When Mami gets drawn back in time with him, she tells Lucius he's not just a copycat—it's his own desire to find new ideas that pulled him to the future. Mami and Lucius fall for each other, but they realize Lucius has subtly influenced Roman politics so that history is changing for the worse. By building a hot-springs spa for the recuperation of injured soldiers, Lucius so impresses the emperor that he's able to steer him back on the right path. Mami heads home, but Lucius promises they'll meet again. Don't all roads lead to Rome?

In the less successful *Thermae Romae II* (2014), Lucius' new task is to build a spa for gladiators. After a trip to a sumo wrestling locker room, he comes back with radical ideas, such as a massage chair, and having gladiators *not* fight to the death. The film continues in the same vein as the first, with Lucius constantly pilfering new ideas from Japan and reuniting with Mami, though the romance doesn't go anywhere.[1]

Fuji TV aired a three-episode anime version of *Therma Romae* in 2012.

The Future Needs Our Help

In *Star Trek IV: The Voyage Home* (1986), Admiral Kirk (William Shatner) and the 23rd century crew of the *Enterprise* are heading for Earth in a Klingon warship to face punishment for their actions in the previous film (including destroying the *Enterprise*). When they arrive, Starfleet and Earth are under siege by an angry alien probe broadcasting what Spock (Leonard Nimoy) recognizes as a humpback whale song. As humpbacks are extinct, the probe gets increasingly destructive when it doesn't hear an answer. Fortunately, the *Enterprise* crew have time travel experience so they take the Klingon ship back to the 20th century. All they need to save their future is to find some humpbacks, redesign the ship to transport them, and find a power source that can get them home.

In between lots of entertaining anachronistic culture-clash humor, the crew finds the whales at a marine biology institute, watched over by Taylor (Catherine Hicks), a cetacean expert. Taylor refuses to believe Kirk's from the future, nor will she entrust her whales to him. After the institute ships the whales off without telling Taylor, she turns to Kirk. The crew locate the humpbacks and rescue them from whalers, then take the whales and Taylor back to the future. Once the hunchbacks start singing, the probe leaves. Taylor resumes working with the whales, and Kirk gets busted back down to captain. He and his crew are assigned to a new *Enterprise*

The Spirit of 76 (1990) opens in 2176 after a magnetic storm erases all digital records, leaving American society devoid of its history (apparently there's nothing left on paper) and therefore without focus, structure or joy. The government recruits Adam-11 (David Cassidy), who's developed a time machine, to carry Heinz-57 (Geoff Hoyle) and uptight Chanel-6 (Olivia d'Abo) back to 1776 to learn the fundamentals of America. Adam's cobbled-together time machine crashlands in 1976.

Adam works to restore the time machine, but has to fit that in between running from the CIA, listening to 1970s music and encountering various far-out characters. Chanel loosens up, hanging with stud Eddie Trojan (1970s teen idol Leif Garrett). Heinz finds a copy of the Constitution printed on a shirt. Adam and Chanel fall in love, and the trio returns to 2176 with not only a copy of the Constitution but a 1970s sense of fun that enlivens the world.

The Drivetime (1999) refers to a channel between Aboriginal Dreamtime and the waking world that allows users to cross the time barrier. The researcher Flux (Michael Douglas but not the famous one) travels back from 2023 to 1999, when the government first began using propaganda to convince people to use the Internet as a substitute for actual human interaction. Flux's presence in the past serves mostly as an excuse for arty footage of poetry slams, religious gatherings and pretentious debate about the Internet before he's told he's extended his stay and has to go home.

The Future Needs Our Genes

Terror from the Year 5000 (1958) has the distinction of being the first feature film to show a time machine. Prof. Erling (Frederic Downs) has built the machine with financing from wealthy Victor (John Stratton), who's hot for Erling's daughter Claire (Joyce Holden). When the machine materializes a mysterious statuette, Claire secretly sends the figurine to Hedges (Ward Costello), an archaeologist. Hedges' carbon-dating tests show the statue is from 3000 years in the future (carbon dating couldn't actually show this) so he drops in on the laboratory. Victor explains they've been trading artifacts with the future, as trade is the standard basis for first contact.

On the next swap, the future sends a written request for help, then a grotesque woman who tries kidnapping Victor. She fails, but her touch inflicts him with radiation poisoning. A nurse (Salome Jens) arrives to care for him, but the future woman kills her and takes her face. The woman eventually reveals that radioactive contamination has turned 20 percent

A radioactive future woman (unidentified) brings *Terror from the Year 5000* (1958) to cowering Joyce Holden, Ward Costello and Frederic Downs.

of future humanity into disfigured mutants like her. She wants Victor's healthy DNA to replenish the gene pool and tries kidnapping him again. The time machine explodes and kills them both. Erling suggests rebuilding it, but Hedges replies that they should devote themselves to changing the present instead.

Millennium (1989) has a similar premise (adapted by John Varley from his "Air Raid"): future humanity sterilized by pollution and snatching people from the past to repopulate. They target passengers about to die in plane crashes, as that reduces the risk of damaging the timeline. Federal investigator Bill Smith (Chris Kristofferson) investigates a crash and discovers oddities such as the passengers' watches all running backwards. He also meets Baltimore (Cheryl Ladd), an airline employee who seduces him. She tries to keep him with her the next day, but he insists on going to the crash site, where he finds pieces of future technology, plus Baltimore in a shiny futuristic jumpsuit. When Baltimore reports this to her superiors, they tell her to go back a day, take Smith to bed, and keep him away from the crash site.

As we already know, that tactic fails. Smith's investigation continues and creates so many time paradoxes it triggers a timequake that wipes out Baltimore's future. Before the apocalypse, her people send the crash survivors they've rescued from the past further into the future to start humanity over. Smith and Baltimore go with them, and it miraculously turns out that Smith's virility has overcome the whole sterility thing and impregnated her. With breathtaking cheesiness, the ending voiceover proclaims this is "the beginning."

In *Official Denial* (1993), future humanity is not only sterile, it's evolved into the "Greys" of UFO legend. Present-day Paul Corliss (Parker Stevenson) is obsessed with the belief he was abducted years earlier by a UFO. His obsession is destroying his marriage to Annie (Erin Gray) because she wants kids, while he refuses to bring them into a world where aliens can abduct you and the government supposedly spies on former abductees.

Although Annie thinks Paul is paranoid, he's right on all counts. A UFO abducts Paul again, but the military gun down the ship after it returns Paul to his bed. The sole surviving ET refuses to communicate with its captors, so Gen. Spalding (Chad Everett) brings Paul to his base to see if the former abductee will have better rapport. Spalding admits to Paul that the military has known about the abductions for years (a popular trope in UFOlogy), but believe it's better to cover things up than admit that the government can't protect us.

The alien telepathically tells Paul it can give him the answers he needs if they return to the crash site, where it can absorb information from its dead comrades' minds. With Spalding's help (the general is desperate to learn the truth), Annie, Paul and the ET reach the crash site, where the alien dies and Paul learns its secrets. As he later explains to Spalding, the aliens are trying to restart humanity by taking DNA from people such as Paul whom history shows didn't contribute to the gene pool. Except a few months later, Paul and Annie have a child, leaving him hopeful that the Greys' sterile future isn't inevitable.

Last Exit to Earth (1996) opens in 2500, long after female geneticists have successfully erased aggression from men, with the side effect of rendering men sterile and sex passionless. The movie informs us that great sex requires male aggression, and the protagonist, Eve (Kimberly Griest), grows rhapsodic at reading de Sade.

Having failed to find a cure for sterility, Eve leads a team of women to 2100 to collect fresh breeding stock. They return with a spaceship captained by two-fisted, heroic Jaid (Costas Mandylor), but also carrying the murderous Bendix (David Groh) and his crew, who planned to use the ship in a bioweapon terrorist attack. Eve tests the men to see if their testosterone can cure fertility, and in the process, falls in love with Jaid. Bendix's gang breaks out and threatens the world with the bioweapon before Jaid's manly manliness stops them. The council exiles Eve and Jaid to the wilderness with other couples who long for the days when men were men. The film ends with Eve pregnant and rugged outdoor life restoring masculine fertility.

While the future humans of *The Last Mimzy* (2007) aren't sterile, centuries of pollution have severely damaged the genome. One brilliant scientist has begun sending "mimzies" back in time to fix this. (The name comes from the source material, Henry Kuttner's classic "Mimsy Were the Borogroves," which deserved a better film.) The final mimzy, disguised as a stuffed rabbit, lands with other future toys in the hands of precocious Emma Wilder (Rhiannon Leigh Wryn). She and her brother Noah (Chris O'Neil) soon exhibit amazing powers (creating energy balls, controlling spiders) and Emma sees flashes of Alice Liddell (the Victorian child fictionalized in *Alice's Adventures in Wonderland*) with a mimzy of her own.

Emma's parents (Timothy Hutton, Joely Richardson) are terrified by all this weirdness. Then the FBI tracks down the family—the toys are affecting the electrical grid—and hauls everyone off to a science center. Agent Broadman (Michael Clarke Duncan) and his team pay no attention to Emma's warnings that if the mimzy breaks down before going back to the future, humanity is doomed. The kids escape and send the tear-stained mimzy through a time gate, which convinces the feds to drop the charges. Back in the future, we learn that the genes in Emma's tears (tears don't actually contain genes) made it possible to heal both humanity's DNA and some unspecified but equally horrible cultural damage. Humanity, once again, is saved.

Time Tourism

Disasters in Time (1992) and *Timeshifters* (1999) both use the concept of tourists from the future traveling through time to witness history's great disasters. The first film is based on C.L. Moore's "Vintage Season," in which the time travelers visit perfect moments in the past, but it reverses the premise: These travelers want decidedly imperfect moments.

Protagonist Ben Wilson (Jeff Daniels) is a small-town innkeeper haunted by guilt: When his wife was injured in a car accident, he panicked and fled instead of finding help. Her father Caldwell (George Murdock) has never forgiven him, and plans to get revenge by taking custody of Ben's daughter Hilary (Ariana Richards). Madame Iovine (Marilyn Lightstone), an eccentric tour guide, books Ben's inn so her equally eccentric tour group can catch "the spectacle." Ben can't understand why the travelers' passports list dates instead of places, but he gets it after a meteorite strikes the town, killing hundreds. The dates are for the Hindenburg crash, Mt. St. Helens, the San Francisco earthquake and other disasters. According to Reeve (Emilia Crow), the future is so stable and safe, this is their only source of excitement. The travel agency chief (Robert Colbert) later tells Ben there's no point in damaging the future's history by trying to save people who died centuries ago.

It turns out the tour is a double event: The town turns its school into a shelter, but a gas explosion kills everyone inside, including Hilary. Reeve feels guilty enough to leave Ben her passport. He uses it to travel back to the past and escape with Hilary, but Caldwell catches them and throws Ben in jail. Ben calls his own past self, who rescues him from jail but refuses to run away and let the town die. Instead they raise an alarm that draws the people away from the strike zone, saving most of the community. In the aftermath, the agency chief tells Ben it would be easy to undo Ben's time tampering. Ben replies that if that were the plan, they wouldn't be talking and suggests any change he's caused to the future will be for the better.

Timeshifters (1999) stars Casper Van Dien as Tom Merrick, a former A-list journalist now reduced to working for tabloids. After discovering photos that show the same person (Julian Richings) at the Hindenburg crash, the *Titanic* and Hurricane Hugo, Merrick spots the man, Trevor, on his plane flight. Realizing what this implies, Merrick hijacks the plane and averts what would have been the most horrifying crash in history.

Trevor, it turns out, is a customer of Thrill Seekers, a 21st century time-tourism firm. The time trips are purely about the travelers' excitement; Merrick compares it to the "if it bleeds it leads" appeal of TV news. With the knowledge gleaned from Trevor's travel brochure, which doubles as a portable time machine, Merrick and co-worker Wintern (Catherine Bell) stop the next disaster, a subway crash. That horrifies Cortez (Theresa Saldana), a Thrill Seekers agent, because it alters the future to the point that her child doesn't exist. To stabilize the time stream, she has to ensure the next disaster, a stadium fire, happens on schedule. Merrick's son is at the stadium so he has to stop it.

Merrick fails. Cortez next tries going back to undo all his interference, but this interacts with Trevor's device and pulls both Merrick and Cortez to the day of the fire. This time Cortez dies trying to stop Merrick, who saves hundreds of people, including his son. But Thrill Seekers is still in business...

The USS Eldridge

According to popular legend, the Navy in World War II used the USS *Eldridge* as the subject of an experiment in either invisibility or teleportation. The "Philadelphia Experiment" technology has been used by multiple movies to explain time travel (*Devil's Pass, 100 Million BC, Triangle* and *Philadelphia Experiment II* elsewhere in this book and *One Way Trip*, which talks about time travel but never actually gets to it).

The Philadelphia Experiment (1984) opens in 1943 with sailors David and Jim (Michael Paré, Bobby Di Cicco) aboard the *Eldridge* as Dr. Longstreet (Miles McNamara) surrounds the ship with a hyperspatial field to turn it invisible. Suddenly the two swabbies find themselves in the desert, pursued by the military. They reach the nearest town, realize they've time-jumped, try to steal a car, discover it has something called an automatic transmission and force the owner, Allison (Nancy Allen), to drive them. When Jim becomes too sick to move, Dave and Allison go it alone, looking for people from David's past, and falling in love in the process.

The couple don't know the problem is bigger than two time-stranded sailors. In the present, Longstreet has repurposed his tech to create an anti-missile shield, but the shield has interacted across time with the original experiment, trapping both the *Eldridge* and Allison's town in a time-space warp. When David and Allison find Longstreet, the scientist tells David that eyewitnesses from 1943 say David's the one who deactivated the hyperspace generator and saved the ship. Despite the risk, David boards the *Eldridge*, turns off the generator, and then jumps off into the present—and Allison's arms—before the ship snaps back to 1943. (A sequel followed, covered in Chapter Six.)

The 2012 remake has present-day scientist Richard Falkner (Ryan Robbins) adapt the original research for a new invisibility device. This pulls the *Eldridge* into the future and sets it teleporting around the globe, demolishing buildings wherever it materializes. During one stop, cop Carl (John Reardon) gets trapped on board while Lt. Gardner (Nicholas Lea) disembarks and gets left behind when the ship teleports again. Gardner meets Carl's girlfriend Molly (Emilie Ullerup), his own grandchild, and learns he never returned after the *Eldridge* vanished from the past.

Molly and Gardner hunt down Salinger (Malcolm McDowell), the original *Eldridge* researcher, but Falkner's sinister sponsor Moore (Gina Holden) sends hitman Hagan (Michael Paré) to kill them all. Moore also calls in an air strike on the *Eldridge*, which has zero effect. As the good guys run from Hagan, Salinger concludes that Gardner's presence is anchoring the ship in the present, so they can save the world by sending him home. They enlist Falkner's help, but Moore just adds Falkner to the hit list. At the climax, Molly shoots Moore before she can kill Falkner; Hagan dies aboard the *Eldridge*; Gardner returns to his ship, while Carl jumps off. When the *Eldridge* returns to the past, it creates a new timeline in which Gardner is still alive in the present as Molly's beloved grandparent.

Bonding Across Time

Some visits from other eras are less about danger or escape than about people in different times forging connections with each other. *Doraemon* (1973–2005) is a hugely popular children's anime that has spun off several movies. The 22nd century Nobi family decides to improve their poverty-stricken lives by sending a robot back in time to help their 20th-century ancestor Nobita (Megumi Oohara) amount to something. Unfortunately the best they can afford is the malfunctioning cat-bot Doraemon (Wasabi Mizuta), whose attempts to help the pre-teen Nobita rarely go as planned. Happily Doraemon has a sack full of advanced tech which lets him pull out a save at the last minute, such as a spice that makes even the worst swill taste delicious, and a comb that makes you float through the air like dandelion fluff (and temporarily turns your hair into fluff).

In *The Adventures of Timothy Pilgrim* (1975), a Canadian children's show, homeless moppet Timothy (Joey Davidson) hides in an abandoned trunk from a bully and emerges a century earlier. The trunk in this era belongs to Zachariah Gibson (David Hemblen), a backwoods patent-medicine huckster who's on the run from an angry local. When he and Tim hide in the trunk again, they emerge back in the present. As Zach struggles to adapt to the modern world, he and Tim become friends, which keeps Zach from making more than occasional trips to the past. Finally he accepts that he can never be happy in Tim's bustling, mechanized age and heads home, but promising to be a more honest salesman.

Come Back Lucy (1978) is a darker variation on the friends-across-time theme. Orphan Lucy (Emma Bahkle) is emotionally shattered by her guardian's death, more so by moving from an old-fashioned, quiet house with nobody else around to her relatives' crowded, modern home. When Lucy explores the attic, Alice (Bernadette Windsor), a Victorian girl, materializes and invites Lucy to play with her. Lucy finds traveling to the past with Alice a welcome break from her cousins, but Alice's possessive insistence that Lucy keep coming back—and eventually that she stay forever—begins to scare her. But disobeying Alice inflicts agonizing pain on Lucy. Finally, on the anniversary of the day in the past that Alice moved from the house, Alice attempts to keep Lucy with her forever by drowning her. (It's unclear whether this would trap Lucy in the past or make them both ghosts.) Lucy's relatives save her, and they all begin bonding into a real family.

In the animated *We're Back: A Dinosaur's Story* (1993), a tyrannosaur, Rex (John Goodman), tells Buster, a young bird, how he came to be a golf-playing dinosaur. Future inventor Captain Neweyes (Walter Cronkite) traveled through time to turn Rex and three other dinos intelligent so that they could journey to the present and bring joy to all the kids who want to see real dinosaurs. Once in the 20th century, the dinosaurs make friends with lonely kids Louie and Cecilia (Joey Shea, Yeardley Smith), turning their lives around.

This enrages the captain's evil brother Screweyes (Kenneth Mars), who turns the kids into monkeys in his circus of fear. To free the children, the dinosaurs have to take treatments that revert them back into savage beasts. Screweyes uses Rex in his dino-taming act at the circus' next show, but soon discovers Rex can't be tamed. The tyrannosaur almost devours the villain but Louie convinces Rex to rise above his animal nature. The dinosaurs regain their intellects and take up residence in New York's Museum of Natural History, where they continue bringing wonder into the lives of children.

The Indian in the Cupboard (1995) adapts Lynne Reid Banks' novel for the story of the friendship between Omri (Hal Scardino) and Little Bear (Litefoot). It begins when Omri receives a plastic Indian figure and an old cupboard for his birthday. When he places the figure in the cupboard, Little Bear, an 18th century Iroquois warrior, materializes at the same size as the figure. (Banks' later novel *The Secret of the Cupboard* explains how it works.)

Omri, thrilled, convinces Little Bear to stay, even though the Iroquois is horrified at living in a world of giants. The two become friends, but Omri still has trouble grasping that the people he summons with the cabinet have real lives elsewhere. After Omri shows his buddy Patrick (Rishi Bhat) the Indian, Patrick sticks a plastic cowboy in the cupboard and gets Boone (David Keith) in return. The cowboy and Iroquois are initially hostile, but slowly become friends. When Boone is injured, Omri finally realizes he has to respect the rights of his "toys" and sends them home. He offers to use a female Indian figure to provide Little Bear with a wife, but the warrior refuses to pluck anyone else out of time. Before leaving, he tells Omri that he regards the boy as family, and both friends agree they'll never forget each other.

In *A Stranger in Time* (1995), present-day tween Andie (Heather Kottek) meets Sarah (Amy Seely), a young girl in a pioneer dress. When they walk to Sarah's home, it's an abandoned farmhouse, even though Sarah insists she left it that morning. It turns out Sarah's been thrown forward from 1890 (the film's opening established there have been other time manifestations from that era). Sarah's horrified at being a century away from her family, but she bonds with Andie and gets to learn about cool things such as TV, rock music and pizza.

With help from Andie's friends, the girls eventually figure they can send Sarah home by duplicating their first meeting. Sarah goes back to 1890, but she's inspired to change history, becoming mayor of the town and organizing its first fire department. As a result, Andie's grandfather, who originally died in a fire, is alive and doting on his granddaughter in the present.

The Sticky Fingers of Time (1997) opens in black-and-white 1953 as writer Tucker Harding (Terumi Matthews) leaves her apartment and her acquaintance Ofelia (Belinda Becker), then suddenly finds herself in the Technicolor present. Isaac (James Urbaniak), who's sleeping with both women, tells Tucker she's one of the rare people with the ability to move nonlinearly through time, though she can never live a given moment over twice.

In the present, Tucker meets Drew (Nicole Zaray), an undisciplined writer targeted by a mysterious killer. The two women learn from old newspapers that Tucker was murdered in the late 1950s. Drew's assailant shoots Tucker in Drew's apartment. The corpse materializes back in the past, dragging Drew with it. Isaac and Ofelia explain that Tucker's death transferred some of her "code," her spiritual DNA, to Drew, and with it the power to time-jump. The attacks on Drew were from someone trying to absorb her own code.

Drew wants to save Tucker with her new powers, but Ofelia—who killed Tucker out of jealousy over Isaac—tells her that altering events is impossible. To prove it, Ofelia forces Drew to watch her parents' marriage end, unable to change anything. Next, Ofelia places Drew's mind in a cactus, planning to collect her code later. Drew escapes, travels to 1953 and prevents Tucker from attending the H-bomb test that altered her code to make her a time traveler. Without her powers, Tucker is no longer fated to die. The two women move in together and Drew gets serious about her writing.

In the Disney family sitcom *Phil of the Future* (2004–06), the Dicks family crashes in the present during a time trip. While trying to repair the time machine, they adapt to 21st century life. Phil (Ricky Ullman), the focus of the series, copes with high school where only his best friend Keeley (Alyson Michalka) knows the truth about him. After two seasons of teen sitcom hijinx enlivened by future tech, Phil and Keeley came to see each other as more than friends, but just when they reached that point, the Dickses went back to the future.

I'll Believe You (2006) is a self-consciously quirky film about Dale Sweeney (David Alan Basche), Melbourne, Florida, host of a late-night radio call-in show on UFOs. The lack of an audience has put the show on the chopping block, but then a mystery man starts calling every night, babbling in an alien tongue. Dale's friends refuse to believe Dale's theory that it's a real ET, but the strange calls draw an audience.

When the caller, Seth (Patrick Warburton), finally appears, he tells Dale he's not an alien but a time traveler from 4162. Seth came to the 21st century to investigate evidence of previous time travelers, only to discover it was his own trip that left the evidence. His time machine broke down, so he's been using Dale's broadcasts to send information to the future in hopes of rescue. A rescuer arrives and reveals that he's devoted his life to becoming part of the legendary story of Seth and Dale. Dale and his friends join Seth on his return to the future, while several other travelers show up a few minutes too late to be Seth's rescuers.

Sengoku Collection (2012) was an anime built around a premise similar to *Battle Girls* and *Ambition of Oda Nobuna*: a feudal Japan where the great warriors and generals are women, or in this case high school–age girls. General Nobunaga (Rumi Ookubo), Masamune Date (Ayumi Tsunematsu) and other famous warriors are drawn to our Earth's present-day Tokyo. They adapt, or don't, to the modern world, becoming singers, martial arts teachers or high school students. Some of them bond together in their new life, while others continue long-standing feuds with each other. Nobunaga is particularly determined to return home, which requires claiming magic treasures from the other warriors. The series ended with everyone still here.

Tenchu (2014) stars Ono Yuriko as Sana, a ninja from Japan's warring states era transported to the present, moments after the death of her sister. She's lost and alone until elderly Murata Seiko (Izumi Pinko) takes her in. Murata's daughter Yukari disappeared years earlier—no trace was ever found—and Murata desperately wants to prevent other people from suffering the same pain. She places Sana under contract to take out bad guys (scam artists preying on the elderly, sex slavers) without killing them, and the two women gather assistants such as a reformed burglar and a martial-arts teacher. Sana discovers that Yukari is an exact look-alike for her sister Yu and wonders if they're somehow the same person.

In the final episode, the two women discover a high government official may have murdered Yukari as part of a serial-killing spree. They set out to kill him, but ultimately realize that their affection for each other outweighs the desire for revenge. With their friends, they bring the killer to justice, and discover that Yukari, though still missing, wasn't one of his victims. Murata and Sana stay together happily as surrogate mother and daughter.

Trading Places

In some stories, past and present change places. *The Jetsons Meet the Flintstones* (1987) brought together two of Hanna-Barbera's best-known cartoon families. The 24th century George and Jane Jetson (George O'Hanlon, Penny Singleton) assume their boy genius son

Elroy (Daws Butler) is kidding when he claims he's invented a time machine. He's not, but instead of taking them further into the future, the machine hurls them back a million years to meet Fred and Wilma Flintstone (Henry Corden, Jean Vander Pyl). Once the families get over their initial shock, they become friends, the Flintstones putting the Jetsons up while Elroy works on the time machine. When it starts running again, it sends the Flintstones and their friends Betty and Barney Rubble (Mel Blanc, Julie McWhirter) to the Jetsons' future, leaving the Jetsons stranded.

Everyone is initially miserable. George, however, becomes a star in the past by using his rocket belt to fly; the Flintstones and the Rubbles, as living history, become equally popular in the future. Soon the Jetsons' wealth becomes a burden and Barney and Fred come to blows when they compete for the spotlight. Fortunately, the Jetsons' friends in the future find a way to bring the family home, pulling the Flintstones' prehistoric car along. George's boss turns driving on the ground—in the future, cars fly—into a new, lucrative craze, and the Flintstones and Rubbles absorb enough temporal energy from the car to make it back to their own "modern Stone Age."

Kappatoo (1990–92) is a nickname for Kappa 29643 (Simon Nash) of 2270. He's about to compete in an elimination contest against the malevolent bully Sigmasix (Felipe Izquierdo), and the odds aren't in his favor. Then his computer (Andrew O'Connor) discovers a look-alike for Kappa in the 20th century, Simon Cashmere (Nash). Kappa goes back in time and proposes they swap places, and Simon agrees. Despite the ever-unpleasant Sigmasix, Simon finds he loves the future. But Kappa feels out of place in the 20th century, even though he can use his future technology to get out of scrapes. In the second season, Simon has to pursue an art thief who jumps through time to steal great works.

The Famous Jett Jackson (1998–2001), a Disney Channel series, starred Lee Thompson Young as a teen actor trying to balance his high school life with his role as teen super-spy Silverstone. In *Jett Jackson—The Movie* (2001), just as Jett contemplates quitting the show, simultaneous freak accidents in two universes cause him and Silverstone to switch realities. (It appears that Silverstone's world is real—he's not just a fictional character brought to life.) Silverstone is thrilled: Even though he suffers the usual confusion of not knowing any of Jett's friends, he loves having a normal teen life for the first time. Jett has a much harder time fitting in, plus he's expected to fulfill Silverstone's latest mission, stopping mad scientist Kragg (Michael Ironside) from shrinking and capturing cities using his molecule-warping technology.

Silverstone learns from the show's next script that Kragg will set a trap for him, and realizes Jett is clueless enough to walk into it. The super-spy finds his way home and sends Jett back to our Earth. Jett discovers that Kragg's trap may kill Silverstone, so he heads back to Earth-Silverstone and saves his counterpart. Together they take Kragg down. Returning home, Jett announces that he's going to stick with playing Silverstone.

Summoned Out of Time

The *Present Time* (1997) series opens with an old man (Jim Bullock) sending a laptop computer to the present, moments before black-clad government agents burst in on him. The computer reaches tween Josh (Steven Harris), whose more computer-savvy friends Emily (Tara Streeter) and Caleb (Philip Bryce Jacobs) get it up and running—after which one of the programs on it pulls Goliath (Renee Stewart) and David (Ryan Devin) from the past. Complicating things, bully Jared (Ryan Domis) brings King Saul (Bryan Kent) to the present, where he tries to kill David. Eventually everyone goes back to their time, but the kids are soon bringing other Biblical figures into the present, for more complications. At the end of the third episode, the old man's hologram reveals he's the Josh of 2074, and that possessing the machine may put the three kids in danger. But as there were no further episodes, that was all the explanation we got.

Mentors (1999–2004), a Canadian TV show, starred Chad Krowchuk as teenage genius Oliver Cates, who can pull anyone out of the past for 36 hours. Oliver and his girlfriend Dee (Sarah Lind) use this information to provide themselves, and the audience, with life lessons such as Anaïs Nin giving advice about love or Elizabeth I teaching about grace under pressure. Oliver's cousin Simon (Stevie Mitchell) inherited the time machine for the last two seasons after Oliver headed off to university.[2]

The title character in *K9* (2009), an intelligent, talking robot dog (John Leeson), traveled with the Doctor of *Doctor Who* for several years, and also appeared in the spin-off *The Sarah Jane Adventures* before his own spin-off series. Prof. Gryffen (Robert Moloney), a scientist in a near-future London, is using a time portal in hopes of bringing his tragically lost family to the present. Instead he brings K9 from the future ... and some alien warriors along with him. As Gryffen continues working with the portal, other aliens show up, and his continued research draws the sinister attention of the powerful government "Department." It turns out in the ending arc that the Department's Thorne (Jared Robinsen) is working with the alien Korven, preparing the time gate to bring an invading Korven army to Earth. Gryffen destroys the time gate at a tragic cost to himself.

Other Visitors

Geoffrey Bayldon is the title character in *Catweazle* (1970–71), a medieval wizard whose magic accidentally hurls him into the 20th century. He's totally agog at modern technology, which he assumes is magic; an electric light, for instance, is "the sun in a bottle" He makes friends with Carrot (Robin Davies), a farmer's son who does his best to steer the mage safely through the confusing modern world and hide his secret until Catweazle can find a way home. The wizard returned to the present for a second season of misadventures, this time with the help of Cedric (Gary Warren), an upper-class boy.

Widowed Andrea (Adrienne Barbeau) and her son Tim (Jeremy Licht) are living on a Greek island in *The Next One* (1984) when they find an amnesiac (Keir Dullea) washed up on the beach after a freak storm. Unable to remember his name or even what a name is, the man eventually takes the name Glenn and shows a strange fascination with images of Jesus. Glenn has two hearts and can perform wonders, such as resurrecting Tim after an accident. Glenn and Andrea become lovers. Eventually Glenn remembers that he came from a future where all humans look identical. He followed his brother across time, but his brother landed 2000 years ago—yes, he became Jesus.

A fisherman who wants Andrea for himself tries to sink Glenn's rowboat. Glenn survives, but the local children with him drown. Members of the community blame Glenn and lock him away, but Tim helps him escape. Glenn worries that like his brother, he's at risk of changing history, so he drowns himself to avoid that. Before dying, he tells Tim another amnesiac, look-alike brother will appear eventually, and Tim should let him take Glenn's place with Andrea. The brother appears, and Tim does so. There's no explanation why the village won't arrest him for the kids' deaths.

The *Outlaws* (1986–87) were Houston bandits (including William Lucking, Charles Napier and Richard Roundtree) who in 1899 have a showdown with Sheriff Grail (Rod Taylor), a former member of their group, in an ancient Native American burial ground. This apparently disturbs the spirits enough that lightning strikes the group and transports them to 1986. After a difficult transition to the new world, the guys settle down and open a "detection agency" to help good folks and thwart the bad ones. They get some help from their new neighbor, Houston Deputy Maggie Randall (Christina Belford).

In *The Secret World of Polly Flint* (1987), imaginative young Polly (Katie Reynolds) lives in a small village with her aunt. Polly discovers she has the ability to see the Time Gypsies of Grimstone, the community that once occupied the village site. Magic allows these travelers to step in and out of time within various limits; eating while traveling, for instance, traps them in whatever time they're in. When a family of Time Gypsies gets stranded in Polly's present-day village, they tell her the only way to return home is if a normal person accompanies them. It turns out that one of the village seniors is actually a trapped, de-powered Gypsy, so his accompanying them does the trick.

Earthfasts (1994) takes place in rural Yorkshire and is based partly on a local legend: A stone circle stands near the hill where Arthur supposedly lies sleeping, to return in Britain's hour of need. Two boys, Keith (Chris Downs) and David (Paul Nicholls), see Nellie Jack John (Bryan Dick), an army drummer from 1742, walk out of the hillside, believing he's only been AWOL a few minutes. After spending a night in the present, Nellie re-enters the hill but leaves behind the cold, constantly burning candle he found within. Bringing out the candle stirs up the past so that boggarts, giants and other folklore creatures appear in the area. David discovers he can see other times when he stares into the candle, which never goes out. Finally David vanishes, apparently disintegrated by lightning.

Keith discovers that the candle is summoning Arthur to our time, which is disastrous, as his hour has not yet come. Keith enters the hill and replaces the candle on the Round Table, ending the time incursions. He finds David in the hill, and also Nellie Jack John, who's been struggling futilely to go home against the flow of time. The three boys return to the present and Nellie settles into the 20th century with his new friends.

Visitors from Parallel Worlds

Screen tales of alternate history usually focus on people from our timeline visiting others. When it's reversed, and travelers from alt-earths visit our world, their intentions aren't usually friendly.

Vexcorp, the corporate villain of *Charlie Jade* (2005), has expanded out of its own dystopian "alphaverse" into our universe ("betaverse") and the idyllic, pre-industrial "gammaverse" with an eye to exploiting both worlds for their natural resources. The eponymous Charlie Jade (Jeffrey Pierce) is a PI operating out of South African Cape City, Vexcorp's home base, until he's caught in a terrorist explosion that blasts him into the betaverse's

Cape Town. The bomb shuts down travel between the universes, so Charlie begins investigating what Vexcorp is up to in the betaverse. Vexcorp is determined to protect its operations there so it sends Boxer (Michael Filipowich), a sociopath who can cross worlds at will, to deal with any threats.

After a season of bad "hardboiled PI" stories, Boxer and Charlie—who's learned he can also cross between worlds—join forces to stabilize Vexcorp's dimensional link before its collapse wrecks both dimensions. They succeed. Then the show was cancelled, so we'll never know what would have happened next.

John Dies at the End (2012) involves an invasion from an alternate timeline that developed computer technology a century earlier than our world. That led first to the invention of artificial intelligence, next to an AI taking over, and now the AI coveting our Earth for conquest. As the film opens, Dave (Chase Williamson) tells reporter Arnie (Paul Giamatti) how he (Dave) and his best friend John (Rob Mayes) acquired the ability to detect entities from the other timeline after taking the hallucinogen "soy sauce." Eventually the invaders kidnap the guys to see if researching their heightened awareness reveals a better way to cross between dimensions. Dave and John (who, inspite of the title of the movie, doesn't actually die) blow up the rogue computer, saving their Earth. They return home, but still have to put down the occasional cross-dimensional incursion.

In *Paradox* (2010), Sean Nault (Kevin Sorbo) is a detective in a parallel world where magic substitutes for science. Magic crystals provide electricity, police necromancers interrogate murder victims, and even guns are magic. Science is crackpot, New Age stuff, but Nault believes it can work as well as sorcery. Nault investigates a series of shootings which show no trace of magic, even though the killer escapes by gargoyle or magic horse. Retired sorcerer Winston Churchill (A.C. Peterson) reveals that the killer uses an ordinary magnum brought from our world, and that Nault is receptive to science because he's a "paradox" with no counterpart on our Earth.

Nault and science buff Lenore (Steph Song) travel to our world with Churchill's help. In their world, success depends entirely on your innate magical talent, so they find our Earth more meritocratic and appealing. Their investigation unearths a blackmail scheme using tape recorders and similar technology to bypass protections against magical eavesdropping. The conspiracy isn't about political power, but about a scheme by Nault's captain (Christopher Judge) to merge both Earths into one, creating a hybrid where magic and science both work. Nault isn't on board with this as millions will die in the transition. He and Lenore defeat the bad guys, even though it costs them their one chance to return to our Earth to stay.

Singularity Principle (2013) opens with the mysterious Cason (William B. Davis) interrogating physicist Peter Tanning (Michael Denis) about Peter's parallel-world research with vanished maverick scientist Jack Brenner (John Diehl). Peter tells Cason that since childhood he's been haunted by glimpses of what he believed might be parallel universes, and that after working with Jack, he found himself shifting between realities. Dealing with counterparts of friends and family was disorienting—he became convinced his wife was cheating on him—but Jack stabilizes Peter, then vanishes. Cason reveals that Jack was from an alternate reality and Peter's world-shifting was a side effect of Jack trying to return home. Peter turns down Cason's offer to work with him on finding other parallel-world visitors and leaves … only to discover he's in Jack's reality, not his own. It's a quite confusing ending.

CHAPTER SIX

Changing History
When Time Is Up for Grabs

"They'll remember Rasputin von Rotten, for history I'll rearrange!"—*Willy McBean and His Magic Machine*

Changing history is a relatively minor part of big- and small-screen time travel stories. The number of films and TV series where people try to change history—the outcome of World War II, the JFK assassination, the fall of Rome, the fall of man—is far fewer than the stories where someone tries to change their personal history. It's also a smaller total than the number of films where someone from the future tries to change events in the present (i.e., *their* history).

Changing personal history or future history is often presented as a change for the better, but tinkering with our own history is not. Films and TV series in this chapter side strongly with keeping history the way it is. Typically, the characters trying to change history are villains (e.g., Nazis who want to win World War II) or they're well-meaning but screw things up.

The What Ifs of World War II

For millions of people, World War II was the "good war," pitting the forces of freedom against the absolute evil embodied by Nazi Germany. A world where the Axis won therefore represents the triumph of absolute evil. With such black-and-white stakes involved, it's not surprising this is the historical event that generates the largest number of history-changing screen stories, as well as many print tales. (Gavriel Rosenfeld's *The World Hitler Never Made* covers many such alternate histories.)

The Yesterday Machine (1963) opens with a college couple searching for help after their car breaks down in the woods. They encounter something incredible (but unseen by viewers), and the boy turns up later, injured and alone. Reporter Jim Crandal (James Britton) learns the kid was shot with a Civil War bullet, which he logically blames on Civil War re-enactors. Lt. Partane (Tim Holt) sees a connection with the infamous scientist Von Hauser (Jack Herman), whose experiments in "super-spectronic relativity" bent time to age children overnight.

Sure enough, when Crandal and the missing girl's sister Sandy (Ann Pellegrino) investigate the wooded area, they find themselves in the middle of the American Revolution, then in Von Hauser's lab. The scientist dominates the remaining film by lecturing on his mastery of time, the genius of Hitler and Nazism and, oh yes, that he plans to change history to ensure Hitler's triumph. After sitting through all the speechifying, Crandal and Sandy escape with her sister, then Partane kills Von Hauser and destroys the machine.

In the 1967 *Star Trek* episode "City on the Edge of Forever," the *Enterprise* crew members come across a sentient time gateway, the Guardian of Forever. When McCoy (DeForest Kelley), temporarily out of his mind from a bad drug reaction, stumbles through the gateway, the crew members around the Guardian discover that the *Enterprise* no longer exists. Kirk (William Shatner) and Spock (Leonard Nimoy) head into time after McCoy to find answers.

It turns out that McCoy's presence in the past will save the life of beautiful visionary Edith Keeler (Joan Collins), whose pacifist views keep the U.S. from entering World War II. Although Kirk falls for Edith, he realizes her survival will transform history for the worse. When McCoy, his sanity returned, tries to save Edith from a car accident, Kirk intervenes to stop him. The decision rips Kirk apart, but history is preserved and the three men return to their own time.

In the utopian 1990s of the loopy Czech comedy *Tomorrow I'll Get Up and Scald Myself with Tea* (1977), nuclear weapons are museum pieces, anti-aging drugs keep seniors youthful and people routinely travel through time to see—but never intervene in—the past. Nazi war criminals Abard, Kraus and Bauer (Jiří Sovák, Vladimir Menšík, Vlastimil Brodský) have struck a deal with time pilot Karel Bures (Petr Kostka) to take them back to 1944, when they will offer Hitler a suitcase nuke stolen from a museum, and thereby change the war's outcome.

Alas for the thousand-year Reich, Karel chokes on a roll and dies. His twin Jan (Kostka again) takes his place rather than break the news to Karel's girlfriend Eva (Zuzana Ondrouchová), whom Jan secretly loves. The Nazis have no idea why their pilot is suddenly clueless about their plans, so they seize control of the time ship. Instead of 1944, they unwittingly steer the ship to December 8, 1941. Hitler is baffled by these strangers begging him to surrender—haven't his allies just crushed the United States?—and sentences them to the firing squad.

Jan and a couple of the Nazis make it back to the present, early enough that Jan hopes he can save Karel from death. Karel dies again, Eva dies too and one Nazi buys it. Jan flies the other Nazis back to the past again, but he tricks Hitler into killing them as assassins. When Jan returns to the present, he again fails to save Karel, so instead he assumes his brother's identity for good and proposes to Eva. He also steers his counterpart in this timeline toward a woman who's interested in him.

The Final Countdown (1980) tackles the question of time-meddling in World War II, and punts. No sooner does the aircraft carrier USS *Nimitz* head out to sea under Capt. Yelland (Kirk Douglas) than a time vortex sucks them back to December 6, 1941. Despite the evidence—the *Arizona*, sunk in the Pearl Harbor bombing, is still afloat, for instance—Yelland and his officers don't believe what's happened until two Japanese planes strafe a nearby civilian yacht. The *Nimitz* takes out the planes, captures one pilot and rescues the yacht's passengers, Senator Chapman (Charles Durning) and his secretary Laurel (Katharine Ross).

The *Nimitz* officers debate whether changing history is possible or even acceptable, until Yelland declares he won't stand by when his country's attacked; tomorrow morning,

The U.S. *Nimitz* goes through time to December 6, 1941, then comes back the next morning without doing anything, in *The Final Countdown* (1980).

they're going in. He assigns Commander Owens (James Farentino) to take Chapman and Laurel (who's fallen for Owens and vice versa) to safety on a nearby island. Once they land, Chapman seizes the helicopter at gunpoint, believing that warning Pearl Harbor about the Japanese attack will win him the White House. In the struggle, a bullet hits the gas tank, blowing Chapman up and stranding Owens and Laurel on the island. The vortex sucks the *Nimitz* home before Yelland can take on the Japanese. Back in the present, we learn that Owens became a wealthy military contractor, happily married to Laurel.

The Philadelphia Experiment II (1993) is set nine years after the original film (see chapter five); David Herdeg (Brad Johnson) is a widowed single father, haunted by living in a time not his own. Meanwhile military researcher Mailer (Gerrit Graham) has used Longstreet's (James Greene) research from the original experiment to create the Phoenix, a teleporting nuclear-armed jet. No sooner does the Phoenix take flight than Herdeg's peaceful suburb becomes a burned-out hellhole occupied by Nazi storm troopers (though the imagery is generic totalitarian rather than distinctively Nazi).

Fleeing the Nazis, Herdeg hooks up with the American resistance, and is taken to Longstreet. The scientist explains the time rift that brought Herdeg to the present also let the Phoenix fly back to World War II. It fell into the hands of Mailer's father Mahler (Graham again), a Nazi scientist who used the plane to nuke Washington and win the war, then killed himself when it turned out the force of the explosion rendered the plane inoperative.

The Mailer of the new timeline plans to go back through the rift and save his father, which requires a sample of Herdeg's DNA, as the sailor's body is attuned to the time rift. Herdeg offers to trade a blood sample for a trip back to his own time, but that's only a ruse. Once inside Mailer's lab, he jumps through the rift, destroys the Phoenix in the past, and kills Mahler. Mailer ceases to exist, history otherwise reverts to normal and Herdeg is happy with his son in the present.

Johnny and the Bomb (2006) deals with time-tampering on a smaller scale. When Johnny Maxwell (George Mackay) and his friends discover elderly Mrs. Tachyon (Zoë Wanamaker) injured in their neighborhood of Paradise Street, they rush her to the hospital—unaware that her shopping cart is full of "bags of time" which transported her away from the Blitz to the present. Once the kids discover the power of the bags, they time-jump back to World War II. Unintentionally they alter events so that when the Luftwaffe bombs Paradise Street that night, there's no warning. A raid with no casualties now caused 19 deaths, including Johnny's future grandmother. His grandfather never married and the present is one where Johnny no longer exists. To put things right, the kids go back to before their arrival and despite suspicion from the authorities, they manage to alert the neighborhood to reach their shelters in the nick of time. When Johnny and his friends return to the present, everything's back to normal.

Much like *The Final Countdown*, *Flight World War II* (2015) uses a convenient time vortex to let a commercial jet fly from 2015 into 1940. The captain (Faran Tahir) and crew refuse to believe this despite evidence including the Luftwaffe strafing them and German bombers wreaking havoc on the coast of France. When crew members contact British radio operator Nigel (Robbie A. Kay), he insists it's 1940 but his version of history doesn't match that of the crew or passengers: Germany has jet fighters and Britain hasn't invented radar yet (the film never really explains the divergence). To help out the Allies, the crew members detach the plane's radar unit and parachute it down to the Brits for them to duplicate, after which the plane returns to the present. As everyone disembarks, the captain discovers that one of the passengers who helped out in the crisis is an older Nigel (Harwood Gordon).

Uchronia: A World We Never Made

A uchronia is an alternate history that stands alone—nobody's actively changing time, it's simply presented as a *fait accompli*. Several movies take this tack in portraying an Axis victory. For instance, the bleak *It Happened Here* (1965) follows the struggles of Pauline (Pauline Murray), an Irish nurse looking for work in the Nazi-occupied Britain of 1944. Pauline does her best to collaborate (most Brits have resigned themselves to obeying the Axis), but the government's oppressive dictates drive her into the arms of the resistance. There's no black-and-white morality here, though: Pauline ends up watching the resistance gun down SS troops after the soldiers surrender.

Germany also occupies Britain in *An Englishman's Castle* (1978), a BBC miniseries set in an alt-1970s. Ingram (Kenneth More) is the creator of a TV drama set during the Blitz and the early occupation. Like most of England, he's complacent about Nazi rule, accepting the velvet glove that hides the iron fist. After events force Ingram to confront the truth, he ultimately sides with the resistance and prepares to fight, though the series ends with his fate and that of Britain uncertain.[1]

Germany also won in *Fatherland* (1994), set in alt-reality in 1962 right before President Joseph Kennedy's (Jack's father) state visit to Germany. A German detective (Rutger Hauer) and an American reporter (Miranda Richardson) investigate the murders of older Nazi officials. It turns out that the killers are eliminating anyone who might give the Americans information about the Holocaust, which in this timeline has been successfully covered up. At the film's end, the reporter delivers the evidence, which convinces Kennedy to cancel the summit. This is a departure from the Robert Harris novel, in which the protagonists wonder if the truth will change anything.

In *Resistance* (2011), the turning point of history was the failure of the D-Day invasion. Germany responded to the attempt by invading Britain, and the battle for control is ongoing at the time of the film. The setting is a small Welsh village where the men have gone to war. The women left behind find themselves caught between the Nazi occupiers and a resistance willing to punish anyone who collaborated.

The Man in the High Castle (2015) was a poor adaptation of Philip K. Dick's classic novel about a 1962 where the Axis controls America (it's an original series on Amazon's video service). Japan and Germany have divided the U.S., but both Axis nations know that once the aging Fuehrer dies, Germany will probably try for all the marbles. Two Americans, Joe (Luke Kleintank) and Juliana (Alexa Davalos), become involved in a resistance operation centering on the film *The Grasshopper Lies Heavy*, which the Nazis banned because it shows a world where the Allies won. It's implied that the film is a documentary from our own world, and in the final scene of the first season, a Japanese official finds himself in what appears to be our San Francisco (the second season aired after this book wrapped).

At time of writing, the BBC is working on adapting Len Deighton's novel *SS-GB*, about a Scotland Yard detective working under the SS in occupied Britain.

The East Asia Perspective

Several Japanese and one Korean screen tale ask, "What if the war in the Pacific had turned out differently?" In most of them, the good guys aren't looking to help Japan win, but to avoid getting into conflict with the U.S. in the first place. This may reflect ambivalence about Japan's imperial past: In *Zipang*, some characters argue that complete defeat was the only way to break Japan's militaristic World War II government and reform the nation.

In the anime *Time Stranger* (1986), Jiro Agino (Keiko Toda), a time traveler from a despotic future, travels back to 1582 to save the life of General Oda Nobunaga, the powerful warrior who united Japan under the shogunate (and appears in *Battle Girls, Ambition of Oda Nobuna, Sengoku Collection* and *Samurai Commando Mission 1549*). Agino believes that if the general lives, Japan will meet the West as an equal, changing history to the point that it will never slide into 20th-century militarism and, eventually, the despotism of Agino's era. Agino stops in the present to charge up his time machine, which results in a busload of teens getting dragged back to the past with him. After several stops at key moments in Japanese history, Agino arrives in 1582. The kids must decide whether to help Agino, while an assassin from the future hunts Agino to preserve the future's status quo.[2]

In *Deep Blue Fleet* (1993–2003), when Isoroku Takano (Yūsaku Yara)—the birth name of the great Japanese leader Admiral Yamamoto—dies in 1943, he wakes up back in his younger body, several years earlier. Joining forces with Otaka (Yuzuru Fujimoto), another time traveler, Takano takes over Japan and changes history. This time when Japan attacks Pearl Harbor, it obliterates the base. With this advantage, Japan dominates the Pacific and prevents the U.S. from using the atom bomb against them. The Nazis are unsettled enough to dissolve their alliance with Japan, thereby giving the Japanese an adversary everyone can root against. The war continues several years longer than in our timeline, with more advanced technology, before Japan finally forces Germany to the peace table.³

South Korea's *2009: Lost Memories* (2002) opens in 2009, when Japan has been governing Chosin, Korea, for decades. The terrorist Chosin Liberation Army fights against Japan's control, most recently by attacking the powerful Inoue Foundation to steal an artifact called the Lunar Soul. The Japanese Bureau of Investigation assigns investigators Sakamoto (Jang Dong-gun) and Saigo (Toru Nakamura), Chosin and Japanese respectively, to the case. Sakamoto realizes he's seen the Lunar Soul in his dreams, around the neck of CLA terrorist Hye-in (Jin-Ho Seo). His investigation displeases the foundation, which has him removed from the case, targets him for death, and frames him for murder when he survives.

Sakamoto turns to the CLA. They reveal that the foundation's Inoue used the Lunar Soul to traverse time and prevent the 1909 assassination of a Japanese diplomat. This gave Inoue enough credibility to convince the government not to ally with Germany or attack the U.S. Japan thereby survived World War II unscathed, and the A-bomb was dropped on Germany. Now the CLA wants to restore the original timeline, and with it Korea's independence. Sato likewise learns about the time tampering from the JBI, which tells him that as his in-laws lived at Hiroshima, restoring the timeline could erase Sato's wife.

Sakamoto heads into the past pursued by his former partner. Neither man wants to kill the other, but at the climax, Sakamoto shoots both Sato and Inoue, restoring the original history but leaving him trapped in the past. Here he meets Hye-in's counterpart, the woman of his dreams, and in the final scene—set in the reunified Korea of 2009—we see the couple in a photo exhibit of the nation's great heroes.

The anime series *Zipang* (2004–05) has a *Final Countdown*-like premise, but handles it better. The aircraft carrier *Mirai* travels through a time anomaly and emerges at the 1942 Battle of Midway. Some of the officers advocate intervening on the side of their country; Captain Umezu (Yūsaku Yara) replies that with the power to demolish an entire fleet, intervention would change history beyond recognition. That sits poorly with crew members who know the massive death toll the U.S. will inflict on the Japanese forces.

Things get more complicated when they rescue the Japanese pilot Kusaka (Hiroki Touchi) from drowning. Kusaka sees the ship as a shining hope: With its power, Japan can hold off the U.S. but move away from a militaristic dictatorship (though Kusaka seems comfortable with Japan staying an empire). He calls his vision "zipang," an archaic word for Japan. As the *Mirai* crew struggles to find fuel and provisions while avoiding both U.S. and Japanese fleets, Kusaka tries to nudge them to change events in the direction he favors. Despite Umeza's intentions, the ship does have to fight and kill to survive. By the series' end it's obvious that history has diverged from the original; what shape it will take and the *Mirai*'s final fate remain open questions.

Samurai Commando Mission 1549 (2005) starts when a Japanese experiment in plasma weaponry goes wrong and hurls Col. Matoba's (Takeshi Kaga) brigade back through time to 1547. In present-day Japan two years later, black holes start manifesting, a sign Matoba is changing history. Kanzaki (Kyoka Suzuki) leads an expedition to bring the troops home with the help of Kashima (Yosuke Eguchi), a veteran who served under Matoba. They head back to 1549, with a three-day window before the vortex closes and strands them.

In 1549, Matoba's forces capture Kanzaki's team with a mix of samurai tactics and modern weaponry. Matoba explains that after the troops arrived, Matoba killed the legendary General Nobunaga, then took his place to preserve history. Eventually he decided that a history that includes Hiroshima, unconditional surrender and postwar pacifism wasn't worth preserving. Instead he plans to detonate a plasma device inside Mt. Fuji, devastating the country so that he can take over and chart a different course. The good guys counter-attack, defeat Matoba's forces and kill the would-be conqueror. Kanzaki and Kashima take the bomb back through the time vortex, which fries its components. History is safe.

Like *Johnny and the Bomb*, *Summer Storm* (2009) is about saving individuals, not altering the grand sweep of history. Sixteen-year-old Arashi (Ryoko Shiraishi) is a ghost from the American bombing of Japan in World War II, now working as a diner waitress. (She has a solid body, not insubstantial.) Middle-schooler Hajime (Yuuko Sanpei) meets Arashi and falls instantly in love; when he touches her, they "connect," creating a power that ghosts can use to travel in time. Using their ability, Hajime and Arashi travel to her past to save lives lost in the bombing, though it turns out those rescues are already part of history rather than truly changing it. Hajime spends the rest of his summer awkwardly crushing on Arashi, helping her with her adventures and encountering other ghostly time travelers.

Un-Killing Kennedy

Running Against Time (1990) stars Robert Hays as David Rhodes, a history professor still haunted by his brother Chris' 1966 death in Vietnam—haunted enough it's poisoning his relationship with his girlfriend Laura (Catherine Hicks). When Rhodes discovers that physicist Koopman (Sam Wanamaker) has perfected time travel, he volunteers himself as a guinea pig: send him back to 1963 and he'll save President Kennedy from Oswald's bullet. David believes JFK will pull the troops out of Nam in his second term, thereby saving his brother.

David materializes on top of the Dallas book depository, right on the edge of the roof and almost falls. (While many movies refer to the physical risks of materializing in the wrong place, this film actually deals with them.) He arrives just a few seconds too late to stop the shooting, then through a twist of fate winds up accused of the assassination himself. Jack Ruby, who originally shot Oswald, kills David. Seeing all this reported in old newspapers, Laura goes back to the day before David arrives. She too is unable to stop the assassination but she gets David away from the cops. They contact 1963's Koopman and convince him they're from the future. Armed with their knowledge, Koopman warns President Johnson what will happen if he sends ground troops to Vietnam. This only inspires Johnson to make the attacks on North Vietnam even more brutal and horrifying, rather than go down in history as losing the Vietnam War.

Present-day Koopman sees the change in history, so he goes back to intercept David and Laura. David accepts that he can't cheat fate, and after he makes a quick visit to his brother, the trio returns to the present. David proposes to Laura at last, then discovers that the conversation with Chris convinced his brother not to enlist—he's still alive.

TimeQuest (2000) has a time traveler (Ralph Waite) appearing in John F. Kennedy's hotel suite on the morning of November 22, 1963. His footage of the assassination and JFK's funeral convinces the family he's for real. The Secret Service captures Oswald, erasing the time traveler's future so he promptly ceases to exist. JFK (Victor Slezak) serves eight years, ends the Cold War, withdraws from Vietnam and dissolves the CIA, making this one film where changing history is unambiguously good. (The film avoids talking about Kennedy's spotty civil rights record.)

After almost losing John, Robert Kennedy (Vince Grant) becomes obsessive about dealing with his brother's enemies. He forces FBI Chief J. Edgar Hoover (Larry Drake) out of office and tries to find the time traveler's counterpart in the new timeline, for fear he might someday change things back. Bobby pegs him as aspiring artist and petty crook Raymond Meade (Joseph Murphy); the family buys up enough of Meade's paintings that he makes art his career and never invents the time machine. After JFK's peaceful death years later, the family tells Meade the truth.

11-22-63 (2016) was an online series based on a Stephen King novel. Terminally ill diner owner Al (Chris Cooper) tells his friend Jake Epping (James Franco) that a time tunnel in Al's office leads to October 1960. He proposes Jake go back in time, find out if Oswald killed Kennedy, and if so, whether he acted as a lone gunman. Al says Epping should use whatever he learns to save Kennedy, which will prevent the Vietnam War and so create a better America. It won't be easy as history resists changing. Al also warns Jake that once he returns to the present, taking another time trip will automatically bring back the original past, erasing all the changes.

In 1960, Jake raises money by betting on events where he already knows the outcome, only to learn the hard way that overly large wins create angry losers. Eventually Jake travels to Jodie, Texas, near Dallas, becomes a teacher to support himself, and begins investigating Oswald. He explores various JFK conspiracy theories before determining Oswald was indeed the assassin. Jake also falls in love with Sadie (Sarah Gadon) a fellow teacher, and eventually tells her the truth about himself. When Nov. 22. 1963 rolls around, Epping and Sadie race to the book depository to stop Oswald. The past tries to stop them — their car suddenly dies, for instance—but the couple save JFK at the last minute. Sadie and Oswald both die in the struggle, and the evidence implicates Jake as the shooter.

After Jake clears himself, he returns to the present. In the new timeline America is a bombed-out ruin: Kennedy served two terms and there was no Vietnam War, but in 1968, race-baiting right-wing politician George Wallace became president, which led to catastrophe (we get no details except vague references to bombings and refugee camps). Jake returns to the past, resetting the original time-line. Back in the present, he discovers Sadie is alive and happy in her eighties in Jodie. He travels to meet her and dances with her one last time.

The Children's Crusade

In 1212, thousands of children, led by a boy prophet, set off to free Jerusalem from Muslim control. It did not go well, and many of the children died, gave up, were sold into slavery or vanished from history. The anime *Sins of the Sisters* (1993) reveals that the leader of the crusade took his life in grief, only to be reincarnated in the present as Aiko (Naoko Matsui), a hermaphrodite attending a convent school. Aiko seduces her fellow students, overthrows the repressive nuns and takes control of their convenient time tunnel. Aiko leads the students back in time to stop Christianity from gaining traction in Japan, then goes on to wipe out religion all over the world. The revolution then heads to 1212 to save Aiko's previous incarnation from the slavers.[4]

Crusade: A March Through Time (2006) is more upbeat. Teen soccer player Dolf Vega (Johnny Flynn) is despondent over a recent loss. When he visits his mother (Emma Watson) who's working on a time machine, Dolf impulsively uses it and lands in the middle of the Children's Crusade. When Dolf tries to return home, pilgrim Jenne (Stephanie Leonidas) assumes the time portal is demonic and holds Dolf back. She tells Dolf that it may be God's will that he stays.

Traveling with the crusade, Dolf does his best to help his companions, saving one drowning victim with mouth-to-mouth resuscitation, keeping fever victims quarantined, trading his music player for enough bread to feed the travelers. This is presented unusually matter-of-factly—no histrionics about whether Dolf has the right to change history, he just helps people when they need it. Dolf knows the Crusade ends tragically and tells Jenne that if he hadn't made the journey easier, more children might have dropped out and survived. Priests accompanying the children are even more certain that Dolf is violating God's will.

Back in the present, Dolf's mother tracks him by the growing body of miracles he's added to the Crusade's history. She sends a message to the past warning Dolf he has one last chance to return, and giving him the location of the time gate. Dolf reaches it with Jenne's help, but when he returns to the present, he realizes he doesn't want to live without Jenne. He returns to the past—recorded as another miracle—and in the final scene, Jenne watches him playing soccer again in the present.

The South Shall Rise Again

A number of print SF stories—*Guns of the South*, *Bring on the Jubilee*, the *Captain Confederacy* comics series—contemplate the possibility of Southern victory in the Civil War. The only film to tackle that idea is the uchronia *CSA: Confederate States of America* (2004). This American-history mockumentary tells how the Confederacy successfully pitched its fight to the European nations as a matter of property rights, not slavery, winning the support of England and France. This led to the South successfully conquering the North, reintroducing slavery there and going on to build a slave empire in South America. In the present, racism is rife: The film includes commercial breaks for products such as Nigger Hair Cigarettes (once a real thing), and you can buy and sell slaves via cable's Slave Shopping Network. Canada is firmly abolitionist and a haven for escaped slaves, glaring at the U.S. from across the "cotton curtain," but slavery in this timeline shows no signs of vanishing.

Accidental Change: Stepping on a Butterfly

In *Timekeeper* (1998), kids Henry, Devon and Mary Beth (Anthony Medwetz, Zachary McLemore, Katie Johnston) discover a time gate to 1880 in their eccentric, clock-collecting neighbor Markham's (Pierrino Mascarino) apartment. After Devon goes through the gate, Markham reveals that he's a Timekeeper, charged with protecting time's stability—and Devon has just destabilized it. Markham browbeats Mary Beth and Henry into going through the gate to fix things.

The kids discover that Devon and the computer book he was reading have fallen into the hands of Brogan (Eugen Cristea), a corrupt businessman forcing Devon to build a computer. That technology in 1880 will rewrite history. To make things worse, time cops from the alternate timeline this creates are hunting for Mary Beth and Henry to stop them changing things back. By the time the kids find Devon, he's already built a working computer, so the kids time-jump back further and collect Devon before Brogan captured him. One of the two Devons vanishes on the way back to the present, and it turns out he became Markham: The Timekeepers recruit temporal duplicates to fill out their own ranks and reduce time paradoxes.

A Sound of Thunder (2005) takes the simple premise of Ray Bradbury's same-name short story—a dinosaur hunter changes history by stepping on a butterfly (which is not the source of the term "butterfly effect")—and mangles it beyond recognition. By the start of the film, Charles Hatton (Ben Kingsley) has made a fortune exploiting Sonia Rand's (Catherine McCormack) time travel research. Hatton's employee Travis Ryer (Edward Burns) takes hunters into the past to gun down a dinosaur, always targeting one on the brink of death from some other cause, to avoid changing history. (The footage makes it look like they all kill the same dinosaur at the same point in time, which makes as much sense as anything else in the movie.) Despite the company's precautions, one hunter steps on a butterfly. After the expedition returns, houseplants become juggernauts capable of growing through concrete, then insects grow bigger, larger and meaner. Sonia deduces that the changes will work their way up the evolutionary ladder until they affect humanity last.

Travis tries to fix things, but the distorted time stream makes it physically impossible to reach the divergence point. As New York becomes a prehistoric hellhole, Sonia figures out how he can correct the divergence. Reality returns to normal and no one even remembers the change. However Travis discovers film of his world-saving efforts and uses that to shut down the time safaris before things go wrong again.

Supercollider (2013) gives us another evil financier in Tarsky (Enzo Cilenti), the backer of Vic Susskind's (Robin Dunne) zero-point collider, a possible source of unlimited energy. Tarsky secretly plans to use the collider to open a time window a few seconds into the future, allowing him to invest with absolute certainty.

Susskind spots a weird time distortion when the supercollider turns on, but Tarsky won't let him stop the test. Suddenly history changes: the world is in an economic depression, storms are destroying the country and Vic learns he divorced his wife Nat (Amy Bailey) when she got their little girl killed in a car accident. Nobody listens to Vic's claims of a time change; after all, millions of people have the same delusional memories of a better world.

Tarsky eventually recruits Vic to fix the supercollider, not to restore time, but so that Tarsky can start seeing the future and getting richer. Vic finds a way to shut down his machine, which dissolves the alternate reality. Vic wakes up to find himself with Nat and their daughter, while the radio announces that Tarsky has been busted for fraud.

Villainous Revisionists

In the stop-motion animated musical *Willy McBean and His Magic Machine* (1965), Rasputin Von Rotten (Larry Mann) plans to become the greatest man in all history by going back in time to design the pyramids, discover the Americas, invent the wheel, and out-draw the fastest gun in the West. His pet monkey Pablo steals a copy of Von Rotten's time machine blueprints and stumbles into the home of Willy (Billie Mae Richards), a 13-year-old tech wiz. Willie is horrified to realize that if Rasputin succeeds, all the facts Willie memorized for history class will be useless. The kid builds a duplicate machine and sets out with Pablo to thwart Von Rotten.

After repeated defeats across time at Willy's hands, Von Rotten arrives in the Neolithic to "invent" fire and the wheel. When a tyrannosaurus destroys his time machine, Willy offers to bring Rasputin back to the present, provided Von Rotten never uses his genius for evil again. Willy now has a much greater appreciation for history, and so does Von Rotten, who becomes Willy's new history teacher.

By contrast, the villain of *Eliminators* (1986) has a modest goal, conquering ancient Rome and building an even greater empire ruled by himself. Would-be emperor Abbott Reeves (Roy Dotrice) tests his time machine using the amnesiac cyborg Mandroid (Patrick Reynolds), then orders the Mandroid disposed of. The cyborg escapes Reeves' Amazon fortress and enlists the help of military scientist Hunter (Denise Crosby) to stop Reeves. Hunter hires charter captain Fontina (Andrew Prine) to ferry them up the Amazon, despite attacks from cavemen, rival captains and Reeves' mercenaries. They survive with the help of Kuji (Conan Lee), a martial artist who has his own score to settle with Reeves.

By the time the boat reaches Reeves' base, the scientist has converted the Mandroid technology into Roman-style battle armor for himself. He kills the Mandroid, then traps the humans in a lethal energy field. Mandroid frees them with his dying breath, but too late to stop Reeves from jumping back through time. History is saved when Fontina accidentally damages the time machine: instead of Rome, Reeves ends up the ruler and only human being in the Silurian Age.

Off the Wall Changes

In the 1976 TV series *Sky*, the eponymous time traveler (Mark Harrison) materializes in the U.K.'s present-day West Country by mistake, as he's actually heading to the distant future. Sky's time traveling people, as we later learn, have been shaping history for millions of years, for example by endowing humanity's ancestors with intelligence. Earth's life force resists Sky's presence as an organism resists bacteria: Leaves and plants spontaneously attack him and nature takes human form as Goodchild (Robert Eddison), who manipulates other humans to kill Sky.

Ultimately Goodchild accepts that it can't kill the intruder, and agrees to let him reach

Stonehenge, the gate that can send him where he needs to be. Sky's human friend Arby (Stuart Lock) follows him through to a future where humanity has rejected technology in favor of psionics, putting them on the track to becoming as cosmic as Sky's own race. Sky sends Arby home with some trace of future humanity's power as a souvenir, along with memories of Sky's presence, which have been wiped from everyone else.

Creation itself is at stake in *Second Time Lucky* (1984) as Satan (Robert Helpmann) challenges God (Robert Morley) to a replay of the Fall of Man, with the winner taking absolute control of the universe. The guinea pig is modern-day Adam (Roger Wilson), a college student we see unsuccessfully flirting with fellow student Eve (Diane Franklin) right before Gabriel (Jon Gadsby) sends them back to the Garden of Eden.

As the serpent seduces Adam and Eve into repeating the Fall, it would seem Satan won. Instead, the students play more rounds in different ages, culminating in the 1960s, where Adam is a politically radical rock star. Eve seduces him into signing with corrupt record mogul "Lew Siffer," but then falls for Adam and sacrifices her life to help him expose Siffer's villainy. God wins, but as Adam is grief-stricken over Eve, the Almighty aborts the entire plotline. Instead of traveling in time, the collegiate Adam and Eve just sleep together.

Mud (1994–95) was a British kids' comedy about the adventures of youngsters Bill (Russell Tovey), Ruby (Brooke Kinsella) and Shane (Russell Brand). In one story arc, they travel back in time to prevent a centuries-old witch from ever taking up the path of magic. When they return, the kids discover Europe never discovered the Americas, bad news for them as they'll never again be able to watch *Baywatch*![5]

Bubble Fiction: Boom or Bust (2007), a Japanese comedy, nostalgically harks back to the booming economy of two decades earlier. Bar hostess Mayumi Tanaka (Ryōko Hirosue) learns from Ministry of Finance official Shimokawaji (Hiroshi Abe) that her recently deceased mother Mariko is actually alive. Japan is facing financial collapse within two years, so Mariko (Hiroko Yakushimaru) went back in time—her washing machine is also a time machine—to prevent the passage of a (fictitious) bill that popped the 1980s boom times. Mayumi reluctantly takes the same trip back to 1989. It's a big culture shock for her to enter a world with no Internet, where everyone spends lavishly in contrast to her penny-pinching lifestyle. The 1989 natives are equally shocked at Mayumi's unbelievably (by their standards) skin-baring outfits. Against this backdrop, Mayumi struggles to find her mother, save Japan's economy and fend off the lecherous younger Shimokawaji. (It's a good thing she succeeds, as it turns out he's her father.)[6]

A found-footage mockumentary, *Lunopolis* (2009) opens in 2012 as Matt (Matt Avant) and Sonny (Sonny Maynor) investigate claims tying Area 51 to a secret lunar city. With help from elderly David James (Dave Potter), they discover that the city exists, built by Lumology (a Scientology parody) because time travel is only possible in a vacuum. At the end of 2012, the church will send hundreds of members into the past to put right everything that's gone wrong in human history.

It turns out that each change only created more problems, requiring more time travelers go back to fix them. The cumulative effects have made reality so mutable that Lumologists carry Polaroid cameras everywhere: hard copy photos remain stable even when time and memory change. Hilliard (Dave Potter), the church founder, now regrets his time tampering and tried unsuccessfully to alert the world by crashing one of the church rockets at Roswell in 1947. When Matt and Sonny finally meet Hilliard, James shows up. He's actually future Hilliard, planning to prevent Lumology's time project by killing his younger self. At the last minute, James remembers living through the same attempt when he was younger, so Hilliard will survive. The film ends with a mysterious Lumology crystal making everyone vanish.

In the animated comedy *Free Birds* (2013), two turkeys try to change the flow of history. Reggie (Owen Wilson) enjoys the life of a pampered pet after the president spares him on Thanksgiving Day. Jake (Woody Harrelson), a revolutionary acting on the orders of the Great Turkey, kidnaps Reggie to help steal a time machine, go back to Pilgrim days and prevent turkeys from going on the menu at the first Thanksgiving.

This proves tougher than they think. Under the leadership of Broadbeak (Keith David), 17th-century turkeys are canny survivors, but the Pilgrim Standish (Colm Meaney) is relentlessly hunting them down to feed the colony. Reggie does meet pretty turkey Jenny (Amy Poehler), who likes him despite his weird talk of time travel. However, Reggie and Jake's efforts to help the flock lead to disaster, getting Broadbeak killed and exposing the turkeys' hiding place to hunters. Jenny becomes the new leader and decides to go to war with the Pilgrims, so Reggie returns home alone. His future selves appear and reveal he's destined to become the Great Turkey who sent Jake on his mission. They also tell him that if he doesn't go back to help Jenny and Jake, the flock is doomed. Reggie returns just as the Pilgrims triumph, offers them pizza as an alternative Thanksgiving dish, and saves the day. He settles down in the past with Jenny while Jake heads off in the time machine to keep fighting for the downtrodden.

Fictional History

A number of fictional settings, just by sticking around for years, develop their own fictional histories. And some time travel stories involve those histories getting rewritten, as in Japan's *Rebirth of Mothra 3* (1998). Godzilla arch-foe King Ghidorah, the three-headed monster that once wiped out the dinosaurs, returns from space to launch another extinction event. In addition to the usual destructive kaijin activities, he also captures children in a gigantic pulsating sphere for some unexplained reason. The tiny sisters Moll (Megumi Kobayashi) and Lora (Misato Tate) summon Mothra, the gigantic, heroic silk moth, to fight Ghidorah. Mothra fails and Ghidorah takes over Lora's mind.

Mothra realizes the only solution is to travel into the past and destroy Ghidorah in the dinosaur age so he can't threaten the present. After a young boy frees Lora, the sisters channel enough power for Mothra to jump across time. In the past, she apparently destroys Ghidorah at the cost of her own life, after which two of her caterpillars cocoon her in silk. Smart move: When Ghidorah, still alive and kicking, renews his attack in the present, Mothra bursts out of the cocoon at peak strength and takes Ghidorah down.

Stargate: Continuum (2008) takes place in the universe of *Stargate: SG-1*, a TV series where Earth soldiers can travel through Stargates to other planets and fight to defend Earth and other worlds against the imperialistic Gou'ald. The SG-1 team attends the execution of the last Gou'ald tyrant, Ba'al (Cliff Simon), only to discover it's a clone, left to distract them while the real Ba'al launches a failsafe plan. It involves going back in time to sink the ship that delivered Earth's Stargate to the U.S. The U.S. never develops a Stargate program, so the team members in the present vanish; only Mitchell (Ben Browder), Carter (Amanda Tapping) and Jackson (Michael Shanks) make it back to Earth. The authorities in the alt-timeline accept their story but refuse to let them alter the lives of millions of people by restoring their own history. After all, Ba'al hasn't attacked Earth, so what's the harm?

The harm begins a year later when Ba'al arrives. He's become supreme among the Gou'ald by using time travel to outmaneuver his rivals, and now plans to neutralize Earth by posing as a friend. His mate Qetesh (Claudia Black), who advocates genocide, double-crosses and kills Ba'al, assumes his throne and prepares to attack. Imminent destruction makes restoring the old timeline seem much more reasonable, so the military recruits SG-1 to set things right. The government preserved the Stargate for emergencies, so SG-1 uses it to reach Ba'al's time machine. Mitchell alone makes it back to the past and ambushes Ba'al's strike force when it attacks the ship. The timeline reverts to normal, and nobody remembers it ever changed.

Pokemon was a wildly popular anime set in a world where humans live alongside the super-powerful Pokemon, whom they capture and train to compete in mock battles. In *Pokemon: Arceus and the Jewel of Life* (2009), protagonist Ash (Rica Matsumoto), his Pokemon Pikachu (Ikue Otani) and their friends visit a beautiful valley kept green and verdant by the magical Jewel of Life. Centuries earlier when the valley was barren, the mighty Pokemon Arceus (Akihiro Miwa) loaned the Jewel to the human Damos (Masahiro Takashima), who then stole it. Sheena (Kie Kitano), Damos' descendant in the present, returns the gem to Arceus, but it turns out to be fake. After Arceus attacks the valley, the time-bending Pokemon Diagli sends Sheela, Ash and his friends back in time to fix things. In the past, they discover the treacherous Marcus (Koichi Yamadera) hypnotized Damos to betray Arceus. Sheela tries to warn Marcus about the consequences, but he exploits her knowledge of the future to destroy Arceus instead.

Ash, Damos and the others save Arceus. When they return to the future, Arceus stops his attack as he acquires memories of the new timeline. Realizing the humans of the valley are his friends, the great Pokemon leaves in peace.

In 2013's animated *Justice League: The Flashpoint Paradox*, Barry Allen, AKA the super-fast Flash (Justin Chambers), suddenly finds himself living in a world where he has no powers and Flash never existed. His long-dead mother is alive, Bruce Wayne died years ago, and it's Bruce's guilt-ridden father Thomas (Kevin McKidd) who fights crime as Batman. Atlantis and the Amazons are at war and Aquaman is about to unleash a doomsday weapon that will wipe out the surface world.

Barry deduces that the changes are side effects of his old adversary Prof. Zoom (C. Thomas Howell) trying to destroy him. Barry contacts Batman, who agrees to help when he realizes that Bruce will live if the timeline is changed back. The two heroes restore Flash's powers, but he still doesn't have the speed to break the time barrier. Zoom confronts the Flash and reveals it was Barry who changed the world, by disrupting the time stream when he saved his mother from a killer. After Batman takes out Zoom, Flash breaks the time barrier and stops his past self saving his mom. (There's a similar plot point takes place in the live-action 2014 *Flash* TV series.) In the restored timeline, Barry takes comfort from his added memories of his mother.

Travels in Alternate History

Visiting parallel worlds provides an easy way to experience different histories. Nobody has to go back and make things change—the alternate universe has always been there, going its own way. And if you don't like the world, you don't have to change things, you just find a way home.

Then again, in the TV series *Sliders* (1995–2000), finding home wasn't so easy. After San Francisco teenage inventor Quinn (Jerry O'Connell) discovers his gravity experiments have created a gateway to parallel Earths, he convinces his best friend Wade (Sabrina Lloyd) and his mentor Prof. Arturo (John Rhys-Davies) to jump through it with him. Faded soul singer Rembrandt Brown (Cleavant Derricks) gets caught in the wormhole and pulled along. The group land in a parallel San Francisco in the grip of an ice age, and Quinn isn't able to get them home. The cast "slid" from dimension to dimension, encountering divergent versions of our world and of themselves. In one world, the government keeps Americans docile by keeping them stoned and Quinn is a radical who opposes the policy. In another world, gender roles are reversed and Arturo runs for president on a "men's liberation" platform. Over time (with the entire cast except Derricks changing), they also became involved with the threat of the Kromaggs, an offshoot of humanity on one parallel world, now seeking to conquer the multiverse. At the series' end, the Kromaggs lost.

In the first episode of *Dual! Parallel Trouble Adventures* (1999), a construction worker finds a strange device at a building site. Two timelines diverge from that moment depending whether he throws the gadget away or pockets it; the first creates our timeline, the second a world of battling mecha. Twenty-two years later, teenager Kazuki (Takayuki Yamaguchi) can't understand why he constantly hallucinates battling robots, but Prof. Sanada (Ryūnosuke Obayashi) realizes Kazuki is seeing the other timeline. The professor's experiments catapult the Kazuki into the other world with the professor's daughter, Mitsuki (Rie Tanaka).

In the alt-world, Sanada's counterpart runs the Earth Defense Forces, which leads the fight against the revolutionary Rara movement. Mitsuki, whose counterpart died, settles in with the professor as a mecha pilot. To everyone's surprise, Kazuki is also able to control the robots, which no other male can do. Between battles, Kazuki becomes the focus of attention for Mitsuki and the other pilots. Eventually the Rara forces triumph, but that's inconsequential compared to the potential for destruction when the two timelines begin to merge. Kazuki finds a way to let them do so without any loss of life, then settles down in the new merged world with the continued attention of his harem.

In *Parallels* (2015), a pilot in the *Sliders* mold, the Carver siblings (Mark Hapka, Jessica Rothe) and their friend Harold (Eric Jungmann) enter an abandoned building in response to a message from the Carvers' father, then emerge into a bombed-out wasteland. The building is a nexus that opens a gate to a different parallel world every 36 hours—and if you stay in one world any longer, you won't be able to leave. The quartet travels from the nuked-out wasteland to a hi-tech world, then meet their father, who tells them they have to find their supposedly dead mother somewhere out in the multiverse. Hidden agendas and mysteries—not to mention divergent versions of themselves—bedevil the travelers before they move on through the nexus to the next adventure.

CHAPTER SEVEN

Shaping the Future by Changing the Past That Is Our Present

"Which future has god—if there is a god—chosen for man's destiny?"—Escape from the Planet of the Apes

From the perspective of a thousand years ahead, or even a year from now, we're history.

Just as screen time travelers from the present go back in time to change history and fix what's wrong, so travelers from the future come to the present to change their history—our future.

From our perspective, that makes a big difference, as noted in the introduction. It's one thing to argue Hitler should be stopped, it's another to argue that someone in the present should be killed for crimes he has yet to commit. Should we even believe the traveler who claims he's acting for the greater good? Surprisingly, yes. Only *Godzilla vs. King Ghidorah* and the *Josh Kirby* films in chapter four have visitors from the future lying about what lies ahead for the world.

The same past good future bad aspect mentioned in previous chapters plays a role in history-changing. Usually characters who want to change the past don't believe the present sucks, they just want to improve it. The futures that people are trying to change are dystopian hellholes incapable of reform. Even so, it still conveniently comes down to changing just one moment, one person, one turning point in the past to eliminate the nightmare future.

I'm Bill S. Preston, Esquire...

Bill & Ted's Excellent Adventure (1989) gives us one of the rare utopian futures in time travel films: People are nice, the music is great, the environment is clean (the sequel reveals that air guitar purifies air pollution). However, as 2688's Rufus (George Carlin) explains at the start of the film, that future isn't guaranteed. Cut to California high schoolers Bill Preston (Alex Winter) and Ted Logan (Keanu Reeves), whose struggling garage band Wyld Stallion is handicapped by their lack of good instruments, skill and talent. And Mr. Logan is preparing to ship Ted to military school in Alaska. The only way to prevent that is for the guys to pass history, which requires staging a killer presentation on how a great historical figure would react to the present. And that's asking a lot of the dimwitted duo.

Rufus materializes in a time traveling phone booth (a *Doctor Who* in-joke) and offers to loan it to Bill and Ted. The guys are skeptical until their future selves appear in a second phone booth and encourage them to go for it. Before long, Bill and Ted have met various great figures—Napoleon, Socrates, Genghis Khan, Joan of Arc—as well as Princesses Joanna (Diane Franklin) and Elizabeth (Kimberly LaBelle), whom the guys invite to the prom. When the phone booth returns to the present, the historical figures get arrested for causing trouble at the mall. Bill and Ted realize they can get them out with the help of their future selves—what if later in the day they steal the keys to the cells, go back in time and leave the keys right ... here! With several such deftly executed paradoxes, they free their historical friends and put on a spectacular presentation.

Rufus shows up that night with the two princesses and explains that Bill and Ted will become the greatest musicians in all history, transforming society with their philosophy of "Be excellent to each other." By preventing them from breaking up, Rufus ensured the utopia will come to be. As a reward, he gets to jam with his heroes.

By the time of *Bill & Ted's Bogus Journey* (1991) the guys still haven't learned to play, which is bad news as their first and possibly last shot at the big time is an imminent battle of the bands. Worse news, 27th century gym teacher De Nomolos (Joss Ackland) plans to replace them with robots who will preach messages of order and obedience, creating a future more to De Nomolos' taste. No sooner do the guys ask the princesses (now Annette Azcuy and Sarah Trigger) to marry them than the robots break up with the girls, then murder Bill and Ted. After a sojourn in a memorably goofy Hell, the guys challenge Death (William Sadler) to a competition for the right to return to life. After they best him at Twister, Battleship and Clue, Death concedes and takes them home, stopping in Heaven on the way. There the team convinces an alien super-genius to come along and build good robots to fight the evil ones.

The improbable team arrives at the concert, destroys the robots and saves the princesses. When De Nomolos appears, the guys pull the same time paradox tricks as before; De Nomolos counters with the same tactics, but Bill and Ted are better at it. They then travel into the past for 18 months of guitar training—not to mention weddings, honeymoons and new babies—and return to deliver a concert so awesome, the future utopia is a slam dunk.

The formula proved easy to adapt for both an animated series (1990) and a live-action one (1992): Confront Bill and Ted with a problem, then have them bop around through time until they stumble over a solution. For example, in the animated episode "A Most Excellent Roman Holiday," the guys wind up in Latin class and realize their only hope of passing is to ace a special assignment by decoding an ancient medallion's inscription. Back the duo go to Rome to get the information from the horse's mouth. After assorted misadventures, they return to reveal the message translates as "Party on, dudes!"

Twelve Monkeys

La Jetée (1962) was a French short whose story is told entirely in a series of stills. Scientists in a post–World War III future send a man (Davos Hanich) across time to find help for their decaying civilization. The man has long dreamed of a woman he met when he was a child, and uses that desire to propel him to the present. He meets the woman (Hélène Chatelain), falls for her and decides not to return home. After a time traveling executioner kills him, it turns out that his younger self saw him die. The sight of the woman sobbing over his body is what made his younger self remember her.

In *12 Monkeys* (1995), a movie loosely inspired by *La Jetée*, the apocalypse is a pandemic unleashed by the terrorist Army of the 12 Monkeys in 1997, wiping out 99 percent of the population and driving the survivors underground. Future scientists send James Cole (Bruce Willis) back to 1996 to stop the terrorists. He arrives in 1990 with his mind disordered by the time jump, gets institutionalized and meets Dr. Railly (Madeleine Stowe). The scientists pull Cole back, send him to World War I, then finally land him in 1996. Cole meets Railly again, kidnaps her and tells her he dreamed of her long before they met. Disregarding the fact that he appears to be an insane kidnapper, Railly melts for him. Together they discover that Goines (Brad Pitt), a fellow inmate from 1990 and the son of a prominent virologist (Christopher Plummer), is the leader of the 12 Monkeys.

As Railly comes to realize that Cole isn't hallucinating his time travel, Cole becomes convinced that he is, because that would free him to stay in 1996. To that end, he encourages the scientists to send him back to 1996 for a sample of the virus they can use to develop a vaccine—but his real agenda is to reunite with Railly and spend time together before the plague starts. Plans change when they learn that Goines is harmless, and the real bioterrorist is his father's assistant Peters (David Morse). Cole dies trying to kill Peters, and as in *La Jetée*, his younger self watches Railly as she weeps over him. Peters proceeds to spread the virus.

The 2015 *12 Monkeys* TV show isn't a sequel to the film but a reboot. Once again Cole (Aaron Stanford) goes back in time from 2043, seeking to destroy the virus that wiped out humanity and may yet wipe out the few survivors (it mutates constantly). Cole and Railly (Amanda Schull) discover that the 12 Monkeys in this version are real, a mysterious organization of time travelers whose agenda includes preserving the bleak future that Cole wants to change. At the end of the first season, the Army of the 12 Monkeys seizes control of the 2043 time travel lab, just as Cole sends an injured Railly to his future to save her life.

Timothy Greenberg offered a lighter take on the whole concept with his student film *La Puppé* (2003), which follows the structure of *La Jetée* except that the protagonist is a dog.

The Terminator Cycle

Movies' most persistent and prolonged struggle to shape the future started in 1984 with *The Terminator*.

Or possibly it started in 1964 with the *Outer Limits* episode "Soldier." SF author Harlan Ellison has said so based on the opening of the two tales; he also says he heard second-hand that *Terminator* director James Cameron acknowledged ripping off *Outer Limits*. Ellison didn't file a lawsuit but now gets an "inspired by" credit on the *Terminator* films.[1]

"Soldier" opens in a war-torn future where soldiers are trained from birth to see everyone as a potential enemy. A time rift sucks soldier Quallo (Michael Ansara) to the present, which he assumes is hostile territory. After the FBI stops his killing spree, philologist Kagan

(Lloyd Nolan) discovers that Quallo's language is a heavily mutated form of English, spiked with future slang such as "peep" for "understand." Once he's able to communicate with Quallo, Kagan takes him into his home despite the soldier's wariness and the FBI's concern. When an enemy soldier comes through the rift and attacks the house, Quallo hurls himself against the man and destroys him. Kagan ponders whether Quallo was protecting the family or reverting to his training.

Another Ellison *Outer Limits* story, "Demon with a Glass Hand," has been cited as a *Terminator* influence, though not by Ellison himself. The excellent episode stars Robert Culp as Trent, a time traveler from the future. For some unknown reason Trent is trapped and hunted by aliens in a modern-day skyscraper. Eventually he learns that all of future humanity has been converted to digital data and hidden within his hand, to protect them from the aliens: If he dies, the human race goes with him. Eventually Trent succeeds in destroying the aliens, then prepares to wait the millennia until his own time, when humanity can be restored.

Neither Ellison protagonist is out to change history, but the Terminators and their adversaries are all about rewriting time. Whether it's possible depends on the film. The *Terminator* characters are already part of the future's history; *Terminator 2* assumes that the future can be changed; *T3* says what lies ahead is inevitable.

The Terminator opens in 2029, at the end of a brutal man vs. machine war. In the present, the naked Terminator (Arnold Schwarzenegger) materializes in Los Angeles, where he beats up some punks and takes their clothes. A second naked man, Kyle Reese (Michael Biehn), materializes but avoids conflict, breaking into a department store to clothe and arm himself. The Terminator uses the LA phone book to hunt down and kill two women named Sarah Connor. When a third Sarah (Linda Hamilton) hears about the deaths and spots Kyle following her, she contacts the police. Kyle is a good guy, though, saving Sarah when the Terminator tracks her down. Despite taking a shotgun blast to the chest, the Terminator gets up and pursues them.

Kyle tells Sarah that in her near future, a military AI called Skynet will trigger a nuclear war, having decided the humans on its own side are as big a problem as the enemy. Skynet's robot army continues wiping out humanity until John Connor, Sarah's future son, turns things around. On the eve of defeat, Skynet sent back the Terminator cyborg—human flesh over a robot core—to kill Sarah before John is even born; John sent Reese back to save her, then blew up the time travel device so Skynet couldn't ever try again. (Later films ignored this, obviously.)

When the police bring in the two humans, Kyle warns the cops that nothing will stop the Terminator. The police aren't impressed until the cyborg attacks the station, killing everyone in its path. Sarah and Kyle escape again. In the aftermath, Reese tells Sarah that in his time she's a legend, the woman who forged John Connor into humanity's champion. He confesses that he fell in love with John's photo of her, which is why he volunteered for the time jump. They make love. The Terminator catches up, pursues them into a factory and kills Reese, after which Sarah crushes it under a mechanical press. Several months later, we see a visibly pregnant Sarah, armed to the teeth, contemplating what to tell her son about all this.

Sarah's voiceover at the start of *Terminator II: Judgment Day* (1991) tells us that 1997 is when we face Judgment Day, Skynet's nuclear attack. She adds that Skynet sent back a second Terminator to kill John in childhood, but adult John also sent back a defender. Once again the Terminator arrives, this time taking clothes and wheels from a biker gang. A second time traveler (Robert Patrick) kills a cop, morphs into the man's double and takes his car and uniform. Using the police computer records he tracks down John Connor (Edward Furlong), a troubled tween with a string of petty crimes on his record. John's in foster care, as Sarah has been institutionalized for her delusions about time traveling cyborgs. Meanwhile, we learn the IT company Cyberdine has salvaged a piece of the original cyborg, which tech genius Dyson (Joe Morton) is using to build Skynet.

Both time travelers close in on John, but now Schwarzenegger is the good guy, reprogrammed to protect the boy. The assassin is the shapeshifter, a T-1000 stronger and more dangerous than the original cyborg. The Terminator saves John, then they find Sarah just as she's breaking out of the mental hospital. The T-1000 shows up, plotting to kill and replace Sarah, but the Connors and the Terminator escape. The cyborg reveals that once Skynet becomes operational, the government decides to shut it down, which is what provokes the AI to go nuclear. Sarah decides the best way to stop this is to kill Dyson.

When the trio confronts the scientist, Sarah discovers she isn't willing to kill an innocent man, even to save the world. Dyson, however, agrees to help them break into his lab and destroy his research. The T-1000 catches up with them at Cyberdine and kills Dyson; then the Terminator destroys the shapeshifter by hurling it into molten metal. That leaves the Terminator as the only source of the technology needed to build Skynet, so he has Sarah destroy him too. The apocalypse ends before it can begin.

Terminator 3: Rise of the Machines (2003) starts ten years later. The year 1997 came and went without Judgment Day, but John (Nick Stahl) is an orphan—Sarah died of leukemia—and he still lives off the grid, alone, with no phone or permanent address. He's not crazy to be cautious, as the military has built a new Skynet, and a new Terminator, TX (Kristanna Loken), has arrived in the present to begin a new killing spree.

TX finds one target, Kate Brewster (Claire Danes), just as Kate meets John Connor for the first time since high school. TX attempts to kill them both but a new model of the original Terminator has come back and saves them, despite TX's superior abilities. The Terminator tells his charges that Judgment Day is inevitable—destroying Dyson's research only delayed Armageddon.

"Iconic" is an overused word but it seems to fit this shot of Arnold Schwarzenegger from *The Terminator* (1984).

The outcome of the war, however, is up for grabs and TX's goal is to kill John's future lieutenants to tilt the balance (Kate is also John's future wife).

After escaping both cops and TX, the trio learn that the military is about to activate Skynet to fight a dangerous Internet virus. Kate's father (David Andrews) runs the Skynet project so John and the others meet with him in the hopes they can still stop Judgment Day. During the trip to Lt. General Brewster, the Terminator reveals that instead of ending in 2029, the war is still ongoing in 2032, when he assassinated John Connor. Kate then reprogrammed the Terminator and sent him back to stop TX.

It turns out Skynet created the virus to force the military to activate Skynet, after which the AI will go nuclear. TX kills Brewster, but not before he sends the kids to Skynet's core to destroy it. TX pursues them, but the Terminator sacrifices himself to blow her up. Kate and John reach the core, but discover it's just a military fallout shelter, Brewster's strategy to keep them safe. As panicked National Guard and civil defense groups call in, John accepts his destiny and takes command.

The 2008–09 TV series *Terminator: The Sarah Connor Chronicles* ignored *T3*. It opens in 1999, two years after the destruction of Skynet, with Sarah (Lena Headey)—a wanted woman after the events of *T2*—still on the move with John (Thomas Dekker), though the only person hunting them is federal agent Ellison (Richard T. Jones). A Terminator, Cromartie (Garret Dillahunt), shows up and attacks, only to be stopped by Cameron (Summer Glau), a good Terminator. (Cameron and Ellison's names pay tribute to Harlan Ellison and James Cameron.)

Sarah wants to vanish again, but John tells her it's time to stand and fight. Cameron convinces them the way to do that is travel with her to 2007—both sides of the war time-jump routinely now—when Skynet's component technologies will come together. (Judgment Day is now scheduled for 2011.) A key component is the Turk, a super-sophisticated chess-playing computer that will become the prototype of Skynet's brain unless the Connors destroy it. Among the complications that crop up are John's unease about living up to his destiny; Kyle's brother Derek (Brian Austin Green) arriving from the future; a resistance cell trying to turn John against Cameron for fear she's a corrupting influence; and a new Terminator (Shirley Manson) seeking to create a Skynet with a sense of ethics, an intriguing development still in play when Fox axed the series.

Several years after the TV series and the dreadful, time travel–free *Terminator Salvation* (2009), Paramount rebooted the franchise with *Terminator Genisys* (2015). This time, when Kyle (Jai Courtney) jumps back to 1984, he finds Sarah (Emilia Clarke) and the Terminator "Pops" (Arnold Schwarzenegger) have already destroyed the Terminator hunting Sarah. Kyle learns that Pops saved Sarah from an attack when she was nine (though neither one knows who sent him to help her), changing history. In 1984, Sarah is already combat-hardened.

What follows is primarily a remake of *T2* with elements of the TV show mixed in. Sarah, Kyle and Pops jump forward to 2017 to destroy Genisys, the computer program that will become Skynet. Instead of the original T1000, they face John (Jason Clarke), who's been transformed by Skynet nannites into an even more powerful shapeshifter. And like John in the TV show, Sarah is burdened by the fear her future is marked out for her and set in stone. Ultimately, Kyle, Sarah and Pops destroy John and Genisys, leaving Sarah free to chart her own course in life. But Genisys has survived after all…

Two sequels have been greenlit at time of writing.

Terminator Wannabes

Nemesis (1992) introduced us to a 21st century in which cyborgs were taking over America. By the 2077 of *Nemesis 2: Nebula* (1995) the cyborgs have won. Scientists genetically engineer Alex, the child of the first film's hero, into a superhuman cyborg-fighter, sent back with her mother to 20th century Africa to grow up safely. After Mom's death, Alex (Sue Price) reaches adulthood as a member of a local tribe. The cyborg assassin Nebula (Chad Stahelski) shows up to kill Alex. The duo spend the rest of the movie chasing, shooting or fighting, with rebels and mercenaries providing extra cannon fodder, before Alex destroys Nebula.

Nemesis 3, Time Lapse (1996) has Alex waking up with amnesia in the desert. She's found by Farnsworth (Tim Thomerson), a superior cyborg sent back to analyze Alex's genes and determine how dangerous the "DNA mutant" is. His probe triggers flashbacks to Alex's meeting with her sister Rain (Ursula Sarcev), one of several other "DNA women" sent to the past: Rain warned Alex that if they don't return to the future within a few hours, it'll be a year before the time gate opens again. After Farnsworth captured Rain, Alex fought through cyborgs and gunmen to rescue her, but failed, and also missed the trip back to the future. (The discontinuous, non-time travel *Nemesis 4* has her in the future without any explanation.)

The title character in *Terminatrix* (1995) comes from a 21st century where sex is outlawed except when the government mandates that suitable individuals reproduce. A T-69 cyborg (Shouko Kudou) travels back to the present to prevent the future resistance leader Hanako from ever being born: She will seduce his future father, Kota Sera (Naofumi Matsuda), then mangle his penis with her vagina dentata (I wish I were kidding about this) so he'll never be able to reproduce. Kaoru (Kei Mizutani) is the Kyle Reese sent back to save Kota. After lots of running, fights and bad softcore sex scenes, Kaoru and Kota destroy the T-69 with an electrified dildo in her vagina (still not kidding). Kaoru stays in the past to become Hanako's mother.

In *Beneath the Bermuda Triangle* (1997), Commander Deakins (Jeff Fahey) is the sole survivor of the mysteriously vanished submarine USS *Alabama*. Deakins claims that a giant vessel from the future destroyed the sub after the *Alabama* went through a time rift. Lance (Jack Coleman), a scientist, believes this and gets his boss Senator Braddock's (Brian Cranston) approval to investigate. Deakins and Lance take another vessel through the rift and arrive in 2077. Braddock now rules the country with an army of shapeshifting cyborg clones, while Deakins' grandson John (Fahey again) leads the resistance. Both sides realize that if Deakins dies, John won't exist, while if Deakins returns home, he may be able to stop Braddock's rise to power.

Deakins does return home, but one of the sub crew members brings back some cloning tech and sells it to Braddock. Lance tries to convince Braddock to listen to the better angels of his nature; when that doesn't work, Lance kills him. Unfortunately it's only a cyborg clone—Braddock's people apparently mastered the tech very fast—and in the subsequent firefight, Deakins' pregnant wife dies. Braddock assumes the future is his now, unaware that it's another woman who will become Deakins' lover and John's grandmother.

Tripping the Rift: The Movie (2008) spun off from an animated series about the sleazy, sex-crazed crew of the Jupiter 42 spaceship. A hulking Arnie-1000 android (a big clown with a German accent) keeps trying to kill Captain Chode (Stephen Root), but another time traveler, Adam-12, saves Chode. He reveals that at Chode's birthday party, the captain will hook up with a drunken Babette—daughter of his old enemy Bobo—and impregnate her, so Bobo's wife sent the android to kill Chode first. Returning to the future, Adam confesses to the Bobos that he's the one who hooked up with Babette. The Bobos agree to call off the android if Adam and Babette break up, though it's clear to the audience that the youngsters are lying.

Defeating Dystopia

Cyborg 2087 (1966) stars Michael Rennie as Garth, a cyborg from the future who arrives in the present the day before Prof. Marx (Eduard Franz) demonstrates his telepathic implants to the military. The professor believes this will benefit the world, but Garth tells Marx's assistant Sharon (Karen Steele) that by 2087, the implants allow the authorities to control every thought. A few minds remain free, and sent Garth back to prevent the demo.

Garth has to contend with cyborgs from the future hunting him in the present, plus local cops who want every cyborg locked up for public safety. Garth perseveres and convinces Marx to abandon his research and miss the demonstration meeting. Once he does, this erases Garth's future and makes everyone forget him. In this altered timeline, Marx does meet the military but only to tell them he's destroying his research.

By the 21st century of *Virgin Hunters* (1994) a multinational corporation has abolished democracy, sex and even sexual thoughts. Two horny guys (Brian Bremer, Christopher Wolf) from the first generation of test tube teens go back to 1994 to stop sexually frustrated, power-hungry prude Camella Swales (Morgan Fairchild) from bringing about the dystopia they came from. They disguise themselves as girls to sneak into Swales' boarding school, which gives them lots of chances to learn about sex, in between trying to get Swales laid and ducking a Terminator knockoff sent to kill them. They solve both problems by reprogramming the cyborg into a super-stud who sleeps with Swales, so the future of sex is saved.

The future of the anime TV series *DNA²* (1994) is insanely overpopulated due to the spread of the "mega-playboy" gene which makes men irresistible and sexually insatiable. The mutation traces back to Junta (Keiichi Nanba), a young man normally so shy that he pukes around girls. Karin (Miina Tominaga), a future scientist, comes to the present to change history with a genetic treatment that will neutralize Junta's mutation. Karin screws up and triggers the mega-playboy gene, which kicks in whenever Junta meets an attractive woman. The only exception is Ami (Hiroko Kasahara), a childhood friend who's in love with Junta; in her presence, he reverts to normal. Another screw-up gives Junta's acquaintance Ryuugi (Takehito Koyasu) amazing powers and drives him insane. When Ryuugi kidnaps Ami, Junta has to become the mega-playboy permanently to defeat him. But after Junta wins, Ami turns him back.

It looks like the future is safe but another time traveler, Mori (Jun Hazumi), turns up to restore Junta's mega-playboy powers. Mori has a method for controlling anyone carrying the gene so curing the mutation will cost him a slave army. Mori transforms Junta back and orders him to kill Karin, but Junta overcomes Mori's control, defeats Mori himself, then returns to normal. Ami and Junta start a normal life together.

In *Total Reality* (1997), 22nd century Earth's Bridgist dictatorship has just crushed the last of the resistance, only to see the rebel leader Tunis (Thomas Kretschmann) escape in a time-ship to the present. The government recruits Rand (David Bradley)—an officer who mutinied to stop his superior from massacring innocents—to lead a team of equally rebellious soldiers into the past after Tunis. As an incentive, they have bombs implanted to kill them if they don't return by deadline.

After the team arrives in the present, Tunis wipes out most of them. Rand realizes that Tunis plans to kill Bridges (Michael Mendelsohn), the self-help guru whose philosophy of success through manipulation will enable power-hungry Jarry (Geof Prysirr) to become dictator. Rand joins forces with Bridges' ex-wife Cathy (Ely Pouget), who has scores of her own to settle. Tunis captures Jarry, who ends up blown to bits; Rand leaves Cathy before his implanted bomb goes off; and the sole survivor from Rand's team returns home and discovers without Jarry's influence, the 22nd century is a good and peaceful place.

In the first episode of *Charmed* (1998–2006), the Halliwell sisters, Prue (Shannon Doherty), Piper (Holly Marie Combs) and Phoebe (Alyssa Milano), learn that they're the Charmed Ones, witches gifted with tremendous powers to fight evil. By the fifth season Prue was dead; half-sister Paige (Rose McGowan) had replaced her; Piper had married Leo (Brian Krause), a "White Lighter" guardian spirit; and Piper and Leo had a son, Wyatt.

At the end of the fifth season, Chris (Drew Fuller), a White Lighter from the future, shows up and saves Piper during a crucial battle. Chris continued helping the Halliwells, but with a secret agenda: He's Piper's second son and in his future Wyatt has become a Voldemort-like tyrant. Chris is determined to either save his brother from turning evil, or kill him. In the sixth season's final episode, Leo saves Wyatt from the events that turned him bad. Chris returns in the series' final episode after Paige and Phoebe have been destroyed battling evil magic. Piper and Leo try going back in time to change events and wind up joining forces with Piper's mother and grandmother, their own future selves, and the grown-up Chris and Wyatt. They win, of course.

In the 2077 of *Continuum* (2012–15), corporations rule the world and freedom is a thing of the past. The Liber8 terrorist movement fought the system and lost—but as the series opens, the revolutionaries escape into the past, dragging policewoman Kiera Cameron (Rachel Nichols) along with them to 2012 Vancouver. Liber8's members set out to prevent their future from ever coming to pass. Cameron sets out to stop them: She believes that the dictatorship keeps the world safe, and fears changing history could erase her son from existence. She presents herself to the Vancouver PD as a federal agent and works against Liber8. Her allies include Detective Carlos Fonnegra (Victor Webster) and teen computer genius Alec Sadler (Erik Knudsen), who will become the Bill Gates of 2077 (William B. Davis).

Things get complicated fast. The cops form an alliance with big business against Liber8, possibly creating the dystopia the terrorists are fighting. New time travelers arrive with their own agendas. Liber8 member Kellogg (Stephen Lobo) becomes a powerful businessman by exploiting his knowledge of the future. At the end of the second season, Alec's girlfriend Emily (Magda Apanowicz) is murdered, so Alec uses a time travel device to save her. Kiera goes with him and discovers someone in the new timeline has killed Kiera's counterpart.

By the end of the third season, Liber8 has erased the future—grandfather paradoxes don't affect time travelers—but invaders from a future war-torn Earth materialize in the present to win the war before it starts. It's implied that Kellogg, the invaders' leader, wants to use his younger self as an organ donor. In the final episode, the invaders lose, Kellogg is trapped in prehistory and Cameron returns home to find 2077 a peaceful, free world. Her son is alive but with the new timeline's Kiera as his mother. All Cameron can do is watch him from a distance.

The protagonists of *DC's Legends of Tomorrow* (2016–) were 20th century superhumans gathered by time traveler Rip Hunter (Arthur Darvill) to stop the conquest of Earth in 2166. Hunter is a Time Master, a member of a league of scholars who watch but never intervene; with Hunter's wife and child killed by the conqueror Vandal Savage, Hunter can no longer live by that code. Savage (Casper Crump) is an immortal Egyptian priest, a master of arcane knowledge and a deadly fighter, with wealth and a cult of devoted disciples backing him up. Hunter's recruits include superheroes White Canary (Caity Lotz) and Atom (Brandon Routh) and villains Heat Wave (Dominic Purcell) and Captain Cold (Wentworth Miller). All chosen because they're non-entities: their death or disappearance won't affect the timeline at all. At time of writing, they've battled Savage in the 1970s, 1980s and the 1950s.

Preventing the Apocalypse

In *The Flight That Disappeared* (1961), passengers on the title plane to Washington include Dr. Morris (Dayton Lummis) who's conceived a new super-bomb; his mathematician assistant Marcia Paxton (Paula Raymond); and Endicott (Craig Hill), a ballistic missile expert. Morris realizes their combined research will give America the power to wipe out any nation with a single super-missile.

The plane suddenly rises higher, defying the pilots and not even stopping when fuel runs out. It lands in a timeless limbo with only Paxton, Morris and Endicott conscious. The residents of the future have summoned them to judgment, for the bomb's power exceeds Morris's calculations to the point that it will wipe out all life on Earth. After a lecture on the horrors of war, the tribunal announces it will strand the researchers in limbo to preserve Earth's future. Then they realize that would change history, which isn't allowed (which makes the whole attempt pointless). The three researchers wake up and assume they had a weird shared dream, but then learn the plane really did vanish for 24 hours. Morris, enlightened, destroys his formula.

Apex (1994) opens in 2073, as time researchers send an **A**dvanced **P**rototype **Ex**ploration **R**obot to an empty area of the Mojave Desert in 1973. A vacationing family comes upon the APEX, triggering a time paradox that shatters the lab. The researchers send a robot "sterilization unit" to fix things by killing the family but lab tech Sinclair (Richard Keats) follows to save them.

When Sinclair returns to 2073, it's a world suffering under a deadly pandemic and ravaged by the sterilization robots trying to erase the altered timeline. Sinclair's wife Natasha (Lisa Ann Russell) is now a soldier with no interest in him. Even so, he convinces her and the rest of their squad to find the ruined time lab so he can return to the previous timeline and fix things. Their efforts cause more time distortion, which draws the killer robots down. Nevertheless, Sinclair makes it back to the original 2073 and aborts the APEX launch, erasing the divergence.

Seven. Shaping the Future by Changing the Past That Is Our Present

Endicott (Craig Hill), Marcia (Paula Raymond) and Morris (Dayton Lummis) (in rear, left to right) learn *The Flight That Disappeared* (1961) wasn't just their imagination.

AI expert Jonathan Driscoll (Giancarlo Esposito) runs into *The Tomorrow Man* (1996) literally: He crashes into the android Ken (Julian Sands) while driving across country. Ken, unharmed, forces Driscoll to drive him to Phoenix, explaining as they travel that an asteroid will wipe out humanity in 400 years unless Ken alters key events in the present. His first, successful change was diverting Driscoll—the only one with the technical know-how to keep Ken running—from his original route, which ended in a fatal crash.

Ken's next mission is to stop a rocket fuel test that triggers a horrifying explosion, turning Earth away from space exploration. Their big obstacle is Berman (Ray Baker), the fuel's developer: the fuel is a fraud, Berman's been lining his pocket with the funds, and the explosion will cover all that up. A secondary obstacle: federal agent Galloway (Craig Wasson), who plans to capture Ken as he did a previous android. Galloway has the first droid's digital information about future events, but needs Ken's computer brain to decipher and exploit it. Despite the opposition, Driscoll and Ken take down Berman, save everyone from the explosion and head off to their next mission, though with Galloway still hunting them.

When Time Expires (1997) is set in a universe where an interstellar alliance uses time travel to avert disasters. That was Travis Beck's (Richard Grieco) job until a disastrous error got him demoted. Beck's now in a small Earth town where he's to drop a quarter into an expired parking meter; this lets the alliance calibrate predictions about Earth's future, after which Earth will be invited to join. While hanging around town, Beck falls for June (Cynthia Geary), a cowgirl whose father is a retired alliance agent, crippled by an injury.

Beck's gets a tip from his ex-partner Thermot (Mark Hamill) that assassins have been sent to stop him from deploying the quarter. Beck discovers his bosses' predictions missed a nuclear war that will wipe out Earth in a year. Using the coin will trigger a chain of events preventing the war, thereby covering up the error. The assassins, and Thermot, work for an alliance faction that will gain politically if Beck's department is discredited. Beck defeats the assassins, but gets beaten to a pulp by a jealous rival for June. June drops the quarter in the meter and saves the world. Once Beck recovers, he goes back through time, prevents June's father's accident, then settles down with her.

By the end of the 21st century in *Nautilus* (1999), ecological collapse has plunged Earth into anarchy, followed by tyranny. In hopes of changing history, Brin (Christopher Kriesa) steers his submarine, the *Nautilus*, back to 1999, when the Prometheus project to tap Earth's core for energy triggered the eco-collapse. Back in 1999, Basim (Victor Eschbach), the businessman behind Prometheus, hires security expert Harris (Richard Norton) to protect the project's oceanic base from the Equinox ecoterrorists. No sooner does Harris capture an Equinox strike force on the drilling platform than the *Nautilus* materializes, demanding custody of Basim and his researchers Levine (Hannes Jaenicke) and Ang (Gloria Mari).

Faced with the sub's firepower, Harris has no choice but to lead the captives to Brin. The captain convinces Levine and Basim to stop drilling in return for Brin sharing his era's alternative energy technology. The two men return to Prometheus with Harris and Brin's daughter Ariel (Miranda Wolfe), but then Basim refuses to shut the drill down. Ang, an Equinox sleeper agent, takes over the *Nautilus* to destroy Prometheus, and Brin realizes that this attack is what destroyed the environment. The captain tells the military how to destroy his sub, Harris kills Basim, and Levine shuts down the drill. With Earth's future safe, Ariel and Harris plan for a future together.

The *Odyssey 5* TV series (2002) opens five years in the future with the crew aboard the Odyssey space shuttle: astronauts Chuck Taggart (Peter Weller), his son Neil (Christopher Gorham) and Angela Perry (Tamara Craig Thomas); scientist Kurt Mendel (Sebastian Roché); and reporter Sarah Forbes (Leslie Silva). They witness Earth's death when the planet is sucked through a shimmering gateway. An alien sends the crew's minds back five years in time to find the cause, which has devastated multiple other planets across the universe.

Five years earlier, the crew discover the existence of Sentients, disembodied intellects that exist in cyberspace and work against humanity; the Synthetics, androids who act as the Sentients' physical agents; and the Cadre, a group of NASA officials working covertly against the Sentients. The five also have to deal with personal dramas. Sarah, for instance, knows that her son will die of a rare disease, but as he has no symptoms, putting him through a risky drug regimen makes her look crazy. Neil, a focused, career-oriented astronaut, has trouble living the life of a high school student with no interests beyond sex, drugs and rock'n'roll. The series ended after one season with all the plotlines unresolved.

In *Retrograde* (2004), Foster (Dolph Lundgren) leads a team from 2204 to the Antarctic of 2004 to avert a pandemic that will wipe out most of humanity. The goal is to destroy the buried meteors that brought the plague to Earth and, if necessary, kill the members of the science expedition that unearthed them. Crew member Dalton (Joe Montana) plans to exploit his knowledge of the future for profit instead, so he and his men kill the rest of the team. Only Foster escapes.

The expedition finds Foster but unfortunately finds the meteors too. The disease begins to spread and the expedition ends up in a shooting war with Dalton, with a high body count on both sides. The fight ends when Foster kills Dalton, destroys the meteors and blows up the expedition's ship. Before returning to 2204, Foster travels back in time to convince a member of the science team, Diaz (Silvia Di Santis), to stay with her child rather than go on the expedition.

Gintama: The Final Chapter: Be Forever Yoruzuya (2013) was a sequel to the *Gintama* anime series about the mercenary Odd Jobs troubleshooters. A time traveling robot kidnaps one Odd Jobs member, the modern-day samurai Gintoki (Tomokazu Sugita), five years into the future. Earth has been ravaged by a pandemic, killing a third of humanity while another quarter left for the stars. Gintoki has been brought through time to find the cause, then go back and avert the plague.

Gintoki learns that the Enma, nanotech sorcerers he destroyed 15 years before, were behind the pandemic. He finds and kills the final surviving Enma, but finds his own future self behind the Enma mask. The dying Future-Gintoki reveals that the Enma infected him with nannites before he destroyed them; the nannites used his body tissue to develop and test the pandemic. To stop the plague, Gintoki must kill his past self before the battle. As soon as Gintoki heads back in time, the future changes for the better and people start forgetting he ever existed. The robot returns to remind them, and takes the future Odd Jobs team back to the battle with the Enma. With their help, Gintoki defeats the Enma without being infected. The bleak future fades for good, so all the time travelers from that timeline vanish with it.

The Next Step in Human Evolution

SF has long played with the idea of a clash between mutants and normal humans, a theme now most associated with Marvel's X-Men. It's an idea that appears in some screen time travel tales.

In *Yesterday's Target* (1996), Paul Harper (Daniel Baldwin) is an amnesiac telekinetic targeted by federal psi-hunter Holden (Malcolm McDowell), his clairvoyant agent Winstrom (LeVar Burton) and Winstrom's team of killers. Winfield (Richard Herd), the leader of a foundation that protects psis, helps Harper escape. The telekinetic regains enough of his memory to realize he came to the present from 30 years ahead. Along with him came the fire-starter Carter (T.K. Carter) and the precog Jessica (Stacey Haiduk), Harper's wife, who are still amnesiac. Harper finds them ahead of Winstrom and steers them to a foundation safe-house. Harper tells Winfield the team's mission is to persuade Winfield—who will make catastrophic mistakes down the road—to step down as leader in favor of one of the younger psis.

The choice becomes moot when Winstrom shows up and kills Winfield. Then Winstrom learns he's another time traveler, the fourth member of Harper's squad. Repentant, he sacrifices himself to protect the safe house, but that doesn't stop Holden from flooding it with nerve gas. The gas doesn't work on the psis' mutated nervous systems, buying Harper time to confront Holden and reveal that he's Holden's son. Stunned, Holden cancels the psi hunt, leaving Harper, Carter and Jessica free to head off for fun.

The animated *Wolverine and the X-Men* (2009) opens when an explosion apparently kills the team's leader, Professor X (Jim Ward), and the mutant Jean Grey (Jennifer Hale). A year later, the team has fallen apart, and the government has become increasingly aggressive about imprisoning mutants and human sympathizers. After Wolverine (Steve Blum) reassembles the X-Men, they discover the professor in a coma. His consciousness now exists two decades in the future, a world in ruins where the mutant-hunting Sentinel androids keep mutants in chains. In the future, Xavier rallies mutants to fight the Sentinels, while feeding information to the X-Men in the past in hopes of averting the apocalypse. Eventually the X-Men discover that Jean Grey triggered the fatal explosion when she tapped into a cosmic entity called the Phoenix. The villainous Hellfire Club's efforts to enslave the Phoenix led to the ravaged future. The X-Men successfully avert the nightmare to come, but in the final episode Professor X reports that in the new timeline, the future Earth is under the tyranny of the mutant Apocalypse.

The title of *The 4400* (2004–07) refers to alien abductees taken away over several decades, then returned to Seattle in the present with super-powers—precognition, telekinesis, healing touch, super-strength. Federal agents Tom Baldwin (Joel Gretsch) and Diana Skouris (Jacqueline McKenzie) are assigned to watch and investigate the 4400 and eventually they learn the reason behind them. As in *Official Denial*, UFOs come from a dying future Earth. By turning the 4400 into superhumans and sending them back to the present, some as programmed sleeper agents, the futurians hope to change history and keep Earth alive. Another future faction opposes this—members believe they'll survive Earth's doom and rule uncontested—and works to keep history unchanged. Tom and Diana were still coping with the schemes of both the futurians and present-day humans when the series expired.

Heroes (2006–10) introduced us to a world of "evos" (super-powered mutants, though the nickname wasn't used until the 2015 sequel series *Heroes Reborn*):

- Claire (Hayden Panettiere), a cheerleader whose body heals from even fatal injuries.
- Hiro (Masi Oka) can transport across time and space.
- Unscrupulous politician Nathan Petrelli (Adrian Pasdar) can fly.
- Nathan's brother Peter (Milo Ventimiglia) duplicates the powers of any evo near him.
- Isaac (Santiago Cabrera) can paint visions of the future, but only when he's high on heroin.

Claire's adoptive father, Noah Bennett (Jack Coleman) works for a covert government agency that traps and imprisons evos. As the series opens, the situation is literally reaching critical mass: Isaac's painting shows an evo going nuclear and destroying New York. Later in the series, Hiro travels five years into the future and discovers the aftermath of the explosion has the government hunting evos even more ruthlessly. The key to preventing the disaster seems to be stopping Sylar (Zachary Quinto), who can steal power from evos he kills. A future version of Hiro warns Peter to "save the cheerleader, save the world," meaning that if Sylar attains Claire's healing ability, he'll be invincible.

At the climax, Hiro takes Sylar out, but Peter has duplicated another evo's explosive power and is about to detonate. Nathan, who previously planned to make political hay from the catastrophe, sacrifices himself to get Peter away from New York before he blows; both Petrellis survived. Time travel continued playing a role in the series. For instance, in the second season, Hiro was temporarily trapped in feudal Japan; Peter traveled a year into the future and discovered a new threat, a dangerous pandemic wiping out most of humanity.

By the time of *Heroes Reborn* (2015–16), evos were "out" and tentatively accepted by normals until a terrorist attack on a human-evo fellowship festival killed hundreds. Once again, evos are on the run, and time travel is key to the plot. CEO Erica Kravid (Rya Kihlstedt), the brains behind the attack, believes evos will inevitably wipe out normal humans. Having learned that a solar storm will wipe out all human life, she plans to use Tommy Clark (Robbie Kay), who duplicates Hiro's time-jumping powers, to create a bridge to the future. A few chosen, non-evo humans will cross the bridge so that they can repopulate the world. Ultimately the good evos and Noah stop the solar flare, erasing the timeline with Erica's future fortress in it, which erases her too. The evos return to the normal lives, but ready to fight again.

2035 Forbidden Dimensions (2014) posits that people born during a 1977 solar eclipse have the ability to time travel. In 1998, Jack Slade (Kyle Morris) finds his powers kicking in, sending him jumping forward to the mutant-ravaged *Road Warrior*–style wasteland of 2035. Blame for the wasteland lies with maniacal Dr. Shector (Mark McGarrey), who in Jack's present creates an anti-aging serum via research on a captive ET. The serum is dangerously mutagenic, transforming millions of humans into monsters and hurling the world into a new dark age. In 2035, Shector rules the ruins, and he'll stop at nothing to destroy the eclipse children for fear they could change history and undo his reign. Shector sets the murderous Tracker (Chris J. Miller) on Jack's trail, but Jack survives long enough to stop Shector from developing the serum. The future is saved, but Jack dies, though another eclipse child, Khadijah (Jamie Katonic), promises this is only the beginning.

The X-Men go time traveling again in *X-Men: Days of Future Past* (2014). In the near future, the Sentinels have wiped out all but a handful of mutants. That handful only survives because when a Sentinel attack is imminent, Kitty Pryde (Ellen Page) can alert her past self so the team has time to retreat. Professor X (Patrick Stewart) suggests that if they use Kitty to send a message to 1973, they can stop Mystique (Jennifer Lawrence) from assassinating the Sentinel designer Trask (Peter Dinklage), the event that led to unleashing the Sentinels. The team sends Wolverine's (Hugh Jackman) mind back, as his healing powers will enable him to survive the shock of such a long jump. Wolverine seeks out young Xavier (Charles Macavoy), an embittered recluse, and convinces him to help bust Magneto (Ian McKellen) out of a military prison. Together they confront Mystique as she's about to kill Trask. Magneto unexpectedly tries to kill Mystique, knowing Trask needs her DNA to create his androids. Mystique escapes, and the fracas convinces President Nixon to authorize Sentinel construction.

When the Sentinels debut, Magneto takes them over with his magnetic powers. He turns them against the government so the X-Men intervene to protect the humans. Mystique guns Magneto down, but Xavier convinces her to let Trask live. Her heroics discredit Trask and convince Nixon to end the Sentinel program. Wolverine wakes up in a world where he's once again a teacher at Xavier's school and mutants aren't being hunted to extinction.

Sending a Message

In *Super Eruption* (2013), park ranger Charlie (Richard Burgi) and vulcanologist Kate (Juliet Aubrey) witness the beginnings of what looks like a Yellowstone volcanic eruption. Kate gets a message from her future self warning her the combination of the magma, the earthquakes and the ash clouds will wipe out North America, as well as warping Earth's magnetic field, which is what makes the cross-time message possible. Future Kate instructs Present Kate how to stop the eruption, Present Kate sells the government on trying it, and she and Charlie save the day.

Life on Earth in *Interstellar* (2014) is doomed when a blight kills off all plants. A series of messages, fashioned as gravity anomalies, lead retired astronaut Cooper (Matthew McConaughey) and his brainy daughter Murph (Mackenzie Foy) to a NASA installation. A professor (Michael Caine) recruits Cooper to join the professor's daughter Brand (Anne Hathaway) on a flight through a wormhole to three distant planets that may be viable new homes for humanity. If the professor can perfect his anti-gravity research, all of Earth's people will emigrate. Otherwise the frozen embryos on the spaceship will give Homo sapiens a fresh start.

The exploration is grim, frustrating work even before Cooper learns that the professor lied: His anti-gravity research is a bust, so everyone still on Earth, including Murph, is doomed. After the exploration ship is critically damaged, Cooper points it at the most likely world, sends it off with Brand, then drops himself into a black hole to gather data on the gravity effects. The same future humans who created the wormhole catch Cooper in a tesseract—a four-dimensional cube in three-dimensional space—which enables Cooper to send the original gravity messages. The grown-up Murphy finally deciphers their meaning, perfects anti-gravity and takes the human race to the stars. Cooper emerges from the tesseract, meets his aging daughter (Ellen Burstyn) and then goes off to join Brand's colony.

Stop the Invasion

In 2022, at the start of *Time Runner* (1993), Earth is overwhelmed by an alien invasion aided by ET infiltrators. One soldier, Raynor (Mark Hamill), escapes into space, where he passes through a wormhole into the present. The aliens have already infiltrated human society, making it that much tougher for Raynor to change Earth's fate, even after the alien spy McDonald (Rae Dawn Chong) joins forces with him. She and Raynor contact the rising politician Neila (Brion James) for help, not noticing that his name spells "alien" backwards.

When McDonald realizes that Neila is one of her people, she tells him her real goal is to milk Raynor's knowledge of the future for their race's benefit. Neila tells McDonald that Raynor's too big a threat and sends her to kill the man's present-day infant self. McDonald helps Raynor save the baby and kill Neila. As Neila was instrumental in destroying Earth's defenses in the future, his death erases the alien victory and the adult Raynor from reality.

A war on Earth between two non-human races from millions of years in the future is depicted in the *Alien Agenda* movies: *Out of the Darkness* (1996), *Endangered Species* (1996) and *Under the Skin* (1997) and the sequel *Alien Conspiracy* films from 2001 (*Beyond the Lost World*) and 2002 (*Time Enough, Grey Skies*). The Greys are mutated fish that evolved to intelligence after humanity nuked itself out of existence. The Morphs are alien colonists who'd like to live on Earth but can't survive the high levels of post-apocalypse radiation. The Morph solution is travel back in time, shapeshift to infiltrate human society, then avert the war. The Greys want their timeline to endure, so they're back in time to ensure Armageddon proceeds on schedule.

In the final film *Beyond the Lost World*, the Morph Callista (Debbie Rochon) tells one of their human agents, Gonzalez (Thomas Nondorf), that the Morphs not only can't win, their struggles with the Greys cause the nuclear war. The Morph solution is to create a massive time vortex that transfers New York City back to the dinosaur age. Callista explains that the city's tech and power sources will last long enough for the residents to jump into space and colonize other worlds, eventually evolving into Morphs. By saving us, the Morphs save themselves.

Returner (2002) starts in 2084 as the invading, *Alien*-esque Daggra demolish humanity's last defenses. Milly (Anne Suzuki) travels back to 2002, two days before the first Daggra visitor summoned the alien fleet, so that she can kill the Daggra and prevent the summons. After recruiting the help of gunman Miyamato (Takeshi Kaneshiro), Milly breaks into the research center holding the Daggra. Instead of an alien point man, they find a helpless alien child who only wants to return home. They also find Mizoguchi (Gorô Kishitani), a vicious crime lord who kidnaps the alien to milk it for advanced technical knowledge. Milly realizes the real cause of the war will be Mizoguchi killing the prisoner once the Daggra serves its purpose.

Milly and Miyamoto rescue the child, which manages to signal its people for help. The aliens arrive in time to save the two humans, who then finish off Mizoguchi. The Daggra take the child home but as this erases Milly's future, she disappears. Miyamoto quits the rackets but an enemy guns him down. Fortunately, if illogically, it turns out that the new future Milly is some sort of time agent who returns to the present and saves Miyamoto's life.

In the anime series *Occult Academy* (2010) it's 1999 and Maya Kumashiro (Yoko Hikasa) has just taken over the prestigious Waldstein Academy after the murder of the principal, her father. New history teacher Uchida Fumiaka (Takahiro Mizumisha) reveals that he's a time traveler from 2012, when Earth is under the brutal control of the alien King of Terror. The invasion starts in just a few weeks, when the creature enters our dimension at the academy. The military sent Uchida back because he's a telekinetic, not knowing that his abilities have faded since they made him a child celebrity.

Although Maya despises everything occult, she agrees to work with Uchida on finding the Nostradamus Key, the object or person that opens the gate. After the pair investigates crop circles, chupacabra and other threats, it turns out that Uchida's giggly girlfriend Mikaze (Minori Chihara) is a sorceress scheming to open the gate. Mikaze unsuccessfully tries using Uchida to kill Maya, but the good guys destroy her instead. The future doesn't change, however: the trigger turns out to be Uchida warping time by meeting his younger self (the "two counterparts of one person can't co-exist" rule). Despite Uchida's best efforts, his two selves meet and the King of Terror comes through. Adult Uchida calls up his old telekinetic abilities and sacrifices himself to close the gate. Maya becomes surrogate mother to his lonely younger self.

Making the Future Worse

Sometimes it's the bad guys who want to change the future, putting wrong what once went right.

In the near future of *The Lathe of Heaven* (1980), the villain thinks he's the hero. Seattle psychiatrist Dr. Haber (Kevin Conway) discovers that his new patient, George Orr (Bruce Davison), can change history with his dreams. Haber programs George to dream a better world into being, but George's unconscious applies a bludgeon rather than a scalpel:

- Seattle is sunny, but that's because of a prolonged, multi-year drought.
- Overpopulation is no longer an issue, because a pandemic wiped out millions.
- Earth's nations no longer wage war on each other because they're united against an alien invasion.

The only dreams that work as Haber wants are the ones that turn him into the head of a powerful research institute. George, horrified by the changes he's wrought, hires attorney Heather Lelache (Margaret Avery) to get him out from under Haber's thumb. After Heather realizes that George is telling the truth, they become lovers. George also meets the aliens, who aren't hostile, and share his powers over reality.

Haber eventually decides to cut out the middle man, duplicating George's ability so he can change reality directly and (he assumes) more efficiently. His first attempt shows him that Earth was destroyed in a nuclear war four years ago; humanity survives only because George dreamed Armageddon away. Haber's sanity snaps, which threatens to wipe out reality completely. George and the aliens somehow fix things (even after multiple viewing, the climax confuses me), creating a new timeline in which George works in a junk shop run by an alien and he's starting a new relationship with Heather. This story was filmed again in 2002 (see chapter nine)

Lazer Tag Academy (1986) was another of those rare tales portraying a utopian future. In 3010, "starlyte" energy has eliminated want, hunger and pollution, Earth is at peace and lazer tag with starlyte-powered guns is the world's most popular sport. (The series was a tie-in with a name-brand version of the game.) Teen Jamie Jaren (Noelle Harling), the lazer-tag champion, has the genetic ability to channel starlyte to create solid-energy constructs, move objects or even travel through time. When scientists at the Starlyte Academy thaw Draxon Drear (Booker Bradshaw) out of suspended animation, he proves to have the same genetic ability. Drear is also a master criminal who'd rather be the sole master of Starlyte, so he travels back in time to assassinate Jamie's ancestor Beth (Christina MacGregor) who invented Starlyte technology.

Jamie saves Beth, then discovers Beth and her siblings can also control Starlyte. Together the Jarens work to thwart Drear's plots which including trying to take out other Jaren ancestors and targeting the kids when they travel through time.

Timestalkers (1987) begins with 26th century scientist Cole (Klaus Kinski) hunting someone in the Old West. We eventually learn that he's hunting the ancestor of Crawford, who established Cole's century's rigid regulations—irrationally oppressive in Cole's view—on scientific research. In the present, widowed historian Scott Mackenzie (William Devane) discovers a photo of Cole in the 1800s packing a modern magnum. Mackenzie can't convince anyone this is evidence of time travel until he meets Crawford's daughter Georgia (Lauren

Hutton), who's come from the future to stop Cole. With Mac's historical knowledge, they're able to figure out that Cole plans to ambush the gunman who will otherwise save Georgia's ancestor from outlaws. They arrive at the right time and place, but Cole has already killed the gunman. Mackenzie, a crack shot, picks up the stranger's gun, saves the ancestral Crawford, then kills Cole in a shoot-out. Georgia finds a loophole in the rules against changing history that allows her to retroactively save Mac's wife and child from the accident that killed them.

Time Trackers (1989) employs many of the same elements as *Timestalkers*: a future technocracy, a rebel scientist (Lee Bergere) and a plan to assassinate the ancestors of key leaders via time travel. The scientist Zandor attempts his initial kill in present-day Los Angeles, then heads back to the medieval era. RJ Craig (Kathleen Beller), daughter of one of the targeted leaders, takes a team in pursuit, picking up hard-nosed Detective Orth (Ned Beatty) in the present.

By the time the team arrives in the past, Zandor has replaced the local lord, giving him the power base to kill Craig's ancestor Edgar (Alex Hyde-White), aka the Red Duke, a heroic outlaw The time travelers defeat Zandor, then return to the future. RJ having fallen for Edgar, she decides to head back to him, even at the risk of changing history. It turns out that she was always destined to be Edgar's wife and her own ancestor.

In *Godzilla vs. King Ghidorah* (1991), time travelers from 2204 arrive in 1992 Japan to warn the government that Godzilla's 21st century rampages will completely destroy the country. They propose traveling back to 1944, before nuclear fallout transformed Godzilla from an ordinary dinosaur into an unstoppable juggernaut, provided the Japanese can pinpoint the right location. Researchers determine that Godzilla was then living on an isolated island. The time travelers capture the dinosaur there, entomb him under water and drop off three genetically engineered creatures on the island to absorb the radiation in Godzilla's place.

The radiation merges the three creatures into what will eventually become the kaiju Ghidorah. The time travelers have been lying: They belong to an organization that believes that no one nation should dominate the world, and in their era Japan is the mightiest country on Earth. By controlling Ghidorah, the time travelers will reduce Japan to ruin. The Japanese fight back by freeing Godzilla, more powerful than ever. Godzilla destroys Ghidorah, but it looks like he'll go on to demolish Japan. This horrifies one of the time travelers, Kano (Anna Nakagawa), a loyal Japanese who didn't know her companions' true agenda. Kano rebuilds Ghidorah as a cyborg under her control, defeats Godzilla and has Ghidorah drop him bound and helpless into the ocean, saving Japan's glorious future.

In *Sailor Moon* (1992–97), one of the most successful "magical girl" animes, Usagi Tsukino (Kotono Mitsuishi) discovers in the first season that she's the reincarnated princess of the ancient Lunar Empire; as Sailor Moon she fights against evil accompanied by the Sailor Scouts (Sailors Mercury, Venus, Mars and Jupiter). Midway through the second season (known as *Sailor Moon R*), a small girl, Chibi (Kae Araki), falls out of the sky on Usagi and her boyfriend Mamoru (Tohru Furuya). Chibi demands that Usagi give up a valuable talisman, the Lunar Crystal, and then worms her way into the Tsukino family, convincing them all she's Usagi's cousin.

In reality, she's Usagi and Mamoru's daughter. In the next century, they'll reign over the utopian metropolis of Crystal Tokyo until the Black Moon Clan conquers the city. Now both Chibi and the clan have moved back to continue the fight in the present. If the Black Moon wins, Crystal Tokyo will never exist. Sailor Moon and the Scouts eventually win.

Sailor Pluto (Chiyoko Kawashima), mistress of the time-space gate, helped Chibi and Sailor Moon from behind the scenes, and became an active member of the team in later seasons.

In *Time Chasers* (1994), Nick (Matthew Bruch) builds a time machine into his personal plane—eliminating the risk of materializing inside anything solid—and takes local reporter Lisa (Bonnie Pritchard) into the utopian future of 2041 (which doesn't look any different from the present). Nick also convinces Robertson (George Woodard), a high-powered businessman, to finance more time travel research.

When Nick and Lisa revisit 2041, they discover that the beautiful city is now a ruined wasteland. Robertson has used Nick's research to build a duplicate time machine, and his abuse of time travel will destroy Earth's future. Nick demands that Robertson shut down the machine; Robertson orders Nick killed. Lisa and Nick go back to stop Past-Nick from showing Robertson his invention, but Robertson and his security team follow them, kill Lisa and drag Present-Nick to 1777 to dispose of as a Revolutionary War casualty. Past-Nick and Past-Lisa notice some of the goings-on, follow along to 1777 and join forces with Present-Nick. Present-Nick and Robertson end up dead. The other Nick and Lisa return to their own time, destroy the time machine, then start a relationship.

Timemaster (1995) reveals that a hedonistic alien race amuses itself by manipulating Earth history for sport, as well as using captured humans in gladiatorial games. The Chairman (Michael Dorn) decides that the ultimate entertainment will be triggering the U.S. nuclear arsenal in 2006 to wipe us out. The good alien Isaiah (Noriyuki "Pat" Morita) opposes this and gets help from pre-teen orphan Jesse (Jesse Cameron-Glickenhaus)—whose supposedly dead parents (Duncan Regehr, Joanne Pacula) are among the aliens' gladiators.

As time rifts aren't linear, Jesse bounces from the 1800s to the present to 2006. In one time jump he meets his sister Veronica (Veronica Cameron-Glickenhaus) in her late teens and learns that she went into a downward spiral after he disappeared into time. When Jesse finally faces the Chairman, the latter proposes settling their differences by using Jesse's parents in a gladiatorial game. If Jesse loses, he dies; if he wins, he can return to Veronica and save her, or he can save the world in 2006—not both. Jesse plays, wins and goes to 2006. No sooner does he avert Armageddon than he wakes up back in the orphanage in the present. Veronica's there and so is Annie (Michelle Williams), the double of a girl Jesse met on his time trip. Isaiah explains that the happy ending is a reward for Jesse's heroism.

Nostradamus (2000) is oddly titled as the seer's famous prophecies play no role in the story. In 1536, a religious order headed by Garamond (Fintan McKeown) sends a Mabus (Peter Jordan) to the 20th century, where his chanting causes a man to spontaneously combust. Detective Nostrand (Rob Estes) learns from FBI psychic Hudson (Joely Fisher) that this is only one of several combustion killings. A mental patient tells Hudson that the Mabus are fallen angels enslaved by the Satanic sect of the Sixth Order. By erasing certain key souls before the millennium, the order hopes to tilt the outcome of the apocalypse in favor of the Antichrist. Nostrand learns that Garamond is a present-day man who used Leonardo da Vinci's time-machine designs to go back to the 1500s, when the stars are perfectly aligned for his evil work.

Nostrand catches and guns down the Mabus after its next killing. When he takes its ring as evidence and absently slides it on, the ring sends him back to the Sixth Order. La Font (Michael C. Gwynne), a spy within the cult, frees Nostrand and returns him to the future to protect Hudson, Garamond's final target. The ring's power has erased Nostrand's original existence in the present, but Hudson's psychic powers enable her to remember him. They defeat the Order's assassins, then kill Garamond when he returns from the past. Nostrand goes back to the 1500s to destroy the Order's time technology, but returns to warn Hudson that the Order is making another try at rewriting Armageddon. Together they set off to save the Order's targets and the world.

The premise of *Looper* (2012) is that by 2072, forensic science makes impossible to hide bodies. Organized crime sends people back to 2042 for execution by Abe's (Jeff Bridges) team of Loopers, so called because eventually the mob "closes the loop" by sending a hit man's future self back in time for his past self to kill. By the start of the film, the Rainmaker, a new crimelord, is purging the killers' ranks, ruthlessly closing all the loops.

One Looper, Joe (Joseph Gordon-Levitt), is ready to kill his future self (Bruce Willis) when he appears, but Future Joe knocks him out and escapes. We learn in flashback that the Rainmaker murdered Future Joe's wife; Future Joe intends to prevent this, *Terminator*-style, by killing the kids who might grow up to be the Rainmaker. Joe tries to redeem himself with Abe by hunting down Future Joe, but Abe orders both Joes killed to minimize the time paradoxes. (It's hard to see how killing Joe 30 years early will do this.) Joe ends up at a farm belonging to Sara (Emily Blunt), a single mother with a telekinetic son, Cid (Pierce Gagnon). Low-level telekinesis is common in 2042, but Cid is actually powerful enough to take out one of Abe's killers.

Future Joe ends up destroying Abe and his gang, then heads out to kill the last child on his list: Cid. He doesn't know that Sara's death defending Cid is what drives the boy to become the Rainmaker and kill all Loopers. When Future Joe shows up, Joe, who's fallen for Sara, realizes there's only one way to save her: He kills himself. Future Joe vanishes, and Cid is free to grow up with his mother like a normal boy.

In *Roborex* (2014), motherless tween James Miller (Kalvin Stinger) and his friend Kara (Maggie Scott) are stunned when a robot dog appears containing the digitized mind of James' golden retriever Rex and carrying a mysterious crystal. James' adult self (Rocky Myers) tells James that the crystal contains their mother's groundbreaking research, with which James has made the future a utopia. He sent the crystal to the past because Mom's embittered colleague Jenkins (Ethan Phillips) wants to find it and use her research to conquer the world. The past isn't safe either, as Jenkins has alerted his past self by sending back another robot, Destructocat.

Despite the kids and Roborex's best efforts, Present-Jenkins obtains the crystal. Rather than send it to the future (he considers his arrogant future self a completely different person), Jenkins decides to power up a time machine that will enable him to recover some lost research from his work with Ms. Miller. The machine, unstable, almost blows up the town before the kids deactivate it. Rex dies in the explosion, and Roborex "dies" putting his mind in Destructocat to tame it. James solves both problems by transferring the dying Rex's mind into Robo.

Where No Man Has Gone Before

Star Trek: First Contact (1996) opens in the 24th century, when the Borg—a cyborg hive-mind that seeks to assimilate all living creatures—attack Earth. The *Enterprise* destroys the Borg ship, but an escape pod vanishes into the past. Instantly Earth is 100 percent Borg, except for the *Enterprise*, which is shielded by proximity to the time rift. Capt. Picard (Patrick Stewart) directs the *Enterprise* through the dwindling rift and arrives on April 4, 2063, the day before Zephram Cochrane's (James Cromwell) rocket makes first contact with the Vulcans.

In their drive to change history, the Borg destroy Cochrane's ship and almost kill Cochrane. The *Enterprise* crew tries to defend Cochrane's small community and rebuild his vessel. The Borg Queen (Alice Krige) sends her forces to seize the *Enterprise*, converting some of the crew, including the android Data (Brent Spiner), into Borg. They can then use the *Enterprise* equipment to summon the Borg of the 21st century to attack Earth. Picard, who was once briefly assimilated into the hive-mind, becomes increasingly unhinged as the fight goes on, to the point where he's willing to sacrifice his crew to stop the Borg. Once Cochran's friend Ellie (Alfre Woodard) makes Picard see how irrational he's become, the captain orders the crew to safety and confronts the Borg Queen alone. Data has resisted assimilation and sabotages the Borg plans from within. Humanity's first contact goes off as planned, so the *Enterprise* can open a time warp and go home.

First Contact led to the Finnish parody *Star Wreck Lost Contact* (1997), the first film in the *Star Wreck* series to use live actors. Captain Pirk (Samuli Torssonen) and his ship *Kickstarter* follow the Korg back in time to 1999, when rocker Jeffrey Cochbrane (Rudi Airisto) gave a concert so loud, it attracted the attention of a Vulgar spaceship. The Korg attack the rock festival Cochbrane is playing at, but Pirk, Dwarf (Timo Vuorensola) and Info (Antti Satama) save the rocker. The concert goes ahead, the Vulgar hear the music, but the Korg take over the *Kickstarter* and try to destroy the Vulgars. Pirk triggers the *Kickstarter* to self-destruct, saving history but stranding him and his crew.

The series picks up eight years later, in *Star Wreck: In the Pirkinning* (2005). Pirk realizes that the timeline is diverging from the history he knows, leading inevitably to a future of "peace, universal language, tights for uniforms" (presumably meaning the real *Star Trek*). To prevent this, Pirk manipulates Russia's moronic president (Kari Väänänen) into building a new *Kickstarter*. Pirk conquers the world with the ship, executes the duped president and builds a space fleet. He then creates a "maggot hole" to a parallel Earth dimension for more conquests, but the space station *Babel 13* (a parody of the TV series *Babylon 5*) sends the *Kickstarter* fleeing home. The unstable maggot hole transports the *Kickstarter* to the ice age, with only Pirk, Info and Dwarf surviving the crash. Info tells the others he'll shut down his system until the 21st century, at which point he'll revive and prevent any of this from happening.

Enterprise (2001–05) took place in the 2150s, 90 years after the events of *Star Trek: First Contact* and more than a hundred years before the original series. The *Enterprise* is Earth's first long-range exploration vessel, captained by Jonathan Archer (Scott Bakula). Along with locking horns with Klingons, Andorians and Vulcans—not as friendly as they would be by Spock's time—the ship's crew members soon find themselves embroiled in a "temporal cold war." As Daniels (Matt Winston), a 31st century time cop, eventually explains to Archer, civilizations with time travel ability live by the Temporal Accords that ban tampering with the past; unsurprisingly, some factions break the rules. The renegades are particularly interested in changing 22nd century history because that's when Archer will inspire the creation of the Federation.

In the first couple of seasons, Archer's adversaries in the war were the alien Suliban, who served one temporal faction in return for genetic upgrades. The *Enterprise's* first mission involved preventing Suliban from fomenting a Klingon civil war. At the end of the second season, another faction—the other-dimensional Sphere Builders—drove the alien Xindi to an attack on Earth that wiped out seven million people. The Sphere Builders know the Federation will block their plans to expand into our dimension; wiping out Earth ensures that the Federation never forms. After a season of fighting, Archer destroys the Xindi's doomsday weapon—the initial attack was a test run—and convinces the aliens to make peace. After the *Enterprise* defeats another faction's attempt to bring about a Nazi win in World War II, Daniels reports to Archer that the time agents can handle any remaining problems without calling in the *Enterprise*.

The most successful time tamperer in the Federation's universe is undoubtedly Nero (Eric Bana), the Romulan antagonist of *Star Trek* (2009): Nero rebooted the entire timeline with an attack on a Federation vessel that killed Jim Kirk's father. In the new timeline, Kirk (Chris Pine) is an embittered, trouble-making brawler. At Captain Pike's (Bruce Greenwood) suggestion, Kirk joins Starfleet, as does Spock (Zachary Quinto), a human/Vulcan hybrid tired of disdain from pureblood Vulcans. When the *Enterprise* investigates a strange disaster on Vulcan, Kirk realizes it's identical to the attack that killed his father.

Sure enough, the long-vanished Nero has returned, and destroys Vulcan with a black hole–generating weapon. He captures Pike and explains that in Nero's future, the Romulan home world died while the Federation and its ambassador, Spock (Leonard Nimoy), did nothing. Now he will destroy the Federation first, and kill the original Spock, who is also back in time.

With Pike gone, Young Spock becomes acting *Enterprise* captain. He deduces that Nero is from the future, but locks horns with Kirk on what to do next. Spock ultimately boots Kirk off the ship, but conveniently Kirk ends up on the same planet where Nero stranded Original Spock. This Spock explains the truth about Romulus: he tried using the black hole device to stabilize and save it, but instead the machine flung him and Nero back in time. With Original Spock's help, Kirk returns to the *Enterprise*, takes over as captain, rescues Pike and destroys Nero. Pike becomes an admiral, Kirk becomes the *Enterprise* captain and Spock becomes Kirk's first officer.

The Fringes of Time

TV's *Fringe* (2008–13) introduced us to the FBI's Fringe Division, which investigates crimes and weird events involving spontaneous combustion, psionics, teleportation and other concepts on the fringes of science. The team includes FBI agent Olivia Dunham (Anna Torv), slightly crazy scientist Walter Bishop (John Noble) and his son Peter (Joshua Jackson), all under the supervision of Agent Broyles (Lance Reddick). The series started as a variation on *The X-Files* but soon grew to encompass war between parallel worlds and an invasion from the future. (This show had an exceptionally complicated backstory, so I can only select a few highlights.)

On "Earth Two" there never was a President Jackson; Nixon's face is on the U.S. silver dollar; zeppelins fly the modern skies. Walter and colleague William Bell (Leonard

Nimoy) discovered Earth Two years ago, and began watching events there. After Peter died of a childhood disease, Walter discovered a cure. Peter's counterpart was dying of the same illness, so Walter traveled to Earth Two to save him—then selfishly brought the boy back home to raise as his own. The cross-dimensional visit disrupted physics on Earth Two, where the Fringe division face far more dangerous freak events. Earth Two Secretary of Defense Walter Bishop—aka "Walternate"—believes his son's kidnapping and the Fringe events are part of a deliberate military assault from Earth One, and must be met with lethal force.

All this took place under the eagle eyes of the Observers, time travelers from the future engineered for advanced intellect at the price of losing their emotions. Peter should have died on the trip between Earths but the Observer September (Michael Cerveris) saved him, believing that Peter was important to the future. That proved wise: At the end of the third season, Peter brought Earths One and Two together before Walternate could trigger a doomsday weapon. Once he'd done so, the Observers removed him from the time stream to reduce the chance that his survival would alter their future. The Fringe team now remembered Peter dying when he was destined to—but Peter somehow survived and returned. He and Olivia were in love, and together they stopped Bell from destroying both Earths to create his own tailor-made timeline from the ashes. Olivia became pregnant and everything looked happy.

In 2015, that changed: The Observers, having polluted their era until it was unlivable, stopped worrying about preserving history, jumped back to the present and took over. The Fringe team escaped by going into suspended animation, thawing out 20 years later. Working with Olivia's daughter Etta (Georgina Haig), they fought back against the seemingly invincible overlords and found a solution. A mutant child had developed even greater mind powers than the Observers, but without losing any emotional capacity. Walter took the boy into the future to show the scientists who created the Observers that they were on the wrong path. The effort succeeded, creating a new 2015 in which Olivia and Peter enjoy a peaceful life with Baby Etta.

Who's the Bad Guy Here?

Although the mutants blew up the world in *Beneath the Planet of the Apes*, in *Escape from the Planet of the Apes* (1971) we learn that Cornelius (Roddy McDowall), Zira (Kim Hunter) and their friend Milo (Sal Mineo) rebuilt one of the human spaceships and retraced Taylor's path through time-space to reach the present (Milo dies shortly afterwards). Implausibly, nobody notices they're physically different from ordinary chimps until Zira loses control and speaks. After initial astonishment, the world turns Cornelius and Zira into celebrities.

Presidential adviser Hasslein (Eric Braeden) sees them as a threat, having figured out from their comments what the future holds for humanity. When Zira becomes pregnant, Hasslein warns the president (William Windom) that if the child breeds with present-day chimps, his descendants could pass on his human-level intelligence. (This would not explain the intelligent gorillas or orangutans.) Hasslein advocates killing the chimps, specifically invoking the "killing Hitler" argument, but the president points out that none of the chimps

Cornelius (Roddy McDowall), Zira (Kim Hunter) and Milo (Sal Mineo) make an *Escape from the Planet of the Apes* (1971) to the present. Astonishingly, nobody realizes they're not regular chimpanzees.

are evil. A government panel concludes that the future apes don't treat future humans any worse than we treat apes today, but nevertheless recommends sterilizing the time travelers and aborting the baby.

Kindly Dr. Dixon (Bradford Dillman) helps the apes hide in ringmaster Armando's (Ricardo Montalban) circus. Armando believes that if it's God's will for apes to rule, then so be it. The military closes in, and Hasslein kills Zira and her newborn baby Milo. Cornelius kills Hasslein, then dies in a hail of bullets. The ape threat is gone ... except that the dead "Milo" was just an ordinary circus chimp. Armando is taking care of the real Milo, who will live to lead the ape revolution in *Conquest of the Planet of the Apes* (1972)

In *Past Perfect* (1996), Dylan Cooper (Eric Roberts) is a former teen hoodlum turned hard, pitiless cop. After arresting teen criminal Rusty Walker (Mark Hildreth), Cooper tries and fails to get Walker to testify against the rest of his gang. Mysterious figures led by Stone (Nick Mancuso) hunt down the other gang members, executing them for crimes the teens swear they haven't committed.

When Stone comes hunting Rusty, Cooper and his partner Marsey (Laurie Holden) refuse to let him execute the boy. After Cooper accidentally kills one of Stone's companions,

Stone outs himself as a time traveler from 25 years ahead. Facing rising violence and anarchy, the government solution is to execute convicted felons before they can commit their crimes—something Stone's mentor Future Cooper actively supports. Stone adds that if they don't kill Rusty pronto, the boy will kill Cooper. When the moment comes, Cooper and Walker talk Rusty into putting down his gun. Stone's sidekick (Saul Rubinek) discovers that by this action Rusty has erased all his future crimes, but Stone attempts to kill him anyway. Cooper and Marsey take out Stone; Cooper vows to change the future that Stone came from. He succeeds: When the government launches the program, the goal is to reform future criminals, not to kill them.

In the 2009 U.K. series *Starhyke*, it's 3034 and humans have shut down their emotions like Vulcans, creating not pacifists but cold-blooded conquerors. After decades of war with humanity, the alien Reptids attempt a last-ditch gambit, traveling back to the 21st century to blow up the Earth. The Terran ship *Nemesis*, under Captain Blowhard (Claudia Christian), travels back in pursuit, but when the ship arrives it's caught in a gas attack. The gas reconnects them with their emotions, leaving everyone on the *Nemesis* feeling off-balance. While dealing with their new feelings, they still have to find and defeat the Reptids. They were still at it when this short-lived series expired.

The Penitent Man (2010) is Darnell (Lance Henriksen), who spends most of the movie pouring out his heart to shrink Jason Pyatt (Lathrop Walker). Darnell claims that he's from the future, where he developed a device for seeing the past. This destroyed civilization as people learned that Jesus was an ordinary man, that the U.S. government killed John and Bobby Kennedy and other shocking revelations. Darnell's own life fell apart, so he's come back in time to avert the timeline.

Although Darnell doesn't come out and say it, it's obvious he's telling Pyatt all this because the psychiatrist is Darnell's past self (but admitting this outright would eliminate all the windy philosophizing). Another, more efficient time traveler tries to kill Pyatt. The shrink survives, and in the aftermath grasps how Darnell's device works. Pyatt decides against building it but his wife (Melissa Roberts) steals the information. The ending implies that the future remains unchanged.

CHAPTER EIGHT

If I Knew Then What I Know Now
Changing Personal History

"It's because the past cannot be undone that people can accept all sorts of pain."—*Stein's;Gate: The Burdensome State of Déja Vu*

Avert Pearl Harbor? Save humanity's future? Good stuff. But fixing our personal dramas packs a much greater emotional punch. Winning back the love you lost, saving someone you care about, averting a timeline in which you turn into a complete jerk.

Most time travel in this chapter is performed by magic or personal wish, rather than a time machine. What drives the trip is typically dissatisfaction with the present, and a belief it can be fixed by rewriting the past. Correct a mistake, or what the protagonist thinks is a mistake. Succeed at what was originally a failure.

Movies in this chapter tend to be optimistic about changing the past. Even though changing the personal past still involves changing other people's lives without their consent—and often requires lying or other unethical acts to get the job done—it's usually presented as morally acceptable. Only a few films such as *Judas Kiss* and *Kristin's Christmas Past* suggest changing personal history is wrong. It rarely has bad outcomes: Even if the travelers fails, that just means they learn to love their lives the way they are. Dr. Tom in *Being Erica* laughs off the idea that changing Erica's personal life could have a butterfly effect on world history.

Set-up is important in "personal change" time travel tales. We can't appreciate how different an alternate timeline is if we haven't seen the original first. If someone wants to change history, we need enough set-up to understand why. Consider, for example, everything the opening of *Back to the Future* (1985) tells us:

- The story of how Marty McFly's parents met.
- Marty's mother disapproves of girls who flirt with boys.
- Biff Tannen has been bullying George McFly his entire life.
- A lightning bolt hit the Hill Valley clock tower in 1955.

All of this is necessary for the rest of the film to work.

Fixing Past Mistakes

The stop-motion *Here Comes Peter Cottontail* (1971) tells how Peter (Casey Kasem), a good-hearted but feckless rabbit, competes with the malevolent Irontail (Vincent Price) to see who delivers the most Easter eggs and thereby becomes the new Easter Bunny. Irontail cheats and wins, though Peter's own foolishness helps. As the new Easter Bunny, Irontail mandates changes such as replacing chocolate bunnies with chocolate tarantulas.

A despondent Peter leaves April Valley in disgrace, then meets vagabond inventor Seymour Sassafras (Danny Kaye). Seymour offers the use of his time machine to go back to Easter and try delivering the eggs again. Irontail's agents sabotage the time machine so Peter goes further back, landing on different holidays. The rules don't require that Peter give away the eggs on Easter, so he keeps remarketing and repainting them to sell as Christmas eggs, Valentine eggs and so forth. Irontail keeps thwarting him, finally using sorcery to turn the Valentine eggs green. But the time machine's next stop is St. Patrick's Day so Peter gives every egg away as the "Blarney Bunny." Peter wins and restores Easter to normal.

Peggy Sue Got Married (1986) has Peggy Sue (Kathleen Turner) attending her 25th high-school reunion with little joy: She's just divorced her husband Charlie (Nicolas Cage) for repeated adultery, caused by his bitterness that his singing career never took off. Peggy Sue passes out suddenly, then awakens in 1960, a few weeks before graduation, and before her marriage. She realizes that if she doesn't get married, she'll escape the pain of the cheating and the divorce.

In the ensuing days, Peggy Sue finds that it isn't easy to go from 43 to 17 (an idea I wish more movies played with). She mouths off to teachers, dips into her father's liquor cabinet and tries seducing Young Charlie—he's so sweet, she can't resist—which completely freaks him out. Peggy Sue also acts out a fantasy by sleeping with brooding poet Michael (Kevin J. O'Connor); she even considers running away with him until she realizes he's a sexist, selfish jerk. Charlie, on the other hand, is so devoted to Peggy Sue that he auditions as a singer professionally; when the agent rejects him, he tells Peggy Sue he's ready to give up his singing dreams and focus on supporting her. (This doesn't appear to be the way the original timeline played out.) Despite Peggy Sue's mixed feelings, she makes love to him, then wakes up in the present, ready to reconcile. Although we see proof the time trip was real, it doesn't appear to have altered anything.

By the start of *Twice Upon a Yesterday* (1998), Victor (Douglas Henshall), a heavy-drinking actor, has already lost his love Sylvia (Lena Headey) after confessing to an affair. He tries and fails to win Sylvia back on her wedding day, but a strange garbage man (Eusebio Lázaro) lets Victor jump back in time to before the breakup. This time around he ends his affair and doesn't admit it to Sylvia. He sets out to be a better boyfriend and to keep her away from David (Mark Strong), the man she married in the original timeline. He fails: Sylvia meets David, has an affair with him, then breaks up with Victor.

Victor's life turns around when he finds new love with Louise (Penélope Cruz) and becomes a TV star. Sylvia's relationship with David falls apart. When she goes back to Victor at the film's end, he rejects her for Louise. (Given what a jerk Victor is, it's hard to see why the movie thinks he deserves happiness.) The end implies that Sylvia will get some sort of do-over herself.

Summer Time Machine Blues (2005) uses time travel to fix a humorously mundane catastrophe. It's a sweltering August in Japan and the collegiate protagonists have just busted the remote that controls their clubhouse air conditioner. They can't replace it, so it looks like an excruciatingly uncomfortable month ahead. Then they discover nerdy Akira (Riki

Honda) in the clubhouse. He runs out, leaving behind what turns out to be a time machine. One member of the group gets transported into the recent past and returns with a photo to prove it.

Naturally the first thing on the group's mind is to travel back and move the remote so it won't get damaged. No sooner do some of them go back in time than Akira meets the others in the present. He reveals he came from 2030, when he and his friends hang out at the clubhouse. He and the others in the present realize that if the past is changed, it will destabilize time, so more of the group head back to prevent that. Things go ludicrously wrong; at one point, the remote winds up lost 90 years in the past. But thanks to some ingenious time-paradoxing, the students are able to stabilize their history, then recover a duplicate remote. Cool days are back.

Time and Again (2005) opens in 1972, when Bobby Jones (Brian Ireland) has spent 16 years in prison for a murder he didn't commit. During a prison break he falls through a time gate into his home town in 1958, the day he was arrested (no, the dates don't add up), giving him a chance to change his past. He meets the pretty flirt Awanda (Jennie Allen) and kills time with her until 10 p.m., when the murder takes place. After Awanda goes out, Bobby discovers proof that she's having an affair with his father. He fails to keep his younger self from reaching the murder scene, and discovers the killer was his own mother, murdering Awanda out of jealousy. As before, young Bobby gets arrested, Mom says nothing, neither does Adult Bobby—and then we learn that Bobby was shot to death in the present-day prison break. The whole time trip was a fantasy along the lines of Ambrose Bierce's "An Occurrence at Owl Creek Bridge."

In *Being Erica* (2009–11), Erica Strange (Erin Karpluk) has four TV seasons of personal problems to fix. Erica blames her miserable life—no boyfriend, dead end job, parental disapproval—on her accumulated bad decisions. Enigmatic therapist Dr. Tom's (Michael Riley) solution is to send Erica back into her past to fix her mistakes, though it rarely works out as she expects. In one episode, Erica tells Tom she regrets not joining a college club because of the networking and connections it would have given her. In the do-over, she joins them only to discover they're arrogant jerks and snobs, just as she originally suspected. Tom tells Erica the lesson to learn is that she can trust her gut, an insight she uses in a current dilemma.

Over the course of the series, Tom sends Erica to multiple points in her past, and also her future and parallel timelines. Erica discovers that Tom is only one in a cadre of time-bending therapists, and she herself is only one of many patients. In the second season she becomes involved with Kai (Sebastian Pigott), a time-therapy patient from the future. In the third season, Erica enters group therapy and discovers a flair for counseling her fellow patients. This leads to her training as and eventually becoming a time therapist herself.

The Miserable Present

Other screen time travelers don't so much have a specific turning point to fix as a miserable present that needs improvement.

In *Chasing Christmas* (2005), dour Jack Cameron (Tom Arnold) has hated Christmas ever since he caught his ex-wife cheating at a Christmas party. Heavenly agent Trevor

(Robert Clarke) sends Christmas Present (Andrea Roth) and Past (Leslie Jordan) to shape him up as they've done so many others. But Past is a burn-out, frustrated that after years of delivering seasonal "guilt trips," the Christmas spirit is still fading from people's hearts. As he and Jack visit Jack's childhood, Past snaps and turns them from ghostly observers into flesh and blood. Jack now has three hours to get back to his rightful time or cease to exist, creating a massive time paradox. Present comes back to help, but when Past leaps into one of Jack's later Christmases (his honeymoon), Jack and Present are dragged along. Present-Jack freaks out when he discovers that his wife was cheating on him even back then.

The trio jumps forward again to the night of Jack's daughter Allison's (Sarah-Jane Redmond) school play (*A Christmas Carol*, of course). Allison's on-stage speech about not being defined by your past hits home and Jack makes peace with his ex, wishing her the best for the future. Trevor intervenes and returns Jack to the present with 15 seconds to spare. Jack celebrates by taking Allison out for some Christmas fun.

At 40, Brad (J. Andrew Keitch), the gay protagonist of *Almost Normal* (2005), is frustrated at having no man in his life. Shortly after telling his best friend Julie (Joan Lauckner) that he wishes he were normal, Brad has a car accident and wakes up back in his senior year of high school. Except now he *is* normal, because gay is normal—the only socially acceptable opposite-sex relationships are to have a child. To Brad's delight, his secret high school crush Roland (Tim Hammer) is now interested in him. When Brad meets Julie, though, they find themselves physically attracted to each other (this comes completely out of the blue). When their classmates catch them doing it, Brad again becomes a sexual outsider. But at the big school dance, Brad turns people's views on heterosexuality around. He wakes up back in the present where he meets a grown-up Roland—and as it turns out, Roland really is both gay and interested.

In *Hot Tub Time Machine* (2010), Adam, Nick and Lou (John Cusack, Craig Robinson and Rob Corddry) are former best friends living sad, miserable lives. Adam's newly divorced; failed singer Nick runs a dog-grooming business; Lou just attempted suicide. To buck Lou up, the guys and Adam's promiscuous sister Kelly (Collette Wolf) repeat a ski-resort trip they took 25 years earlier, accompanied by Kelly's son Jacob (Clark Duke). A freak hot-tub accident transports Adam, Nick and Lou's minds into their younger selves, while Jacob is drawn back physically.

To avoid changing history, Adam has to break up with his hot girlfriend, Nick has to have a one-night stand and Lou lets himself get beaten up by a bully. Adam meets and falls for April (Lizzy Caplan), but he fears that getting involved with her will screw up time. The guys finally reactivate the hot tub time machine, but Lou refuses to return home with them. When the others reach the present, they learn that Lou changed history big-time, marrying Kelly (the time trip revealed that Lou was Adam's unidentified father), inventing the "Lougle" search engine and becoming lead singer for Motley Lou. His changes have rippled out, so Nick's now a music producer and Adam married April. (For *Hot Tube Time Machine II*, see later in this chapter.)

In the oddball comedy *Safety Not Guaranteed* (2012), broody magazine intern Darius (Aubrey Plaza) helps reporter Jeff (Jake Johnson) investigate a recent newspaper ad soliciting a companion for time travel. When they track down the author, Kenneth (Mark Duplass), Darius volunteers. Kenneth tells her that his girlfriend Belinda died in 2001 when a car crashed into her house, so they're going back to save her. Darius thinks Kenneth is crazy, but admits she'd like to save her mother, killed in a robbery while shopping for her demanding daughter.

It turns out that Belinda (Kristen Bell) is still alive and was never Kenneth's girlfriend—it was Kenneth who crashed the car into her boyfriend's house, out of jealousy. When Darius confronts Kenneth with this, he replies that if Belinda's alive, that proves that they'll succeed in saving her. (The movie ignores that he's still a guy who'd crash a car through a house in a jealous rage.) Kenneth and Darius are now in love, so Kenneth offers to take Darius back to save her mother. It turns out he really has a working time machine, so off they go.

Change and Relocation

Most rewriting of personal history relies on limited-duration time trips. The traveler accomplishes the big change, wakes up back in the present and discovers their history is vastly better. As TV series don't need to have a happy ending after two hours' running time, two series have taken the protagonist into the past and left them there.

In *Do Over* (2002), Joel Larsen (Tom Everett Scott) lives a miserable, unmarried life until an electric shock sends him back to his 14-year-old body (Penn Badgely). With his knowledge of the future and the help of his best friend, he sets out to change everything he hates about his life: winning the student council election he lost, stopping his mother from having an affair, trying to steer his sister off her self-destructive path, pursuing the girl of his dreams. Joel also has to deal with the frustration of being a teenager again, and being subject to his parents' rules. Each week he manages to improve things, but there were always more problems to fix.[1]

Hindsight (2015) opens on Becca Brady's (Laura Ramsey) wedding day, as she prepares for an amiable but passionless marriage to her buddy Andy (Nick Clifford). This gets her thinking about her train-wreck first marriage exactly 20 years ago, about the crap job she's had for two decades, and about former best friend Lolly (Sarah Goldberg) whom she hasn't seen in years. Becca passes out, then wakes up in 1995 on her first wedding day.

After convincing Lolly she's come back through time, Becca leaves her groom at the altar, then quits her job. Unlike *Do-Over*'s Joel, there are no further obvious mistakes to fix, so Becca has no idea what the right path is, or how it will change her future; Lolly points out she's no worse off than anyone else. As Becca begins working things out, she meets Lolly's long-time crush, Kevin (Steve Talley). In the original timeline, her affair with Kevin drove Lolly away, so Becca's determined to avoid this. But she falls for Kevin again, and while Lolly's initially okay with that, she changes her mind when she learns about the original affair. This left Becca sobbing, miserable and longing to go back to the present as the first and only season ended.

The only movie that sends someone into their personal past for good is *Stuck in the Past* (2007). Appalachian-born Broadway star Rebecca Role (Margo Smith) lost touch with her family and her faith years ago, and now faces a lonely retirement. She prays for help, then wakes up as her teenage self, Becky (Lesley Bowen). Becky tells her sister Kelly (Sherri Bohlander) she has no memory of her future, therefore no idea what to change.

When the family moves into the neighboring town, the residents mock them as hillbillies. The taunts sting so much, Becky refuses to sing bluegrass in the school talent show, vowing that from now on she's only singing that classy Broadway stuff. Becky also loses her moral bearings, lashing out instead of turning the other cheek, committing petty thefts and rejecting sweet Eb (Josh Moody) when he says he loves her (in the filmmakers' eyes, this is a grave failing). After a local bad boy, Lester (Greg Robbins), tries to rape Becky, she sees the light. Becky realizes she should never have rejected her roots and sings bluegrass in the talent show with her sister Kelly (Sherri Bohlander). Although she's stuck back in her past, she's happy.

Back to the Future

Like *Terminator*, *Back to the Future* (1985) was a standalone film that proved successful enough to spawn sequels. Also like the Terminator films, the *Back to the Future* trilogy vacillates on whether changing history is possible or desirable. In *BTTF II* (1989), Doc Brown (Christopher Lloyd) pulls Marty (Michael J. Fox) into the future to change his children's future history, then lectures Marty against changing history. After the first film changes Marty's family history, the new timeline is treated as if it were the original one: When Marty and Doc discussing restoring the timeline, they never propose restoring Marty's original dysfunctional family (not that you can blame them). Although Doc ends the series telling Marty he can write his own destiny, everyone else in Hill Valley has had their lives rewritten and edited by time-changing multiple times.

At the start of the first film, Marty McFly is saddled with an embarrassment of a family. His father George (Crispin Glover), is a put-upon loser, bullied and exploited by his supervisor Biff (Thomas F. Wilson); mom Lorraine (Lea Thompson) is a drunk and a scold who lectures Marty incessantly on how his sweet girlfriend Jennifer (Claudia Wells) is too slutty for her taste; Marty's siblings are aimless losers. According to Marty's school principal (James Tolkan), no McFly in Hill Valley history has ever amounted to anything.

Marty's friend Doc, an eccentric inventor, astounds Marty by revealing that he's converted a DeLorean into a time machine and wants Marty to videotape Doc traveling to another time. Before Doc can do so, angry terrorists—Doc swindled them out of plutonium to power up the car—attack and kill Doc. A terrified Marty escapes in the DeLorean, unintentionally driving into 1955. With the power exhausted, Marty's trapped in a world of weirdly alien slang, clothes and culture. Worse, his arrival interfered with the meet-cute between his parents, so Lorraine is now crushing on Marty. Having his mother hot for him freaks Marty out, and begins erasing him and his siblings from reality. Marty convinces Doc's younger self that he's really from the future. They figure out that Marty can power the car via an upcoming thunderstorm, but there's no point in going home if they don't bring George and Lorraine together first. Marty also wants to warn Doc about the terrorists, but Doc refuses to tamper with established events.

After repeated failures as a matchmaker and several encounters with teenage Biff (already a bullying jerk), Marty pitches a solution to George, who's become his friend. Marty will hit on Lorraine, who will recoil in horror, and then George will show up and save her virtue. This proves a disastrous idea: Teen Lorraine drinks, smokes and "parks" and she's eager to go all the way with Marty. Then she kisses him and finds it's like kissing her brother. Biff appears, turns Marty over to his hench-bullies, and tries to rape Lorraine. When George arrives, he freaks out at confronting Biff instead of Marty, but his love for Lorraine inspires him to deck Biff. With a little more help from Marty, the McFly parental relationship is back on track.

When Marty returns to 1985, it turns out that Doc listened to Marty's warning and survived the terrorists. Better still, punching Biff changed George's life for the better, boosting his confidence and leading to him becoming a successful businessman and novelist. Lorraine, miserable when George was a wimp, is now happy and sober (Lorraine has no say in her own happiness—apparently it's entirely up to how her husband turns out)[2] and she approves of Jennifer. Marty's siblings are over-achieving professionals. In contrast to the usual teen time travel arc, Marty hasn't come to accept his flawed family, he's made it over into the one he'd like it to be. In a final scene, Doc, having traveled into the future, returns to drag Marty and Jennifer with him to save their children.

This wasn't intended to spark a sequel, but *Back to the Future II* (1989) takes off from there (with Elisabeth Shue now cast as Jennifer). In 2015, Biff's (Thomas F. Wilson) grandson Griff (Wilson) is bullying Marty Jr. (Fox) into helping out in a robbery. This Doc knows will lead to Junior going to jail, then Marty's daughter going to jail for trying to spring him. Doc zaps Jennifer unconscious and leaves her in an alley, then he and Marty successfully save the McFly kids.

Marty also learns that he's become the mirror of his timid, bullied father due to a car accident that crippled his guitar-playing hand and his dreams along with it. Doc warns Marty against tampering with fate, but Marty is determined not to be a loser. He picks up a sports almanac, planning to use the sports history to make can't-lose bets once he's back in the present. Marty doesn't know that Biff has pegged Doc and Marty as time travelers; Biff steals the almanac, drives the DeLorean to 1955 and gives the book to his younger self before returning to the future.

When Marty and Doc arrive back in 1985, it's a nightmare world where Biff's gambling wins have made him the wealthiest man alive. George McFly is dead, Lorraine has married Biff and Hill Valley is a slum. When Marty confronts his stepfather, Biff smugly reveals he killed George and now plans to shoot Marty. With Doc's help, Marty escapes and they head back to 1955 to reclaim the almanac. This requires weaving in and out of events at the climax of *BTTF* without altering them. Marty successfully recaptures and destroys the almanac, then a lightning bolt strikes the DeLorean and apparently destroys Doc.

Moments later, a Western Union messenger gives Marty a message the company has been holding for 75 years. At the start of *Back to the Future III* (1990), the message reveals that Doc is alive in 1885, and content to live out his days there; he's hidden the DeLorean where Marty can find it and return to the present. Marty discovers that "Mad Dog" Tannen (Wilson) gunned Doc down just a few days after Doc wrote the message, so Marty heads to 1885 to save his friend.

When Marty breaks the news, Doc agrees that returning to the present beats dying. The DeLorean is out of gas, and there's no suitable fuel in 1885. The guys finally hit on hijacking a train, placing the car on the cow-catcher and using the train to reach time travel speed. If they fail, the car and train will go off an unfinished bridge and they'll die.

As if that wasn't challenge enough, Doc and the new schoolteacher Clara (Mary Steenburgen) fall instantly in love when they meet, much to Marty's bemusement ("Doc can dance?"). Doc decides to stay in 1885 with Clara, but when he reveals he's a time traveler she rejects him as a liar. The time trip is back on, and despite numerous obstacles, Doc and Marty steal the train and head for the bridge. Clara discovers that Doc was telling the truth and climbs onto the doomed train, forcing Doc to stay and save her while Marty returns to the present.

To Marty's relief, the nightmare 1985 of the second film has been restored to the happy ending of *Back to the Future*. By now, Marty has matured enough to refuse a reckless dare, which averts the accident that crippled his hand. Doc, Clara and their kids arrive on a time traveling steam engine to tell Marty and Jennifer that from this point on, the young couple can write their own future.

Time and Marriage

Back to the Future isn't the only film that has children tampering with their parents' marital history.

Action Replayy (2010) was a Bollywood time travel musical starring Aditya Roy Kapur as Bunty, a man who refuses his girlfriend's proposal because his parents' horrible arguments have left him marriage-phobic. When his parents Kishen and Mala (Akshay Kumar, Aishwarya Rai) decide to divorce, Bunty uses his girlfriend's uncle's time machine to go back in time and make his parents' marriage a happy one.

Marty McFly had it easy. Kishen is a complete wimp while Mala is shrewish, relentlessly strong-willed, and dating someone else. Under Bunty's tutoring, Kishen adopts a strong, tough-guy manner that Mala likes. However, he still has a rival in a local singer, and agrees to compete for Mala's hand with a sing-off. With more coaching from Bunty, Kishen wins, but Bunty's grandparents on both sides oppose the match. Despite their resistance, Bunty gets his parents to the temple on time, returns to the present and discovers that after three decades of marriage, they're a passionate, loving couple. His faith in marriage restored, Bunty pops the question to his woman.

Wizards of Waverly Place: The Movie (2009) spins off a TV series about kid wizards Alex, Max and Justin Russo (Selena Gomez, Jake T. Austin, David Henrie), whose father Jerry (David DeLuise) gave up magic to marry the mortal Theresa (Maria Canals-Barrera). During the family's Caribbean vacation, Alex has an argument with her mother and wishes her parents had never met. The family magic wand turns that wish into a reality: Suddenly both parents are single, Theresa hates kids and Jerry is a party animal. Alex and Justin learn there's a magic stone that can reverse the wish, and hunt for it with the help of ex-wizard Archie (Steve Valentine) and his parrot, the transformed wizard Giselle (Jennifer Alden). Max leads his parents on the same quest, while trying to reunite them. As the altered timeline takes hold, first Max, then Justin disappears from reality. At the last second Alex gets the stone and rewinds time to before the big argument. To her mother's surprise, Alex meekly submits to parental authority. As she never makes the wish, everyone's around.

The Doomed Darkos

Donnie Darko (2001) opens in 1988, when sullen teenager Donnie (Jake Gyllenhaal) is in therapy for his supposed mental problems. When a mysterious half-man, half-rabbit warns Donnie that the world will end in 28 days, his shrink (Katharine Ross) assumes it's a sign that Donnie's schizophrenic. Donnie believes the creature has visited him through a wormhole, which gives him even more to be angsty and miserable about. To further upset him, a plane engine crashes into his bedroom while he's out and nobody can identify the aircraft it belongs to.

More weirdness crops up but everything becomes clear (well, sort of) when the 28-day deadline arrives. The engine belongs to a plane that's sucked through a wormhole into the past. Donnie's own timeline rewinds as a side effect, and when the rewind stops, it drops him in his bedroom just as the engine crashes into it. Donnie dies. His girlfriend never met him and she bicycles past his house, vaguely wondering why his family seems familiar.

The opening of *S. Darko* (2009) reveals that Donnie's sister Sam (Daveigh Chase) ran away from home after her brother's death. She and her best friend Corey (Briana Evigan) wind up in a small Southwestern town after their car dies. Sam has weird visions of apocalypse, then gets killed in a car accident. Then time rewinds so someone else dies instead. Meteors strike the town, which drives an unstable young man to accidentally kill Sam. Time rewinds to the early days of Sam's visit; Sam buys a bus ticket home, erasing the previous timeline. No, there really wasn't a point to it.

Me, Myself and I

It's a common premise in screen time travel that you can't meet your past or future self without triggering catastrophe. In a few stories, however, meeting yourself is part of fixing your history.

In the TV series *Second Chance* (1987), Charles Russell (Kiel Martin) learns at his death in 2011 that he's not bad enough for Hell or good enough for Heaven. St. Peter (Joseph Maher) decides to resolve things by sending Charles back 24 years to meet his teenage self "Chazz" (Matthew Perry) and sway him to the side of virtue. Charles arrives as Chazz is preparing to commit a robbery that will help his divorced mom (Randee Heller) pay the mortgage. Charles can't talk Chazz out of the crime, so he rents out his mother's garage apartment as "Charles Time." The rent takes care of the mortgage so Chazz doesn't have to steal. St. Peter points out that's not enough—Chazz hasn't changed his moral outlook—so Charles needs to keep trying to reform Chazz. He was still at it when the series ended.

After 40 years of marriage, Frank (Ben Gazzara) and Maggie (Rita Moreno) have hit a rough spot in *Blue Moon* (2000): Frank's just retired and neither of them knows how to adjust to the new status quo. During a tense vacation at their Catskills cabin, Maggie wishes they could remember how their love felt, years ago. That night they're awakened by Mac (Brian Vincent) and Peggy (Alanna Ubach), a vacationing unmarried couple (Mac's on the brink of proposing but hasn't found the nerve). They insist it's 1959 and that they're the ones staying in the cabin. Maggie eventually realizes these are their younger selves, and that this is a chance for her and Frank to remember their early years. The quartet talk about their pasts, futures and fears, and Frank reveals his darkest secret, that his father abused him. He tells Peggy that Mac's postponed proposing for fear he'll become the same kind of abusive brute, then tells Mac that's not going to happen. Mac proposes, the younger couple vanish, and Maggie and Frank find themselves in love all over again.

Twice in a Lifetime (1999–2001) took an anthology show approach to the *Second Chance* concept. The recently deceased come before Judge Othniel (Al Waxman) who gives them a chance to avoid damnation by going back and changing their lives. In one episode, bullying IRS agent Stovall (Corbin Bernsen) is sent back to meet his past self (who by heavenly magic can't recognize himself) and teach him to show a little compassion. By convincing Young Stovall to help a dog trainer having a tax crisis, Stovall prevents his own greatest tragedy, the loss of his son: When the kid disappears, the trainer's rescue dogs find the boy.

The Man Who Used to Be Me (2000) opens in 2020 with hard-bitten, hard-drinking cop Sam Ryan (William Devane), still scarred by the murder of his father 20 years earlier. Using a newly developed time machine, he travels back to 2000 to save his father, but arrives a few moments too late. The killer promptly knocks Sam cold and puts the murder weapon in his hand. Barely escaping arrest, Sam realizes the only person he can turn to is his younger self (Rob Estes). Sam presents himself to young Sam as a detective friend of their father's (conveniently nobody sees the resemblance between the two Sams) and together they begin hunting for the real killer.[3]

Disney's The Kid (2000) stars Bruce Willis as Russ, a 40-year-old, emotionally closed-off, work-obsessed image consultant. He wakes up one night to discover an eight-year-old boy has broken into his house; young Rusty (Spencer Breslin), who turns out to be Russ's younger self.

It's not a happy discovery. Russ is contemptuous of his fat, wimpy past self, but Rusty is just as outraged to learn he grew up into an unmarried guy with a boring job (his dream was to be a jet pilot) who doesn't even own a dog. Rusty is, however, very taken by Russ's photographer aide Amy (Emily Mortimer); Amy's charmed enough by the boy to wonder if Russ is less of a jerk than he looks.

Russ eventually decides Rusty has come to the present so they can join forces and change their past. They settle on a bullying incident as the point Russ began closing off the world, and with Russ's coaching, Rusty beats the bully. The school reports the incidents to Rusty's parents, freaking out his terminally ill mother and enraging his father. Russ realizes this, not the fight itself, was what started him down his isolated path so he hasn't changed anything. He promises Rusty he's going to change his future instead, and in the closing shot we learn he'll succeed: He and Rusty meet their 70-year-old self (who apparently set all this up), married to Amy, a pilot, and yes, a dog-owner.

The Tomorrow Man (2001) stars Corbin Bernsen as 1971 carpenter Larry Mackie, frustrated in life and abusive to his son Bryan (Adam Sutton). When the criminal Mack (Morgan Rusler) leads a gang from 2001 back to kidnap Bryan, federal agent Vick (Beth Kennedy) pursues them, accidentally drawing Larry along when she returns to her own time. Vick explains that she works for a government branch changing history for America's benefit—the movie blithely assumes this is a good thing—and that Mack killed her partner to steal a time device. Oh, and Mack is Bryan's future self, determined to take the boy away from Larry to escape years of future abuse.

Mack tries to win over Bryan, even as Larry and Vick race to recover the kid. Mack captures his father, shows him glimpses of how abusive Larry will become, then prepares to kill him. Vick saves Larry and they take out Mack's gang. Mack tries to finish off Larry but Bryan, who doesn't want his father dead, kills Mack first. Vick wipes Bryan's mind of all this and sends the Mackies home. Larry overcomes his dark side to become a good father and when we see Mack again, he's a time travel agent working with Vick.

Judas Kiss (2011) stars Charlie David as Zachary Wells, a washed-up filmmaker turned videographer. When he judges a film festival contest at his alma mater, he discovers that one of the kids, wunderkind Danny Reyes (Richard Harmon)—whom Zach just had a one-night stand with—not only shares Zach's birth name, he's entering the same autobiographical film, *Judas Kiss*, that won Zach the festival grand prize years earlier.

An old man (later revealed to be Zach's future self) reveals that Danny is somehow Zach's younger self (even though Danny has a life in the present with friends and a family) and that if Zach rejects *Judas Kiss* it will break Danny of the arrogance and selfishness that ruined Zach's career. Even after Zach tells Danny they're the same person, Danny rejects his advice and vows to make his own mistakes, not repeat Zach's errors. Danny's father gets *Judas Kiss*, which shows him in a bad light, disqualified on technical grounds, but the festival still airs it. The acclaim gives Danny the strength to stare down his father for the first time. Inspired by the experience, Zach returns to his partner (Tory Fischnaller) and begins writing film scripts again.

Kristin's Christmas Past (2013) stars Shiri Appleby as Kristin, a 34-year-old music producer who hasn't returned home for Christmas in 17 years, spending it with her best friend Jamie (Will Kemp) instead. When Jamie reveals that this year he's visiting his family with his current girlfriend, a despondent Kristin passes out drunk at her apartment, then wakes up in 1996, next to her younger self "Krys" (Hannah Marks).

Kristin convinces Krys who she really is, then they convince their mother (Elizabeth Mitchell) that Kristin is a college recruiter stranded in the area. Kristin knows that after this holiday, Krys and her mother will never speak again—Krys is following her jerk of a boyfriend to NYU and Mom won't accept it—so she sets out to change that. Despite the assistance of young Jamie (Michael-James Olsen), who loves Krys, Kristin fails to break up Krys' relationship, avert the big fight with Mom or convince Jamie to tell Krys his feelings. Finally Kristin accepts that like Danny in *Judas Kiss*, Krys has the right to live her own life and make her own mistakes. Kristin wakes up back in the present and heads home for Christmas. Jamie meets her there, kisses her and finally, as she suggested, tells her he loves her. Together they reunite with Kristin's parents.

In South Korea's excellent *Nine: Nine Time Travels* (2013), reporter Park Sun Woo (Lee Jin Wook) is dying from a recently diagnosed brain tumor as the series kicks off. His goals for the remaining months of his life are to marry fellow reporter Joo Min Young (Jo Yoon Hee)—she's willing even though she knows he's dying—and finally break the power of corrupt businessman Choi (Jeong Dong-Hwan). In the midst of all this, Park discovers that his doctor brother Jung Woo (Jeon No Min) has frozen to death in Nepal, clutching a container of incense sticks.

Lighting one of the sticks transports Park back in time 20 years, returning when the incense burns down (about a half-hour). Park sees his chance to solve multiple problems:

- Warn his younger self about the tumor.
- Save his brother's life.
- Save their father from dying in a fire, which he assumes was his brother's plan for using the incense.
- Reunite Jung Woo with the blue-collar girlfriend their father decided wasn't good enough.

Working both alone and with his younger self, Park is able to save himself and his brother, but not their father. Worse, he discovers that Jung Woo accidentally killed their father, which Choi covered up by starting the fire. Worse still, Jung Woo's lover is Min Young's mother, so when Park reunites her with Jung Woo, Park's fiancée is suddenly his adoring niece. Park's heart breaks, but he can't see how to change things back without killing his brother.

On a later time trip, Park convinces his brother to turn himself in to the police over their father's death, and to implicate Choi in the cover-up. The new change leaves Jung Woo doing medical charity work, Choi impoverished and powerless and Min Young and Park a couple again. On their wedding day, the last incense stick strands Park in the past when it burns out, instead of returning him home. Young Choi recognizes Park as the man behind his troubles and kills him. The dying Park encounters Min Young, creating a new timeline in which she and Park meet and eventually fall for each other again. In the final scene, Jung Woo dies again in Nepal, but an older, bearded Park appears to save him. (What this means is anybody's guess.)

Based on Robert Heinlein's "All You Zombies," *Predestination* (2015) stars Ethan Hawke as Leonard, a time traveling federal agent whose failed attempt to stop a time traveling terrorist leaves him so badly injured he's undergone major plastic surgery. Now working undercover in the 1970s, Leonard meets John (Sarah Snook), who reveals he was born Jane, a hermaphrodite. An orphan, Jane grew up into a math and science whiz. She joins NASA as a sex worker—men in space need to get laid, you see—but gets canned when her bosses learn she's a hermaphrodite. Jane takes a lover, becomes pregnant, has her baby stolen and become sterile due to complications from the birth. Doctors decide that's grounds to surgically turn her male.

Leonard recruits John as a time agent and takes him back to 1963. There John becomes Jane's lover and the father of her child. Leonard kidnaps the baby and takes it back to the orphanage, where it will grow up into Jane. Leonard—John's future self—hates doing this to himself, but his boss reminds him that it's already happened. When Leonard finally locates that bomber, he discovers that the man is his own future self. The bomber claims he committed the attacks to save lives by changing history. Leonard shoots him but the dying man declares he did exactly the same when he was Leonard, when he was Leonard's future is now inevitable.

Love and Death

Repeat Performance (1947) opens with actor Sheila Page (Joan Leslie) gunning down her husband Barney (Louis Hayward) in self-defense on New Year's Eve. As she staggers to a friend's New Year's Eve party to call the cops, she wishes she could rewrite the previous hellish year like a bad script. When Sheila arrives at the party, it's the previous New Year's Eve and she has her chance.

Over the next year, Sheila sets out to save not only Barney but also her best friend William (Richard Basehart), whose wealthy mistress (Natalie Schafer) will have him committed when their relationship sours. Neither fate nor human nature cooperate: Despite Sheila's best efforts, Barney once again meets and falls for the scheming Paula (Virginia Field) and William winds up in the asylum. Paula dumps Barney when he can no longer help her career, leaving him full of anger. When Barney confronts Paula on New Year's Eve, Paula accuses Sheila of driving her away. Barney, insanely angry, attacks Sheila once again. William, newly released from the madhouse, shoots Barney to save Sheila the pain of killing him. As the police drag William away, he tells Sheila that while they can't thwart destiny, they can fudge the details. *Repeat Performance* was faithfully remade in 1989 as *Turn Back the Clock* with Connie Sellecca in the lead.

One Magic Christmas (1985) stars Mary Steenburgen as Ginny, for whom Christmas is anything but magical. She's stressed out from her salesclerk job, from being the only income in her family, from having no money and from giving up all hope. The Christmas angel Gideon (Harry Dean Stanton) engages in some cold-blooded shock therapy by having a desperate thief kill Ginny's husband Jack (Gary Basaraba). It's the bleakest Christmas possible for Ginny, until Gideon and Santa Claus (Jan Rubes) help reconnect Jennie with her childhood faith in Christmas and in dreams of the future. Once her heart embraces hope again, Jack returns—the tragic timeline has been erased—and Jennie digs into her savings to finance Jack's dream of opening a bicycle store.

In *Another Day* (2001), just as Kate's (Shannon Doherty) years of study and saving pay off with med school admission, she learns that she's pregnant. Boyfriend Paul (Max Martini) offers to marry her, but Kate leans toward an abortion. After Paul dies in a factory fire that police suspect he caused, Kate goes ahead with the pregnancy. She builds a new life with little Meghan (Courtney Kidd) and David (Julian McMahon), a lifelong friend who happens to be in love with her. Kate can't let go of Paul's memory, so David decides to move away. Then Kate drowns trying to pull Meghan out of a river.

Instead of Heaven, Kate wakes up in the past, before Paul's death. She agrees to marry Paul and tries to keep him out of the factory on the day of the fire. Despite Kate's efforts, Paul dies, but she learns he didn't start the fire, and also gets to give him a proper goodbye. She wakes up in the present, at peace with her past and ready to start a new relationship with David.

In *Three Days* (2001), Andrew Farmer (Reed Diamond) has been married to sweet, sunny Beth (Kristin Davis) for 20 years. During that time he's become a clone of the father he hates, increasingly obsessed with work, neglecting Beth and contemplating an affair. When Beth dies in a Christmas Eve car accident, Andrew realizes how much he loved her. The angel Lionel (Tim Meadows) lets Andrew relive the last three days with Beth so he can make her final Christmas magical and—if he gives her the perfect gift—prevent her death.

Andrew's renewed devotion knocks Beth for a loop, but rather than the glamorous Christmas vacation he suggests, she asks him to visit their home town. Andrew has to deal with his father, come to terms with Beth's pregnancy announcement and somehow find the perfect gift. When the moment of her death comes round again, Andrew realizes that the perfect gift is to sacrifice himself to save her. Lionel saves Andrew too so the Farmers and their new baby will live happily ever after.

In *If Only* (2004), Ian (Paul Nicholls) is a less than focused boyfriend to Sam (Jennifer Love Hewitt), an insecure singer-songwriter. After Ian confesses to mixed feelings about their relationship, Sam breaks things off, then dies a few minutes later in a car accident. A grieving Ian wakes up the next morning to discover the day has rebooted and Sam's alive. He sets out to make it a good day for her, and possibly change her fate. Over the course of the day, he opens up to Sam as he's never done before and truly knows love. When the fatal crash comes, Ian sacrifices his own life to save Sam. Unlike *Three Days*, he stays dead, but his heroism inspires Sam to overcome her insecurity and begin performing her music.

Fetching Cody (2005) also starts with tragedy: Drug dealer Art (Jay Baruchel) discovers that his junkie girlfriend Cody (Sarah Lind) is comatose from an overdose. His friend Harvey (Jim Byrnes) has found an old recliner he claims can magically transport anyone sitting in it across time and space. It works. Art begins jumping back to crucial points in Cody's life to fix the events—school bullying, sexual assault, her brother's suicide—that put her in a downward spiral, but nothing changes her fate. Finally Art accepts that he and his drugs destroyed Cody, so he goes back to the day they met and calls the cops on himself. His past self never meets Cody, so back in the present she's okay, although Art no longer remembers her.

The anime *Future Diary* (2011–12) starts off focused on precognition rather than time travel. Yuki (Misuzu Togashi), a shy 14-year-old and perpetual outsider, records impressions around him on his cell phone diary. Then the time god Deus ex Machina (Norio Wakamoto) drafts Yuki and 11 others in a competition to replace the aging deity. The players' diaries record different aspects of future events, which they must use to outmaneuver and kill each other. One player, Yuki's classmate Yuno (Misuzu Togashi), is so obsessed with him that she'll kill anyone, in the game or out of it, that she sees as a threat to him or their relationship. Her insane devotion horrifies Yuki but charms him at the same time.

As bodies pile up, Yuno convinces Yuki that his only hope is to become Deus, then rewind time to resurrect everyone. Yuki goes along, then learns that Yuno knows this won't work—because she *is* Deus. In the world's original timeline she killed the other players, including Yuki, then discovered that even Deus can't raise the dead. The new timeline is her chance to set things right by saving Yuki. Now that Yuki knows the truth, Yuno seals him in an idyllic pocket universe where his parents are alive, then reboots the timeline again. In the reboot universe, though, the counterparts of the original players are happy and at peace, with no desire to seize power by killing people. When Yuki escapes his prison, Yuno stabs herself so that Yuki can survive to become the new Deus. Yuki reigns as lord of time for millennia, alone, but then the rebooted timeline's non-homicidal version of Yuko finds him.

Panic Time (2007) turns the usual formula on its head: Elisa (Emily Lockhart) doesn't want to save her husband James (Russell Reynolds), she wants to kill him before he murders her. Using a time device stolen from the company she works for, Elisa goes back in time and kills him while she has a perfect alibi. Her friend Jack (Kirk Extrell) knows the truth because he got caught in her time wake and dragged back with her. Then Elisa discovers that she's pregnant, so she jumps back a month to prevent it by dosing her past self with sleeping pills on the night she and James made love. Jack gets dragged along again, goes home and discovers his wife cheating on him.

Elisa loses the device, trapping her and Jack in the past. When they try to swipe a second unit, security man Garrett (Lawrence Sutherland) catches them in the act. Someone helps Jack and Elisa escape and the next morning they find the device in their motel room. Elisa makes another time trip to arrange the escape and drop off the device, tying up the time paradoxes. She also gets Garrett busted by the contractor's other security people. Back in the present, she and Jack become a couple.

In *Cruel and Unusual* (2014), Edgar (David Richmond-Peck) finds himself in what appears to be a recovery group meeting, with no memory of how he got there. When he enters his room at the facility, he relives the last day of his life, when he murdered his live-in girlfriend Maylon (Bernadette Saquibal). Edgar's group-mates explain this is Hell, or *a* hell, where they relive their crimes, then publicly rehash and repent them. Edgar protests that he only killed Maylon because she poisoned him and tried to stop him calling 911. The Facilitator (Mary Black) says that as Maylon died first, it's only Edgar who gets damned.

A determined Edgar escapes the facility, but that only forces him to relieve that fatal day from the viewpoints of Maylon and her son Gogan (Monsour Cataquiz). To Edgar's horror he discovers that instead of being a swell guy supporting a cheating girlfriend and her psycho kid, he's a controlling, bullying creep whose treatment of Gogan drove Maylon to poison him. Edgar vows to change events rather than just relive them, so he convinces Doris (Michelle Harrison)—damned since her suicide in 1972—to enter his room with him, so she'll be drawn back with him and can save Maylon. The trick works, but Edgar realizes Maylon will now be damned for killing him. When Doris is sucked back to her own death-day, Edgar saves her from killing herself, then commits suicide, getting Maylon off the hook. In the present, Maylon and Doris are both alive and mourning Edgar; back in Hell, Edgar is at peace with himself.

Dimensions (2011) focuses on brothers Stephen (Henry Lloyd-Hughes) and Conrad (Sean Hart) and their friend Jane (Camilla Rutherford), who dies in 1921, when they're all kids. Stephen grows up to become a physicist, working on a machine that will take him to a parallel timeline where it's still 1921 and he can save Jane. His student Annie (Olivia Llewellyn) helps the brothers build their time machine because she's in love with Stephen. He, however, can't let go of Jane enough to love anyone.

Robert (Edward Halsted), a British agent, contrives to steal the machine and exploit its power, but on his first trip he gets lost between dimensions. When he returns, he kills himself from horror. Stephen figures a way to travel without getting lost, but he admits to Annie it's still a one-way trip. Conrad heroically takes the first world-jump, then Stephen confesses to Annie that he loves her. Annie says nothing (for no reason other than plot requirements) so Stephen assumes she doesn't love him and jumps after Conrad. The brothers save Jane, or maybe an alternate Jane, from her death.

Children Saving (Grand)Parents

In *Blue Yonder* (1985), young Jonathan (Huckleberry Fox) has grown up on eccentric Henry's (Art Carney) stories of Jonathan's late grandfather Max (Peter Coyote), an inventor and aviator who died in 1927 trying to make the first transatlantic crossing. Jonathan feels closer to the grandfather he never met than to his own super-sensible father, who remembers Max as an impractical dreamer. Henry has designed a time machine to go back and save Max but when he falls ill, he asks Jonathan to build the machine and take the trip.

Jonathan meets and bonds with Max in the past. He tries to delay Max's flight until after Lindbergh's crossing, so Max will no longer have a reason to make the attempt. When Max becomes suspicious, Jonathan confesses that he's from the future and eventually convinces him. Max can't let go of the dream, however, and attempts the flight, though by a different route. Jonathan returns to the present where he learns that Max reached Europe before crashing and dying, the most successful pre–Lindbergh attempt. Max has a place in history and Jonathan is inspired to follow his own dream, trying out for Little League.

In 1990's *Future Zone*, John Tucker (David Carradine, reprising a role he played in 1989's *Future Force*) is a near-future bounty hunter somewhat annoyed that Billy (Ted Prior), a hot new rival, seems determined to hang out with him. When one of Tucker's jobs turns out to be a trap, Billy saves Tucker's life and lets slip he's from Tucker's future.

The bad guys blow up Tucker's house, which makes Billy realize he's changing history, as the house was still intact in his era. The crooks take Tucker's wife Mary (Gail Jensen) hostage but Tucker and Billy rescue her. Tucker realizes that if Billy hadn't saved him, he'd have died in that battle. Billy departs for his own time, but tells the Tuckers they'll see him in about seven months, when Mary gives birth.

Tenchi Muyo in Love (1996) spun off from the *Tenchi Muyo* anime series. Tenchi (Masami Kikuchi), seemingly a typical Japanese boy, is actually descended from galactic royalty—the Jurai—and constantly surrounded by beautiful ET women competing for his heart. The film opens with Kain (Ryuzaburo Otomo), a planet-wrecking super-villain, escaping his subspace prison and traveling back to 1970, where he plans to kill Tenchi's mother, Achika (Megumi Hayashibara). The super-scientist Wasshu (Yuko Kobayashi) shields Tenchi from the effect of any history changes, then sends him and his harem back to the past. Tenchi gets to watch his parents meet and connect—particularly poignant for him as his mother died when he was a kid—but then Kain arrives and attacks. Wasshu's genius imprisons the fiend in a dimensional trap, but he drags Tenchi's parents down with him. Tenchi follows them inside the trap where Achika uses her full Jurai power to annihilate Kaine. The parents' memories of the events are erased and Tenchi and his crew return to the future.

The 2001 video game adaptation *Lara Croft Tomb Raider* starred Angelina Jolie as a live-action version of the archaeologist adventuress. The Illuminati cult plans to use an upcoming planetary alignment to activate the Triangle of Light, which will give them control of time itself. Illuminati member Powell (Ian Glen) wants that power for himself, so he recruits Croft to help steal the Triangle. Croft agrees in the hope she can use the Triangle to save her father (Jon Voight) from his death some years ago. After lots of violence, action and tomb raiding, Crofts gets control of the Triangle and meets her father in the past. He warns her against changing history, so Croft returns to the present, smashes the Triangle and finishes off Powell.

At the opening of *Enter Nowhere* (2011), Jody (Sara Paxton) and Kevin (Christopher Denham) hold up a convenience store. At Jody's insistence, the store attendant (Jesse Perez) opens the safe, but tells her she won't like what's inside.... Cut to pregnant Sam

(Katherine Waterston), wandering in the woods after her car dies. At a small cabin she meets Tom (Scott Eastwood), stranded by a car accident of his own, then Jody turns up on the front step. They're all wary of each other, more so when they realize they disagree on where they are (New Hampshire? Wisconsin? South Dakota?) or even what year it is: Sam comes from 1962, Jody from 1985, Tom from 2011 and there's a bunker near the cabin with World War II German maps and equipment. The occupant, Hans (Shaun Sipos), shows up and demands to know why Americans are interfering with his mission in Poland.

Eventually the Americans realize they're four generations of one family, cursed by a chain of events: Hans dies in a bombing raid which leads to Sam dying in childbirth, the orphaned Jody growing up abused and Tom growing up in an orphanage. Saving Hans may save all of them, but he refuses to abandon his mission. Jody finally convinces Hans to hide in the bunker, then we return to 2011, where Jody and Sam are mourning Hans' recent death. Kevin shows up at the convenience store with a different girlfriend, and once again the attendant opens the safe…

Friends, Siblings and Others

The first segment of the anthology film *Dead of Night* (1977), "Second Chance," introduces us to college student and car buff Frank Cantrell (Ed Begley, Jr.). Frank painstakingly restores a classic 1920s car, destroyed when its owner crossed railroad tracks a little too slowly. When Frank test-drives his baby, he winds up back in 1926, where someone drives off in the car despite Frank's protests. Frank returns to the present, then to school, where he falls for a fellow student, Helen (Christine Hart), he'd somehow never noticed before. When he visits her grandparents, he learns that her grandfather Vince (E.J. Andre) was the driver who died at the railroad crossing, until Frank's protests delayed him by a few seconds. Until Frank gave Vince his second chance, Helen didn't exist.

In *Change of Life* (2010), the tragedy that needs fixing is the death of Nova (Alexis Palfrey), a lesbian whose friends don't know she's the daughter of anti-gay, hate-mongering preacher Gary Cattell (Denny Day). Nova's lover Erin (Alyson Schacherer) walks out after learning the truth, which drives Nova to suicide. A shell-shocked Gary tells God he'd do things differently if he had a second chance, then wakes up a few days earlier as one of Nova's gay friends. Hanging with Nova, Gary sees her as she really is, as well as hearing how she sees him. Transformed by what he learns, Gary sacrifices his life to save one of Nova's friends from a fatal gay-bashing. He wakes up back in the present with his daughter still alive, and wastes no time showing he now accepts her relationship with Erin.

In *Time Again* (2011) the bond is sisterhood. Waitresses Marlo (Angela Rachelle) and Sam (Tara Smoker) run from an attack on their diner by Way (Scott F. Evans), a ruthless crime lord seeking four coins that one of his flunkies gave to Sam as a tip. In the aftermath of the attack, Sam's body is gone, so everyone but Marlo assumes she's dead. Six months later a mysterious woman (Gigi Perreau) shows up and uses the same coins to send Marlo back in time to save Sam. The coins are Roman talismans used by Augustus Caesar to travel through time and thereby thwart assassins. Way plans to use them to become world emperor.

After two failures, Marlo succeeds in saving Sam and returns with her to the present.

Way and his gunman New (Fred Anderson) trap the girls by using their father as a hostage, but Way is blown up by his own bomb. The old woman vanishes into time, the implication being she's some alt-version of Sam come to see everything works out right.

The bond between the aspiring mad scientist Okarin (Mamoru Miyano) and his best friend Mayuri (Kana Hanazawa) is what's at stake in the excellent anime *Stein's;Gate* (2011). With their computer-nerd porn-loving buddy Daru (Tomokazu Seki), they're trying to invent a phone-operated microwave, but instead discover a way to send emails back in time. Okarin tests the Dmail—for DeLorean Mail—by letting various friends contact their past selves. The changes that result are always bigger than expected, but only Okarin notices them. He's good at sensing temporal divergences, aka "reading Stein."

After Okarin uses a Dmail warning to save the life of physicist Cristina Makuse (Asami Imai), she joins the lab. The research also draws the attention of SERN (a fictionalized version of the CERN physics research organization), which is plotting to conquer the world. When SERN tries to capture Okarin and his research, they kill Mayuri. To save her, Okarin and Cristina adapt the Dmail technology to send Okarin's mind back in time. He tries to save Mayuri, but fails … and fails … and fails … pushing himself to the emotional brink. Amane (Yukari Tamura), Daru's daughter from the SERN-ruled future, arrives in the present and tells Okarin that in this timeline, Mayuri's death is fixed and unchangeable. The only way to save her is to undo all the changes wrought by Dmail, restoring the original timeline—but that requires letting Cristina die. Okarin eventually finds a way to undo his Dmail *and* make sure that both women live. While Cristina no longer remembers working with Okarin, she's drawn to him when they meet again.

The sequel *Stein's;Gate: The Burdensome State of Déja Vu* (2013) takes place a year later. Everything seems great for the gang, but Okarin is increasingly troubled by his memories of Mayuri's multiple deaths. Amane tells Cristina that the trauma of seeing Mayuri die repeatedly has left Okarin unable to believe in the current happy timeline, so he's starting to slip out of reality. With Amane's help, Cristina recovers enough time travel knowledge to go back and try to prevent this. After repeated failures, Cristina gives the teenage Okarin his first kiss, inspiring him to believe in happiness again.

Puella Magi Madoka Magica (2011) is another story of a time traveler trying and failing to save a friend, though that isn't obvious at first. Eighth-graders Madoka (Aoi Yuki) and her best friend Sayaka (Eri Kitamura) are blown away when they meet Mami (Kaori Mizuhashi), a witch-slaying magical girl, and her familiar-mentor Kyubey (Emiri Kato). Kyubey offers to grant a wish for both Madoka and Sayaka in return for which they will each become witch hunters. Magical girl Homura (Chiwa Saito) warns them not to accept.

After Mami dies, Sayaka signs up in return for a wish restoring an injured friend to full health. Then she and Madoka learn that to make Sayaka a magical girl, Kyubey removed her soul and placed it in an enchanted gem. The soul gems inevitably become corrupted, turning the witch hunters into witches. That emotional cycle generates energy Kyubey's people are using to stave off the entropic death of the universe.

Homura knows this because she's lived it before: after seeing Madoka and Mami die fighting witches, Homura became a magical girl in return for rewinding time so she could prevent the deaths. When she failed, she rewound time again, and again, and again … but Madoka always becomes a magical girl. Kyubey realizes this has made Madoka into a true being of destiny, a nexus of multiple timelines. When she becomes a witch, she'll destroy the world, generating all the power Kyubey's people will ever need.

Homura tells Madoka the truth, but when the super-witch Walpurgisnacht defeats Homura, Madoka makes her own wish. The wish is to prevent the creation of any witches, past, present or future. Madoka disappears from reality, becoming a cosmic concept; Homura and other magical girls are spared from becoming witches; and instead of witches, magical girls battle the evil Wraiths. A sequel film, *Puella Magi Madoka Magica: The Movie—Rebellion* (2013) followed up on the new reality, but without time travel.

The 2014 anime *In Search of the Lost Future* spends most of the season focused on the whimsical doings of a high school Astronomy Club. However there are odd things piling up in their lives, such as ghost sightings, classmates in comas and a mysterious black cube. Plus, of course, there's their newest member, Yui (Akane Tomonaga), an amnesiac transfer student. But all of that becomes unimportant when Kaori (Hatsumi Takada), involved in a traffic accident, ends up vegetative despite Yui's efforts to save her. Yui collapses into sleep and doesn't wake up.

Sou (Takuma Terashima), Kaori's childhood buddy—she wanted to be lovers, he wasn't sure—is devastated by Kaori's condition. He becomes a medical researcher in hopes of finding a cure, without success. A former classmate reveals that her own research on Yui shows the girl is an android. Attempts to place Kaori's mind into Yui's body fail, so Sou finds a way to send Yui back in time to save Kaori. He knows that in his timeline, Kaori will stay comatose, but he hopes the new timeline he's creating will eventually merge back.

It turns out the accident we saw was only the latest of Yui's repeated failures to save Kaori. The ghosts and comas are quantum side-effects of her previous time-jumps. Finally Yui realizes the real issue is that Sou never gave Kaori an honest answer about their relationship. Without that, Kaori can't move on emotionally, which is anchoring the timeline in place. Yui nudges Sou to give Kaori an answer. He does, telling her he's in love with Yui—and finally Yui can save Kaori. As that eliminates the need to send Yui back, in the new timeline she ceases to exist or ever have existed. (In the old timeline, Kaori eventually wakes up.) However, Sou retains enough buried memories of his lost love that it becomes clear someday he will build her again.

My Evil Twin

Visiting a parallel world is another way to see how your life could have ended up differently. In several parallel-world films, the protagonists learn that their lives could have ended up with them being evil.

In *Nightmare Street* (1998), one of the darker parallel-world tales, the constant confusion over recognizing people and places comes off as a sign of disorientation or madness rather than wacky comedy. Widowed Joanna Burke (Sherilyn Fenn) gets hit on the head shoving her toddler away from an oncoming truck, then wakes up to find she's now Sara Randolph—or so everyone around her and her driver's license says. And she has no daughter. And she's a manipulator, a backstabber and a suspect in her son's murder.

Joanna seriously worries she's insane but Dr. Matt Westbrook (Thomas Gibson), who treated her after the accident, suggests she might have crossed over from a parallel world.

They fall in love, but Joanna's determined to find a way home. A dying man who's capable of seeing both worlds tells Joanna to repeat the incident that brought her over. Before trying this, Joanna discovers that Sara did indeed murder her child. She sends the police a taped confession, duplicates the accident before the police can arrest her for Sara's crimes, then wakes back in her own world. The film ends with her meeting Matt's counterpart.

A 1998 TV movie *The Lake*, has Jackie Ivers (Yasmine Bleeth) visiting her estranged, dying father, Steve (Stanley Anderson). Things get weird fast: Steve suddenly becomes warm and loving, a man Jackie saw die turns up alive, and a neighbor claims that her husband is an imposter, then denies it. Jackie and her old boyfriend Jeff (Linden Ashby) discover the mayor throwing people into a vortex in a nearby lake.

Steve finally admits that the vortex is a gate for town residents from a dying parallel Earth to emigrate and replace their counterparts here. Steve—apparently the only good counterpart—sacrifices himself so that Jackie and Jeff can escape their doppelgangers and reach the state police. The cops scoff until their own duplicates turn up. But new vortexes are opening everywhere—is it too late?

Yulaw (Jet Li), the villain of the action movie *The One* (2001), kicks things off by murdering the 123rd of his parallel-world counterparts. Parallels are linked at a quantum level so each kill enhances Yulaw's strength and intellect, as well as that of the last surviving counterpart, good-hearted Gabe (Li). Yulaw believes once he kills Gabe he'll become a god. The trans-dimensional agents pursuing Yulaw (Delroy Lindo, Jason Statham) worry that he'll create a quantum imbalance that destroys everything.

Yulaw kills one of the agents as well as Gabe's wife (Carla Gugino), so Gabe joins forces with the surviving cop against him. Eventually Gabe takes down his counterpart in a spectacular Li vs. Li martial arts battle. The authorities seal Yulaw away in another dimension while Gabe finds his wife's unmarried counterpart in another parallel world.

In *Undermind* (2003), attorney Derrick Hall (Sam Trammell) is irresponsible and self-destructive, reluctant to marry his girlfriend Lucy (Susan May Pratt) or in general to grow up. Suddenly he finds that he's Zane (Trammell again), a wannabe musician and occasional criminal, caught up in an elaborate, dangerous crime scheme. Zane likewise finds himself in Derrick's life. Derrick doesn't exist in Zane's world, so presumably they've swapped timelines, not just bodies. Zane's low-life knowledge makes it easy for him to solve the murder case Derrick is defending. He also clears out a lot of detritus from Derrick's life, and finally expresses Derrick's love for Lucy. Derrick meanwhile navigates the shoals of Zane's life and escapes, accompanied by Zane's girlfriend Anya (Tara Subkoff). At the climax, both men jump back into their bodies and discover their lives have improved substantially.

In the animated *Justice League: Crisis on Two Earths* (2010), the heroic Lex Luthor (Chris Noth) of a parallel world recruits the Justice League to fight against the Crime Syndicate, evil versions of the superheroes (Ultraman for Superman, Owlman for Batman, etc.). The Syndicate already runs its world behind the scenes but anticipates using the quantum bomb that Owlman (James Woods) has developed to seize open control. Neither side realizes that Owlman is frustrated with a multiverse where every Syndicate victory splits off a divergent timeline where they lost, and vice versa. Owlman believes this renders all actions meaningless except one: detonating the quantum bomb on the original root Earth to erase the multiverse completely.

When Owlman heads to Earth Prime with the bomb, the Justice League and the Syndicate join forces to stop him. Flash and his Syndicate counterpart Johnny Quick use their speed to open a gateway for Batman to pursue his duplicate. The Caped Crusader reaches Owlman, then shifts him and his bomb to a different, lifeless Earth. The quantum bomb takes out Owlman and that one Earth, reality survives, and the JLA finishes off the Syndicate.

In *Phineas and Ferb: Across the 2nd Dimension* (2011), it isn't the eponymous genius kids (Vincent Martella, Thomas Sangster) who face their evil counterpart, but the inept evil scientist Dr. Doofenshmirtz (Dan Povenmire), who dreams of ruling the "tri-state area." After the kids help him perfect a dimensional gateway, they all go through along with the boys' platypus Perry (a secret agent dedicated to thwarting Doofenshmirtz). The 2nd Dimension's Doofenshmirtz has been eptly evil since losing his favorite toy as a kid, and now tyrannizes the tri-state area. The double Doofenshmirtzes join forces to invade the kids' Earth. Phineas and Ferb hook up with the 2nd Dimension's resistance, led by the counterpart of their sister Candace (Ashley Tisdale). The invasion triumphs until Doofenshmirtz-1 gives his counterpart a copy of the toy he lost. The happy Doofenshmirtz-2 cancels the invasion and goes home, where the resistance captures him and puts him on trial.

Coherence (2013) is more about the fear that your counterpart is evil than the reality. Four couples are having dinner when a comet passes overhead, blacking out the neighborhood except one house. When they explore, they discover it's identical to the house they're eating in, with counterparts of themselves inside, a quantum effect caused by the comet. There's no evidence the counterparts are hostile, but the couples take a worst-case approach, preparing for a fight and worrying some of the duplicates have already infiltrated them. To make matters worse, they discover there are multiple counterparts of the house and themselves in the area.

After much worry and talk, Em (Emily Foxler) slips over to one of the duplicate houses, kills her counterpart and replaces her. It seems to succeed, but the next morning her husband gets a call from another of Emily's counterparts, and the film ends with him staring at Em suspiciously.

"Mirror, Mirror"

The "mirror universe" of *Star Trek* is an evil-counterpart parallel world that's cropped up on three different *Trek* series. In the original series' "Mirror, Mirror," a freak transporter accident throws Kirk (William Shatner) and some of his crew into an alternate timeline. The Federation's counterpart is the Empire, which kills all who refuse to submit to its rule. Starfleet discipline is brutal and sadistic, officers rise by assassinating their superiors—alt-Kirk has a secret super-weapon for that—and alt-Spock (Leonard Nimoy) has a beard. Kirk & Co. eventually replicate the accident and go home, but not before Kirk urges alt-Spock to reform the Empire, using alt-Kirk's weapon if force is required.

The mirror universe next appeared in *Star Trek: Deep Space Nine*'s (1993–99) episode "Crossover." (For more on the series, see Appendix IV.) Bajoran officer Kira Nerys (Nana Visitor) and DS9 doctor Julian Bashir (Alexander Siddig) accidentally enter the mirror universe, where Kira's counterpart is "the Intendant," the absolute authority in their section of space. The Intendant explains that Spock steered the Empire onto a peaceful path, after which a Klingon-Cardassian alliance conquered it. Kira and Bashir escaped back to DS9, but other members of the crew would be abducted to the mirror universe in several more episodes scattered throughout the series' run. In the seventh and final season, the human resistance overthrew the Alliance's ruler, Worf (Michael Dorn), hopefully leading to a free Terra.

Enterprise (2001–05) contributed the two-part episode "In a Glass Darkly," set entirely in the mirror universe. The story reveals that in the mirror universe, Zephram Cochrane's first contact with the Vulcans (see the previous chapter) ended with Cochrane and his friends killing the Vulcans and seizing their ship. Ninety years later, Archer (Scott Bakula) seizes the captaincy of the *Enterprise* and captures a ship that had crossed over from the 23rd century of the main *Trek* series. Archer believes the ship's superior technology will give him power to rule the Empire. Instead his mistress Hoshi Sato (Linda Park) poisons him and becomes Empress Sato.

A Fifth Dimension Beyond Those Known to Man

Starting in 1959, Rod Serling's *The Twilight Zone* used the concept of changing personal history for several episodes.

- "Walking Distance" While visiting his old home town, a stressed-out businessman finds himself back in his past, the perfect summer he remembers from boyhood (though in this case, he's still an adult, not in his old body). In the end, his efforts to see his parents one final time result in tragedy.
- "The Last Flight." A World War I pilot is shocked to find himself landing at a 1959 military base. When the base commander interrogates him, the pilot eventually confesses that he abandoned a dogfight against overwhelming odds, even though that meant letting his wingman die. When he learns his friend survived, the pilot realizes that somehow he must find a way back to save him.
- "The Trouble with Templeton." A brilliant actor who's never recovered from the death of his adored wife finds himself back with her in the 1920s. When he realizes she's nothing but a cheating drunk, he flees back to the present, where he discovers a script in his hand, detailing every minute of their encounter. He realizes his wife drew him back in time to force him to start living his life again instead of living in the past with her.
- "Static." A lonely old man, bored out of his head watching TV, discovers he can use an old radio to tune in the long-cancelled radio shows he enjoyed. His repeated listening eventually draws him back to his youth, where he recovers an old love.
- "The Incredible World of Horace Ford." Horace returns to the world of his childhood, for which he has great nostalgia. Unfortunately he's forgotten how bullied he was in his youth…

Serling took up the same themes again in "They're Tearing Down Tim Riley's Bar," a 1971 episode of his TV series *Night Gallery*. Randy Lane (William Windom), a burned-out executive approaching the end of his career, jumps back to his youth, when his wife was alive and everyone hung out at Tim Riley's. In the original script, the story ends with Lane sobbing as a wrecking ball demolishes the bar; in the version that aired, Lane's devoted secretary convinces his boss to give him another chance and Lane discovers his life isn't over.

Bad Guys, Bad Changes

Villains can have just as much reason to upgrade their pasts as the heroes. And upgrading their pasts often means downgrading someone else's.

In the anime series *Emblem Take Two* (1993–95), dimwitted Yakuza thug Joji Akutsu (Toshiyuki Morikawa) is a loser married to a woman he can't stand and constantly undercut by his subordinates. When his crime family has him whacked as a liability, he wakes up ten years earlier, in the middle of a street fight he humiliatingly lost. Now, though, with a decade of experience, Akutsu easily intimidates his adversaries. With his knowledge of who will rise and fall in the Yakuza hierarchy over the next decade, Akutsu sets out to outmaneuver and destroy his enemies. But his ability to change events is still limited, making it an uphill struggle.[4]

In *Kim Possible: A Sitch in Time* (2003), teen troubleshooter Kim Possible (Christy Carlson Romano) is dismayed when her best friend and sidekick Ron Stoppable (Will Friedle) moves overseas because his mom got a job in Norway. When their arch-enemies—mad scientist Drakken (John DiMaggio), martial artist Shego (Nicole Sullivan), cyborg golfer Duff Killigan (Brian George) and man-monkey ninja Monkey Fist (Tom Kane)—join forces to obtain an ancient "time monkey" idol, Kim's unable to stop them without Ron.

Using the idol, the villains attempt to destroy Kim by attacking her at various points in her past. In each case they fail thanks to the strength of the Kim-Ron team. Shego's future self warns her the plan to destroy Kim is futile, so Shego should take the time monkey for herself.

Ron reunites with Kim and together they defeat the remaining villains. Then a descendant of Ron's pet mole rat warns them that in the near future, Shego will conquer the world. When the teens arrive in the future, Shego captures them along with their friends and family, who have become the core of the resistance. Shego reveals that in addition to making a fortune in investments through time travel and building an arsenal of super-weapons, she arranged the Stoppables' move to Norway, having realized that Kim and Ron were unbeatable together. Ron's so outraged at this that he breaks free and shatters the idol. The timeline, including the Stoppable move, is wiped out and the kids are back in school together.

The Santa Clause 3: The Escape Clause (2006) was the third in a series about Scott Calvin (Tim Allen), an ordinary man forced to become Santa after accidentally killing his predecessor. The upcoming Christmas is particularly stressful: Carol Claus (Elizabeth Mitchell) is close to having a baby, her parents (Alan Arkin, Ann-Margret) are visiting, and Scott's trying to hide his identity by telling them the North Pole is a Canadian toy factory.

Enter Jack Frost (Martin Short), bitterly jealous that he isn't the star of the winter season. Learning that Scott can wish himself free of Santa-hood with the "escape clause," Jack tricks him into making the wish, then seizes the red suit for himself. Scott finds himself in an alternate timeline where his counterpart is still a ruthless businessman, his kids are miserable and Frost's North Pole is a tacky theme park. Scott tricks Jack into unwishing the change, regains his old reality and reveals the truth to his in-laws. Scott's daughter Lucy (Liliana Mumy) reforms Jack by melting his heart with affection.

In *Cinderella III: A Twist in Time* (2007), Cindy's Stepmother (Susanne Blakeslee) acquires the fairy godmother's wand and uses it to rewrite history. Now when Cinderella's (Jennifer Hale) stepsister Anastasia (Tress MacNeille) tries on the shoe, it fits. Prince Charming (C.D. Barnes) assumes that Anastasia is the woman he loves, which pleases Stepmother but not Anastasia; she wants true love and knows this isn't it. Both Cindy and the prince eventually realize what's happened and try to put things right. Stepmother counters by turning Anastasia into Cindy's double so the wedding will go through, then arranging for Cinderella to die in a trap. Cindy escapes and reaches the wedding in time to see Anastasia refuse to go through with it. Stepmother attempts to destroy both girls, but the magic boomerangs and turns her into a frog. The Fairy Godmother (Russi Taylor) reclaims her wand but, as the royal couple has already reunited, she doesn't bother changing the timeline back. Anastasia soon finds her own true love.

Lewis (Daniel Handson/Jordan Fry), the protagonist of *Meet the Robinsons* (2007), is a brilliant but nerdy orphan and inventor. His science fair entry, a memory scanner, draws the attention of both a time traveling criminal (Matthew Josten) who wants to steal it, and Wilbur Robinson (Wesley Singerman), a boy from the future hunting the thief. The thief's interference trashes the science fair and leaves Lewis with no invention to show. He gives up on science, but Wilbur knows the scanner is vital to history, so he offers to take Lewis on a time trip if he rebuilds it. Arguing over which direction to go, they crash the machine in Wilbur's time. His eccentric family welcome Lewis and even offer to adopt him until they learn he's from the past.

The burglar kidnaps Lewis to make him repair the damaged scanner. Lewis learns that the scanner is the first of his many great inventions, and that he's also Wilbur's future father. The thief is Lewis' fellow orphan Mikey, whose life Lewis unintentionally ruined. In return, Mikey plans to destroy the Robinsons' happy timeline by taking over the world with one of Lewis' discarded future inventions, a mind-controlling hat. When Mikey starts deploying the hats, they seize power for themselves, turning the future into a hat-enslaved dystopia. Lewis saves the future by repairing the time machine, going home and deciding never to invent the hat. Reality returns to normal, Lewis returns to inventing and with his help, Mikey gets a happy future too.

Prince of Persia: The Sands of Time (2010) harks back to the sword-and-sandal Arabian Nights films of the 1950s. Dastan (Jake Gyllenhaal), a street orphan adopted by Persian King Sharaman (Ronald Pickup), has grown into a doughty warrior who has now conquered Princess Tamina's (Gemma Arterton) city. Sharaman's brother Nizam (Ben Kingsley) murders the king and frames Dastan, forcing the prince to flee. Dastan learns from Tamina that her city holds a giant hourglass full of magic sand that can rewind time. Nizam plans to rewind the years to the day he saved his brother's life, let Sharaman die and become king years earlier. Tamina warns Dastan that using that much stand could trigger a curse on the hourglass and bury the world in sand. Dastan uses the sand to rewind time, save Sharaman and expose Nizam as a traitor. Tamina no longer remembers Dastan, but agrees to marry him anyway.

In *Ticking Clock* (2011), hard-drinking journalist Hicks (Cuba Gooding, Jr.) finds his girlfriend dead, chases the killer (Neal McDonough) and sees the man disappears into thin air, leaving behind a journal predicting more killings. Hicks tries to prevent the killing spree, but as he keeps appearing at crime scenes—nobody else ever sees the killer—police begin to suspect him. There's a fingerprint on the manuscript, but it belongs to an 11-year-old orphan, James (Austin Abrams). Hicks befriends the kid, a lonely, creepy boy who dreams of building a time machine to make his life better.

The reporter eventually figures out what the audience has already grasped, that the killer, Keech, is James' adult self. Hicks wonders if murdering young James would be as justified as killing Hitler. The police arrest Hicks for the murders. Keech abducts him from the police station to explain himself: He's a hero, saving his younger self from the abusive caregivers who warped his life. But his murders haven't changed his past enough, for which Keech blames Hicks, first for interfering, then for befriending James and never returning. Keech's solution is to have James capture Hicks, becoming a hero. Instead at the climax, Keech kills Hicks, James attacks Keech, and Keech reflexively kills James. That erases Keech from existence; his victims are alive and James is a happy kid with a normal life. How that came about is left unexplained.

In *The Caller* (2011), Mary (Rachelle Lefevre) moves into a new apartment after divorcing abusive Steve (Ed Quinn). When a woman calls on the apartment's landline looking for her boyfriend, Mary's annoyed, then really annoyed when the woman, Rose (Lorna Raver), claims it's 1979. Rose proves it by painting a rose on the wall that Mary suddenly discovers in the present. The two women bond, and Mary encourages Rose to break away from her own abusive boyfriend. In the original timeline, Rose broke it off by strangling herself with the phone cord; now, though, things change and she kills the guy. Mary, horrified, tells Rose to stop calling; Rose retaliates by finding Mary's present-day friends in 1979 and killing them. Rose also meets young Mary and "accidentally" pours boiling water over her (the scars suddenly appear on Mary's present-day body).

Mary tries to trick Rose into visiting a bowling alley Mary knows will burn down. Rose survives and comes after Mary in both 1979 and the present. Mary talks to her younger self over the phone and convinces her to stab Rose to death in the past. Young Mary succeeds, ending the threat, but the killing changes Mary: When Steve shows up and assaults her, she kills him without a qualm.

Agents K and J (Tommy Lee Jones, Will Smith) are Men in Black, part of a super-secret agency dealing with extraterrestrials on Earth. In *Men in Black 3* (2012), one of K's former busts, Boris the Animal (Jemaine Clement), escapes prison, time travels to 1969 and kills K before the agent originally arrested him. Although J remembers K, agency boss Agent O (Emma Thompson) scoffs until she sees J craving chocolate milk, a side effect of temporal distortion. When Boris in the present summons an invasion fleet, O discovers that K died without deploying the Arcnet, Earth's ultimate defense against invasion.

To save K, J has to time jump—quite literally, as the device triggers by jumping of a skyscraper. On arrival, J almost kills Young Boris but Young K (Josh Brolin, doing an amazing Tommy Lee Jones impersonation) intervenes. J convinces K to work with him, and discovers that in 1969, his somber, stone-faced partner is friendly and flirtatious. K acquires the Arcnet, but it has to be deployed on the Apollo 11 mission—and Cape Canaveral is where Boris will kill K. A clairvoyant warns the agents that in every possible timeline, Boris will bring death. The heroes forge ahead, defeat the two Borises and deploy the Arcnet, but the dying alien guns down a military officer. J realizes this is his own father, who vanished in J's childhood (as established earlier in the film). Back in the present, J discovers Earth is safe and K is alive.

The Flash (2014–) was a superhero TV series starring Grant Gustin as Barry Allen, a young forensic scientist with the Central City police department. As a child, Barry witnessed a superhumanly fast yellow figure murder his mother, but no one believed him. Instead his father (John Wesley Shipp) went to jail for the crime.

When tech genius Harrison Wells' (Tom Cavanagh) particle accelerator overloads, it endows Barry with super-speed, which he uses to fight crime as the Flash. He doesn't know that Wells is really Eobard Thawne, the time traveling Reverse-Flash—his costume reverses Flash's red-and-yellow color scheme—from a century in the future. Even though Thawne's ancestor Eddie (Rick Cosnett) is Barry's friend, the Reverse-Flash will become one of the Scarlet Speedster's deadliest foes. Thawne went back and murdered Nora Allen in hopes of traumatizing Barry so that he'd never become the Flash. Thawne's speed powers faded on his trip home, so ironically his only hope to reach the 22nd century is to give Barry super-speed sooner than in the original timeline (he succeeds) and steal some of that power.

At the end of the first season, Barry and Thawne strike a deal: Thawne will show Barry how to open a wormhole that allows Reverse-Flash to go home and lets Barry go back to save his mother. When Barry arrives in the past, however, another version of himself warns him not to intervene. After a final goodbye to his mother, Barry returns to the present for a showdown with Thawne. It ends unexpectedly when Eddie shoots himself, erasing his descendant's existence. (Reverse-Flash returns in the second season, with the time paradoxes dropped).

"The Monkey's Paw"

Some movies make it very clear that even if you're not a villain, changing your past is tampering with God's domain. No matter how bad your situation, it can always be worse.

Case in point, Travis (James Bulliard), protagonist of the TV series *That Was Then* (2002), has a mess of a life. He lost his dream girl Claudia (Kiele Sanchez) to his brother, lives with his widowed mother and his only joy in life is his adorable young nephew. Travis blamed everything that went wrong on one single week in high school when he blew it with Claudia and publicly humiliated himself. When lightning strikes the house while Travis listens to the Kinks' "Do It Again," he finds himself a 16-year-old again. He immediately and successfully changes everything that went wrong, but when he returns to the present his life is even worse: He's married, but not to Claudia, and his nephew was never born. Putting on the Kinks once more, he headed back into the past ... but his second attempt only made things worse yet. Presumably the downhill path would have continued had this lasted longer than two weeks.

Always Will (2006) stars Andrew Baglini as Will, a typically miserable movie high schooler. His childhood best friends Danny (John Schmidt) and Jacob (Mark Schroeder) are no longer pals; his dream girl Julie (Noelle Meixell) does no more than nod to him in passing; and his stepfather Al (Bart Mallard) verbally abuses both Will and his mom Lydia (Jody Seymour). Then Will discovers that a fifth-grade time capsule that he and his friends stole gives him the power to change his past. A few judicious tweaks to his history and he's one of the cool kids—football star, academic wiz, Julie's boyfriend.

Jacob realizes what's happening and warns Will he did the same thing in middle school, until his time-tampering led to his brother losing an eye. Will isn't convinced until he sees how miserable Al makes Will's mother. As Al met Lydia at the time capsule dedication, Will goes back and steals the capsule before the ceremony. In the new timeline, Al and Lydia never meet, and Lydia completes her education and becomes an architect. Will lets history revert to the original timeline, except now he stays friends with Danny and Jacob.

Primer (2004) is a low-key do-over film stylistically reminiscent of found-footage movies. Aaron (Shane Carruth) and Abe (David Sullivan), wannabe tech entrepreneurs, discover that the strange effects generated by "the box," a device they've built, are due to the box unmooring anything inside it in time. With a little more tinkering, they're able to use the box to travel back in time. They start making stock picks and sports bets in the past, always avoiding time paradoxes and awkward questions: If they're going back to Monday, for instance, they spend Monday the first time in a hotel room away from everyone they know.

The careful, cautious plan rapidly unravels. An acquaintance uses the box and turns up vegetative. Aaron and Abe secretly build backup boxes they use independently of each other. Aaron tapes conversations, then jumps back in time so he can steer the discussion in the direction he wants. Sometimes he even drugs his past self to replace him. As the two former friends and their temporal counterparts continue working against each other, Aaron suggests that he and Abe leave the country for a clean break. Abe stays behind, determined to stop their past selves from developing the machine.

In *The Butterfly Effect* (2004), Evan Treborn (Ashton Kutcher) has spent his life suffering from odd memory gaps. In college Evan discovers he can project his mind into his past body—causing the memory lapses—and change events. After Evan's best friend Kayleigh (Amy Smart) kills herself, Evan goes back to his childhood and forces Kayleigh's father (Eric Stoltz) to stop abusing her (the movie assumes a kid saying "no!" is all it takes), changing her life for the better. Evan and Kayleigh become a happy couple in the present, but her father kept on abusing her brother Tommy (William Lee Scott), so he's now an unstable, jealous psycho. Evan goes to jail for killing Tommy in self-defense so he tries another time fix, then another ... until Kayleigh's dead, Evan's mother has terminal cancer (she never quit smoking) and Evan's brain is frying from holding multiple conflicting memories from different timelines.

Evan eventually learns that if not for their friendship with him, Tommy and Kayleigh would have moved away to live with their mother. Evan goes back in time, ends their friendship and sees the siblings move away to grow up happy. He also gets his mom to quit smoking. The director's cut went darker, having Evan leap into the womb and make his mother miscarry so Kayleigh never met him. ("Butterfly effect" refers to big results from minor changes, but Evan makes great big changes.)

In *The Butterfly Effect 2* (2006), Nick (Eric Lively) suffers headaches and brain spasms after a car crash kills his girlfriend Julie (Erica Durance) and their friends Trevor and Amanda (Dustin Milligan, Gina Holden). When he stares at a photo from right before the crash, he finds himself back there and prevents the accident, then returns to a present where Julie's alive and Trevor's working with Nick at a tech company.

Dave (David Lewis), the firm's arrogant VP, fires Trevor. Nick sticks up for his friend and gets canned too. Nick retaliates by going back in time and stealing the deal that won Dave his promotion. Back in the present, Nick now has Dave's job, but he and Julie are no longer together. Worse, one of the new investors is a mob boss who kills Trevor for losing the syndicate's money. Nick's drastic solution is to go back again to the day of the crash and break up with Julie. When she drives off, Nick remembers she's going to die and saves her at the cost of his own life. At the end, we learn Julie's baby by Nick has inherited Daddy's powers.

By the start of *The Butterfly Effect 3: Revelations* (2009), Sam (Chris Carmack) has already learned that changing the past has costs: He saved his sister Jenna (Rachel Miner) from a fire, but in this new timeline his parents died instead. Sam now uses his powers to watch murders in the past without intervening, then claim a reward by identifying the killer with his "psychic" abilities.

Sam's true love Elizabeth (Sarah Habel) was murdered some time ago; her sister Rebecca (Mia Serafino) convinces Sam the man convicted for the killing is innocent. Sam uses his powers to save Elizabeth and identify the murderer, but things go very wrong. When Sam returns to the present, Rebecca and Elizabeth are both dead, the first victims of the "Pontiac Killer," and the police suspect Sam. As more murders occur, Sam identifies Jenna as the Pontiac Killer. She's had an incestuous obsession with Sam since he saved her, so she uses her own time-jumping powers to kill his girlfriends before he meets them. Sam erases the entire timeline by going back to the night of the fire and stopping himself from saving Jenna. At the film's end, Sam and Elizabeth are married, but their child may have inherited Jenna's madness.

Spy Kids: All the Time in the World (2011) opens with pregnant spy Marissa Wilson (Jessica Alba) taking down the time-stopping criminal Tick-Tock. She then retires to family life with husband Wilbur (Joel McHale) and stepkids Rebecca and Cecil (Rowan Blanchard, Mason Cook), none of whom know about her spy work. A year later, Tick-Tock escapes and allies with another villain, the Timekeeper. Together, they activate the Armageddon Device, which will accelerate time until the universe achieves total entropy and time stops forever.

Marissa goes back into the field, which leads to Rebecca and Cecil learning about her spy career. The kids subsequently discover that Marissa's boss D'Amo (Jeremy Piven) is the Timekeeper. The Wells Project, an earlier chrono-experiment, left D'Amo frozen in time for decades, while his father and friends died. By deploying the Armageddon Device, D'Amo intends to open a time gate to save his father's life. (Dad died of old age, so it's unclear how that's going to work.) The kids somehow deduce that this is not only impossible but D'Amo's henchmen and Tock-Tock are divergent versions of D'Amo created by previous failures. The Timekeeper tries again, but when his father tells him life should go forward instead of back, D'Amo listens and gives up his mad plan.

I'll Follow You Down (2014) is more about the drama surrounding time travel than the journey itself. When Erol (Haley Joel Osment) is a child, his physicist father Gabriel (Rufus Sewell) disappears on a business trip. Erol's mother Marika (Gillian Anderson) has a breakdown, then years later kills herself. Erol's grief makes him receptive to his grandfather Sal (Victor Garber), who has a crazy theory that Gabriel disappeared because he went back in time. Evidence that Gabriel died in 1946 in a mugging seems to prove Sal right.

Erol and Sal set out to duplicate Gabriel's time travel theories so that they can bring him back before Marika kills herself. This doesn't sit well with Erol's girlfriend Grace (Susanna Fournier), who fears that a change to the family history will erase their relationship. Erol insists that no matter what, he'll find her again. Finally Erol makes it back to confront his father in 1946. Gabriel explains that he came back to get Albert Einstein's advice on using time travel for the public good. Erol replies their family's suffering shows time is too dangerous to tamper with. As Gabriel is unwilling to return home, Erol plays a trump card: He shoots himself. The only way to save his son is to abort the entire timeline, so Gabriel returns to his family just a couple of days after he left.

In the found-footage film *Project Almanac* (2015), teenage David (Jonny Weston) discovers video footage of his seventh birthday party, with his present-day self visible in the background. Searching the house further, David finds his father's plans for a time machine. With his friends he develops an improved model they can control via a cell phone app. Despite the app's limits—they can't go back far and meeting yourself is fatal—the kids use it to rewrite embarrassing moments, win the lottery (they get one number wrong, so they're not millionaires) and to crash a rock concert (they buy old backstage passes online, then go back to use them). David and cute fellow traveler Jessie (Sofia Black-D'Elia) almost hook up after the concert but David blows his chance. Despite a pact with his friends that they'll never time travel alone, David uses the app for a do-over and wins Jessie.

The group's activities on concert night trigger a series of cascading disasters and deaths. David blames himself and tries fixing things secretly. He only makes things worse, culminating in Jessie meeting herself and vanishing. Devastated, David prunes the timeline by going back to his seventh birthday and destroying his father's research, erasing everything that happened, including his time traveling self. Miraculously the camera with all the footage of their adventures survives, and everything starts over.

If You Were Never Born...

Frank Capra's *It's a Wonderful Life* (1946) is easily the best known film about changing your past. As it opens, apprentice angel Clarence (Henry Travers) learns that George Bailey (Jimmy Stewart) is on the brink of drowning himself and reviews George's life to learn why. George, it turns out, has spent most of his life hoping to blow the dust of his hometown, Bedford Falls, off his shoes and see the world. Time and again, though, he puts duty—to family, to his father's savings and loan, to the community—before self and stays: His honeymoon with Mary (Donna Reed), for example, never gets beyond city limits so they can use their travel budget to keep the S&L afloat in the Depression.

Just by offering an alternative to the covetous Potter (Lionel Barrymore) and his unreasonable slums-for-rent, George becomes Potter's nemesis. Potter gets his revenge on Christmas Eve when George's nitwit uncle (Thomas Mitchell) loses $8,000 in S&L money—Potter finds and hides it—right before a bank examiner arrives for an audit. Without the money, George faces business failure, ruin and prison. Jeering, Potter gloats that with $15,000 in life insurance, George is worth more dead than alive.

To stop George's suicide, Clarence jumps into the river first. George saves him, but refuses to believe that Clarence is an angel, or that his (George's) own life matters. Clarence proves otherwise by erasing George from history. Suddenly Bedford Falls is Potterville, a cheap slum with a garish red-light district. People George helped over the years are dead, ruined or in despair; Mary is an old maid librarian. Once George accepts what a wonderful life he had, Clarence restores the old timeline. Everything works out fine as George's friends raise enough money to cover the deficit.

The premise has been much imitated. *It Happened One Christmas* (1977) is an outright remake, but with genders reversed, so Marlo Thomas plays Mary Bailey (the James Stewart role), Wayne Rogers is her husband and Cloris Leachman is the guardian angel.

Most imitators simply take the never-been-born concept and adapt it to their own needs, as in *Richie Rich's Christmas Wish* (1998), one of several films based on the comic book about the world's wealthiest boy. After Richie's (David Gallagher) malicious cousin Reggie (Jake Richardson) pulls off a prank that makes Richie look like the world's wealthiest jerk, Richie wishes he'd never been born. As he made the wish next to scientist Keenbean's (Eugene Levy) wish-granting machine, it comes true: Richie's in a timeline where he never existed and Reggie controls the Rich billions.

A Reggie-ruled world is a nightmare for everyone, so Richie enlists the counterparts of his friends to fight back, plus his butler Cadbury (Keene Curtis), now a rock'n'roll roadie. They capture the wishing machine and the giant wishbone that powers it, but Reggie's security team recaptures Richie and the machine. Before Reggie can make a wish, his dog, which understandably likes Richie better, steals the wishbone. That buys Richie enough time to bring his old reality back.

It's a Very Merry Muppet Christmas Movie (2002) follows in the same tradition: As the Muppets ramp up for their big Christmas Eve show, corrupt banker Bitterman (Joan Cusack) calls in their loan, then alters the contract so that she can foreclose on their theater. Kermit becomes convinced that his dreams of show business ruined the Muppets until a guardian angel (David Arquette) shows him how miserable everyone would be without him. Kermit returns home in high spirits, and discovers one of his friends has saved the theater by getting it declared a historic landmark.

Shrek Forever After (2010), the fourth and to date final Shrek film, is an animated fantasy in which the once terrifying ogre (Mike Myers) is now happily married to ogress Fiona (Cameron Diaz), father of three toddlers, surrounded by friends and treated like a cuddly, harmless grouch. All of which brings on a midlife crisis that the sorcerer Rumpelstiltskin (Walt Dohrn) is happy to exploit. He offers to give Shrek one day of living as the terrifying ogre he used to be, in return for a day from Shrek's babyhood the ogre won't even remember. Shrek agrees, only to discover the day he gave up was the day he was born. He never existed; after his day of freedom, he'll fade away. This creates a timeline where Rumpelstiltskin's cabal of witches rules the kingdom. To undo the new timeline, Shrek needs to win true love's kiss from alt-Fiona, leader of the ogre resistance.

Shrek's efforts to woo Fiona not only fail, they get the resistance captured. Shrek trades himself for their freedom but Rumpole keeps Fiona prisoner on a technicality, and doesn't let the two ogres lock lips. Shrek's sacrifice inspires the resistance to storm the castle, after which Fiona kisses Shrek, restoring reality at the last minute. Shrek now appreciates that he, too, had a wonderful life.

Doonby (2013) is a conservative Christian *Wonderful Life* (the creators acknowledged the influence). Drifter Sam Doonby (John Schneider) enters a small town, takes a job as a bartender and stuns the locals with his good looks, charm and talent. He saves a boy from being hit by a truck; saves the bar owner (Ernie Hudson) from a gunman and saves spoiled doctor's daughter Laura Reaper (Jenn Gotzon) from a crazy stalker. The eruption of violent incidents sets the town wondering if Sam could be responsible for them. Even though he and Laura are dating, she freaks out about this and, after a big argument, she tells Sam she wishes he'd never been born. The next second, she has her wish. Now everyone San saved is dead (except, illogically, Laura herself), and her father Dr. Reaper (Joe Estevez), whom Sam cleared of a fake rape charge, is ruined. Laura discovers that Sam's mother aborted him (it seems this was the original reality and the movie took place in a divergent timeline) and Dr. Reaper performed the procedure. Weeping, Laura realizes that Doonby is just an anagram for "nobody."

In *The Disappearance of Haruhi Suzu* (2010), high schooler Kyon (Tomokazu Sugita) starts to appreciate his wonderful life when he wakes up without it: He's in a world where Haruhi (Aya Hirano) never dragged him into her club, the SOS Brigade (see *The Melancholy of Haruhi Susimaya* in chapter eleven), so he doesn't know her or any of the other members. Haruhi exists in this timeline, but she attends a different school and never met Kyon. Fortunately the SOS Brigade's living computer, Nagato (Minori Chihara), who's human in the new timeline, left a software program for Kyon that sends him back three years in the past, before things changed. Past-Nagato explains that her future self developed emotions, which left her unable to deal with the overbearing Haruhi; in the new timeline, she doesn't have to. Past-Nagata gives Kyon "liquid data" that will restore the old timeline if he injects her future self. That proves tougher than expected, but Kyon finally succeeds. The alternate timeline became the basis for the reboot series *The Disappearance of Nagato Yuki-Chan*.

Change Your Personal Future

A few time travel movies and series tackle changing the protagonist's future rather than his past.

W.E.I.R.D. World (1995) was an anthology TV movie based on stories in old EC Comics. In one story, an industrial spy (Marshall Bell) orders Bob (Miguel Nunez), the corrupt security chief at the Wilson Emery Institute for Research and Development, to steal his sister Pat's (Gina Ravera) prototype time machine. It looks like a slam-dunk when Pat shows Bob a near-future newspaper with her obituary; but the newspaper got the facts wrong and it's actually Bob who ends up dead. At the end of the movie, W.E.I.R.D's director announces that a combination of genetic research and time travel has enabled the institute to recruit Albert Einstein as a new team member.

In *Ditto* (2000) a Korean movie reminiscent of *Frequency*, two students at an exclusive school make contact over an old ham radio—even though one of them, So-eun (Kim Ha-Neul), lives in 1979 while Jee In (Yoo Ji-Tae) lives in 2000. The 21-year gap highlights the changes in South Korea: So-eun lives in an authoritarian era about to slide into military dictatorship, In lives under a democratic government. In has a comfortable, upscale lifestyle where So-eun has to settle for austerity. In the course of chatting, So-eun realizes In's parents are the man she loves and her best friend. Rather than erase In, So-eun gives up her man.

Tragically she gets no reward beyond personal satisfaction: In discovers that she vanishes, presumably dead, during the years of military dictatorship.[5]

Against Time (2001) is unusual in that the viewpoint character is the one who has to change, not the one effecting the change. ZT (Ean Mering), a high school inventor and baseball player, is thrown for a loop when a man claiming to be his future self (Robert Loggia) shows up and calls him a murderer. "Zach" explains that he volunteered for a time travel experiment to stop a terrible mistake his younger self will make soon … but years of drink leave Zach too confused to remember what must be undone. Even so, the two guys bond and Zach nudges ZT to start dating cute classmate Delena (Emilie Jacobs).

Eventually Zach remembers that ZT will invent a defective water purification process that kills 23 kids, including his son. ZT's terrible mistake is winning a baseball scholarship by playing with an amped-up bat he designed, establishing a life-long habit of cutting corners to succeed. After Delena dies in an accident (a side effect of Zach's time tampering), ZT decides to honor her faith in him and play the game straight. He still wows the scouts, and making the right choice changes everything: There's no future tragedy, Zach is a happy grandfather who never had to change his past, and Delena's alive.

In *5ive Days to Midnight* (2004), widowed physics professor J.T. Neumeyer (Timothy Hutton) has a good life with his daughter Jesse (Gage Golightly) and his new girlfriend Karla (Kari Macht). Then, by his wife's grave, he discovers a locked briefcase containing a police file referencing his own unsolved murder, five days hence. He brings this to Detective Sikorsky (Randy Quaid) who dismisses it as a hoax, but reconsiders as events begin conforming to the predictions in the briefcase. JT tries to use the suspect list from the file to identify the murderer but everyone around him has a motive. JT's brother is financially desperate, Karla's on the run from her mobster husband and JT's student Carl (Hamish J. Linklater) believes JT has to die to preserve the stability of time.

It turns out that Sikorsky is the killer, hoping to steal some land deeds Karla stole from her husband. The cop's attempt to kill Karla and JT fails, and JT shoots Sikorsky with the original murder bullet. The case file now reflects the changes and Carl theorizes that Jesse sent the case back to save JT.

The Jacket (2005) opens in 1991. Jack Sparks (Adrien Brody) is a Desert Storm veteran with a brain injury that leaves him with memory gaps. When he goes on trial for shooting a policeman, he can't even remember if he did it. After he's committed to Dr. Becker's (Kris Kristofferson) asylum, the doctor subjects him to a sensory deprivation therapy that unmoors Sparks' mind in time. He materializes in the present and meets Jackie (Keira Knightley) whom he befriended as a child. After Sparks learns that he died in 1993, he begins hunting for a way to avoid death. Traveling between time, he also falls in love with Jackie and prevents her mother from dying in a fire. Sparks fails to stop the accident that kills him, but he projects himself back to the future as he dies and begins a new relationship with Jackie.

13 Going on 30 (2004) starts in 1987, as the cool girls at Jenna Rink's (Christa B. Allen) thirteenth birthday party humiliate her. As a sobbing Jenna wishes she were grown up, she knocks over the vial of "wishing dust" her best friend Matt gave her. Suddenly it's 17 years in the future and Jenna's (Jennifer Garner) the adult editor of the women's magazine *Poise*. As she's mentally still 13, she's overwhelmed at dealing with naked men, cell phones ("Do you hear that?") and adult responsibilities.

When she turns to the grown-up Matt (Mark Ruffalo) for support, she learns they haven't spoken since the party, as Jenna dumped him in favor of winning over the cool girls. Jenna also learns that her grown-up self is a horrible person who fires subordinates on a whim, treats people like dirt, seduces married men and is giving insider tips to a rival magazine in return for an eventual editorship. She realizes Matt loves her and reciprocates, but he's engaged and won't break it off. To cap off a crappy future, Jenna's best friend Lucy (Judy Greer) steals the editor's job adult Jenna wanted and destroys *Poise* in the process. Jenna discovers more wishing dust, which returns her to the night of the party. She settles her score with the mean girls and kisses Matt ... and when we see her at 30 again, she and Matt are happily married.

In *Zathura* (2005), quarreling brothers Danny (Jonah Bobo) and Walter (Josh Hutcherson) play the eponymous board game while alone at home. The reality-bending game hurls them into outer space where they encounter menaces ranging from meteorites to robots to aliens, plus rescuing "the Astronaut" (Dax Shepard) from a time warp. When Walter contemplate using a Zathura card to wish Danny had never existed, the Astronaut reveals that he did the same thing to his own brother. That trapped him in the game forever, because there was nobody to take the next turn. Walter passes on the card, and later uses another card to wish the Astronaut's brother back, and it turns out to be Danny. The Astronaut is an older version of Walter, in a timeline that no longer exists because Walter didn't use the card. The counterparts disappear and the brothers finish the game, return home and have a much greater appreciation of each other.

The anime series *Noien* (2005) takes place in a world where multiple futures exist as alternate dimensions. In the present, young Haruka (Haruka Kudo) thinks she's an ordinary schoolgirl until world-shifters from Lachryma, an Earth 15 years ahead of hers, arrive searching for something called the Dragon Torque. The dimension of Shangri-La is beginning to absorb Lachryma and only the torque can prevent this.

The visitors, it turns out, are older versions of Haruka's own friends; for example, the brooding Karasu (Kazuya Nakai) is Haruka's timid best friend Yuu (Fujiko Takimoto). Haruka isn't among them because her counterpart chose to save Lachryma by becoming the Dragon Torque. Haruka runs from the hunters, slides into other worlds, and periodically seems to explode with power. Finally the entity Noein (Nakai again) draws Haruka to Shangri-La, where Noien reveals himself as another adult version of Yuu. After Haruka and his other friends died in a car crash, this Yuu began crossing world after world, but found only unhappiness in every timeline—though it's implied he found despair because he no longer believed there was anything else. Yu now intends to absorb all dimensions into Shangri-La and return the multiverse to nothingness, from which he hopes a better world will emerge.

Haruka fights against Noein, forcing him to confront his positive memories. Her world's Yuu, who followed Haruka to Shangri-La, tells Noein he will never give in to despair and become such a monster. With no one to affirm his reality, Noein begins to decohere and vanish—the series offers a quantum-mechanics rationale—ending the threat of Shangri-La and stabilizing the multiverse.

Click (2006) stars Adam Sandler as Michael Newman, an overstressed architect neglecting his family in his zeal for his career. Disguised as a sales clerk, the angel Morty (Christopher Walken) sells Michael a remote that lets him control time, fast-forwarding through the boring parts or going back to rewatch key moments. He can also put in twice as much time at work, and soon makes partner at his firm. The catch: The remote tries to anticipate Michael's needs and begins fast-forwarding through large chunks of his life without being asked. Suddenly it's 16 years in the future, Michael's marriage has collapsed and his son has become the same kind of workaholic as Michael himself. Fortunately Morty lets Michael wake up back in the past and avert the bleak future, devoting himself to his family instead of his job.

The Sarah (Rebecca St. James) of *Sarah's Choice* (2009) is an ambitious career woman and lapsed Christian who discovers she's accidentally pregnant. Everyone in the secular world around her—her friends, her doctor, her co-worker—assures her the only logical thing to do is to abort the baby; her doctor compares it to removing a wart. Then an old woman (Judy Lewis) shows up and gives Sarah glimpses of what a wonderful, beautiful life she'll have if she goes through with the pregnancy. The woman eventually reveals she's Sarah's older self, that she did get the abortion and that not a day passes when she doesn't regret it. Sarah re-dedicates herself to God and has the baby, and it all works out.

In *A Thousand Kisses Deep* (2011), Londoner Mia Selva (Jodie Whittaker) has never gotten over her ne'er-do-well musician lover Ludwig (Dougray Scott) dumping her to move to America. When an elderly recluse in Mia's apartment building commits suicide, Mia discovers that the woman possesses all Mia's photos and mementos. The woman is Mia's future if she can't get Ludwig out of her system.

Building manager Max (David Warner) tells Mia that snooping in the apartment has thrown time out of joint, so now Mia must fix it. The building elevator shifts Mia to different points in her past, giving her a chance to warn her younger self away from Ludwig. Mia fails, as Ludwig is irresistible sex catnip (not that Scott pulls this off) and Young Mia wants him desperately. Present-day Mia grows more disgusted as she continues to learn about Ludwig, including that he was her mother's lover and possibly her own father. Finally she confronts Ludwig before he meets Young Mia, and shoots him. When she returns to the present, Mia learns that the old recluse she was going to become no longer exists—the timeline is erased.

In *Hot Tub Time Machine 2* (2015), the buddies' transformed lives from the end of the first film are floundering: Lou's struggling to keep his marriage and Lougle afloat, Nick's only keeping his singing career going by stealing other writers' future hit songs, and Jacob is miserable (Adam is off on a spiritual retreat and doesn't appear). Lou has rebuilt the time machine so when someone castrates him with a gunshot, Jacob and Nick take him back in time to save his penis. Instead they arrive in 2025—somehow this restores his lost member anyway—where Lou is a lonely old fart, Nick is a desperate has-been and Jacob is as self-destructively selfish as Lou used to be.

Figuring the gunman came from 2025, the trio hunt for him with the help of Adam Jr. (Adam Scott). The hunt devolves into self-indulgent behavior, cheating and anal rape (it's meant to be funny), all of which Lou justifies as just being the way guys are. It turns out that Adam Jr. shot Lou for sleeping with Junior's fiancée, but when the other guys figure this out, they talk Adam out of it. A second Lou, dressed in Revolutionary garb, shows up via the hot tub, shoots his counterpart and reveals that he's from an alternate timeline. The guys follow alt-Lou through the tub into more adventures, including saving Lincoln and bedding Marilyn Monroe.

A Few Minutes Ago

Some "personal history" time travel films focus on very short jumps.

In the mindless action movie *Retroactive* (1997), police psychologist Karen's (Kylie Travis) car dies and she makes the mistake of hitching a ride with Frank (James Belushi) and Rayanne (Shannon Whirry). A small-time crook and a complete psycho, Frank explodes into violence when he's stopped by a deputy, killing the cop and Rayanne. Fleeing Frank, Karen stumbles into Brian's (Frank Whaley) time travel lab and has him send her back 20 minutes—the maximum safe jump—to fix things. Instead events erupt into more violence with a higher body count, then worse still on her next go-round. Finally Brian sends her back two hours, destroying his machine in the process. Karen changes everything by refusing Frank's offer of a ride, then tipping off the cops to arrest him.

In *Slipstream* (2005), Stuart Conway (Sean Astin) is an obnoxious government scientist who's stolen Slipstream, a hand-held time travel device that can send the user back up to ten minutes. When his attempt to flirt with bank teller Margaret (Verity Price) goes astray, he uses the device to send his consciousness back in time several minutes and start over, with no better luck.

FBI agents (and lovers) Tanner (Ivana Milicevic) and Jake (Kevin Otto) attempt to bust Conway. Then Briggs (Vinnie Jones) and his crew of robbers arrive and everything goes haywire. Conway is fatally shot, rewinds time and lives; Tanner, because she was touching Conway, goes back too. This changes things just enough that now Jake dies in the robbery and Briggs steals Slipstream. Hoping to save Jake, Tanner drags Conway along in her effort to recover Slipstream, even though he tells her that Jake's death is too far back to be changeable.

As the film progresses, the gang takes a city bus hostage, Briggs learns what Slipstream can do and his girlfriend (Victoria Bartlett) gets shot. Like Tanner, Briggs wants Conway to rewind time to save his love, but faces the same ten-minute barrier. After further misadventures, Conway licks the time limit and rewinds back to before the robbery. He gets a date with the teller, Tanner and Briggs have their loves back, and Briggs calls off the robbery.

Timescrimes (2007) stars Karra Elejalde as Hector, a happily married man who can't resist using his binoculars to check out a naked woman in the woods. After Hector's wife goes out, he gets a strange call, goes into the woods and finds the woman apparently unconscious. Now a man with a grotesque pink bandage covering his face stabs Hector. Fleeing, Hector stumbles across a strange laboratory where the sole worker directs him to hide in a tank. When Hector climbs out again, he discovers it's one hour earlier. The technician (Nacho Vigalondo) tells Hector he's now the world's first time traveler.

Hector calls home—the strange call he already received—then takes a car from the lot and drives back to his house. Pausing when he sees the young woman bicycling by, he's rear-ended and crashes into the woods. He takes the bandage from his stab wound to cover his face and realizes he's the bandage-faced man who already attacked him. The technician has warned him that changing events could be disastrous, so Hector re-enacts them, waiting for his past self and then stabbing him. With history secure, Hector returns home, pursues what he thinks is an intruder up to the roof and sends his own wife falling to her death. Desperate to save her, he returns to the lab and jumps back once again. To avoid changing history, he brings the cyclist to his house and dresses her up like his wife, then waits for his earlier self to send her running up to the roof to die. Hector's wife is saved and everything's fine, if you overlook the murder.

The teen heroes of *Minutemen* (2008)—nice guy Virgil (Jason Dolley), brainy Charlie (Luke Benward), surly Zeke (Nicholaus Braun) and motormouth Jeanette (Kara Crane)—are ordinary high school outcasts until Charlie invents a time machine that can go back up to 48 hours. Disguised as the masked Minutemen, the guys start jumping back and changing things whenever a fellow nerd makes a social gaffe or becomes the victim of a cool-kid prank. Steph (Chelsea Staub) and Derek (Steven R. McQueen), former friends of Virgil before they joined "the in crowd," peg Virgil as one of the Minutemen. Derek asks Virgil to help him by jumping back to prevent Steph from learning that Derek cheated on her. Virgil, hoping to hang with his old friends again, agrees.

Before Virgil can jump, Charlie discovers that their time trips have created a destructive wormhole. The Minutemen go through the wormhole to close it, landing on the day Virgil saved Charlie from bullies and thereby joined him as an outcast. Virgil realizes he can stay a cool kid if he stops himself from saving Charlie; after Charlie tells him how much their friendship matters, Virgil leaves the past unchanged. The guys close the wormhole and return to the present, where Steph dumps Derek for Virgil.

In *Misfits* (2009–13) we find a much less lovable group. Young adults are performing community service when a freak storm gives them superpowers: telepathy, invisibility or, in Curtis' (Nathan Stewart-Jarrett) case, the power to rewind time. When the storm turns their probation officer into a super-strong berserker, he kills the other Misfits. Curtis reboots the past few minutes to bring them back and kill their attacker. In another episode, Curtis jumps back to the night he and his girlfriend got busted for drugs—her life completely fell apart afterwards—and eventually changes things so only he gets arrested. As the storm super-charged a lot of people, several other characters with different time-warping power cropped up throughout the series. In the final episode, Jess (Karla Crome) is kidnapped by a stalker who pulls her a year into the future, when they're married with a baby. Jess's escape gets most of the cast killed, but before dying she sends a message back to her present-day self enabling her to change things.

The animated *Saving Santa* (2013) stars Martin Freeman as Bernard, an inept, insecure elf inventor. When his latest tinkering shuts down the North Pole's cloaking field, shipping magnate Neville Baddington (Tim Curry) locates Santa's workshop. He hopes to capture Santa's sleigh and use its tech for shipping, thereby impressing his odious mother Vera (Joan Collins). Baddington captures the Pole and Santa but Bernard uses the sleigh's time travel tech—how do you think Santa can be so many places in a single night?—to go back and warn everyone. Nobody believes him so Bernard goes back again and again, with no more success. Bernard does, however, gain confidence and finally saves the day with a device that gives perfect recall of Christmas memories. Subjecting Neville to the memory machine makes the businessman remember he loves Christmas and doesn't want to hurt it. Another Bernard invention wipes Vera's memory, after which Neville takes her away. Bernard finally has respect as an inventor and a hero.

Eureka!

Eureka (2006–12) was a SyFy Channel show set in the eponymous secret community where the government has gathered the country's greatest geniuses to work on the fringes of science. Lawman Jack Carter (Colin Ferguson) serves as sheriff, relying on common sense and nerve to make up for his utter cluelessness about science and technology.

At the start of the fourth season, an experimental wormhole generator accidentally contacts a similar device built by Trevor Grant (James Callis) in Eureka in 1947. Carter, Eureka administrator Allison Blake (Salli Richardson), engineer Henry Deacon (Joe Morton), deputy Jo Lupo (Erica Cerra) and nerdy Douglas Fargo (Neil Grayston) are all hurled back to the past. When they return, they discover that their actions in the past—not to mention bringing Grant forward with them—have changed Eureka in multiple ways. Allison's autistic son is completely normal; Jo is now head of security but her former boyfriend hates her; Fargo is Eureka's top man. Negotiating the new status quo took everyone several episodes, complicated by not being able to reveal it without triggering government protocols for time tampering (nothing pleasant). In the final episode, after the government shuts down Eureka's funding, Grant—now a tech billionaire—buys up the town to keep it running.

The Girls Who Leapt Through Time

Yasutaka Tsutsui's 1967 novella *The Girl Who Leapt Through Time* is the story of Kazuko, a junior high school student who catches someone in the school science lab, inhales a lavender-scented gas, and passes out. The next day, she and her friend Goro are hit by a truck; Kazuko wakes up two days earlier, which enables her to save Goro from the truck and prevent a fire from destroying his house. Kazuko feels that her powers make her more a freak than a hero, so she time-jumps back to the lab to find out what happened. She finds her friend Kazuo there; he tells her he's a time traveler, synthesizing the chemical that will return him to the future. Kazuo tells Kazuko he'll have to make everyone, including her, forget his existence, but promises he'll return someday to stay.

The story has been adopted multiple times in Japan, but only a couple of adaptations are available in the U.S. *The Little Girl Who Conquered Time* (1983), starring Tomoyo Harada as Kazuko, follows the opening of Tsutsui's story fairly closely: accidental exposure in the lab, saving Goro (Toshinori Omi), discovering that Kazuo Fukamachi (Ryoichi Takayanagi) is involved in what happened to her. Visiting Kazuo exposes her to the gas again and she bounces through time before returning. Kazuo explains he's from 2660, gathering pharmaceutical plants unavailable in his time. Kazuko's memories of him as a lifelong friend were only a mental implant, and now he erases them along with all other evidence he was there. The treatment doesn't erase Kazuko's feelings: As an adult, her heart can't make room for any other man. When she sees Kazuo walk past on another time visit, she pauses a second, then goes on with her lonely life.

In 2006, the story went anime as *The Girl Who Leapt Through Time*. Here, unlike the source novel, Makoto (Riisa Naka) discovers her powers—which require literally leaping to activate—and she's thrilled. She can sleep as late as she wants, then jump back to arrive at school on time; when her friend Chiaki (Takuya Ishida) asks her out, she makes repeated jumps back until she manages to duck the conversation. These indulgences eventually exhaust her power, which she regrets when she needs it to save her friend Kosuke's (Mitsutaka Itakura) life. Chiaki, the visitor from the future in this version, time-jumps to save Kosuke instead. This exhausts his own chronal power, so he's trapped in the present. Makoto realizes she loves Chiaki, and that due to the changes caused by his last jump, she has one leap left. She uses it to go back and prevent herself acquiring her powers, so Chiaki's power isn't exhausted. He tells Makoto he'll be waiting for her when she reaches his time the normal way.

Time Traveller—The Girl Who Leapt Through Time (2010) was more a sequel to the novella than an adaptation. Kazuko (Narumi Yasuda), now an adult scientist, has recreated the time travel formula even though she doesn't remember traveling in time. After an accident puts her in the hospital with severe injuries, she sends her daughter Akari (Riisa Naka) back to 1972 to deliver a message to Kazuo, reminding him of his promise to visit her again. Unfortunately, Akari lands in 1974. Amateur filmmaker Ryota (Akiyoshi Nakao) takes in the time-lost girl and helps her hunt for Kazuo, falling in love in the process. None of Kazuko's friends remember Kazuo, of course. Akari does meet her future father, but discovers she can't do anything to prevent her parents from separating.

Kazuo (Kanji Ishimaru) returns from the future to tell Akari that he'll take her home, after which he'll make everyone, including her, forget her presence in the past. He allows Akari to say goodbye to Ryota, but won't let her save him from dying in an accident. When he and Akari return to the present, Kazuo visits Kazuko, restoring her to full health before leaving again. Later, Akari discovers a copy of Ryota's 8mm film in her pocket. She can't remember where it came from, nor can she understand why watching it makes her cry so much.

Long-Distance Calls

In *Frequency* (2000), John Sullivan (Jim Caviezel) is a dour Queens cop whose love life is in the toilet. When he tinkers around with his late firefighter father's old ham radio, the decrepit vacuum-tube set picks up a signal from some weirdo in Queens who talks as if the 1969 World Series were happening right now. The weirdo is incredulous when John perfectly predicts the outcome of the first game. Finally John realizes he's talking to his father Frank (Dennis Quaid), a day before he died in a fire in 1969 (freak atmospheric conditions in both times make this possible). Frank doesn't believe a word of this, but while making a rescue the next day, he remembers John's prediction, adjusts his tactics and lives. In the present, John suddenly remembers two more decades of life with Frank, before his death from lung cancer in 1989.

Frank and John talk endlessly about John's life in the present, and bond as they never could before. However Frank's survival accidentally triggers other minor changes, one of which saves the life of the man who's secretly the "Nightingale Killer." The killer took the life of three nurses, but now John remembers a body count of ten, including John's mother Julie (Elizabeth Mitchell). Frank wants to take Julie and leave town but John tells him they have a duty to save the other victims. Working across time, the Sullivans identify cop Jack Shepard (Shawn Doyle) as the killer, but like so many other investigators in time travel stories, Frank winds up looking like the prime suspect. Frank does expose Shepard, then apparently kills him. Shepard survives to attack Frank and Julia in 1969 and John in the present. Frank drives off Shepard in the past, then older Frank shows up in the present to save John. In the final timeline, Frank and Julia are alive in the present and John is a happily married man. This became a TV series in 2016.

In *Cryptic* (2009), Jessie's (Jadin Gould) ninth-birthday gift from her mother (Jodi Thelen) is her first cell phone. After her mother's death in a freak electrical accident, Jessie stuffs the phone away. She comes across it by chance as she approaches 18 (played by Julie Carlson), sullen, angry and recovering from her father's (Toby Huss) physical abuse. On impulse Jessie dials her old number and gets a young girl she seems to have a lot in common with ... and after a couple more calls, realizes it's herself, though she doesn't tell Past-Jessie this. Every time she makes a call, Present-Jessie remembers receiving it in the past. She warns Past-Jessie about Mom's upcoming accident and realizes as they talk that their father arranged the "accident."

Past-Jessie saves Mom's life, but Mom winds up comatose. This ripples through Jessie's life so at 18 she's living with her boyfriend Damon (Johnny Pacar), formerly her platonic best friend, and never called her past self. When she stumbles across the phone, she realizes who the mystery caller in her childhood was and dials Past-Jessie again, despite a warning voice on the phone telling her not to. Past-Jessie discovers her father and his girlfriend trying to murder Mom. Dad tries to kill Jessie to cover things up, but a cop arrests him. Time ripples again: in the present, Jessie lives with her mom and everything's happy ... until Dad gets out of prison and shoots Jessie. Damon saves the day by using the phone to call Past-Jessie. This time when Dad arrives, Jessie's waiting with a gun ("This was the right ending!").

College student Haley Simmons' (Steffany Huckaby) life falls apart in *Disconnect* (2010) when her mother Sonya (Devorah Richards) dies of a heart attack. Three months later, playing with her mother's old toy phone, Haley and her best friend Cathy (Amanda Troop) discover they can call the past on it. After making prank calls to 1960, Haley calls her mother a few months in the past and warns her to go to the hospital. Nothing changes.

When Haley sees that the autopsy indicated a drug-and-alcohol overdose—something very out of character for Sonya—contributed to the death, she begins to suspect foul play. She starts calling people in the past to get their help, but each attempt makes things worse: Her boyfriend Dylan (Michael Muhney) gets arrested for killing Sonya, Haley's father is murdered and so is Cathy. Finally Haley calls Past-Haley, who arrives in time to save her mother from a crazy stalker strangling her. That saves Cathy, Dylan and Haley's father as well.

CHAPTER NINE

Love in a Time of Time Travel

"There is someone ... it's kind of a long-distance relationship."—The Lake House

The pain of being separated from the one you love is a classic romantic plot element. And what can separate two lovers more than time itself? Boy loves girl, girl loves boy back, but with 50 or 500 years separating them, how do they make it work?

Sometimes it doesn't. When it does, it usually requires that one of them give up their own time and move. Nobody has followed the concept of Lisa Goldstein's novel *The Dream Years*, in which the time-separated protagonists decide to keep to their own times but visit each other regularly.

As with most movie genres, many time travel films and TV series have a romantic subplot of some sort. The screen stories in this chapter put the romance front and center.

Romance movies frequently adopt an "all's fair in love and war" attitude toward characters' romantic tricks and tactics. That's reflected in the ethics most of these movies take to time-tampering. Like changing personal history, it's okay to change the past if you're a good person and it gets you the one you love. In *My Future Boyfriend* (2011), for instance, the time traveler's big obstacle is that the woman he loves is engaged—until he goes back in time to meet her first. That's a rough deal for her fiancé, but it's for true love, so the movie doesn't care.

Love and Death

In *Berkeley Square* (1933)—already mentioned in chapter three—American Peter Standish (Leslie Howard) is thrilled to move into the same London house his ancestor, namesake and look-alike owned in the Georgian era, an age Standish considers far superior to the modern world. Standish believes that on the anniversary of his ancestor's arrival in 1784, the two of them will trade places—and of course, he's right.

To avoid altering history, Standish proposes to his ancestor's future wife, Kate (Valerie Taylor). She accepts, but like the rest of London society she's soon alienated by Standish's strange slang, peculiar ways (he bathes every day!) and his uncanny knowledge of coming events. Kate's family worries that Standish is insane or possessed, except for Kate's sister Helen (Heather Angel), whom Peter eventually tells all to. They forget a connection so strong she can see the future through his eyes, but the modern world horrifies her. She tells Peter to return home: they can't be happy in each other's time, so they must trust they'll come together in "God's time." Peter snaps back to the present, where he learns that Helen, instead of marrying as in the original family history, chose to die a spinster. Peter likewise ends his own engagement, vowing to spend the rest of his life alone in the house where he loved Helen.

Most other cross-time love stories aspire to a union this side of the grave, but there are exceptions. In *Portrait of Jennie* (1948), frustrated painter Eben Adams (Joseph Cotten) is talented but uninspired until he meets Jennie (Jennifer Jones), a charming teenager. Despite the girl's odd habits—she refers to the New York of 30 years ago as if it were now—Eben is intrigued and sketches her, the first work he's done that rises above mere competence. Eben keeps meeting Jennie, but each time she's several years older. He begins work on a portrait of her that an art dealer (Ethel Barrymore) tells him has greatness in it. The evidence she really is from another time barely registers on Eben's love-smitten brain.

After Jennie leaves New York to stay with an aunt in Maine, Eben learns from one of Jennie's former teachers that he's in love with a woman who died years ago, in a Maine hurricane. Fearing the worst, Eben goes to Maine, rents a boat and goes out to save Jennie. A sudden storm dashes Eben's boat upon the rock; Jennie gets shipwrecked too, but as Eben pulls her to shore, she says he can't save her. Jennie tells him not to worry: There's no life until you find love, but once you do, there's no death. The storm sweeps Jennie to her death in the past, but Eben's portrait of his beloved will enshrine him in art history.

Somewhere in Time (1980) begins with college playwright Richard Collier (Christopher Reeve) meeting an elderly woman (Jane Seymour) who hands him a pocket watch and tells him to come back to her. Eight years later Collier spots a photograph of once-legendary actress and beauty Elise McKenna (Seymour) and falls in love. He learns that McKenna, a recluse since she left the theater in 1912, was the one who gave him the watch, dying immediately afterwards.

Collier consults Prof. Finney (Patrick Billingsley), who believes that Collier can hypnotize himself into crossing time by surrounding himself with clothes and items from 1912. (The professor's name is an in-joke on Jack Finney, whose *Time and Again* uses a similar method of travel.) Collier succeeds in crossing time, but winning Elise isn't easy. She resists Collier's charms and her manager (Christopher Plummer) tries driving him away before he distracts Elise from her career. Collier wins out, and Elise abandons her current tour to stay with him. They make love, but the next morning Collier finds a modern penny left in one pocket. His hypnotic spell snaps, sending him back to the present where he dies of heartbreak. (In the source novel, Collier was already terminally ill.) Elise greets him in the afterlife, where they depart into eternity together.

You Look Just Like Her

The House in the Square (1951) is a remake of *Berkeley Square*, keeping the basic plot but adding some new wrinkles. A lightning bolt is responsible for the time jump to 1784 and Standish (Tyrone Power) is a scientist who tries introducing future inventions to the past, *Connecticut Yankee*–style. The big change, though, is that after Standish leaves Helen (Ann Blyth) behind in the past, he meets Martha, Helen's exact double (Blyth again), in the present. He hasn't lost his love after all.[1]

Jane Seymour as Elise McKenna, the woman for whom Richard Collier (Christopher Reeve) gives up first his own time, then his life, in *Somewhere in Time* (1980).

This is a popular solution to loving someone in another time, first used in Bing Crosby's 1949 *Connecticut Yankee* and in many other films since; you'll find multiple examples such as *Forbidden Kingdom* and *Prehistoric Women* scattered through previous chapters. It doesn't make much sense, as a woman of Georgian England, Camelot or ancient China isn't going to be the same person as a modern-day look-alike. The gambit simply hopes that the visuals

("Look, she's identical! It's the very same actor!") will convince us to suspend any rational objections.

Usually the twist is just implausible. Sometimes it's worse than that, as in *Forbidden Kingdom*, which has the protagonist meet the double right after the original woman dies in his arms. Or consider *The Edge of the Garden* (2011) in which the male lead is paired up with the granddaughter of his lost love. Workaholic Brian Connor (Rob Estes) takes a job in rural Maine to slow down. He discovers a locket in an old house, then meets the owner, Nora (Sarah Manninen), in the garden that night. Nora's hand passes through the locket when she reaches for it, not because she's a ghost but because she's living in 1960. The two connect emotionally even though Nora's married to the abusive Tom (David Lewis) in her own time. When Nora takes ill, Brian's able to get a modern diagnosis of Lyme disease and recommend the right treatment.

Brian begins researching Nora and learns from local legend that Tom, who's still alive, supposedly burned down the house with her inside it. What really starts the fire is the locket falling into Brian's fireplace and channeling the flames into 1960. Brian saves Nora—Tom dies—and meets her in the present as a happily married grandmother. Who it turns out has been grooming her look-alike granddaughter to take her place in Tom's heart.

Relocation Solution

The simple solution to the time-divided couple staying together is for one of them to relocate. Invariably, the relocation involves one partner moving to the past, or if from the future, to our present. Only the *Bill & Ted* films have the partner from the past move to the present. Some examples:

In *Cavegirl* (1985), Rex (Daniel Roebuck), a nerdy student studying *homo erectus*, is the butt of endless jokes by his brain-dead classmates. During a field trip, Rex stumbles out of an excavation into prehistory. He meets and falls hard for sexy cave girl Eba (Cindy Ann Thompson), who seems equally charmed by him. Rex has to cope with her baffled tribe, the language barrier, his own awkwardness, and finally Eba getting kidnapped by a tribe of cannibals. Rex saves her by using his present-day technology to scare off the tribe, then returns through a time rift to the present. Nobody believes Rex's tale, but he doesn't really care. He bids his classmates goodbye and returns to Eba's loving embrace.

In *Kate & Leopold* (2001), Leopold (Hugh Jackman) is an 1876 duke and science buff being pressured by his uncle into a wealthy marriage. When he finds a stranger (Liev Schreiber) ruffling through his papers, Leopold pursues him and ends up in the 21st century. The stranger explains that he's Leopold's descendant Stuart, a physicist who's figured out how to predict when wormholes open into the past. Stuart adds that there won't be a return wormhole to 1876 for another week, so Leopold's stuck in modern New York. That's quite time enough for Stuart's cynical ex-girlfriend Kate (Meg Ryan) to meet Leopold as he explores the city (Jackman does a wonderful job conveying the duke's alternating delight and bafflement). Kate's attracted to Leopold, but more focused on winning a promotion at her marketing firm and negotiating a possible relationship with her boss (Bradley Whitford). Nevertheless she and Leopold eventually fall in love.

The duke agrees to lend his elegant presence to a butter-substitute commercial that will seal Kate's promotion, but quits when he actually tastes the product. He lectures Kate on the immorality of marketing products she doesn't believe in, and they break up. Leopold returns to 1876, resigned to marrying rich, while Kate accepts the promotion. Stuart, however, discovers old photographs that show Kate in 1876. Realizing her future lies in the past, Kate races through the wormhole and reconciles with Leopold.

Secret (2007) is a Chinese film in which piano student Ye Xiang Lun (Jay Chou) falls for Lu (Lun Mei Gwei), a shy pianist nobody else seems to know. After Lu mysteriously vanishes from his life, Ye learns the truth: Lu attended the school 20 years ago, and came to the present via a magical piece of music. It also made her invisible to everyone else. Lu cannot return to the present, so Ye finds the magic musical score before it's buried in a demolished building. He uses it to join her.

The Past Is a Better Place

In some films, protagonists relocate because they've not only fallen in love with someone in the past, they've fallen in love with the past itself. It's nicer. Sweeter. More innocent. More moral. Of course, the sweetness and niceness of past eras depends a lot on your money, class and race, but nostalgic films avoid pointing that out.

This also has a tradition in print fiction: Jack Finney's classic *Time and Again* has the hero relocate as much out of fondness for the 1890s as for the girl he loves. Ditto *Second Sight* by David Williams, the basis for the 1979 film *The Two Worlds of Jennie Logan* (1979)

A 1954 film adaptation of the Broadway musical, *Brigadoon* stars Gene Kelly and Van Johnson as Tommy and Jeff, vacationers in the Scottish Highlands who stumble onto a curiously old-fashioned village. Tommy loves quaint little Brigadoon, and he's particularly taken with lovely Fiona (Cyd Charisse), but he's puzzled why she fears leaving the village boundaries. Eventually the guys learn that two centuries ago, Brigadoon's saintly pastor vowed to save his village from the corruption of modernity. God granted the pastor's prayers, so every night Brigadoon leaps 100 years into the future; the town doesn't exist the rest of the century, so the modern world will never touch it. As Brigadoon can accept new residents, Tommy contemplates staying with Fiona despite his engagement back in New York.

Disgruntled villager Archie (Tudor Owen) doesn't see the magic as a gift. He's lost the woman he loves to another man, and he'll never be able to start over elsewhere. Archie decides to leave even though any villager doing so will cause Brigadoon to vanish forever. Jeff accidentally kills Archie, saving Brigadoon, but unsettling Tommy, who returns with Jeff to New York. Tommy can't forget Fiona, though, so he returns to Scotland. The power of love brings the village back from beyond, and Tommy joins Fiona forever.

A 1966 TV version with Robert Goulet and Peter Falk as Tommy and Jeff included more of the original score than the film did, and offered a different reason for the magic (fleeing the witch-hunting hysteria of the 1600s).

Unusually it's the time traveler in *The Two Worlds of Jennie Logan* who's someone's exact double. Jennie (Lindsay Wagner) is struggling to rebuild her marriage after her husband Michael's (Alan Feinstein) affair when she discovers an 1890s dress in the attic of their Victorian home. When Jennie puts it on, it transports her to the 19th century where she meets her home's former owner, widowed artist David Reynolds (Marc Singer). As she's a dead ringer for David's dead wife, David assumes she's a ghost (curiously nobody else ever notices a resemblance). After repeated visits, David realizes otherwise.

The two fall in love to the displeasure of David's sister-in-law Elizabeth (Linda Grey), who wants David for herself. Back in the present, Michael thinks Jennie's going crazy. Researching David, Jennie learns he died dueling with his father-in-law over Elizabeth's honor. David refuses to avoid the duel, but on the day of his death, Jennie meets the aged Elizabeth in the present. She confesses she's the one who shot David, out of jealousy. Jennie rushes into the past and takes the bullet for her love; in the present, Michael finds Jennie dead in the dress in the attic. Later, though, he discovers paintings hidden behind the walls that prove Jennie survived to live a long, happy life with David.

For All Time (2000) is an intensely nostalgic film in the Jack Finney tradition, though nominally based on *The Twilight Zone*'s "A Stop at Willoughby." In that episode, a stressed-out commuter (James Daly) finds his train stopping at Willoughby, an old-fashioned small town where everyone knows him; when stress finally kills the man, he's able to stay in Willoughby for good (so it's an afterlife rather than time travel). In *For All Time*, Charlie Lattimer (Mark Harmon) is a stressed-out, miserable St. Louis commuter. Charlie buys a conductor's pocket watch from antiques dealer (Bill Cobbs), who next turns up as the conductor of Charlie's train. The conductor invites Charlie to get off at Summerville, an 1896 town that appears when Charlie checks the watch.

Once in Summerville, Charlie falls in love with the low-key, slow-paced life there, and with newspaper editor Laura Brown (Mary McDonnell). He returns to his life in the present with his careerist wife Chris (Catherine Hicks) but keeps visiting Summerville. The conductor warns Charlie the train won't stop there forever.

When Charlie tells Laura he's married, she rejects him. Charlie returns to the present, smashes the watch, but also leaves his job and his marriage. He then learns his time trips changed history so Laura will die in a gas main explosion. Charlie gets the watch working again, boards the train and reaches Summerville in time to save her. In the timeline that results, Chris is a happy, contented mother with a different husband. A historical photo in one of her books shows Charlie and Laura as husband and wife.

Future Lovers

In a few films, the time traveler is someone from the future falling in love with a protagonist in the present and eventually relocating to Now.

In *Happy Accidents* (2000), the relocation has already happened when the story starts. Ruby Weaver (Marisa Tomei) is delighted when she meets sweet, charming Sam (Vincent D'Onofrio), so different from the usual screwed-up men she falls for. Within a week she lets him move in with her, though she can't understand why the mundane details of life seem to astonish him. (D'Onofrio does an amazing job portraying someone out of step with the present.) Eventually Sam tells her that he's from 2471, fell in love with her photo and used illegal technology to time travel back and find her. By a "happy accident" he succeeded.

Ruby knows he must be crazy or lying, but the fantasy charms her enough to stay with him. She's also supportive during his occasional bouts of nausea, which Sam blames on time briefly rewinding around him as a time-travel side effect. Ruby tells her therapist (Holland Taylor) she worries that she's picked the wrong man again. Even though the therapist is another time traveler (there are lots of them living among us), she doesn't tell Ruby that Sam's on the level. Sam finally tells Ruby he came to her hoping to save her from her imminent death in a traffic accident. Changing the past requires powerful emotion, so they can succeed if their love is strong enough. Despite promising to stay in the apartment when the time rolls around, Ruby ends up running out and gets hit. Sam has another time-rewind attack which buys him the seconds to save her life and cheat fate.

The future visitor in *11 Minutes Ago* (2009) is Pack (Ian Michaels), a scientist from 48 years ahead. Visiting the present for an air sample he needs, he's bemused to find his laboratory is now a family home and the scene of a big wedding reception. Stranger still, everyone there already knows him from earlier in the evening. Pack can't figure out why he'd bother to jump back there again, as it takes months to prep for a time trip, and each jump only lasts 11 minutes.

It becomes clearer when he meets Cynthia (Christina Mauro) who remembers him very well. As Pack keeps jumping back in time, he finds himself falling in love with her (and having a quickie in a closet) even though with each jump back, Cynthia knows him less. After Pack introduces himself to Cynthia at the beginning of the evening, he realizes he doesn't want to leave her. He stays past his 11-minute window, stranding him in the present, and hides until all his previous time jumps have finished. At the evening's end he meets Cynthia again to begin a life together.

In *My Future Boyfriend* (2011), PAX 497 (Barry Watson), an inhabitant of the ultra-rational 32nd century, discovers an ancient romance novel by Elizabeth Barrett (Sara Rue) which fascinates him with its unknown (to him) concepts such as "sex" and "love." He travels to her time to ask her what these things are, and of course falls in love with her. While Elizabeth assumes that Pax is nuts, she starts reciprocating his feelings, even though she's already engaged.

The 21st century money Pax brought with him comes from post–2011, which gets him arrested for counterfeiting. Pax's superior Bob (Fred Willard) frees Pax, who returns to Elizabeth and asks her to join him in the future. Elizabeth still thinks he's crazy so she refuses. Both men disappear in front of her, but it's too late to take Pax back. Except it isn't: Pax goes back to several months before he first met Elizabeth and wins her heart before she meets her fiancé.

Please Mr. Postman

In some time travel love affairs, the lovers can't physically cross the years, they can only communicate. (*The Caller* and *Frequency* in previous chapters employ the same premise.)

The first such film is *The Love Letter* (1998), based on a Jack Finney short story. Scotty Corrigan (Campbell Scott) buys an antique desk and in a secret compartment discovers an unmailed letter from 1863. The writer, aspiring poet Elizabeth Whitcomb (Jennifer Jason Leigh), is being pressured into a loveless marriage and has addressed the letter to the fantasy lover she longs to meet. Scotty, intrigued, writes a response, mailing it through the town's

Civil War–era post office. The letter reaches Elizabeth, who puts her answer in the desk, where Scotty finds it. In the Finney story, the exchange lasts a couple of letters; in the film, they become regular correspondents and fall in love. Scotty's fiancée Deborah (Daphne Ashbrook) realizes she's losing him but doesn't understand why.

After an accident renders Scotty comatose, Elizabeth finds love in her own time with a Union officer, Denby, Scotty's double. (It's implied that the two men are in some fashion one.) After Scotty recovers, he researches Denby and discovers that he dies at Gettysburg. Scotty tries to warn Elizabeth in time to save Denby, but fails. Scotty breaks up with Deborah; then the post office burns down, ending the correspondence with Elizabeth. Scotty learns his letters inspired Elizabeth to reject her unwanted suitor, live single and become a poet. While visiting her grave, Scott meets her look-alike, Beth (Leigh). A new romance blooms.

The Korean film *Il Mare* (2000) has less trouble bringing the lovers together as they're only two years apart. In 1999, Kim Eun-joo (Jun Ji-hyun), who recently lost her boyfriend when she refused to follow him to the U.S., moves out of her waterfront home. She leaves a note in the mailbox asking the next tenant to forward her mail. Han Sung-hyun (Lee Jung-jae) replies with a letter saying he found her note in the mailbox, but in 1997. Both suspect a trick, both come to realize otherwise, and both lonely people start falling in love. Han runs into Kim in 1997, but she's still with her boyfriend and doesn't notice him.

Kim and Han make a date to meet—two years in the future for Han—but Han never shows. In Kim's next letter she ends the relationship, but asks Han to convince Past-Kim to stay with her boyfriend. Kim then discovers the reason Han missed their date is that he was killed in a car accident while going to see Past-Kim. Kim realizes she loves him and returns to the lake house to leave him a warning about the accident. She spends the night by the mailbox waiting ... and in the morning, Han arrives. (It would surely make more sense to have him make the original date, but that's admittedly less dramatic.)

If this sounds familiar, that's probably because in 2006 it became *The Lake House* with Sandra Bullock and Keanu Reeves as the correspondents, Dr. Kate Forster and architect Alex Wyler. This packs in a lot more subplot about Kate's relationship issues and Alex's troubled relationship with his arrogant father (Christopher Plummer). The temporal games are more complicated, too. For instance, when Alex meets Kate in her past, his knowledge of her helps him connect and they have a make-out session. Early in the film, Kate spends Valentine's Day 2000 trying and failing to save an accident victim; she realizes at the end of the film it was Alex, and again saves him with a final letter.

The Filipino *Moments of Love* (2006) goes with phone calls rather than snail mail. Shortly after elderly Rosa (Gloria Romero) saves Marco (Dingdong Dantes) from being hit by a car—she gets hit instead and becomes comatose—Marco begins chatting on the phone with someone named Divina (Iza Calzado). They fall for each other despite Divina's impending marriage to brutal Juancho (Paolo Contis) and Marco's interest in Rosa's granddaughter Lianne (Karylle). When Marco and Divina agree to meet at a nearby lake, neither one shows—and Marco discovers it's because Divina lives in 1957. She scoffs until Marco correctly predicts the death of the Filipino president.

Marco urges Divina to flee Juancho to Manila and wait for Marco there, despite the age difference she'll have in the present. When Marco learns she drowned on the trip to Manila during a storm, he tells Lianne the whole story. He adds that while he loved Davina, he's now ready to love a woman he can actually be with.

When Rosa recovers, Lianne takes Marco to meet her—and, of course, Rosa is Divina. Surviving the sinking, she let the world think her dead to escape Juancho. Although she eventually fell in love and married (now widowed), she remembered Marco's story about his accident and went to the site of the accident to save him. She embraces Marco and gives her blessing to his relationship to Lianne.

Lovers in Two Times

Two television series feature a cross-time love where one partner is an adulterer. In *Goodnight Sweetheart* (1993–99), Gary Sparrow (Nicholas Lyndhurst) walks down a London alley in the present and emerges, without explanation, in 1940. He soon figures out how to travel back and forth, and after meeting Phoebe (Dervla Kirwan) in the past he begins making regular trips, even though he's married to Yvonne (Michelle Holmes) in the present. Stories involve Gary protecting Phoebe and her family with his knowledge of World War II events, bringing Phoebe chocolates and nylons unavailable in wartime Britain, and selling items from the past as collectibles in the present. In the final episode, the time portal closes, trapping Gary in the past with Phoebe for good.

Diana Gabaldon's best-selling *Outlander* adventures, which came to TV in 2014, broke a great many romance conventions: Her protagonist, nurse Claire Randall (Caitriona Balfe), is older and more experienced than the virginal hero, Jamie Fraser (Sam Heughan), and Claire is married to another man, Frank (Tobias Menzies). During the Randalls' belated honeymoon in post–World War II Scotland, Claire steps inside a stone circle and steps out in the 1700s. With no way home, she uses her healing skills to join the local Mackenzie clan, which convinces Black Jack Randall (Menzies again), Frank's ancestor, that she's working with the Scots rebels against England. Jamie marries Claire to give her legal protection against Randall, but their feelings soon go beyond a marriage of convenience. Claire does indeed becomes involved in the Jacobite rebellion, while Frank, back in the present, struggles to find out what happened to her. If the series lasts and follows the books, he'll learn eventually.

Weird Love

Unlike the 1980 adaptation of *The Lathe of Heaven*—see chapter seven—the 2002 version is a love story. As in the book and first adaptation, George Orr (Lukas Haas) is a young man in an overpopulated future whose dreams can alter reality. George's court-appointed psychiatrist, Haber (James Caan), begins controlling George's dreams to "improve" the world—reduce overpopulation, for instance—with unforeseen side effects (the population is low because of a pandemic). Haber also uses the dreams to make himself head of the now world-famous Haber Institute.

Unlike the previous versions of *Lathe*, George knew his public defender Heather (Lisa Bonet) before they met, because she was his lover until a time shift made them strangers. Even so, she feels a connection with George, who tells her they're always drawn together, no matter how the timeline changes. When another time change makes Heather an A-list attorney who's never met George, they're brought together again and go on the run from

Haber. The psychiatrist uses the institute's technology to duplicate George's powers so he can shape the world himself, but his mind snaps, sending reality sliding into chaos. Heather dies, but when time stabilizes, she's alive again as a waitress. Once again she and George are attracted to each other.

From top to bottom, **the core cast of the 2002** *Lathe of Heaven*: **James Caan as Haber, Lisa Bonet as Heather, Lukas Haas as George, and David Straitharn as Mannie.**

A Necklace for Julia (2006) has a man traveling through time hunting his vanished lover. Despite its recent vintage, this low-budget indie film isn't on DVD at time of writing and there's no information available beyond the names of the cast and crew.[2]

The Time Traveler's Wife (2009) unsuccessfully adapts the best-selling novel about Henry Detamble (Eric Bana), who, starting in childhood, randomly jumps in time due to a genetic abnormality. When he materializes naked in a library—clothes don't travel—and meets Clare (Rachel McAdams), she invites him to dinner, then into her bed. Clare reveals that she's known and loved Henry since he materialized next to her when she was a child (that scene, cute in the novel, looks creepy onscreen). They end up marrying despite the problems of living their lives out of synch.

When Clare has a miscarriage, Henry worries that this was a side effect of his genetics and gets a vasectomy to prevent another pregnancy. He doesn't consult Clare first and she's furious—so much so that when Henry's pre-vasectomy self turns up in the present, Clare sleeps with him and becomes pregnant again. Henry's worries vanish when their daughter Alba (Hailey McCann) arrives from the future: She's not only healthy, she can control her time jumps. The family lives happily until a time trip leads to Henry accidentally getting shot and killed. Several years later, his younger self visits Clare and Alba for a proper farewell.

In *Love & Teleportation* (2013), Brian Owens (Jan Van Sickle) is a former big-shot physicist reduced to teaching who unexpectedly falls in love with fellow teacher Shelly (Robin DeMarco). Brian has two problems, one being that his experimental teleporter destroys whatever he sends through it; the other, that the loan shark who financed his research wants the money back, and Brian doesn't have it. As an object lesson, the lender's goons force Shelly into the teleporter. Her apparent destruction leaves Brian grief-stricken until his elderly neighbor (Adair Jameson) reveals that she *is* Shelly. The teleporter is actually a time machine that materialized Shelly in 1971. She had a good enough life in the past she didn't want to intervene and prevent herself going back. Now that the time-jump has happened, she gives Brian enough money to pay off the loan shark. Instead of continuing his research, Brian ignores Shelly's request not to tamper with her new life and heads back into the past for her.

Tim (Domhnall Gleeson) learns at the start of *About Time* (2013) that the men in his family can travel back into their own past simply by finding somewhere dark and quiet and wishing (though unlike most do-overs, they travel back physically, after which their past body disappears or something). His father (Bill Nighy) admits he's never done anything much with it except to find time to read, but Tim's determined to use the power to find love. He discovers that if you're dating the wrong person, doing the date over won't magically create romance.

When Tim meets Mary (Rachel McAdams), they have the right stuff, but it still isn't easy. They meet in the normal way, and hit it off, but then Tim goes back to help out a friend on the same night, erasing his encounter with Mary. He finds her again, but now she has a boyfriend. After repeated jumps and do-overs, Tim wins her love again and they marry. While Tim keeps tinkering with time—to see his dying father more often, to help his sister straighten out her life—he eventually stops, deciding life with Mary is too wonderful to tamper with.

In *Juko's Time Machine* (2011), Juko (Nathan Cozzolino) has been in love with Rory

(Zibby Allen) since third grade, but they're now in their twenties and he's always frozen up when the time comes to tell her. Now that she's newly married, it seems the time has gone for good. Juko's best friend Jed (Alex Moggridge) builds a time machine so that Juko can go back one year and tell Rory he loves her.

The first attempt is a social disaster, so Jed and Juko try again ... and again ... which is tricky as making eye contact with their counterparts would be fatal. ("The exponent goes to infinity!") Finally Juko has the perfect opportunity to kiss Rory—and freezes. Rory kicks him out, and Jed declares that he's done waiting for Juko to grow up and get his act together. As Jed storms away, he locks eyes with one of his counterparts and both vanish.

Jed's wife Nina (Katie Sigismund) is furious when Juko tells her this. Juko doesn't believe he can work the time machine by himself, but realizing how much Jed means to him, he figures it out. He and Nina go back and with her running interference between counterparts, they save Jed. Juko finally delivers that kiss and wins Rory. Jed and Nina return to the present, but Juko stays in the past until the happy couples meet up a year later. (It's unclear what happened to Juko's past self.)

The Infinite Man (2014) is another romance with multiple copies running into each other. Dean (Josh McConville), an awkward, nervous control freak, dumps his girlfriend Lana (Hannah Marshall) in the erroneous belief she's cheating on him with her ex (Alex Dimitriades). A year later he's still regretting that mistake, so he asks Lana to join him on a time trip that will let them fix their last day together.

Despite having to dodge their past selves, things go well until another version of Dean shows up and steals Lana away. Dean-2 assures Dean-1 that a year later, he'll be Dean-2 and get Lana back. When Dean-1 does come back in time with Lana again, he tells her all they have to do to avoid further paradoxes is hole up for a year until their various past selves have all jumped into time. More counterparts show up, including Alex's ex, and Dean's problems multiply. Ultimately his obsessiveness at trying to make it work out perfectly drives Lana away. Dean realizes he's not ready for a relationship, but tells Lana he'll be back when he's matured. As Dean walks away, another Dean shows up with flowers and chocolates, finally ready for love.

The One That Got Away

Several movies focus on an alternate timeline where the protagonist picks a different spouse, or makes a different choice between marriage and career. As this is often stereotyped as a woman's issue, it's not surprising that only a few of these films confront men with that dilemma. Most of them don't involve actual travel to the past; instead, history is magically realigned to create a new reality.

In *Turn Back the Clock* (1933), Joe (Lee Tracy) is a New York druggist and World War I veteran married to Mary (Mae Clarke), whom he chose over the wealthy Elvina (Peggy Shannon). When Joe meets Elvina's husband, his old buddy Ted (Otto Kruger), the foursome go out together, which reminds Joe how rich marrying Elvina would have made him. A car hits Joe and he wakes up 20 years earlier, and now seizes the chance to marry Elvina and go into business with her father. While Joe's anachronisms confound people (he assumes "the war" means World War I rather than the Spanish-American War), his knowledge of future trends makes him even wealthier. Joe also tries to improve society, but fails: His efforts to expose corruption and profiteering in World War I are dismissed as "defeatist"; he warns people that the stock market is going to crash, but nobody believes him. Elvina cheats on him, just as she cheated on Ted. When Joe wakes up—it was just a dream—he realizes Mary was always his true soulmate.

In *Eve's Christmas* (2004), Eve (Elisa Donovan) breaks up with her fiancé Scott (Sebastian Spence) on the eve of their 1996 wedding so that she can take a Manhattan job. Eight years later, she's a marketing superstar but single and lonely, and her adulterous boss just ended their relationship. Her guardian angel (Peter Williams) misinterprets Eve's drunken Christmas wish and sends her back eight Christmases to do things over.

Eve's amazed by how different things seem—was her mother always this awesome?—and rediscovers how wonderful Scott is. Even so, when she gets the job offer, she contemplates taking it, although she knows Scott will never walk away from his family's local bookstore. Finally accepting the fact that she loves Scott more than her career, she puts her marketing skills in the store's service, with the help of some new technology called the Internet. Scott and Eve get married, then she wakes up in the present to discover she helped turn the store into a successful national retail chain.

In the opening scene of *Family Man* (2000) we see Jack (Nicolas Cage) promising his girlfriend Kate (Téa Leoni) that spending a year apart working on their respective careers won't affect their marriage plans. Fast-forward to the present when Jack is single and loving it, a ruthless Wall Street shark, who has no qualms about ordering his staff in for a Christmas Day meeting. On Christmas Eve he impulsively talks an armed punk, Cash (Don Cheadle), out of shooting a store owner, then discovers that the punk is an angel. Cash repays Jack's act of decency by changing his life: He's now married to Kate and running his father-in-law's (Harve Presnell) tire store.

Jack's horrified to learn he lives a life of middle-class income, retail sales, domestic duties and non-bespoke clothes, but he also finds himself falling in love with Kate all over again. By the time Cash takes him home, Jack doesn't want to leave, but nevertheless he wakes up in his old life on Christmas morning. Jack hunts down Kate and finds she's an A-list lawyer leaving for a job in Paris. The movie makes it clear this Kate is not the same person as alt-Kate (a refreshing insight in films like this), but Jack's still interested. By the ending credits, it looks like some type of romance will resume.

In *Me Myself I* (1999), successful freelance writer Pamela (Rachel Griffiths) is single at 30 and still wondering what would have happened if she hadn't broken up with boyfriend Robert (David Roberts). After a car hits Pamela, she wakes up in the home of an alt-Pamela who did marry Robert—and who then vanishes into Pamela's timeline, leaving the writer saddled with a husband and three kids. Like *Family Man*'s Jack, Pamela eventually learns to enjoy her new life, but that life is much less ideal. Pam and Robert have both strayed, Robert frequently acts like a jerk. Pam returns to writing and has an affair with fellow writer Ben (Sandy Winton). She breaks it off in guilt and begins working to fix her new life. Just as Robert rediscovers his love for her, alt-Pam returns, apologizing for wanting to explore her own road not taken. The two women resume their old lives with new enthusiasm, and Pam finds love with Ben's double.

Comfort and Joy's (2003) corporate powerhouse, Jane Berry (Nancy McKeon), returns to consciousness after a car crash to discover she's suddenly a stay-at-home mother of two, married to Sam (Steven Eckholdt). Having no way back to her real life, she gradually adapts, then comes to enjoy her new lifestyle. (Unlike *Family Man*'s Jack, Jane was clearly miserable when she was unmarried.) After Sam sticks up for Jane against her overbearing mother (Dixie Carter), Jane finally falls in love with him—at which point she finds herself back in her wrecked car, single again. But Sam, seeing the wreck, stops and helps her out...

In *The Christmas Clause* (2008), attorney Sophie Kelly (Lea Thompson) already has the family, but between the kids, husband Dave (Andrew Airlie) and a demanding boss, she's burning out. When she wishes she could have an unmarried friend's life, an apprentice angel (Doug Abrahams) grants her wish: Sophie's now single, a senior partner at her high-powered firm, and her kids no longer exist. That last part horrifies her, but the angel says he can't undo the wish until Sophie realizes what she truly values. Finally Sophie sees that her children are her greatest treasure, and that in trying to have it all, she's been neglecting them. (From what we saw of her life, that isn't true.) That insight restores the original timeline. Sophie quits her job to open a small private practice.

Before You Say "I Do" (2009) works a variation on the formula as ad man George Murray (David Sutcliffe) wants to fix someone else's marital mistake. His girlfriend Jane's (Jennifer Westfeldt) first marriage to womanizing Doug (Jeff Roop) was so painful that when George proposes, Jane breaks up with him rather than marry again. George wishes he could save Jane from ever having married Doug, and after yet another convenient car accident, he wakes up in 1999, shortly before Jane's wedding.

George goes to work for the same alternative newspaper as Jane, who's astonished how well the two of them mesh. Still, she's not about to dump Doug for a guy she just met. George tries to expose Doug's cheating, but Doug covers it up. At the last minute, George crashes Jane's wedding and opens her eyes to the truth. She agrees to marry George, and after another accident he wakes up back in the present, on his tenth anniversary with Jane.

What If… (2010) puts a Christian spin on *Family Man*, following most of the plot beats exactly. Ben (Kevin Sorbo) and Wendy (Kristy Swanson) separate after college so he can get his professional career under way, after which they'll marry and found a ministry. Fifteen years later, Ben's a lapsed Christian and successful businessman. Then he meets angel Mike (John Ratzenberger) and wakes up as a minister married to Wendy with two kids. Ben isn't happy about the changes, but Mike informs him this is God's plan for his life, a plan Mike rejected when he dumped Wendy and turned secular. Like *Family Man*'s Jack, Ben eventually comes to love his new life, at which point God sends him back to the old. Ben rushes to reunite with Wendy and eight years later Ben's a happily married father who's finally living his life in harmony with God's wishes.

Holidaze (2013) stars Jennie Garth as Melody, a rising executive at the Save More big-box chain. To land a big promotion, Melody has to sell her home town on approving the chain's 100th store. She heads home for Thanksgiving, only to discover that Save More will have to demolish her ex-fiancé Carter's (Cameron Mathison) bed-and-breakfast to build a store. After a nasty fall (no car accident this time), Melody wakes up married to Carter. Unlike *Comfort and Joy*'s Jane. Melody didn't lose her ambitions in the alternate life—she's running her mother's cafe as a locally sourced organic business about to go to franchise. After coming to love her new life, Melody uses her inside knowledge of Save More to spike the corporation's plans when they apply for a building permit. Returning to the original timeline, Melody wins Carter back and once again thwarts Save More's plans. Her savvy impresses the chain's CEO, who agrees to cancel the store if Melody sets up a chain of organic cafes in partnership with Save More.

A Snow Globe Christmas (2013) dips the *Family Man* premise in Christmas treacle. Meg (Alicia Witt) is a hard-driving TV-movie producer who won't ease up her staff's workload at the holidays, but secretly longs for a perfect Christmas like the one captured in her favorite snow globe. The mysterious Sal (Christina Milian) grants Meg's wish, transporting her to a timeline where Meg stayed with her old boyfriend Ted (Douglas Faison), has two kids and lives in an idyllic Christmas community.

Although Meg begins enjoying her new life, her cynical ways soon ruin the community. For example she unintentionally inspires a businessman to sell off the local forest land for a ski resort. Meg almost quits the fantasy world in dismay, but finds a way to fix things instead. Sal then returns her to the old timeline where Meg meets Ted for real; ten years later, they indeed have two kids. We learn that Sal is Ted's mother's ghost, giving the couple the life they were supposed to have.

95ers: Time Runners (2014) has a lot of subplots jumbled together. The core story involves Sally (Alesandra Durham), an FBI profiler and control freak who can rewind time by a few seconds at a shot, and her husband Horatio (Joel Bishop), a government physicist who's secretly investigating her powers. After Horatio's death, Sally discovers that he was tracking various other freak events, and that he was forced by his mysterious employer to test out a time travel project.

Widowed and pregnant, Sally feels her life spiraling out of control and wishes she'd never met Horatio. Her boss Grandon (Terence Goodman) invites her to use the time travel project to make that happen. She does so and immediately regrets it, but Grandon won't let her undo the undoing. Sally now finds herself fading from existence in favor of her alternate never-married self. In between all this, people in a hi-tech control room shout intensely about how Sally is the nexus of a dangerous time paradox.

Reading Horatio's journal, Sally learns she acquired her powers from a time rift created by the project. When Sally reads how Horatio, despite his agenda, genuinely loved her, she's inspired to break into the time project and restore her marriage. With the help of one of the control room guys, Sally succeeds, so Horatio is alive and there for her when the baby is born. Sally's timeline is now so convoluted, Grandon's people don't dare tamper with her past again. We close in the control room, where it turns out that Future Sally is running the show.

Back to Christmas (2014) has yet another lonely woman—Allie (Kelly Overton)—working on Christmas Eve and wishing she hadn't dumped her boyfriend Cam (Michael Muhney) a year earlier when he didn't give her the ring she expected. Christmas angel Ginny (Jennifer Elise Cox) sends Allie back to Christmas Eve Past to do it over. Events don't play out exactly the same and Allie begins to see that Cam has none of Allie's passion for Christmas with family or having kids, plus he's irrationally jealous of Alison's childhood friend Nick (Jonathan Patrick Moore). Ultimately Allie realizes that she and Nick are meant to be. She dumps Cam, kisses Nick, then wakes up in the present with him, living a life she loves.

Like Sophie in *Christmas Clause*, the problem for Sharon Holden (Olivia D'Abo) in *A Christmas Eve Miracle* (2015) is that kids plus husband plus career (advertising) is burning her out. And that's before she loses her phone during Christmas vacation, misses a key teleconference, and blames herself for her son's injuries when he goes hunting for the phone. Sharon wishes she'd never had kids and, presto!, her husband is a Wall Street wizard instead of a stay-at-home dad, and the Holdens are so wealthy they can indulge their every whim. Their kids turn up as another couple's children, but far more spoiled and selfish. Eventually Sharon comes to appreciate her old life, which gives her the power to undo the wish. She tells her boss she's taking extra holiday time and discovers she's such a valued employee that her boss is okay with that.

Other Timelines, Other Loves

Based on John Wyndham's "Random Quest," the parallel world film *Quest for Love* (1971) uses the "fall in love with your previous love's exact double" twist to let the hero have a tragic love affair that still ends happily. Physicist Colin Trafford (Tom Bell), knocked cold during an experiment, wakes up in a London club where everyone, including his best friend Tom (Denholm Elliott), insists that Colin's a brilliant though obnoxious writer, not a scientist. In this timeline, World War II and the Vietnam War never happened; Mt. Everest has never been climbed; and John F. Kennedy is still alive, heading the League of Nations.

Colin perks up when he meets "his" stunning wife Ottilie (Joan Collins) only to discover she despises his counterpart for years of drinking, cruelty and womanizing. Colin tries to show he's changed, but Ottilie assumes it's another of alt-Colin's mind games. Even when Colin convinces her he's from another timeline, his physics explanations don't heal Ottilie's battered heart. Finally, though, she realizes that Colin is everything she thought his counterpart was, and falls in love.

Ottilie has a terminal heart condition and her world, unlike ours, has no cure. She dies telling Colin how much their time together has meant to her (1970's *Love Story* may have influenced the script—the death isn't in the Wyndham original) and urging him to find her counterpart in his own world. Colin breaks into a physics lab and sends himself home (his body has been comatose so his counterpart hasn't been able to wreak any mischief). When he hunts for Ottilie, he discovers she died in the Blitz; further research indicates she survived, adopted under another name. Colin finds Ottilie just as her heart gives out and gets her to the hospital in the nick of time. When she recovers, it's obvious their love will begin again.

The 2006 adaptation *Random Quest* follows Wyndham more faithfully: Ottilie-1 (Kate Ashfield) doesn't die, Colin (Samuel West) simply loses her when he returns to his own world. This version does update the divergence point to the 1980s: The Cold War didn't end until the USSR and United States exhausted their resources and collapsed, leaving China and Japan as the dominant world powers.

In *Last Lives* (1997), it's a man from another world who finds his lost love here. Malakai (Billy Wirth) is an imprisoned parallel-world terrorist, grieving since the oppressive government killed his wife (Jennifer Rubin). Government scientist Merkhan (Judge Reinhold) taps that grief for parallel-world research, projecting Malakai's mind across dimensions to find his wife's counterpart. When Malakai finds his wife's double, Adrienne, on our Earth, he uses Merkhan's device to travel here with his followers. He kidnaps Adrienne from her wedding, murders everyone there, and flees—killing pretty much anyone they encounter—

with Merkhan and Adrienne's fiancé Aaron (C. Thomas Howell) in hot pursuit. After an interminable series of explosions and car crashes, Malakai dies and Aaron reunites with Adrienne.

Brain surgeon Ben Creed (Tate Donovan) has lost his love Melody (Grace Phillips) to another man by the time *Tempting Fate* (1998) starts. When his scientist friend Emmett (Matt Craven) opens a dimensional gateway into a utopian parallel world—no crime, no pollution, much happiness—Ben discovers that his counterpart there married alt-Melody before dying in a war. Ben world-jumps, passes himself off as his counterpart (he explains the body was misidentified) and finally has his happy ending. His buddy John (Abraham Benrubi) comes along so he can start over in a world where he's not facing bankruptcy.

There's a catch; in fact, several catches. The world is crime-free because society channels destructive impulses into murderous games. Everyone's happy because unhappy people get brain surgery. Melody underwent the operation voluntarily when she couldn't get over alt-Ben's death. Overweight people are also unacceptable, so hefty John ends up exiled to the wilderness. And the building holding the gateway has been demolished so there's no way home.

John finds a sort of peace with other misfit exiles in the wilderness, but Ben's miserable. Then he meets scientist Ellen Moretti (Ming-Na Wen), a colleague of Emmett's who came to Earth-2 by building her own gateway. She's been sentenced to brain surgery at Ben's counterpart's hospital, but Ben helps her escape. The government makes them the quarry in one of the murder games, but they reach Ellen's gate and make it home in one piece.

In *Twice Upon a Time* (1998), Beth (Molly Ringwald) is having a miserable Thanksgiving. She lost out on a big promotion and her ex, Nick (Rob Youngblood), is a baseball superstar, making Beth's steady Joe (George Newbern) look dull by comparison. As she and Joe pull on the Thanksgiving turkey wishbone, Beth wishes she could have the life she wants. Next morning she's in a parallel world where she's married to Nick, landed the promotion—and better cancer treatment has saved her mother's life.

Beth has no wish to ever go home ... until she catches Nick cheating on her, and jealously watches Joe in a relationship with someone else. After Beth's efforts to win Joe back fall flat, she realizes how selfish she's being and instead plays Cupid for him and his girlfriend. Another wishbone sends her back to the real world, finally appreciating her life. In a nice touch, we see the spoiled, shallow alt-Beth is just as happy to go home to her life.

In the dull *Holiday Switch* (2007), Nicole Eggert plays Paula, a housewife frustrated because her husband Gary's (Bret Anthony) dwindling income has left the family broke at Christmas. The magic power of an old Christmas ornament draws Paula through her clothes dryer into a parallel world where she married wealthy Nick (Brett Le Bourveau), her other high school boyfriend. Her initial joy fades when she learns that in this timeline she's never treated Nick as anything but a cash cow—and now she's divorcing him to move on to greener pastures.

Realizing how much she loves her family, Paula tries to get together with alt-Gary, but he's married to someone else and doesn't cheat. Fortunately, when he gives her a duplicate of her magic ornament, she's able to return home.

Chapter Ten

Time Cops
Policing the Time Stream (or) Putting Right What Once Went Wrong

"Time is fluid and I'm the guy who makes sure the glass doesn't get knocked over."—*Trancers IV*

When someone changes history, there are winners and losers.

If Nazis change history to win World War II or the South wins the Civil War, future generations are immeasurably worse off. If the United States changes history to win the Vietnam War (an idea tossed off in 2001's *Tomorrow Man*), that's great for America, lousy for Vietnam. Or consider *Escape from the Planet of the Apes*: Hasslein's scheme to kill the ape time travelers will save future generations of Homo sapiens from slavery but it erases the existence of millions of innocent intelligent apes.

The purpose of time police is to stop individuals from taking the kind of high-handed actions that transform history and reshape millions of lives. It's an idea with a long pedigree in print SF, including Poul Anderson's Time Patrol and DC Comics' Linear Men. This chapter looks not only at the time police who preserve history but individuals who do the opposite, working for God or the government to change history for the better.

The Trancers Series

Trancers (1985) are mind-controlled berserkers serving the psionic Whistler (Michael Stefani) in 24th century Los Angeles. (Most references say 23rd, but *Trancers III* says otherwise.) LA Detective Jack Deth (Tim Thomerson) has been hunting the Trancers since one murdered his wife. The city's ruling triumvirate tells Deth that Whistler has sent his mind back into the 20th century, where he's possessed his ancestor's body with an eye to killing the triumvirate's ancestors. With Los Angeles leaderless, Whistler will return to the future and rule. Deth ensures that won't happen by shooting Whistler's comatose body, then jumps back into his own ancestor (Thomerson again).

Baffled by present-day L.A., Deth recruits his ancestor's lover Leena (Helen Hunt) to help. She thinks he's crazy, until her first encounter with a Trancer proves otherwise. The two discover that Whistler's ancestor is a cop, so Whistler wields the power of the badge, and is also Trancing other cops. He kills two of the ancestors, causing their descendants in the future to disintegrate. Jack and Leena beat Whistler to number three, Skid Row derelict

In *Trancers II* (1991), Jack Deth (Tim Thomerson) discovers he's married to both Lena (Helen Hunt, left) and Alice (Megan Ward, right) due to an innocent time-travel mistake.

Hap Ashby (Biff Manard), but Whistler captures Leena; he tells her she's Deth's ancestor, so if she dies, Jack dies. Deth saves her and kills Whistler at the cost of the device that would have sent his mind home. Jack and Leena settle down in the present together.

In *Trancers II* (1991), Jack and Lena (the credits now spell it that way) are married and living with the dried-out, newly wealthy Hap. A message from the future alerts Jack to the fact that Whistler's brother Wardo (Richard Lynch) is in the past creating more Trancers. Also in the past: Jack's wife Alice (Megan Ward), who time-jumped into her ancestor before the Trancers killed her. Alice arrived six months ago only to discover that her ancestor was confined to a mental hospital.

Wardo sends Trancers after a terrified Hap, but his real goal is creating a Trancer army from patients at the mental hospital he runs. Alice is one of the patients, but she escapes and joins Jack, unaware he's now a bigamist. Lena decides to be noble and leaves Jack so he and Alice can fight Wardo together. Wardo imprisons Lena in his asylum but Alice and Jack storm the place to free her. Hap finds the courage to confront and kill Wardo, ending the threat. Jack chooses Lena and sends Alice back to the future.

Alas, by *Trancers III* (1992), Jack and Lena are divorcing. Then the android Shark (R.A. Mihailoff) shows up and drags Jack back to the future, where a new mastermind has created enough Trancers to overwhelm Los Angeles. The embattled city's only hope is for Jack to go back to 2005, when the very first Trancers were created, and destroy the plague at the source.

In 2005, Col. Muthuh (Andrew Robinson) is brainwashing soldiers into Trancers, creating an army to purge America of anyone Muthuh objects to. Lena, now a reporter, puts Jack in touch with Garrett (Melanie Smith), a refugee from the Trancer project. Garett and Deth break into Muthuh's base where Garrett succumbs to her programming and tries to kill Deth. Jack kills her and Muthuh, pruning the Trancers from history and saving the 24th century. L.A.'s new leaders assign Jack and Shark to police the time stream against all future threats to the city—and it looks like Jack will get Alice back as a consolation prize.

After *Trancers IV* and *V* (see Appendix IV), the series rebooted *sans* Thomerson with *Trancers 6* (2002). The L.A. council discovers that someone is trying to kill Jack by killing Jo (Zette Sullivan), his daughter by Lena and thereby his ancestor. To prevent that, they send Jack (stock footage of Thomerson) back into Jo's body. Investigating, Deth discovers that scientists are using meteorite energy to turn runaway teens into what the film calls Trancers, though they're nothing like the originals. Deth shuts down the operation, but learns that one of the scientists is an alien, one of hundreds working to create Trancers and take over. Deth decides that until the threat is destroyed, he'll have to stay in Jo's body

British Time Cops

The first time cops to appear on screen were on British TV. The title characters in *Sapphire and Steel* (1979–82) were time agents sent to Earth whenever the forces of chaos broke through from outside time. Steel (David McCallum) was hard, ruthless and exceptionally strong. Sapphire (Joanna Lumley) had more charm, at least on the surface, and some psychic ability. In a typical adventure, a photographer combined old photos with contemporary images, thereby opening a gateway by which the Victorian children in the photos emerge

***Sapphire and Steel* (1979–82) didn't make much sense but David McCallum and Joanna Lumley offered viewers some eye candy.**

into the present as agents for an alien force. The eerie but usually illogical storylines tended to trigger a love-it-or-hate-it reaction from viewers.

In the final story arc, Sapphire and Steel show up at a present-day diner to confront a stranded party of 1920s motorists. They discover that one of the factions in their own organization has set this up to trap them as part of an internal power struggle. In the final scene, the diner floats through an infinite starry void with the two agents inside.

Crime Traveller (1997) was a flop BBC series in which Detective Jeff Slade (Michael French) discovers that police scientist Holly Turner (Chloë Annett) possesses a time machine developed by her father. Turner tells Slade it's impossible to prevent crimes—you can't change the past—but Slade shows that investigating in the past can help solve crimes. Despite the risk of being trapped in the past if they stay too long, Holly and Jeff begin cracking cases together *and* develop a romantic relationship.

The U.K. TV series *Primeval* (2007) begins when a series of magnetic anomalies rip open time, dropping dinosaurs and super-evolved future horrors into the present. The government forms a team including scientists Cutter (Douglas Henshall), Connor (Andrew-Lee Potts) and Abby (Hanna Spearritt) to capture the creatures. Cutter also hopes to find his missing wife Helen (Juliet Aubrey), whom he believes vanished through an anomaly. It turns out he's right: Helen is exploring Earth's past, and also scheming to change it. The anomalies make it easy: A minor change at the end of the first season turns the team's tiny operation into the massive Anomaly Research Center (ARC).

Helen ultimately decides the only way to prevent humanity ruining the planet is to wipe out so many of our ancestors that the modern world never exists. She dies trying, but stopping her leaves Abby, Connor and Danny (Jason Flemyng) trapped in prehistory. By the time they return, a year has passed and ARC is now financed by Burton (Alexander Siddig), an entrepreneur who hopes to use the anomalies as a power source. Multiple time travelers show up, the most important being Matt Anderson (Ciarán McMenamin), a traveler from the future sent to abort an apocalypse revolving around ARC. He averts the disaster, the result of Burton's experiments.

In *Primeval: New World* (2012–13), a new batch of anomalies opens in Vancouver, where one of the first dinos to appear eats tech entrepreneur Evan Cross's (Niall Matter) wife. Cross believes the death of even one dinosaur could butterfly-effect history, so he devotes his company's resources to capturing the creatures and sending them home. A covert branch of the Canadian military eventually takes over the operation, believing it can change the past to create a better present. In the final episode, it's obvious that something has gone wrong with that plan, but we'll never know what.

Frequently Asked Questions About Time Travel (2009) offers a light-hearted British take on time policing. Ray (Chris O'Dowd), an SF and time travel nerd, is hanging with his friends Toby (Marc Wootton) and would-be writer Pete (Dean Lennox Kelly) at their local pub when he meets Cassie (Anna Farris), a time cop there to close a rift. She's thrilled to meet Ray, one of her heroes; he's charmed even though he assumes this is all a joke his buddies set up. When Ray tells his friends about Cassie, Toby assumes Ray's the one making stuff up. Then Toby walks into the rest room, emerges into the future and finds everyone in the pub dead.

Returning to the present, he convinces Ray and Pete to go through the rift with him, stumbling first into the recent past, then into an apocalyptic future, then into a party where everyone's dressed like Toby, Ray and Pete, the legendary Imagineers. Cassie keeps showing up, though from her perspective their encounters are months apart.

After Cassie's colleague Millie (Meredith MacNeill) helps the guys home from the Imagineers party, Pete realizes which of his many ideas—based on suggestions by the others—will make them legends. The guys are thrilled until Cassie tells them Millie belongs to the Editors, assassins who murder artists after their greatest triumph to avoid the inevitable years of lesser work. Pete finally destroys the paper with his idea written on it, sacrificing future fame but getting the guys off Millie's hit list. As the friends leave the pub, Cassie—who from her perspective has been dating Ray for two years now—recruits them for another mission.

American Time Cops

The first U.S. time cops appeared in the plodding TV series *Voyagers* (1982–83). This took as its premise that history wouldn't come out right if the time traveling Voyagers didn't nudge events in the right direction. Voyager Phineas Bogg (Jon-Erik Hexum) is a clueless hunk of beefcake who fortunately picks up orphaned history buff Jeffrey (Meeno Peluce) on one of his trips. Bogg has no idea what to do when he finds the Wright brothers not speaking to each other or a basket washed up along the Nile with a baby in it, but Jeffrey knows the answers: patch up the quarrel in time for the first airplane flight, get baby Moses downstream to Pharaoh's daughter. Taking Jeffrey through time violates Voyager protocol, but it turns out that Jeffrey was destined to join the Voyagers. The adventures could keep going.

Time Trax (1993–94) reversed the premise of *Alcatraz* by sending outlaws from the future to the present, rather than from the past. By 2193 Dr. Sahmbi (Peter Donat) has invented TRAX, a time travel device he uses to send wanted men two centuries into the past (technically a parallel world where it was still 1993). Investigator Darien Lambert (Dale Midkiff)—a man of exceptional ability even by the standards of his age—exposes Sahmbi's operation and captures him. Sahmbi escapes into the past himself, killing Darien's lover Elissa (Mia Sara) in the process, so Darien follows Sahmbi into 1993. In between learning such anachronistic arts as driving and ordering a hamburger, Darien hunts down the chronal fugitives and thwarts Sahmbi's various schemes, such as shipping present-day nuclear waste into the future. Darien's main ally was Selma (Elizabeth Alexander), an AI with a holographic interface, manifesting from a super-computer the size of a credit card.

In *Timecop* (1994), scientists develop time travel and criminals immediately begin exploiting it. After a terrorist group loots the past to finance their operations, the government creates a watchdog Time Enforcement Commission, overseen by Senator McComb (Ron Silver). After Walker (Jean-Claude Van Damme) becomes one of the first TEC field agents, killers blow up his house and murder his wife (Mia Sara).

A decade later, Walker learns that McComb is a power-hungry schemer using time travel to eliminate his enemies and raise money for a presidential bid. The Senator goes back to 1994 to kill his one-time business partner, who in the original timeline bought McComb out and became a millionaire. Walker and his partner Fielding (Gloria Reuben) follow the Senator, but Fielding is on McComb's payroll and turns on Walker. He fights back, Fielding goes down, but the fight buys McComb enough time to complete his mission. When he returns to 2004, he's too wealthy and powerful for the TEC or anyone else to cross, and nobody but Walker remembers it differently.

The Senator imposes a moratorium on time travel but Walker sneaks back to 1994 to

Time-enforcement agent Walker (Jean-Claude Van Damme, right) tackles a hired killer (James Lew) in *Timecop* (1994).

question the dying Fielding. She tells Walker that McComb was responsible for the attack on his home, an attempt to eliminate Walker before he became a threat. Walker rushes to his house and helps his younger self take down McComb's killers. The Senator arrives from the future, gloating that he's set a bomb to kill both Walkers; McComb will die too, but his younger self will survive to take the presidency. Walker trumps this by tricking Young McComb into showing up, then shoves the two Senators together. Physical contact destroys temporal counterparts, so when Walker returns to the future McComb is long dead and Walker's wife is alive.

The short-lived 1997 *Timecop* TV series starred T.W. King as temporal agent Jack Logan, operating from the near future of 2007. In each episode, he tackled some criminal attempting to tamper with history—murdering the mother of a future president, helping the Nazis win World War II, replacing Jack the Ripper to become an even greater serial killer. Jack trusted in his gut instincts to crack cases despite technician Hemmings (Cristi Conaway) nudging him to rely on technology and number crunching.

Timecop: The Berlin Decision (2003) takes place in 2025, but the TEC oversight is just as faulty as in the first film. Miller (Thomas Ian Griffith), the TEC's top watchdog, is remaking history for the better, for example by assassinating Hitler. TEC agent Chang (Jason Scott Lee) saves Hitler, but Miller's wife Sasha (Tricia Barry) dies in the firefight. Two years later, Miller escapes from prison and begins traveling to the past to kill or erase TEC agents. Chang saves his own ancestors from Miller, but otherwise keeps running one step behind; the bodies pile up in the past, leading to the present changing for the worse. Chang realizes his childhood self will be Miller's next target, and that saving him is what caused Chang's father's death. The time agent intercepts Miller in the past, kills him, then tells Miller's past self not to go down the same route. Miller listens, so 2025 is back to normal when Chang returns.

Like *Voyagers*, the animated heroes of *Time Squad* (2001–03) were devoted to fixing history when it went off the rails, with two professional cops—Buck Tuddrussel (Rob Paulsen) and robotic Larry 3000 (Mark Hamill)—assisted by a history-wise orphan, Otto (Pamela Segall). Their adventures were more entertaining; for example, an episode in which Eli Whitney is building flesh-eating robots instead of his cotton gin. In other episodes, the squad straightens out Leonardo da Vinci, who's turned into a Renaissance beatnik, and President Abe Lincoln, who's running wild as "Dishonest Abe."

Japanese Time Cops

The title characters in the live-action Japanese TV series *Time Keepers* (1997) were a group of young time cops. After Japan creates the first artificial wormhole—between 2040 and 1997—it's the time police who see that nobody abuses the potential power of traveling to the past. In the first episode, a squad goes back through the wormhole to stop a time traveler from killing a boy in 1997 and thereby altering history. Only two young agents make it through, but they realize they have to be enough.[1]

Flint the Time Detective (1998–99) had the premise that a mysterious Dark Lord has scattered entities from the Land of Time through history, hoping they'll become corrupted enough for him to exploit. Each "time shifter" has an amazing power, and can transform, Pokemon-like, into a more powerful form. The Time Police of the 25th century seek to collect the shifters before the Dark Lord's agents do.

During one trip to the past, the villainous Aino (Yumi Touma) petrifies the young caveman Genshi (Akiko Suzuki)—the English-language Flint—and his father, intending to thaw them out in the 25th century. Instead, the Time Police thaw Genshi, though his father remains petrified as a sentient stone hammerhead. Flint joins the time cops, which works well for them as his friendly personality can often win over the time shifters. In a typical episode the Time Police locate a time shifter in the past, Aino activates its evil and more powerful form, but the good guys eventually return it to normal. In the ending episodes, Flint took the fight to the Dark Lord, who ultimately lost.

Mirai Sentai Time Rangers (2000) was one in a long series of "Super Sentai" characters who became America's *Power Rangers* franchise. All Sentai dress in similar uniforms and battle similar monsters but have different backstories and goals. This version of the franchise opens in the 30th century where time travel has been outlawed to avoid time paradoxes. The Dolnero gang trick the Time Protection Department's new recruits into letting the gang travel back to the 20th century to steal. The recruits follow and, joined by a 20th century martial artist, fight the villains as the Time Rangers. The Rangers eventually realize that both they and the Dolneros are destabilizing history, so they return everyone to their own time.[2]

In the U.S. this became the *Power Rangers Time Force* (2001). This opens in the 30th century, one of the rare utopian futures ... except for deformed, malevolent mutants. (The series waffles on whether mutants are pure evil or reacting to discrimination.) The mutant Ransik (Vernon Wells) kills Alex (Jason Faunt), the leader of the Time Force Power Rangers, then travels back to the present with his daughter Nadira (Kate Sheldon) and an army of mutants and robots. Alex's fiancée Jen (Erin Cahill) leads the Rangers in pursuit. The Time Force finds a present-day ally in Alex's double Wes Collins (Faunt), who eventually assumes Alex's Red Ranger role. The Rangers fight Ransik's mutant menaces despite the disapproval of Wes' father (Edward Laurence Albert) and Wes' jealous former friend Eric (Daniel Southworth); Eric eventually becomes the Quantum Ranger but doesn't join the team. Jen begins falling for Wes, even after it turns out that Alex is somehow still alive in the future. Like the Sentai team, the Rangers discover their presence is altering the time stream, but the series promptly forgets about this.

In the three-part series finish, Alex orders the time travelers home before Ransik's ultimate robot, Doomtron, annihilates the city. Rather than see Wes die, the team fights beside him against Doomtron. When Nadira tries to shield a human baby, her father accidentally injures her. Horrified that he hurt the one person he loves, Rasnik surrenders. The Rangers return home, leaving Wes and Eric, their friendship restored, to protect the city.

Like the Super Sentai, the Kamen Rider franchise similarly reboots the basic premise—ordinary human who can turn into an armored biker—into multiple versions. The 2007–08 version, *Kamen Rider Den-O*, stars Takeru Satoh as Ryotaro Nogami, a young man with bad luck but a good heart. When he's possessed by an Imagin—time travelers from an alternate future, seeking to manipulate history—Ryotaro fights back against the bullies picking on him, but reins in the Imagin before it does them serious harm. That impresses the crew of the Denliner, a time traveling train, which recruits Ryotaro to help them fight against the Imagin time-change plans as Kamen Rider Den-O. By staying in control while different Imagin possess him, Ryotaro is able to select from a palette of different Imagin powers to use. Time and again he thwarts the Imagin, eventually erasing them from history.[3]

This was one of the most successful incarnations of the series and generated an anime spinoff, *Imagin*, and several movies, starting with *Cho Kamen Rider and Decade* (2009) in which the disruptions caused by the series' battle allow oni, Japanese demons, to slip through time and try to prevent their own extinction. The Denliner crew and the Kamen Rider put a stop to that.

Putting Right What Once Went Wrong

The short-lived 1979 series *Time Express* was an anthology built around the premise that God—or whoever the "head of the line" might be—grants some people a magical second chance. Each week, two guest stars arrive at Track 13, where a special train run by Jason and Margaret Winters (Vincent Price and Coral Browne) picks the passengers up and drops them back in time at a personal turning point. In various episodes, a skater gets another chance at the romance she walked away from; a man who built a fortune on money he found and kept turns it in to the cops; a boxer finds out if he could have won the fight he threw; and a cop investigates whether a man he put away was really innocent.[4]

Most other supernatural time-cop stories are even less clear about who the boss is.

Gary Hobson (Kyle Chandler) of *Early Edition* (1996–2000) receives a copy of the next day's newspaper every morning, but nobody on the show knows where it came from. (One episode establishes that Gary is neither the first nor the last person to get the early edition.) A good-hearted guy, Gary uses this foreknowledge to avert tragedies, despite his friend Chuck (Fisher Stevens) insisting they should use it to make money.

Quantum Leap (1989–93) was like the polar opposite of *The Time Tunnel*: The focus was on ordinary people and personal crises rather than big events, changing the past was the point of the show and it was actually good. Genius researcher Sam Beckett (Scott Bakula) learns that funding for Project Quantum Leap—which he believes will let a man time travel within his own lifespan—may be cut off, so he decides to test it first. He wakes up in the body of a 1950s Air Force pilot (we see Sam's face, everyone else sees the pilot). Al (Dean Stockwell), Sam's best friend and colleague, uses the project supercomputer Ziggy to project a hologram of himself into the past. Al warns Sam that within a few days, the pilot will die in a crash. With Al's guidance and Ziggy's research, Sam saves the pilot, then "leaps" into another body in another time to avert another tragedy. Ziggy concludes that God himself is moving Sam through time "to put right what once went wrong."

Over the course of the series, Sam leapt into men, women, blacks, whites, rich and poor. In later episodes, the formula varied: Sam leapt into the Civil War era, leapt into Lee Harvey Oswald, and battled an evil leaper trying to undo all the changes Sam and Al had made. Through it all, Sam kept hoping the project would someday bring him home, until the last episode. After an encounter with what might be God, Sam realizes that helping people with time travel is his true calling, and he chooses to keep leaping: "Sam Beckett never returned home."

Seven Days (1998–2001) involved a time cop improving events for the U.S. government rather than the Almighty. The military's Operation Backstep has figured out how to send a man back in time one week. When terrorists or other enemies pull off a successful attack on America, Backstep sends Lt. Frank Parker (Jonathan LaPaglia)—chosen because his mind can withstand the shock of time travel—back to prevent the catastrophe. Unlike many time travelers, he never has to worry about people believing him. Once in the past, all Frank has to do is call Operation Backstep and give his superiors the right code phrase. The project then provides whatever assistance he needs.

Tru Calling (2003–05) stars Eliza Dushku as Tru Davies, a med student and night-shift morgue attendant. In the first episode, a newly arrived corpse opens its eyes and asks Tru for help. Time rewinds and Tru's at the start of the day, knowing a murder will occur but not why, or by whom, or the name of the victim. She figures it out and saves the victim, but more corpses begin asking for help. Tru's brother Harrison (Shawn Reaves) came to realize that she wasn't crazy and did his best to help, though he also kept his eye out for ways to profit off knowing the future. Davis (Zach Galifianakis), Tru's boss, was her right hand; he eventually revealed that Tru's late mother possessed the same power, and had saved his life with it.

Tru also had an adversary, Jack (Jason Priestley), who relives days but seeks to keep events as unchanged as possible. In Tru's eyes, Jack's an accomplice to murder; in Jack's eyes, he's the time cop preserving reality against Tru's time-tampering. Jack had his own allies, notably Tru's father (Cotter Smith) who had played Jack's part against Tru's mother, and eventually murdered her. The battle was ongoing when the series ended.

In *Déjà Vu* (2006), ATF agent Doug Carlin (Denzel Washington) investigates a terrorist bombing that killed 500-plus Navy personnel and their families. Carlin discovers a connection between the bombing and one of the apparent victims, Claire Kuchever (Paula Patton). Then FBI agent Pryswarra (Val Kilmer) invites him to work on a special counter-terrorism task force. It turns out the task force is a team of physicists who accidentally created a wormhole that allows them to peer four days, six hours into the past.

Physical travel through the wormhole is supposedly impossible, but Carlin convinces the team to send his past self a written warning of the attack. The note reaches another agent, who tries to catch the terrorist and dies; this, however, gives the task force a glimpse of the killer, Oerstadt (Jim Caviezel). Carlin tracks Oerstadt down in the present, closing the case, but he then uses the time window to go back physically and save Claire. Carlin rescues Claire and together they kill Oerstadt and stop the bombing, at the cost of Carlin's life. The agent's counterpart in the past shows up as the film ends, and Claire tells her his story.

Journeyman (2007) protagonist Dan Vassar (Kevin McKidd) was a newspaperman, recovered gambling addict and husband to Katie (Gretchen Egolf)—and then he became a time traveler. Like Sam Beckett and Tru Davies, his mission was to go back in time and change people's lives: a trial witness marked for execution, two abused siblings, a family on the brink of driving off a cliff. (Unlike Sam, he physically materialized in the past.) At first Dan wondered if he was going crazy; Katie wasn't too happy either as from her perspective her husband was just up and disappearing without warning.

Eventually Katie learned that Dan was on the level, but there was still a problem: his deceased ex Livia (Moon Bloodgood) was still alive, traveling in time and mentoring Dan on his missions. Dan eventually learns that Livia came from 1948; they would never have met except she was stranded in the future for several years. The series didn't last long enough to learn what was behind all the time-jumping.

In the British series *Paradox* (2009), Detective Inspector Flint (Tamzin Outhwaite) is stunned when noted physicist Christian King (Emun Elliott) presents her with images he received in his computer showing the results of a terrorist attack—one that won't happen for several hours yet. Although skeptical and suspicious, Flint and her team investigate. While they fail to stop the attack, which is actually a freak accident, they save most of the people. When King receives more warnings, Scotland Yard assigns Flint's team to work with King on stopping the events before they happen. King theorized that the warnings came from a parallel Earth slightly ahead of ours in time, but the short run neither confirmed nor disproved this.

Chapter Eleven

Déjà Vu All Over Again
Time Loop Films

"Is time relative? That is, does time warp back in on itself, and if so ... why?"
—*12 Days of Christmas Eve*

The freedom from causality in time-loop movies lets some characters claim to be completely free of morality. In *Christmas Do-Over*, Jay Mohr brushes off his jerkish behavior on the grounds nobody will remember come the reboot. A character in *Repeaters* justifies rape and murder by the same logic. The protagonists of *Repeaters* and *Day Break* insist on doing the right thing, even though the time loop will also erase their good deeds.

Time-loop movies involve a variant form of time travel where at the end of the day (or the hour, or whatever), time reboots to the start of the day, then does it again when the day ends. And again. And again. Everything happens exactly as before, day after day, except when the protagonist changes things.

This sets up the ultimate violation of causality: Nothing the protagonist does has any consequence. When Phil Connors gets turned down by a woman in *Groundhog Day* (1993), he uses what he's learned to do better the next day, and the next, and the next, with no penalty for past failures. But the same applies to Barry Thomas in *12:01*: He finally makes love to his dream girl, but next morning he's back to square one with her.

Some characters see the lack of causality as a get-out-of-jail-free card for acting unethically. Kevin in *Christmas Do-Over* excuses acting like a jerk to his son on the grounds that nobody will remember it the next day. One of the leads in *Repeaters* justifies rape by the same logic; his adversary argues that rebooting the day doesn't get you off the hook morally.

Almost all time loops films are fantasy; only four films (both versions of *12:01*, *Source Code* and *Edge of Tomorrow*) qualify as science fiction. Usually what powers the time loop is the need for personal growth: Time resumes its normal course when the protagonist learns to love or conquers fear.

Set-up is vitally important in time-loop films. The events of the first day (before the universe hits the reset button) repeat and recycle over and over unless the protagonist changes them. If there's not enough recycling, the film loses the feeling of time repeating, but events have to be interesting enough, or at least tolerable enough, that we don't mind seeing them play out multiple times. Predicting the day's events is the standard way to prove to other characters that the reboot is real. *12:01* works a nice twist on that: Barry doesn't pay enough attention to what's going on to predict things.

Some sources have cited William Dean Howell's "Christmas Every Day" (1892) as the earliest time-loop story, but that's incorrect: Time passes normally in the story, with magic forcing everyone to celebrate Christmas no matter what the date is. The time-loop concept goes back at least as far as 1922's *Worm Ouroboros*: At the end of a great war, the protagonists opt to have time recycle endlessly rather than settle into postwar lives of peace and comfort. In Malcolm Jameson's 1941 story "Doubled and Redoubled," a more conventional time loop, a man experiences the best day of his life, and wishes every day could be like that, and a witch overhears…

The first time-loop film is the short *12:01 P.M.* (1990), based on Richard Lupoff's story of the same name. Shortly after noon, Myron (Kurtwood Smith) strikes up a conversation with an attractive young woman (Laura Harrington) and tells her that at 1 p.m. the universe will rewind back to 12:01. Although Myron can change his actions and alter events around him, when time reboots everything he does is canceled out. Myron learns from Prof. Rosenbluth (Don Amendolia) that the world is trapped in a "time bounce" that keeps resetting everything. Myron's consciousness has become unmoored from time so he alone remembers previous cycles, but neither he nor Rosenbluth can end the bounce. Myron shoots himself in despair, but he's alive again at the next 12:01.

12:01 P.M. director-co-writer Jonathan Heap produced the more upbeat TV film *12:01* in 1993. Barry Thomas (Jonathan Silverman), an HR staffer at a physics institute, has a god-awful day. He's raked over the coals by brilliant particle physicist Moxley (Martin Landau); he makes a disastrous attempt to flirt with physicist Lisa Fredericks (Helen Slater); he sees Lisa gunned down in a drive-by after work; and at 12:01 a.m., he gets an electric shock. The day then reboots, but Barry doesn't realize it. When he gets to work and starts talking about Lisa's murder, everyone wonders what the joke is. Barry discovers that despite federal safety mandates, Moxley hasn't shut down his unstable particle accelerator, but nobody listens. Lisa refuses to believe his talk about killers targeting her, and winds up dead again.

On the next loop Barry saves her, and they go on the run. While hiding out, they make love; talking afterwards, Lisa deduces that the accelerator triggered the time bounce at the exact instant Barry received the electric shock, which unmoored his mind from the cycle. Next morning, Lisa's forgotten she ever knew Barry, but he uses what he's learned about her ("37.1. Oysters. Brie. The Carpenters.") to prove the time loop is real. Working together, they learn that Moxley won't shut down the accelerator because he anticipates millions in tech breakthroughs if he goes ahead—and he's willing to kill anyone who might interfere. At the climax, Moxley holds Lisa and Barry at gunpoint, but in the subsequent struggle, Moxley falls into the particle beam. That blocks the ray from starting the time bounce, so Lisa and Barry can resume their regular lives.

The Archetype: Groundhog Day

In between the two *12:01* films came *Groundhog Day* (1993), which established itself as the definitive time-loop film. After it became a hit, TV shows such as *Xena: Warrior Princess* and *Stargate: SG-1* did episodes knocking off the plot.

As the film starts, it's February 1 and egocentric, unpleasant TV weatherman Phil Connors (Bill Murray) reluctantly joins producer Rita (Andie McDowell) and cameraman Larry (Chris Elliott) on a trip to Puxatawney, Pennsylvania. There, legendary groundhog Puxatawney Phil will look for his shadow and predict whether winter will last. Phil sneers at the assignment and condescends towards Rita and everyone in Puxatawney. He's even less happy when a blizzard stops the trio from returning home ... and then the time-loop starts.

As the day keeps rebooting and rebooting, Phil has trouble coping. At various points he indulges in massive over-eating, manipulates a woman into bed (learns about her one day, seduces her the next), attempts suicide and tries seducing Rita, without success. In a later iteration he convinces Rita what's happening, and when they talk honestly, the seeds of change begin. Phil starts using his time to learn—piano—and helps out people around town. He feels his foreknowledge makes him a god, but discovers he still can't save one old vagrant from death; he has to settle for buying him a great last meal. After Phil spends an entire day helping people and delivering an incredible performance for the news shoot, Rita falls for him for real. They spend the night together and the next day, time is back to normal.

Phil Connors (Bill Murray) prepares to commit suicide and take Puxatawney Phil with him in *Groundhog Day* (1993).

Christmas Looping

Although *Groundhog Day* could be considered the preeminent holiday-themed time-loop film, Christmas may be the most popular time-loop film holiday. Much like New Year's Day in *Repeat Performance*, Christmas is a time when magic seems plausible, at least in movies. It's also a day that brings family and friends together, giving writers plenty of emotional material to mine for drama. And particularly on TV, there are so many Christmas movies every year, that it's not hard to squeeze in a time-loop here and there.

As *Christmas Every Day* (1996) opens, young Billy Jackson (Erik von Detten) is frustrated with duties at his father's (Robert Hays) general store, life in his small town and his father constantly pushing him to play basketball. After an awful Christmas Day involving bullies, a disastrous Christmas pageant and his uncle's (Robert Curtis-Brown) plans to open a local big-box store—which would kill the Jacksons' store—Billy wishes it would just stay Christmas, as the coming days will only get worse.

Christmas magic obliges. When Billy realizes what's happening, his responses include self-interest (hitting on a pretty girl, mastering the jump shot), helping his family (convincing his uncle to drop his plans and come to work in the family store) and matchmaking two elderly neighbors (a subplot that reoccurs in several of these movies). Now that Billy's learned the virtue of helping others and the importance of the family business, the time loop ends.

Mickey's Once Upon a Christmas (1999) is an anthology film whose first segment, "Stuck on Christmas," spotlights Donald Duck's nephews Huey, Dewey and Louie. They have a fabulous (but selfish) Christmas, grabbing food ahead of everyone and blowing off the adults for their own amusement. They go to bed wishing it could be Christmas every day— and when it comes true, they're delighted. Before long, though, the boys are sick of eating turkey and hanging with relatives. That makes them more selfish until they realize how much they're hurting everyone else. Remorseful, they help Donald, Daisy Duck and the others have a perfect Christmas, which breaks the spell

12 Days of Christmas Eve (2004) is unusual for giving heartless retail CEO Calvin Cooper (Steven Weber) a set limit on the number of loops he gets. After a freak Christmas Eve accident kills Cooper, Angie (Molly Shannon), his guardian angel, warns him that if he doesn't figure out where his life went wrong before the end of his twelfth Christmas Eve, he's dead for good.

Calvin tries becoming more charitable, more Christmassy, and spending time with his family, but it's all insincere, and doesn't help him. As the last day dawns with no hope of reprieve, Calvin suddenly gets genuine Christmas spirit. He gives his staff the day off, breaks up with his girlfriend, whom he's learned would be happier without him, and reconnects with his family. At the fatal moment, he suffers a heart attack—but wakes up Christmas Day to learn it was only heartburn.

Christmas Do-Over (2006) stars Jay Mohr as Kevin, a failed singer-songwriter and grade-A

Heartless Calvin (Steven Weber), left, learns from his guardian angel Angie (Molly Shannon) that he if he doesn't turn his life around, he's going to lose it in *12 Days of Christmas Eve* (2004).

jerk spending Christmas with his ex, Jill (Daphne Zuniga), their son Ben (Logan Grove) and Jill's boyfriend Todd (David Millbern). Jay's selfishness makes Christmas miserable for everyone, though he's miserable himself when he sees Jill accept Todd's proposal. When the looping starts, Kevin becomes an even bigger jerk, even to Ben, rationalizing that it doesn't count because Ben won't remember. He also tries using his foreknowledge to humiliate Todd and win Jill back, without success. Finally Kevin works to ensure that everyone except Todd has an incredible Christmas Day, wins Jill back and breaks the loop. Too bad it still feels like he's gaming the system rather than genuinely a better person.

In *12 Dates of Christmas* (2011), businesswoman Kate (Amy Smart) reluctantly goes on a blind Christmas Eve date with Miles (Mark-Paul Gosselaar). She blows him off in hopes of winning back her ex, only to discover that the latter has proposed to someone else. When time starts repeating, Kate assumes she's been given a second chance with her ex, but she still fails. Kate also discovers she likes Miles more with each repeat date, but he's uncomfortable by the fact that Kate seems ready to get serious within minutes of meeting him.

Eventually, Kate pulls together everything she's learned about the people around her: She plays matchmaker for both her elderly neighbor and an IT geek, stops a homeless teen from running away and brings everyone together for a Christmas Eve party. At midnight, she and Miles kiss … and Christmas arrives.

Pete's Christmas (2013) is the worst ever for 13-year-old Pete (Zachary Gordon): His parents didn't give him a present, he's humiliated in the neighborhood touch football game, gets unfairly blamed for his jock brother ruining Christmas dinner, and has to give up his bed to visiting grandfather (Bruce Dern), who later walks out after a furious fight with Pete's father (Rick Roberts). When the time loop begins, Pete starts exploiting it, which makes everyone more miserable. For instance, Pete wins at touch football as he knows every player's moves, but his performance leaves his brother feeling like a loser. Eventually Pete figures a way to make everyone happy, such as winning the game with a double play that makes his brother the star. Lessons have been learned, and December 26 arrives.

Non-Christmas Time Loops

Camp Slaughter (2005) starts with four college friends, including loudmouthed Jen (Anika McFall) and shy Angela (Joanna Suhl), getting lost in the Maine woods and arriving at Camp Hiawatha. Cell phones don't work, everyone uses 1980s slang (which the visitors have apparently never heard before)—and someone's slashing up the campers *a la Friday the 13th*, which the movie references repeatedly in case we miss the point. By day's end, the campers and staff are dead, but they're fine the next morning.

Camp counselors Daniel and Ivan (Kyle Lupo, Jon Fleming) explain that the time loop has been happening since the original murder spree in 1981. The four friends agree to help catch the killers, but it turns out the counselors are the villains, manipulating two campers to do their dirty work. Further complicating things, groundskeeper Lou (Jim Marlow) has been murdering the murderers in every time loop to punish himself for not stopping the original killings. (He doesn't attempt to save or protect the victims, just avenge them.) The end result of all this slasher-ness is that everyone dies except Jen, who escapes. Three years later, Daniel and Ivan find a way out of the loop and begin hunting her.

Day Break (2006) has more tension and less comedy than most time loops due to the stakes. In the first episode Detective Brett Hopper (Taye Diggs) is framed for murder. A mysterious figure (Jonathan Banks) shows Hopper footage of his girlfriend Rita's (Moon Bloodgood) murder and tells Hopper that he either confesses to the murder or his sister and niece die too.

When time reboots, Hopper begins putting together a piece of the mystery each day. He's aware that the magic could vanish as fast as it came, before he's cleared himself, saved Rita or brought down the people behind the frame-up. At one point he tells his ex-partner Chad (Adam Baldwin) that he won't kill people gratuitously out of the same fear the day might not reboot—plus he's still a cop and he wants to play it by the book as much as possible. In several iterations Hopper meets Pryor (Clayton Rohner), a mentally disturbed homeless man who claims he's also reliving days.

Hopper finally exposes and busts the political conspiracy that framed him, but the day reboots again. He puts together a few missing pieces: His father's suicide was faked by the conspiracy and Chad is working for the bad guys. The reboots stop before everything's resolved. Nonetheless, Hopper successfully cracks the case and gets back to his everyday life, while Pryor—now sane and professionally dressed—watches from the sidelines. Was it really Pryor's loop and Hopper got caught up in it? Was Pryor some sort of guardian angel helping Hopper out? Feel free to speculate.

In *The Melancholy of Haruhi Suzumaya* (2006), an off-the-wall, often parodic anime, headstrong, restless high schooler Haruhi (Aya Hirano) forms a school club, the SOS Brigade, to seek out the wonders Haruhi believes will make life worthwhile. She's unaware that the club members include an ET, a telepath and time traveler Mikuru (Yuuko Gotou), all drawn by Haruhi's unconscious power to manipulate events. In the second season opener, Haruhi's best friend Kyon (Tomokazu Sugita) goes back in time, then the SOS Brigade becomes trapped in a time loop at the end of summer vacation. The same events recycle thousands of times before Kyon deduces that Haruhi's fear of starting school unprepared is causing the loop. The club has a big cram session on the last day of summer, which gives Haruhi the confidence to break the loop.

The Last Day of Summer (2007) likewise finds Luke Malloy (Jansen Panettiere) on Labor Day terrified that he's not ready to enter middle school. Even though his Labor Day experiences include getting bullied, feuding with his sister and stage fright about the school talent show, Luke wishes he could live it over instead of facing school tomorrow. When the time loop starts, Luke exploits his situation—he makes cool friends and dumps his old ones—before learning better. He reconnects with his sister, reforms a bully and gives a great performance with his band, after which the loop ends.

Triangle (2009) is unusual in that the time-loop premise isn't immediately obvious. It opens with a series of initially confusing scenes involving Florida single-mom Jess (Melissa George) and her mentally handicapped son Tommy (Joshua McIvor) before Jess joins Greg (Michael Dorman) and his friends for an afternoon's yachting. A storm rips off the mast and overturns the yacht, which drifts until it encounters the liner *Aeolus* (in Greek mythology, Aeolus' son was Sisyphus, who endlessly rolls a boulder up a hill in the afterlife). Once aboard, Jess spots a lurking figure who soon kills everyone else. Jess throws the hooded killer overboard, but not before the attacker warns Jess that everyone must die for her to see Tommy again. As soon as the killer drowns, Jess sees a battered yacht show up, with her and her friends alive on board. She attempts to save them but fails, then the yacht shows up again and again ... and in one scene we see a pile of corpses to indicate how long the cycle's been repeating.

In the "final" loop, Jess becomes the killer herself as part of a desperate plan to fix things, only to have her counterpart throw her overboard. She washes up on the coast hours earlier, goes home and sees her past self abusing Tommy. Jess kills Past-Jess in a moment of rage and drives away with Tommy, only to see him die when a car hits them. Jess (who may be dead herself) wanders to the marina to restart the cycle.

Repeaters (2010) puts the ethical questions of time looping—does what you do matter if it "never" happened?—front and center. Addicts Kyle (Dustin Milligan), Sonia (Amanda Crew) and Michael (Richard de Klerk) are enduring their time in a treatment center when the movie begins. When their counselor tells them it's time to apologize to those they've wronged, none of the trio does. The next day, they're looping.

Kyle's initial impulse is to save a suicidal jumper they heard about on the news, but the effort fails. The following days, the threesome steal, try crack and get drunk. Michael rapes a 15-year-old, arguing that tomorrow she'll be unraped so why not? In a later loop, the same thinking drives him to kill two cops for the hell of it. The time loop also wipes out Kyle's efforts to reconnect with his sister (Alexia Fast) but Kyle insists that doing the right thing matters. Sometimes Kyle tries capturing Michael to prevent him from hurting anyone; Michael sometimes tries capturing Kyle to end his interference.

Eventually Kyle apologizes to his sister and promises to do better. Sonia tells her abusive, terminally ill father that she doesn't hate him, but she's no longer letting him affect her life. The next day, Michael hunts his former friends down to kill them, kills two people in the process, then discovers it's the real next day—the time loop has stopped. Kyle confronts Michael, who accepts his guilt and kills himself. Sonia and Kyle move on with their healing but Michael wakes up and begins a new solo loop.

Source Code (2011) opens with Capt. Colter Stevens (Jake Gyllenhaal) finding himself on a commuter train, flirting with Christina (Michelle Monaghan). As Stevens' last memory is of being shot down in Afghanistan, this is confusing, especially as he doesn't recognize his own face. After eight minutes, a bomb destroys the train, then Stevens wakes up in a tiny space with Goodwin (Vera Farmiga), a military officer, grilling him about the bomber's identity. He has no clues, so Goodwin makes him relive the train trip to find some.

As we and Stevens eventually learn, Goodwin's boss Rutledge (Jeffrey Wright) is using memories from one of the bombing victims' brains to create a "source code" for a pocket universe that exists for just eight minutes, then reboots. By inserting Stevens' mind into this world, Rutledge hopes to identify the bomber, after which he'll shut down the time loop and use Stevens in other investigations. (Stevens is so badly maimed, Rutledge considers him useless otherwise.)

Stevens becomes convinced the pocket universe exists independently. After he identifies the bomber, he persuades Goodwin to send him back one more time, then allow his body to die. Inside the loop he captures the bomber, saves the train, gets the girl ... and when the eight minutes are up, the universe continues existing. Stevens can enjoy a new life with Christina, and asks that universe's Goodwin to help Stevens' counterpart out.

College graduates take a road trip to celebrate in *Mine Games* (2012). Things start to go south when they hit someone on the road but can't find the body, then end up at an

Cage and Vrataski (Tom Cruise, Emily Blunt) are Earth's only hope of survival in *Edge of Tomorrow* (2014).

abandoned house near an eerie mine, with an apparent serial killer stalking them. Mysterious written warnings tell them to "break the cycle" and they find their own corpses. It turns out they're in a time loop: The person they hit was one of their own group who'd arrived on the previous loop, one of them left the warnings, etc. This being a horror movie, nothing does any good and it all repeats—but at the end, one of the victims survives to warn her friends when they arrive for the next iteration.

The sexist, unfunny *Premature* (2014) gives raunch a time-loop twist. Rob (John Karna), a high school virgin, blows off a platonic evening with his best friend Gaby (Katie Findlay) after hot blonde Angela (Carlson Young) invites him to her house for sex. When he comes prematurely while making out, the day reboots, starting at the point where his mother wakes him out of a wet dream. (*Premature* recycles fewer incidents than most time loops, but it can't get enough of that scene.) Rob realizes he can get away with anything, such as squeezing a teacher's breasts, as long as he jerks off afterwards.

Rob decides that making love to Angela will end the loop, so he goes to see her again. When it turns out she only wants to trade sex for him doing her schoolwork, he dumps her and apologizes to Gaby. She and Rob realize they feel more than friendship and wind up in bed together. Having chosen the virgin over the slut (the movie drives this home with sledgehammer subtlety), Rob escapes the loop.

Edge of Tomorrow (2014) combines time looping with an alien invasion for spectacular effect. The alien Mimics have swarmed over Europe, crushing the opposition, but Rita Vrataski (Emily Blunt) achieves a virtual one-woman victory over them at Verdun. As the Earth forces prepare to fly into Europe for a final battle, shallow PR officer Major Cage (Tom Cruise) annoys a general so much that he gets shanghaied into the frontline troops. It goes badly and Cage dies fighting, only to wake up the previous day.

After multiple do-overs, Cage is a tougher and smarter fighter, but the battle still ends every time with the humans massacred where they land. Vrataski learns the reason Cage is fighting so well and reveals that she won at Verdun the same way. The aliens are a hive mind with the power to reboot time whenever they lose a fight. When human blood mingles with a Mimic—as happened to Vrataski, then Cage—the human gets the power, which Vrataski lost after a blood transfusion.

The duo attempts to reach the Omega, the alien queen, but fail repeatedly; Vrataski kill Cage several times rather than risk him getting a transfusion. When they finally succeed in locating the lair, it turns out to be a trap. Cage and Vrataski press on and locate the real base, but Cage suffers heavy blood loss and this time he gets a transfusion. With the Omega able to use its do-over power again, Cage recruits his squad to join a suicide attack on the Mimic queen. Everyone dies but Cage kills the Omega and bathes in her blood. This gives him enough do-over juice to reboot time back before Cage locked horns with the general. To everyone's surprise but his and Vrataski's, the queen's death ripples back through time, causing the Mimics to die off before the big assault begins. Earth is saved.

Appendices

Films in each appendix are listed alphabetically; foreign films are alphabetized by English-language title, if they have one. Anime series often come in multiple versions—*Haruka* has multiple sequel and reunion series—but in most cases I've only listed one main series or film rather than try to provide credits for all of them.

Films made for television are identified by the channel on which they aired, rather than production company.

Appendix I
Film Credits

This section lists credits for films covered in the body of the text.

About Time (2013)
United Kingdom; 123 minutes; Working Title, Translux
Cast: Domhnall Gleeson, Rachel McAdams, Bill Nighy
Credits: Director-Writer: Richard Curtis

Action Replayy (2010; aka *Flash Forward*)
India; 129 minutes; Sunshine Pictures
Cast: Aditya Roy Kapur, Akshay Kumar, Aishwarya Rai
Credits: Director-Producer: Vipul Amrutlal Shah; Story-Screenplay: Suresh Nair, Aatish Kapadia, based on Shobhana Desai Gusatrata's play *Action Replay*

Against Time (2001; aka *All Over Again*)
USA; 96 minutes; Second Images Studio
Cast: Ean Mering, Robert Loggia, Craig T. Nelson, Emilie Jacobs
Credits: Director-Writer: Cleve Nettles

Age of the Great Dinosaurs (1979)
Japan; 73 minutes; animated; Toei Animation
Cast: Chikao Otsuka, Hiroku Suzuki, Ichiro Nagai
Credits: Directors: Shotaro Ishinomori, Hideki Takayama; Writers: Ishinomori, Makoto Naito

Aladdin and the Adventure of All Time (2000)
USA; 81 minutes; animated; Concorde
Cast: Cathy Cavadini, Danny Mann, Jim Cummings, Claudette Nevins
Credits: Director: Cirio H. Santiago; Writers: Craig J. Nevius, Ferris Ellen Gluck

Ali Baba Goes to Town (1937)
USA; 81 minutes; Twentieth Century–Fox
Cast: Eddie Cantor, Tony Martin, Roland Young, Virginia Field
Credits: Director: David Butler; Writers: Harry Tugend, Jack Yellend; Story: Gene Towne, Graham Baker, Gene Fowler

Alien Agenda: Endangered Species (1996)
USA; 102 minutes; Brimstone Media
Cast: Debbie Rochon, Joel D. Wynkoop, Joseph Zaso, Candice Meade
Credits: Director-Writers: Gabriel Campisi, Ron Ford, Kevin J. Lindenmuth, Tim Ritter

Alien Agenda: Out of the Darkness (1996)
USA; 85 minutes; Brimstone Media
Cast: Mick McCleery, Candice Meade, John Collins
Credits: Director-Writers: Kevin J. Lindenmuth, Mick McCleery

Alien Agenda: Under the Skin (1997)
USA; 68 minutes; Brimstone Media
Cast: Leslie Body, Arthur Lundquist
Credits: Director-Writers: Tom Vollman, Mike Legge, Kevin Lindenmuth

The Alien Conspiracy: Beyond the Lost World (2001)
USA; 86 minutes; Brimstone Media
Cast: Debbie Rochon, Thomas Nondorf
Credits: Directors: John Bowker, Tim Ritter, Kevin J. Lindenmuth; Writers: Tim Ritter, Kevin J. Lindenmuth, Stephen C. Seward

Almost Normal (2005)
USA; 91 minutes; Tenure Track Productions
Cast: J. Andrew Keitch, Joan Lauckner, Tim Hammer
Credits: Director-Writer: Marc Moody

Always Will (2006)
USA; 95 minutes; Windermere Pictures
Cast: Andrew Baglini, John Schmidt, Mark Schroeder, Noelle Meixell
Credits: Director-Writer: Michael Sammaciccia

The Amazing Mr. Blunden (1972)
United Kingdom; 99 minutes; Hemdale Group
Cast: Garry Miller, Lynne Frederick, Laurence Naismith, Diana Dors, Dorothy Allison
Credits: Director-Writer: Lionel Jeffries, based on *The Ghosts* by Antonia Barber

An Angel for May (2002)
United Kingdom; 99 minutes; Portman Film, Spice Factory, Barzo
Cast: Matthew Beard, Charlotte Wakefield, Julie Cox, Tom Wilkinson, Anna Massey
Credits: Director: Harley Cokeliss; Writer: Peter Milligan, based on the novel by Melvin Burgess

Another Day (2001)
USA; 90 minutes; USA Network
Cast: Shannon Doherty, Max Martini, Julian McMahon, Courtney Kidd
Credits: Director: Jeffrey Reiner; Writer: Helen Frost, Don MacLeod

Apex (1994)
USA; 98 minutes; Green Communications

Cast: Richard Keats, Mitchell Cox, Lisa Ann Russell, David Jean Thomas
Credits: Director: Phillip J. Roth; Writer: Roth, Ronald Schmidt; Story: Roth, Gian-Carlo Scandiuzzi

Army of Darkness (1993)
USA; 81 minutes; Universal, Dino De Laurentiis Communications, Renaissance Pictures
Cast: Bruce Campbell, Embeth Davidtz, Marcus Gilbert, Ian Abercrombie
Credits: Director: Sam Raimi; Writers: Sam Raimi, Ivan Raimi

Arthur's Quest (1999)
USA; 87 minutes; Crystal Sky Communications
Cast: Eric Christian Olsen, Alexandra Paul, Arye Gross, Catherine Oxenberg, Zach Galligan
Credits: Director: Neil Mandt; Writers: Gregory Poppen, Clint Hutchison, Lance W. Dreesen

Austin Powers: The Spy Who Shagged Me (1999)
USA; 95 minutes; New Line Cinema
Cast: Mike Myers, Heather Graham, Seth Green, Verne J. Troyer, Michael York, Robert Wagner
Credits: Director: Jay Roach; Writers: Mike Myers; Michael McCullers

Back to Christmas (2014)
USA; 85 minutes; Marvista Entertainment
Cast: Kelly Overton, Michael Muhney, Jonathan Patrick Moore, Jennifer Elise Cox
Credits: Director: Tim O'Donnell; Writer: Rachel Stuhler

Back to the Future (1985)
USA; 116 minutes; Universal
Cast: Michael J. Fox, Christopher Lloyd, Lea Thompson, Crispin Glover, Thomas F. Wilson
Credits: Director: Robert Zemeckis; Writers: Zemeckis, Bob Gale

Back to the Future II (1989)
USA; 108 minutes; Universal
Cast: Michael J. Fox, Christopher Lloyd, Thomas F. Wilson, Lea Thompson, Elizabeth Shue
Credits: Director: Robert Zemeckis; Writer: Bob Gale; Story: Zemeckis, Gale

Back to the Future Part Three (1990)
USA; 118 minutes; Universal
Cast: Michael J. Fox, Christopher Lloyd, Mary Steenburgen, Thomas F. Wilson, Lea Thompson, Elizabeth Shue
Credits: Director: Robert Zemeckis; Writer: Bob Gale; Story: Zemeckis, Gale

Back to the Jurassic (2012; aka *Dino Time*)
South Korea; 86 minutes; animated; CJ Entertainment.
Cast: Pamela Adlon, Tara Strong, Melanie Griffith, Jane Lynch, Rob Schneider, Yuri Lowenthal
Credits: Directors: Yoon S. Choi, John Kafka; Writer: Adam Beechen, Jae Woo Park, James Greco, Zack Rosenblatt; Story: Joon B. Heo, Yoon S. Choi

Before You Say "I Do" (2009)
USA; 90 minutes; Hallmark Channel
Cast: David Sutcliffe, Jennifer Westfeldt, Lauren Holly, Brad Borbridge
Credits: Director: Paul Fox; Writer: Elena Krupp

Ben 10: Race Against Time (2007)
USA; 67 minutes; Cartoon Network
Cast: Graham Phillips, Haley Ramm, Lee Majors, Christien Anholt
Credits: Director: Alex Winter; Writer: Mitch Watson; Story: Thomas Pugsley, Greg Klein

Beneath the Bermuda Triangle (1997; aka *Time Under Fire*)
USA; 94 minutes; Royal Oaks Entertainment
Cast: Jeff Fahey, Richard Tyson, Jack Coleman, Brian Cranston, Chick Vennera, Linda Hoffman
Credits: Director: Scott Levy; Writers: Tripp Reed, Sean McGinly

Beneath the Planet of the Apes (1970)
USA; 95 minutes; Twentieth Century–Fox
Cast: James Franciscus, Kim Hunter, Maurice Evans, Linda Harrison, Charlton Heston
Credits: Director: Ted Post; Writer: Paul Dehn; Story: Dehn, Mort Abrahams, based on characters created by Pierre Boulle

Berkeley Square (1933)
USA; 87 minutes; Fox
Cast: Leslie Howard, Heather Angel, Valerie Taylor
Credits: Director: Frank Lloyd; Writers: Sonya Levien, John L. Balderston, from the Balderston stage play

Between Time and Timbuktu: A Space Fantasy (1972)
USA; 90 minutes; PBS
Cast: William Hickey, Dortha Duckworth, Ray Goulding, Bob Elliott, Kevin McCarthy, Ariane Munker
Credits: Director: Fred Barzyk; Writers: Barzyk, David Loxton, David Odell, based on stories by Kurt Vonnegut

Beyond the Time Barrier (1960)
USA; 75 minutes; Miller Consolidated Pictures
Cast: Robert Clarke, Darlene Tompkins, Vladimir Sokoloff, Boyd Morgan
Credits: Director: Edgar G. Ulmer; Writer: Arthur C. Pierce

Biggles (1986; aka *Biggles: Adventures in Time*)
United Kingdom; 108 minutes; Compact Yellowbill, Tambarle
Cast: Alex Hyde-White, Neil Dickson, Fiona Hutchison, Peter Cushing
Credits: Director, John Hough; Writers: John Groves, Kent Walwin, based on characters created by W.E. Johns

Bill and Ted's Bogus Journey (1991)
USA; 93 minutes; Nelson Entertainment

Cast: Alex Winter, Keanu Reeves, George Carlin, Joss Ackland, William Sadler, Pam Grier
Credits: Director: Pete Hewitt; Writers: Chris Matheson, Ed Solomon

Bill and Ted's Excellent Adventure (1989)
USA; 90 minutes; Nelson Entertainment
Cast: Alex Winter, Keanu Reeves, George Carlin, Terry Camilleri, Dan Shor, Tony Steedman, Rod Loomis, Diane Franklin, Kimberly LaBelle
Credits: Director: Stephen Herek; Writers: Chris Matheson, Ed Solomon

Black Knight (2001)
USA; 96 minutes; 20th Century-Fox, Regency
Cast: Martin Lawrence, Tom Wilkinson, Marsha Thomason
Credits: Director: Gil Junger; Writers: Darryl J. Quarles, Peter Gaulke, Gerry Swallow

Blue Moon (2000)
USA; 89 minutes; Paradise Pictures
Cast: Ben Gazzara, Rita Moreno, Brian Vincent, Alanna Ubach
Credits: Director-Writer: John Gallagher; Story: Stephen Carducci

The Blue Yonder (1985; aka *Time Flier*)
USA; 95 minutes; Disney Channel
Cast: Peter Coyote, Huckleberry Fox, Art Carney
Credits: Director-Writer: Mark Rosman

The Boy and the Pirates (1960)
USA; 84 minutes; United Artists
Cast: Charles Herbert, Murvyn Vye, Joseph Turkel
Credits: Director-Story: Bert I. Gordon; Writers: Lillie Hayward, Jerry Sackheim

Bridge Across Time (1985; aka *Terror at London Bridge*)
USA; 96 minutes; NBC
Cast: David Hasselhoff, Stepfanie Kramer, Randolph Mantooth, Adrienne Barbeau, Clu Gulager
Credits: Director: E.W. Swackhamer; Writer: William F. Nolan

Brigadoon (1954)
USA; 108 minutes; MGM
Cast: Gene Kelly, Van Johnson, Cyd Charisse
Credits: Director: Vincente Minnelli; Writer: Alan Jay Lerner, based on the play by Lerner and Frederick Loewe

Brother Future (1991)
USA; 120 minutes; PBS
Cast: Phill Lewis, Carl Lumbly, Michael Burgess, Akosua Busia
Credits: Director: Roy Campanella II; Writer: Ann E. Eskridge

Bubble Fiction: Boom or Bust (2007; aka *Baburu e go!! Taimu Mashin Wa Doramu Shiki*)
Japan; 116 minutes; Toho
Cast: Ryôko Hirosue, Hiroshi Abe, Hiroko Yakushimaru
Credits: Director: Yasuo Baba; Writer: Ryôichi Kimizuka

The Butterfly Effect (2004)
USA; 120 minutes; New Line Cinema, FilmEngine
Cast: Ashton Kutcher, Melora Walters, Amy Smart
Credits: Director-Writers: Eric Bress, J. Mackye Gruber

The Butterfly Effect 2 (2006)
USA; 92 minutes; New Line Cinema, FilmEngine
Cast: Eric Lively, Erica Durance
Credits: Director: John R. Leonetti; Writer: Michael Weiss

The Butterfly Effect 3: Revelations (2009)
USA; 90 minutes; After Dark Films, Infinity Features, FilmEngine
Cast: Chris Carmack, Rachel Miner, Melissa Jones
Credits: Director: Seth Grossman; Writer: Holly Brix

The Caller (2011)
USA; 91 minutes; Pimienta Film Company, Salt Film Company, Alcove Entertainment
Cast: Rachelle Lefevre, Stephen Moyer, Lorna Raver
Credits: Director: Matthew Parkhill; Writer: Sergio Casci

Camp Slaughter (2005; aka *Camp Daze*)
USA; 95 minutes; Lightning Entertainment, Screamking Productions
Cast: Kyle Lupo, Anika McFall, Eric McIntire
Credits: Director-Story: Alex Pucci; Writer: Draven Gonzalez

Cavegirl (1985)
USA; 81 minutes; Crown International Pictures
Cast: Daniel Roebuck, Cindy Ann Thompson
Credits: Director-Writer: David Oliver, adapted from the screenplay *Primal Urge* by Phil Groves

Change of Life (2010)
USA; 93 minutes; Agent Provocateur Films, Blue Wave Productions
Cast: Denny Day, Alexis Pelfrey, Vince Mollica, Alyson Schacherer
Credits: Director: Amy McClung; Writers: McClung, Jon Weimer

Chasing Christmas (2005)
USA; 90 minutes; ABC Family, Insight Film Studios
Cast: Tom Arnold, Andrea Roth, Leslie Jordan
Credits: Director: Ron Oliver; Writer: Todd Berger

The Christmas Clause (2008)
USA; 84 minutes; Cinamour Entertainment, Insight Films
Cast: Lea Thompson, Andrew Airlie, Rachel Hayward, Doug Abrahams
Credits: Director: George Erschbamer; Writer: Sheri Elwood

Christmas Do-Over (2006)
USA; 89 minutes; ABC Family
Cast: Jay Mohr, Daphne Zuniga, David Millbern, Adrienne Barbeau, Tim Thomerson, Ruta Lee
Credits: Director: Catherine Cyran; Writers: Trevor Reed Cristow, Jacqueline David

A Christmas Eve Miracle (2015)
USA; 80 minutes; Crystal Sky
Cast: Olivia D'Abo, Anthony Starke, Jon Voight, Josh Reid
Credits: Director: R. Michael Givens; Writer: Jon Young; Story: Steven Paul

Christmas Every Day (1996)
USA; 86 minutes; ABC Family
Cast: Erik von Detten, Robert Hays, Bess Armstrong
Credits: Director: Larry Peerce; Writer: Stephen Alix, Nancey Silvers; Story: Stephen Alix

Cinderella III: A Twist in Time (2007)
USA; 74 minutes; animated; Disney
Voices: Jennifer Hale, C.D. Barnes, Susanne Blakeslee
Credits: Director: Frank Nissen; Writers: Dan Berendsen, Margaret Heidenry, Colleen Ventimilia, Eddie Guzelian

Cleopatra (1970; aka *Cleopatra, Queen of Sex*)
Japan; 112 minutes; animated; Mushi Productions
Cast: Yoshiro Kato, Jitsuko Yoshimura, Nobuo Tsukamoto, Tsubame Yanagiya, Chinatsu Nakayama, Hajime Hana
Credits: Directors: Osama Tezuka, Eichi Yamamoto; Writer: Shigemi Satoyoshi

Click (2006)
USA; 107 minutes; Columbia, Revolution Studios, Happy Madison Productions
Cast: Adam Sandler, Kate Beckinsale, Christopher Walken, David Hasselhoff, Henry Winkler
Credits: Director: Frank Coraci; Writers: Steve Koren, Mark O'Keefe

Clive Barker Presents Saint Sinner (2002; aka *Saint Sinner*)
USA; 86 minutes; SciFi Channel
Cast: Greg Serano, Gina Ravera, Mary Mara
Credits: Director: Joshua Butler; Writer: Doris Egan, Hans Rodionoff; Story: Clive Barker

Coherence (2013)
USA; 88 minutes; Oscilloscope Films
Cast: Emily Foxler, Maury Sterling, Nicholas Brendon, Elizabeth Gracen
Credits: Director: James Ward Byrkit; Writer: James Ward Byrkit; Story: Byrkit, Alex Manugian

Comfort and Joy (2003)
USA; 99 minutes; Lifetime Channel
Cast: Nancy McKeon, Steven Eckholdt, Dixie Carter
Credits: Director: Maggie Greenwald; Writer: Judd Parkin

A Connecticut Yankee (1931; aka *A Connecticut Yankee in King Arthur's Court*)
USA; 95 minutes; Fox
Cast: Will Rogers, Myrna Loy, William Farnum, Maureen O'Sullivan
Credits: Director: David Butler; Writer: William Conselman, based on the Mark Twain novel

A Connecticut Yankee in King Arthur's Court (1921)
USA; 80 minutes; Fox
Cast: Harry Myers, Pauline Starke, Rosemary Theby, Charles Clary
Credits: Director: Emmett J. Flynn; Writer: Bernard McConville, based on the Mark Twain novel

A Connecticut Yankee in King Arthur's Court (1949)
USA; 107 minutes; Paramount
Cast: Bing Crosby, Rhonda Fleming, Cedric Hardwicke, William Bendix, Murvyn Vye
Credits: Director: Tay Garnett; Writer: Edmund Beloin, based on the Mark Twain novel

A Connecticut Yankee in King Arthur's Court (1970)
USA; 74 minutes; animated; API
Cast: Orson Bean
Credits: Director: Zoran Janjic; Writer: Michael Robinson, based on the Twain novel

A Connecticut Yankee in King Arthur's Court (1989)
USA; 94 minutes; NBC
Cast: Keshia Knight Pulliam, Bryce Hamnet, Michael Gross, Emma Samms, Jean Marsh
Credits: Director: Mel Damski; Writer: Paul Zindel, based on the Mark Twain novel

Cruel and Unusual (2014)
Canada; 92 minutes; CFC Features
Cast: David Richmond-Peck, Bernadette Saquibal, Michelle Harrison, Monsour Cataquiz
Credits: Director-Writer: Merlin Dervisevic

Crusade: A March Through Time (2006; aka *Crusade in Jeans, Kruistocht in Spijkerbroek*)
Netherlands; 101 minutes; Kasander Film Company, Intuit Pictures
Cast: Johnny Flynn, Stephanie Leonidas, Emily Watson
Credits: Director: Ben Sombogaart; Writer: Bill Haney, based on screenplay by Jean-Claude van Rijckeghem, Chris Craps, based on the novel *Kruistocht in Spijkerbroek* by Thea Beckman

Cryptic (2009)
USA; 86 minutes; Compendium Entertainment Group
Cast: Julie Carlson, Jadin Gould, Jodi Thelen, Toby Huss, Johnny Pacar
Credits: Director-Writers: Danny Kuchuck, John Weiner

C.S.A.: Confederate States of America
(2004)
USA; 89 minutes; Hodcarrier Films
Cast: Greg Kirsch, Renee Patrick, Molly Graham
Credits: Director-Writer: Kevin Willmott

Cyborg 2087 (1966)
USA; 86 minutes; Harold Goldman Associates, United Pictures
Cast: Michael Rennie, Karen Steele, Wendell Corey, Warren Stevens
Credits: Director: Franklin Adreon; Writer: Arthur C. Pierce

Daleks' Invasion Earth 2150 AD (1966)
United Kingdom; 80 minutes, AARU Productions
Cast: Peter Cushing, Bernard Cribbins, Ray Brooks, Roberta Tovey
Credits: Director: Gordon Flemyng; Writers: Terry Nation, Milton Subotsky, David Whitaker

Dead of Night (1977)
USA; 88 minutes; NBC
Story: "Second Chance"
Cast: Ed Begley, Jr., E.J. Andre, Ann Doran, Christine Hart
Credits: Director: Dan Curtis; Writer: Richard Matheson, based on the story by Jack Finney

Déjà Vu (2006)
USA; 126 minutes; Touchstone Pictures
Cast: Denzel Washington, Paula Patton, Val Kilmer, Jim Caviezel
Credits: Director: Tony Scott; Writers: Bill Marsilli, Terry Rossio

The Devil's Arithmetic (1999)
USA; 101 minutes; Showtime
Cast: Kirsten Dunst, Brittany Murphy, Paul Freeman, Mimi Rogers, Louise Fletcher
Credits: Director: Donna Deitch; Writer: Robert J. Averch, based on the Jane Yolen novel

Dimension 5 (1966)
USA; 90 minutes; United Pictures
Cast: Jeffrey Hunter, France Nuyen, Harold Sakata, Donald Woods
Credits: Director: Franklin Adreon; Writer: Arthur C. Pierce

Dimensions (2011)
United Kingdom; 101 minutes; Mousetrap Films, Sculptures of Dazzling Complexity
Cast: Henry Lloyd-Hughes, Camilla Rutherford, Patrick Godfrey, Olivia Llewellyn, Sean Hart, Edward Halsted
Credits: Director: Sloane U'Ren; Writer: Antony Neely

Dinosaur Valley Girls (1997)
USA; 94 minutes; Frontline Entertainment
Cast: Jeff Rector, Denise Ames, Griffin Drew, William Marshall, Ed Fury, Karen Black
Credits: Director-Writer: Donald F. Glut

The Disappearance of Haruhi Suzumiya
(2010)
Japan; 163 minutes; animated; Kadokawa Pictures
Cast: Ayo Hirano, Tomokazu Sugita, Minori Chihara, Yuuko Gotou
Credits: Directors: Tatsuya Ishihara, Yasuhiro Takemoto; Writer: Fumhiko Shimo, based on the manga novel by Nagaru Tanigawa

Disasters in Time (1992; aka *Grand Tour, Timescape*)
USA; 95 minutes; HBO
Cast: Jeff Daniels, Ariana Richards, Emilia Crow, Marilyn Lightstone, George Murdock, Robert Colbert
Credits: Director-Writer: David N. Twohy, based on "Vintage Season" by Henry Kuttner and C.L. Moore

Disconnect (2010)
USA; 112 minutes; Osiris Entertainment
Cast: Steffany Huckaby, Amanda Troop, Eddie Jones, Holmes Osborne, Michael Muhney
Credits: Director-Writer: Robin Christian

Disney's the Kid (2000; aka *The Kid*)
USA; 101 minutes; Disney
Cast: Bruce Willis, Spencer Breslin, Emily Mortimer, Lily Tomlin, Jean Smart
Credits: Director: Jon Turteltaub; Writer: Audrey Wells

Ditto (2000; aka *Donggam*)
South Korea; 110 minutes; Tai Seng
Cast: Kim Ha-Neul, Yoo Ji-Tae
Credits: Director: Kim Jeong-kwon; Writer: Jin Jang

Doctor Who (1996; aka *Doctor Who—The Movie*)
USA; 89 minutes, Fox TV
Cast: Paul McGann, Daphne Ashbrook, Eric Roberts
Credits: Director: Geoffrey Sax; Writer: Matthew Jacobs

Dr. Who and the Daleks (1965)
United Kingdom; 85 minutes; AARU Productions
Cast: Peter Cushing, Roy Castle, Jennie Linden
Credits: Director: Gordon Flemyng; Writers: Terry Nation, Milton Subotsky

Donnie Darko (2001)
USA; 113 minutes; Pandora, Newmarket.
Cast: Jake Gyllenhaal, Holmes Osborne, Maggie Gyllenhaal, Mary McDonnell
Credits: Director-Writer: Richard Kelly

Doomsday (2015)
United Kingdom; 95 minutes; Still Night Monster Movies, Empire Motion Pictures
Cast: Alain Terzoli. Amy Pemberton, Darren Jacobs, Richard Lawrence, Helen Soraya
Credits: Director-Writer: Neil Johnson

Doonby (2013)
USA; 104 minutes; Gravitas Ventures, Riverhorse Entertainment, MTM Entertainment
Cast: John Schneider, Jenn Gotzon, Ernie Hudson, Robert Davi, Joe Estevez, Jennifer O'Neill
Credits: Director-Writer: Peter Mackenzie

The Drivetime (1995)
USA; 86 minutes; ParaTheatrical ReSearch, Tele-Visionary Oracle
Cast: Michael Douglas, Michael George, Susan Mansfield, Kristen Kosmas
Credits: Director: Antero Alli; Writers: Alli, Rob Brezsny

Durango Kids (1999)
USA; 91 minutes; Good Friends Productions
Cast: Larry Drake, Curtis Williams, Brendon Ryan Barrett, Caitlin Lara Barrett
Credits: Director: Ashton Root; Writers: Root, William Brennan

Edgar Rice Burroughs' The Land That Time Forgot (2009; aka *The Land That Time Forgot*)
USA; 89 minutes; The Asylum
Cast: C. Thomas Howell, Timothy Bottoms, Lindsey McKeon, Darren Dalton
Credits: Director: C. Thomas Howell; Writer: Darren Dalton, based on the Edgar Rice Burroughs novel

The Edge of the Garden (2011)
USA; 84 minutes; Hallmark Channel
Cast: Rob Estes, Sarah Manninen, David Lewis
Credits: Director: Michael M. Scott; Writer: Duane Poole

Edge of Tomorrow (2014)
USA; 113 minutes; Warner Brothers
Cast: Tom Cruise, Emily Blunt, Brendan Gleeson, Bill Paxton
Credits: Director: Doug Liman; Writers: Christopher McQuarrie, Jez Butterworth, John-Henry Butterworth, based on *All You Need Is Kill* by Hiroshi Sakurazaka

11 Minutes Ago (2009)
USA; 83 minutes; Fly High Films
Cast: Ian Michaels, Christina Mauro, Evan Lee Dahl
Credits: Director-Writer: Bob Gebert

Eliminators (1986)
USA; 95 minutes; Empire Pictures
Cast: Denise Crosby, Andrew Prine, Patrick Reynolds, Conan Lee, Roy Dotrice
Credits: Director: Peter Manoogian; Writers: Paul De Meo, Danny Bilson

Enter Nowhere (2011)
USA; 89 minutes; Caliber Media
Cast: Katherine Waterston, Scott Eastwood, Sara Paxton, Shaun Sipos, Christopher Denham, Jesse Perez
Credits: Director: Jack Heller; Writers: Shawn Christensen, Jason Dolan

Escape from the Planet of the Apes (1971)
USA; 98 minutes; Twentieth Century–Fox
Cast: Roddy McDowall, Kim Hunter, Bradford Dillman, Natalie Trundy, Ricardo Montalban, Sal Mineo
Credits: Director: Don Taylor; Writer: Paul Dehn, based on characters created by Pierre Boulle

Escape Through Time (1992)
USA; 96 minutes; Linn Productions
Cast: Jill Killinger, Kirsten Meyer, Carl Schoenborn
Credits: Director: Michael Linn; Writers: Michael and Marc Linn

Escape to Grizzly Mountain (1999)
USA; 95 minutes; Tomorrow Films
Cast: Miko Hughes, Dan Haggerty, Ellina McCormick, Nik Winterhawk, Cynthia Palmer
Credits: Director: Anthony Dalesandro; Writer: Boon Collins, based on a story by George Furla

Eve's Christmas (2004)
USA; 96 minutes; Shavick/Insight Studios, Regent Entertainment
Cast: Elisa Donovan, Sebastian Spence, Peter Williams
Credits: Director: Timothy Bond; Writer: Peter Sullivan; Story: Jeffrey Schenck, Peter Sullivan

The Excalibur Kid (1999)
USA; 81 minutes; Moonbeam Films
Cast: Jason McSkimming, François Klanfer, Mak Fyfe, Francesca Scorsone, Natalia Ester
Credits: Director: James Head; Writer: Antony Anderson

Family Man (2000)
USA; 126 minutes; Universal, Beacon Pictures
Cast: Nicolas Cage, Téa Leoni, Don Cheadle, Jeremy Piven, Saul Rubinek
Credits: Director: Brett Ratner; Writers: David Diamond, David Weissman

Fatherland (1994)
USA; 106 minutes; HBO
Cast: Rutger Hauer, Miranda Richardson, Jean Marsh
Credits: Director: Christopher Menaul; Writers: Stanley Weiser, Ron Hutchinson, based on the Robert Harris novel

Fetching Cody (2005)
USA; 88 minutes; Cheap and Dirty Productions
Cast: Jay Baruchel, Sarah Lind, Jim Byrnes
Credits: Director-Writer: David Ray; Story: Ray, Carolyn Allain

Fiddlers Three (1944; aka *While Nero Fiddled*)
United Kingdom; 88 minutes; Ealing Studios
Cast: Tommy Trinder, Frances Day, Sonnie

Hale, Francis L. Sullivan, Diana Decker, Elisabeth Welch
Credits: Director: Harry Watt; Writers: Angus MacPhail, Diana Morgan

The Final Countdown (1980)
USA; 102 minutes; Tallmantz Aviation, Optical House
Cast: Kirk Douglas, Martin Sheen, Katharine Ross, James Farentino, Ron O'Neal, Charles Durning
Credits: Director: Don Taylor; Screenplay: David Ambrose, Gerry Davis, Thomas Hunter, Peter Powell; Story: David Ambrose, Thomas Hunter, Peter Powell

Fire Tripper (1985)
Japan; 50 minutes; animated; Shogakugan
Cast: Sumi Shimamoto, Yuu Mizushima, Mayumi Tanaka
Credits: Director: Motosuke Takahashi; Writer: Tomoku Konparu

The Flight That Disappeared (1961)
USA; 72 minutes; United Artists, Harvard Film Corporation
Cast: Craig Hill, Paula Raymond, Dayton Lummis, Gregory Morton
Credits: Director: Reginald LeBorg; Writers: Ralph Hart, Judith Hart, Owen Harris

Flight World War II (2015)
USA; 86 minutes; The Asylum
Cast: Faran Tahir, Robbie A. Kay, Harwood Gordon
Credits: Director: Emile Edwin Smith; Screenplay: Jacob Cooney, Bill Hanstock

For All Time (2000)
USA; 86 minutes; Lifetime Network
Cast: Mark Harmon, Mary McDonnell, Catherine Hicks
Credits: Director: Steven Schachter; Writer: Vivienne Radkoff, based on the *Twilight Zone* TV episode "A Stop at Willoughby"

The Forbidden Kingdom (2008)
USA; 104 minutes; Casey Silver Productions
Cast: Michael Angarano, Jackie Chan, Jet Li, Morgan Benoit, Liu Yifei
Credits: Director: Rob Minkoff; Writer: John Fusco

Found in Time (2012)
USA; 90 minutes; Chaotic Sequence
Cast: MacLeod Andrews, Mina Vesper Gokal, Kelly Sullivan, Derek Morgan, Eric Martin Brown
Credits: Director-Writer: Arthur Vincie

Frankenstein Unbound (1990; aka *Roger Corman's Frankenstein Unbound*)
USA; 90 minutes; 20th Century-Fox, Mount Company
Cast: John Hurt, Raul Julia, Nick Brimble, Bridget Fonda
Credits: Director, Roger Corman; Writers: Roger Corman, F.X. Feeney, based on *Frankenstein Unbound* by Brian W. Aldiss

Free Birds (2013)
USA; 91 minutes; animated; Relativity Media
Cast: Owen Wilson, Woody Harrelson, Amy Poehler, George Takei, Colm Meaney
Credits: Director: Jimmy Hayward; Writers: Scott Mosier, Hayward; Story: David I. Stern, John J. Strauss

Freejack (1992)
USA; 108 minutes; Morgan Creek
Cast: Emilio Estevez, Mick Jagger, Rene Russo, Anthony Hopkins, Jonathan Banks, Amanda Plummer
Credits: Director: Geoff Murphy; Writers: Steven Pressfield, Ronald Shusett, Dan Gilroy; Story: Pressfield, Shusett, based on *Immortality, Inc.* by Robert Sheckley

Frequency (2000)
USA; 119 minutes; New Line
Cast: Jim Caviezel, Dennis Quaid, Shawn Doyle, Elizabeth Mitchell, Andre Braugher
Credits: Director: Gregory Hoblit; Writer: Toby Emmerich

Frequently Asked Questions About Time Travel (2009)
United Kingdom; 83 minutes; HBO, BBC
Cast: Chris O'Dowd, Anna Farris, Marc Wootton, Dean Lennox Kelly, Meredith MacNeill
Credits: Director: Garth Carrivick; Writer: Jamie Mathieson

From Time to Time (2009)
United Kingdom; 96 minutes; Ealing Studios
Cast: Alex Etel, Maggie Smith, Timothy Spall, Eliza Hope Bennett, Kwayedza Kureya
Credits: Director-Writer: Julian Fellowes, based on *Chimneys of Greene Knowe* by Lucy M. Boston

Futurama: Bender's Big Score (2007)
USA; 88 minutes, animated, Curiosity Co.
Voices: Billy West, Katey Segal, John DiMaggio, Lauren Tom, Phil LaMarr
Credits: Director: Dwayne Carey-Hill; Writer: Ken Keeler; Story: Keeler and David X. Cohen

Future War (1997)
USA; 82 minutes; 20th Century-Fox, Silver Screen International, Cine Excel Entertainment
Cast: Daniel Bernhardt, Robert Z'Dar, Travis Brooks Stewart
Credits: Director: Anthony Doublin; Writer: Dom Magwilli; Story: David Hue, Magwilli

Future Zone (1990)
USA; 79 minutes; AIP Entertainment
Cast: David Carradine, Ted Prior, Patrick Culliton, Gail Jensen, Charles Napier
Credits: Director-Writer: David A. Prior

G.I. Samurai (1979; aka *Time Slip*, *Sengoku Jietai*)
Japan; 139 minutes; Kadokawa Films
Cast: Sonny Chiba, Isao Natsuyagi, Jun Etō

Credits: Directors: Mitsumasa Saito; Writer: Toshio Kamata, based on Ryo Hanmura's novel *Sengoku Jietai*

Gintama: The Final Chapter: Be Forever Yoruza (2013; aka *Gekijouban Gintama Kanketsu-hen: Yorozuyayo Eien Nare*)
Japan; 110 minutes; animated; Shueisha, Aniplex
Cast: Tomokazu Sugita, Rie Kugimiya, Daisuke Sakaguchi
Credits: Director: Yoichi Fujita; Writer: Akatsutki Yamatoya

The Girl Who Leapt Through Time (2006; aka *Toki o Kakeru Shoujo*)
Japan; 96 minutes; animated; Mad House, Happinet Pictures, Kadokawa Pictures
Voices: Riisa Naka, Takuya Ishida, Mitsutaka Itakura, Ayami Kakiuchi
Credits: Director: Mamoru Hosada; Writer: Satoko Okudera, based on the novel by Yasutaka Tsutsui

Godzilla vs. King Ghidorah (1991; aka *Gojira Buiese Kingu Gidora*)
Japan; 101 minutes; Toho Studios
Cast: Kosuke Toyohara, Anna Nakagawa, Megumi Odaka
Credits: Director-Writer: Kazuki Omori

Grey Skies: The Alien Conspiracy (2002)
USA; 64 minutes; Brimstone Media
Cast: Nathan King, Meredith Levers, Autumn Lucas
Credits: Director-Writers: Tom Nondorf, Kevin J. Lindenmuth, Les Sekely

Grizzly Mountain (1997)
USA; 96 minutes; Mega Communications, Napor Kids
Cast: Dan Haggerty, Dylan Haggerty, Nicole Lund, Kim Morgan Greene, Perry Stephens
Credits: Director: Jeremy Hart; Writer: Hart, Peter White; Story: Eric Parkinson

Groundhog Day (1993)
USA; 101 minutes; Columbia Pictures
Cast: Bill Murray, Andie McDowell, Chris Elliott
Credits: Director: Harold Ramis; Writers: Danny Rubin, Ramis; Story: Rubin

The Halloween Tree (1993)
USA; 70 minutes; animated; TBS
Cast: Ray Bradbury, Leonard Nimoy
Credits: Director-Producer: Mario Piluso; Writer: Ray Bradbury, based on his story

Happy Accidents (2000)
USA; 110 minutes; IFC Films
Cast: Marisa Tomei, Vincent D'Onofrio, Holland Taylor
Credits: Director-Writer: Brad Anderson

A Hitch in Time (1978)
United Kingdom; 57 minutes; Children's Film Foundation
Cast: Patrick Troughton, Michael McVey, Pheona McLellan, Jeff Rawle
Credits: Director: Jan Darnley-Smith; Writer: T.E.B. Clarke

Holiday Switch (2007)
USA; 89 minutes; Lifetime Network
Cast: Nicole Eggert, Patricia Mayen-Salazar, Bret Anthony, Brett Le Bourveau
Credits: Director: Bert Kish; Writer: Gayl Decoursey

Holidaze (2013)
USA; 86 minutes; ABC Family
Cast: Jennie Garth, Cameron Mathison, Kristin Booth
Credits: Director: Jerry Ciccoritti; Writer: Michael Vickerman

Hot Tub Time Machine (2010)
USA; 100 minutes; Paramount, MGM
Cast: John Cusack, Clark Duke, Craig Robinson, Rob Corddry, Chevy Chase
Credits: Director: Steve Pink; Writers: Josh Heald, Sean Anders, John Morris; Story: Heald

Hot Tub Time Machine 2 (2015)
USA; 93 minutes; Paramount, MGM
Cast: Rob Corddry, Craig Robinson, Clark Duke, Adam Scott, Gillian Jacobs, Chevy Chase, Collette Wolfe
Credits: Director: Steve Pink; Writer: Josh Heald

House II: The Second Story (1987)
USA; 88 minutes; New World Pictures
Cast: Arye Gross, Jonathan Stark, Royal Dano, Bill Maher, John Ratzenberger, Devon DeVasquez
Credits: Director-Writer: Ethan Wiley

The House in the Square (1951; aka *I'll Never Forget You*)
USA; 91 minutes, Twentieth Century–Fox
Cast: Tyrone Power, Ann Blyth, Michael Rennie
Credits: Director: Roy Baker; Writer: Ranald MacDougall, based on *Berkeley Square*

I Love You, I Love You (1968; aka *Je t'aime Je t'aime*)
France; 92 minutes; 20th Century-Fox
Cast: Claude Rich, Olga Georges-Picot
Credits: Director: Alain Resnais; Screenwriter: Jacques Sternberg

Idaho Transfer (1971)
USA; 85 minutes; Pando Co.
Cast: Kelley Bohanan, Kevin Hearst, Caroline Hildebrand, Keith Carradine, Dale Hopkins
Credits: Director: Peter Fonda; Writer: Thomas Matthiesen

If Only (2004)
USA; 96 minutes; Intermedia Films, Outlaw Productions, Love Spell Entertainment
Cast: Jennifer Love Hewitt, Paul Nicholls, Tom Wilkinson
Credits: Director: Gil Junger; Writer: Christina Welsh

Il Mare (2000)
South Korea; 96 minutes; Sidus
Cast: Lee Jung-jae, Jeon Ji-hyun
Credits: Director: Lee Hyun-seung; Writer: Yeoh Jina

I'll Believe You (2006)
USA; 80 minutes; Stand Up Films, Boy in the Drain
Cast: David Alan Basche, Patrick Warburton, Siobhan Fallon Hogan, Patrick Gallo
Credits: Director: Paul Francis Sullivan; Writers: Sullivan, Sean McPharlin, Ted Sullivan

I'll Follow You Down (2014)
Canada; 93 minutes; Resolute Films
Cast: Haley Joel Osment, Susanna Fournier, Rufus Sewell, Gillian Anderson, Victor Garber
Credits: Director-Writer: Richie Mehta

In His Father's Shoes (1997)
USA; 105 minutes; Showtime, Hallmark Channel
Cast: Robert Ri'chard, Louis Gossett, Jr., Barbara Eve Harris
Credits: Director: Vic Sarin; Writer: Gary Gelt

In the Name of the King 2: Two Worlds (2011)
USA; 96 minutes; Brightlight Pictures, Event Film, Pistoleros
Cast: Dolph Lundgren, Lochlyn Munro, Natassia Malthe, Christina Jastrzembska
Credits: Director: Uwe Boll; Writer: Michael C. Nachoff

In the Name of the King 3: The Last Mission (2014)
USA; 85 minutes; Event Film
Cast: Dominic Purcell, Ralitsa Paskaleva, Daria Simeonova, Petra Gocheva
Credits: Director: Uwe Boll; Writer: Joel Ross

The Indian in the Cupboard (1995)
USA; 98 minutes; Columbia Pictures, Paramount Pictures
Cast: Hal Scardino, Litefoot, Rishi Bhat, Lindsay Crouse, David Keith
Credits: Director: Frank Oz; Writer: Melissa Mathison, based on the Lynne Reid Banks novel

The Infinite Man (2014)
Australia; 85 minutes; Invincible Pictures, Bonsai Films
Cast: Josh McConville, Hannah Marshall, Alex Dimitriades
Credits: Director-Writer: Hugh Sullivan

Interstellar (2014)
USA; 168 minutes; Paramount, Warner Brothers, Legendary
Cast: Matthew McConaughey, Mackenzie Foy, Jessica Chastain, Ellen Burstyn, John Lithgow, Anne Hathaway, Michael Caine, Matt Damon
Credits: Director: Christopher Nolan; Writers: Jonathan and Christopher Nolan

It Happened Here (1965)
United Kingdom; 96 minutes; Milestone Films
Cast: Pauline Murray, Sebastian Shaw, Fiona Leland, Bart Allison, Reginald Marsh
Credits: Director-Writers: Kevin Brownlow, Andrew Mollo, from an idea by Brownlow

It Happened One Christmas (1977)
USA; 109 minutes; ABC
Cast: Marlo Thomas, Orson Welles, Wayne Rogers, Cloris Leachman
Credits: Director: Donald Wrye; Writers: Lionel Chetwynd, Lloyd J. Schwartz, based on *It's a Wonderful Life*

It's a Very Merry Muppet Christmas Movie (2002)
USA; 88 minutes; NBC
Cast: Steve Whitmire, Eric Jacobson, David Arquette, Joan Cusack, Whoopi Goldberg, William H. Macy
Credits: Director: Kirk B. Thatcher; Writers: Tom Martin, Jim Lewis

It's a Wonderful Life (1946)
USA; 130 minutes; Liberty Films
Cast: James Stewart, Donna Reed, Lionel Barrymore, Henry Travers, Gloria Grahame
Credits: Director-Producer: Frank Capra; Writers: Frances Goodrich, Albert Hackett, Frank Capra, Jo Swerling; Based on *The Greatest Gift* by Philip Van Doren Stern

Ivan Vassilyevich Changes Occupation
(1973; aka *Ivan Vassilyevich Back to the Future, Ivan Vassilyevich Menyaet Professlyu*)
USSR; 87 minutes; Experimental Artistic Association
Cast: Yuri Yakovlev, Aleksandr Demyanenko, Leonid Kuravlyov, Natalya Seleznyova
Credits: Director: L. Gaidai; Writers: V. Bakhnov, L. Gaidai, from the play by Mikhail A. Bulgakov

Izo (2004)
Japan; 127 minutes; KSS
Cast: Kazuya Nakayama
Credits: Director: Takashi Miike; Writer: Shigenori Takechi

The Jacket (2005)
USA; 103 minutes; Warner Independent Pictures, Mandalay Pictures
Cast: Adrien Brody, Keira Knightley, Kris Kristofferson, Jennifer Jason Leigh
Credits: Director: John Maybury; Writer: Massy Tadjedin; Story: Tom Bleecker, Marc Rocco

The Jetsons Meet the Flintstones (1987)
USA; 92 minutes; animated; Hanna-Barbera
Voices: Henry Corden, Mel Blanc, Julie McWhirter, George O'Hanlon, Penny Singleton
Credits: Supervising Director: Ray Patterson; Writers: Don Nelson, Arthur Alsberg

Jett Jackson—The Movie (2001)
USA; 89 minutes; Disney Channel

Cast: Lee Thompson Young, Kerry Duff, Lindy Booth, Michael Ironside
Credits: Director: Shawn Levy; Writer: Bruce Kalish, based on the series created by Fracaswell Hyman

John Dies at the End (2012)
USA; 99 minutes; Magnet, Silver Sphere, M3 Creative, Touchy Feely Films
Cast: Chase Williamson, Rob Mayes, Paul Giamatti, Clancy Brown
Credits: Writer-Director: Don Coscarelli, based on the David Wong novel

Johnny Mysto Boy Wizard (1997)
USA; 82 minutes; Full Moon Entertainment
Cast: Toran Caudell, Russ Tamblyn, Michael Ansara, Amber Tamblyn, Ian Abercrombie
Credits: Director: Jeff Burr; Writer: Benjamin Carr

Josh Kirby ... Time Warrior (1995–96)
USA; 96 minutes; Kushner-Locke, Full Moon Entertainment
Installments: Planet of the Dino-Knights (91 minutes), The Human Pets (96 minutes), Trapped on Toy World (87 minutes), Eggs from 70 Million BC (93 minutes), Journey to the Magic Cavern (93 minutes), Final Battle for the Universe (86 minutes)
Cast: Corbin Allred, Jennifer Burns, Derek Webster, Barrie Ingham
Credits: Directors: Frank Arnold, Mark Manos, Ernie Farino; Writers: Cy Voris, Ethan Reiff

Journey to the Center of Time (1967)
USA; 77 minutes; Borealis Enterprises, Dorad Corporation, American General
Cast: Scott Brady, Anthony Eisley, Gigi Perreau, Abraham Sofaer
Credits: Director: David L. Hewitt; Writer: David Prentiss [Hewitt]

Judas Kiss (2011)
USA; 94 minutes; Blue Seraph Productions, Border2Border Entertainment
Cast: Charlie David, Richard Harmon
Credits: Director: J.T. Tepnapa; Writer: Carlos Pedraza

Juko's Time Machine (2011)
USA; 73 minutes; Young Barney
Cast: Nathan Cozzolino, Alex Moggridge, Katie Sigismund, Zibby Allen
Credits: Director-Writer: Kai Barry

Jules Verne's Mysterious Island (2012)
USA; 91 minutes; SyFy Channel
Cast: Gina Holden, Lochlyn Munro, Pruitt Taylor Vince, Mark Sheppard, W. Morgan Sheppard
Credits: Director: Mark Sheppard; Writer: Cameron Larson, based on the novel by Jules Verne

Just Visiting (2001)
USA; 88 minutes; Gaumont
Cast: Jean Reno, Christina Applegate, Christian Clavier, Tara Reid, Malcolm McDowell
Credits: Director: Jean-Marie Gaubert; Writers: Christian Clavier, Jean-Marie Poiré, John Hughes, based on Les Visiteurs by Jean-Marie Poiré and Christian Clavier

Justice League: Crisis on Two Earths (2010)
USA; 75 minutes; animated; Warner Brothers Animation
Cast: William Baldwin, Mark Harmon, Chris Noth, Gina Torres, James Woods
Credits: Directors: Sam Liu, Lauren Montgomery; Writer: Dwayne McDuffie

Justice League: The Flashpoint Paradox (2013)
USA; 81 minutes; animated; Warner Brothers Animation
Cast: Justin Chambers, C. Thomas Howell, Michael B. Jordan, Kevin McKidd, Kevin Conroy, Sam Daly, Dana Delany
Credits: Director: Jay Oliva; Writer: Jim Krieg, based on Flashpoint by Geoff Johns and Andy Kubert

Kate & Leopold (2001)
USA; 121 minutes; Miramax
Cast: Meg Ryan, Hugh Jackman, Liev Schreiber
Credits: Director: James Mangold; Writers: Mangold, Steven Rogers, Story: Rogers

A Kid in Aladdin's Palace (1997)
USA; 89 minutes; Tapestry Films, Trimark Pictures
Cast: Thomas Ian Nicholas, Rhona Mitra, Nicholas Irons, James Faulkner, Taylor Negron, Aharon Ipalé
Credits: Director: Robert L. Levy; Writer: Michael Part; Story: Part, Levy

A Kid in King Arthur's Court (1995)
USA; 90 minutes; Disney
Cast: Thomas Ian Nicholas, Joss Ackland, Ron Moody, Art Malik, Paloma Baeza, Kate Winslet, Daniel Craig
Credits: Director: Michael Gottlieb; Writers: Michael Part, Robert L. Levy

Kim Possible: A Sitch in Time (2003)
USA; 66 minutes; Disney Channel
Voices: Christy Carlson Romano, Will Friedle
Credits: Director: Steve Loter; Writers: Bill Motz, Bob Roth

A Knight in Camelot (1998)
USA; 88 minutes; ABC
Cast: Whoopi Goldberg, Michael York, Amanda Donohoe, Paloma Baeza
Credits: Director: Roger Young; Writer: Joe Wiesenfeld, inspired by A Connecticut Yankee in King Arthur's Court by Mark Twain

Kristin's Christmas Past (2013)
USA; 87 minutes; Lifetime Network
Cast: Shiri Appleby, Hannah Marks, Elizabeth Mitchell, Will Kemp
Credits: Director: Jim Fall; Writer: Rachel Stuhler

La Jetée (1963)
France; 28 minutes; Argos Films
Cast: Héléne Chatelain, Davos Hanich
Credits: Director-Writer: Chris Marker

The Lake (1998)
USA; 95 minutes; NBC
Cast: Yasmine Bleeth, Linden Ashby
Credits: Director: David S. Jackson; Writers: Alan Brennert, J.D. Feigelson; Story: Feigelson

The Lake House (2006)
USA; 98 minutes; Warner Brothers
Cast: Sandra Bullock, Keanu Reeves, Christopher Plummer, Dylan Walsh
Credits: Director: Alejandro Agresti; Writer: David Auburn, based on *Il Mare*

Lancelot, Guardian of Time (1997)
USA; 90 minutes; Alpine Pictures, Anubis Productions
Cast: Marc Singer, Claudia Christian, John Saxon
Credits: Director: Rubiano Cruz; Writer: Patricia Monville; Story: Ryan Carroll

Land of the Lost (2009)
USA; 102 minutes; Universal, Relativity Media
Cast: Will Ferrell, Anna Friel, Danny McBride, Leonard Nimoy
Credits: Director: Brad Silberling; Writers: Chris Henchy, Dennis McNicholas, based on Sid and Marty Krofft's *Land of the Lost* series

Lara Croft Tomb Raider (2001)
USA; 100 minutes; Paramount, Mutual Film Company
Cast: Angelina Jolie, Jon Voight, Noah Taylor, Ian Glen, Daniel Craig
Credits: Director: Simon West; Writers: Patrick Massett, John Zinman; Adaptation: West; Story: Sara B. Cooper, Mike Werb, Michael Colleary

The Last Day of Summer (2007)
USA; 86 minutes; Nickelodeon
Cast: Jansen Panettiere, Jon Kent Ethridge, Eli Vargas, Alexandra Krosney
Credits: Director: Blair Treu; Writer: Kent Pierce

Last Exit to Earth (1996)
USA; 87 minutes; Showtime Channel
Cast: Costas Mandylor, Kimberly Griest, David Groh
Credits: Director: Katt Shea; Writer: Shea, Katherine Martin; Story: Rachel Samuels

Last Lives (1997)
USA; 96 minutes; Sci-Fi Channel
Cast: Billy Wirth, C. Thomas Howell, Jennifer Rubin, Judge Reinhold
Credits: Director: Worth Keeter; Writer: Dan Duling

The Last Mimzy (2007)
USA; 100 minutes; New Line Cinema, Time Warner
Cast: Chris O'Neil, Rhiannon Leigh Wryn, Joely Richardson, Timothy Hutton
Credits: Director: Bob Shaye; Writers: Bruce Joel Rubin, Toby Emmerich; Story: James V. Hart, Carol Skilken, based on "Mimsy Were the Borogroves" by Henry Kuttner

The Lathe of Heaven (1980)
USA; 103 minutes; PBS
Cast: Bruce Davison, Kevin Conway, Margaret Avery, Peyton Park
Credits: Director-Producers: David Loxton, Fred Barzyk; Writers: Roger E. Swaybill, Diane English, based on the Ursula K. Le Guin book

The Lathe of Heaven (2002)
USA; 100 minutes; A&E
Cast: Lukas Haas, James Caan, David Straitharn, Lisa Bonet
Credits: Director: Philip Haas; Writer: Alan Sharp, based on the novel by Ursula K. Le Guin

Legend of the Millenium Dragon (2011; aka *Onigamiden*)
Japan; 99 minutes; animated; Pierrot
Cast: Kenshō Ono, Satomi Ishihara
Director: Hirotsugu Kawasaki, Writers: Naruhisa Arakawa, Hirotsugu Kawasaki, based on the novel by Takafumi Takada.

The Little Girl Who Conquered Time (1983; aka *Toki o Kakeru Shoujo*)
Japan; 104 minutes; Kadokawa Pictures
Cast: Tomoyo Harada, Ryoichi Takayanagi, Toshinori Oki
Credits: Director: Nobuhiko Obayashi; Writer: Wataru Kenmochi, based on the novel *The Girl Who Leapt Through Time* by Yasutaka Tsutsui

Looper (2012)
USA; 119 minutes; Tristar
Cast: Joseph Gordon-Levitt, Bruce Willis, Emily Blunt, Paul Dano, Noah Segan, Piper Perabo, Jeff Daniels
Credits: Director-Writer: Rian Johnson

The Lords of Magick (1988)
USA; 98 minutes; Marsh International Films
Cast: Jarrett Parker, Mark Gauthier, Brendan Dillon, Jr., David Snow, Ruth Zackarian, Candace Galvane, John Clark
Credits: Director: David Marsh; Writers: Marsh, Sherman Hirsh

Lost in Space (1998)
USA; 130 minutes; Prelude Pictures
Cast: William Hurt, Mimi Rogers, Heather Graham, Lacey Chabert, Gary Oldman, Matt LeBlanc
Credits: Director: Stephen Hopkins; Writer: Akiva Goldsman

The Lost Medallion: The Adventures of Billy Stone (2013)
USA; 98 minutes; Freestyle Digital Media, Methinx Entertainment
Cast: Billy Unger, Sammi Hanratty, James Hong, Jansen Panettiere
Credits: Director-Writer: Bill Muir

Love & Teleportation (2013)
USA; 93 minutes; McGatlin Films
Cast: Jan Van Sickle, Robin DeMarco, Adair Jameson
Credits: Director-Writer: Troy McGatlin

The Love Letter (1998)
USA; 100 minutes; CBS
Cast: Campbell Scott, Jennifer Jason Leigh
Credits: Director-Producer: Dan Curtis; Writer: James Henerson, based on the Jack Finney short story

Lunopolis (2009)
USA; 97 minutes; Media Savant
Cast: Dave Potter, Jed Himel, Matt Avant, Sonny Maynor, Nathan Avant, Sarah Avant
Credits: Director-Writer: Matthew J. Avant

Lurid Tales: The Castle Queen (1997)
USA; 76 minutes; Torchlight Entertainment
Cast: Shannon Dow Smith, Kim Dawson, Christi Harris, Betsy Lynn George
Credits: Director: Ellen Cabot; Writer: Randall Fontana

The Man Who Used to Be Me (2000; aka *Race Through Time*)
USA; 88 minutes; Fox Family
Cast: William Devane, Rob Estes, Laurie Holden
Credits: Director: Jeff Woolnough; Writer: James Fryman; Story: Bruce Nash

Marching out of Time (1993; aka *Back to the Fuehrer, Dr. Zemo's Zeitmachine*)
USA; 74 minutes; International Venture Consult Trust
Cast: Frederick Anderson, Matthew Henerson
Credits: Director-Writer: Anton Vassil

Me Myself I (1999)
Australia; 104 minutes; Gaumont
Cast: Rachel Griffiths, David Roberts, Sandy Winton
Credits: Director-Writer: Pip Karmel

Medieval Park (1999; aka *Teen Knight*)
USA; 82 minutes; Kushner-Locke, Canarom Films, Castel Films
Cast: Kristopher Lemche, Caterina Scorsone, Benjamin Plener, Paul Soles, Kimberly Pullis
Credits: Director: Phil Comeau; Writer: Antony Anderson

Meet the Robinsons (2007)
USA; 96 minutes; animated; Disney
Voice Cast: Daniel Hansen, Jordan Fry, Matthew Josten, Angela Bassett, Laurie Metcalf
Credits: Director: Stephen Anderson; Writers: Jon Bernstein, Michelle Spitz, Don Hall, Nathan Greno, Aurian Redson, Joe Mateo, Anderson, based on "A Day with Wilber Robinson" by William Joyce

Men in Black 3 (2012)
USA; 105 minutes; Columbia
Cast: Tommy Lee Jones, Will Smith, Josh Brolin, Jemaine Clement, Michael Stuhlbarg, Emma Thompson
Credits: Director: Barry Sonnenfeld; Writer: Etan Cohen, based on the Malibu Comic by Lowell Cunningham

Mickey's Once Upon a Christmas (1999)
USA; 96 minutes, animated; Disney
STORY: "Stuck on Christmas"
Cast: Tony Anselmo, Diane Michelle, Russi Taylor, Tress MacNeille, Alan Young
Credits: Director: Bradley Raymond; Writer: Charlie Cohen, inspired by "Christmas Every Day" by William Dean Howells

Midnight in Paris (2011)
USA; 100 minutes; Mediapro
Cast: Owen Wilson, Rachel McAdams, Marion Cotillard, Kathy Bates, Tom Hiddleston, Corey Stoll
Credits: Director-Writer: Woody Allen

Millennium (1989)
USA; 108 minutes; Gladden Entertainment
Cast: Kris Kristofferson, Cheryl Ladd, Daniel J. Travanti
Credits: Director: Michael Anderson; Writer: John Varley, based on his short story "Air Raid'"

Millennium Actress (2001; aka *Sennen Joyuu*)
Japan; 87 minutes; animated; Bandai Visual Company
Cast: Fumiko Orikasa, Kōichi Yamadera, Masaya Onosaka, Shōzō Iizuka
Credits: Director: Satoshi Kon; Writers: Sadayuki Murai, Satoshi Kon

Mine Games (2012)
USA; 93 minutes; Phase 4 Films
Cast: Briana Evigan, Julianna Guill, Joseph Cross, Alex Meraz
Credits: Director: Richard Gray; Writers: Michele Davis-Gray, Gray, Ross McQueen; Story: Robert Cross, Gray, McQueen

Minutemen (2008)
USA; 92 minutes; Disney Channel
Cast: Jason Dolley, Luke Benward, Nicholaus Braun, Chelsea Staub, Steven R. McQueen, Kara Crane
Credits: Director: Lev L. Spiro; Teleplay: John Killoran; Story: David Diamond, David Weissman

Mr. Peabody and Sherman (2014)
USA; 92 minutes; animated; Dreamworks
Cast: Ty Burrell, Max Charles, Ariel Winter, Allison Janney
Credits: Director: Rob Minkoff; Writer: Craig Wright, Michael McCullers, based on *Peabody's Improbable History*

Moments of Love (2006)
Philippines; 104 minutes; GMA Films
Cast: Dingdong Dantes, Iza Calzado, Karylle, Paolo Contis, Gloria Romero, Sandy Andolong
Credits: Director: Mark A. Reyes; Writer: Gina Marissa Tagasa; Story: Annette Gozon-Abrogar

Morlocks (2011; aka *Time Machine: Rise of the Morlocks*)
USA; 86 minutes; SyFy Channel
Cast: Robert Picardo, David Hewlett, Christina Cole
Credits: Director: Matt Codd; Writers: Adam J. Karp, Royal McGraw, based on H.G. Wells' *The Time Machine*

My Future Boyfriend (2011)
USA; 116 minutes; ABC Family
Cast: Sara Rue, Barry Watson, Justin Smith, Fred Willard
Credits: Director: Michael Lange; Writers: James Orr, Jim Cruickshank

My Science Project (1985)
USA; 94 minutes; Touchstone Films, Silver Screen Partners II
Cast: John Stockwell, Danielle von Zerneck, Fisher Stevens, Dennis Hopper, Raphael Sbarge, Richard Masur
Credits: Director-Writer: Jonathan R. Betuel

Mysterious Museum (1999)
USA; 90 minutes; Kushner-Locke Company
Cast: A.J. Trauth, Brianna Brown, Megan Lusk, Michael Lee Gogin, John Duerler, Adrian Neil
Credits: Director: David Schmoeller; Writer: Adam Wohl

Naruto Shippuden the Movie: The Lost Tower (2010)
Japan; 85 minutes; animated; TV Tokyo
Cast: Junko Takeuchi, Toshiyuki Morikawa, Saori Hayami
Credits: Director: Masahiko Murata; Writer: Junki Takegami, based on Masashi Kishimoto's *Naruto Shippuden* manga

Nautilus (1999)
USA; 100 minutes; Royal Oaks Entertainment
Cast: Richard Norton, Hannes Jaenicke, Miranda Wolfe, Christopher Kriesa, Gloria Mari
Credits: Director: Rodney McDonald; Writer: C. Courtney Joyner

The Navigator: A Medieval Odyssey (1988)
New Zealand; 92 minutes; Arenafilm
Cast: Hamish McFarlane, Bruce Lyons, Chris Haywood, Marshall Napier, Noel Apleby
Credits: Director: Vincent Ward; Writers: Ward, Kely Lyons, Geoff Chapple, from an idea by Ward

A Necklace for Julia (2006)
USA; 86 minutes, Tamarack Road Productions
Cast: Kerry Palmer, David Dietrich, Glenn Norgren, Christine Brookes
Credits: Director-Writer: David Dietrich

Nemesis 2: Nebula (1995)
USA; 85 minutes; Filmwerks
Cast: Sue Price, Chad Stahelski
Credits: Director-Writer: Albert Pyun

Nemesis 3: Time Lapse (1996; aka *Nemesis 3: Prey Harder*)
USA; 91 minutes; Filmwerks
Cast: Sue Price, Tim Thomerson
Credits: Director-Writer: Albert Pyun

The Next One (1984; aka *The Time Traveller*)
USA; 105 minutes; Allstar Productions
Cast: Keir Dullea, Adrienne Barbeau, Jeremy Licht, Peter Hobbs
Credits: Director-Writer: Nico Mastorakis

Nightmare Street (1998)
USA; 83 minutes; ABC
Cast: Sherilyn Fenn, Rena Sofer, Thomas Gibson
Credits: Director: Colin Bucksey; Writers: Rama Laurie Stagner, Dan Witt, from the Margaret Tabor novel

95ers: Time Runners (2014; aka *95ers: Echoes*)
USA; 97 minutes; Inception Media Group
Cast: Alesandra Durham, Joel Bishop, Terence Goodman, Ian Paul Freeth, Chris Laird, Danor Gerald
Credits: Director-Writer: Thomas Gomez Durham; Story: Durham, James Durham

Norman's Awesome Experience (1987)
USA; 90 minutes; Norstar Entertainment, Salter Street Films
Cast: Tom McCamus, Laurie Paton, Jacques Lussier, Gabriela Salos
Credits: Director-Writer: Paul Donovan

Nostradamus (2000; aka *End of Century*)
USA; 88 minutes; Regent Entertainment, John Aaron Productions
Cast: Rob Estes, Joely Fisher, Fintan McKeown, Michael C. Gwynne, Peter Jordan
Credits: Director: Tibor Takács; Writer: David Bourla, Brian Irving

Official Denial (1993)
USA; 98 minutes; Sci-Fi Channel
Cast: Parker Stevenson, Erin Gray, Chad Everett, Dirk Benedict
Credits: Director: Brian Trenchard-Smith; Writer: Bryce Zabel

The One (2001)
USA; 87 minutes; Revolution Studios
Cast: Jet Li, Carla Gugino, Delroy Lindo, Jason Statham
Credits: Director: James Wong; Writers: Glen Morgan, Wong

100 Million BC (2008)
USA; 85 minutes; The Asylum
Cast: Michael Gross, Christopher Atkins, Greg Evigan, Marie Westbrook
Credits: Director: Louis Myman; Writer: Paul Bales

One Magic Christmas (1985)
USA; 88 minutes; Disney

Cast: Mary Steenburgen, Gary Basaraba, Harry Dean Stanton, Elizabeth Harnois
Credits: Director: Phillip Borsos; Writer: Thomas Meehan; Story: Meehan, Borsos, Barry Healey

Out of Time (1988)
USA; 92 minutes; NBC
Cast: Bruce Abbot, Adam Ant, Bill Maher, Rebecca Schaeffer
Credits: Director: Robert Butler; Writers: Brian Alan Lane, John J. Sakman, Kerry Lenhart; Story: Lane

Panic Time (2007)
USA; 71 minutes; Panic Time Productions
Cast: Emily Lockhart, Kirk Extrell, Russell Reynolds, Lawrence Sutherland
Credits: Director-Writer: John Carstarphen

Paradox (2013)
USA; 87 minutes; Bron Studios
Cast: Kevin Sorbo, Steph Song, Christopher Judge
Credits: Director: Brenton Spencer; Writer: Christos N. Gage, Ruth Fletcher Gage, based on the *Paradox* comic book created by Christos N. Gage

Parallels (2015)
USA; 83 minutes; Zero Day Fox
Cast: Mark Hapka, Jessica Rothe, Eric Jungmann, Constance Wu, Yorgo Constantine
Credits: Director-Writer: Christopher Leone; Story: Leone, Laura Harkcom

Past Perfect (1996)
USA; 89 minutes; Nu Image, Shavick Entertainment
Cast: Eric Roberts, Laurie Holden, Nick Mancuso, Saul Rubinek, Mark Hildreth, Marcie Mellish
Credits: Director: Jonathan Heap; Writer: John Penney

Peggy Sue Got Married (1986)
USA; 103 minutes; Tri-Star Pictures
Cast: Kathleen Turner, Nicolas Cage, Barry Miller, Catherine Hicks, Joan Allen
Credits: Director: Francis Coppola; Writer: Jerry Leichtling, Arlene Sarner

The Penitent Man (2010)
USA; 93 minutes; Mirror Images
Cast: Lance Henriksen, Lathrop Walker, Andrew Keegan, Melissa Roberts
Credits: Director: Nicholas Gyeney; Writer: Gyeney; Story: Gyeney, Trevor Tillman

Pete's Christmas (2013)
USA; 88 minutes; Arc Entertainment
Cast: Zachary Gordon, Molly Parker, Rick Roberts, Wesley Morgan
Credits: Director: Nisha Ganatra; Writers: Peter McKay, Gregg Rossen, Brian Sawyer; Story: McKay

The Philadelphia Experiment (1984)
USA; 101 minutes; New World Pictures
Cast: Michael Paré, Nancy Allen, Eric Christmas, Bobby Di Cicco, Louise Latham
Credits: Director: Stewart Raffill; Writers: William Gray, Michael Janover; Story: Wallace Bennett, Don Jakoby

The Philadelphia Experiment (2012)
USA; 89 minutes; SyFy Channel
Cast: Nicholas Lea, Emilie Ullerup, Ryan Robbins, Gina Holden, Michael Paré, Malcolm McDowell
Credits: Director: Paul Ziller; Writer: Andy Briggs

The Philadelphia Experiment II (1993)
USA; 98 minutes; Trimark Pictures
Cast: Brad Johnson, Marjean Holden, Gerrit Graham
Credits: Director: Stephen Cornwell; Writers: Kevin Rock, Nick Paine; Story: Kim Steven Ketelsen, Rock

Phineas and Ferb the Movie—Across the 2nd Dimension (2011)
USA; 76 minutes; animated; Disney Channel
Cast: Vincent Martella, Thomas Sangster, Ashley Tisdale, Caroline Rhea, Richard O'Brien, Dan Povenmire
Credits: Director: Dan Povenmire, Robert F. Hughes; Writers: Jon Colton Barry, Povenmire, Jeff "Swampy" Marsh

Pirates of the Plain (1999)
USA; 89 minutes; Coast Entertainment
Cast: Tim Curry, Seth E. Adkins, Dee Wallace Stone, Charles Napier
Credits: Director-Writer: John Cherry

The Pirates Who Didn't Do Anything: A Veggie Tales Movie (2008)
USA; 84 minutes; animated; Big Idea, Universal
Cast: Phil Vischer, Mike Nawrocki, Cam Clarke, Laura Gerow, Yuri Lowenthal
Credits: Director: Mike Nawrocki; Writer: Phil Vischer

Planet of the Apes (2001)
USA; 120 minutes; Twentieth Century–Fox
Cast: Mark Wahlberg, Tim Roth, Helena Bonham Carter, Michael Clarke Duncan, Paul Giamatti
Credits: Director: Tim Burton; Writer: William Broyles, Jr., Lawrence Konner, Mark Rosenthal, based on Pierre Boulle's *Monkey Planet*

+1 (2013)
USA; 100 minutes; Process Productions
Cast: Rhys Wakefield, Logan Miller, Ashley Hinshaw, Natalie Hall
Credits: Director-Story: Dennis Iliadis; Writer: Bill Gullo

Pokemon: Arceus and the Jewel of Life (2009)
Japan; 106 minutes; animated; Oriental Light and Magic
Cast: Rica Matsumoto, Ikue Ôtani, Akihiro Miwa, Kie Kitano
Credits: Director: Kunihiko Yuyama; Writer: Hideki Sonoda

Portrait of Jennie (1948)
USA; 87 minutes; Selznick Studios
Cast: Joseph Cotten, Jennifer Jones
Credits: Director: William Dieterle; Writers: Paul Osborne, Peter Berneis, adaptation by Leonardo Bercovici, based on the novel by Robert Nathan

Predestination (2015)
USA; 98 minutes; Stage 6
Cast: Ethan Hawke, Sarah Snook
Credits: Director-Writer: The Spierig Brothers, based on "All You Zombies" by Robert A. Heinlein

Prehistoric Women (1967; aka *Slave Girls*)
United Kingdom; 91 minutes; Hammer
Cast: Michael Latimer, Martine Beswick, Edina Ronay
Credits: Director: Michael Carreras; Writer: Henry Younger [Carreras]

Premature (2014)
USA; 89 minutes; FilmNation Entertainment, AI Film
Cast: John Karna, Katie Findlay, Carlson Young
Credits: Director: Dan Beers; Writers: Beers, Mathew Harawitz

Premonition (2007)
USA; 96 minutes; TriStar, MGM, Hyde Park Entertainment
Cast: Sandra Bullock, Julian McMahon
Credits: Director: Mennan Yapo; Writer: Bill Kelly

Primer (2004)
USA; 77 minutes, ERBP
Cast: Shane Carruth, David Sullivan, Casey Gooden, Anand Upadhyaya, Carrie Crawford
Credits: Director-Writer: Shane Carruth

Prince of Persia: The Sands of Time (2010)
USA; 116 minutes; Disney
Cast: Jake Gyllenhaal, Gemma Arterton, Ben Kingsley, Alfred Molina
Credits: Director: Mike Newell; Writer: Boaz Yakin, Doug Miro, Carlo Bernard; Screen Story: Jordan Mechner; based on the *Prince of Persia* video game series created by Mechner

Project Almanac (2015)
USA; 106 minutes; Insurge Pictures, MTV Films, Platinum Dunes
Cast: Jonny Weston, Sofia Black-D'Elia, Sam Lerner, Allen Evangelista, Virginia Gardner
Credits: Director: Dean Israelite; Writers: Jason Harry Pagan, Andrew Deutschman

Quest for Love (1971)
United Kingdom; 87 minutes; The Rank Organization
Cast: Tom Bell, Joan Collins, Denholm Elliott, Laurence Naismith
Credits: Director: Ralph Thomas; Writer: Terence Feely, based on John Wyndham's "Random Quest"

Rebirth of Mothra 3 (1998; aka *Mothra 3: King Ghidora Attacks*, *Mosura Suri Kingu Gidora Raishu*)
Japan; 100 minutes; Toho
Cast: Megumi Kobayashi, Misato Tate, Aki Hano
Credits: Director: Okihiro Yoneda; Writer: Masumi Suetani

Repeat Performance (1947)
USA; 93 minutes; Eagle-Lion Films
Cast: Joan Leslie, Richard Basehart, Louis Hayward
Credits: Director: Alfred Werker; Writer: Walter Bullock, based on the novel by William O'Farrell

Repeaters (2010)
Canada; 89 minutes; Rampart Films
Cast: Dustin Milligan, Amanda Crew, Richard de Klerk, Alexia Fast
Credits: Director: Carl Bessai; Writer: Arne Olsen

Resistance (2011)
United Kingdom; 82 minutes; Big Rich Films
Cast: Andrea Riseborough, Tom Wlaschiha, Stanislav Ianevski
Credits: Director: Amit Gupta; Writers: Gupta, Owen Sheers, based on Sheers' novel

Retroactive (1997)
USA; 87 minutes; Cohiba Pictures
Cast: James Belushi, Kylie Travis, Frank Whaley, Shannon Whirry
Credits: Director: Louis Morneau; Writers: Michael Hamilton-Wright, Robert Strauss, Phillip Badger

Retrograde (2004)
USA; 92 minutes; First Look Pictures
Cast: Dolph Lundgren, Silvia Di Santis, Joe Montana, Gary Daniels
Credits: Director-Story: Christopher Kulikowski; Writers: Tom Reeve, Gianluca Curti

The Return of the Time Machine (1984; aka *Die Rückkehr der Zeitmaschine*)
Germany; 116 minutes; Telefilm Saar Film Production
Cast: Klaus Schwarzkopf, Nikolas Lansky
Credits: Director: Jurgen Klauss; Writer: Günter Kunert

Returner (2002)
Japan; 106 minutes; Amuse
Cast: Anne Suzuki, Takeshi Kaneshiro, Gorô Kishitani
Credits: Director: Takashi Yamazaki; Writers: Yamazaki, Kenya Hirata

Richie Rich's Christmas Wish (1998)
USA; 84 minutes; Saban Entertainment
Cast: David Gallagher, Eugene Levy, Keene Curtis, Jake Richardson, Martin Mull, Lesley Ann Warren, Michelle Trachtenberg
Credits: Director: Jon Murlowski; Writer: Mark Furey; Story: Bob Kerchner, Jason Teffer

The Ride (2003)
USA; 93 minutes; Third Reef Pictures

Cast: Scot Davis, Sean Kaawa, Mary Paalani
Credits: Director-Writer: Nathan Kurosawa

Roborex (2014; aka *The Adventures of Roborex*)
USA; 90 minutes; Kaboom entertainment, Wolf/Gourley Productions, Escapology
Cast: Kalvin Stinger, Ethan Phillips, Maggie Scott, Ben Browder
Credits: Director: Stephen Shimek; Writers: Kristi Shimek, Stephen Shimek

Roman Scandals (1933)
USA; 93 minutes; Howard Productions
Cast: Eddie Cantor, Edward Arnold, David Manners, Willard Robertson
Credits: Director: Frank Tuttle (production numbers by Busby Berkeley); Writer: William Anthony McGuire; Story: George S. Kaufman, Robert E. Sherwood

The Ruby Ring (1997)
USA; 90 minutes; Showtime Channel
Cast: Emily Hamilton, Christien Anholt, Rutger Hauer
Credits: Director: Harley Cokeliss; Writers: Lin Oliver, Alan Moskowitz, based on *Secret of the Ruby Ring* by Yvonne MacGrory

Running Against Time (1990)
USA; 92 minutes; USA Network
Cast: Robert Hays, Catherine Hicks, Sam Wanamaker
Credits: Director: Bruce Seth Green; Writers: Stanley Shapiro, Robert Glass, based on Shapiro's *A Time to Remember*

S. Darko (2009)
USA; 103 minutes; Silver Nitrate Productions
Cast: Daveigh Chase, Briana Evigan, Ed Westwick
Credits: Director: Chris Fisher; Writer: Nathan Atkins

Safety Not Guaranteed (2012)
USA; 84 minutes; Big Beach, Filmdistrict
Cast: Aubrey Plaza, Mark Duplass, Jake Johnson, Karan Soni, Mary Lynn Rajskub
Credits: Director: Colin Trevorrow; Writer: Derek Connolly

Samurai Commando Mission 1549 (2005; aka *Sengoku Jieitai* 1549)
Japan; 87 minutes; Kadokawa Eiga KK, Nippon Television Network
Cast: Yôsuke Eguchi, Kyôka Suzuki, Haruka Ayase
Credits: Director: Masaaki Tezuka; Writer: Harutoshi Fukui, based on the novel by Ryo Hanmura

The Santa Clause 3: The Escape Clause (2006)
USA; 92 minutes; Disney
Cast: Tim Allen, Elizabeth Mitchell, Martin Short, Eric Lloyd, Judge Reinhold, Wendy Crewson
Credits: Director: Michael Lembeck; Writers: Ed Decter, John J. Strauss

Sarah's Choice (2009)
USA; 86 minutes; Pure Flix
Cast: Rebecca St. James, Judy Lewis, Dick Van Patten, Brad Stine
Credits: Director: Chad Kapper; Writers: Sean Paul Murphy, Timothy Ratajczak

Saving Santa (2013)
United Kingdom; 83 minutes; animated; Gateway Films
Cast: Martin Freeman, Tim Conway, Tim Curry, Joan Collins
Credits: Directors: Leon Joosen, Aaron Seelman; Writers: Rick Roxburgh; Story: Antony Nottage

Second Time Lucky (1984)
USA; 101 minutes; United International Pictures
Cast: Diane Franklin, Roger Wilson, Robert Helpmann, Jon Gadsby, Robert Morley
Credits: Director: Michael Anderson; Writers: Ross Dimsey, David Sigmund, Howard Grigsby; Story: Sigmund, Dimsey

Secret (2007)
Taiwan; 102 minutes; Avex Asia
Cast: Jay Chou, Gwei Lun-Mei
Credits: Director: Jay Chou; Writer: Chou, Chi-long To

Shrek Forever After (2010)
USA; 93 minutes; animated; Dreamworks
Cast: Mike Myers, Cameron Diaz, Eddie Murphy, Walt Dohrn
Credits: Director: Mike Mitchell; Writers: Josh Klausner, Darren Lemke

Shuffle (2011)
USA; 82 minutes; Screen Media, Theatre Junkies
Cast: T.J. Thyne, Paula Rhodes, Chris Stone, Meeghan Holaway, Tamara Taylor
Credits: Director-Writer: Kurt Kuenne

Singularity Principle (2013)
USA; 88 minutes; Big Screen Entertainment
Cast: William B. Davis, John Diehl, Michael Denis, Kallie Sorensen
Credits: Directors: David Deranian, Austin Hines; Writer: Deranian, Hines, Michael Denis

Slaughterhouse-Five (1972)
USA; 103 minutes; Universal
Cast: Michael Sacks, Ron Leibman, Eugene Roche, Sharon Gans, Valerie Perrine
Credits: Director: George Roy Hill; Writer: Stephen Geller, based on the Kurt Vonnegut novel

Slipstream (2005)
USA; 89 minutes; ApolloProMedia
Cast: Sean Astin, Ivana Milicevic, Vinnie Jones, Kevin Otto, Victoria Bartlett
Credits: Director: David van Eyssen; Writer: Phillip Badger; Story: Badger, Louis Morneau

A Snow Globe Christmas (2013)
USA; 94 minutes; The Asylum
Cast: Alicia Witt, Donald Faison, Christina Milian
Credits: Director: Jodi Binstock; Writer: Naomi Selfman; Story: Selfman, Delondra Williams

Somewhere in Time (1980)
USA; 103 minutes; Universal
Cast: Christopher Reeve, Jane Seymour, Christopher Plummer
Credits: Director: Jeannot Szwarc Writer: Richard Matheson, based on his novel *Bid Time Return*

A Sound of Thunder (2005)
USA; 110 minutes; Franchise Pictures
Cast: Edward Burns, Ben Kingsley, Catherine McCormack
Credits: Director: Peter Hyams; Writers: Thomas Dean Donnelly, Joshua Oppenheimer, Gregory Poirier; Story: Donnelly, Oppenheimer, based on "A Sound of Thunder" by Ray Bradbury

Source Code (2011)
USA; 94 minutes; Summit Entertainment, Vendome Pictures
Cast: Jake Gyllenhaal, Michelle Monaghan, Vera Farmiga, Jeffrey Wright
Credits: Director: Duncan Jones; Writer: Ben Ripley

Sphere (1998)
USA; 134 minutes; Warner Brothers
Cast: Dustin Hoffman, Sharon Stone, Samuel L. Jackson, Peter Coyote, Liev Schreiber
Credits: Director: Barry Levinson; Writers: Stephen Hauser, Paul Attanasio; Adaptation: Kurt Wimmer, based on *Sphere* by Michael Crichton

The Spirit of 76 (1990)
USA; 81 minutes; Commercial Pictures
Cast: David Cassidy, Olivia d'Abo, Geoff Hoyle, Leif Garrett
Credits: Director-Writer: Lucas Reiner; Story: Roman Coppola, Reiner

Split Infinity (1992)
USA; 87 minutes; Feature Films for Families
Cast: Melora Slover, Trevor Black, H.E.D. Redford
Credits: Director: Stan Ferguson; Writer, Leo Paur; Story Concept: Sharon Baker

Spy Kids: All the Time in the World (2011; aka *Spy Kids 4D*)
USA; 87 minutes, Troublemaker Studios, Dimension Films
Cast: Jessica Alba, Joel McHale, Rowan Blanchard, Mason Cook, Jeremy Piven, Alexa Vega
Credits: Director-Writer: Robert Rodriguez

Star Trek (2009)
USA; 126 minutes; Paramount
Cast: Chris Pine, Zachary Quinto, Leonard Nimoy, Eric Bana, Bruce Greenwood, Karl Urban, Zoé Saldana, Simon Pegg
Credits: Director, Producer: J.J. Abrams; Writer: Roberto Orci, Alex Kurtzman

Star Trek: First Contact (1996)
USA; 111 minutes; Paramount
Cast: Patrick Stewart, Jonathan Frakes, Brent Spiner, LeVar Burton, Michael Dorn, Gates McFadden, Marina Sirtis, Alfre Woodard, James Cromwell, Alice Krige
Credits: Director: Jonathan Frakes; Writer: Brannon Braga, Ronald D. Moore; Story: Rick Berman, Brannon Braga, Moore

Star Trek IV: The Voyage Home (1986)
USA; 118 minutes; Paramount
Cast: William Shatner, Leonard Nimoy, DeForest Kelley, James Doohan, George Takei, Walter Koenig, Nichelle Nichols, Catherine Hicks, Mark Lenard
Credits: Director: Leonard Nimoy; Writers: Steve Meerson, Peter Krikes, Harve Bennett, Nicholas Meyer; Story: Nimoy, Bennett

Star Wreck: In the Pirkinning (2005; aka *Star Wreck*)
Finland; 105 minutes; Energia
Cast: Samuli Torssonen, Antti Satama, Tiina Routamaa, Timo Vuorensola
Credits: Director: Timo Vuorensola; Writer: Rudi Airisto, Jarmo Puskala, Samuli Torssonen

Star Wreck Lost Contact (1997)
Finland; 34 minutes; ST Movies
Cast: Samuli Torssonen, Antti Satama, Timo Vuorensola, Rudi Airisto, Nina Karppinen
Credits: Director: Rudy Airisto; Writers: Airisto, Samuli Torssonen

Stargate: Continuum (2008)
USA; 98 minutes; MGM
Cast: Ben Browder, Amanda Tapping, Christopher Judge, Claudia Black, Richard Dean Anderson, William Devane, Beau Bridges, Michael Shanks, Cliff Simon
Credits: Director: Martin Wood; Writer: Brad Wright

Stein's;Gate: The Burden of Déjà Vu (2013; aka: *Stein's;Gate: Fuka Ryoiki no Déjà Vu*)
Japan; 90 minutes; animated; AT-X
VOICES: Mamoru Miyano, Asami Imai, Kana Hanazawa
Credits: Directors: Hiroshi Hamazaki, Takuya Sato, Kanji Wakabayashi; Writer: Jukki Hanada

Stephen King's the Langoliers (1995)
USA; 179 minutes; ABC
Cast: Patricia Wettig, Dean Stockwell, David Morse, Bronson Pinchot, Kate Maberly, Mark Lindsay Chapman, Christopher Collet
Credits: Director-Writer: Tom Holland

The Sticky Fingers of Time (1997)
USA; 82 minutes; Crystal Pictures, Good Machine
Cast: Terumi Matthews, Nicole Zaray, Belinda Becker, James Urbaniak
Credits: Director-Writer: Hilary Brougher

A Stranger in Time (1995)
USA; 85 Minutes; Framework Productions
Cast: Heather Kottek, Amy Seely
Credits: Director-Writer: Dennis Rockney

Stuck in the Past (2007)
USA; 77 minutes; Uplifting Entertainment
Cast: Lesley Bowen, Sherri Bohlander, Eddie Mekka, Laura Romeo, Josh Moody
Credits: Director: Greg Robbins; Writer: Owen Smith; Story: Timothy Craig

Summer Time Machine Blues (2005; aka *Sama Taimu Mashin Burusu*)
Japan; 96 minutes; Robot Communications
Cast: Eita, Juri Ueno, Kuranosuke Sasaki, Riki Honda
Credits: Director: Katsuyuki Motohiro; Writer: Makota Ueda

Super Eruption (2011)
USA; 89 minutes; SyFy Channel
Cast: Richard Burgi, Juliet Aubrey
Credits: Director: Matt Codd; Writer: Rafael Jordan

Supercollider (2013)
USA; 87 minutes; SyFy Channel
Cast: Robin Dunne, Amy Bailey, Brendan Beiser, Enzo Cilenti
Credits: Director: Jeffery Lando; Writers: Lando, Phillip Roth

Teenage Mutant Ninja Turtles III (1993)
USA; 96 minutes; New Line Cinema
Cast: David Fraser, Jim Raposa, Matt Hill, Mark Caso, James Murray, Paige Turco, Stuart Wilson, Sab Shimono, Vivian Wu, Henry Hayashi
Credits: Director-Writer: Stuart Gillard, based on characters created by Kevin Eastman and Peter Laird

Tempting Fate (1998)
USA; 94 minutes; ABC
Cast: Tate Donovan, Abraham Benrubi, Ming-Na Wen
Credits: Director: Peter Werner; Writer: Gerald DiPego, Justin DiPego

Tenchi Muyo in Love (1996; aka *Tenchi Muyou! in Love*)
Japan; 95 minutes; Anime International
Cast: Masami Kikuchi, Megumi Hayashibara, Yuko Kobayashi, Ryuzaburo Otomo
Credits: Director: Hiroshi Negishi; Writers: Hiroshi Negishi, Ryoe Tsukimura

The Terminator (1984)
USA; 107 minutes; Pacific Western
Cast: Arnold Schwarzenegger, Linda Hamilton, Michael Biehn, Paul Winfield, Lance Henriksen
Credits: Director: James Cameron; Writer: Cameron, Gale Anne Hurd, with acknowledgment to the works of Harlan Ellison

Terminator 2: Judgment Day (1991
USA; 152 minutes; Pacific Western, Lightstorm Entertainment
Cast: Arnold Schwarzenegger, Linda Hamilton, Edward Furlong, Robert Patrick, Earl Boen, Joe Morton
Credits: Director: James Cameron; Writer: Cameron, William Wisher

Terminator 3: Rise of the Machines (2003)
USA; 110 minutes; Warner Brothers, Intermedia, C2 Pictures
Cast: Arnold Schwarzenegger, Nick Stahl, Claire Danes, Kristanna Loken
Credits: Director: Jonathan Mostow; Writers: John Brancato, Michael Ferris; Story: Brancato, Ferris and Tedi Sarafian

Terminator Genisys (2015)
USA; 125 minutes; Paramount, Sky Dance Productions
Cast: Emilia Clarke, Arnold Schwarzenegger, Jai Courtney, Jason Clarke
Credits: Director: Alan Taylor: Writers: Laeta Kalogridis, Patrick Lussier, based on characters created by James Cameron and Gale Ann Hurd

Terminatrix (1995)
Japan; 75 minutes; TMC
Cast: Kei Mizutani, Naofumi Matsuda, Shouko Kudou, Saeko Ichijou, Yuuki Fujisawa, Yasunori Matsuda
Credits: Director-Writer: Mikio Hirota

Terror from the Year 5000 (1958; aka *Cage of Doom*)
USA; 74 minutes; La Jolla Productions
Cast: Ward Costello, Joyce Holden, John Stratton, Frederic Downs, Salome Jens
Credits: Director-Writer: Robert J. Gurney, Jr.

Therma Romae—Roman Baths (2012; aka *Terumae Romae*)
Japan; 108 minutes; Filmmakers
Cast: Hiroshi Abe, Masachika Ichimura, Aya Ueto, Kazuki Kitamura
Credits: Director: Hideki Takeuchi, Writer: Shogo Muto, based on Mari Yamazaki manga

Therma Romae II (2014; aka *Terumae Romae II*)
Japan; 113 minutes; Filmmakers
Cast: Hiroshi Abe, Masachika Ichimura, Aya Ueto, Kazuki Kitamura
Credits: Director: Hideki Takeuchi, Writer: Hashimoto Hiroshi, based on Mari Yamazaki manga

13 Going on 30 (2004)
USA; 97 minutes; Revolution Studios
Cast: Jennifer Garner, Mark Ruffalo, Judy Greer, Andy Serkis
Credits: Director: Gary Winick; Writers: Josh Goldsmith, Cathy Yuspa

A Thousand Kisses Deep (2011)
United Kingdom; 84 minutes; Tomori Films
Cast: Jodie Whittaker, Dougray Scott, Emilia Fox, Jonathan Slinger, David Warner
Credits: Director: Dana Lustig; Writer: Alex Kustanovich, Vadim Moldovan

Three Days (2001)
USA; 86 minutes; ABC Family

Cast: Kristin Davis, Reed Diamond, Tim Meadows, Danielle Britt
Credits: Director: Michael Switzer; Writers: Robert Tate Miller, Eric Tuchman

The Three Stooges Meet Hercules (1962)
USA; 89 minutes; Columbia
Cast: Larry Fine, Moe Howard, Joe De Rita, Quinn Redeker, George N. Neise, Samson Burke, Vicki Trickett
Credits: Director: Edward Bernds; Writer: Elwood Ullman; Story: Norman Maurer

The Time Crystal (1981; aka *Tut and Tuttle, Through the Majic Pyramid*)
USA; 94 minutes; NBC
Cast: Chris Barnes, Vic Tayback, Eric Greene, Kario Salem, Hans Conried, Olivia Barash
Credits: Director: Ron Howard; Writer: Rance Howard; Herbert J. Wright

Ticking Clock (2011)
USA; 101 minutes; Stage 6 Films
Cast: Cuba Gooding, Jr., Neal McDonough, Nicki Aycox, Austin Abrams, Yancey Arias, Dane Rhodes, Veronica Berry
Credits: Director: Ernie Barbarash; Writer: John Turman

Time After Time (1979)
USA; 112 minutes; Warner Brothers
Cast: Malcolm McDowell, David Warner, Mary Steenburgen
Credits: Director-Writer: Nicholas Meyer; Story: Karl Alexander, Steve Hayes

Time Again (2011)
USA; 88 minutes; Nasty Strangers
Cast: Scott F. Evans, John T. Woods, Angela Rachelle, Tara Smoker, Gigi Perreau
Credits: Director: Ray Karwel; Writers: Karwel, C.S. Hill, Debbie Glovin; Story: Karwel

Time and Again (2004)
USA; 60 minutes; Quantus Pictures
Cast: Brian Ireland, Jennie Allen, Bob Darby, Andrew Zehnder
Credits: Director: Jason J. Tomaric; Writers: Robert T. Noll, Tomaric

Time at the Top (1999)
Canada; 92 minutes; Taurus 7 Film Corporation
Cast: Elisha Cuthbert, Timothy Busfield, Gabrielle Boni, Lynne Adams
Credits: Director: Jimmy Kaufman; Writers: Linda Brookover, Alain Silver, based on the novel by Edmond Ormondroyd

Time Bandits (1981)
USA; 115 minutes; Anchor Bay Entertainment, Hand Made Films
Cast: David Rappaport, Kenny Baker, Malcolm Dixon, Mike Edmonds, Jack Purvis, Tiny Ross, Craig Warnock, Sean Connery, David Warner
Credits: Director: Terry Gilliam; Writers: Michael Palin, Gilliam

Time Barbarians (1990)
USA; 96 minutes; Vista Street Entertainment
Cast: Deron Michael McBee, Jo Ann Ayres, Daniel Martine, Ingrid Vold
Credits: Director-Writer: Joseph J. Barmettler

Time Changer (2002)
USA; 99 minutes; Five & Two Pictures
Cast: D. David Morin, Gavin MacLeod, Hal Linden, Jennifer O'Neill, Paul Rodriguez
Credits: Director-Writer: Rich Christiano

Time Chasers (1994)
USA; 89 minutes; Edgewood Entertainment
Cast: Matthew Bruch, Bonnie Pritchard, Peter J. Harrington, George Woodard
Credits: Director-Writer: David Giancola

Time Enough: The Alien Conspiracy (2002)
USA; 99 minutes; Brimstone Productions
Cast: Chris Mack, Sarah K. Lippman, Ron Ford, Paula Pointer-Ford, John Fallon, Gordon Linzner
Credits: Directors-Writers: Ron Ford, Alexander Michaud, Kevin Lindenmuth

Time Flies (1944)
United Kingdom; 84 minutes; Gainsborough
Cast: Tommy Handley, Evelyn Dall, Felix Aylmer
Credits: Director: Walter Forde; Writers: J.O.C. Orton, Ted Kavanagh, Howard Irving Young

Time Kid (2003)
USA; 74 minutes; animated; MGM, DIC
Cast: Michael Monroe Heyward, Danielle Young, Jerry Longe, Jon Kodera
Credits: Director: Will Meugniot; Writers: Mark Edward Edens, Michael Edens, based on *The Time Machine* by H.G. Wells

The Time Machine (1960)
USA; 103 minutes; MGM
Cast: Rod Taylor, Yvette Mimieux, Alan Young
Credits: Director: George Pal; Writer: David Duncan, based on the H.G. Wells novel

The Time Machine (1978)
USA; 99 minutes; NBC
Cast: John Beck, Priscilla Barnes, Andrew Duggan, Rosemary DeCamp
Credits: Director: Henning Schellerup; Writer: Wallace Bennett, based on the H.G. Wells novel

The Time Machine (2002)
USA; 96 minutes; Dreamworks, Warner Brothers
Cast: Guy Pearce, Samantha Mumba, Jeremy Irons, Mark Addy, Phyllida Law, Sienna Guillory
Credits: Director: Simon Wells; Writer: John Logan, based on the H.G. Wells novel

Time Machine: The Journey Back (1993)
USA; 48 minutes; 7th Voyage Productions
Cast: Rod Taylor, Alan Young,
Credits: Director: Clyde Lucas; Writers: David Duncan, Bunky Young

Time Runner (1993)
Canada; 93 minutes; North American Pictures, Excalibur Pictures
Cast: Mark Hamill, Rae Dawn Chong, Brion James, Marc Baur, Gordon Tipple
Credits: Director: Michael Mazo; Writers: Chris Hyde, Greg Derochie, Ron Tarrant, Ian Bray, Michael Mazo, John Curtis

Time Stranger (1986; aka *Toki No Tabibito*)
Japan; 91 minutes; animated; Madhouse
Cast: Keiko Toda, Tadashi Yokouchi
Credits: Director: Mori Masaki; Writers: Atsushi Yamatoya, Masaki, Yashio Takeuchi

Time Trackers (1989)
USA; 86 minutes; Concorde Pictures
Cast: Wil Shriner, Ned Beatty, Kathleen Beller, Alex Hyde-White, Lee Bergere, Robert Cornthwaite
Credits: Director-Writer: Howard R. Cohen

The Time Travelers (1964; aka *Time Trap*)
USA; 84 minutes; Dobil Productions
Cast: Preston Foster, Philip Carey, Merry Anders, John Hoyt, Joan Woodbury, Dolores Wells
Credits: Director-Writer: Ib Melchior; Story: Melchior, David L. Hewitt

The Time Travelers (1976)
USA; 78 minutes; ABC
Cast: Sam Groom, Tom Hallick, Richard Basehart
Credits: Director: Alexander Singer; Writer: Jackson Gillis; Story: Rod Serling

The Time Traveler's Wife (2009)
USA; 107 minutes; New Line Cinema
Cast: Eric Bana, Rachel McAdams, Brooklynn Proulx, Hailey McCann, Tatum McCann, Ron Livingston, Jane McLean
Credits: Director: Robert Schwentke; Writer: Bruce Joel Rubin, based on the novel by Audrey Niffenegger

Time Traveller—The Girl Who Leapt Through Time (2010; aka *Time Traveller, Toki o Kakeru Shojo*)
Japan; 121 minutes; Aniplex
Cast: Riisa Naka, Akiyoshi Nakao, Kanji Ishimaru, Munetaka Aoki
Credits: Director: Masaaki Taniguchi; Writer: Tomoe Kanno based on *The Girl Who Leapt Through Time* by Yasutaka Tsutsui

Timecop (1994)
USA; 99 minutes; Universal
Cast: Jean-Claude Van Damme, Mia Sara, Ron Silver, Bruce McGill, Gloria Reuben, Scott Bellis
Credits: Director: Peter Hyams; Writer: Mark Verheiden; Story: Mike Richardson, Verheiden, based on their comic book

Timecop: The Berlin Decision (2003)
USA; 81 minutes; Universal
Cast: Jason Scott Lee, Thomas Ian Griffith, Mary Page Keller, John Beck, Tava Smiley, Tricia Barry
Credits: Director: Stephen Boyum; Writer: Gary Scott Thompson, based on the comic book by Mike Richardson and Mark Verheiden

Timecrimes (2007; aka *Los Cronocrimenes*)
Spain; 89 minutes; Karbo Vantas Entertainment
Cast: Karra Elejalde, Candela Fernandez, Barbara Goenaga, Nacho Vigalondo, Ion Inciarte
Credits: Director-Writer: Nacho Vigalondo

Timekeeper (1998; aka *Clockmaker*)
USA; 89 minutes; Pulsepounders, Kushner-Locke, Moonbeam
Cast: Anthony Medwetz, Katie Johnston, Zachary McLemore, Pierrino Mascarino, Daisy Nystul, Tom Gulager
Credits: Director: Christopher Rémy; Writer: Benjamin Carr

Timeline (2003)
USA; 115 minutes; Paramount Pictures
Cast: Paul Walker, Frances O'Connor, Gerard Butler, Billy Connolly, David Thewlis, Anna Friel, Neal McDonough
Credits: Director: Richard Donner; Screenplay: Jeff Maguire, George Nolfi, based on the Michael Crichton novel

Timemaster (1995)
USA; 101 minutes; SGE Entertainment
Cast: Jesse Cameron-Glickenhaus, Veronica Cameron-Glickenhaus, Noriyuki "Pat" Morita, Michael Dorn, Michelle Williams
Credits: Director-Writer: James Glickenhaus

Timequest (2000)
USA; 94 minutes; Destination Earth
Cast: Victor Slezak, Caprice Benedetti, Joseph Murphy, Ralph Waite, Vince Grant, Larry Drake, Bruce Campbell
Credits: Director-Writer: Robert Dyke

Timerider: The Adventures of Lyle Swann (1983)
USA; 93 minutes; MGM
Cast: Fred Ward, Belinda Bauer, Peter Coyote
Credits: Director: William Dear; Writers: Dear, Michael Nesmith

The Timeshifters (1999; aka *The Thrill Seekers*)
USA; 88 minutes; TBS
Cast: Casper Van Dien, Catherine Bell, Theresa Saldana, Mimi Kuzyk, Martin Sheen
Credits: Director: Mario Azzopardi; Writer: Kurt Inderbitzin, Gay Walch

Timeslingers (1999; aka *Aliens in the Wild, Wild West*)
USA; 89 minutes; Moonbeam Films, Kushner-Locke Company, Canarom Productions Castel Films
Cast: Taylor Locke, Carly Pope, Barna Moricz, Markus Parilo, George Ilie
Credits: Director: George Erschbamer; Writer: Alon Kaplan

Timestalkers (1987)
USA; 94 minutes; CBS

Cast: William Devane, Lauren Hutton, Klaus Kinski, John Ratzenberger
Credits: Director: Michael Schultz; Writer: Brian Clemens; Story: Ray Brown, Clemens

Tomorrow I'll Get Up and Scald Myself with Tea (1977; aka *Zitra Vstanu a Oparim se Cajem*)
Czechoslovakia; 90 minutes; Filmové Studio Barrandov
Cast: Petr Kostka, Jiří Sovák, Vladimir Menšík, Vlastimil Brodský, Zuzana Ondrouchová
Credits: Director: Jindřich Polák; Writer: Miloš Macourek, Polák; Story: Josef Nesvadba

The Tomorrow Man (1996)
USA; 96 minutes; 20th Century-Fox
Cast: Julian Sands, Giancarlo Esposito, Craig Wasson, Ray Baker
Credits: Director: Bill D'Elia; Writer: Alan Spencer

The Tomorrow Man (2001)
USA; 93 minutes; Elsinore Pictures
Cast: Corbin Bernsen, Morgan Rusler, Beth Kennedy, Jeanne Cooper, Adam Sutton
Credits: Director-Writer: Doug Campbell

Tom's Midnight Garden (1999)
United Kingdom; 107 minutes; Hyperion
Cast: Anthony Way, Florence Hoath, Greta Scacchi, James Wilby, Joan Plowright
Credits: Director-Writer: Willard Carroll, based on the Philippa Pearce novel

Total Reality (1997)
USA; 92 minutes; United Film Organization
Cast: David Bradley, Ely Pouget, Misa Koprova, Thomas Kretschmann, Michael Mendelsohn, Geof Prysirr
Credits: Director: Phillip Roth; Writers: Roth, Rob Trenton; Story: Roth

Trancers (1984)
USA; 76 minutes; Empire Pictures
Cast: Tim Thomerson, Helen Hunt, Michael Stefani, Biff Manard, Telma Hopkins, Art La Fleur
Credits: Director: Charles Band; Writer: Danny Bilson, Paul De Meo

Trancers II (1990)
USA; 88 minutes; Full Moon Entertainment
Cast: Tim Thomerson, Helen Hunt, Alyson Croft, Megan Ward, Biff Manard, Martine Beswick, Jeffrey Combs, Richard Lynch, Telma Hopkins
Credits: Director: Charles Band; Writer: Jackson Barr; Story: Barr, Band

Trancers III (1993)
USA; 74 minutes; Full Moon Entertainment
Cast: Tim Thomerson, Melanie Smith, R.A. Mihailoff, Andrew Robinson, Tony Pierce, Helen Hunt, Megan Ward, Stephen Macht, Telma Hopkins
Credits: Director-Writer: C. Courtney Joyner

Trancers 6 (2002)
USA; 80 minutes; Full Moon Pictures, Young Wolf Productions

Cast: Zette Sullivan, Jennifer Capo, Robert Donavan, Timothy Prindle
Credits: Director: Jay Woelfel; Writer: Gene Yarbrough

Triangle (2005)
USA; 173 minutes; Sci-Fi Channel
Cast: Eric Stoltz, Catherine Bell, Lou Diamond Phillips, Bruce Davison, Michael Rodgers, Sam Neill
Credits: Director: Craig R. Baxley; Writer: Rockne S. O'Bannon; Story: O'Bannon, Bryan Singer, Dean Devlin

Triangle (2009)
USA; 98 minutes; Icon Entertainment International
Cast: Melissa George, Joshua McIvor, Jack Taylor, Michael Dorman, Henry Nixon, Rachael Carpani, Emma Lung, Liam Hemsworth, Bryan Probets
Credits: Director-Writer: Christopher Smith

Tripping the Rift: The Movie (2008)
Canada; 75 minutes; animated; Cinegroupe
Cast: Stephen Root, Maurice Lamarche, Jenny McCarthy, John Melendez, Gayle Garfinkle
Credits: Director: Bernie Denk; Writers: Jon Minnis, Ken Goin, Mark Amato, Terry Sweeney, Lanier Laney

Turn Back the Clock (1933)
USA; 81 minutes; MGM
Cast: Lee Tracy, Mae Clarke, Otto Kruger, George Barbier, Peggy Shannon, C. Henry Gordon, Clara Blandick
Credits: Director: Edgar Selwyn; Writers: Selwyn, Ben Hecht

Turn Back the Clock (1989)
USA; 91 minutes; NBC
Cast: Connie Sellecca, Jere Burns, Wendy Kilbourne, David Dukes
Credits: Director: Larry Elikann; Writers: Lee Hutson, Lindsay Harrison, based on *Repeat Performance*

12:01 (1993)
USA; 94 minutes; Fox TV
Cast: Jonathan Silverman, Helen Slater, Martin Landau, Jeremy Piven
Credits: Director: Jack Sholder; Writer: Philip Morton; Story: Jonathan Heap, based on *12:01 P.M.*

12:01 PM (1990)
USA; 28 minutes; Chanticleer Films
Cast: Kurtwood Smith, Laura Harrington, Don Amendolia
Credits: Director: Jonathan Heap; Writer: Stephen Tolkin, Heap, based on the Richard A. Lupoff short story

12 Dates of Christmas (2011)
USA; 86 minutes; ABC Family
Cast: Amy Smart, Mark-Paul Gosselaar
Credits: Director: James Hayman; Writer: Aaron Mendelsohn, Janet Brownell; Story: Mendelsohn, Blake Harris

12 Days of Christmas Eve (2004)
USA; 88 minutes; USA Network
Cast: Steven Weber, Patricia Velasquez, Molly Shannon, Stefanie von Pfetten
Credits: Director: Martha Coolidge; Writer: J.B. White; Story: Jean Abounader, White

12 Monkeys (1995)
USA; 130 minutes; Atlas Entertainment
Cast: Bruce Willis, Madeleine Stowe, Brad Pitt, Christopher Plummer, David Morse
Credits: Director: Terry Gilliam; Writer: David Peoples, Janet Peoples

Twice Upon a Time (1998)
USA; 91 minutes; Lifetime Network
Cast: Molly Ringwald, George Newbern, Rob Youngblood
Credits: Director: Thom Eberthardt; Writer: Scott A. Fifer

Twice Upon a Yesterday (1998; aka *If Only, The Man with Rain in His Shoes*)
UK-Spain; 91 minutes; CLT, Ecsima, Handmade Films
Cast: Douglas Henshall, Lena Headey, Penélope Cruz, Gustavo Salmeron, Eusebio Lázaro
Credits: Director: Maria Ripoll; Writer: Rafa Russo

Twilight Zone: The Movie (1983)
USA; 101 minutes; Warner Brothers
Story "Time Out"
Cast: Vic Morrow, Doug McGrath, Charles Hallahan
Credits: Director-Writer: John Landis

2009 Lost Memories (2002 aks Loseutu Memorijeu)
South Korea; 136 minutes; ADV Films, CJ Entertainment
Cast: Jang Dong-gun, Toru Nakamura, Seo Jin-Ho, Ahn Kil-kang
Credits: Director: Lee Si-myung; Writers: Lee Sang-hak, Lee Si-myung

2035 Forbidden Dimensions (2014)
USA; 87 minutes; Z Sky Productions, Razorwire Pictures
Cast: Kyle Morris, Mark McGarrey, Jamie Katonic, Carl Crew, Chris J. Miller, Todd Brown
Credits: Director-Writer: Chris J. Miller

The Two Worlds of Jennie Logan (1979)
USA; 95 minutes; CBS
Cast: Lindsay Wagner, Marc Singer, Alan Feinstein, Linda Gray
Credits: Director-Writer: Frank De Felitta, based on David Williams' *Second Sight*

The Twonky (1953)
USA; 72 minutes; Arch Oboler Productions, United Artists
Cast: Hans Conried, Billy Lynn, Janet Warren, Gloria Blondell
Credits: Director-Writer: Arch Oboler, based on "The Twonky" by Henry Kuttner

The Undead (1957)
USA; 71 minutes; American International Pictures
Cast: Pamela Duncan, Richard Garland, Allison Hayes, Val Dufour, Maurice Manson
Credits: Director-Producer: Roger Corman; Writers: Charles Griffith, Mark Hanna

Undermind (2003)
USA; 113 minutes; Vertical Pictures
Cast: Sam Trammell, Erik Jensen, Susan May Pratt
Credits: Director-Writer: Nevil Dwek

Unidentified Flying Oddball (1979)
USA; 93 minutes; Disney
Cast: Dennis Dugan, Jim Dale, Ron Moody, Kenneth More, Sheila White
Credits: Director: Russ Mayberry; Screenwriter: Don Tait, based on the novel *A Connecticut Yankee in King Arthur's Court* by Mark Twain

Virgin Hunters (1994; aka *Test Tube Teens from the Year 2000*)
USA; 74 minutes; Torchlight Entertainment
Cast: Brian Bremer, Sara Suzanne Brown, Christopher Wolf, Michele Matheson, Don Dowe, Ian Abercrombie, Morgan Fairchild
Credits: Director: Ellen Cabot; Writer: Kenneth J. Hall

The Visitors (1993; aka *Les Visiteurs*)
France;107 minutes; Gaumont
Cast: Jean Reno, Christian Clavier, Valérie Lemercier, Marie-Anne Chazel
Credits: Director: Jean-Marie Poiré; Writers: Poiré, Christian Clavier

The Visitors 2: The Corridors of Time (1998; aka *Les Couloirs du Temps: Les Visiteurs II*)
France; 118 minutes; Gaumont
Cast: Christian Clavier, Jean Reno, Muriel Robin, Marie-Anne Chazel
Credits: Director: Jean-Marie Poiré; Writers: Poiré, Christian Clavier

Warlock (1991)
USA; 103 minutes; New World Pictures
Cast: Julian Sands, Lori Singer, Richard E. Grant
Credits: Director: Steve Miner; Writer: D.T. Twohy

Waxwork (1988)
USA; 97 minutes; Artisan Entertainment, Vestron Pictures
Cast: Zach Galligan, Deborah Foreman, Michelle Johnson, David Warner, Eric Brown, Clare Carey, Dana Ashbrook, Patrick Macnee
Credits: Director-Writer: Anthony Hickox

Waxwork: Lost in Time (1992)
USA; 104 minutes; Artisan Entertainment
Cast: Zach Galligan, Monika Schnarre, Martin Kemp, Bruce Campbell, Michael Des Barres, Patrick Macnee
Credits: Director-Writer: Anthony Hickox

W.E.I.R.D. World (1995)
USA; 89 minutes; Fox TV
Cast: Miguel Nuñez, Gina Ravera, Marshall Bell
Credits: Director: William Malone; Writers: Gilbert Adler, A.L. Katz, Scott Nimerfro, based on stories in *Weird Science* and *Weird Fantasy* comics

We're Back: A Dinosaur's Story (1993)
USA; 71 minutes; animated; Universal
Cast: John Goodman, René Le Vant, Felicity Kendal, Charles Fleischer, Joey Shea, Yeardley Smith, Walter Cronkite, Kenneth Mars
Credits: Director: Dick Zondag, Ralph Zondag; Writer: John Patrick Shanley, based on the book by Judson Talbot

What If … (2010)
USA; 118 minutes; Pure Flix, Jenkins Entertainment
Cast: Kevin Sorbo, Kristy Swanson, John Ratzenberger, Debby Ryan, Kristin Minter
Credits: Director: Dallas Jenkins; Writer: Cary Solomon, Chuck Konzelman, Andrea Gyertson Nasfell; Story: David A.R. White, Michael Scott

When Time Expires (1997)
USA; 93 minutes; Showtime
Cast: Richard Grieco, Cynthia Geary, Mark Hamill, Tim Thomerson
Credits: Director-Writer: David Bourla

Where Do We Go From Here? (1945)
USA; 78 minutes; Twentieth Century–Fox
Cast: Fred MacMurray, Joan Leslie, June Haver, Gene Sheldon
Credits: Director: Gregory Ratoff; Writer: Morrie Ryskind; Story: Ryskind, Sid Herzig

Willy Mcbean and His Magic Machine (1965)
USA; 100 minutes; Videocraft International; animated
Cast: Billie Mae Richards, Larry Mann
Credits: Director-Writer: Arthur Rankin, Jr.

The Winning Season (2004)
USA; 91 minutes; TNT
Cast: Shawn Hatosy, Matthew Modine, Kristin Davis
Credits: Director: John Kent Harrison; Writer: Steve Bloom, based on *Honus and Me* by Dan Gutman

Wizards of Waverly Place: The Movie (2009)
USA; 94 minutes; Disney Channel
Cast: Selena Gomez, Jake T. Austin, David Henrie, Jennifer Stone, Maria Canals-Barrera, David DeLuise
Credits: Director: Lev L. Spiro; Writer: Dan Berendsen

World Without End (1956)
USA; 80 minutes; Allied Artists
Cast: Hugh Marlowe, Rod Taylor, Nancy Gates, Nelson Leigh
Credits: Director-Writer: Edward Bernds

X-Men: Days of Future Past (2014)
USA; 130 minutes; 20th Century-Fox
Cast: Hugh Jackman, Patrick Stewart, James McAvoy, Michael Fassbender, Jennifer Lawrence, Halle Berry, Nicholas Hoult, Anna Paquin, Ellen Page, Peter Dinklage, Shawn Ashmore
Credits: Director: Bryan Singer; Writer: Simon Kinberg; Story: Jane Goldman, Kinberg, Matthew Vaughn

The Yesterday Machine (1964)
USA; 78 minutes; Carter Films
Cast: Tim Holt, James Britton, Ann Pellegrino, Jack Herman
Credits: Director-Writer: Russ Marker

Yesterday Was a Lie (2008)
USA; 87 minutes; Helicon Arts Cooperative
Cast: Kipleigh Brown, Chase Masterson, John Newton
Credits: Director-Writer: James Kerwin

Yesterday's Target (1996)
USA; 80 minutes; Showtime
Cast: Daniel Baldwin, Stacy Haiduk, T.K. Carter, Richard Herd, LeVar Burton, Malcolm McDowell
Credits: Director: Barry Samson; Writer: David Bourla

A Young Connecticut Yankee in King Arthur's Court (1995)
Canada-France; 92 minutes; Filmline International, Images Television International, Screen Partners
Cast: Philippe Ross, Michael York, Theresa Russell, Nick Mancuso, Polly Shannon
Credits: Director: R.L. Thomas; Writer: Frank Encarnacao, Thomas, based on the novel *A Connecticut Yankee in King Arthur's Court* by Mark Twain

Zathura (2005)
USA; 101 minutes; Columbia, Radar Pictures
Cast: Jonah Bobo, Josh Hutcherson, Dax Shepard, Kristen Stewart,
Credits: Director: Jon Favreau; Writer: David Koepp, John Kamps, based on the Chris Van Allsburg book.

Appendix II

Television and Direct-to-Video Series Credits

This section lists credits for all series covered in the text.

Adventures of Brisco County Jr. (1993–94)
USA; Fox TV
Cast: Bruce Campbell, Billy Drago, Julius Carry, Christian Clemenson, John Astin

The Adventures of Timothy Pilgrim (1975)
Canada; TV Ontario
Cast: Joey Davidson, David Hemblen

Alcatraz (2012)
USA; Fox TV
Cast: Sarah Jones, Jorge Garcia, Sam Neill, Johnny Coyne

Ambition of Oda Nobuna (2012; aka *Oda Nobuna no Yabou*)
Japan; TV Tokyo; animated
Cast: Takuya Eguchi, Kanae Itou

Ashes to Ashes (2008–10)
United Kingdom; BBC
Cast: Keeley Hawes, Philip Glenister

Atlantis (2013–15)
United Kingdom; BBC
Cast: Jack Donnelly, Mark Addy, Robert Emms, Alysha Hart, Juliet Stevenson

Back to Sherwood (1998)
Canada; CBC
Cast: Aimée Castle, Larry Day

Back to the Future (1991–92)
USA; CBS; animated
Cast: David Kaufman, Dan Castellaneta, Mary Steenburgen, Thomas F. Wilson, Joshua Wiener, Troy Davidson

Battle Girls: Time Paradox (2011; aka *Sengoku Otome: Momoiro Paradox*)
Japan; TV Tokyo; animated
Cast: Rina Hidaka, Megumi Toyoguchi, Yuka Hirata, Mariya Ise

Being Erica (2009–11)
Canada; CBC
Cast: Erin Karpluk, Michael Riley

Best Friends Whenever (2015)
USA; Disney Channel
Cast: Landry Bender, Lauren Taylor, Gus Kamp, Ricky Garcia

Bill & Ted's Excellent Adventures (1990–91)
USA; CBS; animated
Cast: Alex Winter, Keanu Reeves, George Carlin

Bill & Ted's Excellent Adventures (1992)
USA; Fox TV
Cast: Evan Richards, Christopher Kennedy, Rick Overton

The Box of Delights (1984)
USA; United Kingdom; BBC
Cast: Devin Stanfield, Robert Stephens, Patrick Troughton

Captain Z-Ro (1955–56)
USA; Syndicated
Cast: Roy Steffens, Bruce Haynes

Catweazle (1970–71)
United Kingdom; LWT
Cast: Geoffrey Bayldon, Robin Davies, Gary Warren

Charlie Jade (2005)
Canada; Space
Cast: Jeffrey Pierce, Michael Filipowich, Patricia McKenzie, Tyrone Benskin

Charmed (1998–2006)
USA; WB
Cast: Holly Marie Combs, Alyssa Milano, Brian Krause, Rose McGowan

Come Back Lucy (1978)
United Kingdom; ATV
Cast: Emma Bakhle, Bernadette Windsor, Phyllida Law

Continuum (2012–15)
Canada; Showcase
Cast: Rachel Nichols, Victor Webster, Erik Knudsen, Stephen Lobo, Lexa Doig, Omari Newton, Luvia Peterson, William B. Davis

Crime Traveller (1997)
United Kingdom; BBC
Cast: Michael French, Chloë Annett, Sue Johnston

Dark Shadows (1966–1971)
USA; ABC
Cast: Jonathan Frid, Thayer David, Kathryn Leigh Scott, Grayson Hall, David Selby, Lara Parker

Dark Shadows (1991)
USA; NBC
Cast: Ben Cross, Joanna Going, Jean Simmons, Roy Thinnes, Joseph Gordon-Levitt

Day Break (2006)
USA; ABC
Cast: Taye Diggs, Moon Bloodgood, Meta Golding, Clayton Rohner, Adam Baldwin

DC's Legends of Tomorrow (2016–)
USA; CW
Cast: Victor Garber, Brandon Routh, Arthur Darvill, Wentworth Miller, Caity Lotz, Casper Crump

Deep Blue Fleet (1993–2003; aka *Konpeki no Kantai*)
Japan; direct-to-video; animated
Cast: Yusaku Yara, Yuzuru Fujimoto

DNA² (1994)
Japan; Nippon TV; animated
Cast: Miina Tominaga, Keiichi Nanba, Hiroko Kasahara, Takehito Koyasu

Do Over (2002)
USA; WB
Cast: Penn Badgley, Angela Goethals, Natasha Melnick, Michael Milhoan

Doctor Who (1962–)
United Kingdom; BBC
Cast: William Hartnell, Patrick Troughton, Jon Pertwee, Tom Baker, Christopher Eccleston, David Tennant, Matt Smith, Peter Capaldi

Doraemon (1973–2005)
Japan; Nippon TV; animated
Cast: Megumi Oohara, Wasabi Mizuta

Dual! Parallel Trouble Adventures (1999)
Japan: WOWOW Network; animated
Cast: Takayuki Yamaguchi, Rie Tanaka, Chie Nakamura, Ryūnosuke Ōbayashi

Early Edition (1996–2000)
USA; CBS
Cast: Kyle Chandler, Fisher Stevens

Earthfasts (1994)
United Kingdom; BBC
Cast: Chris Downs, Paul Nicholls, Bryan Dick

11-22-63 (2016)
USA; Hulu; streaming
Cast: James Franco, Sarah Gadon, Chris Cooper

Emblem Take Two (1993–95)
Japan; direct-to-video; animated
Cast: Toshiyuki Morikawa, Daiki Nakamura

An Englishman's Castle (1978)
United Kingdom; BBC
Cast: Kenneth More

Enterprise (2001–05)
USA; UPN
CST: Scott Bakula, Jolene Blalock, John Billingsley, Dominic Keating, Connor Trinneer

Erasmus Microman (1998–99)
United Kingdom; Granada Television
Cast: Ken Campbell, Lee B. McPlank

Eureka (2006–12)
USA; SyFy
Cast: Colin Ferguson, Salli Richardson, Joe Morton, Erica Cerra, Neil Grayston

Fantastic Journey (1977)
USA; NBC
Cast: Jared Martin, Roddy McDowall, Ike Eisenmann, Katie Saylor, Carl Franklin

Fantasy Island (1977–84)
USA; ABC
Cast: Ricardo Montalban, Hervé Villechaize

Fantasy Island (1998–99)
USA; ABC
Cast: Malcolm McDowell

5ive Days to Midnight (2004)
USA; Sci-Fi Channel
Cast: Timothy Hutton, Randy Quaid, Kari Matchett, Hamish J. Linklater, Gage Golightly

The Flash (2014–)
USA; CW
Cast: Grant Gustin, Jesse L. Martin, Candice Patton

Flint the Time Detective (1998–99; aka *Jikuu Tantei Genshi-Kun*)
Japan; TV Tokyo; animated
Cast: Akiko Suzuki, Chiaka Morita, Yuji Ueda

The Fonz and the Happy Days Gang (1980–82)
ABC; animated
Cast: Henry Winkler, Ron Howard, Didi Conn, Donny Most, Frank Welker

The 4400 (2004–07)
USA; USA Network
Cast: Joel Gretsch, Jacqueline McKenzie, Laura Allen, Patrick Flueger, Chad Faust

Fringe (2008–13)
USA; Fox TV
Cast: Anna Torv, Joshua Jackson, John Noble, Lance Reddick

Future Diary (2011–12; aka *Mirai Nikki*)
Japan; Chiba TV; animated
VOICES: Misuzu Togashi, Tomosa Murata

The Future Is Wild (2007–08)
USA; Discovery Kids; animated
Cast: Marc Donato, Miranda Jones, Taylor Abrahamse, Ashley Peters

The Georgian House (1976)
United Kingdom; ITV
Cast: Spencer Banks, Adrienne Byrne, Brinsley Forde

Goodnight Sweetheart (1993–99)
United Kingdom; BBC
Cast: Nicholas Lyndhurst, Dervia Kirwan, Michelle Holmes

Haruka: Beyond The Stream of Time
(2004–05; aka *Harukanaru Toki no Naka de*)
Japan; TV Tokyo; animated
VOICES: Tomoko Kawakami, Tomokazu Seki, Kouki Miyata, Ryotaro Okiayu

Heroes (2006–10)
USA; NBC
Cast: Masi Oka, Hayden Panettiere, Greg Grunberg, Ali Larter, Milo Ventimiglia, Adrian Pasdar, Jack Coleman

Heroes Reborn (2015–6)
USA; NBC
Cast: Jack Coleman, Zachary Levi, Robbie Kay, Kiki Sukezane

Hindsight (2015)
USA; VH1
Cast: Laura Ramsey, Sarah Goldberg, Craig Horner, John Patrick Amedori, Jessy Hodges, Drew Sidora, Nick Clifford

In Search of the Lost Future (2014; aka *A la Recherche du Futur Perdu*, *Ushinawareta Mirai o Motomete*)
Japan; AT-X; animated
Cast: Takuma Terashima, Akane Tomonaga, Hatsumi Takada

Into the Labyrinth (1981–82)
United Kingdom; HTV
Cast: Ron Moody, Pamela Salem, Simon Beal, Simon Henderson, Lisa Turner, Chris Harris

Inuyasha (2000–04)
Japan; NNS; animated
Cast: Kappei Yamaguchi, Satsuki Yukino

It's About Time (1966–67)
USA; CBS
Cast: Jack Mullaney, Frank Aletter, Joe E. Ross, Imogene Coca

Jimmy Green and His Time Machine (1968)
United Kingdom; Yorkshire Television; puppets
Cast: Juliet Cooke

Johnny and the Bomb (2006)
United Kingdom; BBC
Cast: George Mackay, Zoë Wanamaker, Jazmine Franks, Keith Barron

Journeyman (2007)
USA; NBC
Cast: Kevin McKidd, Gretchen Egolf, Moon Bloodgood, Reed Diamond

Kamen Rider Den-O (2007–08)
Japan; TV Asahi
Cast: Takeru Satoh, Yuriko Shiratori, Rina Akiyama

Kappatoo (1990)
United Kingdom; ITV
Cast: Simon Nash, Felipe Izquierdo

King Arthur and the Knights of Justice (1992)
USA; Syndicated; animated
Cast: Andrew Kavadas, Jim Byrnes, Kathleen Barr

Kiteretsu Encyclopedia (1988–96; aka *Kiteretsu Daihyakka*)
Japan; Fuji TV; animated.
Cast: Toshiko Fujita, Yuuji Mitsuya, Naoki Tatsuta

K9 (2009)
Australia; Network Ten
Cast: Robert Moloney, Keegan Joyce, John Leeson, Philippa Coulthard, Daniel Webber

Land of the Lost (1974–76)
USA; NBC
Cast: Spencer Milligan, Wesley Eure, Kathy Coleman

Land of the Lost (1991–94)
USA; ABC
Cast: Timothy Bottoms, Jennifer Drugan, Robert Gavin, Ed Gale, Shannon Day

Lazer Tag Academy (1986)
USA; NBC; animated
Cast: Noelle Harling, Billy Jayne, Christina MacGregor, Booker Bradshaw

Legion of Super-Heroes (2006–08)
USA; CW, animated.
Cast: Yuri Lowenthal, Andy Milder, Heather Hogan, Kari Wahlgren, Adam Wylie, Wil Wheaton

Life on Mars (2006–07)
United Kingdom; BBC
Cast: John Simm, Philip Glenister, Liz White

Life on Mars (2008–09)
USA; ABC
Cast: Jason O'Mara, Harvey Keitel, Gretchen Mol

Lost (2004–10)
USA; ABC
Cast: Matthew Fox, Evangeline Lilly, Terry O'Quinn, Yunjin Kim

The Lost Saucer (1975–76)
USA; ABC
Cast: Jim Nabors, Ruth Buzzi, Alice Playten, Jarrod Johnson

Man Dog (1972)
United Kingdom; BBC
Cast: Carol Hazell, Jane Anthony, Adrian Shergold

The Man In the High Castle (2015–)
USA; Amazon streaming
Cast: Alexa Davalos, Luke Kleintank, Rufus Sewell, Rupert Evans, Cary-Hiroyuki Tagawa

Mary Shelley's Frankenhole (2010–12)
USA; Adult Swim; animated
Cast: Jeff Bryan Davis

Megas XLR (2004–05)
USA; Cartoon Network; animated

Cast: David DeLuise, Wendee Lee, Steven Jay Blum, Scott Rienecker

The Melancholy of Haruhi Suzumiya (2006, 2009)
Japan; Chiba TV; animated
Cast: Tomokazu Sugita, Aya Hirano, Yuuko Gotou, Daisuke Ono

Mentors (1999–2004)
Canada; Family Channel
Cast: Chad Krowchuk, Sarah Lind, Stevie Mitchell, Samantha Krutzfeld

Mira Sentai Time Rangers (2000–01)
Japan; TV Asahi
Cast: Ryūzaburō Ōtomo, Hikaru Midorikawa

Misfits (2009–13)
United Kingdom; E4
Cast: Lauren Socha, Nathan Stewart-Jarrett, Antonia Thomas, Iwan Rheon, Robert Sheehan

The Mr. Peabody and Sherman Show (2015–)
USA; Netflix; animated.
Cast: Chris Parnell, Max Charles

Moondial (1988)
United Kingdom; BBC
Cast: Siri Neal, Tony Sands, Helena Avellano

Mud (1994–95)
United Kingdom; CBBC
Cast: Russell Brand, Brooke Kinsella, Russell Tovey

Nine: Nine Time Travels (2013; aka *Nain: Ahob Beonui Shiganyeohaeng*)
South Korea; TVN
Cast: Lee Jin Wook, Jo Yoon Hee, Jeon No-Min

Noein (2005–06; aka *Noien: To Your Other Self, Noein: Toward Another You, Noein: Mou Hitori no Kimi e*)
Japan; CTC; animated
Cast: Haruka Kudo, Fujiko Takimoto, Akemi Okamura, Kazuya Nakai

Occult Academy (2010; aka *Seikimatsu Occult Gakuin*)
Japan, TV Tokyo; animated
Cast: Yoko Hikasa, Takahiro Mizumisha, Minori Chihara

Odyssey 5 (2002)
Canada; Space, Showtime
Cast: Peter Weller, Sebastian Roché, Christopher Gorham, Leslie Silva, Tamara Craig Thomas

Outlander (2014–)
USA; Starz
Cast: Caitriona Balfe, Sam Heughan, Tobias Menzies

Outlaws (1986–87)
USA; CBS
Cast: Rod Taylor, William Lucking, Charles Napier, Richard Roundtree, Christina Belford

Paradox (2009)
United Kingdom; BBC
Cast: Tamzin Outhwaite, Emun Elliott, Mark Bonnar, Chiké Okonkwo

Peabody's Improbable History (1959–64)
A segment of *Rocky and His Friends/The Bullwinkle Show*.
USA; ABC, NBC; animated
VOICES: Bill Scott, Walter Tetley

The Peter Potamus Show (1964–65)
USA; syndicated; animated
Cast: Daws Butler, Don Messick

Phil of the Future (2004–06)
USA; Disney Channel
Cast: Ricky Ullman, Amy Bruckner, Craig Anton, Lise Simms

Planet of the Apes (1974)
USA; CBS
Cast: Ron Harper, James Naughton, Roddy McDowall, Booth Colman, Mark Lenard

Power Rangers Time Force (2001)
USA; Fox Kids
Cast: Jason Faunt, Michael Copon, Kevin Kleinberg, Deborah Estelle Philips, Erin Cahill, Vernon Wells, Kate Sheldon

Prehistoric Park (2006)
United Kingdom; ITV
Cast: Nigel Marven, Rod Arthur, Suzanne McNabb

Present Time (1997–98)
USA; Direct-to-video
Cast: Steven Harris, Tara Streeter, Philip Bryce Jacobs, Ryan Devin, Jim Bullock

Primeval (2007–11)
United Kingdom; ITV
Cast: Andrew-Lee Potts, Hannah Spearritt, Ben Miller, Juliet Aubrey

Primeval: New World (2012–13)
Canada; Space
Cast: Niall Matter, Sara Canning, Crystal Lowe, Miranda Frigon, Geoff Gustafson

Puella Magi Madoka Magica (2011)
Japan; TBS, MSBS; animated
Cast: Aoi Yuki, Emiri Kato, Chiwa Saito, Kaori Mizuhashi, Eri Kitamura

Quantum Leap (1989–93)
USA; NBC
Cast: Scott Bakula, Dean Stockwell

Red Dwarf (1988–2012)
United Kingdom; BBC
Cast: Craig Charles, Chris Barrie, Danny John-Jules

Return to the Planet of the Apes (1975)
USA; NBC; animated
Cast: Austin Stoker, Philippa Harris, Henry Corden, Richard Blackburn, Edwin Mills, Tom Williams, Claudette Nevins

Sailor Moon (1992–97; aka *Bishojo Senshi Sailor Moon*)
Japan; TV Asahi; animated.
Cast: Kotono Mitsuishi, Kae Araki, Tohru Furuya, Chiyoko Kawashima

Samurai Jack (2001–2004)
USA; Cartoon Channel; animated
Cast: Phil LaMarr, Mako

Sapphire and Steel (1979–82)
United Kingdom; ATV
Cast: Joanna Lumley, David McCallum

Second Chance (1987)
USA; Fox TV
Cast: Kiel Martin, Matthew Perry, Randee Heller

The Secret World of Polly Flint (1987)
United Kingdom; Central Independent TV
Cast: Katie Reynolds, Don Henderson, Daniel Pope

Sengoku Collection (2012; aka *Parallel World Samurai*)
Japan; TV Tokyo; animated
Cast: Akeno Watanabe, Rumi Ookubo, Kana Hanazawa, Ayumi Tsunematsu

Seven Days (1998–2001)
USA; UPN
Cast: Jonathan LaPaglia, Don Franklin, Norman Lloyd, Justina Vail

Shazzan (1967–68)
USA; CBS; animated
Cast: Jerry Dexter, Janet Waldo, Barney Phillips

Sins of the Sisters (1993; aka *Sei Michaela no Gakuen Hyoryuki*, Tales of Saint Michaela's Academy)
Japan; direct-to-video; animated
Cast: Naoko Matsui, Hirotaka Suzuoki, Kumiko Watanabe

Sir Arthur Conan Doyle's The Lost World (1999–2002)
USA; syndicated
Cast: Peter McCauley, Rachel Blakely, Will Snow, Jennifer O'Dell

Sky (1976)
United Kingdom; HTV
Cast: Mark Harrison, Stuart Lock, Robert Eddison

Sliders (1995–2000)
USA; Fox TV, Sci-Fi Channel
Cast: Jerry O'Connell, Sabrina Lloyd, Cleavant Derricks, John Rhys-Davies

Starhyke (2009)
United Kingdom; Showcase TV
Cast: Claudia Christian, Suanne Braun, Jeremy Bulloch

Starship Girl Yamamoto Yohko (1995–96, 1999; aka *Soreyuke! Uchuusenkan Yamamoto Youko*)
Japan; direct-to-video, TV Osaka, TV Tokyo; animated
Cast: Minami Takayama, Megumi Yahashibara, Shiho Niiyama

Steins;Gate (2011)
Japan; AT-X PLUS; animated
Cast: Mamoru Miyano, Kana Hanazawa, Tomokazu Seki

Strange Days at Blake Holsey High (2002–06)
USA; NBC
Cast: Emma Taylor-Isherwood, Shadia Simmons, Michael Seater, Tony Munch, Lawrence Bayne

Summer Storm (2009; aka *Natsu no Arashi*)
Japan; TV Tokyo; animated
Cast: Ryoko Shiraishi, Chiaki Omigawa, Yuuko Sanpei, Kaori Nazuka

Tenchu (2014)
Japan; Fuji TV
Cast: Ono Yuriko, Izumi Pinko

Terminator: The Sarah Connor Chronicles (2008–09)
USA; Fox TV
Cast: Lena Headey, Thomas Dekker, Summer Glau, Brian Austin Green, Garret Dillahunt, Shirley Manson

Terra Nova (2011)
USA; Fox TV
Cast: Jason O'Mara, Shelley Conn, Stephen Lang, Christine Adams

That Was Then (2002)
USA; ABC
Cast: James Bulliard, Bess Armstrong, Jeffrey Tambor, Kiele Sanchez

Time Express (1979)
USA; CBS
Cast: Vincent Price, Coral Browne, James Reynolds, William Phipps

Time Fighters (1975–2000; aka *Time Bokan*)
Japan; Fuji TV; animated
Cast: Mari Okamoto, Yoshiko Oota, Ryuuji Saikachi, Noriko Ohara

Time Is the Enemy (1958)
United Kingdom; ITV
Cast: Clifford Elkin, Nigel Arkwright, Betty Huntley-Wright

Time Keepers (1997)
Japan
Cast: Mikihisa Azuma, Emiri Nakayama, Hideaki Takizawa

Time Riders (1991)
United Kingdom; Thames Television.
Cast: Haydn Gwynne, Clive Merrison, Kerry Shale, Brinley Jenkins, Kenneth Hall

Time Squad (2001–03)
USA; Cartoon Network; animated
Cast: Rob Paulsen, Pamela Segall, Mark Hamill

Time Travel Tondekeman (1989–90; aka *Time Quest*)
Japan; Fuji; animated
Cast: Kumiko Nishihara, Shigeru Chiba, Yuuji Mitsuya, Junpei Takiguchi

Time Trax (1993–94)
USA; Syndicated
Cast: Dale Midkiff, Elizabeth Alexander, Peter Donat

The Time Tunnel (1966–67)
USA; ABC
Cast: James Darren, Robert Colbert, Lee Meriwether, Whit Bissell

Time Warp Trio (2005–06)
USA; Discovery Kids; animated
Cast: Mark Rendall, Scott McCord, Darren Frost, Sarah Gadon, Sunday Muse, Laurie Elliott

Timecop (1997–98)
USA; ABC
Cast: T.W. King, Cristi Conaway, Don Stark, Kurt Fuller

Timeslip (1970–71)
United Kingdom; ATV
Cast: Cheryl Burfield, Spencer Banks, Denis Quilley

Tom's Midnight Garden (1989)
United Kingdom; BBC
Cast: Jeremy Rampling, Caroline Waldron

A Traveller In Time (1978)
United Kingdom; BBC
Cast: Sophie Thompson

Tru Calling (2003–05)
USA; Fox TV
Cast: Eliza Dushku, Shawn Reaves, Zach Galifianakis, Jason Priestley

12 Monkeys (2015–)
USA; SyFy
Cast: Aaron Stanford, Amanda Schull, Emily Hampshire, Kirk Acevedo, Barbara Sukowa

Twice In a Lifetime (1999–2001)
USA; Pax
Cast: Gordie Brown, Paul Popowich, Al Waxman

The Twilight Zone (1959–64, 1985–89, 2002–03)
USA; CBS, Syndicated, UPN
Host: Rod Serling

Voyagers (1982–83)
USA; NBC
Cast: Jon-Erik Hexum, Meeno Peluce

Wolverine and the X-Men (2009)
USA; Nicktoons; animated
Cast: Steve Blum, Jim Ward, Kari Wahlgren, Fred Tatasciore

Zipang (2004–05)
Japan; animated; Tokyo Broadcasting
Cast: Hiroki Touchi, Tetsu Inada, Yuusaku Yara, Takanori Hoshino

Appendix III
Television Specials

Brigadoon (1966)
USA; CBS
Cast: Robert Goulet, Peter Falk, Sally Ann Howes

Bugs Bunny in King Arthur's Court (1978)
USA; CBS; animated
Cast: Mel Blanc

Here Comes Peter Cottontail (1971)
USA; ABC; animated.
Voices: Casey Kasem, Vincent Price, Danny Kaye

Random Quest (2006)
USA; 59 minutes; BBC
Cast: Samuel West, Kate Ashfield, David Burke, Shaun Parkes
Credits: Director: Luke Watson; Writer: Richard Fell, from "Random Quest" by John Wyndham

Rudolph's Shiny New Year (1976)
USA; ABC; animated
Cast: Red Skelton, Billie Mae Richards, Paul Frees

The Time Machine (1949)
United Kingdom; 60 minutes; BBC
Cast: Russell Napier, Mary Dorn
Credits: Director-Writer: Robert Barr

Appendix IV

Films and Television Series with Minor Time Travel Elements

Adventure Kid (1992; aka *Adventure Duo*)
Japan, video series
An anime mixing porn and comedy, involving two Japanese who died in World War II and are now reincarnated as present-day teens. Their exploits include an adventure in a parallel world.

Amityville: It's About Time (1992)
USA, film
A clock from the accursed house of *The Amityville Horror* unleashes new evil when it's placed in a new home. At the end, an attack on the clock resets time so that none of the deaths ever happen.

Army of Apes (1974; aka *Saru no Gundan*)
Japan, TV series
Three humans wake from suspended animation to find themselves in an ape-ruled future. At the end of the series, they return to cryosleep at such low temperatures time rewinds and they return to the present. This was re-edited into the 1984 film *Time of the Apes*.

Arthur, the King (1985)
USA, TV movie
A tourist discovers Merlin and his lover Nimue imprisoned at Stonehenge. After they tell her the history of Camelot, she convinces them they have the power to change the Fall of Camelot so that the ideals of King Arthur don't die completely.

The Atomic Man (1955)
USA, movie
A nuclear scientist involved in a murder case gives incomprehensible answers when he's questioned. It's because a freak accident has placed his mind several seconds in the future, so he's answering questions that haven't been asked yet.

Austin Powers in Goldmember (2002)
USA, movie
Dr. Evil (Mike Myers) hides super-spy Austin Powers' (Myers) kidnapped father (Michael Caine) in 1975 at the villainous Goldmember's (Myers) disco. Powers fails to rescue his father but brings FBI agent Foxxy Cleopatra (Beyoncé Knowles) back to the present with him.

Awake (2012)
USA, TV series
A man believes he exists in two timelines, divided by whether his wife or his son died in an accident. Or is it just a hallucination to deal with his grief?

Battle Royale High School (1987)
Japan, movie
Demons square off in battle in a modern-day Japanese high school in fulfillment of an ancient prophecy. A time-patrolman joins in the mindless action.

Beasties (1991)
USA, movie
Alien monstrosities escape a spaceship and start eating small-town teens. It turns out the ship is from the future, piloted by the protagonist's mutated future self to change his history.

Bewitched (2005)
USA, movie
Will Farrell plays an actor making a big-screen adaptation of the 1960s TV show *Bewitched*; Nicole Kidman is his co-star, a real witch. After she casts a love spell on Farrell, she decides to win his heart for real and rewinds time to cancel the spell.

Beyond the Bermuda Triangle (1975)
USA, TV movie
Fred MacMurray investigates the Bermuda Triangle and becomes convinced it's a time rift. He vanishes mysteriously while searching for proof.

Blue Flame (1993)
USA, movie
A man hunting the aliens who abducted his little girl finds her in an alien dreamscape, grown to adulthood. At the end of the film, the girl kills her abductor, which enables her to change time and cancel out the kidnapping.

Brick Bradford (1947)
USA, movie serial
Based on a comic strip, this serial has Brick (Kane Richmond) battling villains for control of a missile-defense ray. At one point, Brick uses a time top to travel into the past and acquire a scientific formula that will improve the ray's effectiveness.

C (2011)
Japan, TV series
Anime in which battles in a limbo called the Financial District change the players' futures. The duels can also erase people and things from reality.

Century Falls (1993)
United Kingdom, TV series
TV thriller about a small town blighted because of a botched 1953 effort to summon a demon. Some

of the villagers plan to bring 1953 into the present so they can fix things.

Conceiving Ada (1997)
USA, movie
A modern-day computer programmer finds a way to peer through time at 19th century mathematician Ada Lovelace (Tilda Swinton). Eventually she clones Lovelace's mind and implants it in her newborn daughter.

Cube²: Hypercube (2002)
USA, movie
A group of human guinea pigs are trapped inside a tesseract. Time in the cube constantly shifts so the prisoners keep encountering past, future and alternate versions of themselves. Almost everyone dies.

The Day Time Ended (1980)
USA, movie
A "time space war" causes UFOs and monsters to show up at a family's home in the Southwest before transporting the family to another world.

Devil's Pass (2013)
USA, movie
Teens exploring a mysterious incident in the USSR discover a secret Philadelphia Experiment–based lab in the mountains. At the film's end, the two surviving explorers are hurled back to 1959 and turned into monsters.

Dimension (2006)
USA, movie
Charming film in which God gives residents of a small community the option to change their lives by three inches. The film watches different people interpret this different ways: one woman goes back in time to save her baby from a fall (she missed him by a couple of inches), another gets to be born in New York instead of Alabama (three inches apart on the map).

Dreamland (2007)
USA, movie
A young couple traveling near Roswell encounter weird phenomena, some of which may involve time travel but might be hallucinations.

Eerie, Indiana: The Other Dimension (1998)
USA, TV series
Eerie, Indiana was a story about a young boy living in a town haunted by the paranormal. In the first episode of this reboot, a dimensional rift shifts the weirdness to the Eerie Indiana of a parallel world, where a new kid protagonist has to deal with it all.

Far-Out Space Nuts (1975–76)
USA, TV series
This live-action Saturday-morning series involved a couple of NASA workers accidentally launched into space. In the season ender, they travel through time and end up on Earth right before the launch. They decide their adventures were fun, so they allow events to play out as they originally did.

Flashback (2011)
USA, movie
A 32nd-century movie studio plans to use a time machine to loot realistic props and historical figures from the past. A janitor tries using the time machine to fix a disastrous first date, then to save his girlfriend from a bomb.

Flight of the Navigator (1986)
USA, movie
After an overnight flight on an alien spaceship, a young boy discovers that because of FTL time dilation, eight years have passed. Eventually the ship breaks the time barrier and returns the boy to eight years in the past, so he can resume his old life.

1408 (2007)
USA, movie
After enduring a supernatural hell in a haunted hotel room, writer John Cusack learns the hour will repeat, over and over until he kills himself. He sets fire to the room with a Molotov cocktail, escapes and survives.

Foxfur (2012)
USA, movie
In this arty film, the protagonist wanders through a shifting reality before getting what's either a time trip back to 1982, or recovering her memories of 1982.

Galaxy Quest (1999)
USA, movie
Aliens recruit actors from a *Star Trek*–like series to save them from an alien warlord. After the actors succeed and head home, the warlord attacks and kills them. A time-displacement device rewinds events by 30 seconds so one of the actors can take out the warlord before the attack.

Great Revolution (2014; aka *Dai Shogun*)
Japan, TV series
Anime set in an alternate timeline where Onigami, a giant mecha, enabled Japan to remain closed to foreign visitors.

Green Lantern (2011–13)
USA, TV series
Superhero Green Lantern fights evil in space accompanied by aliens and the computer-intelligence Aya. By the end of the series, Aya becomes convinced emotions are dangerous. She uses a time travel device to return to the moment of creation, plotting to eliminate emotions by preventing the existence of life.

Halloweentown II: Kalabar's Revenge (2001)
USA, TV movie
A teenage witch trapped by an evil teen warlock uses a time travel spell to go back before he imprisoned her. She escapes successfully but then faces the challenge of returning to the present.

Harry Potter and the Prisoner of Azkaban (2004)
USA, movie

In this film adaptation of J.K. Rowling's third novel, Hermione uses a "time turner" to travel back in time and take extra classes. At the climax, Harry and his friends use the turner to prevent multiple tragedies.

Hercules and the Amazon Women (1994)
USA, TV movie

When the arrogant Hercules (Kevin Sorbo) goes up against the Amazons, he and their leader (Roma Downey) fall in love. An angry Amazon kills the queen, so Hercules convinces Zeus to wind back time and save her.

Hyperfutura (2013)
USA, movie

A mad scientist attempts to turn a human test subject into a "trans human" with time travel powers. At the end of the film, the human guinea pig escapes into time.

The Illustrated Man (1969)
USA, movie

A drifter discovers he sees Ray Bradbury stories when he stares at Rod Steiger's tattoos. Steiger claims tattoo artist Claire Bloom was able to create the mysterious "skin illustrations" because she was from the future.

Jubilee (1978)
United Kingdom, movie

Punks in modern-day England party down, break out into violence and waffle on pretentiously about society. A time traveling Queen Elizabeth I periodically stands around in the present wringing her hands over the state of England.

Jumanji (1995)
USA, movie

Two children are trapped into playing the eponymous game alongside Robin Williams, who was sucked into the game world back in 1969. When Williams finally wins, he returns to 1969, which enables him to avert tragedy for both his family and, years later, for the two kids.

The Lovers (2015)
USA, movie

Josh Hartnett falls into a coma. We flash back to interminable past-life adventures in 1700s India, then his past-life lover arrives in the present to magically bring him back to consciousness.

Lucy (2014)
USA, movie

A drug gives Scarlet Johansson reality-altering powers. She time travels briefly.

Malice in Wonderland (2009)
United Kingdom, movie

A young woman loses her memory after an accident and wanders into a wonderland peopled with various unsavory criminals. She's about to die when a mysterious deejay lets her relive the moments before the accident. She avoids the accident and thereby erases the events of the film.

The Man Who Could Work Miracles (1936)
United Kingdom, movie

In this H.G. Wells adaptation, the gods see how an ordinary mortal (Roland Young) handles the power to work miracles. After Young accidentally destroys the world, he rewinds time to the moment before he received the power and wishes never to acquire it.

Mask of Zeguy (1993)
Japan, TV series

Two-episode anime in which travelers from another dimension cross "cloud roads" to enter our universe at different points in time, hunting the Mask of Zeguy.

Masters of the Universe (1987)
USA, movie

In the aftermath of the epic battle between heroic He-Man and evil Skeletor, Earth teen Courtney Cox goes home from their world of Eternia. She arrives back in time before the death of her parents and saves their lives.

The Meeksville Ghost (1999)
USA, movie

A ghost (Judge Reinhold) cursed for accidentally shooting the woman he loved enlists a young drifter to help break the curse. Near the end of the film, the drifter goes back in time and stops the shooting. Everything in the present becomes better.

Memoirs of a Survivor (1981)
United Kingdom, movie

Julie Christie, living in a dreary, post-apocalyptic world, escapes by entering into the Victorian past. At the end, she take her family into the past with her.

The Place Promised in Our Early Days
(2004; aka *Kumo no Mukou, Yakusoku no Basho*)
Japan, movie

In this anime, Japan has been divided like Korea in our world. A mysterious tower on Hokkaido threatens to absorb Earth into a parallel reality, but a comatose young girl's mind keeps the world stable.

Pokemon 4ever (2001)
Japan, movie

The cast of the *Pokemon* TV show help a time-displaced boy and his Pokemon friend escape from an evil villain. It turns out the boy grew up to be one of the series' regular characters.

Possible Worlds (2000)
Canada, movie.

A man pursues his wife through multiple parallel worlds. At the end it turns out these are the dreams of his disembodied brain, stored in a laboratory.

Premonition (2004; aka *Yogen*)
Japan, movie

A mysterious newspaper page warns a man of his daughter's death in a car accident. After she dies, he undergoes many bizarre incidents before finally he gets to go back in time and exchange his life for hers.

Rows (2015)
USA, movie
After a young woman serves eviction papers on an old woman, she finds herself sliding back and forth through time, confronting increasingly nightmarish situations. Eventually history changes so the eviction never happens. Life returns to normal.

Samurai Girls (2010; aka *Hyakka Ryouran*)
Japan, TV series
Anime set in a world where the shogunate survived into the 20th century. A teenage boy rebels against his oppressive school council with the help of several fellow students named for great samurai.

Scooby-Doo: Mystery Incorporated (2010–13)
USA, TV series
One of several series about a group of mystery-solving teens and their Great Dane, Scooby-Doo. After they destroy a demon that's manipulated their small town for centuries, history changes, leaving the kids living entirely different lives.

The Seeker: The Dark Is Rising (2007)
USA, movie
In this flat adaptation of Susan Cooper's novel, a teenage boy jaunts through time to collect six sigils that will stop darkness overwhelming the world. The time trips make little difference to the story.

666 Park Avenue (2012–13)
USA, TV series
The Drake is a sinister apartment building run by Satan's agents. A tenant exploring its secrets repeatedly travels through a basement gateway into the building's past.

Southland Tales (2007)
USA, movie
Primarily a muddled film about a chaotic dystopian future, but it does have Dwayne Johnson and Justin Timberlake falling through rifts in time. Timberlake touches his past counterpart which threatens to destabilize all time, but nothing actually happens.

Spider-Man (1994–1998)
USA, TV series
At the end of this animated series, Spider-Man travels through multiple dimensions fighting a threat to all reality. He enters one dimension where he's a comic book character and gets helpful advice from his "creator," Stan Lee.

Star Trek: Deep Space Nine (1993–99)
USA, TV series
Adventures centering on the eponymous space station, positioned next to a wormhole that contains "gods" living outside linear time. The wormhole gods and the time-bending Orbs they created cropped up as a running thread through the series.

Star Trek: Generations (1994)
USA, movie
Battling the mad scientist Zorin (Malcolm McDowell), Captain Picard (Patrick Stewart) is swept into the Nexus, a realm outside time and space, while the *Enterprise* and several planets are destroyed. Finding James Kirk (William Shatner) inside the Nexus, Picard re-emerges with him before the *Enterprise* is blasted and together they defeat Zorin.

The Strange World of Planet X (1956)
United Kingdom, TV series
In this British TV serial, scientists master a formula for crossing the fourth dimension but rather than time travel they take a quick trip to Planet X.

Super Capers (2009)
USA, movie
An inept wannabe superhero (Justin Whalin) reluctantly joins the third-rate Super Capers team. Near the end of the movie, after everything's gone wrong, he goes back in time and saves his team from the villain.

Superman (1978)
USA, movie
At the climax of the film, earthquakes unleashed by Lex Luthor (Gene Hackman) kill Lois Lane (Margot Kidder). Superman (Christopher Reeve) super-speeds back through time to prevent her death.

Teen Beach 2 (2015)
USA, TV-movie
In *Teen Beach Movie*, two surfing teens were drawn into a 1960s beach-party film; in this sequel, the movie characters escape into the present. This eventually erases the movie which changes the past so the two surfers never meet. By the end of the film, they're back together in the new timeline.

Termination Point (2007)
USA, TV-movie
A stolen time-space teleporter sucks a plane into an interdimensional limbo and creates a wormhole that threatens to suck up the entire Earth.

Throg (2004)
USA, movie
A medieval dimwit becomes the champion of the gods and wanders through centuries of unfunny adventures. At the end, his triumphant reward is to be sent back to his own past.

Time Warrior (2012)
USA, movie
The "lord of war" recruits two teens to fight in battles throughout history so as to prolong the bloodshed and conflict. However, there's almost no actual time travel in the film.

Trancers IV (1994)
USA, movie
Jack Deth starts a trip through time only to be hurled into an alternative world ruled by Trancer-like vampires.

Trancers V (1994)
USA, movie
After bringing peace to the vampire world, Deth returns to his own timeline.

The Triangle (2001)
USA, movie
Three friends experience a nightmarish adventure on a ghost ship in the Bermuda Triangle. When they return to civilization after what they think is a few days, they discover four years have passed.

Vampire Time Travelers (1998)
USA, movie
Bad horror comedy about vampires terrorizing a sorority. The heroine uses magic to hurl a vampire forward in time, exposing the undead to daylight. Later the heroine magically travels back in time to erase the events of the movie.

Webs (2003)
USA, TV-movie
Richard Grieco and his friends are transferred to a parallel Earth that has been invaded by murderous spider-creatures.

Wishmaster (1997)
USA, movie
A woman unleashes a djinn that will summon its people to destroy the world once the woman makes three wishes. Her third wish is to rewind time so the djinn was never freed to work its magic.

Young Justice (2010–13)
USA, TV series
In the second season of this superhero series, Bart Allen, the Flash's grandson, travels back from a future Earth oppressed by the alien Reach. His mission: to change history to save the Flash and prevent the superhero Blue Beetle from becoming the Reach's top enforcer.

APPENDIX V

The Rest of the World

The focus of this book is on time-travel stories from the U.S., Canada, the United Kingdom and Japan. While I have included a few films and TV shows from the rest of the world in the text, most of them are placed in this appendix.

Adventurers: Masters of Time (2005; aka *Adventurers Mission Zeitreise*)
German TV series. Students at a private school discover that one of their teachers has gone back in time to stop the sinister Hacker from tampering with history. The teens follow to help in the fight.

Adventures in Time (2001; aka *Aventuras en el Tiempo*)
Mexican TV series. An orphan girl discovers that one of her relatives has an old time machine hidden away. The girl and her family begin to explore the time stream.

Amapola (2014)
Argentinian movie. A young woman in the 1960s gets a look at her family in 1982. When she returns to her own time, she uses what she's learned to find love and prevent tragedy.

Ancient Relic (2002; aka *Das Jesus Video*)
German TV miniseries. Archaeologists discover that a time traveler went back to the first century and recorded Jesus on video. Catholic assassins attempt to find and destroy the video for fear it will undermine the faith.

Argai: The Prophecy (2000; aka *Argai: La Prophétie*)
France. Animated TV series in which a medieval hero battles a villainous sorceress from the 21st century to save the life of the woman he loves.

As Time Goes By (1988)
Australian film. A surfer seeking the truth about the father he never knew meets an alien at a diner in the Outback. The alien sends the surfer back in time to recover a piece of technology that would enable Japan to win World War II.

Brødrene Dal og Spektralsteinene (1982)
Norwegian TV series. An alien sends the adventurous Dal Brothers through time to gather valuable energy crystals for his home world. Their travel includes visits to Robinson Crusoe, the Three Musketeers and World War II Norway.

Brothers Dal and the Mystery of Karl XII's Gaiters (2005; aka *Brødrene Dal og Mysteriet med Karl XIIs Gamasjer*)
Norwegian series. The brothers Dal once again travel through time, hitting different events in history

Carnivale (2000)
France. Animated fantasy film about children playing in an abandoned amusement park. They're drawn back through time to when the park was open—and full of evil.

Chinese Odyssey (1995; aka *Sai Yau Gei*)
Chinese film. In this two-part version of *Journey to the West*, the legendary hero Monkey is reincarnated in the present as the outlaw Joker. When his lover is injured, he uses Pandora's Box to travel back in time and attempts to save her.

Deja Vu (2013–14; aka *Hui Dao Ai Yi Qian*)
Taiwanese TV series. After the death of her husband, a woman goes back in time and changes his fate by preventing their first meeting. When life throws them together anyway, she has to decide whether to try to win his love again.

Déjà Vu Darling (2013)
France. TV miniseries involving a feuding family that includes witches, mesmerists and mad scientists. A time travel potion is just one of the plot elements in play.

Don't Fool with Love (1990)
Mexico. In one segment of this anthology film, a couple separated by time see each other in an antique mirror. Eventually the woman of the present steps into the past to join her man.

Dr. Jin (2012)
South Korea. TV series about a 21st century doctor who gets drawn back to 1860 and uses his modern knowledge to heal the people of the past.

Dr. Plonk (2007)
Australian film. In 1907, a super-scientist discovers the world will end in 2008 and builds a time machine to visit the future and confirm his theory. A comedy shot as a black-and-white silent movie.

Dream of a Warrior (2001)
South Korean film. After a scientist projects his daughter into her past life, he recruits a police detective to follow her into the past.

El Ministerio del Tiempo (2015–)
Spanish TV series. The country's ultra-secret Ministry of Time guards the gates of time to prevent anyone altering the past, or coming to the present from another time.

11 A.M. (2013; aka *Yeolhansi*)
South Korea. Film in which a scientist tests his time machine by jumping 24 hours ahead, only to discover the lab destroyed and his colleagues missing. Can he avert the future?

Eternity (2006)
Philippines film. Two lovers discover their romance is doomed by a curse cast on them in a past life. By risking death in the present, the female lead changes the past so that the curse is never cast.

Faith (2012; aka *The Great Doctor, Shinui*)
South Korean TV series. A general travels from 1351 to bring back a modern-day doctor for an injured princess. The female doctor falls for the general and becomes caught up in court intrigue.

The Fog (2010; aka *Tuman*)
Russian film. A squad of young Russian soldiers enters a fog and emerges in World War II. Now instead of drills and mock combat, they have to face the real thing.

Frenchman's Farm (1987)
Australian film. A woman jumps back in time to World War II where she witnesses a murder. When she returns to the present, she becomes a target for the killer's ghost.

Fun2shh (2003)
Indian film. Three comic goofballs are accused of stealing a priceless antique crown. When they flee the cops, a car accident sends them back to the tenth century. They realize that if they can steal the ancient crown in the past, then return to the present, they can clear their names.

Future Cops (1993; aka *Cha-Oji Xuexiao Bawan*)
Hong Kong movie. When a master criminal goes on trial in 2043, his henchmen travel back to 1993 to turn the judge into a brainwashed sleeper agent. The title future cops go back too, and get involved in wacky comic adventures in the present.

Future Past (1987)
Australian movie. A freak accident brings a video clerk's ruthless future self to the present where he plans to exploit his knowledge of coming events. The present-day clerk sets out to stop himself, even though his future self already knows everything the clerk will attempt.

Future Hunters (1986)
Philippines. Film in which a time traveler from Earth's dystopian future uses the Spear of Destiny to travel to the present. He recruits a couple (Robert Patrick, Linda Carol) to unmake the dystopia, which sets them against a scheming neo–Nazi.

The Girl from Tomorrow (1991)
Australia. TV series about Alana, a teenager from the year 3,000 who's kidnapped and dragged back to the present. She has to find the kidnapper and the time machine before it automatically returns home, or she'll be trapped here.

Glorious Times at the Spessart Inn (1967; aka *Herrliche Zeiten im Spessart*)
Germany. The third film in a popular series about the title tavern, this has characters (including ghosts) transported to the past and future by a lever in a castle.

God's Gift—14 Days (2014; aka *Shinui Sunmool*)
South Korean TV series. After a serial killer murders a little girl, the girl's mother drowns herself. She finds herself 14 days in the past and sets out to avert the tragedy.

Guest from the Future (1985; aka *Gostya iz Budushchego*)
USSR TV series. A grade-school boy finds an abandoned time machine and travels to the future. When he returns to the present, various future characters follow.

He Ain't Heavy, He's My Father (1993; aka *Xin Nan Xiong Nan Di*)

Hong Kong film. A covetous young man is contemptuous of his sweet, generous father. Then he falls into a wishing well and meets his father as a young man.

Heaven's Soldiers (2005; aka *Cheon Gun*)
South Korean film. A strike force protecting a nuclear warhead gets pulled back to 1572. They have to find a way home before the warhead goes off, and also turn a local lowlife into the great military leader he's destined to be.

Hero Beyond the Boundary of Time (1993; aka *Wei Xiao Bao: Feng Zhi Gou Nu*)
Hong Kong movie. A pot-smoking Chinese emperor sends his envoy to the 20th century to find a virgin queen. The envoy finds a virgin, then falls for her.

House at the End of Time (2013)
Venezuelan film. A woman convicted of murdering her family leaves prison years later to return home under house arrest. She discovers the reason for the strange events at the time of the murder: The house distorts time. Using its power, she saves her children's lives and returns with them to the present.

House of Clocks (1989)
Italy. This movie has three punks break into an elderly couple's home and kill them. The old man's clocks rewind time magically, allowing the couple to return to life and attack the intruders.

Hu-Man (1975)
French movie. Mass emotion can be used to power time travel. Terence Stamp competes on a game show where the emotions of the audience determine whether he'll be sent to the past or the future.

Hourglass Sanatorium (1973)
Polish film. A man visits his father in a crumbling mental hospital where time and reality seem to slide out of joint.

I Killed Einstein, Gentleman (1970; aka *Zabil Jsem Einsteina Pánové*)
Czechoslovakian film. Nuclear radiation has made all women sterile and bearded. A time traveler goes back to murder Einstein in the hope that without his theories, atomic weapons will never be developed.

Indru Netru Naalai (2015)
Indian movie. A scientist in 2065 tests his time machine by sending it back 50 years. In the present, two guys find the machine and begin using it. Comedy results.

The Invisible Boy (1995; aka *El Niño Invisible*)
Spanish film. Children discover a magic stone that transports them to the 12th century.

Journey to the Beginning of Time (1967; aka *Cesta do Pravěku*)
Czechoslovakian film. Four kids travel down a river that takes them from the present through prehistory to the dawn of creation. There are lectures on paleontology the whole way. More documentary than fiction.

The King of Yesterday and Tomorrow (2003)
Hong Kong TV series. A Chinese emperor and the female assassin seeking to kill him are transported to the present, where they have to get day jobs.

Kin-Dza-Dza! (1986)
USSR. Movie in which an alien accidentally teleports two Russians to the Kin-Dza-Dza galaxy. After various satirical adventures, the Russians return across time to the moment they arrived in Kin-Dza-Dza. Their foreknowledge lets them outmaneuver the aliens and return home.

La Edad de Piedra (1964)
Mexican film. A scientist sends comedy team Viruta and Capulina back to the Stone Age, where they befriend a baby dinosaur and hook up with hot cavewomen. When they return to the present, they decide they prefer the past and go back to the Stone Age.

Liebe in der Warteschleife (2004)
German movie. A man uncertain about his future finds the time for making a decision has come—and then the day starts repeating.

Lilovy Shar (1987)
USSR film. Space travelers discover that centuries ago, aliens infected humans with a deadly virus that induces hostility. The travelers go back to medieval times and destroy the virus.

Love in the Time of Twilight (1995; aka *Hua Yue Jia Qi*)
Hong Kong film. A woman's ghost joins forces with a living man to travel back in time, solve her murder and resolve other problems in the past.

Love Story 2050 (2008)
Indian movie. After the tragic death of the woman he loves, a young man travels to 2050 Mumbai to find and win her in another incarnation.

Magic Müller (1993)
German film. An actor who never has time for his little daughter decides he can use his roommate's time machine to arrange his life better. Things get worse instead.

Hungarian Vagabond (2004; aka *Magyar Vandor*)
Hungary. Comedy film in which seven Magyar chieftains wander through Hungarian history, seeing their nation under the boots of different conquerors. At the end, they arrive in the 21st century, when Hungary is free.

The Man from the Future (2011; aka *O Homem do Futuro*)
Brazilian film. A scientist who has never gotten over the night his girlfriend publicly dumped him goes back 20 years and warns his younger self what's

about to happen. When he returns to the present, he finds that in the new timeline he's powerful and corrupt. Horrified, he tries to restore the original reality.

The Milky Way (1969; aka *La Voie Lactée*)
French film. As two modern-day pilgrims travel to the shrine of St. James in Spain, they seem to slip back in time to encounter heretics from different Christian eras.

The Miracle in Valby (1989; aka *Miraklet i Valby*)
Denmark. Film wherein kids go through a time gate into a grimy, violent Middle Ages. After one of them is kidnapped, the others are forced to return to the present, but they make their way back to the past for a rescue mission.

Mirror for a Hero (1988; aka *Zerkalo Dlya Geroya*)
USSR movie. Two Russians go back to 1949 where they relive the same day over and over. The experience helps one of the men come to understand his father's generation.

Mirror, Mirror (1995–98)
Australian TV series. An enchanted mirror allows a present-day girl and a girl from 1919 to visit each other's times. Their adventures include efforts to change history to prevent a toxic waste incident. In the second season, a modern boy uses the mirror to befriend a boy from 1867.

Mr. Rossi Looks for Happiness (1976; aka *Il Signor Rossi Cerca la Felicità*)
Italian animated film. A bullied worker uses a magic whistle to travel through time to find happiness. Eventually he gives up and returns home, but then his boss uses the whistle and disappears. Happiness achieved!

My Mother the Mermaid (2004; aka *Ineo Gongju*)
South Korean movie. A young woman finds she's gone back in time to the fishing village where her mother grew up. She makes friends with her mother and finally comes to understand her.

Myth (2010; aka *Shen Hua*)
China. A TV series about two modern-day men transported back to the Qin dynasty, where they become entangled in the politics of the era.

Nem Sansao Nem Dalila (1955)
Brazilian film. In a sendup of the film *Samson and Delilah*, two men crash a Jeep into a scientist's time machine. The machine hurls the trio back to Old Testament times, where one of them acquires Samson's wig and becomes super-strong.

Nothing Left to Do but Cry (1984; aka *Non ci Resta Che Piangere*)
Italian film. Two men spend the night lost in the country and wake the next morning in the 15th century. They meet Leonardo da Vinci and try to stop Christopher Columbus from leaving on his trip.

Palace (2012; aka *Gong 2*)
Chinese TV series. In a metafictional sequel to *Palace—Lock Heart*, the protagonist of that TV series, returned to the present, adapts her adventures into a successful TV series.

Palace—Lock Heart (2011; aka *Gong, Gong Suo Xin Yu*)
Chinese TV series. A modern girl transported back to the Qing Dynasty era becomes involved in a struggle for the throne as her heart is caught between two princes.

Paul's Awakening (1985; aka *Il Risveglio di Paul*)
Italian movie. A time machine whisks characters into the future to participate in a great competition.

Peut-Être (1999)
French film. A man who doesn't want to have kids is pulled into the future through a time gate in his bathroom. He meets his aged son and grandchildren, who beg him to change his mind.

Pirates en el Callao (2005)
Peruvian film. A boy falls through a hole in time and winds up in the 17th century fighting pirates.

Playing Beatie Bow (1986)
Australian film. A modern-day Sydney teenager meets a girl time traveling from the past, and gets pulled back to 1870s Sydney. The teen discovers she's part of a prophecy the girl's psychic family must fulfill to pass on their gifts to future generations.

The Queen and I (2012; aka *Queen In-Hyun's Man, Inhyeonwanghooui Namja*)
South Korea. TV series about a Chosin court official helping a former queen survive political intrigue. A magic charm shifts him from the 1600s to 2012, where he becomes involved with an actor playing the queen in a historical drama series.

Quest Beyond Time (1985)
Australian film. A hang-glider travels 500 years into the future where he helps a post-apocalypse community survive a mysterious sickness.

Rooftop Prince (2012; aka *Oktab Bang Wangseja*)
South Korean TV series. After the death of his bride, a Korean prince is transported to the 21st century with his honor guard. He replaces his present-day reincarnation, becomes embroiled in that man's family dramas, and falls in love.

Ruby Red (2013; aka *Rubinrot*)
German film. A teenage girl discovers she's inherited her family's time travel gene when she jumps back to the 19th century.

Russian Ark (2002)
Russia. A film showing a modern-day Russian and a Frenchman wandering through the Hermitage, occasionally falling into different art scenes.

Sapphire Blue (2014; aka *Saphirblau*)
German film. The time traveling protagonist of *Ruby Red* must balance her love life with her new duties as a time traveler.

Scarlet Heart (2011; aka *Bu Bu Jing Xin, Startling By Each Step*)
Chinese TV series. After a car crash, a modern-day Chinese woman finds herself back in the past as the daughter of a Manchu general. She struggles to return to her own time and to survive amidst the era's dangerous political intrigues.

Second Time Around (2002; aka *Mou Han Fou Wut*)
Chinese movie. A gambler acquires magic stones that give him the power to go back through time. When his best friend is killed in a car accident, the gambler and a female cop go back three days and try to alter events.

Shree (2013)
Indian film. A man desperate for money agrees to take part in a secret experiment. He doesn't remember what happens, but when he leaves the lab he learns he's wanted for murder. The secret behind the frame involves time travel.

Signal (2016; aka *Sigeunol*)
South Korea. TV drama about a police profiler in 2016 who comes into walkie-talkie contact with a detective in 2000. The detective is investigating an unsolved murder that took the life of the profiler's high-school classmate.

Simon of the Desert (1965; aka *Simon del Desierto*)
Mexico. Short film by Luis Buñuel in which Satan, after repeatedly failing to seduce an ascetic from his pillar-sitting, transports him to a modern-day nightclub.

A Spasso nel Tempo (1996)
Italian film. Two men discover that a theme park's time machine actually works. They have comical adventures in multiple time periods.

A Spasso nel Tempo—L'Avventura Continua (1997)
Italian film. Sequel to *A Spasso nel Tempo* in which the protagonists continue their time travels. In a *Highlander* parody, a Scots immortal concludes that anyone who can show up in so many eras must be immortal, and tries to kill them.

Spellbinder (1995-97)
Australian TV series. A boy enters a parallel world where the Industrial Revolution never happened and the tyrannical Spellbinders use technology to control the population.

Sport Billy (1979-80)
Germany. Animated television series about the humanoid ET Sport Billy, who promotes sportsmanship, and evil Queen Vanda, who wants to destroy it. Billy's spaceship is a time machine so he can battle Vanda in any era as well as any place.

Stork Day (2004; aka *È Gia Ieri, Already Yesterday*)
Italian film. The protagonist gets trapped in a time loop while filming a documentary about storks.

Supermenler (1979)
Turkish film. A superhero team assists a German scientist when criminals try to capture him and exploit his time travel research.

3rd After the Sun (1973)
Bulgaria. This film chronicles the effect of alien visitors on various characters. In the future, one alien discovers that humans can travel in time. A young woman goes back to the 13th century, falls in love with a prince and gets accused of witchcraft.

Thunderstone (1999-2000)
Australia. TV series about a boy who travels from his underground home in a post-apocalypse future to a future in which Earth is green again. He starts bringing animals from the 20th century to repopulate the future. At the end of the second season he prevents the catastrophe that ruined Earth. The third season explores the new timeline that results.

Tiger Stripe Baby Is Waiting for Tarzan (1998; aka *Tigerstreifenbaby Wartet auf Tarzan*)
German film. A man from a future when women are extinct travels back to the present to meet the author of the eponymous novel. They begin an affair, but another woman makes it a *menage a trois*.

De Tijdscapsule (1963-64)
Belgium. In this TV series, a time traveler from our future explores history. On one of his trips he saves a young woman accused of witchcraft, and she becomes his companion.

Time and Again (2007; aka *Cheating Fate*)
Australian film. After the death of her husband and child, a woman discovers a music box that rewrites the past when she plays it. The changes are not under her control, and usually for the worse.

The Time Guardian (1987)
Australian movie. A city flees the war-ravaged world of 4039 by traveling back in time, pursued by bloodthirsty cyborgs. When the city's advance man arrives in the present to prepare a landing site, the cyborgs attack.

Time Masters (1982; aka *Les Maîtres du Temps*)
France. Animated film about a space pilot's attempt to rescue a young boy on a distant planet. As the spaceship approaches the world, the cosmic Time Masters warp the planet back 60 years in the past. It turns out one of the spaceship passengers is that same young boy, 60 years older.

Time Trackers (2008)
Australian TV series. Three teens—a spaceship captain, a cave girl and a present-day boy—join forces to

fight a time virus that could erase the wheel, the printing press and other inventions from history.

Timetrip: Curse of the Viking Witch (2009; aka *Vølvens Forbandelse*)
Danish film. A teenager volunteers to help a scientist test his new time machine. The boy doesn't know the scientist is an immortal hoping to go back in time and end the curse that left him unable to die.

Tomorrow's End (1993)
Australia. Sequel television series to *The Girl from Tomorrow* has Alana and a 20th-century friend try to stop a villain from causing a catastrophe that destroys Alana's future.

The Trip (1996; aka *Der Trip*)
German film. When an aspiring singer kisses an engaged woman, they're magically transported to 1972, but arrive separately. The singer sets out to find the woman and win her love.

The 25th Reich (2012)
Australian film. The Allies send a military platoon back in time to obtain a crashed spaceship that can turn the tide of the war. One of the men is a Nazi agent who steals the ship for the Axis and changes history. Given the premise, it's amazingly dull.

2046 (2004)
Hong Kong film. A womanizing author's reminiscences of the 1960s are mixed with scenes from his book about a man traveling by train to 2046, an era when lost memories can be recovered.

Valerian & Laureline (2007–08; aka *Time Jam*)
French TV series, animated. Valerian, a time traveler from 2417, rescues Laureline from peril in the year 912. This somehow erases Earth's subsequent existence. Back in 2417, the two last Terrans hunt for their world while supporting themselves by taking jobs anywhere in known space.

We Are from the Future (2008; aka *My Iz Budushchego, Black Hunters*)
Russian film. Four young men are hurled back from present-day St. Petersburg to the Nazi siege of 1942 during the Great Patriotic War.

We Are from the Future 2 (2010; aka *My Iz Budushchego 2, Amongst Heroes, Paradox Soldiers*)
Russian film. Four more Russians get time-shifted from the present to World War II.

A Witch Without a Broom (1967)
Spanish film. A college professor discovers a beautiful woman in his class is a witch. She proceeds to transport him back and forth across time, including 15th century Toledo and the post–World War IIII future.

Zärtliche Chaoten II (1988)
German movie. Patent office workers in 2043 use a time machine that's up for a patent to prevent the birth of their rotten boss. They fail, and discover their office has become even less fun to work in, so they return to the past to stay.

Zentrix (2003–04)
Hong Kong. In this TV series, robots seize control of a future Earth. Princess Megan travels back seven years to avert the catastrophe.

Appendix VI

Interesting Short Films

Barbie and the Rockers: Out of This World (1987)
USA. An unsuccessful animated pilot in which Barbie and her rock band are hurled back to the 1950s during a space-shuttle ride. This justifies a crash course in 1950s slang ("Zowie!"), fashions, music and culture (visits to a malt shop!) before a scientist figures out how to send the band home.

The Chronology Protection Case (2002)
USA. A forensic scientist investigates several mysterious deaths tied to a time travel project. It turns out the universe is preserving the time stream by destroying anyone who researches time travel.

Dexter's Laboratory: Ego Trip (1999)
USA. Animated spinoff of the TV cartoon. Child genius Dexter travels ahead in time and winds up meeting himself at multiple ages. He discovers that the survival of Earth depends on defeating his longtime rival Mandarrk.

Elmo Saves Christmas (1996)
USA. Elmo gets his wish that it could be Christmas every day. After a few months, everyone's sick of turkey dinners and *It's a Wonderful Life* so Elmo goes back in time and wishes for a teddy bear instead.

Eyes of a Cowboy (1998)
In this Canadian short film, a down-and-out country singer rides a horse back into the Old West.

Hoops and Yoyo Ruin Christmas (2011)
USA. On Christmas Eve, Hoops and Yoyo—characters created for Hallmark cards—hitch a ride on Santa's time-traveling sleigh. They fall off in the past, accidentally disrupt the events that turn Kris Kringle into Santa, then struggle to fix their mistake.

JLA Adventures: Trapped in Time (2014)
USA. Lex Luthor sends a team of villains back through time to send the infant Superman back into space before the Kents find his rocket.

Kung Fury (2015)
Swedish action-film parody in which a 1980s cop with superhuman kung fu abilities discovers Hitler, the "Kung Fuhrer," has traveled from the 1930s to kill him. "Kung Fury" travels back to the 1930s to return the favor.

My Mother Was Never a Kid (1981)
USA. An *ABC Afterschool Special* in which a teenager gets flung back in time to meet her mother as a teen and discover how different she used to be.

Path in Time (2005)
USA. A Christian short film in which a teen questioning his faith is recruited to stop a future tyrant from erasing Christianity from history to secure his rule.

Time Slip (1953)
United Kingdom. BBC drama in which a medically dead man is revived with his mind 4.7 seconds in the future. By the end of the 30 minute show, he's cured. Based on the same book as *The Atomic Man*.

Yu-Gi-Oh! Bonds Beyond Time (2010)
Japan. Anime special celebrating the tenth anniversary of the *Yu-Gi-Oh!* TV series. A time traveler who blames the series' "duel monsters" for destroying his world seeks to change history to erase the game.

Appendix VII

Movies About Parallel Lives

Some films, while not claiming to deal with parallel timelines, do show the divergent lives that result from the protagonist's making different choices.

All About Christmas Eve (2012)
USA. A woman's life changes depending on whether she catches a plane.

And Then Came Lola (2009)
USA. A tribute to *Run Lola Run* has a lesbian photographer struggling to carry out a favor for her girlfriend, an effort that plays out three different ways.

Blind Chance (1987)
A Polish film following a medical student after he has an encounter with a beer-drinking man. Their interaction determines whether the student becomes a Communist Party member, a revolutionary or apolitical, though none of the options work out well for him.

Clue (1985)
USA. The original film inspired by the murder-mystery board game has three different endings. The DVD edition has all three included in one movie.

Dangerous Corner (1934)
USA. The truth about a death comes out at a dinner party some months later, leading to a second death. The same events play out differently when one of the guests proposes marriage to his girlfriend.

Run Lola Run (1998; aka *Lola Rennt*)
Germany. Lola (Famke Potenta) struggles to reach her boyfriend, who will be killed if he doesn't pay off a debt. Events play out three different ways.

Sliding Doors (1998)
USA. Gwyneth Paltrow's life diverges along two parallel tracks depending on whether she catches a train.

Appendix VIII
Time Travel Porn Films

Electric Blue 37 (1986)
   USA. A time machine sends a nerd back to the 1950s.

Exotic Time Machine (1998)
   USA. After two scientists develop a time machine, one of them gets lost in the past. His partner follows and erotic adventures in different eras result.

Exotic Time Machine II: Forbidden Encounters (2000)
   USA. The two scientists travel through time planting beacons that will block any attempt to steal the technology.

50,000 B.C. (Before Clothing) (1963)
   USA. A "nudie"—a pre-porn skin-flick with lots of topless beauties. The nominal plot involves a man stumbling into a time machine, then out into pre-history.

New Barbarians (1990)
   USA. A thief steals a gem that can arouse people sexually, then flees into another era, pursued by a hot female warrior.

Quantum Deep (1993)
   USA. In this takeoff on *Quantum Leap*, a scientist bounces around in time and puts things right that once went wrong—but there are big-breasted women and sex involved.

Sex Slider Shag-A-Rama (1999)
   USA. Protagonists bounce between parallel worlds until they land in one where sex is forbidden. They join up with the resistance; the beautiful but sex-hating tyrant eventually gets turned on.

Time Adventure Zeccho 5-Byo Mae (1986)
   Japan. A girl travels forward in time 15 years and has sexual misadventures.

Timegate: Tales of the Saddle Tramps (1991)
   USA. Two sexually frustrated housewives are drawn through a magic mirror into the Old West where they become hookers at a local whorehouse.

Tits a Wonderful Life (1994)
   USA. A well-endowed guardian angel shows a man what it would be like if he were never born.

Vortex (1998)
   USA. Scientists open a time vortex which enables a villain to get laid in different time streams.

Chapter Notes

See Bibliography for publication details

Preface

1. *Time Travelers in Old Time Radio*, Old Time Radio Catalog.
2. Bud Foote, *The Connecticut Yankee in the Twentieth Century* (1991), 10–12, 37–39.
3. *Ibid.*
4. *Ibid.*
5. Alicia Lutes, "*Hindsight* to Explore Space-Time Continuum in Season Two" (2015).

Chapter One

1. Jeffrey Richards, *Swordsmen of the Screen* (1977), 4–5.

Chapter Three

1. David Lowenthal, *The Past Is a Foreign Country* (1985), 22.
2. Fred Patten, "Tezuka's Adult Features: 'Cleopatra' (1970)."
3. Roger Fulton and John Betancourt, *The Sci-Fi Channel Encyclopedia of TV Science Fiction* (1998), 180.
4. Tim Brooks and Earle Marsh, *The Complete Directory* (2003), 587.
5. Andrew Pragasam, *Age of the Great Dinosaurs*.
6. Turner Classic Movies, *Ali Baba Goes to Town*, www.tcm.com/tcmdb/title/66991/Ali-Baba-Goes-to-Town/.
7. David Lewis, "Cult Box: Rewind: 1978's BBC Drama 'A Traveller in Time' Revisited."
8. Alex J. Geairns, "Georgian House on DVD."
9. Fulton and Betancourt, 667.
10. H. Bruce Franklin, "Don't Look Where We're Going" (1983): 70–80.

Chapter Four

1. Turner Classic Movies, *Where Do We Go from Here*: www.tcm.com/tcmdb/title/95529/Where-Do-We-Go-from-Here.

Chapter Five

1. Maggie Lee, *Film Review: "Therma Romae II"* (2014).

2. Andy Taylor, *Mentors*, Andy's Anachronism: www.timetravelreviews.com/tv_reviews/mentors.html.

Chapter Six

1. Gavriel D. Rosenfeld, *The World Hitler Never Made* (2005), 62–64.
2. Jonathan Clements and Helen McCarthy, *The Anime Encyclopedia* (2001), 402–3.
3. *Ibid.*, 84–5.
4. *Ibid.*, 357–8.
5. America Pink, *Mud (TV Series)* america.pink/mud-series_3103472.html.
6. Bryan Hartzheim *Bubble Fiction*.

Chapter Seven

1. David Brennan, *When Ellison Attacks*.

Chapter Eight

1. Brooks and Marsh, *The Complete Directory* (2003), 315.
2. Katharine Farrimond "Mom! You Look So Thin!"
3. Richard Scheib, *Race Through Time*.
4. Clements and McCarthy, *The Anime Encyclopedia* (2001), 113–4.
5. Gunner, SPC Net, *Ditto*.

Chapter Nine

1. Turner Classic Movies, *I'll Never Forget You*, http://www.tcm.com/tcmdb/title/78984/I-ll-Never-Forget-You/.
2. *A Necklace for Julia*, directed by David Dietrich, 2006, Tamarack Road Productions.

Chapter Ten

1. IMDB: *Time Keepers*.
2. Ranger Wiki, *Mirai Sentai Timeranger* (http://kamenrider.wikia.com/wiki/Kamen_Rider_Den-O).
3. Kamen Rider Wiki, *Kamen Rider Den-O* (http://kamenrider.wikia.com/wiki/Kamen_Rider_Den-O).
4. Brooks and Marsh, *The Complete Directory* (2003), 1204.

Bibliography

Brennan, David. *James Cameron Online:* "When Ellison Attacks." www.jamescamerononline.com/Ellison.htm

Brooks, Tim, and Earle Marsh. *The Complete Directory to Prime Time Network and Cable TV Shows 1946–Present* (Eighth Edition). New York: Ballantine Books, 2003.

Clements, Jonathan, and Helen McCarthy. *The Anime Encyclopedia: A Guide to Japanese Animation since 1917*. Berkeley: Stone Bridge Press, 2001.

Dolgopolov, Greg. "Andrei Maliukov: We Are from the Future (My iz budushchego, 2008)." *KinoKultura*, September 30, 2008.

Erickson, Hal. *Sid and Marty Krofft: A Critical Study of Saturday Morning Children's Television, 1969–1993*. Jefferson: McFarland, 1998.

Farrimond, Katharine. "'Mom! You Look So Thin!': Constructions of Femininity Across the Space-Time Continuum in Worlds of Back to the Future," in Ní Fhlainn, Sorcha (ed.) *The Worlds of Back to the Future: Critical Essays on the Films* (Jefferson, NC: McFarland) 165, 169.

Foote, Bud. *The Connecticut Yankee in the Twentieth Century: Travel to the Past in Science Fiction*. Westport, CT: Greenwood Press, 1991.

Franklin, H. Bruce. "Don't Look Where We're Going: Visions of the Future in Science-Fiction Films, 1970–82." *Science Fiction Studies* 10, no. 1 (1983): 70–80.

Fulton, Roger. *The Encyclopedia of TV Science Fiction*. Bungay: Boxtree Limited, 1990.

_____, and Betancourt, John. *The Sci-Fi Channel Encyclopedia of TV Science Fiction*. New York: Warner Books, 1998.

Geairns, Alex J. "Cult TV: Georgian House on DVD." cult.tv/index.php/component/content/article/34-articles-v15–10000000005/tvdvd-v15–34/589-the-georgian-house-dvd-v15–589.

Glenn, Edward. "The Time Machine Project," *TV Zone*, Issue 17, April 1991.

Gunner. *Ditto*. SPC Net: Asian Movies and TV Series Reviews. www.spcnet.tv/Movies/Ditto-review-r672.html.

Hartzheim, Bryan. "Bubble Fiction: Boom or Bust." *Midnight Eye*: www.midnighteye.com/reviews/bubble-fiction-boom-or-bust/

Hirsch, David. *TV Episode Guides Vol. 2: Science Fiction, Adventure and Superheroes*. New York: Starlog Press, 1982.

Lee, Maggie. "Film Review: *Therma Romae II*." *Variety*, June 9, 2014.

Lewis, David. "Cult Box: Rewind: 1978's BBC Drama 'A Traveller in Time' Revisited." www.cultbox.co.uk/features/rewind/rewind-1978s-bbc-drama-a-traveller-in-time-revisited_

Lowenthal, David. *The Past Is a Foreign Country*. Cambridge: Cambridge University Press, 1985.

Lutes, Alicia. "*Hindsight* to Explore Space-Time Continuum in Season Two," *Hollywood Reporter*, March 25, 2015.

Maltin, Leonard. *Leonard Maltin's Movie Guide 2014 Edition: The Modern Era*. New York: Signet, 2013.

Ní Fhlainn, Sorcha, ed. *The Worlds of Back to the Future: Critical Essays on the Films*. Jefferson, NC: McFarland, 2010.

Obskura. "Stalin's ghost in *perestroika* cinema: Mirror for the Hero." Nov. 29, 2014.

Patten, Fred. "Tezuka's Adult Features: 'Cleopatra' (1970), Cartoon Research: cartoonresearch.com/index.php/tezukas-adult-features-cleopatra-1970/.

Pragasam, Andrew. "*Age of the Great Dinosaurs*." The Spinning Image: www.thespinningimage.co.uk/cultfilms/displaycultfilm.asp?reviewid=3913.

Richards, Jeffrey. *Swordsmen of the Screen from Douglas Fairbanks to Michael York*. London: Routledge and Kegan Paul Ltd., 1977.

Rogers, Dave. *The ITV Encyclopedia of Adventure*. London: Boxtree Limited, 1988.

Rosenfeld, Gavriel D. *The World Hitler Never Made: Alternate History and the Memory of Nazism*. Cambridge: Cambridge University Press, 2005.

Scheib, Richard. "*Race Through Time*." Moria: Science Fiction, Horror and Fantasy Film Reviews moria.co.nz/sciencefiction/racethroughtime.htm.

Schow, David J., and Jeffrey Frentzen. *The Outer Limits: The Official Companion*. New York: Ace Science Fiction, 1986.

Sherman, Fraser. *Cyborgs, Santa Claus and Satan: Science Fiction, Fantasy and Horror Films Made for Television*. Jefferson, NC: McFarland, 2000.

Westfahl, Gary, George Edgar Slusser, and David Leiby. *Worlds Enough and Time: Explorations of Time in Science Fiction and Fantasy*. Westport: Greenwood Press, 2002.

Index

Numbers in ***bold italics*** refer to pages with photographs.

A&E 212
A La Recherche du Futur Perdu 227
AARU Productions 206
Abbott, Bruce 67, 215
ABC 210, 211, 214, 219, 221, 225, 226, 227, 228, 229, 230
ABC Family Channel 204, 205, 209, 214, 219, 222
Abe, Hiroshi 71, 95, 204, 219
Abercrombie, Ian 203, 211, 223
Abounader, Jean 223
About Time 174, 202
Abrahams, Doug 177, 203, 204
Abrahams, Mort 203
Abrahamse, Taylor 44, 226
Abrams, Austin 149, 220
Abrams, J.J. 218
Abromeit, Susie 57
Acevedo, Kirk 230
Ackland, Joss 11, 100, 204, 211
Action Replay 202
Action Replayy 132, 202
Adams, Christine 229
Adams, Don 49
Adams, Lynne 36, 220
Addie, Robert 10
Addy, Mark 28, 220, 225
Adkins, Seth E. 66, 215
Adler, Gilbert 224
Adlon, Pamela 27, 203
Adreon, Franklin 205, 206
Adult Swim 227
ADV Films 223
Adventure Duo 231
Adventure Kid 231
Adventurers: Masters of Time 235
Adventurers Mission Zeitreise 235
Adventures in Time 235
The Adventures of Brisco County Jr. 64–65, 225
The Adventures of Roborex 217
The Adventures of Timothy Pilgrim 77, 225
After Dark Films 204
Against Time 3, 156, 202
Age of the Great Dinosaurs 202
Agent Provocateur Films 204
Agresti, Alejandro 212
Ahn, Kil-Kang 223
AI Film 216
AIP 223
AIP Entertainment 208
"Air Raid" 73 213

Airisto, Rudi 120, 218
Airlie, Andrew 177, 204
Akiyama, Rina 227
Aladdin and the Adventure of All Time 23, 202
Alba, Jessica 152, 218
Albert, Edward Laurence 189
Albertson, Frank 8
Alcatraz 67, 225
Alcove Entertainment 204
Alden, Jennifer 132
Aldiss, Brian W. 208
Aletter, Frank 25, 227
Alexander, Elizabeth 186, 230
Alexander, Karl 220
The Alexei Sayle Show 54
Ali Baba Goes to Town 28, 202
Alien Agenda: Endangered Species 114–15, 202
Alien Agenda: Out of the Darkness 114–15, 202
Alien Agenda: Under the Skin 115, 202
Alien Conspiracy: Beyond the Lost World 115, 202
Aliens in the Wild, Wild West 221
Alix, Stephen 205
All About Christmas Eve 241
All Over Again 202
All You Need Is Kill 207
"All You Zombies" 136, 216
Allain, Carolyn 207
Allen, Christa B. 156
Allen, Irwin 35
Allen, Jennie 127, 220
Allen, Joan 215
Allen, Laura 226
Allen, Nancy 76, 215
Allen, Tim 147, 217
Allen, Woody 24, 213
Allen, Zibby 175, 211
Alli, Antero 207
Allied Artists 224
Allison, Bart 210
Allison, Dorothy 35, 202
Allred, Corbin 52, 211
Allstar Productions 214
Almost Normal 128, 202
Alpine Pictures 212
Already Yesterday 239
Alsberg, Arthur 210
Always Will 150–51, 202
Amapola 150–51, 235

Amato, Mark 222
The Amazing Mr. Blunden 35, 202
Amazon streaming 227
The Ambition of Oda Nobuna 32–33, 79 225
Ambrose, David 208
Amedori, John Patrick 227
Amendolia, Don 193, 222
American General 211
American International Pictures *see* AIP
Ames, Denise 26, 206
Amityville: It's About Time 231
Amongst Heroes 240
Amuse 216
Anchor Bay Entertainment 220
Ancient Relic 235
And Then Came Lola 241
Anders, Merry 221
Anders, Sean 209
Anderson, Antony 207, 213
Anderson, Brad 209
Anderson, Fred 141
Anderson, Frederick 66, 213
Anderson, Gillian 152, 210
Anderson, Michael 213, 217
Anderson, Richard Dean 218
Anderson, Stanley 144
Anderson, Stephen 213
Andolong, Sandy 213
Andre, E.J. 141, 206
Andrews, David 103
Andrews, MacLeod 63, 208
Angarano, Michael 29, 208
Angel, Heather *21*, 164, 203
An Angel for May (film) 40, 202
An Angel for May (novel) 202
Anholt, Christien 36, 66, 203, 217
Anime International 219
Aniplex 209, 221
Ann-Margret 147
Annett, Chloë 185, 225
Another Day 137, 202
Ansara, Michael 25, 101, 211
Anselmo, Tony 213
Ant, Adam 67, 215
Anthony, Bret 180, 209
Anthony, Jane 67, 227
Anton, Craig 228
Anubis Productions 212
Aoki, Munetaka 221
Apanowicz, Magda 107
Apex 108, 202

245

API 205
Apleby, Noel 214
ApolloProMedia 217
Appleby, Shiri 135, 211
Applegate, Christina 69, 211
Arakawa, Naruhisa 212
Araki, Kae 117, 229
Arc Entertainment 215
Arch Oboler Productions 223
Arenafilm 214
Argai: The Prophecy 235
Argai: La Prophétie 235
Argentina 235
Argos Films 212
Arias, Yancey 220
Arkin, Alan 147
Arkwright, Nigel 229
Armstrong, Bess 205, 229
Army of Apes 231
Army of Darkness 11–12, 203
Arnold, Edward 27, 211, 217
Arnold, Frank 211
Arnold, Tom 127, 204
Arquette, David 154, 210
Arterton, Gemma 148, 216
Arthur (English King) 7–12, 24–25, 68, 70, 231
Arthur, Rod 228
Arthur, the King 231
Arthur's Quest 70, 203
Artisan Entertainment 223
As Time Goes By 235
Ashbrook, Dana 171, 223
Ashbrook, Daphne 206
Ashby, Linden 144, 212
Ashes to Ashes 41 225
Ashfield, Kate 179, 230
Ashmore, Shawn 224
Astin, John 225
Astin, Sean 159, 217
The Asylum 207, 208, 214, 217
Atkins, Christopher 26, 214
Atkins, Nathan 217
Atlantis 28, 225
Atlas Entertainment 223
The Atomic Man 231
Attanasio, Paul 218
ATV 225, 229, 230
AT-X 218, 227
AT-X Plus 229
Auberjonois, Rene 11
Aubrey, Juliet 114, 185, 219, 228
Auburn, David 212
Austin, Jake T. 132, 224
Austin Powers in Goldmember 231
Austin Powers: The Spy Who Shagged Me 40, 203
Australia 210, 227, 235, 236, 238, 239, 240
Avant, Matt 95, 213
Avant, Matthew J. 213
Avant, Nathan 213
Avant, Sarah 213
Avellano, Helena 35, 228
Aventuras en el Tiempo 235
Averch, Robert J. 206
Avery, Margaret 116, 212
Avex Asia 217
Awake 231

Ayase, Haruka 217
Aycox, Nicki 220
Aylmer, Felix 33, 220
Ayres, Jo Ann 68, 220
Azcuy, Annette 100
Azuma, Mikihisa 229
Azzopardi, Mario 221

Baba, Yasuo 204
Baburu e go!! Taimu Mashin Wa Doramu Shiki 204
Back to Christmas 178, 203
Back to Sherwood 23, 225
Back to the Fuehrer 213
Back to the Future 2, 4, 5, 125, 130–31, 203
Back to the Future (TV cartoon) 51, 225
Back to the Future II 130, 131, 203
Back to the Future III 131–2, 203
Back to the Jurassic 27, 203
Badgely, Penn 129, 226
Badger, Phillip 216, 217
Baeza, Paloma 11, 211
Baglini, Andrew 150, 202
Bahkle, Emma 77, 225
Bailey, Amy 219
Baker, Graham 202
Baker, Kenny 220
Baker, Ray 109, 209, 222
Baker, Roy 209
Baker, Sharon 218
Baker, Tom 226
Bakhle, Emma 225
Bakhnov, V. 210
Bakula, Scott 120, 146, 190, 226, 228
Balderston, John L. 203
Baldwin, Adam 197, 226
Baldwin, Daniel 111
Baldwin, Stephen 27
Baldwin, William 27, 211
Bales, Paul 214
Balfe, Caitriona 172, 228
Ball, Angeline 40
Bana, Eric 174, 218, 221
Band, Charles 222
Bandai Visual Company 213
Banks, Jonathan 197, 208
Banks, Lynne Reid 77, 210
Banks, Spencer 34, 43, 226, 230
Barash, Olivia 220
Barbarash, Ernie 220
Barbeau, Adrienne 81, 204, 205, 214
Barber, Amanda 202
Barbie and the Rockers: Out of This World 240
Barbier, George 222
Baresh, Olivia 22
Barker, Clive 205
Barmettler, Joseph J. 220
Barnes, C.D. 148, 205
Barnes, Chris 22, 220
Barnes, Priscilla 14, 220
Barr, Jackson 222
Barr, Kathleen 24, 227
Barr, Robert 230
Barrett, Brendon Ryan 207
Barrett, Caitlin Lara 207
Barrie, Chris 55, 228

Barron, John 43
Barron, Keith 227
Barry, Jon Colton 215
Barry, Kai 211
Barry, Tricia 187, 221
Barrymore, Ethel 165
Barrymore, Lionel 153, 210
Bartlett, Victoria 159, 217
Baruchel, Jay 138, 207
Barzo 202
Barzyk, Fred 203, 212
Basaraba, Gary 137, 215
Basche, David Alan 79, 210
Basehart, Richard 35, 137, 216, 221
Bassett, Angela 213
Bates, Kathy 24, 213
Battle Girls: Time Paradox 32, 79, 225
Battle Royale High School 231
Bauer, Belinda 37, 221
Baur, Marc 221
Baxley, Craig R. 222
Bayldon, Geoffrey 81, 225
Bayne, Lawrence 59, 229
BBC 13. 87, 88, 185, 208, 225, 226, 227, 228, 230, 241
Beacon Pictures 207
Beal, Simon 50, 227
Bean, Orson 9, 205
Beard, Matthew 40, 202
Beasties 231
Beastmaster 2 6
Beatty, Ned 117, 221
Beck, John 14, 220, 221
Becker, Belinda 78, 218
Beckinsale, Kate 205
Beckman, Thea 205
Beechen, Adam 203
Beers, Dan 216
Before You Say "I Do" 2, 4, 177, 203
Begley, Ed, Jr. 141, 206
Being Erica 127, 225
Beiser, Brendan 219
Belford, Christina 82, 228
Belgium 239
Bell, Catherine 75, 221, 222
Bell, Kristen 129
Bell, Marshall 155, 224
Bell, Tom 179, 216
Beller, Kathleen 117, 221
Bellis, Scott 221
Beloin, Edmund 205
Belushi, James 159, 216
Ben 10 66
Ben 10: Race Against Time 66, 203
Bender, Landry 52, 225
Bendix, William 8, 205
Beneath the Bermuda Triangle 105, 203
Beneath the Planet of the Apes 45, 122, 203
Benedetti, Caprice 221
Benedict, Dirk 214
Bennett, Eliza 36, 208
Bennett, Eliza Hope *see* Bennett, Eliza
Bennett, Harve 218
Bennett, Wallace 215, 220
Benoit, Morgan 208

Benrubi, Abraham 180, 219
Benskin, Tyrone 225
Benton, Anya 57
Benward, Luke 160, 213
Bercovici, Leonardo 216
Berendsen, Dan 205, 224
Berger, Melissa 38
Berger, Todd 204
Bergere, Lee 117, 221
Berkeley, Busby 217
Berkeley Square (1933) 2, 20, *21*, 25, 164–65, 203
Berkeley Square (play) 203, 209
Berman, Rick 218
Bermuda Triangle, 56–57, 197–98, 231, 235
Bernard, Carlo 216
Bernds, Edward 220, 224
Berneis, Peter 216
Bernhardt, Daniel 68, 208
Bernsen, Corbin 134, 222
Bernstein, Jon 213
Berry, Halle 224
Berry, Veronica 220
Bessai, Carl 216
Best Friends Whenever 52, 225
Beswick, Martine 26, 216, 222
Betuel, Jonathan R. 214
Between Time and Timbuktu 47, 55–56, 203
Bewitched 231
Beyond the Bermuda Triangle 231
Beyond the Time Barrier 17, 203
Bhat, Rishi 78, 210
Bid Time Return 218
Biehn, Michael 102, 219
Big Beach 217
Big Idea 215
Big Rich Films 216
Big Screen Entertainment 217
Biggles 38–39, 203
Biggles: Adventures in Time see *Biggles*
Bill & Ted's Bogus Journey 100, 203–4
Bill & Ted's Excellent Adventure 99–100, 204
Bill & Ted's Excellent Adventures (cartoon series) 100, 225
Bill & Ted's Excellent Adventures (live-action series) 100, 225
Billingsley, John 226
Billingsley, Patrick 165
Bilson, Danny 207, 222
Binstock, Jodi 217
Bishojo Senshi Sailor Moon 229
Bishop, Joel 178, 214
Bissell, Whit 230
Black, Claudia 97, 218
Black, Karen 206
Black, Mary 139
Black, Trevor 218
Black-D'Elia, Sofia 153, 216, 222
Black Hole High see *Strange Days at Blake Holsey High*
Black Hunters 240
Black Knight 30, 204
Blackburn, Richard 229
Blakely, Rachel 229

Blakeslee, Susanne 148, 205
Blalock, Jolene 226
Blanc, Mel 9, 80, 210, 230
Blanchard, Rowan 152, 218
Blandick, Clara 222
Bleecker, Tom 210
Bleeth, Yasmine 144, 212
Blick, Hugo E 10
Blind Chance 241
Blondell, Gloria 223
Bloodgood, Moon 191, 197, 226, 227
Bloom, Claire 233
Bloom, Steve 224
Blue Flame 231
Blue Moon 133–34, 204
Blue Seraph Productions 211
Blue Wave Productions 204
Blue Yonder 139–40, 204
Blum, Steve 112, 230
Blum, Steven Jay 68, 228
Blunt, Emily 119, **199**, 200, 207, 212
Blyth, Ann 165, 209
Bobo, Jonah 157, 224
Body, Leslie 202
Boen, Earl 219
Bohanan, Kelley 43, 209
Bohlander, Sherri 129, 219
Boll, Uwe 210
Bond, Timothy 207
Bonet, Lisa 172, **173**, 212
Boni, Gabrielle 36, 220
Bonnar, Mark 228
Bonsai Films 210
Booth, Kristin, 209
Booth, Lindy 210
Borbridge, Brad 203
Border2Border Entertainment 211
Borealis Enterprises 211
Borsos, Philip 215
Boston, Lucy M. 36, 208
Bottoms, Timothy 207, 227
Boulle, Pierre 203, 207, 215
Bourla, David 214, 224
Bowen, Lesley 129, 219
Bowker, John 202
The Box of Delights 50, 225
The Boy and the Pirates 20–1, 204
Boy in the Drain 210
Boylan, John 62
Boyum, Stephen 221
Bradbury, Ray 93, 209, 218, 233
Bradley, David 107, 222
Bradley, Leslie 33
Bradshaw, Booker 116, 227
Brady, Scott 54, 211
Braeden, Eric 122
Braga, Brannon 218
Brancato, John 219
Brand, Russell 95, 228
Braugher, Andre 208
Braun, Nicholas 160, 213
Braune, Suanne 229
Bray, Ian 221
Brazil 237, 238
Bremer, Brian 106, 223
Brendon, Nicholas 205
Brennan, William 207
Brennert, Alan 212
Breslin, Spencer 134, 206

Bress, Eric 204
Brezsny, Rob 207
Brick Bradford 2, 231
Bridge Across Time 65, 204
Bridges, Beau 218
Bridges, Jeff 119
Brigadoon (1954) 168, 204
Brigadoon (1966) 168, 230
Brigadoon (play) 204
Briggs, Andy 215
Brightlight Pictures 210
Brimble, Nick 23, 208
Brimstone Media 202, 209, 220
Bring on the Jubilee 92
Britt, Danielle 220
Britton, James 84 , 224
Brix, Holly 204
Brødrene Dal og Mysteriet med Karl XIIs Gamasjer 235
Brødrene Dal og Spektralsteinene 235
Brodský, Vlastimil 85, 222
Brody, Adrien 156, 210
Brolin, Josh 149, 213
Bron Studios 215
Brookes, Christina 214
Brookover, Linda 220
Brooks, Ray 206
Brother Future 35, 204
Brothers Dal and the Mystery of Karl XII's Gaiters 235
Brougher, Hilary 218
Browder, Ben 97, 217, 218
Brown, Brianna 30, 214
Brown, Clancy 211
Brown, Eric 223
Brown, Eric Martin 208
Brown, Gordie 230
Brown, Kipleigh 62
Brown, Pat Crawford 25
Brown, Ralph 41
Brown, Ray 222
Brown, Sara Suzanne 223
Brown, Todd 223
Browne, Coral 189, 229
Brownell, Janet 222
Brownlow, Kevin 210
Broyles, William, Jr. 215
Bruch, Matthew 118, 220
Bruckner, Amy 228
Bu Bu Jing Xin 239
Bubble Fiction: Boom or Bust 95, 204
Bucksey, Colin 214
Bugs Bunny in King Arthur's Court 9–10, 230
Bulgakov, Mikhail A. 210
Bulgaria 239
Bulliard, James 150, 229
Bulloch, Jeremy 229
Bullock, Jim 80, 228
Bullock, Sandra 62, 171, 212, 216
Bullock, Walter 216
The Bullwinkle Show 47, 228
Burfield, Cheryl 43, 230
Burgel, Patrick 69
Burgess, Melvin 202
Burgess, Michael 35, 204
Burgi, Richard 114, 219

Burke, David 230
Burke, Samson 21, 220
Burns, Edward 93, 218
Burns, Jennifer 52, 211
Burns, Jere 222
Burr, Jeff 211
Burrell, Ty 48, 213
Burstyn, Ellen 114, 210
Burton, LeVar 111, 218
Burton, Tim 215
Busfield, Timothy 36, 220
Busia, Akosua 35, 204
Butler, David 202, 205
Butler, Daws 49, 80, 228
Butler, Gerard 30, 221
Butler, Joshua 205
Butler, Robert 215
The Butterfly Effect 151, 204
The Butterfly Effect 2 151–52, 204
The Butterfly Effect 3: Revelations 153, 204
Butterworth, Jez 207
Butterworth, John-Henry 207
Buzzi, Ruth 54 227
Byrkit, James Ward 205
Byrne, Adrienne 34, 226
Byrnes, Jim 24, 138, 207, 227

C 231
Caan, James 172, **173**, 212
Cabot, Ellen 213, 223
Cabrera, Santiago 112
Cage, Nicolas 126, 176, 207, 215
Cage of Doom 219
Cahill, Erin 189, 228
Cain, Dean 19
Caine, Michael 114, 210
Caliber Media 207
The Caller 149, 204
Callis, James 161
Calzado, Iza 171, 213
Cameron, James 101 219
Cameron-Glickenhaus, Jesse 118, 221
Cameron-Glickenhaus, Veronica 118, 221
Camilleri, Terry 204
Camp Daze 204
Camp Slaughter 196, 204
Campanella, Roy, II 204
Campbell, Bruce 11, 65, 203, 221, 223, 225
Campbell, Doug 222
Campbell, Ken 22, 226
Campisi, Gabriel 202
Canals-Barrera, Maria 132, 224
Canarom Films 213, 221
Canning, Sara 228
Cantor, Eddie 27, 28, 202, 217
Capaldi, Peter 226
Caplan, Lizzy 128
Capo, Jennifer 222
Capra, Frank 153, 210
Captain Confederacy 92
Captain Z-Ro 47, 225
Carducci, Stephen 204
Carey, Clare 223
Carey, Philip 221
Carey-Hill, Dwayne 208

Carlin, George 99, 204, 225
Carlson, Julie 163, 205
Carlson, Kim 220
Carmack, Chris 152, 204
Carney, Art 139, 204
Carnivale 235
Carpani, Rachael 222
Carr, Benjamin 211, 221
Carradine, David 140, 208
Carradine, Keith 209
Carreras, Michael, 216
Carrivick, Garth 208
Carroll, Ryan 212
Carroll, Willard 222
Carruth, Shane 151, 216
Carry, Julius 225
Carstarphen, John 215
Carter, Adam 68
Carter, Dixie 177, 205
Carter, Helena Bonham 45, 215
Carter, T.K. 111
Carter Films 224
Cartoon Network 203, 227, 230
Casci, Sergio 204
Casey Silver Productions 208
Caso, Mark 219
Cassidy, David 72, 218
Castel Films 213, 221
Castellaneta, Dan 51, 225
Castle, Aimée 23, 225
Castle, Roy 206
Cataquiz, Monsour 139, 205
Catweazle 81, 225
Caudell, Toran 25, 211
Cavadini, Cathy 202
Cavanagh, Tom 150
Cavegirl 167, 204
Caviezel, Jim 162, 191, 206, 208
CBBC 228
CBC 225
CBS 213, 221, 223, 225, 226, 227, 228, 229, 230
Central Independent Television 229
Century Falls 231–32
Cerra, Erica 161, 226
Cerveris, Michael 122
Cesta do Praveku 237
CFC Features 205
Cha-Oji Xuexiao Bawan 236
Chabert, Lacey 212
Chambers, Justin 97, 211
Chan, Jackie 29, 208
Chandler, Kyle 190, 226
Change of Life 141, 204
Chanticleer Films 222
Chaotic Sequence 208
Chapman, Mark Lindsay 42, 218
Chapple, Geoff 214
Charisse, Cyd 168, 204
Charles, Craig 55, 228
Charles, Max 48, 213, 228
Charlie Jade 82–83, 225
Charmed 107, 225
Chase, Chevy 209
Chase, Daveigh 133, 217
Chasing Christmas 127–28, 204
Chastain, Jessica 210

Chatelain, Héléne 101, 212
Chazel, Marie-Anne 69, 223
Cheadle, Don 176, 207
Cheap and Dirty Productions 207
Cheating Fate 239
Cheon Gun 237
Cherry, John 215
Chetwynd, Lionel 210
Chiba, Shigeru 28, 230
Chiba, Sonny 31, 209
Chiba TV 226, 228
Chihara, Minori 115, 155, 206, 228
Children's Film Foundation 209
Chimneys of Green Knowe 208
China 235, 238, 239
Chinese Odyssey 235
Cho Kamen Rider and Decade 189
Choi, Yoon S. 203
Chong, Rae Dawn 114, 221
Chou, Collin 29
Chou, Jay 168, 217
Christensen, Shawn 207
Christian, Claudia 68, 124, 212, 229
Christian, Robin 206
Christian films 34, 70, 80–81, 154–55, 158, 241
Christiano, Rich 220
Christie, Julie 233
Christmas, Eric 215
A Christmas Carol 2
The Christmas Clause 177, 204
Christmas Do-Over 192, 195–96, 205
A Christmas Eve Miracle 178, 205
Christmas Every Day (movie) 194–95, 205
"Christmas Every Day" (short story) 193, 213
Christmas films 127–28, 147–48, 160, 176, 177, 178–9, 193, 194–96, 241
"The Chronic Argonauts" 2
The Chronology Protection Case 240
Ciccolella, Jude 62
Ciccoritti, Jerry 209
Cilenti, Enzo 93, 219
Cinderella III: A Twist in Time 148, 205
Cine Excel Entertainment 208
Cinegroupe 222
CJ Entertainment 203, 223
Clark, John 212
Clarke, Cam 34, 215
Clarke, Emilia 104, 219
Clarke, Jason 104, 219
Clarke, Mae 175, 222
Clarke, Robert 17, 128, 203
Clarke, T.E.B. 209
Clary, Charles 205
Clavier, Christian 69, 211, 223
Cleese, John 56
Clemens, Brian 222
Clemenson, Christian 225
Clement, Jemaine 149, 213
Cleopatra 21–2, 205
Cleopatra, Queen of Sex see *Cleopatra*
Cleverdon, Dean 58
Click 157–58, 205
Cliff, John 21

Clifford, Nick 129, 227
Clive Barker Presents Saint Sinner 70–71, 205
Clockmaker 221
CLT 223
Clue 241
Coast Entertainment 215
Cobbs, Bill 169
Coca, Imogene 25, 227
Codd, Matt 214, 219
Cohen, Charlie 213
Cohen, David X. 208
Cohen, Etan 213
Cohen, Howard R. 221
Coherence 145, 205
Cohiba Pictures 216
Cohn, Didi 55
Cokeliss, Harley 202, 217
Colbert, Robert 54, 75, 206, 230
Cole, Christina 18, 214
Coleman, Jack 105, 112, 203, 227
Coleman, Kathy 60, **61**, 227
Colleary, Michael 212
Collet, Christopher 218
Collins, Boon 207
Collins, Joan 85, 160, 179, 216, 217
Collins, John 202
Colman, Booth 17, 45, 228
Columbia Pictures 205, 209, 210, 224
Combs, Holly Marie 107, 225
Combs, Jeffrey 222
Come Back Lucy 77, 225
Comeau, Phil 213
Comfort and Joy 176–77, 205
Commercial Pictures 218
Compact Yellowbill 203
Compendium Entertainment Group 205
Conaway, Cristi 187, 230
Conceiving Ada 232
Concorde Pictures 202, 221
Conn, Didi 226
Conn, Shelley 26, 229
A Connecticut Yankee 8, 205
A Connecticut Yankee in King Arthur's Court (1910) 2, 8
A Connecticut Yankee in King Arthur's Court (1921) 8, 205
A Connecticut Yankee in King Arthur's Court (1931) see *A Connecticut Yankee*
A Connecticut Yankee in King Arthur's Court (1949) 8–9, **9**, 166, 205
A Connecticut Yankee in King Arthur's Court (1970) 9, 205
A Connecticut Yankee in King Arthur's Court (1989) 10–11, 205
A Connecticut Yankee in King Arthur's Court (novel) 2, 7, 165, 205, 211, 223, 224
Connery, Sean 56, 220
Connolly, Billy 30, 221
Connolly, Derek 217
Conquest of the Planet of the Apes 123
Conried, Hans 64, 220, 223
Conroy, Kevin 211

Conselman, William 205
Constantine, Yorgo 215
Continuum 3, 107–8, 225
Contis, Paolo 171, 213
Conway, Kevin 30, 116, 212
Conway, Tim 217
Cook, Mason 152, 218
Cooke, Juliet 227
Coolidge, Martha 223
Cooney, Jacob 208
Cooper, Chris 91, 226
Cooper, Jeanne 222
Cooper, Jenny 59
Cooper, Sara B. 212
Cooper, Susan 234
Copon, Michael 228
Coppola, Francis 215
Coppola, Roman 218
Coraci, Frank 205
Corddry, Rob 128, 209
Corden, Henry 45, 80, 210, 229
Corey, Wendell 205
Corman, Catherine 23
Corman, Roger 208, 223
Cornthwaite, Robert 221
Cornwell, Stephen 215
Coscarelli, Don 211
Cosnett, Rick 150
Costello, Ward 72, **73**, 219
Cotillard, Marion 24, 213
Cotten, Joseph 165, 216
Les Couloirs du Temps: Les Visiteurs II 223
Coulthard, Philippa 227
Courtney, Jai 104, 219
Cox, Courtney 233
Cox, Jennifer Elise 178, 203
Cox, Julie 40, 202
Cox, Mitchell 203
Coyne, Johnny 225
Coyote, Peter 37, 139, 204, 218, 221
Cozzolino, Nathan 174, 211
Craig, Daniel 11, 211, 212
Craig, Timothy 219
Crane, Kara 160, 213
Cranston, Brian 105, 203
Craps, Chris 205
Craven, Matt 180
Crawford, Carrie 216
Crew, Amanda 198, 216
Crew, Carl 223
Crewson, Wendy 217
Cribbins, Bernard 206
Crichton, Michael 218, 221
Crime Traveller 185, 225
Cristea, Eugen 30, 93
Cristow, Trevor Reed 205
Croft, Alyson 222
Crome, Karla 160
Cromwell, James 120, 218
Cronkite, Walter 77, 224
Los Cronocrímenes 221
Crosby, Bing 8, **9**, 205
Crosby, Denise 94, 207
Cross, Ben 225
Cross, Joseph 213
Cross, Robert 213
Crouse, Lindsay 210
Crow, Emilia 75, 206

Crown International Pictures 204
Cruel and Unusual 139, 205
Cruickshank, Jim 214
Cruise, Tom **199**, 200, 207
Crump, Casper 108, 226
Crusade: A March Through Time 92, 205
Crusade in Jeans see *Crusade: A March Through Time*
Cruz, Penélope 126, 223
Cruz, Rubiano 212
Cryptic 163, 205
Crystal Pictures 218
Crystal Sky Communications 203, 205
CSA: Confederate States of America 3, 92, 206
CTC 228
C2 Pictures 219
Cube²: Hypercube 232
Culliton, Patrick 208
Culp, Robert 102
Cummings, Jim 202
Cunningham, Lowell 213
Curiosity, Co. 208
Curry, Tim 66, 160, 215, 217
Curti, Gianluca 216
Curtis, Dan 59, 206, 213
Curtis, John 221
Curtis, Keene 154, 216
Curtis, Richard 202
Curtis-Brown, Robert 194
Cusack, Joan 154, 210
Cusack, John 128, 209
Cushing, Peter 39,**53**, 203, 206
Cuthbert, Elisha 36, 220
CW 226, 227
Cyborg 2087 106, 206
Cyran, Catherine 205
Czechoslovakia 85, 222, 237

D'Abo, Olivia 72, 178, 205, 218
Daehan-Minguk 236
Dahl, Evan Lee 207
Dai Shogun 232
Dale, Jim 10, 223
Daleks' Invasion Earth 2150 AD 54, 206
Dalesandro, Anthony 207
Dall, Evelyn 33, 220
Dalton, Darren 207
Daly, James 169
Daly, Sam 211
Damon, Matt 210
Damski, Mel 205
Danes, Claire 103, 219
Dangerous Corner 241
Daniels, Gary 216
Daniels, Jeff 75, 206, 212
Dano, Paul 212
Dano, Royal 58, 209
Dantes, Dingdong 171, 213
Darby, Bob 220
Dark Shadows (1966–71) 59–60, 225
Dark Shadows (1991) 60, 225
Darnley-Smith, Jan 209
Darren, James 54, 230
Darvill, Arthur 108, 226
Davalos, Alexa 88, 227

Davi, Robert 207
David, Charlie 135, 211
David, Jacqueline 205
David, Keith 96
David, Thayer 60, 225
Davidson, Joey 77, 225
Davidson, Troy 225
Davidtz, Embeth 12, 203
Davies, Lane 19
Davies, Robin 81, 225
Davis, Gerry 208
Davis, Jeff Bryan 37, 227
Davis, Kristin 23, 137, 220, 224
Davis, Scot 23, 217
Davis, William B. 83, 107, 217 225
Davis-Gray, Michele 213
Davison, Bruce 116, 212, 222
Dawson, Kim 34, 213
Day, Denny 141, 204
Day, Frances 27, 207
Day, Larry 23, 225
Day, Shannon 227
Day Break 192, 197, 226
The Day Time Ended 232
A Day with Wilbur Robinson 213
DC's Legends of Tomorrow 1, 108, 226
De Tijdcapsule 239
Dead of Night 141, 206
Dear, William 221
DeCamp, Rosemary 220
Decker, Diana 208
Decoursey, Gayl 209
Decter, Ed 217
Deep Blue Fleet 2, 89, 226
De Felitta, Frank 223
Dehn, Paul 203, 207
Deitch, Donna 206
Déja Vu (film) 191, 206
Deja Vu (TV series) 236
Deja Vu Darling 236
Dekker, Thomas 104, 229
De Klerk, Richard 198, 216
Delany, Dana 211
D'Elia, Bill 222
DeLuise, David 68, 132, 224, 228
DeMarco, Robin 174, 213
De Meo, Paul 207, 222
"Demon with a Glass Hand"
Demyanenko, Aleksandr 22, 210
Dengel, Suzanne 42
Denham, Christopher 140, 207
Denis, Michael 83, 217
Denk, Bernie 222
Denmark 238, 240
Deranian, David 217
De Rita, Joe 21, 220
Dern, Bruce 196
Derochie, Greg 221
Derricks, Cleavant 98, 229
Dervisevic, Merlin 205
Des Barres, Michael 223
Destination Earth 221
Deutschman, Andrew 216
Devane, William 116, 134, 213, 218, 222
Devasquez, Devin 58, 209
The Devil's Arithmetic (film) 40, **41**, 206

The Devil's Arithmetic (novel) 206
Devil's Pass 232
Devin, Ryan 81, 228
Devlin, Dean 222
Dexter, Jerry 28, 229
Dexter's Laboratory: Ego Trip 240
Diamond, David 207, 213
Diamond, Reed 137, 220, 227
Diaz, Cameron 154, 217
DIC 220
Di Cicco, Bobby 76, 215
Dick, Bryan 82, 226
Dick, Philip K. 88
Dickens, Charles 2
Dickson, Neil 39, 203
Diehl, John 83, 217
Dieterle, William 216
Dietrich, David 214
Diggs, Taye 197, 226
Dillahunt, Garret 229
Dillman, Bradford 123, 207
Dillon, Brendan, Jr. 67, 212
DiMaggio, John 65, 147, 208
Dimension 232
Dimension Films 218
Dimension 5 49, 206
Dimensions 139, 206
Dimitriades, Alex 175, 210
Dimsey, Ross 217
Dinklage, Peter 113, 224
Dino De Laurentis Communications 203
Dino Time 203
Di Santis, Silvia 110, 216
Dinosaur Valley Girls 26, 206
DiPego, Gerald 219
DiPego, Justin 219
The Disappearance of Haruhi Suzumiya (anime) 155, 206
The Disappearance of Haruhi Suzumiya (manga) 206
The Disappearance of Nagato Yuki-Chan 155
Disasters in Time 75, 206
Disconnect 163, 206
Discovery Kids 51, 226, 230
Disney 205, 206, 211, 213, 214, 216, 217, 223
Disney Channel 52, 78, 80, 204, 210, 211, 213, 215, 224, 225. 228
Disney's The Kid 134, 206
Ditto 155–56, 206
Dixon, Malcolm 220
Dixon, McIntyre 56
DNA^2 106, 226
Do Over 19, 226
Dobil Productions 221
Dr. Jin 236
Dr. Plonk 236
Doctor Who (1996 TV film) 54, 206
Doctor Who (TV series) 1, 52–54, 226
Doctor Who and the Daleks **53**, 54, 206
Doctor Who—The Movie 206
Dr. Zemo's Zeitmachine 213
Doherty, Shannon 107, 137, 202
Dohrn, Walt 154
Doig, Lexa 225

Dolan, Jason 207
Dolley, Jason 160, 213
Domis, Ryan 81
Don't Fool with Love 236
Donat, Peter 186, 230
Donato, Marc 44, 226
Donavan, Robert 222
Donggam see *Ditto*
Donnelly, Jack 28, 225
Donnelly, Thomas Dean 218
Donner, Richard 221
Donnie Darko 133, 206
D'Onofrio, Vincent 169, 209
Donohoe, Amanda 211
Donovan, Elisa 176, 207
Donovan, Paul 214
Donovan, Tate 180, 219
Doohan, James 218
Doomsday 69, 206
Doonby 154–55, 207
Dorad Corporation 211
Doraemon 77, 226
Doran, Ann 206
Dorman, Michael 197, 222
Dorn, Mary 13, 230
Dorn, Michael 118, 218, 221
Dors, Diana 35, 202
Dotrice, Roy 94, 207
"Doubled and Redoubled" 193
Doublin, Anthony 208
Douglas, Kirk 85, 208
Douglas, Michael 72, 207
Dowe, Don 223
Downey, Roma 233
Downs, Chris 82, 226
Downs, Frederic 72, **73**, 219
Doyle, Shawn 162, 208
Drago, Billy 65, 225
Drake, Larry 38, 91, 207, 221
Dream of a Warrior 236
The Dream Years 164
Dreamland 232
Dreamworks 213, 217, 220
Dreesen, Lance W. 203
Drew, Griffin 206
The Drivetime 72, 207
Drugan, Jennifer 227
Drunk in Time 54
Dual! Parallel Trouble Adventures 98, 226
Duckworth, Dortha 203
Duerler, John 30, 214
Duff, Kerry 211
Dufour, Val 29, 223
Dugan, Dennis 10, 223
Duggan, Andrew 220
Duke, Clark 128, 209
Dukes, David 222
Duling, Dan 212
Dullea, Keir 81, 214
Dumbrille, Douglas 28
Duncan, David 220
Duncan, Michael Clarke 74, 215
Duncan, Pamela 29, 223
Dunham, Joanna 35
Dunn, Nora 52
Dunne, Robin 93, 219
Dunst, Kirsten 40, **41**, 206
Duplass, Mark 128, 217

Durance, Erica 151, 204
Durango Kids 38, 207
Durham, Alesandra 178, 214
Durham, James 214
Durham, Thomas Gomez 214
Durning, Charles 85, 208
Dushku, Elisha 190, 230
Dwek, Nevil 223
Dyke, Robert 221

E4 228
Eagle-Lion Films 216
Ealing Studios 207, 208
Early Edition 190, 226
Earthfasts 82, 226
Eastman, Kevin 219
Eastwood, Scott 141, 207
Eberthardt, Thom 223
Eccleston, Christopher 226
Eckholdt, Steven 177, 205
Ecsima 223
La Edad de Piedra 237
Eddison, Robert 94, 229
Edens, Mark Edward 220
Edens, Michael 220
Edgar Rice Burroughs' The Land That Time Forgot 57, 207
The Edge of the Garden 167, 207
Edge of Tomorrow 192, ***199***, 200, 207
Edgewood Entertainment 220
Edmiston, Walker 60
Edmonds, Mike 220
Eerie Indiana: The Other Dimension 232
Egan, Doris 205
Eggert, Nicole 180, 209
Eggs from 70 Million BC 211
Egolf, Gretchen 191, 227
Eguchi, Takuya 32, 225
Eguchi, Yōsuke 90, 217
Egypt 2102
Eight Men Out 23
Eisenmann, Ike 57, 226
Eisley, Anthony 54, 211
Eita 219
S.S. *Eldridge* see Philadelphia Experiment
Electric Blue 37 242
Elejalde, Karra 159, 221
11 A.M. 236
11 Minutes Ago 170, 207
11-22-63 (novel) 91
11-22-63 (series) 91, 226
Elikann, Larry 222
Eliminators 94, 207
Elkin, Clifford 34, 229
Elliott, Bob 203
Elliott, Chris 194, 209
Elliott, Denholm 179, 216
Elliott, Emun 191, 228
Elliott, Laurie 51, 230
Ellison, Harlan 101–2, 219
Elmo Saves Christmas 240
Elsinore Pictures 222
Elwood, Sheri 204
Emblem Take Two 147, 226
Emerson, Michael 59
Emmerich, Toby 208, 212

Emms, Robert 28, 225
Empire Motion Pictures 206
Empire Pictures 207, 222
Encarnacao, Frank 224
End of Century 214
Energia 218
English, Diane 212
An Englishman's Castle 87–88, 226
Enter Nowhere 140–41, 207
Enterprise 120–21, 146, 226
Erasmus Microman 22, 226
ERBP 216
Erschbamer, George 204, 221
Escape 13
Escape from the Planet of the Apes 45, 99, 122–23, ***123***, 181, 207
Escape Through Time 55, 207
Escape to Grizzly Mountain 38, 207
Escapology 217
Eschbach, Victor 110
Eskridge, Ann E. 204
Esposito, Giancarlo 109, 222
Ester, Natalia 207
Estes, Rob 118, 134, 167, 207, 213, 214
Estevez, Emilio 44, 208
Estevez, Joe 155, 207
Etel, Alex 36, 208
Eternity 236
Ethridge, Jon Kent 212
Etō, Jun 208
Eure, Wesley 60, ***61***, 227
Eureka 160–61, 226
Evangelista, Allen 316
Evans, Maurice 203
Evans, Rupert 227
Evans, Scott F. 141, 220
Event Film 210
Everett, Chad 74, 214
Eve's Christmas 176, 207
Evigan, Briana 133, 213, 217
Evigan, Greg 214
Evil Dead 11
Evil Dead II 11
The Excalibur Kid 25, 207
Excalibur Pictures 221
Exotc Time Machine 242
Exotic Time Machine II: Forbidden Encounters 242
Experimental Artistic Association 210
Extrell, Kirk 138, 215
Eyes of a Cowboy 240

Fahey, Jeff 105, 203
Fairchild, Morgan 106, 223
Faison, Donald 217
Faison, Douglas 178
Faith 236
Falconer, Ian 11
Falk, Peter 168, 230
Fall, Jim 211
Fallon, John 220
Family Channel (Canada) 228
Family Man 176, 177, 207
The Famous Jett Jackson 80, 211
Fantastic Journey 56–57, 226
Fantasy Island (1977–84) 49–50, 226
Fantasy Island (1998) 50, 226

Far-Out Space Nuts 232
Farentino, James 86, 208
Farino, Ernie 211
Farmiga, Vera 198, 217
Farnum, William 8, 205
Farris, Anna 185, 208
Fassbender, Michael 224
Fast, Alexia 198, 216
Fatherland (movie) 88, 207
Fatherland (novel) 88, 207
Faulkner, James 211
Faunt, Jason 189, 228
Faust, Chad 226
Favreau, Jon 224
Feature Films for Families 218
Feely, Terence 216
Feeney, F.X. 208
Feigelson, J.D. 212
Feinstein, Alan 168, 223
Fell, Richard 230
Fellowes, Julian 208
Fenn, Sherilyn 143, 214
Fenton, Simon 10
Ferguson, Colin 161, 226
Ferguson, Stan 218
Fernandez, Candela 221
Ferrell, Will 60, 212
Ferris, Michael 219
Fetching Cody 138, 207
Fiddlers Three 27, 207–8
Field, Virginia 137, 202
Fifer, Scott A. 223
50,000 B.C. (Before Clothing) 242
Filipowich, Michael 83, 225
Filmdistrict 217
FilmEngine 204
Filmline International 224
Filmmakers 219
FilmNation Entertainment 216
Filmové Studio Barrandov 222
Filmwerks 214
Final Battle for the Universe 211
The Final Countdown 85–86, ***86***, 208
Findlay, Katie 200, 216
Fine, Larry 21, 220
Finland 218
Finney, Jack 165, 170, 206, 213
Fire Tripper 31, 208
First Look Pictures 216
Fischnaller, Tory 135
Fisher, Chris 217
Fisher, Joely 118, 214
Five & Two Pictures 220
5ive Days to Midnight 156, 226
The Flash 5, 97, 150, 226
Flash Forward 202
Flashback 232
Flashpoint 211
Fleischer, Charles 224
Fleming, Jon 196
Fleming, Rhonda 8, ***9***, 205
Flemyng, Gordon 206
Flemyng, Jason 185
Fletcher, Louise 40
Flight of the Navigator 232
The Flight That Disappeared 4, 108, ***109***, 208
Flight World War II 87, 208

Flint the Time Detective 188, 226
Flueger, Patrick, 226
Fly High Films 207
Flynn, Emmett J. 205
Flynn, Johnny 92, 205
The Fog 236
Fonda, Bridget 22, 208
Fonda, Peter 209
Fontana, Randall 213
The Fonz and the Happy Days Gang 55, 226
Foote, Bud 4
For All Time 5, 169, 208
The Forbidden Kingdom 5, 29, 166, 167, 208
Ford, Carole Ann 53
Ford, Ron 202, 220
Forde, Brinsley 34, 226
Forde, Walter 220
Foreman, Deborah 50, 223
The 4400 112, 226
Foster, Preston 221
Found in Time 63, 208
Fournier, Susanna 153, 210
1408 232
Fowler, Gene 202
Fox 203, 205
Fox, Emilia 219
Fox, Emily 4
Fox, Huckleberry 139, 204
Fox, Matthew 59, 227
Fox, Michael J. 130, 131, 203
Fox, Paul 203
Fox-Brenton, David 66
Fox Family 213
Fox Kids 228
Fox-TV 67, 206, 222, 224, 225, 226, 228, 229, 230
Foxfur 232
Foxler, Emily 145, 205
Foy, Mackenzie 210
Frakes, Jonathan 218
Framework Productions 218
France 69, 212, 224, 235, 236, 237, 238, 240
Franchise Pictures 218
Franciscus, James 45, 203
Franco, James 91, 226
Franken, Steve 17
Frankenstein Unbound (film) 22–3, 208
Frankenstein Unbound (novel) 22, 208
Franklin, Carl 57, 226
Franklin, Diane 100, 204, 217
Franklin, Don 229
Franklin, H. Bruce 43
Franks, Jazmine 227
Franz, Eduard 106
Fraser, David 219
Frederick, Lynne 35, 202
Free Birds 96, 208
Freejack 44, 208
Freeman, Martin 160, 217
Freeman, Paul 206
Frees, Paul 49
Freestyle Digital Media 212
Freeth, Ian Paul 214
French, Michael 185, 225

Frenchman's Farm 236
Frequency 155, 162, 208
Frequently Asked Questions About Time Travel 185–86, 208
Frid, Jonathan 59, 225
Friedle, Will 147, 211
Friel, Anna 30, 61, 212, 221
Frigon, Miranda 228
Fringe 121–22, 226
From Time to Time 36–37, 208
Frontline Entertainment 206
Frost, Darren 51, 230
Frost, Helen 202
Fry, Jordan 148, 213
Fryman, James 213
Fuji TV 71, 227, 229, 230
Fujimoto, Yuzuru 89, 226
Fujisawa, Yuuki 219
Fujita, Toshiko 50, 227
Fujita, Yoichi 209
Fukui, Harutoshi 217
Full Moon Entertainment 211, 222
Fuller, Drew 107
Fuller, Kurt 230
Fun2shh 236
Furey, Mark 216
Furla, George 207
Furlong, Edward 103, 219
Furuya, Tohru 117, 229
Fury, Ed 206
Fusco, John 208
Futurama 65
Futurama: Bender's Big Score 65, 208
Future Cops 236
Future Diary 138, 226
Future Force 140
Future Hunters 236
The Future Is Wild 44, 226
Future Past 236
Future War 68, 208
Future Zone 140, 208
Fyfe, Mak 25, 207

Gabaldon, Diana 172
Gadon, Sarah 51, 91, 226, 230
Gadsby, Jon 95, 217
Gage, Christos, N. 215
Gage, Ruth Fletcher 215
Gagnon, Pierce 119
Gaidai, L. 210
Gainsborough 220
Galager, Clu 204
Galaxy Quest 232
Gale, Bob 203
Gale, Ed 227
Galifianakis, Zach 190, 230
Gallagher, David 154, 216
Gallagher, John 204
Galligan, Zach 50, 203, 223
Gallo, Patrick 210
Galvane, Candace 212
Ganatra, Nisha 215
Gans, Sharon 217
Garber, Victor 152, 210, 226
Garcia, Jorge 67, 225
Garcia, Ricky 225
Gardner, Virginia 216
Garfinkle, Gayle 222

Garland, Richard 29, 223
Garner, Jennifer 156, 219
Garnett, Tay 205
Garrett, Leif 72, 218
Garth, Jennie 177, 209
Gates, Nancy 16, 224
Gateway Films 217
Gaubert, Jean-Marie 211
Gaulke, Peter 204
Gaumont 211, 223
Gauthier, Mark 67, 212
Gavin, Robert 227
Gazzara, Ben 133, 204
Geary, Cynthia 110, 224
Gebert, Bob 207
Gekijouban Gintama Kanketsu-hen: Yorozuvavo Eien Nare 209
Geller, Stephen 217
Gelt, Gary 210
George, Betsy Lynn 34, 213
George, Brian 147
George, Melissa 197, 222
George, Michael 207
The Georgian House 34, 226
Georgs-Picot, Olga 62, 209
Gerald, Danor 214
Germany 235, 236, 237, 238, 239, 240, 241
Gerow, Laura 34, 215
Gerrold, David 60
The Ghosts 202
G.I. Samurai 31, 208–9
E Gia Leri 239
Giamatti, Paul 83, 211, 215
Giancola, David 220
Gibson, Thomas 143, 214
Gilbert, Marcus 11, 203
Gillard, Stuart 219
Gilliam, Terry 56, 220, 223
Gillis, Jackson 221
Gilroy, Dan 208
Gintama 111
Gintama: The Final Chapter: Be Forever Yoruza 111, 209
The Girl from Tomorrow 236
The Girl, the Gold Watch and Everything 6
The Girl Who Leapt Through Time (novella) 161, 209, 212, 221
The Girl Who Leapt Through Time (2006 anime) 161–62, 209
Givens, R. Michael 205
Gladden Entertainment 213
Glass, Robert 217
Glau, Summer 104, 229
Gleeson, Brendan 207
Gleeson, Domhnall 174, 202
Glen, Ian 140, 212
Glenister, Philip 41, 225, 227
Glickenhaus, James 221
Glorious Times at the Spessart Inn 236
Glover, Crispin 130, 203
Glovin, Debbie 220
Gluck, Ferris Ellen 202
Glut, Donald F. 206
GMA Films 213
Gocheva, Petra 210
Godfrey, Patrick 206

God's Gift—14 Days 236
Godzilla vs. King Ghidorah 117, 209
Goenaga, Barbara 221
Goethals, Angela 226
Gogin, Michael Lee 214
Goin, Ken 222
Going, Joanna 225
Gojira Buiese Kingu Gidora 209
Gokal, Mina Vesper 63, 208
Goldberg, Sarah 129, 227
Goldberg, Whoopi 10, 210, 211
Golding, Meta 226
Goldman, Jane 224
Goldsman, Akiva 212
Goldsmith, Josh 219
Goldstein, Lisa 164
Golightly, Gage 156, 226
Gomez, Selena 132, 224
Gong 238
Gong 2 238
Gonzalez, Draven 204
Good Friends Productions 207
Good Machine 218
Gooden, Casey 216
Gooding, Cuba, Jr. 148, 220
Goodman, John 77, 224
Goodman, Terence 178, 214
Goodnight Sweetheart 172, 226
Goodrich, Frances 210
Gordon, Bert I. 204
Gordon, C. Henry 222
Gordon, Harwood 208
Gordon, Zachary 196, 215
Gordon-Levitt, Joseph 119, 212, 225
Gorham, Christopher 110, 228
Gosselaar, Mark-Paul 196, 222
Gossett, Louis, Jr. 39, 210
Gostya iz Budushchego 236
Gotou, Yuuko 197, 206, 228
Gottlieb, Michael 211
Gotzon, Jenn 155, 207
Gould, Jadin 163, 205
Goulding, Ray 203
Goulet, Robert 168, 230
Gozon-Abrogar, Annette 213
Gracen, Elizabeth 205
Graham, Gerrit 86, 215
Graham, Heather 40, 203, 212
Graham, Molly 205
Graham, Spencer 43
Grahame, Gloria 210
Granada Television 226
Grand Tour 206
grandfather paradox 3
Granger, Marc 35
Grant, Richard E. 68, 223
Grant, Vince 91, 221
Gravitas Ventures 207
Gray, Erin 74, 214
Gray, Linda 223
Gray, Richard 213
Gray, William 215
Grayston, Neil 161, 226
The Great Doctor 236
Great Revolution 232
"The Greatest Gift" 210
Greco, James 203
Green, Brian Austin 104, 229
Green, Bruce Seth 217

Green, Seth 203
Green Communications 202
Green Lantern 232
Greene, Eric 22, 220
Greene, James 86
Greene, Kim Morgan 37, 209
Greenwald, Maggie 205
Greenwood, Bruce 121, 218
Greer, Judy 157, 219
Greno, Nathan 213
Gretsch, Joel 112, 226
Grey Skies: The Alien Conspiracy 115, 209
Grey, Linda 168
Grieco, Richard 109, 224
Grier, Pam 204
Griest, Kimberly 74, 212
Griffith, Charles 223
Griffith, Melanie 27, 203
Griffith, Thomas Ian 187, 221
Griffiths, Rachel 176, 213
Grigsby, Howard 217
Grizzly Mountain 37–38, 209
Groh, David 74, 212
Groom, Sam 35, 221
Gross, Arye 58, 70, 203, 209
Gross, Michael 26, 214
Gross, Stephen 10, 205
Grossman, Seth 204
Groundhog Day 3, 192, 193–94, **194**, 209
Grove, Logan 196
Groves, John 203
Groves, Phil 204
Gruber, J. Mackye 204
Grunberg, Greg 227
Guest from the Future 236
Gugino, Carla 144, 214
Guill, Julianna 213
Guillory, Sienna 14, 220
Gulager, Clu 204
Gulager, Tom 221
Gullo, Bill 215
The Guns of the South 92
Gupta, Amit 216
Gurney, Robert J., Jr. 219
Gusatrata, Shobhana Desai 202
Guslistaya, Natalia 31
Gustafson, Geoff 228
Gustin, Grant 150, 226
Gutman, Dan 224
Guzelian, Eddie 205
Gwei, Lun-Mei 168, 217
Gwynne, Haydn 33, 230
Gwynne, Michael C. 118, 214
Gyeney, Nicholas 215
Gyllenhaal, Jake 133, 148, 198, 206, 216, 217
Gyllenhaal, Maggie 206

Haas, Lukas 172, **173**, 212
Haas, Philip 212
Habel, Sarah 152
Hackett, Albert 210
Hackman, Gene 234
Haggerty, Dan 37, 207, 209
Haggerty, Dylan 37, 209
Haiduk, Stacey 111
Haig, Georgina 122

Hale, Jennifer 112, 148, 205
Hale, Sonnie 27, 207–8
Hall, Don 213
Hall, Grayson 225
Hall, Kenneth 34, 230
Hall, Kenneth J. 223
Hall, Natalie 215
Hallahan, Charles 223
Hallick, Tom 35, 221
Hallmark Channel 203, 207, 210
The Halloween Tree (movie) **51**, 209
The Halloween Tree (story) 209
Halloweentown II: Kalabar's Revenge 232
Halsted, Edward 139, 206
Hamazaki, Hiroshi 218
Hamill, Mark 110, 114, 188, 221, 224, 230
Hamilton, Emily 36, 217
Hamilton, Linda 102, 219
Hamilton-Wright, Michael 216
Hammer, Tim 128, 202
Hammer Films 216
Hamnet, Bryce 10, 205
Hampshire, Emily 230
Hana, Hajime 21, 205
Hanada, Jukki 218
Hanazawa, Kana 142, 218, 229
Hand Made Films 220
Handley, Tommy 33, 220
Handmade Films 223
Handson, Daniel 148
Haney, Bill 205
Hanich, Davos 100, 212
Hanmura, Ryo 209, 217
Hanna, Mark 223
Hanna-Barbera 210
Hano, Aki 216
Hanratty, Sammi 37, 212
Hansen, Daniel 213
Hanstock, Bill 208
Hapka, Mark 98, 215
Happy Accidents 169–70, 209
Happy Days 55
Happy Madison Productions 205
Harada, Tomoyo 161, 212
Harawitz, Mathew 216
Hardwicke, Cedric 8, 205
Hardy, Jonathan 67
Harkcom, Laura 215
Harling, Noelle 116, 227
Harmon, Mark 169, 208, 211
Harmon, Richard 135, 211
Harnish, Dustin 26
Harnois, Elizabeth 215
Harold Goldman Associates 206
Harper, Ron 45, 228
Harrell, Rebecca 70
Harrelson, Woody 96, 208
Harrington, Laura 193, 222
Harrington, Peter J. 220
Harris, Barbara Eve 210
Harris, Blake 222
Harris, Chris 227
Harris, Christi 34, 213
Harris, Owen 208
Harris, Philippa 45, 229
Harris, Robert 88, 207

Harris, Steven 80, 228
Harrison, John Kent 224
Harrison, Linda 45, 203
Harrison, Lindsay 222
Harrison, Mark 94, 229
Harrison, Michelle 139, 205
Harry Potter and the Prisoner of Azkaban 232-33
Hart, Alysha 225
Hart, Christine 141, 206
Hart, James V. 212
Hart, Jeremy 209
Hart, Judith 208
Hart, Ralph 208
Hart, Sean 139, 206
Hartnell, William 53, 226
Hartnett, Josh 233
Haruka: Beyond the Stream of Time 32, 227
Harukanaru Toki no Naka de 227
Harvard Film Corporation 208
Hasselhoff, David 66, 204, 205
Hatcher, Teri 19
Hathaway, Anne 114, 210
Hatosy, Shawn 24, 224
Hauer, Rutger 36, 88, 207, 217
Hauser, Stephen 218
Haver, June 224
Hawes, Keeley 41, 225
Hawke, Ethan 136, 216
Hayami, Saori 42, 147, 214
Hayashi, Henry 31, 219
Hayashibara, Megumi 140, 219
Hayes, Allison 29, 223
Hayes, Steve 220
Hayman, James 222
Haynes, Bruce 47, 225
Hays, Robert 90, 194, 205, 217
Hayward, Jimmy 208
Hayward, Lillie 204
Hayward, Louis 136, 216
Hayward, Rachel 204
Haywood, Chris 214
Hazell, Carol 67, 227
Hazumi, Jun 106
HBO 206, 207, 208
He Ain't Heavy, He's My Father 236-37
Head, James 207
Headey, Lena 104, 126, 223, 229
Heald, Josh 209
Healey, Barry 215
Heap, Jonathan 215, 222
Hearst, Kevin 209
Heaven's Soldiers 237
Hecht, Ben 222
Heidenry, Margaret 205
Heinlein, Robert 136, 216
Helicon Arts Cooperative 224
Heller, Jack 207
Heller, Randee 133, 228
Helpmann, Robert 95, 217
Hemblen, David 77, 225
Hemdale Group 202
Hemsworth, Liam 222
Henchy, Chris 212
Henderson, Don 229
Henderson, Simon 50, 227
Henerson, James 213

Henerson, Matthew 66, 213
Henesy, David 60
Henrie, David 132, 224
Henriksen, Lance 124, 215, 219
Henshall, Doug 126, 185, 223
Heo, Joon B. 203
Herbert, Charles 20, 204
Hercules and the Amazon Women 233
Herd, Richard 111
Here Comes Peter Cottontail 125-26, 230
Herek, Stephen 204
Herman, Jack 84
Hero Beyond the Boundary of Time 237
Heroes 112-13, 227
Heroes Reborn 113, 227
Herrliche Zeiten im Spessart 236
Herzig, Sid 224
Heston, Charles 203
Heston, Charlton 44
Heughan, Sam 172, 228
Hewitt, David L. 211, 221
Hewitt, Jennifer Love 138, 209
Hewitt, Pete 204
Hewlett, David 18, 214
Hexum, Jon-Erik 186, 230
Heyward, Michael Monroe 17, 220
Hickey, William 55, 203
Hickox, Anthony 223
Hicks, Catherine 72, 90, 169, 208, 215, 217, 218
Hidaka, Noriko 32
Hidaka, Rina 32, 225
Hiddleston, Tom 24, 213
Hikasa, Yoko 115, 228
Hildebrand, Caroline 209
Hildreth, Mark 123, 215
Hill, Craig 108, **109**, 208
Hill, C.S. 220
Hill, George Roy 217
Hill, Jacqueline 53
Hill, Matt 219
Himel, Jed 213
Hindsight 1, 2, 4, 5, 129, 227
Hines, Austin 217
Hinshaw, Ashley 42, 215
Hirano, Aya 155, 197, 206, 228
Hirata, Kenya 216
Hirata, Yuka 32, 225
Hiroshi, Hashimoto 219
Hirosue, Ryōko 95 204
Hirota, Mikio 219
Hirsh, Sherman 212
A Hitch in Time 50, 209
Hoath, Florence 36, 222
Hobbs, Peter 214
Hoblit, Gregory 208
Hodcarrier Films 206
Hodges, Jessy 227
Hoffman, Dustin 65, 218
Hoffman, Linda 203
Hogan, Heather 227
Hogan, Siobhan Fallon 210
Holaway, Meeghan 217
Holden, Gina 57, 76, 151, 211, 215
Holden, Joyce 72, **73**, 219
Holden, Laurie 123, 213, 215

Holden, Marjean 215
Holiday Switch 180, 209
Holidaze 177-78, 209
Holland, Tom 218
Holly, Lauren 203
Holm, Ian 56
Holmes, Michelle 172 226
Holt, Tim 84, 224
O Homem Do Futuro 237-38
Honda, Riki 127, 219
Hong, James 212
Hong Kong 236, 237, 240
Honus and Me 224
Hoops & Yoyo Ruin Christmas 241
Hopkins, Anthony 44, 208
Hopkins, Dale 209
Hopkins, Stephen 212
Hopkins, Telma 222
Hopper, Dennis 57, 214
Horner, Craig 227
Hosada, Mamoru 209
Hoshino, Takanori 230
Hot Tub Time Machine 128, 209
Hot Tub Time Machine 2 158, 209
Hough, John 203
Hoult, Nicholas 224
Hourglass Sanatorium 237
House at the End of Time 237
The House in the Square 165, 209
House of Clocks 237
House II: The Second Story 58, 209
Howard, Leslie 20, 164, 203
Howard, Moe 21, 220
Howard, Rance 220
Howard, Ron 55, 220 226
Howard Productions 217
Howell, C. Thomas 57, 97, 180, 207, 211, 212
Howells, William Dean 193, 213
Howes, Sally Ann 230
Hoyle, Geoff 72, 218
Hoyt, John 221
HTV 227, 229
Hua Yue Jia Qi 237
Huckaby, Steffany 163, 206
Hudson, Ernie 155, 207
Hue, David 208
Hughes, John 211
Hughes, Miko 38, 207
Hughes, Robert F. 215
Hui Dao Ai Yi Qian 236
Hulu 226
Hu-Man 237
The Human Pets 211
Hungarian Vagabond 237
Hungary 237
Hunt, Helen 181, **182**, 222
Hunter, Jeffrey 49, 206
Hunter, Kim 45, 122, **123**, 203, 207
Hunter, Thomas 208
Huntley-Wright, Betty 229
Hurd, Gale Anne 219
Hurt, John 22. 208
Hurt, William 58, 212
Huss, Toby 163, 205
Hutcherson, Josh 157, 224
Hutchinson, Ron 207
Hutchinson, Clint 203
Hutchison, Fiona 39, 203

Hutson, Lee 222
Hutton, Lauren 116–17, 222
Hutton, Timothy 74, 156, 212, 226
Hyakka Ryouran 234
Hyams, Peter 218, 221
Hyde, Chris 221
Hyde Park Entertainment 216
Hyde-White, Alex 38–39, 117, 203, 221
Hyman, Fracaswell 211
Hyperfutura 233
Hyperion 222

I Killed Einstein, Gentlemen 237
I Love You, I Love You 209
Ichijou, Saeko 219
Ichimura, Masachika 71, 219
Icon Entertainment International 222
Idaho Transfer 43, 209
If Only 138, 209
IFC Films 209
Iizuka, Shōzō 213
Iliadis, Dennis 215
Ilie, George 38, 221
I'll Believe You 79, 210
I'll Follow You Down 152–53, 210
I'll Never Forget You 209
The Illustrated Man 233
Images Television International 224
Imagin 189
Imai, Asami 142, 218
Immortality Inc. 44, 208
In His Father's Shoes 39–40, 210
In Search of the Lost Future 3, 4, 143, 227
In the Name of the King 2: Two Worlds 31, 210
In the Name of the King 3: The Last Mission 31, 210
Inada, Tetsu 230
Inception Media Group 214
Inciarte, Ion 221
Inderbitzin, Kurt 221
India 202, 236, 237, 239
The Indian in the Cupboard (movie) 77–78, 210
The Indian in the Cupboard (novel) 77, 210
Indru Netru Naalai 237
Ineo Gongju 238
The Infinite Man 175, 210
Infinity Features 204
Ingham, Barrie 52, 211
Inhyeonwanghooui Namja 238
Insight Film Studios 204
Insurge Pictures 216
Intermedia Films 209, 219
International Venture Consult Trust 213
Interstellar 114, 210
Into the Labyrinth 50, 227
Intuit Pictures 205
Inuyasha 32, 227
Inuyasha: The Final Act 32
Invincible Pictures 210
The Invisible Boy 237
Ipalé, Aharon 28, 211

Ireland, Brian 127, 220
Irons, Jeremy 15, 220
Irons, Nicholas 28, 211
Ironside, Michael 80, 211
Irving, Brian 214
Ise, Mariya 32, 225
Ishida, Takuya 161, 209
Ishihara, Satomi 33, 212
Ishihara, Tatsuya 206
Ishimaru, Kanji 162, 221
Ishinomori, Shotaro 202
Israelite, Dean 216
It Happened Here 87, 210
It Happened One Christmas 154, 210
Itakura, Mitsutaka 161, 209
Italy 237, 238, 239
Itou, Kanae 32, 225
It's a Very Merry Muppet Christmas Movie 154, 210
It's a Wonderful Life 153–54, 210
It's About Time 25, 227
ITV 226, 227, 228, 229
Ivan Vassilyevich Back to the Future see *Ivan Vassilyevich Changes Occupation*
Ivan Vassilyevich Changes Occupation 22, 210
Ivan Vassilyevich Menyaet Professlyu see *Ivan Vassilyevich Changes Occupation*
Izo 71, 210
Izquierdo, Felipe 80, 227
The Jacket 156, 210

Jackman, Hugh 113, 167, 211, 224
Jackson, David S. 212
Jackson, Joshua 121, 226
Jackson, Samuel L. 65, 218
Jacobs, Darren 69, 206
Jacobs, Emilie 156, 202
Jacobs, Jillian 209
Jacobs, Matthew 206
Jacobs, Philip Bryce 80, 228
Jacobson, Eric 210
Jaenicke, Hannes 110, 214
Jagger, Mick 44, 208
Jakoby, Don 215
James, Brion 114, 221
Jameson, Adair 174, 213
Jameson, Malcolm 193
Jang, Dong-gun 9, 223
Jang, Jin 206
Janjic, Zoran 205
Janney, Allison 48, 213
Janover, Michael 215
Jastrzembska, Christina 31, 210
Jayne, Billy 227
Je t'aime, Je t'aime 62, 209
Jeffries, Lionel 202
Jenkins, Brinley 230
Jenkins, Dallas 224
Jenkins Entertainment 224
Jens, Salome 72, 219
Jensen, Erik 223
Jensen, Gail 140, 208
Jeon, Ji-hyun 171, 210
Jeon, No-min 135, 228
Jeong, Dong-Hwang 135
Das Jesus Video 235

La Jetée 100–101m 212
The Jetsons Meet the Flintstones 79–80, 210
Jett Jackson—The Movie 80, 210–11
JFK assassination 3, 90–91
Jikuu Tantei Genshi-Kun 226
Jimmy Green and his Time Machine 49, 227
Jina, Yeoh 210
JLA Adventures; Trapped in Time 241
Jo, Yoon Hee 135, 228
Johansson, Scarlet 233
John Aaron Productions 214
John Dies at the End 83, 211
John-Jules, Danny 55, 228
Johnny and the Bomb 87, 227
Johnny Mysto Boy Wizard 5, 24–5, 211
Johns, Geoff 211
Johns, W.E. 38, 203
Johnson, Brad 86, 215
Johnson, Dwayne 234
Johnson, Jack 58
Johnson, Jake 128, 217
Johnson, Jarrod 54, 227
Johnson, Michelle 50, 223
Johnson, Neil 206
Johnson, Page 56
Johnson, Rian 212
Johnson, Van 168, 204
Johnston, Katie 70, 93, 221
Johnston, Sue 225
Jolie, Angelina 140, 212
Jones, Duncan 218
Jones, Eddie 206
Jones, Jennifer 165, 216
Jones, Melissa 204
Jones, Miranda 44, 226
Jones, Richard T. 104
Jones, Sarah 67, 225
Jones, Tommy Lee 149, 213
Jones, Vinnie 159, 217
Joosen, Leon 217
Jordan, Leslie 128, 204
Jordan, Michael B. 211
Jordan, Peter 118, 214
Jordan, Rafael 219
Josh Kirby ... Time Warrior 52, 211
Josten, Matthew 148, 213
Journey to the Beginning of Time 237
Journey to the Center of Time 54, 211
Journey to the Magic Cavern 211
Journey to the West 235
Journeyman 191, 227
Joyce, Keegan 227
Joyce, Wilbur 213
Joyner, C. Courtney 214, 222
Jubilee 233
Judas Kiss 135, 211
Judge, Christopher 83, 215, 218
Juko's Time Machine 3, 174–75, 211
Jules Verne's Mysterious Island 57, 211
Julia, Raul 22, 208
Jumanji 233
Junger, Gil 204, 209

256　Index

Jungmann, Eric 98, 215
Just Visiting 69, 211
Justice League: Crisis on Two Earths 144–45, 211
Justice League: The Flashpoint Paradox 97, 211

K 9 54, 81, 227
Kaawa, Sean 23, 217
Kaboom Entertainment 217
Kadokawa Eiga KK 217
Kadokawa Pictures 206, 209, 212
Kafka, John 203
Kaga, Takeshi 90
Kakiuchi, Ayama 209
Kalish, Bruce 210
Kalogridis, Laeta 219
Kamata, Toshio 209
Kamen Rider 189
Kamen Rider Den-O 189, 227
Kamiya, Akira 28
Kamp, Gus 225
Kamps, John 224
Kane, Tom 147
Kaneshiro, Takeshi 115, 216
Kapadia, Aatish 202
Kaplan, Alon 221
Kappatoo 80, 227
Kapper, Chad 217
Kapur, Aditya Roy 132, 202
Karbo Vantas Entertainment 221
Karmel, Pip 213
Karna, John 200, 216
Karp, Adam J. 214
Karpluk, Erin 127, 225
Karppinen, Nina 218
Karwel, Ray 220
Karylle 171, 213
Kasahara, Hiroko 106, 226
Kasander Film Company 205
Kasem, Casey 125, 230
Kate & Leopold 167–68, 211
Kato, Emiri 142, 228
Kato, Yoshiro 21, 205
Katonic, Jamie 113, 223
Katz, A.L. 224
Kaufman, David 51, 225
Kaufman, George S. 217
Kaufman, Jimmy 220
Kavadas, Andrew 24, 227
Kavanagh, Ted 220
Kawakami, Tomoko 32, 227
Kawasaki, Hirotsugu 212
Kawashima, Chiyoko 118, 229
Kay, Robbie 113, 208, 227
Kay, Robbie A. 87
Kaye, Danny 126, 230
Keating, Dominic 226
Keats, Richard 108, 203
Keegan, Andrew 215
Keeler, Ken 208
Keeter, Worth 212
Keitch, J. Andrew 128, 202
Keitel, Harvey 41, 227
Keith, David 78, 210
Keller, Mary Page 221
Kelley, DeForest 85, 218
Kelly, Bill 216
Kelly, Dean Lennox 185, 208

Kelly, Gene 168, 204
Kelly, Richard 206
Kemp, Martin 223
Kemp, Will 135, 211
Kendal, Felicity 224
Kendrick, Alex 37
Kenmochi, Wataru 212
Kennedy, Beth 134, 222
Kennedy, Christopher 225
Kent, Bryan 81
Kerchner, Bob 216
Kerwin, James 224
Ketelsen, Kim Steven, 215
The Kid see *Disney's The Kid*
A Kid in Aladdin's Palace 28–29, 211
A Kid in King Arthur's Court 11, 28, 211
Kidd, Courtney 137, 202
Kidder, Margot 234
Kihlstedt, Rya 113
Kikuchi, Masami 140, 219
Kilbourne, Wendy 222
Killinger, Jill 55, 207
Killoran, John 213
Kilmer, Val 191, 206
Kim, Ha-Neul 206
Kim, Jeong-kwon 206
Kim, Yunjin 227
Kim Possible: A Stich in Time 147, 211
Kimizuka, Ryôichi 204
Kin-Dza-Dza! 237
Kinberg, Simon 224
King, Nathan 209
King, Stephen 42, 218
King, T.W. 187, 230
King Arthur and the Knights of Justice 24, 227
King Arthur's Court see *A Kid in King Arthur's Court*
The King of Yesterday and Tomorrow 237
Kingsley, Ben 93, 148, 216, 218
Kinsella, Brooke 95, 228
Kinski, Klaus 116, 221
Kirkwood, David 38
Kirsch, Greg 206
Kirwan, Dervla 172, 226
Kiser, Terry 19
Kish, Bert 209
Kishimoto, Masashi 214
Kishitani, Gorô 216
Kitamura, Eri 142, 228
Kitamura, Kazuki 219
Kitano, Kie 97, 215
Kiteretsu Daihyakka 227
Kiteretsu Encyclopedia 50, 227
Klanfer, François 25
Klausner, Josh 217
Klauss, Jurgen 216
Klein, Greg 203
Kleinberg, Kevin 228
Kleintank, Luke 88, 227
A Knight in Camelot 10, 211
Knight-Mare Hare 9
Knightley, Keira 156, 210
Knudsen, Erik 107, 225
Kobayashi, Megumi 96, 216
Kobayashi, Yuko 140, 219

Kodera, Jon 17, 220
Koenig, Walter 218
Koepp, David 224
Kon, Satoshi 213
Konner, Lawrence 215
Konparu, Tomoku 208
Konpeki no Kantai 226
Konzelman, Chuck 224
Koprova, Misa 222
Koren, Steve 205
Kosmas, Kristen 207
Kostka, Petr 85, 222
Kottek, Heather 78, 218
Koyasu, Takehito 106, 226
Kramer, Stepfanie 66, 204
Krause, Brian 107, 225
Kretschmann, Thomas 107, 222
Krieg, Jim 211
Kriesa, Christopher 110, 214
Krige, Alice 120, 218
Krikes, Peter 218
Kristin's Christmas Past 135, 211
Kristofferson, Kris 73, 156, 210, 213
Krofft, Marty 212
Krofft, Sid 212
Krosney, Alexandra 212
Krowchuk, Chad 81, 228
Krupp, Elena 203
Krutzfeld, Samantha 228
KSS 210
Kubert, Andy 211
Kuchuck, Danny 205
Kudo, Haruka 157, 228
Kudou, Shouko 219
Kuenne, Kurt 217
Kugimiya, Rie 209
Kulikowski, Christopher 216
Kumar, Akshay 132, 202
Kumo no Mukuo, Yakusoku no Basho 233
Kunert, Günter 216
Kung Fury 240
Kuravlev, Leonid 22, 210
Kureya, Kwayedza 36, 208
Kurosawa, Nathan 217
Kurtzman, Alex 218
Kushner-Locke 211, 213, 214, 221
Kustanovich, Alex 219
Kutcher, Ashton 151, 204
Kuttner, Henry 64, 74, 206, 212, 223
Kuzyk, Mimi 221

LaBelle, Kimberly 100, 204
Ladd, Cheryl 73, 213
La Fleur, Art 222
Laird, Chris 214
Laird, Peter 219
La Jolla Productions 219
The Lake 144, 212
The Lake House 164, 171, 212
Lamarche, Maurice 222
LaMarr, Phil 44, 208, 229
Lancelot, Guardian of Time 68, 212

Land of the Lost (movie) 60–62, 212
Land of the Lost (1974–6) 60, **61**, 212, 227
Land of the Lost (1991–2) 60, 227
The Land That Time Forgot (movie) 207
The Land That Time Forgot (novel) 207
Landau, Martin 193, 222
Landis, John 223
Lando, Jeffery 219
Landor, Rosalyn 35
Lane, Brian Alan 215
Laney, Lanier 222
Lang, Stephen 27, 229
Lange, Michael 214
Langedijk, Jack 11
The Langoliers (novel) 218
The Langoliers (TV) see *Stephen King's The Langoliers*
Lansky, Nikolas 16, 216
LaPaglia, Jonathan 190, 229
Lara Croft Tomb Raider 140, 212
Larson, Cameron 211
Larter, Ali 227
The Last Day of Summer 197, 212
Last Exit to Earth 64, 74, 212
Last Lives 179–80, 212
The Last Mimzy 74–75, 212
Latham, Louise 215
The Lathe of Heaven (novel) 172, 212
The Lathe of Heaven (1980) 116, 212
The Lathe of Heaven (2002) 172–73, **173**, 212
Latimer, Michael 26, 216
Lauckner, Joan 128, 202
Law, Phyllida 220, 225
Lawrence, Jennifer 113, 224
Lawrence, Martin 30, 204
Lawrence, Richard 69, 206
Lázaro, Eusebio 126, 223
Lazer Tag Academy 116, 227
Lea, Nicholas 76, 215
Leachman, Cloris 154, 210
LeBlanc, Matt 212
LeBorg, Reginald 208
Le Bourveau, Brett 180, 209
Lee, Conan 207
Lee, Hyun-seung 210
Lee, Jason Scott 187, 221
Lee, Jin Wook 135, 228
Lee, Jung-jae 171, 210
Lee, Ruta 205
Lee, Sang-hak 223
Lee, Si-myung 223
Lee, Wendee 68, 228
Leeson, John 81, 227
Lefevre, Rachelle 149, 204
Legend of the Millenium Dragon 33, 212
Legendary 210
Legge, Mike 202
Legion of Super-Heroes 44, 227
Leguin, Ursula K. 212
Leibman, Ron 62, 217
Leichtling, Jerry 215
Leigh, Jennifer Jason 170, 210, 213
Leigh, Nelson 224

Leland, Fiona 210
Lembeck, Michael 217
Lemche, Kristopher 213
Lemercier, Valérie 69, 223
Lemke, Darren 217
Lenard, Mark 45, 218, 228
Lenhart, Kerry 215
Leone, Christopher 215
Leonetti, John R. 204
Leoni, Téa 176, 207
Leonidas, Stephanie 92, 205
Lerner, Alan Jay 204
Lerner, Sam 216
Leslie, Joan 47, 136, 216, 224
Le Vaillant, Nigel 36
Le Vant, René 224
Levers, Meredith 209
Levi, Zachary 27
Levien, Sonya 203
Levinson, Barry 218
Levy, Eugene 154, 216
Levy, Robert L. 211
Levy, Scott 203
Levy, Shawn 211
Lew, James **187**
Lewis, David 152, 167, 207
Lewis, Jim 210
Lewis, Judy 158, 217
Lewis, Phill 35, 204
Li, Jet 29, 144, 208, 214
Liberty Films 210
Licht, Jeremy 81, 214
Liebe in der Warteschleife 237
Life on Mars (UK) 41, 227
Life on Mars (US) 41–42, 227
Lifetime Network 205, 208, 209, 211, 223
Lightning Entertainment 204
Lightstone, Marilyn 75, 206
Lightstorm Entertainment 219
Lilly, Evangeline 227
Lilovy Shar 237
Liman, Doug 207
Lind, Sarah 81, 138, 207, 228
Linden, Hal 220
Linden, Jennie **53**, 206
Lindenmuth, Kevin J. 202, 209, 220
Lindo, Delroy 144, 214
Lindo, Olga 33
Linklater, Hamish J. 156, 226
Linn, Marc 207
Linn, Michael 207
Linn Productions 207
Linzner, Gordon 220
Lippman, Sarah K. 220
Litefoot 78, 210
Lithgow, John 210
The Little Girl Who Conquered Time 161, 212
Liu, Sam 211
Lively, Eric 151, 204
Livingston, Ron 221
Llewellyn, Olivia 139, 206
Lloyd, Christopher 130, 203
Lloyd, Eric 217
Lloyd, Frank 203
Lloyd, Norman 229
Lloyd, Sabrina 98, 229
Lloyd-Hughes, Henry 139, 206

Lobo, Stephen 107, 225
Lock, Stuart 95, 229
Locke, Taylor 38, 221
Lockhart, Emily 138, 215
Loewe, Frederick 204
Logan, John 220
Loggia, Robert 156, 202
Lois and Clark: The New Adventures of Superman 19
Loken, Kristanna 103, 219
Lola Rennt 241
Longe, Jerry 17, 220
Loomis, Rod 204
Looper 119, 212
The Lords of Magick 67, 212
Loseutu Memorijeu 223
Lost 59, 227
Lost in Austen 6
Lost in Space 58, 212
The Lost Medallion: The Adventures of Billy Stone 37, 212
The Lost Saucer 54–55, 227
Loter, Steve 211
Lotz, Caity 108, 226
Love & Teleportation 213
Love in the Time of Twilight 237
The Love Letter (film) 170–71, 213
"The Love Letter" (short story) 170–71, 213
Love Spell Entertainment 209
Love Story 2050 237
The Lovers 233
Lowe, Crystal 228
Lowenthal, David 20
Lowenthal, Yuri 27, 34, 44, 203, 215, 227
Loxton, David 203, 212
Loy, Myrna 8, 205
Lucas, Autumn 209
Lucas, Clyde 220
Lucking, William 82, 228
Lucy 233
Lumbly, Carl 35, 204
Lumley, Joanna 183, **184**, 229
Lummis, Dayton 108, **109**, 208
Lund, Nicole 37, 209
Lundgret, Dolph 31, 110, 210, 216
Lundquist, Arthur 202
Lung, Emma 222
Lunopolis 95–96, 213
Lupo, Kyle 196, 204
Lupoff, Richard A. 193, 222
Lurid Tales: The Castle Queen 34, 213
Lush, Valerie 35
Lusk, Megan 30, 214
Lussier, Jacques 28 214, 219
Lussier, Patrick 219
Lustig, Dana 219
LWT 225
Lynch, Jane 27, 203
Lynch, Richard 183, 222
Lyndhurst, Nicholas 172, 226
Lynn, Billy 64, 223
Lyons, Bruce 70, 214
Lyons, Kely 214

M3 Creative 211
Maberly, Kate 42, 218

Index

Macavoy, Charles 113
MacDougall, Ranald 209
MacGregor, Christina 116, 227
MacGrory, Yvonne 217
Macht, Kari 156
Macht, Stephen 222
Mack, Chris 220
Mackay, George 87, 227
Mackenzie, Peter 207
MacLeod, Don 202
MacLeod, Gavin 70, 220
MacMurray, Fred 47, 224
Macnee, Patrick 50, 223
MacNeill, Meredith 185, 208
MacNeille, Tress 213
Macourek, Miloš 222
MacPhail, Angus 208
Macy, William 210
Mad House 209
Madhouse 221
Magic Müller 237
Magnet 211
Maguire, Jeff 221
Magwilli, Dom 208
Magyar Vandor 237
Maher, Bill 67, 209, 215
Maher, Joseph 133
Les Maîtres du Temps 239
Majors, Lee 66, 203
Mako 44, 229
Malice in Wonderland 233
Malik, Art 11, 211
Mallard, Bart 150
Malone, William 224
Malthe, Natassia 210
Man Dog 67, 227
The Man from the Future 237–38
The Man in the High Castle (film) 88, 227
The Man in the High Castle (novel) 88
The Man Who Could Work Miracles 233
The Man Who Used to Be Me 134, 213
The Man with the Rain in His Shoes 223
Manard, Biff 183, 222
Mancuso, Nick 11, 123, 215, 224
Mandalay Pictures 210
Mandt, Neil 203
Mandylor, Costas 74, 212
Mangold, James 211
Mann, Danny 202
Mann, Larry 94, 224
Manners, David 27, 217
Manninen, Sarah 167, 207
Manoogian, Peter 207
Mansfield, Susan 207
Manson, Maurice 29, 223
Manson, Shirley 104, 229
Mantooth, Randolph 204
Manugian, Alex 205
Mara, Mary 70, 205
Marching Out of Time 66, 213
Il Mare 171, 210, 212
Mari, Gloria 110, 214
Marker, Chris 212
Marker, Russ 224

Marks, Hannah 135, 211
Marlow, Jim 196
Marlowe, Hugh 224
Mars, Kenneth 77, 224
Marsh, David 212
Marsh, Jean 205, 207
Marsh, Jeff "Swampy" 215
Marsh, Reginald 210
Marsh International Films 212
Marshall, Hannah 175, 210
Marshall, William 206
Marsilli, Bill 206
Martella, Vincent 145, 215
Martin, Jared 56, 226
Martin, Jesse L. 226
Martin, Katherine 212
Martin, Kiel 133, 228
Martin, Tom 210
Martin, Tony 202
Martine, Daniel 68, 220
Martini, Max 137, 202
Marven, Nigel 26, 228
Marvista Entertainment 203
Mary Shelley's Frankenhole 37, 227
Mascarino, Pierrino 93, 221
Masefield, John 50
Mask of Zeguy 233
Massett, Patrick 212
Massey, Anna 40, 202
Masters of the Universe 233
Masterson, Chase 62
Mastorakis, Nico 214
Masur, Richard 214
Matchett, Kari 226
Mateo, Joe 213
Matern, Anik 23
Matheson, Chris 204
Matheson, Michele 223
Matheson, Richard 206, 218
Mathieson, Jamie 208
Mathison, Cameron 177, 209
Mathison, Melissa 210
Matsuda, Naofumi 219
Matsuda, Yasunori 219
Matsui, Naoko 92, 229
Matsumoto, Rica 97, 215
Matter, Niall 185, 228
Matthews, Terumi 78, 218
Matthiesen, Thomas 209
Maurer, Norman 220
Mauro, Christina 170, 207
Mayberry, Russ 223
Maybury, John 210
Mayen-Salazar, Patricia 209
Mayes, Rob 83, 211
Maynor, Sonny 95, 213
Mazo, Michael 221
McAdams, Rachel 24, 174, 202, 213, 221
McAvoy, James 224
McBee, Deron Michael 67, 220
McBride, Danny 60, 212
McCallum, David 183, **184**, 229
McCamus, Tom 27, 214
McCann, Hailey 174, 221
McCann, Tatum 221
McCarthy, Jenny 222
McCarthy, Kevin 56, 203
McCauley, Peter 58, 229

McCleery, Mick 202
McClung, Amy 204
McConaughey, Matthew 114, 210
McConville, Bernard 205
McConville, Josh 175, 210
McCord, Scott 51, 230
McCormack, Catherine 93, 218
McCormick, Ellina 38, 207
McCullers, Michael 203, 213
McDonald, Rodney 214
McDonnell, Mary 169, 206, 208
McDonough, Neal 149, 220, 221
McDowall, Roddy 45, 57, 122, **123**, 207, 226, 228
McDowell, Andie 194, 209
McDowell, Malcolm 18, 50, 76, 111, 211, 215, 220, 226, 234
McDuffie, Dwayne 211
McFadden, Gates 218
McFall, Anika 196, 204
McFarlane, Hamish 70, 214
McGann, Paul 54, 206
McGarrey, Mark 113, 223
McGatlin, Troy 213
McGatlin Films 213
McGill, Bruce 221
McGinly, Sean 203
McGowan, Rose 107, 225
McGrath, Doug 223
McGraw, Royal 214
McGuire, William Anthony 217
McHale, Joel 152, 218
McIntire, Eric 204
McIvor, Joshua 197, 222
McKay, Peter 215
McKellan, Ian 113
McKenzie, Jacqueline 112, 226
McKenzie, Patricia 225
McKeon, Lindsey 207
McKeon, Nancy 176, 205
McKeown, Fintan 118, 214
McKidd, Kevin 97, 191, 211, 227
McLeAn, Jane 221
McLellan, Pheona 50, 209
McLemore, Zachary 93, 221
McMahon, Julian 62, 137, 202, 216
McMenamin, Ciarán 185
McNabb, Suzanne 228
McNamara, Miles 76
McNicholas, Dennis 212
McPharlin, Sean 203
McPlank, Lee B. 22, 226
McQuarrie, Christopher 207
McQueen, Ross 213
McQueen, Steven R. 160, 213
McSkimming, Jason 25, 207
McVey, Michael 50, 209
McWhirter, Julie 80, 210
Me Myself I 176, 213
Meade, Candice 202
Meadows, Tim 137, 220
Meaney, Colm 96, 208
Mechner, Jordan 216
Media Savant 213
Mediapro 213
Medieval Park 29–30, 213
Medwetz, Anthony 93, 221
Meehan, Thomas 215
The Meeksville Ghost 233

Meerson, Steve 218
Meet the Robinsons 148, 213
Mega Communications 209
Megas XLR 68, 227–28
Mehta, Richie 210
Meixell, Noelle 150, 202
Mekka, Eddie 219
The Melancholy of Haruhi Suzumaya 197, 228
Melchior, Ib 221
Melendez, John 222
Mellish, Marcie 215
Melnick, Natasha 226
Memoirs of a Survivor 233
Men in Black (comic book) 213
Men in Black 3 149–50, 213
Menaul, Christopher 207
Mendelsohn, Aaron 222
Mendelsohn, Michael 107, 222
Menšík, Vladimír 85, 222
Mentors 81, 228
Menzies, Tobias 172, 228
Meraz, Alex 213
Mering, Ean 156, 202
Meriwether, Lee 54, 230
Merrison, Clive 33, 230
Messick, Don 49,228
Metcalf, Laurie 213
Methinx Entertainment 212
Meugniot, Will 220
Mexico 235, 236, 237, 239
Meyer, Kirsten 55, 207
Meyer, Nicholas 218, 220
MGM 204, 209, 216, 218, 220, 221, 222
Michaels, Ian 170, 207
Michalka, Alyson 79
Michaud, Alexander 220
Michelle, Diane 213
Mickey's Once Upon a Christmas 195, 213
Midkiff, Dale 186, 230
Midnight in Paris 20, 24, 213
Midorikawa, Hikaru 228
Mihailoff, R.A. 183
Miike, Takashi 210
Milano, Alyssa 107, 225
Milder, Andy 227
Milestone Films 210
Milhoan, Michael 226
Milian, Christina 178, 217
Milicevic, Ivana 159, 217
The Milky Way 238
Millbern, David 196, 205
Millennium 73, 213
Millennium Actress 52, 213
Miller, Barry 215
Miller, Ben 228
Miller, Chris J. 113, 223
Miller, Garry 35, 202
Miller, Logan 42, 215
Miller, Marvin 60
Miller, Robert Tate 220
Miller, Wentworth 108, 226
Miller Consolidated Pictures 203
Milligan, Dustin 151, 198, 216
Milligan, Peter 202
Milligan, Spencer 60, 227
Mills, Edwin 45, 229

Mimieux, Yvette 13, **14**, 16, 220
"Mimsy Were the Borogroves" 74, 212
Mine Games 198–200, 213
Mineo, Sal 122, **123**, 207
Miner, Rachel 152, 204
Miner, Steve 223
El Ministerio del Tiempo 236
Minkoff, Rob 208, 213
Minnelli, Vincente 204
Minnis, Jon 222
Minter, Kristin 224
Minutemen 160, 213
Mira Sentai Time Rangers 188, 228
The Miracle in Valby 238
Mirai Nikki 226
Mirai Sentai Time Rangers 188, 228
Miraklet I Valby 238
Miramax 211
Miro, Doug 216
Mirror for a Hero 238
Mirror Images 215
Mirror, Mirror 238
mirror universe in *Star Trek* series 145–146
Misfits 160, 228
Mr. Peabody and Sherman 48, **48**, 213
The Mr. Peabody and Sherman Show 48–49, 228
Mr. Rossi Looks for Happiness 238
Mitchell, Elizabeth 135, 147, 162, 208, 211, 217
Mitchell, Mike 217
Mitchell, Stevie 81, 228
Mitchell, Thomas 153
Mitra, Rhona 28, 211
Mitsuishi, Kotono 117,229
Mitsuya, Yuuji 28, 227, 230
Miwa, Akihiro 97, 215
Miyano, Mamoru 142, 218, 229
Miyata, Kouki 32 227
Mizuhashi, Kaori 228
Mizumisha, Takahiro 115, 228
Mizushima, Yuu 31, 208
Mizuta, Wasabi 77, 226
Mizutani, Kei 105, 219
Modine, Matthew 24, 224
Moffat, Jan 36
Moggridge, Alex 175, 211
Mohr, Jay 195, 205
Mol, Gretchen 227
Moldovan, Vadim 219
Molina, Alfred 216
Mollica, Vince 204
Mollow, Andrew 210
Moloney, Robert 81, 227
Moltke, Alexandra 59
Moments of Love 171–72, 213
Monaghan, Michelle 198, 217
Monkey Planet 215
Montalban, Ricardo 49, 123, 207, 226
Montana, Joe 110, 216
Montgomery, Lauren 211
Monville, Patricia 212
Moody, Josh 219
Moody, Marc 202
Moody, Ron 10, 11, 50, 211, 223, 227

Moon, George 33
Moonbeam Films 207, 221
Moondial 35, 228
Moore, C.L. 75, 206
Moore, Jonathan Patrick 178, 203
Moore, Ronald D. 218
morality and time travel 164,
More, Kenneth 10, 87, 223, 226
Moreno, Rita 133, 204
Morgan, Boyd 203
Morgan, Derek 208
Morgan, Diana 208
Morgan, Glen 214
Morgan, Wesley 215
Morgan Creek 208
Moricz, Barna 38, 221
Morikawa, Toshiyuki 147, 214, 226
Morin, D. David 70, 220
Morita, Chiaka 226
Morita, Noriyuki "Pat" 118, 221
Morley, Robert 95, 217
Morlocks 18, 214
Morneau, Louis 216, 217
Morris, John 209
Morris, Kyle 113, 222
Morrow, Vic 39, 223
Morse, David 42, 101, 218, 223
Mortimer, Emily 134, 206
Morton, Gregory 208
Morton, Joe 103, 161, 219, 226
Morton, Philip 222
Mosier, Scott 208
Moskowitz, Alan 217
Most, Donny 55, 226
Mostow, Jonathan 219
Mosura Suri Kingu Gidora Raishu 216
Mothra 3: King Ghidora Attacks 216
Motohiro, Katsuyuki 219
Motz, Bill 211
Mount Company 208
Mousetrap Films 206
Moyer, Stephen 204
MSBS 228
MTM Entertainment 207
MTV Films 216
Mud 95, 228
Muhney, Michael 163, 178, 203, 206
Muir, Bill 212
Mull, Martin 216
Mullaney, Jack 25, 227
Mumba, Samantha 15, 220
Mumy, Liliana 148
Munch, Tony 229
Munker, Ariane 56, 203
Munro, Lochlyn 57, 210, 211
Murai, Sadayuki 213
Murata, Masahiko 214
Murata, Tomosa 138, 226
Murdock, George 75, 206
Murlowski, Jon 216
Murphy, Brittany 40, 206
Murphy, Eddie 317
Murphy, Geoff 208
Murphy, Joseph 91, 221
Murphy, Sean Paul 217
Murray, Bill 194, **194**, 209
Murray, James 219

Murray, Pauline 87, 210
Muse, Sunday 51, 230
Mushi Productions 205
Muto, Shogo 219
Mutual Film Company 212
My Future Boyfriend 170, 214
My Iz Budushchego 240
My Iz Budushchego 2 240
My Mother the Mermaid 238
My Mother Was Never a Kid 240
My Science Project 57–58, 214
Myers, Harry 8, 205
Myers, Mike 40, 154, 203, 217
Myers, Rocky 119
Myman, Louis 214
The Mysterious Island 211
Mysterious Museum 30–31, 214
Myth 238

Nabors, Jim 54, 227
Nachoff, Michael C. 210
Nagai, Ichiro 25, 202
Nain: Ahob Beonui Shiganyeohaeng 228
Nair, Suresh 202
Naismith, Laurence 35, 202, 216
Naito, Makoto 202
Naka, Riisa 161, 162, 209, 221
Nakagawa, Anna 117, 209
Nakai, Kazuya 157, 228
Nakajima Toshihiko 32
Nakamura, Chie 226
Nakamura, Daiki 226
Nakamura, Toru 89, 223
Nakao, Akiyoshi 162, 221
Nakayama, Chinatsu 21, 205
Nakayama, Emiri 229
Nakayama, Kazuya 71, 210
Nanba, Keiichi 106, 226
Napier, Charles 66, 82, 208, 215, 228
Napier, Marshall 214
Napier, Russell 13, 230
Napor Kids 209
Naruto Shippuden (anime) 42
Naruto Shippuden (manga) 214
Naruto Shippuden the Movie: The Lost Tower 42
Nasfell, Andrea Gyertson 224
Nash, Bruce 213
Nash, Simon 80, 227
Nasty Strangers 220
Nathan, Robert 216
Nation, Terry 206
Natsu no Arashi 229
Naughton, James 45, 228
Nautilus 110, 214
The Navigator: A Medieval Odyssey 69–70, 214
Nawrocki, Mike 215
Nazuka, Kaori 229
NBC 204, 205, 206, 210, 212, 220, 222, 225, 226, 227, 228, 229, 230
Neal, Siri 35, 228
A Necklace for Julia 174, 214
Neely, Antony 206
Negishi, Hiroshi 219
Negron, Taylor 28, 211
Neil, Adrian 30, 214
Neill, Sam 57, 67, 222, 225

Neise, George N. 21, 220
Nelson, Craig T. 202
Nelson, Don 210
Nelson Entertainment 203
Nem Sansao Nem Dalila 238
Nemesis 105
Nemesis 2: Nebula 105, 214
Nemesis 3: Prey Harder 214
Nemesis 3: Time Lapse 105, 214
Nemesis 4 105
Nesmith, Michael 221
Nesvadba, Josef 222
Netflix streaming 48, 228
Netherlands 205
Nettles, Cleve 202
Network Ten 227
Nevins, Claudette 45, 202, 229
Nevius, Craig J. 202
New Barbarians 242
New Line Cinema 203, 204, 208, 212, 219, 221
New World Pictures 209, 215
New Zealand 69, 214
Newbern, George 180, 223
Newell, Mike 216
Newmarket 206
Newton, John 62, 225
Newton, Omari 225
The Next One 81–82, 214
Nicholas, Thomas Ian 11, 28, 211
Nicholls, Paul 82, 138, 209, 226
Nichols, Austin 38
Nichols, Nichelle 218
Nichols, Rachel 107, 225
Nickelodeon 212
Nicktoons 230
Niffenegger, Audrey 221
Nightmare Street 143–44, 214
Nighy, Bill 174, 202
Niiyami, Shiho 229
Nimerfro, Scott 224
Nimoy, Leonard 51, 62, 71, 85, 121, 122, 145, 209, 212, 218
Nine: Nine Time Travels 135–36, 228
95ers: Echoes 214
95ers: Time Runners 178, 214
El Niño Invisible 237
Nippon TV 217, 226
Nishihara, Kumiko 28, 230
Nissen, Frank 205
Niven, Larry 60
Nixon, Henry 222
NNS 227
Noble, John 121, 226
Nobunaga, Oda 32, 33, 79, 88, 90
Noein 157, 228
Noein: Mou Hitori no Kimi e see *Noien*
Noein: To Your Other Self see *Noien*
Noein: Toward Another You see *Noien*
Nolan, Christopher 210
Nolan, Jonathan 210
Nolan, Lloyd 102
Nolan, William F. 204
Nolfi, George 221
Noll, Robert T. 220
Non ci Resta Che Piangere 238

Nondorf, Thomas 115, 202, 209
Nondorf, Tom see Nondorf, Thomas
Norgren, Glenn 214
Norman's Awesome Experience 27–28, 214
Norstar Entertainment 214
North American Pictures 221
Norton, Richard 110, 214
Norway 235
Nostalgia in time-travel 4–5, 20, 146–47, 168–69
Nostradamus 118–19, 214
Noth, Chris 144, 211
Nothing Left to Do But Cry 238
Nottage, Antony 217
Nu Image 215
Nuñez, Miguel 224
Nuyen, Frances 49, 206
Nystul, Daisy 221

O'Bannon, Rockne S. 222
Obayashi, Nobuhiko 212
Ōbayashi, Ryūnosuke 98, 226
Oboler, Arch 223
O'Brien, Richard 215
Occult Academy 115 228
"Occurence at Owl Creek Bridge, An"
O'Connell, Jerry 98, 229
O'Connor, Andrew 80
O'Connor, Frances 221
O'Connor, Kevin 126
Oda Nobuna no Yabou 225
Odaka, Megumi 209
Odell, David 203
O'Dell, Jennifer 58, 229
O'Donnell, Tim 203
O'Dowd, Chris 185, 208
Odyssey 5 110, 228
O'Farrell, William 216
Official Denial 73–74, 112, 214
O'Hanlon, George 79, 210
Ohara, Noriko 51, 229
Oka, Masi 112, 227
Okamoto, Mari 51, 229
Okamura, Akemi 228
O'Keefe, Mark 205
O'Keeffe, Miles 50
Oki, Toshinori 212
Okiayu, Ryotaro 32, 227
Okonkwo, Chiké 228
Oktab Bang Wangseja 238
Okudera, Satoko 209
Oldman, Gary 58, 212
Oliva, Jay 211
Oliver, David 204
Oliver, Lin 217
Oliver, Ron 204
Olsen, Arne 216
Olsen, Eric Christian 70, 203
Olsen, Michael-James 135
O'Mara, Jason 26, 41, 227, 229
Omigawa, Chiaki 229
Omori, Kazuki 209
The Once and Future King 25
Ondrouchová, Zuzana 85, 222
The One 144, 214
One Magic Christmas 137 214–5

100 Million BC 26, 214
O'Neal, Ron 208
O'Neil, Chris 74, 212
O'Neill, Jennifer 207, 220
Onigamiden 212
Ono, Daisuke 228
Ono, Kenshō 33, 212
Onosaka, Masaya 52, 213
Oohara, Megumi 77, 226
Ookubo, Rumi 79, 229
Oota, Yoshiko 51, 229
Oppenheimer, Joshua 218
Optical House 208
O'Quinn, Terry 227
Orci, Roberto 218
Oriental Light and Magic 215
Orikasa, Fumiko 213
Ormondroyd, Edmond 220
Orr, James 214
Orton, J.O.C. 220
Osborne, Holmes 206
Osborne, Paul 216
Oscilloscope Films 205
Osiris Entertainment 206
Osment, Haley Joel 152, 210
O'Sullivan, Maureen 8, 205
Ōtani, Ikue 97, 215
Ōtomo, Ryūzaburō 42, 140, 219, 228
Otsuka, Chikao 25, 202
Otto, Kevin 159, 217
Out of Time 67, 215
Outer Limits: "Demon with a Glass Hand" 102; "Soldier" 101–2
Outhwaite, Tamzin 191,228
Outlander (book) 172
Outlander (TV series) 1, 172, 228
Outlaw Productions 209
Outlaws 82, 228
Overton, Kelly 178, 203
Overton, Rick 225
Owen, Tudor 168
Oxenberg, Catherine 70, 203
Oz, Frank 210

Paalani, Mary 23, 217
Pacar, Johnny 163, 205
Pacific Western 219
Packard, Nicholas 22
Pacula, Joanne 118
Pagan, Jason Harry 216
Page, Ellen 113, 224
Paine, Nick 215
Pal, George 220
Palace 238
Palace—Lock Heart 238
Palfrey, Alexis 141
Palin, Michael 220
Palmer, Cynthia 207
Palmer, Kerry 214
Paltrow, Gwyneth 241
Pando Co. 209
Pandora 206
Panettiere, Hayden 112, 227
Panettiere, Jansen 37, 197, 212, 212
Panic Time 138–39, 215
Panic Time Productions 215
Paquin, Anna 224
Paradise Pictures 204
Paradox (comic book) 215

Paradox (film) 83, 215
Paradox (TV series) 191, 228
Paradox Soldiers 240
Parallel World Samurai 229
Parallels 98, 215
Paramount 205, 209, 210, 212, 218, 219, 221
ParaTheatrical ReSearch 207
Paré, Michael, 76, 215
Parilo, Markus 38, 221
Parish, Sarah 28
Park, Jae Woo 203
Park, Linda 146
Park, Peyton 212
Parker, Jarrett 67, 212
Parker, Lara 59, 225
Parker, Molly 215
Parkes, Shaun 230
Parkhill, Matthew 204
Parkin, Judd 205
Parkinson, Eric 209
Parnell, Chris 48, 228
Part, Michael 211
Pasdar, Adrian 112, 227
Paskaleva, Ralitsa 210
The Past Is a Foreign Country 20
Past Perfect 123, 215
Path in Time 241
Paton, Laurie 27–28, 214
Patrick, Dennis 17
Patrick, Renee 205
Patrick, Robert 103, 219
Patterson, Ray 210
Patton, Candace 226
Patton, Paula 191, 206
Paul, Alexandra 70, 203
Paul, Steven 205
Paul's Awakening 238
Paulsen, Rob 188, 230
Pax 230
Paxton, Bill 207
Paxton, Sara 140, 207
PBS 203, 204, 212
"Peabody's Improbable History" 47–48, 213, 228
Pearce, Guy 14, 220
Pearce, Philippa 222
Pedraza, Carlos 211
Peerce, Larry 205
Pegg, Simon 218
Peggy Sue Got Married 2, 126, 215
Pelfrey, Alexis 204
Pellegrino, Ann 84, 224
Peluce, Meeno 186, 230
Pemberton, Amy 69, 206
The Penitent Man 124, 215
Penney, John 215
Peoples, David 223
Peoples, Janet 223
Perabo, Piper 212
Perez, Jesse 140, 207
Perreau, Gigi 54, 141, 211, 220
Perrine, Valerie 62, 217
Perry, Matthew 133, 228
Pertwee, Jon 226
Peru 238
The Peter Potamus Show 49, 228
Peters, Ashley 44, 226
Peterson, A.C. 83

Peterson, Luvia 225
Pete's Christmas 196, 215
Peut-Etre 238
Phase 4 Films 213
Phil of the Future 78–79, 228
Philadelphia Experiment (legend) 26, 57, 76, 86–87, 232
The Philadelphia Experiment (1984) 76, 215
The Philadelphia Experiment (2012) 76, 215
The Philadelphia Experiment II 86–87, 215
Philippines 213, 236
Philips, Deborah Estelle 228
Phillips, Barney 28, 229
Phillips, Ethan 119, 217
Phillips, Grace 180
Phillips, Graham 66, 203
Phillips, Lou Diamond 222
Phineas and Ferb the Movie— Across the 2nd Dimension 145, 215
Phipps, William 229
Picardo, Robert 18, 214
Pickup, Ronald 148
Pierce, Arthur C. 203, 205, 206
Pierce, Jeffrey 82, 225
Pierce, Kent 212
Pierrot 212
Pigott, Sebastian 127
Pill, Alison 24
Piluso, Mario 209
Pimienta Film Company 204
Pinchot, Bronson 42, 218
Pine, Chris 121, 218
Pink, Steve 209
Pinko, Izumi 79, 229
Pirates en el Callao 238
Pirates of the Plain 66, 215
The Pirates Who Didn't Do Anything 34, 215
Pistoleros 210
Pitt, Brad 101, 223
Piven, Jeremy 152, 207, 218, 222
The Place Promised in Our Early Days 233
Planet of the Apes (1968) 44–45
Planet of the Apes (TV series) 45, 228
Planet of the Apes (2001) 45–46, 215
Planet of the Dino-Knights 211
Platinum Dunes 216
Playing Beatie Bow 238
Playten, Alice 54, 227
Plaza, Aubrey 128, 217
Plener, Benjamin 213
Plowright, Joan 36, 222
Plummer, Amanda 208
Plummer, Christopher 101, 165, 171, 212, 218, 223
+1 42, 215
Poehler, Amy 96, 208
Pointer-Ford, Paula, 220
Poiré, Jean-Marie 211, 223
Poirier, Gregory 218
Pokemon 97, 233
Pokemon: Arceus and the Jewel of Life 97, 215

Index

Pokemon4Ever 233
Polák, Jindřich 222
Poland 237, 241
Poole, Duane 207
Poots, Andrew-Lee,
Pope, Carly 38, 221
Pope, Daniel 229
Popowich, Paul 230
Poppen, Gregory 203
Portman Film 202
Portrait of Jennie (film) 165, 216
Portrait of Jennie (novel) 216
Possible Worlds 233
Post, Ted 203
Potenta, Famke 241
Potter, Dave 95 213
Potts, Andrew-Lee 185, 228
Pouget, Ely 107, 222
Povenmire, Dan 145, 215
Powell, Peter 208
Power, Tyrone 165, 209
Power Rangers Time Force 188–89, 228
Pratt, Susan May 144, 223
Predestination 136, 216
Prehistoric Park 26, 228
Prehistoric Women 26, 166, 216
Prelude Pictures 212
Premature 200, 216
Premonition 62, 216
Premonition (Japan) 233
Prentiss, David 211
Present Time 80–81, 228
Presnell, Harve 176
Pressfield, Steven 208
Preston, Mary 43
Price, Sue 105, 214
Price, Verity 159
Price, Vincent 125, 189, 229, 230
Priestley, Jason 190, 230
Primal Urge 204
Primer 151, 216
Primeval 185, 228
Primeval: New World 185, 228
Prince of Persia 216
Prince of Persia: The Sands of Time 148, 216
Prindle, Timothy 222
Prine, Andrew 94, 207
Prior, David A. 208
Prior, Ted 140, 208
Pritchard, Bonnie 118, 220
Probets, Bryan 222
Process Productions 215
Project Almanac 153, 216
Proulx, Brooklynn 221
Prysirr, Geof 107, 222
Pucci, Alex 204
Puella Magi Madoka Magica 142–43, 228
Puella Magi Madoka Magica: The Movie—Rebellion 143
Pugovkin, Mikhail 22
Pugsley, Thomas 203
Pulliam, Keshia Knight 10, 205
Pullis, Kimberly 213
Pulsepounders 221
La Puppé 101
Purcell, Dominic 31, 108, 210

Pure Flix 217, 224
Purvis, Jack 220
Puskala, Jarmo 218
Pyun, Albert 214

Quaid, Dennis 162, 208
Quaid, Randy 156, 226
Quantum Leap 190, 228, 242
Quantus Pictures 220
Quarles, Darryl J. 204
The Queen and I 238
Queen In-Hyun's Man 238
Quest Beyond Time 238
Quest for Love 179, 216
Quilley, Denis 43, 230
Quinn, Ed 149
Quinto, Zachary 112, 121

Rabett, Catherine 23
Race Through Time 213
Rachelle, Angela 141, 220
Radar Pictures 224
Radford, H.E.D. 39, 218
Radkoff, Vivienne 208
Raffill, Stewart 215
Rai, Aishwarya 132, 202
Raimi, Ivan 203
Raimi, Sam 203
Rajskub, Mary Lynn 217
Ralston, John 59
Ramis, Harold 209
Ramm, Haley 203
Rampart Films 216
Rampling, Jeremy 230
Ramsey, Laura 129, 227
"Random Quest" 179, 216, 230
Random Quest (TV) 179, 230
The Rank Organization 216
Rankin, Arthur, Jr. 224
Raposa, Jim 219
Rappaport, David 220
Ratajczak, Timothy 217
Ratner, Brett 207
Ratoff, Gregory 224
Ratzenberger, John 177, 209, 222, 224
Raver, Lorna 149, 204
Ravera, Gina 71, 155, 205, 224
Rawle, Jeff 50, 209
Ray, David 207
Raymond, Bradley 213
Raymond, Paula 108, **109**, 208
Razorwire Pictures 223
Reardon, John 76
Reaves, Shawn 190, 230
Rebirth of Mothra 3 96, 216
Rector, Jeff 26, 206
Red Dwarf 55, 228
Reddick, Lance 121, 226
Redeker, Quinn 21, 220
Redmond, Sarah-Jane 128
Redmond, Thea 22
Redson, Aurian 213
Reed, Donna 153, 210
Reed, Tripp 203
Reeve, Christopher 165, 166, 218, 234
Reeve, Tom 216
Reeves, Keanu 98, 171, 204, 212, 225

Regehrt, Duncan 118
Regency 204
Regent Entertainment 207, 214
Reid, Josh 205
Reid, Tara 211
Reiner, Jeffrey 202
Reiner, Lucas 218
Reinhold, Judge 179, 212, 217, 233
Relativity Media 208, 212
Rémy, Christopher 221
Renaissance Pictures 203
Rendall, Mark 51, 230
Rennie, Michael 106, 205, 209
Reno, Jean 69, 211, 223
Repeat Performance (movie) 2, 3, 4, 136–37, 216, 222
Repeat Performance (novel) 216
Repeaters 192, 198, 216
Resistance (film) 88, 216
Resistance (novel) 88, 216
Resnais, Alain 209
Resolute Films 210
Retroactive 159, 216
Retrograde 110–11, 216
The Return of the Time Machine 15–16, 216
Return to the Planet of the Apes 45, 229
Returner 115, 216
Reuben, Gloria 186, 221
Revolution Studios 205, 214, 219
Reyes, Mark A. 213
Reynolds, James 215, 229
Reynolds, Katie 82, 229
Reynolds, Patrick 94, 207
Reynolds, Russell 138
Rhea, Caroline 215
Rheon, Iwan 228
Rhodes, Dane 220
Rhodes, Paula 63, 217
Rhys-Davies, John 98 229
Rich, Claude 62, 209
Ri'chard, Robert 39, 210
Richards, Ariana 75, 206
Richards, Billie Mae 49, 94, 224
Richards, Devorah 163
Richards, Evan 225
Richards, Jeffrey 7–8
Richardson, Ian 10
Richardson, Jake 154, 216
Richardson, Joely 74, 212
Richardson, Mike 221
Richardson, Miranda 88, 207
Richardson, Ralph 56
Richardson, Salli 226
Richie Rich's Christmas Wish 154, 216
Richings, Julian 75
Richmond, Kane 231
Richmond-Peck, David 139, 205
The Ride 23, 216–17
Reiff, Ethan 211
Rienecker, Scott 228
Riley, Michael 127, 225
Ringwald, Molly 180, 223
Ripley, Ben 218
Ripoll, Maria 223
Riseborough, Andrea 216
Il Risveglio di Paul 238

Ritter, Tim 202
Riverhorse Entertainment 207
Roach, Jay 203
Robbins, Greg 219
Robbins, Ryan 76, 215
Roberts, David 176, 213
Roberts, Eric 123, 206, 215
Roberts, Melissa 124, 215
Roberts, Rick 196, 205
Robertson, Willard 27, 207
Robin, Muriel 223
Robinsen, Jared 81
Robinson, Andrew 183
Robinson, Craig 128, 209
Robinson, Marc 29
Robinson, Michael 205
Roborex 119, 217
Robot Communications 219
Rocco, Marc 210
Roche, Eugene 217
Roché, Sebastian 110, 228
Rochon, Debbie 115, 202
Rock, Kevin 215
Rockney, Dennis 218
Rocky and His Friends 47, 228
Rodgers, Michael 222
Rodionoff, Hans 205
Rodriguez, Paul 220
Rodriguez, Robert 218, 220
Roebuck, Daniel 167, 204
Roger Corman's Frankenstein Unbound see *Frankenstein Unbound*
Rogers, Mimi 58, 206, 212
Rogers, Steven 211
Rogers, Wayne 154, 210
Rogers, Will 8, 205
Rohner, Clayton 197, 226
Roman Scandals 27, 217
Romano, Christy Carlson 147, 211
Romeo, Laura 219
Romero, Gloria 171, 213
Ronay, Edina 26, 216
Rooftop Prince 238
Roop, Jeff 177
Root, Ashton 207
Root, Stephen 106, 222
Rosenblatt, Zack 203
Rosenfeld, Gavriel 84
Rosenthal, Mark 215
Rosman, Mark 204
Ross, Joe E. 25, 227
Ross, Joel 210
Ross, Katharine 85, 133, 208
Ross, Matthew 69
Ross, Philippe 11, 224
Ross, Tiny 220
Rossen, Gregg 215
Rossilli, Paul 65
Rossio, Terry 206
Roth, Andrea 128, 204
Roth, Bob 211
Roth, Philip J. 202, 219, 222
Roth, Tim 46, 215
Rothe, Jessica 98, 215
Roundtree, Richard 82, 228
Routamaa, Tiina 218
Routh, Brandon 108, 226
Rows 234

Roxburgh, Rick 217
Royal Oaks Entertainment 203, 214
Rubes, Jan 137
Rubin, Bruce Joel 212
Rubin, Danny 209
Rubin, Jennifer 179, 212
Rubinek, Saul 124, 207, 215
Rubinrot 238
Ruby Red 238
The Ruby Ring 36, 217
Die Rückkehr der Zeitmaschine 216
Rudolph's Shiny New Year 49
Rue, Sara 170, 214
Ruffalo, Mark 157, 219
Run, Lola Run 241
Running Against Time 3, 90–91, 217
Rusler, Morgan 134, 222
Russell, Lisa Ann 108, 203
Russell, Theresa 11, 224
Russell, William 53
Russia 236, 238, 240
Russian Ark 238
Russo, Rafa 223
Russo, Rene 44, 208
Rutherford, Camilla 139, 206
Ryan, Debby 224
Ryan, Meg 167, 211
Ryskind, Morrie 224

S. Darko 133, 217
Saban Entertainment 216
Sackheim, Jerry 204
Sacks, Michael 62, 217
Sadler, William 100, 204
Safety Not Guaranteed 128–29, 217
Sai Yau Gei 235
Saikachi, Ryuuji 51, 229
Sailor Moon 117–18, 229
Sailor Moon R 117–18
St. James, Rebecca 158, 217
Saint Sinner see *Clive Barker Presents Saint Sinner*
Saito, Chiwa 228
Saito, Mitsumasa 209
Sakaguchi, Daisuke 209
Sakata, Harold 206
Sakman, John J. 215
Sakurazaka, Hiroshi 207
Sakuma, Rei 28
Saldana, Theresa 75, 221
Saldana, Zoé 218
Salem, Kario 22, 220
Salem, Pamela 50, 227
Salmeron, Gustavo 223
Salos, Gabriela 28, 214
Salt Film Company 204
Salter Street Films 214
Sama Taimu Mashin Burusu 219
Sammaciccia, Michael 202
Samms, Emma 10, 205
Samson, Barry 224
Samuels, Rachel 212
Samurai Commando Mission 1549 88, 89–90, 217
Samurai Girls 234
Samurai Jack 20, 44, 229
Sanchez, Kiele 150, 229
Sandler, Adam 157, 205
Sands, Julian 68, 109, 222, 223

Sands, Tony 35, 228
Sangster, Thomas 145, 215
Sanpei, Yuuko 90, 229
The Santa Clause 3: The Escape Clause 147–48, 217
Santiago, Cirio H. 202
Saphirblau 239
Sapphire and Steel 183–85, **184**, 229
Sapphire Blue 239
Saquibal, Bernadette 139, 205
Sara, Mia 186, 221
Sarafian, Tedi 219
The Sarah Jane Adventures 54, 81
Sarah's Choice 158, 217
Sarcev, Ursula 105
Sarin, Vic 210
Sarner, Arlene 215
Saru no Gundan 231
Satama, Antti 120, 218
Sato, Takuya 218
Satoh, Takeru 189, 227
Satoyoshi, Shigemi 205
Saving Santa 160, 217
Sawyer, Brian 215
Sax, Geoffrey 206
Saxon, John 68, 212
Saylor, Katie 57, 226
Sbarge, Raphael 214
Scacchi, Greta 36, 222
Scandiuzzi, Gian-Carlo 203
Scardino, Hal 78, 210
Scarlet Heart 239
Schacherer, Alyson 141, 204
Schachter, Steven 208
Schaeffer, Rebecca 67, 215
Schafer, Natalie 137
Schellerup, Henning 220
Schenck, Jeffrey 207
Schmidt, John 150, 202
Schmidt, Ronald 202
Schmoeller, David 214
Schnarre, Monika 50, 223
Schneider, John 154, 207
Schneider, Rob 203
Schoenborn, Carl 207
Schreiber, Liev 65, 167, 211, 218
Schroeder, Mark 150, 202
Schull, Amanda 101, 230
Schultz, Michael 222
Schwarzenegger, Arnold 102, 103, **103**, 104, 219
Schwarzkopf, Klaus 15, 216
Schwentke, Robert 221
Sci-Fi Channel see SyFy Channel
Scieszka, Jon 51
Scooby-Doo: Mystery Incorporated 234
Scorsone, Caterina 213
Scorsone, Francesca 25, 207
Scott, Adam 158, 209
Scott, Bill 48, 228
Scott, Campbell 170, 213
Scott, Dougray 158, 219
Scott, Kathryn Leigh 59, 225
Scott, Maggie 119, 217
Scott, Michael 224
Scott, Michael M. 207
Scott, Tom Everett 129
Scott, Tony 206

264 Index

Scott, William Lee 24, 151
Screamking Productions 204
Screen Media 217
Screen Partners 224
Sculptures of Dazzling Complexity 206
Seater, Michael 229
"Second Chance" (film segment) see Dead of Night
"Second Chance" (short story) 206
Second Chance (TV series) 133, 228
Second Images Studio 202
Second Sight 168, 223
Second Time Around 239
Second Time Lucky 95, 217
Secret 168, 217
The Secret of the Cupboard 78
Secret of the Ruby Ring 217
The Secret World of Polly Flint 82, 229
The Seeker: The Dark Is Rising 234
Seelman, Aaron 217
Seely, Amy 78, 218
Segal, Katey 65, 208
Segall, Pamela 188, 230
Segan, Noah 212
Sei Michaela no Gakuen Hyoryuki 229
Seikimatsu Occult Gakuin 228
Sekely, Les 209
Seki, Tomokazu 32, 142 227, 229
Selby, David 60, 225
Seleznyova, Natalia 22, 210
Selfman, Naomi 217
Sellecca, Connie 137, 222
Selwyn, Edgar 222
Selznick Studios 216
Sengoku Collection 79, 229
Sengoku Jieitai 1549 (book) 209, 217
Sengoku Jieitai 1549 (film) 208, 217
Sengoku Otome: Momoiro Paradox 225
Sennen Joyuu 213
Seo, Jin-Ho 89, 223
Serafino, Mia 152
Serano, Greg 70, 205
Serkis, Andy 219
Serling, Rod 146, 221, 230
Seven Days 190, 229
7th Voyage Productions 220
Seward, Stephen C. 202
Sewell, Rufus 152, 210, 227
Sex Slider Shag-a-Rama 242
Seymour, Jane 165, **166**, 218
Seymour, Jody 150
SGE Entertainment 221
Shah, Vipul Amrutlal 202
Shale, Kerry 230
Shanks, Michael 97, 218
Shanley, John Patrick 224
Shannon, Molly 195, **195**, 223, 224
Shannon, Peggy 175, 222
Shannon, Polly 11, 224
Shapiro, Stanley 217
Sharp, Alan 212
Shatner, William 71, 85, 145, 218, 234
Shavick Entertainment 215
Shavick/Insight Studios 207

Shaw, Sebastian 210
Shaye, Bob 212
Shazzan 28, 229
Shea, Joey 77, 224
Shea, Katt 212
Sheckley, Robert 44, 208
Sheehan, Robert 228
Sheen, Martin 208, 221
Sheers, Owen 216
Sheldon, Gene 47, 224
Sheldon, Kate 189, 228
Shen Hua 238
Shepard, Dax 157, 224
Sheppard, Mark 211
Sheppard, W. Morgan 57, 211
Shergold, Adrian 67, 227
Sherwood, Robert E. 217
Shidō, Nakamura II 33
Shimamoto, Sumi 31, 208
Shimek, Kristi 217
Shimek, Stephen 217
Shimo, Fumhiko 206
Shimono, Sab 31, 219
Shinui 236
Shinui Sunmool 236
Shipp, John Wesley 150
Shiraishi, Ryoko 90, 229
Shiratori, Yuriko 227
Shogakugan 208
Shoji, Miyoko 52
Sholder, Jack 222
Shor, Dan 204
Short, Martin 147, 217
Showcase 225
Showcase-TV 229
Showtime 206, 210, 212, 217, 224, 228
Shree 239
Shrek Forever After 154, 217
Shriner, Wil 221
Shue, Elizabeth 131, 203
Shueisha 209
Shuffle 63, 217
Shusett, Ronald 208
Siddig, Alexander 145, 185
Sidora, Drew 227
Sidus 207
Sigeunol 239
Sigismund, Katie 175, 211
Sigmund, David 217
Signal 239
Il Signor Rossi Cerca la Felicità 238
Silberling, Brad 212
Silva, Leslie 110, 228
Silver, Ron 186, 221
Silver Nitrate Productions 217
Silver Screen International 208
Silver Screen Partners II 214
Silver Sphere 211
Silver, Alain 220
Silverman, Jonathan 193, 222
Silvers, Nancey 205
Simeonova, Daria 210
Simm, John 41 227
Simmons, Jean 58, 225
Simmons, Shadia 22
Simms, Lise 228
Simon, Cliff 96, 218
Simon del Desierto 239

Simon of the Desert 239
Singer, Alexander 221
Singer, Bryan 222, 224
Singer, Lori 68, 223
Singer, Marc 68, 168, 212, 223
Singerman, Wesley 148
Singleton, Penny 79, 210
Singularity Principle 83, 217
Sins of the Sisters 91, 229
Sipos, Shaun 141, 207
Sir Arthur Conan Doyle's The Lost World 58, 229
Sirtis, Marina 218
666 Park Avenue 234
Skelton, Red 49
Skilken, Carol 212
Sky 94–95, 229
Sky Dance Productions 219
Slater, Helen 193, 222
Slaughterhouse-Five (movie) 62, 217
Slaughterhouse-Five (novel) 62, 217
Slave Girls 216
Slezak, Victor 91, 221
Sliders 98, 229
Sliding Doors 241
Slinger, Jonathan 219
Slipstream 159, 217
Slover, Melora 39, 218
Smart, Amy 151, 196, 204, 222
Smart, Jean 206
Smiley, Tava 221
Smith, Christopher 222
Smith, Cotter 190
Smith, Emile Edwin 208
Smith, Justin 214
Smith, Kurtwood 193, 222
Smith, Lane 66
Smith, Maggie 36, 208
Smith, Margo 129
Smith, Matt 226
Smith, Melanie 183
Smith, Owen 219
Smith, Shannon Dow 34, 213
Smith, Will 149, 213
Smith, Yeardley 77, 224
Smoker, Tara 141, 220
Snook, Sarah 136, 216
Snow, David 67, 212
Snow, Will 220, 229
A Snow Globe Christmas 178, 217
Socha, Lauren 228
Sofaer, Abraham 54, 211
Sofer, Rena 214
Sokoloff, Vladimir 203
Soles, Paul 30, 213
Solomon, Cary 224
Solomon, Ed 204
Sombogaart, Ben 205
Somewhere in Time 165, **166**, 218
Song, Steph 83, 215
Soni, Karan 217
Sonnenfeld, Barry 213
Sonoda, Hideki 215
Soraya, Helen 69, 206
Sorbo, Kevin 83 177, 215, 224, 233
Sorensen, Kallie 217
Soreyuke! Uchuusenkan Yamamoto Youko 229

A Sound of Thunder (movie) 93, 218
"A Sound of Thunder" (short story) 93, 218
Source Code 192, 198, 218
South Korea 89, 135, 155, 206, 210, 223, 236, 237, 238, 239
Southland Tales 234
Southworth, Daniel 189
Sovák, Jiří 85, 222
Space Channel 225, 228
Spain 221, 223, 236, 237, 240
Spall, Timothy 208
A Spasso nel Tempo 239
A Spasso nel Tempo—L'Avventura Continua 239
Spearritt, Hannah 185, 228
Speer, Hugo 40
Spellbinder 239
Spence, Sebastian 176, 207
Spencer, Alan 222
Spencer, Brenton 215
Sphere (movie) 65, 218
Sphere (novel) 65, 218
Spice Factory 202
Spider-Man (cartoon) 234
The Spierig Brothers 216
Spiner, Brent 120, 218
The Spirit of 76 5, 72, 218
Spiro, Lev L. 213, 224
Spitz, Michelle 213
Split Infinity 39, 218
Sport Billy 239
Spy Kids 4D 218
Spy Kids: All the Time in the World 152, 218
The Spy Who Shagged Me see *Austin Powers: The Spy Who Shagged Me*
SS-GB 88
Stage 6 216, 220
Stagner, Rama Laurie 214
Stahelski, Chad 214
Stahl, Nick 103, 219
Stamp, Terence 237
Stand Up Films 210
Stanfield, Devin 50, 225
Stanford, Aaron 101, 230
Stanton, Harry Dean 137, 215
Star Trek (2009) 121, 218
Star Trek (TV series) 85, 145
Star Trek: Deep Space Nine 145–46, 234
Star Trek: First Contact 119–20, 218
Star Trek IV: The Voyage Home 71–72, 218
Star Trek: Generations 234
Star Wreck: In the Pirkinning 120, 218
Star Wreck Lost Contact 120, 218
Star Wreck series 120, 218
Stargate: Continuum 96–97, 218
Stargate: SG-1 96
Starhyke 124, 229
Stark, Don 230
Stark, Jonathan 58, 209
Starke, Anthony 205
Starke, Pauline 8, 205
Starship Girl Yamamoto Yohko 44, 229

Startling by Each Step 239
Starz 228
Statham, Jason 144, 214
Staub, Chelsea 160, 213
Steedman, Tony 204
Steele, Karen 106, 205
Steenburgen, Mary 18, 51, 132, 137, 203, 215, 220, 225
Stefani, Michael 181, 222
Steffens, Roy 47, 225
Steiger, Rod 233
Stein;s Gate 142, 229
Stein;s Gate: Burdensome State of Deja Vu 125, 142, 218
Stein's;Gate: Fuka Ryoiki no Déja Vu 218
Stephen King's The Langoliers 42, 218
Stephens, Perry 37, 209, 225
Stephens, Robert 225
Sterling, Maury 205
Stern, David I. 208
Stern, Philip Van Doren 210
Sternberg, Jacques 209
Stevens, Fisher 57, 190, 214, 226
Stevens, Warren 205
Stevenson, Juliet 225
Stevenson, Parker 74, 214
Stewart, Jimmy 153, 210
Stewart, Kristen 224
Stewart, Patrick 113, 120, 218, 224, 234
Stewart, Renee 81
Stewart, Travis Brooks 68, 208
Stewart, Trish 35
Stewart-Jarret, Nathan 160, 228
The Sticky Fingers of Time 78, 218
Still Night Monster Movies 206
Stine, Brad 217
Stinger, Kalvin 119, 217
Stockwell, Dean 42, 190, 218, 228
Stockwell, John 57, 214
Stoker, Austin 45m 229
Stoll, Corey 24
Stoltz, Eric 151, 222
Stone, Chris 63, 217
Stone, Dee Wallace 66, 215
Stone, Jennifer 224
Stone, Sharon 65, 218
"A Stop at Willoughby" 169, 208
Stork Day 239
Stowe, Madeleine 101, 223
Straitharn, David *173*, 212
Strange Days at Blake Holsey High 58–59, 229
The Strange World of Planet X 234
A Stranger in Time 78, 218
Stratton, John 72, 219
Strauss, John J. 208, 217
Strauss, Robert 216
Streeter, Tara 80, 228
Strong, Mark 126
Strong, Tara 203
Stuck in the Past 129–30, 219
"Stuck on Christmas" 195
Stuhlbarg, Michael 213
Stuhler, Rachel 203, 211
Sturgeon, Theodore 60
Subkoff, Tara 144

Subotsky, Milton 206
Suetani, Masumi 216
Sugita, Tomokazu 111, 155, 197, 206, 209, 228
Suhl, Joanna 196
Sukezane, Kiki 227
Sukowa, Barbara 230
Sullivan, David 151, 216
Sullivan, Francis L. 27, 208
Sullivan, Hugh 210
Sullivan, Kelly 63, 208
Sullivan, Nicole 147
Sullivan, Paul Francis 210
Sullivan, Peter 207
Sullivan, Ted 210
Sullivan, Zette 183, 222
Summer Storm 90, 229
Summer Time Machine Blues 126–27, 219
Summit Entertainment 218
Sunshine Pictures 202
Super Capers 234
Super Eruption 114, 219
Super Sentai 188
Supercollider 93–94, 219
Superman 3, 234
Supermenier 239
Sutcliffe, David 177, 203
Sutherland, Lawrence 139, 215
Sutton, Adam 134, 222
Suzuki, Akiko 188,226
Suzuki, Anne 115, 216
Suzuki, Hiroku 25, 202
Suzuki, Kyōka 90, 217
Suzuoki, Hirotaka 229
Swackhamer, E.W. 204
Swallow, Gerry 204
Swanson, Kristy 177, 224
Swaybill, Roger E. 212
Sweden 241
Sweeney, Terry 222
Swerling, Jo 210
Switzer, Michael 220
SyFy Channel 160, 205, 211, 212, 214, 215, 219, 222, 226, 229, 230
Szwarc, Jeannot 218

Tabor, Margaret 214
Tadjedin, Massy 210
Tagasa, Gina Marissa 213
Tagawa, Cary-Hiroyuki 227
Tahir, Faran 87, 208
Tai Seng 206
Tait, Don 223
Taiwan 217, 236
Takács, Tibor 214
Takada, Hatsumi 143, 227
Takada, Takafumi 212
Takahashi, Motosuke 208
Takahashi, Rumiko 31
Takashima, Masahiro 97
Takayama, Hideki 202
Takayama, Minami 44, 229
Takayanagi, Ryoichi 161, 212
Takechi, Shigenori 210
Takegami, Junki 214
Takei, George 208, 218
Takemoto, Yasuhiro 206
Takeuchi, Hideki 219

Takeuchi, Junko 42, 214
Takeuchi, Yashio 221
Takiguchi, Junpei 28, 230
Takimoto, Fujiko 157, 228
Takizawa, Hideaki, 229
Talbot, Judson 224
Tales of Saint Michaela's Academy 229
Talley, Steve 129
Tallmantz Aviation 208
Tamarack Road Produtions 214
Tambarle 203
Tamblyn, Amber 25, 211
Tamblyn, Russ 25, 211
Tambor, Jeffrey 229
Tamura, Yukari 142
Tanaka, Mayumi 31, 208
Tanaka, Rie 98, 226
Tanigawa, Nagaru 206
Taniguchi, Masaaki 221
Tapestry Films 211
Tapping, Amanda 97, 218
Tarrant, Ron 221
Tatasciore, Fred 27, 230
Tate, Misato 96, 216
Tatsuta, Naoki 227
Taurus 7 Film Corporation 220
Tayback, Vic 22, 220
Taylor, Alan 219
Taylor, Don 207, 208
Taylor, Holland 170, 209
Taylor, Jack 222
Taylor, Lauren 52, 225
Taylor, Noah 212
Taylor, Rod 13 **14, 15, 16**, 16, 82, 220, 224, 228
Taylor, Russi 148, 213
Taylor, Tamara 217
Taylor, Valerie 164, 203
Taylor-Isherwood, Emma 58, 229
TBS 209, 221, 228
Teen Beach 2, 234
Teen Beach Movie 6
Teen Knight 213
Teenage Mutant Ninja Turtles III 31–32, 219
Teffer, Jason 216
Telefilm Saar Film Production 216
TeleVisionary Oracle 207
Tempting Fate 180, 219
Tenchi Muyo 140
Tenchi Muyo in Love 140, 219
Tenchi Muyou in Love! 219
Tenchu 79, 229
Tennant, David 226
Tenure Track Productions 202
Tepnapa, J.T. 211
Terashima, Takuma 143 227
Termination Point 234
The Terminator 101–2, **103**, 219
Terminator Genisys 104, 219
Terminator Salvation 104
Terminator: The Sarah Connor Chronicles 104, 229
Terminator 2: Judgment Day 102–103, 219
Terminator 3: Rise of the Machines 102, 103, 219
Terminatrix 105, 219

Terra Nova 26–27, 229
Terror at London Bridge see *Bridge Across Time*
Terror from the Year 5000 72–73, **73**, 219
Terumae Romae 219
Terumae Romae II 219
Terzoli, Alain 69, 206
Test Tube Teens from the Year 5000 223
Tetley, Walter 48, 228
Tezuka, Masaaki 217
Tezuka, Osama 205
Thames Television 230
That Was Then 150, 229
Thatcher, Kirk B. 210
Theatre Junkies 217
Theby, Rosemary 205
Thelen, Jodi 163, 205
Therma Romae (TV series) 71
Therma Romae—Roman Baths 71, 219
Therma Romae II 71, 219
Thewlis, David 30, 221
"They're Tearing Down Tim Riley's Bar" 146–47
Thinnes, Roy 225
3rd After the Sun 239
Third Reef Pictures 216
13 Going on 30 156–57, 219
Thomas, Antonia 228
Thomas, David Jean 203
Thomas, Marlo 154, 210
Thomas, Ralph 216
Thomas, R.L. 224
Thomas, Tamara Craig 110, 228
Thomason, Marsha 30, 204
Thomerson, Tim 105, 181, **182**, 205, 214, 222, 224
Thompson, Cindy Ann 167, 204
Thompson, Emma 149, 213
Thompson, Gary Scott 221
Thompson, Lea 130, 177, 203, 204
Thompson, Sophie 33, 230
A Thousand Kisses Deep 158, 219
Three Days 137–38, 219–20
Three Stooges 21, 220
The Three Stooges Meet Hercules 21, 220
The Thrill Seekers 221
Throg 234
Through the Magic Pyramid 220
Thunderstone 239
Thyne, T.J. 63, 217
Ticking Clock 148–49, 220
Tiger Stripe Baby Is Waiting for Tarzan 239
Tigerstreifenbaby Wartet auf Tarzan 239
Tillman, Trevor 215
Timberlake, Justin 234
Time Adventure Zeccho 5-Byo Mae 242
Time After Time 18–19, 220
Time Again 141–42, 220
Time and Again (2004) 127, 220
Time and Again (2007) 239
Time at the Top (film) 36, 220
Time at the Top (novel) 220

Time Bandits 56, 220
Time Barbarians 67–68, 220
Time Bokan 51, 229
Time Bokan: Royal Revival 51
Time Bokan Yatterman 51
Time Bokan Zendarman 51
Time Changer 70, 220
Time Chasers 118, 220
The Time Crystal 22, 220
Time Enough: The Alien Conspiracy 115, 220
Time Express 189, 229
Time Fighters 229
Time Flier 204
Time Flies 33, 220
The Time Guardian 239
Time Is the Enemy 34–35, 229
Time Jam 240
Time Keepers 188, 229
Time Kid 17–18, 220
The Time Machine (1949) 13, 230
The Time Machine (1960 film) 13–14, **14, 15, 16**, 220
The Time Machine (1978 film) 14, 220
The Time Machine (novel) 2, 13, 214, 220
The Time Machine (radio drama) 2, 13
The Time Machine (2002 film) 14–15, 220
Time Machine: Rise of the Morlocks 214
Time Machine: The Journey Back 15, 220
Time Masters 239
Time of the Apes 231
"Time Out" see *Twilight Zone: The Movie*
Time Riders 33–34, 230
Time Runner 114, 221
Time Slip see *G.I. Samurai*
Time Slip (1953) 241
Time Squad 188, 230
Time Stranger 88, 221
A Time to Remember 217
Time Trackers (film) 117, 221
Time Trackers (TV) 239–40
Time Trap 221
Time Travel Tondekeman 28, 230
The Time Traveler (1976) 35, 221
The Time Travelers (1964) 17, 54, 221
The Time Traveler's Wife (film) 174, 221
The Time Traveler's Wife (novel) 174, 221
The Time Traveller (1984) see *The Next One*
Time Traveller—The Girl Who Leapt Through Time 162, 221
Time Trax 4, 186, 230
The Time Tunnel 35, 54, 190, 230
Time Under Fire 203
Time Warner 212
Time War Trio (books) 51
Time Warp Trio (TV) 51–52, 230
Time Warrior 234
Timecop (comic book) 221

Timecop (movie) 4, 186–87, **187**, 221
Timecop (TV) 187, 230
Timecop: The Berlin Decision 187–88, 221
Timecrashers 3
Timecrimes 159, 221
Timegate: Tales of the Saddle Tramps 242
Timekeeper 93, 221
Timeline (movie) 30, 221
Timeline (novel) 221
Timemaster 118, 221
Timequest 91, 221
Timerider: The Adventures of Lyle Swann 37, 221
Timescape 206
The Timeshifters 75–76, 221
Timeslingers 38, 221
Timeslip 43, 230
Timestalkers 116–17, 221–22
Timetrip: Curse of the Viking Witch 240
Tipple, Gordon 221
Tisdale, Ashley 145, 215
Tits a Wonderful Life 242
TMC 219
TNT 224
To, Chi-Long 217
Toda, Keiko 88, 221
Togashi, Misuzu 138, 226
Toho Studios 204, 209, 216
Toki No Tabibito 221
Toki O Kakeru Shojo 209, 221
Tokyo Broadcasting 230
Tolkan, James 130
Tolkin, Stephen 222
Tom, Lauren 208
Tomaric, Jason J. 220
Tomei, Marisa 169, 209
Tominaga, Miina 106, 226
Tomlin, Lily 206
Tomonaga, Akane 143, 227
Tomori Films 219
Tomorrow Films 207
Tomorrow I'll Get Up and Scald Myself with Tea 85, 222
The Tomorrow Man (1996) 109, 222
The Tomorrow Man (2001) 134–5, 181, 222
Tomorrow's End 240
Tompkins, Darlene 17, 203
Tom's Midnight Garden (1999) 36, 222, 230
Tom's Midnight Garden (novel) 36, 222
Torchlight Entertainment 213, 223
Torchwood 54
Torres, Gina 211
Torssonen, Samuli 120, 218
Torv, Anna 121, 226
Total Reality 107, 222
Touchi, Hiroki 89, 230
Touchstone Pictures 206, 214
Touchy Feely Films 211
Touma, Yumi 188
Tovey, Roberta 206
Tovey, Russell 95, 228
Towne, Gene 202
Toyoguchi, Megumi 32, 225

Toyohara, Kosuke 209
Trachtenberg, Michelle 216
Tracy, Lee 175, 222
Trammell, Sam 144, 223
Trancers 3, 4, 181–83, 222
Trancers 6 183, 222
Trancers II **182**, 183, 222
Trancers III 183, 222
Trancers IV 181, 234
Trancers V 234
Trandafir, Claudiu 29
Translux 202
Trapped on Toy World 211
Trauth, A.J. 30, 214
Travanti, Daniel J. 213
A Traveller in Time 33, 230
Travers, Henry 153, 210
Travis, Kylie 159, 216
Trenchard-Smith, Brian 214
Trenton, Rob 222
Treu, Blair 212
Trevorrow, Colin 217
The Triangle (2001) 235
Triangle (2005) 57, 222
Triangle (2009) 197–98, 222
Trickett, Vicki 21, 220
Trigger, Sarah 100
Trimark Pictures 211, 215
Trinder, Tommy 27, 207
Trinneer, Connor 226
Der Trip 5, 240
The Trip 240
Tripping the Rift 105
Tripping the Rift: The Movie 105–6, 222
Tristar 212, 216
Tri-Star Pictures 215
Troop, Amanda 163, 206
Troublemaker Studios 218
Troughton, Patrick 50, 209, 225, 226
Troyer, Verne J. 203
Tru Calling 190, 230
Trundy, Natalie 207
Tsukamoto, Nobuo 21, 205
Tsukimura, Ryoe 219
Tsunematsu, Ayumi 79, 229
Tsutsui, Yasutaka 161, 209, 212, 221
Tuchman, Eric 220
Tugend, Harry 202
Tuman 236
Turco, Paige 31, 219
Turkel, Joseph 20, 204
Turkey 239
Turman, John 220
Turn Back the Clock (1933) 2, 3, 175–76, 222
Turn Back the Clock (1989) 137, 222
Turner, Kathleen 126, 215
Turner, Lisa 50, 227
Turteltaub, Jon 206
Tut and Tuttle 220
Tuttle, Frank 217
TV Asahi 227, 228, 229
TV Ontario 225
TV Osaka 229
TV Tokyo 214, 225, 226, 227, 228, 229
TVN 228

Twain, Mark 2, 7–8, 25, 211, 223, 224
12 Dates of Christmas 196, 222
12 Days of Christmas Eve 192, 195, **195**, 223
12 Monkeys (movie) 101, 223
12 Monkeys (TV series) 101, 230
12:01 192, 193, 222
12:01 P.M. (film) 193, 222
12:01 P.M. (short story) 193, 222
20th Century-Fox 202, 203, 204, 207, 208, 209, 215, 222, 224
The 25th Reich 240
Twice in a Lifetime 134, 230
Twice Upon a Time 180, 223
Twice Upon a Yesterday 126, 223
The Twilight Zone 2, 146, 169, 208, 230
Twilight Zone the Movie 39, 223
2046 240
2009: Lost Memories 89, 223
2035 Forbidden Dimensions 113, 223
The Two Worlds of Jennie Logan 5, 168–69, 223
Twohy, David N. 206
Twohy, D.T. 223
"The Twonky" (short story) 64, 223
The Twonky (film) 64, 223
Tyson, Richard 203

Ubach, Alanna 133, 204
Ueda, Makota 219
Ueda, Yuji 226
Ueno, Juri 219
Ueto, Aya 71, 219
Ullerup, Emilie 76, 215
Ullman, Elwood 220
Ullman, Ricky 79, 228
Ulmer, Edgar G. 203
The Undead 29, 223
Undermind 144, 223
Unger, Billy 37, 212
Unidentified Flying Oddball 7, 10, 223
United Artists 204, 208, 223
United Film Organization 222
United International Pictures 217
United Kingdom 202
United Pictures 206
Universal 203, 207, 212, 215, 217, 218, 221, 224
Upadhyaya, Anand 216
Uplifting Entertainment 219
UPN 226, 229, 230
Urban, Karl 218
Urbaniak, James 78, 218
U'Ren, Sloane 206
USA Network 202, 223, 226
Ushinawareta Mirai o Motomete 227
USSR *see* Russia

Väänänen, Kari 120
Vail, Justina 229
Valentine, Steve 132
Valerian & Laureline 240
Valev, Marian 31
Vampire Time Travelers 235
Van Allsburg, Chris 224

Van Damme, Jean Claude 186, *187*, 221
Vander Pyl, Jean 80
Van Dien, Casper 75, 221
Van Dreelen, John 17
Van Eyssen, David 217
Van Patten, Dick 217
Van Rijckeghem, Jean-Claude 205
Van Sickle, Jan 174, 213
Vargas, Eli 212
Varley, John 73, 213
Vassil, Anton 213
Vaughn, Matthew 224
Vega, Alexa 218
Veggie Tales 34
Velasquez, Patricia 223
Vendome Pictures 218
Venezuela 237
Vennera, Chick 203
Ventimiglia, Milo 112, 227
Ventimiglia, Colleen 205
Verheiden, Mark 221
Vertical Pictures 223
Vestron Pictures 223
VH 1 227
Vickerman, Michael 209
Videocraft International 224
Vigalondo, Nacho 159, 221
Villechaize, Hervé 226
Vince, Pruitt Taylor 211
Vincent, Brian 133, 204
Vincie, Arthur 208
"Vintage Season" 75, 206
Virgin Hunters 106, 223
Vischer, Phil 215
Les Visiteurs 211, 223
Visitor, Nana 145
The Visitors 4, 69, 223
The Visitors 2—The Corridors of Time 69, 223
Vista Street Entertainment 220
La Voie Lactée 238
Voight, Jon 140, 205, 212
Vold, Ingrid 220
Vollman, Tom 202
Vølvens Forbandelse 240
Von Detten, Erik 194, 205
Vonnegut, Kurt 55, 62, 203, 217
Von Pfetten, Stefanie 223
Von Zerneck, Danielle 57, 214
Voris, Cy 211
Vortex 242
Voyagers 186, 230
Vuorensola, Timo 120, 218
Vye, Murvyn 8, 20, 204, 205

Wagner, Honus 24
Wagner, Lindsay 168, 223
Wagner, Robert 203
Wahlberg, Mark 45, 215
Wahlgren, Kari 227, 230
Waite, Ralph 91, 221
Wakabayashi, Kanji 218
Wakamoto, Nori 138
Wakefield, Charlotte 40, 202
Wakefield, Rhys 42, 215
Walch, Gay 221
Waldo, Janet 28, 229
Waldron, Caroline 230

Walken, Christopher 157, 205
Walker, Lathrop 124, 215
Walker, Paul 30, 221
Walking with Dinosaurs 26
Walsh, Dylan 212
Walters, Melora 204
Walwin, Kent 203
Wanamaker, Sam 90, 217
Wanamaker, Zoë 87, 227
Warburton, Patrick 79, 210
Ward, Fred 37, 221
Ward, Jim 112, 230
Ward, Megan *182*, 183, 222
Ward, Vincent 214
Warlock 68, 223
Warlock II 68
Warner, David 18, 50, 56, 158, 219, 220, 223
Warner Brothers 207, 210, 212, 218, 219, 220, 223
Warner Brothers Animation 211
Warner Independent Pictures 210
Warnock, Craig 56, 220
Warren, Gary 81, 225
Warren, Janet 223
Warren, Lesley Ann 216
Washington, Denzel 191, 206
Wasson, Craig 109, 222
Watanabe, Akeno 229
Watanabe, Kumiko 229
Waterston, Katherine 141, 207
Watson, Barry 170, 214
Watson, David 45
Watson, Emily 205
Watson, Emma 92
Watson, Luke 230
Watson, Mitch 203
Watt, Harry 208
Waxman, Al 134, 230
Waxwork 50, 223
Waxwork: Lost in Time 51, 223
Way, Anthony 36, 222
WB 225, 226
We Are from the Future 240
We Are from the Future 2 240
Webber, Daniel 227
Weber, Steven 195, *195*, 223
Webs 235
Webster, Derek 52, 211
Webster, Victor 107, 225
Wei Xiao Bao: Feng Zhi Gou Nu 237
Weimer, Jon 204
Weiner, John 205
W.E.I.R.D. World 155, 224
Weird Fantasy 224
Weird Science 224
Weiser, Stanley 207
Weiss, Michael 204
Weissman, David 207, 213
Welch, Elisabeth 27, 208
Welker, Frank 226
Weller, Peter 110, 228
Welles, Orson 210
Wells, Audrey 206
Wells, Claudia 130
Wells, Dolores 221
Wells, H.G. 2, 13, 214, 220, 233; as fictional character 18–19

Wells, Simon 14, 220
Wells, Vernon 189, 228
Welsh, Christina 209
Wen, Ming-Na 180, 219
We're Back: A Dinosaur's Story (book) 224
We're Back: A Dinosaur's Story (film) 77, 224
Werker, Alfred 216
Werner, Peter 219
West, Billy 65, 208
West, Samuel 179, 230
West, Simon 212
Westbrook, Marie 214
Westfeldt, Jennifer 177, 203
Weston, Jonny 153, 216
Westwick, Ed 217
Wettig, Patricia 218
Whaley, Frank 159, 216
Whalin, Justin 234
What If... 177, 224
Wheaton, Wil 227
When Time Expires 109–10, 224
Where Do We Go from Here? 47, 224
While Nero Fiddled 207
Whirry, Shannon 159, 216
Whitaker, David 206
White, David A.R. 224
White, J.B. 223
White, Liz 227
White, Peter 209
White, Sheila 10, 223
White, T.H. 25
Whitford, Bradley 167
Whitmire, Steve 210
Whittaker, Jodie 158, 219
Wiener, Joshua 225
Wiesenfeld, Joe 211
Wilby, James 36, 222
Wiley, Ethan 209
Wilkinson, Tom 40, 202, 204, 209
Willard, Fred 170, 214
Williams, Curtis 207
Williams, David 168, 223
Williams, Delondra 207
Williams, Michelle 118, 221
Williams, Peter 176, 207
Williams, Robin 233
Williams, Tom 45, 229
Williamson, Chase 83, 211
Willis, Bruce 101, 119, 134, 206, 212, 223
Willmott, Kevin 206
Willy McBean and His Magic Machine 84, 94, 224
Wilson, Owen 24, 96, 208, 213
Wilson, Roger 95, 217
Wilson, Stuart 32, 219
Wilson, Thomas F. 51, 130, 131, 203, 225
Wimmer, Kurt 218
Windermere Pictures 202
Windom, William 122, 146
Windsor, Bernadette 77, 225
Winfield, Paul 219
Winick, Gary 219
Winkler, Henry 55, 205, 226
The Winning Season 5, 23–4, 224

Winslet, Kate 211
Winslette, Kate 11
Winston, Matt 120
Winter, Alex 99, 203, 204, 225
Winter, Ariel 48, 213
Winterhawk, Nik 38, 207
Winton, Sandy 176, 213
Wirth, Billy 179, 212
Wisher, William 219
Wishmaster 235
A Witch Without a Broom 240
Witt, Alicia 178, 217
Witt, Dan 214
Wizards of Waverly Place 132
Wizards of Waverly Place: The Movie 132, 224
Wlaschiha, Tom 216
Woelfel, Jay 222
Wohl, Adam 214
Wolf, Christopher 106, 223
Wolf/Gourley Productions 217
Wolfe, Collette 128, 209
Wolfe, Miranda 110, 214
Wolverine and the X-Men 112, 230
Wong, David 211
Wong, James 214
Wood, Martin 218
Woodard, Alfre 120, 218
Woodard, George 118, 220
Woodbury, Joan 221
Woods, Donald 206
Woods, James 144, 211
Woods, John T. 220
Woolnough, Jeff 213
Wootton, Marc 185, 208
Working Title 202
The World Hitler Never Made 84
World War II 40, **41**, 84–90, 236, 240
World Without End, 2, 16, 43, 224
The Worm Ouroboros 193
WOWOW Network 226
Wright, Brad 218
Wright, Craig 213
Wright, Herbert J. 220

Wright, Jeffrey 198, 218
Wrye, Donald 210
Wryn, Rhiannon Leigh 74, 212
Wu, Constance 215
Wu, Vivian 32, 219
Wylie, Adam 227
Wyndham, John 179, 216, 230
Wynkoop, Joel D. 202

X-Men: Days of Future Past 113, 224
Xin Nan Xiong Nan Di 236–37

Yahashibara, Megumi 229
Yakin, Boaz 216
Yakovlev, Yuri 22, 210
Yakushimaru, Hiroku 95, 204
Yamadera, Kōichi 52, 97, 213
Yamaguchi, Kappei 32, 227
Yamaguchi, Takayuki 99, 226
Yamamoto, Eichi 205
Yamatoya, Akatsutki 209, 221
Yamazaki, Takashi 216, 219
Yanagiya, Tsubame 21, 205
Yapo, Mennan 216
Yara, Yūsaku 89, 226, 230
Yarbrough, Gene 222
Yasuda, Narumi 162
Yellend, Jack 202
Yeolhanshi 236
The Yesterday Machine 84–85, 224
Yesterday Was a Lie 4, 62–63
Yesterday's Target 111–12
Yifei, Liu 29, 208
Yogen 233
Yokouchi, Tadashi 221
Yolen, Jane 206
Yoneda, Okihiro 216
Yoo, Ji-Tae 155, 206
York, Michael 10, 40, 203, 211, 224
Yorkshire Television 227
Yoshimura Jitsuko 21, 205
Young, Alan 13, 213, 220
Young, Bunky 220
Young, Carlson 200, 216
Young, Danielle 17, 220

Young, Howard Irving 220
Young, Jon 205
Young, Lee Thompson 80, 211
Young, Roger 211
Young, Roland 202, 233
Young Barney 211
A Young Connecticut Yankee in King Arthur's Court 11, 224
Young Justice 235
Young Wolf Productions 222
Youngblood, Rob 180, 223
Younger, Henry 216
Yu-Gi-Oh! Bonds Beyond Time 241
Yuki, Aoi 142, 228
Yukino, Satsuki 32, 227
Yuriko, Ono 79, 229
Yuspa, Cathy 219
Yuyama, Kunihiko, 215

Z Sky Productions 223
Zabel, Bryce 214
Zabil Jsem Einsteina Panova 237
Zackarian, Ruth 67, 212
Zaray, Nicole 78, 218
Zaremba, John 54
Zartliche Chaoten II 240
Zaso, Joseph 202
Zathura (book) 224
Zathura (film) 157, 224
Z'Dar, Robert 208
Zehnder, Andrew 220
Zemeckis, Robert 203
Zentrix 240
Zerkalo Dlya Geroya 238
Zero Day Fox 215
Ziller, Paul 215
Zindel, Paul 205
Zinman, John 212
Zipang 89, 230
Zitra Vstanu a Oparim se Cajem 222
Zondag, Dick 224
Zondag, Ralph 224
Zukerman, Ashley 27
Zuniga, Daphne 196, 205

www.ingramcontent.com/pod-product-compliance
Lightning Source LLC
Chambersburg PA
CBHW081546300426
44116CB00015B/2766